BOB GREENE'S AMERI

Bob Greene's America

AMERICAN BEAT

CHEESEBURGERS

Galahad Books • New York

Published in 1993 by

Galahad Books
A division of Budget Book Service, Inc.
386 Park Avenue South
New York, NY 10016

Galahad Books is a registered trademark of Budget Book Service, Inc.
Published by arrangement with the author.

Library of Congress Catalog Card Number: 93-70260
ISBN: 0-88365-818-6

Printed in the United States of America.

Contents

American Beat

For Rob Fleder and Marilyn Johnson

Contents

xii   *Contents*

Introduction

I have a job that I like. I make my living by going out and seeing things. Then I write stories about what I saw. If that sounds like an enviable line of work . . . well, I agree. I'm lucky to be doing it.

The stories that appear here were written between the middle of the 1970s and the present. They originally appeared three different places: in my "American Beat" column in *Esquire* magazine; in the *Chicago Tribune*, where my syndicated newspaper column has been based since 1978; and in the *Chicago Sun-Times*, where I worked before that.

I am neither a pundit nor a political philosopher. I try to be a storyteller; I try to go out and explore something that interests me, and then—after hanging around and watching and listening and asking questions—I try to give the reader some sense of what it was like to have been there.

Some of the stories here were written "off the news," in the course of covering breaking events. The Atlanta murders, the Super Bowl, the death of Elvis Presley—on those stories I was one of many reporters on the scene, trying to carve out a piece of the action for myself.

Much more often, I was the only writer around, trying to tell a story that otherwise wouldn't get told. A lone conscientious teacher in an Arizona classroom, a young woman who got fired from her job because she dropped her pants and sat on a Xerox machine, two fifteen-year-old boys growing up in a sprawling suburban shopping mall, a father begging someone to help his wayward son before it became too late . . .

those are the kinds of things that don't really qualify as "news," but that seem to me to have as much to do with the way we live as most of the events that warrant bold banner headlines.

Sometimes I visited someone with whom I just felt like spending time. Once in a while it was a person who was a prime target for other journalists, as in the case of Richard Nixon. Most of the time, though, it was someone who, at the time I made my call, was not especially sought after by the rest of the press: Fess Parker twenty years after "Davy Crockett"; Ingemar Johansson; Frank Sinatra, Jr. I was seldom in search of news; what exactly drew me is hard for me to define. I hope it shows up in the stories.

I found myself on the road much of the time. The experiences I came across differed widely; but whether I was flying across the country watching Ella Fitzgerald trying to perform on a DC-10, or picking out the prettiest girl in Kanawha County, West Virginia, or sitting with mass murderer Richard Speck in his prison cell, all of those experiences eventually translated into stories.

In a strange way, though, the stories weren't the main reason for the journeys; the journeys themselves were the reason. One of the men I write about in this book—Bob Seger, the singer—once wrote a song that included the line: "Such a fine memory, I think I'm going to take it with me." That's what all of this has been about: a never-ending trip in search of memories, all of them there for the taking.

Before we get on with the book itself, I'd like to say thank you to a few people.

At *Esquire,* Phillip Moffitt enthusiastically embraced the idea of "American Beat," and gave me the encouragement, the resources, and the forum to expand the newspaper reporting I had been doing for years into a format without editorial limits, with the entire country as my "hometown."

At the *Chicago Tribune,* the people with whom I work most closely every day have given me a genuine sense of family. No matter where I may travel in pursuit of my stories, the *Tribune* is where I return to sort them out and to write them; the people who work with me—they are my bosses, my colleagues, and my friends—make coming to work a pleasure. I am indebted to Jim Squires, Max McCrohon, the late Bill Jones, Dick Ciccone, Colleen Dishon, Mike Argirion, and Randy Curwen; and at the Tribune Company Syndicate, Bob Reed, Walter Mahoney, Don Michel, and Evelyn Smith.

At the *Chicago Sun-Times*, where the earliest pieces in this book first appeared, some of my fondest thoughts still reside. Of Jim Hoge— editor while I was at the paper, now publisher—I can only say: outside of my own family, no one has been more important to my life.

BOB GREENE
March 1983

American Beat

That's Entertainment

Steve Caudill, a twenty-three-year-old airfreight handler, bled from his nose, mouth, and eyes. The blood formed a mask over his face; with each breath he took, the bleeding grew worse. As he moved to avoid getting hit one more time, a paper cup full of beer dropped from the darkness and splashed his legs.

"Kill somebody!" came a voice from high in the arena, but it was hard to make out individual voices amid the animal chant. More beer was thrown into the ring. Caudill's opponent—David Guidugli, twenty-six, a construction worker—was also losing blood, but the sound of the crowd seemed to make him afraid to stop.

This was in a place called Hara Arena, a converted ice rink on the outskirts of Dayton, Ohio. The evening had not been promoted as a boxing match, and indeed it was something . . . different. These two contestants were not boxers; neither were the thirty-four other local men who were providing the entertainment for the audience of almost four thousand.

The crowd was excited to see Caudill and Guidugli spill their blood, yes, but if the truth be told, they had been even happier several minutes earlier, when Stanton Long, a machine operator, had staggered to the side of the ring and, in great pain, vomited the entire contents of his stomach onto the concrete floor below. And they had laughed mightily when Raymond Morris, a forty-five-year-old bartender, had convulsed on the mat after taking a beating from a man twenty-two years his junior.

The arena had been chilly before the people had arrived, but now it was steaming. You could feel the heat.

Three weeks earlier, the posters had gone up in the bars and factories around Dayton. "HOW TOUGH ARE YOU?" read the headline that stood next to a large drawing of a man's fist. The subhead: "We're looking for the toughest man in the Southwest Ohio area. Could it be you?"

The poster solicited "bar bouncers, construction workers, bar brawlers, truck drivers, policemen, factory workers, firemen, farmers, etc., etc." Professional boxers were not welcome. Tickets for the two evenings would be scaled from $6 to $10. The winner would receive $1,000, the runner-up $500. The others would receive nothing.

This was the Toughman Contest. If you live in New York or Chicago or Los Angeles, you may have never heard of this phenomenon; it does not travel to most major metropolitan areas. But virtually every weekend of the year, a Toughman Contest is held somewhere in the United States—in Wheeling, West Virginia; in Savannah, Georgia; in Grand Rapids, Michigan; in Green Bay, Wisconsin.

The premise—as devised by Arthur Dore, the entrepreneur from Bay City, Michigan, who invented Toughman in 1979—is simple. People in towns that have not been able to support professional boxing for years will pack the nearest arenas and fairgrounds coliseums to see the local braggarts and barroom bullies try to hurt one another. And the meanest men in these towns will fight—most of them for free—out of some vague dream of glory.

The word *boxing* is almost never used in promoting the Toughman Contest. It's too tame a phrase and would turn off potential customers; besides, it doesn't come close to describing what goes on in the Toughman ring. Sure, there are boxing gloves and three two-minute rounds and a panel of judges to select a winner if both contestants go the distance. But almost no one does. Most matches end with one contestant either on the floor or begging for someone to stop the beating. There is fear and cruelty and humiliation in that ring. There are 300-pound men punching 175-pound men to the canvas and then snorting aloud as they punch them some more. There are men who, finding themselves unable to back up the bravado that brought them there in the first place, weep as they are repeatedly slammed against the ropes. There are painfully out-of-shape men being tortured by men tough enough to maim them. On the final night, a contestant who continues to win his matches may be required to fight four different opponents. These elimination bouts go on until there is only one man left.

No, *boxing* doesn't cover it. The Toughman competition has more to do with professional wrestling, except that this is not the illusion of blood and violence but the fact of blood and violence; it has more to do with *The Music Man*, except that the local pride that Art Dore has come to town to exploit comes from a darker side of the human spirit.

"This is what people want to see," Dore said. A bearded man of forty-three, he was sitting in a room in the concrete bowels of Hara Arena a few hours before the Dayton show was to begin. "It's a macho thing. It's for real. They know it's not fake. There's no bobbing or weaving or dancing. These people want action. They want to see a guy who's always boasting that he can whip someone's ass go out and prove it.

"I don't try to analyze it," Dore said with a shrug. "I just try to sell it."

And the men who would do the bleeding? They had sent résumés to the arena, listing their physical dimensions and their occupations: carpenter, Frigidaire worker, city parks maintenance man, Pepsi delivery agent. Many had simply noted "Unemployed." For two nights they would step into the ring with strangers, while other strangers screamed at them from the seats and Art Dore, at the microphone, egged them on with insults and exhortations.

Between elimination bouts they waited in a small room on the arena's first floor. The men wore cut-off Levi's and tank tops, T-shirts and swimming trunks. Some looked like motorcycle gang members; others would have seemed more at home next to a gas station pump. Here was a man with a ring in his left ear; there was another with an obscenity tattooed on the back of his hand. Most of the Toughman contestants waiting backstage could not precisely define what made them want to do this. They seemed to be drawn by the promise of the one thing that had eluded them all their lives: success. They were all small-town, small-job boys; none had attempted to make it in the larger world. They had accepted that, and lived with it. Since grade school they had known they had certain . . . limitations. And then Art Dore had come to town with his promise: You don't need talent. You don't need grace. You don't need ambition. All you need is the meanness that has been your little secret all your life, and if you're mean enough, you're going to be a star. Success? Bleed for it, and it can finally be yours.

"I don't know," said Harlan Glassburn, a twenty-five-year-old construction worker, whose entry form listed him at six feet five inches and 245 pounds. "I just want to see what I can do in there. I've been in a few barroom brawls, but you get hit with a pool stick and you ain't going to be standing up too long. I know I ain't going to make it all the way to the end of this, but at least I got more guts than the people sitting up in the stands. They just want to see blood, and I ain't afraid to bleed."

Stanton Long, the twenty-three-year-old machine operator who would later vomit before the delighted crowd, said, "All my buddies at work were talking about this. You know, there's a lot of crazy people walking around Dayton, a lot of people carrying guns. I've beat up many guys with my fists, but I don't carry a gun. I'm a pretty mellow guy, but if there's a fight, someone's got to do the fighting."

After winning his first-round match, Bruce Niles, thirty-two years old and 330 pounds, a stockman for International Harvester, came into the room. The noise from the crowd followed him in.

"The fights I've been in on the street, there's been a lot of kicking and biting," he said. "You know, you drink a lot of beer and your head gets all buzzed up. Out there just now, I knocked the guy over the ropes, and I don't know what got into me . . . I wanted to kill him. The referee kept pulling me off, but I got on top of the guy. I don't know what it is . . . when you get excited . . . you just want to blow it out of your gourd . . . finish the job. . . ."

High in the arena, fueled by beer, the crowd was on its feet and screaming. This was the second night of the Toughman Contest. Although the fighters were being led into the ring one pair after another, the pace was not fast enough for some members of the audience. "Bring on the meat!" a voice called out. A number of fistfights had broken out in the stands, the frequency of these brawls increasing as the night grew longer.

"Those are everyday people out there," said Jerry Johnson, a carpenter who had paid his way into both nights of the contest. "They're people just like us, mashing each other's noses and mouths up. There's no rules, just good action."

Johnson's tone was flat and even, betraying not a trace of irony. He seemed to be enjoying a casual night out. If another visitor to Hara Arena felt a different set of emotions—a sick creeping in the pit of the stomach, an unclean film on the soul that seemed to grow thicker with each new roar from the crowd, with each new bloodletting—that visitor was clearly in the minority. The people in the arena seemed to feel no revulsion. They felt only an urgent tingling.

The crowd was mostly male, but the women who were in the audience seemed to be enjoying the show even more than the men. "I think
it must be exciting to hit someone like that," said Rosa Ginter, thirty-
three, a nursing-home employee. "I don't think it's true that women
don't like violence. I'd like to see even more action, if you want to know
the truth."

About halfway back on the main floor, a twenty-year-old woman
named Tonya Hopkins—a cashier at a local K mart—sat with her husband, watching a particularly bloody exchange. Her eyes were alive.
Asked if she wanted to sit at ringside, she left her husband to accompany a reporter to the card table that had been set up against the ring.
Up close, she could hear each punch tear at flesh, watch each spurt of
blood spatter from the mouths and noses of the fighters. She did not
take her eyes away from them; her breathing became irregular, and her
chest heaved.

"I like it," she said, her eyes still on the men. "I really like it. These
guys can really take a lot of stuff. I didn't realize . . . I like the way
they look in each other's eyes. It's so physical . . . I think it's more
the taking that gets to me than the giving. I can't stop looking in their
faces. It's so beautiful."

"There's almost seven hundred pounds of men in that ring," Art Dore
shouted into the ringside microphone as two huge contestants belted
each other toward the end of the evening.

The Dayton Toughman Contest was nearly over. It had played itself
out almost without incident. Oh, there was one problem when a group
of men from the audience lured an arena security guard into a men's
rest room, where their companions waited for him, split his head open,
beat him, and left him on the floor. But generally, Dore was happy
with the way the two evenings had gone.

David Guidugli won the title of Toughest Man in Southwest Ohio;
he was presented with a check for $1,000, and Dore played a cassette
tape of the theme from *Rocky* into the microphone as Guidugli stood,
cut and weary, in the center of the ring.

Hara Arena emptied as quickly as it had filled. Several of the Toughman contestants stayed around, as if there might be something else
waiting for them, but when no one spoke to them they quietly departed.

The heat was gone, too. Once again, the arena was just a chilly ice
rink that for some reason had a boxing ring set up in the middle.
Streaks of blood remained on the white floor of the ring, but other than

that there was no reminder of what had occurred during the past two nights.

Art Dore closed his briefcase. He walked toward the box office of the arena to check the night's receipts. In the morning he would be on a plane; he had work to do. Dayton was over; he was on his way to find the toughest man in Sioux City, Iowa.

A Wolf in Wolf's Clothing

It is nearing midnight in the $800,000 condominium of Nick Nickolas. We are on the sixty-eighth floor of an elegant high-rise near Lake Michigan in Chicago.

Nickolas, who is forty-one, drinks a Stolichnaya with an orange peel. Across the room, banging balls across the brown felt top of Nickolas's pool table, is one Claudia Mendron. Miss Mendron has been a Playboy Bunny, a Chicago Bears Honey Bear, and a model in a *Playboy* magazine layout entitled "Pro Football's Main Attractions." She is twenty-five and very tan; her blond hair cascades to her shoulders, which are bare. She wears a pair of tight white jeans and a tighter white top. Nickolas pays no attention to her. He is telling a story.

"People talk about women aging worse than men," Nickolas says. "It's the truth! I went back to Oakland, to my twenty-three-year high school reunion. My date happened to be a young lady who was Miss California. And I got to the reunion, and I saw the girl I took to the senior prom back when I was in high school. She looked terrible! I was so embarrassed, I wouldn't even introduce my date to her. I didn't want to admit that I ever actually went out with her. She looked terrible, and me—I never looked better."

Nickolas directs his eyes across the room at Miss Mendron.

"Let's face it," he says. "I wouldn't be with Claudia here if she weighed a hundred and sixty-five pounds. I don't care how pretty she is or how pretty she kisses."

Miss Mendron stops shooting pool and gazes over at Nickolas.

"Right?" Nickolas says.

"Right," she says, beaming.

*   *   *

The nation's social fabric has been embellished in recent years by the arrival of something called the New American Man. In his extreme and exotic form, the New American Man drinks white wine and cries a lot and is so achingly sensitive that he often finds himself quivering. He is constantly searching for the feminine side of his own personality. He is a staunch supporter of feminist theology; in many cases, his wife has left him, but he is secretly proud that she was able to show such strength.

It is instructive and somehow perversely comforting, then, to know that in isolated pockets of male America, men like Nick Nickolas exist. Nickolas is not the New American Man. To be blunt, he is a dinosaur. If the feminine side of Nickolas's personality were ever to reveal itself, Nickolas would probably stomp on it until it was dazed and bleeding.

Nickolas owns a chain of high-ticket fish restaurants, each called Nick's Fishmarket, in Beverly Hills, Honolulu, and Chicago, with another under construction in Houston. He is a burly man (six feet two inches, 225 pounds) with dark hair and brown eyes; he favors western clothes, cowboy hats, and gold jewelry. In a time when even Hugh Hefner supports the Equal Rights Amendment and is showing signs of something of a feminist consciousness, Nickolas is a total throwback to the days of leering playboys and ladies' men; the fantasy he is living out is one that millions of men once openly embraced but have since forsaken out of resignation or what they perceive as heightened awareness. Nickolas seems stuck in the 1950s, and yet his approach appears to be working to perfection for him.

He is constantly surrounded by stunning young women, most of them in their early twenties (Nickolas estimates the number of women he has been romantically involved with to be in the "high hundreds"). He lives in limousines and mirror-walled homes and first-class airplane cabins. He is fond of saying such things as "The reason I like my women young is that the older ones are offended if you call them at three in the morning and say 'Let's go to Hawaii.'"

Men like Nickolas aren't supposed to exist anymore. When he asks a young woman out, he will often put her in his limousine first, give her $500, and tell her to buy some new clothes. ("So she doesn't embarrass me or herself," Nickolas explains. What happens when an outraged modern woman turns him down on such an offer? "It's never happened yet.")

Nickolas is a man with a fifteenth-century sense of honor and a rather wicked temper. If someone insults a woman in his presence, Nickolas has been known to deck the offender, and unfriendly food critics foolish enough to step into a Nick's Fishmarket after writing a negative review have found themselves dragged across their dinner by Nick himself and tossed out into the street. But Nickolas prides himself on being gentle with his women. "I never need to meet another woman in my life," he says. "I get enough new ones coming in just on referrals."

None of this would be of interest, perhaps, if women felt unanimous scorn for Nickolas or simply found him pathetic. But all evidence indicates that plenty of women do not. The women around Nick Nickolas—almost all of them beautiful and, by most objective standards, desirable—seem to want nothing to do with the New American Man, at least as long as Nick is around. On paper, none of Nickolas's routine should work in the new age; in reality, it seldom fails.

"Half of the people who hear about me don't like me," Nickolas says. "We are dealing with envy here. Let's face it, a man who hears about me isn't going to say, 'That Nick Nickolas is a hell of a guy.'"

We are having a late-afternoon drink in Nickolas's condominium. Johnny Paycheck is blasting out of speakers that are built into the walls. Nickolas has gone into his closet (sixty suits, ninety shirts, five hundred ties) and changed from a business suit to jeans, a western shirt open to the waist, and hand-tooled leather cowboy boots that have been cut into bedroom slippers.

"The modern man is a sissy," Nickolas says. "He is defensive, he can't feel good inside about himself, so he becomes afraid of women. He's come to the point where he can't even walk up to a woman and say, 'Hey, how you doin'?' He feels so bad about himself that a little rejection from a woman is going to defeat him.

"You see what I mean? The modern man takes a wimpy approach. He comes on soft, like he's going to get shot down. So he will.

"I'll be in one of my restaurants, and I'll see a pretty lady at the bar. I'll say to the bartender, 'Hi, David, anyone here *Nick* should meet?' I only say it so the woman will know I'm Nick, and I'll see the people who work for me smiling at each other and saying, 'All right! Here he comes! Watch out!'"

Nickolas understands that this kind of talk will generally bring raised eyebrows from people who did not believe that men with his attitudes still exist at this late date. He enjoys eliciting that reaction, and once he is rolling it is difficult to slow him down.

Nickolas on romance: "I don't let a woman move in with me, but I'm not afraid to tell 'em I love 'em. Hell, I've told a woman I love her four hours after I met her. And it's true. What are you supposed to do, wait a year before you tell her? Are you supposed to tell her you 'like her a lot'? We've suppressed the phrase 'I love you' because we're afraid of it. It's one of the prettiest, nicest things you can say to a woman."

Nickolas on the way women gravitate to him: "They hear about me. One of their friends says, 'You may not fall in love with him, but you'll have a good time. You'll go first class, he'll treat you nice, and if you don't want him to jump in your skivvies, he won't.' I've never won any beauty contests, but women tell me, 'When I first met you I never thought I'd end up in the sack with you, but here I am.' I hear that a lot."

Nickolas on the oft-repeated charge that he is afraid of bright women: "Bring 'em on. What am I supposed to do, ask them to fill out a questionnaire before I take them to dinner? I'll admit it, the first thing I'm attracted to is beauty. My life is not centered around what I think. I'm not afraid to say it: I don't need a whole lot of mental stimulation from a woman. Who needs the pressure? You want to debate about Southeast Asia? I don't give a —— about Southeast Asia. Come on, baby, we're going to Greece for two weeks."

And what about the times when Nickolas makes a mistake, when he brings a woman home only to find that they're not hitting it off, that his efforts have been wasted?

"'Sorry, darling, aloha,'" Nickolas says. "'You want to go somewhere, Frankie here will take you in the car. Later.'"

It is considered correct these days to reflexively criticize the world of Nick Nickolas, but it is questionable how wise such a reaction is. In a society that has apparently rejected his values, Nickolas appears to have found delirious happiness. It is easy to denounce Nickolas's way of life and to condemn him for going against the grain of every ideal that enlightened people have come to embrace. It is another thing to admit grudgingly that maybe he has something here. In today's social atmosphere, where everything, at times, seems to have gone wrong between the sexes, most men and women would automatically say that Nickolas does not have the answers—but do *they*?

A more reasonable response to Nickolas is probably a sort of puzzled ambivalence. Yes, he seems too basic and simple to be real, a kind of cutout doll, ready to be propped up to receive the assaults of the people he offends. But how many men can deny—in all honesty— that they would welcome the company of the women to be found at

Nickolas's side? And how many women can deny—when no one's listening—that they feel a sort of fascination at the idea of stepping, however briefly, into Nickolas's strange world, where all the rules are reversed? Sure, it's safe to claim these days that you are repelled by Nickolas's excesses and extremes; it is a little chancier to admit that, after all, you wouldn't mind sharing in some of the things he's managed to give himself. What Nickolas has finally given himself is a private universe that shouldn't work at all but does. And how many people who rail against that are really doing so out of a genuine sense of moral outrage and not out of a frustrated desire to have their share of the pleasures he gets?

Claudia Mendron, the Playboy Bunny and NFL cheerleader, is a woman who has been asked out perhaps a thousand times a year since she was a teenager. Turning men down is a way of life for her. Of Nickolas she says, "I love him the way he is. He's a man's man. He's handsome and gallant and charming and playful and a conglomeration of everything put together.

"Yes, he's macho and aggressive. He's the leader in the relationship. Deep down, I think every woman wants a man like Nick Nickolas. If he were like Phil Donahue or Alan Alda, I don't think I would be interested."

Someone who knows Nickolas well says, "People who hear about Nick thirdhand can be very critical of the way he is. But it's funny: you go into one of his restaurants, and all the men who work there—the waiters, the bartenders—they all seem to be imitating him. I think it's unconscious: they walk the way he walks, talk the way he talks . . . it's as if they're all trying to be little Nicks."

There are people who say that Nickolas really hates women. "Hate them?" he replies. "Women are the greatest motivation in my life. The woman I base all my relationships on is my mother. The way I was raised, in my house the woman was always superior. I wanted my mother to have all the niceties. I had the greatest respect for my mother, and that's carried over to the way I feel about women today."

And now we are at a party in the condominium, given by Nickolas for guests at the National Restaurant Show. Nickolas is in a chocolate-brown tuxedo, with no tie; the ever-present cowboy boots are on his feet.

A woman, slightly tipsy, makes her way across the room until she is at Nickolas's side. It is clear that they have met before.

"I've thought about it, Nick, and I've decided it's worth the ten pounds," she says.

"Hey," Nickolas says with a smile, "great."

"I mean it," she says. "It's absolutely worth the ten pounds."

"Terrific," Nickolas says.

Someone else, overhearing this, looks puzzled.

"Nick told me that I could stay here with him some night," the woman explains. "But he said that I'd have to lose ten pounds first."

There is, for the moment, total silence.

"So I'm going to lose the ten pounds, Nick," she says.

"Hey," Nickolas says with a shrug and the flash of a grin. "Make it eight."

Song of the Powder Room

It was early in the evening, still before the dinner hour. The place is called Zorine's, a fancy private club that gets regular mention in the gossip columns. On this, a weeknight, business was slow; the crowds would come later, after nine o'clock, when the solid wall of sound caused by disco dancing records would wash over the club.

Now, though, it was almost deserted. At a piano by the bar, a musician named Jim Burke played cocktail music. He, too, would leave when it was time for the disco records to begin.

A visitor, who had never been inside Zorine's before, sat nursing a drink at the bar. He looked over the empty tables, trying to decide whether to stay and wait for the throngs. And then it happened.

A woman came out of the ladies' room. She was wearing a uniform and an apron; it was obvious that she was the washroom attendant. She looked around the club, as if to confirm that there weren't too many people she might bother.

She whispered something to the piano player. He nodded. He began to play a light jazz tune. The washroom attendant started to sing along with him. Softly at first, and then she picked up his rhythm and began to sing louder. The song was "It Ain't Necessarily So," and by the middle of the first chorus she was standing with her feet spread apart, her arms stretched outward, and she was belting out the lyrics in a most astonishing manner.

There is only one word to describe the purity and sweetness of that lady's voice: perfect. The visitor at the bar had heard Ella Fitzgerald in live performance once, and he had heard Billie Holiday on records. Outside of Miss Fitzgerald and Miss Holiday, though, he had never heard a voice in a class with this washroom lady who was wailing out her song in the empty club.

She completed the song, and said something quietly to the piano player. He hit a note, and she began "Summertime." It was the same thing all over again; beyond her raw talent there was something else; there was that artist's sense of what it means to be a star. She wasn't merely singing, she was performing. The range and authority and clarity of her voice were astounding. She sang "Summertime," and "Georgia on My Mind," and "Bye Bye Blackbird," and "God Bless the Child," and as the magnificence of her voice rebounded off the walls in the vacant club, the only thing to do was to stare at her and wonder how this could be happening.

After about fifteen minutes, she halted. She thanked the piano player, and headed back toward the washroom.

The visitor at the bar stopped her and introduced himself. He thanked her for her songs.

"Oh, that was just for myself," she said. "I do it sometimes if it's not crowded, before the dance records start."

The visitor asked her who she was.

"I'm Millie Gay," she said. "I hope I didn't bother you. It's just that sometimes I'll be sitting there in the ladies' room, and I'll hear the piano and I'll have to come out. I really can't help it."

She talked some more with the visitor, and she looked as if she was weighing whether to tell him something. Finally she did, and her story came pouring out.

Back in the early 1950s, Millie said, she and her sister Evelyn were under contract to Savoy Records. They were gospel singers, and they put out a dozen singles and one album.

"In 1951, I performed in Carnegie Hall," she said. "It was the first time gospel singers had ever sung in Carnegie Hall. I was on the bill with Mahalia Jackson and the Clara Ward Singers. It was quite an evening. I'll never forget it."

Like many black performers in those days, however, Millie Gay never received the money that was due her. She is forty-seven years old now, and when her husband—who was working as a doorman in the Rush Street area—heard about the opening of Zorine's, he arranged for Millie to get the 6:30 P.M.-to-1:00 A.M. job as ladies' room attendant.

"It's a nice job," she said. "My responsibilities are to keep the ladies' room straight, all neat and tidy for the girls who come in. I keep the toilet tissues in order, and make sure that there are towels nice and handy, and make sure that the toilets are tidy."

She noticed that some people were beginning to come into the club.

"I'd better get back to the ladies' room," Millie said. "It's going to be crowded soon, and I'm supposed to stay in there. The records will be playing before too long, and the people are going to want to start dancing."

The visitor asked Millie how she passed the hours and hours when the disco records were playing and she was sitting in the ladies' room.

She looked out over the dance floor.

"It's all right," she said. "When they're dancing out here, I'm singing in there."

Something Blue

She was supposed to get married. This was the afternoon. She had planned it all. The ceremony, the guests, the reception— Jeannie was going to be a bride, and as corny as it may sound these days, that is all she ever wanted to be.

Then he walked out on her. His name was John; he was a medical student, and she had come to Chicago six years ago to be with him. "When I get done with school," he had said, and she had waited. She had gone to work at Sears, as a copywriter for the catalog, and although she was not in love with Chicago, she was in love with John. Everything she did pointed to this day.

So the afternoon was here, and Jeannie was not in a church. Instead, she was in her one-room studio apartment on the fifth floor of an apartment building in New Town. It was a sultry day; she had pulled the white shades down, to keep out the heat and to block out the view of Broadway to the west.

"It was supposed to be kind of funny," Jeannie said.

That's what it was supposed to be. She had sent out invitations to her closest women friends at Sears, saying that she "requests the humiliation of your presence" on the occasion of her "jilting at the altar. . . . There will be a reception only, as the church ceremony originally scheduled at this time has been canceled."

Explaining it later, she would say, "It seemed like a good way to avoid being by myself and crying all afternoon. . . . I know it sounds like kind of a sick idea, but I thought maybe I could laugh about it. If I made fun of it, I wouldn't have time to cry."

The guests had arrived; Kim was there, and Louise, and Zahava, and Jo, and Sheila. They were all, like Jeannie, in their mid-twenties (Jeannie was twenty-four); she greeted them at the door wearing a bridal bonnet. New York State pink champagne was in Jeannie's refrigerator.

Linda Ronstadt, on Jeannie's stereo, sang "I Guess It Doesn't Matter Anymore." The women arranged themselves on the couch, on the chairs, on the floor. One, Zahava, was wearing a bridesmaid's dress, and flowers in her hair. There was a wedding cake, with figurines of a bride and groom; the head of the groom had been cut off. It had seemed funny, during the planning.

The women drank.

"Here," said Kim, handing Jeannie a gift-wrapped package.

"You weren't supposed to do this," Jeannie said, but all of the women had.

She started to open the present.

"If you break the ribbon, that's how many kids you're going to have," Kim said.

"You're supposed to line your drawers with this paper," one of the other women said.

"You guys . . ." Jeannie said.

There were more presents. Each had a card attached. "In the Loss of Your Loved One," said one card. "Thoughts of Sympathy." "Wedding Wishes for the Bride Not to Be," the word "Not" written in with ball-point pen.

"I had to cancel my subscription to *Bride's Magazine* . . ." Jeannie said.

"Oh, Jeannie," said Shelia.

". . . but it was too late," Jeannie said. She lifted up her champagne glass. "Here's to my poor mother. She had to cancel her subscription to *Bride's Magazine*, too. My mother feels like such a loser."

For the first hour or so, there were plenty of laughs, as the presents were opened. Then the laughter died as the women stayed together in the little room.

"When did he leave town?" Jo asked.

"John?" Jeannie said. "He left on Tuesday. But he called me this morning."

"He did?" three of the women said at once.

Jeannie nodded.

"What did he say?" Louise said.

Jeannie shrugged, and began talking about something else.

There were more Ronstadt songs: "When Will I Be Loved," "You're No Good," "Time Heals." Zahava, the only married woman in the room, said:

"Being married is fun, in its own way. Being single is fun, in its own way too."

"You guys don't have to say that," Jeannie said.

"No, really," Zahava said.

Jeannie went to the kitchen to bring out some food. By the wall telephone was a list of numbers: "John's Folks," "John's Hospital." Taped to the refrigerator was a picture of an attractive woman in a bikini, with the handwritten notation, "Soon! You Can Resemble This!!! Stop, Think, and Don't Eat!"

Jeannie went back to the main room, where the other women were waiting with a serious present for her, complete with a serious card:

"He's the fool. He doesn't know what he's missing. Maybe someday he'll realize his BIG error."

"You guys have made this one of the nicest days of my life," Jeannie said.

"We're going to miss you," Louise said.

"I'll miss you, too," Jeannie said. "I can't really believe I'm leaving."

"Well, Jeannie," Louise said, "when you marry some famous senator, we'll all come down to Washington for the wedding."

"Really," Jeannie said. "I don't want to let you guys down twice."

"It's too hot today for a wedding, anyway," Kim said.

There was silence.

"You know, I was born and raised to be an independent woman, a career woman," Jeannie said. "But who wants to be alone for the rest of their lives?"

"Stop it, Jeannie," Zahava said. "You'll get married."

The women toasted one another.

"I heard there's a good Gary Cooper movie on tonight," Jeannie said.

Limo

Somewhere on the Indiana Toll Road, heading east, the sound of the FM radio station began to fade. This was a disappointment; the disc jockey for WVPE in Elkhart had just been exhorting his listeners to send in ten dollars each in an effort to help the station go stereo, and I was listening for an address so I could mail my money.

"Julius, we'd better find another station," I said.

My voice echoed in the vast back seat of the double-length, jet-black Lincoln Continental limousine. Outside the windows of the limo, the cornfields of Indiana were whizzing by.

"Yes, sir," came the voice of Julius Person, my chauffeur. A Toyota pulled up next to us, like a Cessna buzzing a 747, and its occupants tried to stare into our window. But I did not look back; I just read my *Wall Street Journal* while Julius searched for another rock station.

It had started as one of those dares that you give to yourself.

The air traffic controllers' strike was in its first days; I had a reporting trip scheduled to central Ohio, and getting there from Chicago in the confusion of the strike's beginning was not an appetizing thought.

It was to be a four-day trip; an eight-hour drive from Chicago. The situation called for something to break the monotony of the Indiana Toll Road and the Ohio Turnpike. My idea of the greatest luxury in this life has always been the chauffeured limousine; once in a while I would even treat myself to a limo ride to O'Hare International Airport. But a limousine for eight straight hours through heartland Illinois, Indiana, and Ohio? And for four days in central Ohio during the trip?

The owners of Chicago Limousine Service said the tariff would be $1,200, plus the chauffeur's hotel and meal expenses in Ohio, plus a suitable tip.

You live once.

*   *   *

Julius Person, fifty-five, was a dapper, compact man in a black suit and a chauffeur's cap who would have looked perfect as a host at Harlem's Cotton Club in the Twenties. He had my newspaper waiting on the back seat when I came out the door of my apartment building. He opened the trunk; his own suitcase was already there.

The car was enormous; it had been lengthened at a custom body shop that specializes in stretch limousines. If you lay down with your head against the back seat, your feet would not reach all the way to the front seat. All during our drive out of Chicago we were the object of gapers. But it was not until we hit the Indiana Toll Road—"Main Street of the Midwest," as its slogan goes—that the delirious ridiculousness of this excess became clear. Virtually every car on the road tried to check us out; it was as if Lyndon Johnson had suddenly been set down on the pavement of northern Indiana.

I looked out the windows, and the scenery told me that this was something out of *Penrod*. Pure farmland all around; two lanes this way, two lanes that way, and the Knute Rockne Service Area looming up ahead. But Julius's radio jarred me back to the Eighties. A disc jockey had asked his listeners to suggest a name for the station's women's softball team, and those listeners, on an open line, were responding:

"The Bush Leaguers."

"The Ball Busters."

"The Pitching Mounds."

"The Periods."

Julius turned around in the front seat. "That air conditioning cool enough for you, Mr. Greene?" he said.

If you have never pulled up for lunch at the Holiday Inn in Perrysburg, Ohio, with your chauffeur at the wheel of your limo, there is no preparing you for it.

The folks at the front desk lined up and stared as Julius and I made our way into the dining room. All during the trip thus far, Julius had been as silent as possible; I understood instinctively that part of his professionalism was maintaining the psychic distance between himself and his passenger. And he was even extending this to our lunch; we might be sharing a table, but he was not going to impose himself unless asked.

Finally I realized this was getting absurd. "So Julius," I said. "How is that tuna fish sandwich?"

"It's very good," Julius said. He nodded for emphasis.

I asked him if an out-of-town assignment like this one was unusual for him.

"I do it once in a while," he said. "The last one was taking Pearl Bailey down to St. Louis, and then over to Indianapolis."

"Was she singing or something?" I said.

"No," Julius said. "She was promoting a movie. I believe she played a duck."

We passed through Fostoria, Ohio, on Route 23. Ace's Body Shop and the Fraternal Order of Eagles lodge and Ron Smith Realty came lazily into view; Julius had slowed down to heed the speed limit. There was some construction on the road. The flagman was a teenage girl; she saw us and said something into a hand radio, and when we reached the end of the construction three minutes later the other flag-man—also a girl—was smiling and waving at us.

We were going to be coming close to the place where my parents live. I had Julius detour to their neighborhood. He carefully backed the limousine into their driveway. He waited in the car while I visited inside.

Later, I would learn that one of my parents' neighbors had tele-phoned another:

"Is everything all right at the Greene house? No, I know every-thing's not all right at the Greene house. There's a hearse in the drive-way, and young Bob is in from Chicago looking very grim."

Why I will never be a good rich person, Part One:

Every time a carful of people would look in the back seat to see whose limo it was, I would feel guilty for letting them down. Of all the people they might have hoped for, I felt it was my fault that it was only me.

Why I will never be a good rich person, Part Two:

When we reached our destination and stopped for the night, Julius dropped me at the Hyatt Regency and told me that he was going to go get a room at a cheap hotel that I knew to be in a seedy part of town. He told me he would call me in my room as soon as he got there. I watched him drive away in that big limo, and all I could think about all evening was what a crummy deal it was that I got to stay at the Hyatt and Julius had to look for a dump. It was clearly what he was used to on trips like these; he accepted it, and if I really belonged in a limousine, I would have too.

In the morning Julius was waiting outside the Hyatt with the *Wall Street Journal* and the local newspaper in the back seat. He was smiling.

"Mr. Greene," he said, "I believe I have found us the hardest rock station in the entire United States." And as we cruised through central Ohio, the sound of Foreigner singing "Women" reverberated inside the car.

In the course of my reporting, I met two working mothers named Elaine Shayne and Beanie Weiss. They were admiring the limousine; Mrs. Shayne said she had to go to the K mart, and Julius and I exchanged glances. Why not?

So it was that Mrs. Shayne and Mrs. Weiss pulled up to the local K mart in the Lincoln Continental limousine. Julius stopped at the front door of the store. He fairly leapt from the driver's seat, circled around to the back seat, opened the door, and, with a flourish, helped the women alight from the car.

A crowd was gathering. For a moment they were silent, but soon shouts broke out.

"Where are you from?" a voice demanded.

"'Queen for a Day,'" said Beanie Weiss. The two of them entered the store.

Julius stood sentinel by the limo. "Those women don't own this limousine," someone said. "If they could afford a limousine like this, they wouldn't shop at the K mart."

Julius smiled. "The reason they can afford a limousine like this is that they shop at the K mart," he said.

I don't know what the best moment of the four days was. It may have been when I was dropping in at the local newspaper office and there was a commotion at the window of the city room. I thought that someone must have dropped dead on the street down below, but when I joined the others at the window I saw that everyone was looking out at Julius, who was being interviewed by a young reporter the city editor had sent.

It may have been at a bar late at night when, at closing time, I walked out with the other customers and Julius was waiting—in that suit and cap—with the back door open.

It may have been when a local cop cruised by Julius's parked car four times, going slower every time. Because Julius was a black stranger in a white Ohio town, I thought he might be in for some petty harassment. But the policeman finally pulled to a stop and, in a voice full of politeness, said:

"Sir, what kind of mileage does that car get?"

"Very good," Julius said, in a serious tone. "Very good."

It was a little like being a kid at an amusement park. I suppose if you got to ride the roller coaster every day, you would get jaded by it. But when you're new at it, you think the kick will never go away. I suppose, somewhere, there are men who step into their limousines every morning and truly don't give it a second thought. And I suppose I will never be one of them.

On the way back to Chicago, Julius said from the front seat:

"Did you see that pretty girl back there who was hitchhiking?"

For a moment I considered it. But we had a long way to go through Indiana, and this was supposed to be my fantasy, not hers.

I had to call my office. So, at a truck stop outside of Indianapolis, Julius pulled up to a phone booth and, beside the highway, I made the call as traffic slowed down to look at the limo.

When I got back in and we were on our way again, I asked Julius if he ever got used to every person he passed gawking at him.

"It doesn't take you long to get used to it," he said. "I've been doing this a long time. And you learn right away that they're not looking at you. They just want to see who's in the back seat."

I asked him if he didn't ever just drive the limo around on his own, so that he could savor in relative privacy some of whatever it was the car gave off.

"I can't do that," he said. "The car doesn't belong to me. It belongs to the company."

"Then you don't drive this on your own?" I asked.

I could only see the back of his head.

"No," he said. "I drive a Gremlin."

The last few hours through Indiana were smooth. Julius's radio continued to provide a sound track; an Indianapolis newscaster informed us that a local man had just been arrested and charged with murdering his wife and children, and then John Lennon was singing "A Day in the Life."

On the outskirts of Chicago, traffic began to back up on the express-way. It was rush hour.

"Julius," I said, "do you ever run into any of your passengers again?"

He was still staring straight ahead. "I just drive wherever they tell me to drive, sir," he said.

We rode in silence to my home; I ran in and dropped off my suit-case, and then Julius headed in the direction of my office. I still had time to check the phone messages.

We both got out in front of the office building. I signed the receipt for the trip, and then Julius and the limousine were back in Michigan Avenue traffic, and soon they were lost. You would think after all these years you would forget what it feels like when the roller-coaster ride is over. You'd be surprised how quickly it comes back to you.

Night Callers

Loneliness is the great American epidemic. More than any disease, it insinuates itself into the lives of people wealthy and poor, old and young. It is an affliction of which people are ashamed; they are willing to admit almost anything before they will admit they are lonely.

It makes itself known in many ways, and probably no way is seen more graphically than Audrey Loehr sees it.

Mrs. Loehr is sixty-two years old; she is an employee of one of the giant oil companies—a company with its name on the pumps of gas stations all over the world.

Mrs. Loehr lives and works in Tulsa. Her job is a simple one. It is this:

The oil company has a policy that, on any charge over thirty-five dollars, a gas station attendant must call a toll-free number to get the credit card approved. The attendant has the 800 number posted inside the station; he calls it, and someone on the other end answers, and he reads the card number and the person on the other end punches that number into a computer to make sure the card has not been lost or stolen.

Mrs. Loehr is one of the people on the other end. The credit card center is located in Tulsa; it is open twenty-four hours a day, 365 days a year, so there are always employees—almost all of them women— available to answer the phone when a gas station attendant anywhere in the country has a big charge to check out.

Mrs. Loehr says that there is a pattern to the calls. Most of the time they are straightforward business calls—gas dealers dialing to confirm a charge card.

But on weekends—Fridays, Saturdays, and Sundays—late at night, the obscene calls will begin.

Mrs. Loehr will answer the phone, and, from off in the distance, a man's voice will say something aggressively sexual to her. The voice will make lewd suggestions, will ask improper questions. The voice will say things that most people would never say to other people face-to-face.

She has figured it out:

"At that time of the night, most gas stations are manned by only one person," she said. "It's usually a young man who has been assigned to work all night. He's alone there, and it's dark, and there's no one to talk to."

So what the attendants will do—in Los Angeles, in Houston, in St. Louis, in New York, in Chicago—is call the toll-free number, the one that is posted at the station. And when they hear a woman's voice, they will speak of sex to it.

"It's very sad," she said. "Some of the young girls who work here think it's funny, but I don't think they really understand what loneliness is. When I pick up the phone and hear one of these men start up again, all I can think about is how alone they must be to resort to something like that."

She said there is often a tone of desperation in the men's voices; the men want the female voice to stay on the line.

"They will say, 'Keep talking, keep talking, don't hang up,'" she said. "They know so little about women; the idea of women frustrates them so much that the only contact they can have is to say these things to a stranger's voice.

"If they need professional help, we can't help them. We're just credit-card checkers, and our supervisor has told us to hang up as soon as we know it's that kind of a call. He says that they need guidance, and it would do us no good to try to talk to them, and I know he's probably right."

Mrs. Loehr feels that she has come to understand something about the young men: "They must have so little in their lives; can you imagine standing in a gas station somewhere and dialing that number, just so they can say those things to a female voice?

"I am sixty-two years old, and I don't sound like a young girl. The men must know that. And yet just because I'm a woman, that's enough. It makes you so sad.

"There's nothing humorous about it, and there's nothing sexual, other than the words. It's just such a sign of their loneliness. They are so unimaginative in the things they say, and their voices tell you more than the words do. The voices are voices of men who are so unsure of themselves that they have to resort to this."

She has sometimes thought what the lonely young men might do other than mouth the obscenities: recite a love poem, a proverb from a foreign philosopher, a quote from the Bible. As far as she knows, none ever has; one caller, though, always whispers "I love you" just before he hangs up.

"I'm just sorry about it," she said. "I wish in their own lives they had a way to get a woman's attention. It would be nice if the gas stations could afford to hire couples to work the all-night shifts; it would make me feel glad to think each of those men had a real, live woman to talk to.

"Sometimes they will try to personalize you. One man said to me, 'You sound tall.' I could imagine him, alone in that gas station somewhere, fantasizing about a tall woman who would talk to him."

She said that she fears something has happened to the masculinity of American men; something that makes them so afraid of women that the only way they can deal with them is to make such a call, over the miles.

She said that there is no real answer; loneliness is a part of so many lives, and it is her fate to work in a job where it comes ringing so often. "I just answer the calls," she said. "When I find out that it's one of those calls, I hang up. But I always silently wish that the men find inner peace, and that they somehow get better."

We Will Pay Cash for Your Class Ring

The advertisement in the newspaper caught her eye. Perhaps it was the drawing of the high school class ring; perhaps it was the headline:

WANTED . . . 25,000 class rings needed . . . We pay cash! Paying up to $125, all cash!!!

The ad had been placed by the American Gold and Silver Co., Inc., of St. Louis; the company's representatives had come to town and set up shop, for four days, in twelve motels around the city. The rest of the ad copy explained why:

We have a buyer who has put in an order for 25,000 class rings. We desperately need to fill this order as soon as possible, so for the remaining part of this week and weekend American Gold and Silver will be offering a special premium on all class rings. . . .

She read the ad twice. She is thirty-seven years old; her name is Carol Andrysiak. She went to her closet.

The ring was in an old box, near the bottom of a pile of other boxes. A gold band, with a blue stone surrounded by white mother-of-pearl, and the school crest in the center. Bremen Community High School, Class of '61.

"Sell the old class ring," she said to herself. "A hundred twenty-five bucks. Okey doke."

She put it in her purse.

On the weekend, she drove to the Holiday Inn in a nearby suburb. The desk clerk said the American Gold and Silver people were in room 107.

There were perhaps fifteen people lined up in the corridor. She stood at the end of the line.

The woman in front of her was holding a baby in her arms. They started a conversation. The woman with the baby said that she had been divorced, and now she had to raise the child. She said she had been a pompom girl in high school; "I thought life was going to be a piece of cake," she said.

Up a few feet in the line was a young couple. She talked to them, too; the man had just been laid off his job, and now the two of them were going to sell their class rings. They wanted the rings, they said, but the recession made this day necessary.

She began to roll the ring around in her hand. Slowly she moved closer to the door. All the while she was thinking.

She had had the dream back in high school, too. Back when she had bought that ring, she was going to get married and live in the suburbs and have two children and somehow, in her spare time, become a famous writer.

She had married, but that was long over. There had never been children. Now she lived alone in a studio apartment in the city. The novels had never quite got written; she worked as a secretary in a busy office building.

She clutched the ring in her palm, and she started to wonder what had happened to all of these people in line. What had happened to the hopeful boys and girls in high school, who had purchased their class rings with such pride? Here they all were, well into the mainstream of their lives, having to sell a piece of yesterday to make it today.

Her thoughts were interrupted. She was first in line. The door to room 107 opened, and she was escorted in. The door closed again behind her.

There was a man at a table, a jeweler's scale in front of him. Another man—a plainclothes security guard—stood to one side.

It took maybe three minutes. The man weighed her ring, then examined it through an eyepiece. He offered her $45.

She asked him about the $125 offer, and he said the ring was not heavy enough.

She took the $45 in cash. The man had her sign a receipt. When she returned to the hallway, the line had grown.

Now that the ring was gone, she couldn't stop thinking of high school. The romantic dreams that all seemed possible; the endless opportunities she had seen ahead . . . she wondered what would become of her ring.

It was a good thing she did not wonder too hard. For the newspaper advertisement had not been quite accurate. "We have a buyer who has put in an order for 25,000 class rings. . . ." Yes, but the buyer did not want to use them to make new class rings.

The rings were going to be melted down. It was as simple as that. Gold has gone up so much in price since the days that people now in their thirties and forties and fifties bought class rings that it is worth it for American Gold and Silver to travel around the country buying them up. This four-day trip to Chicago would bring in some 3,000 class rings; all to be melted, all to be sold to a gold refinery.

Sometimes, the day after a man or woman has sold a ring, they will call the American Gold and Silver offices in St. Louis and say they made a terrible mistake. The memories of the ring meant too much; could they buy it back?

And Irwin J. Reif, the vice-president of the company, would have to tell them that it was not possible. All the rings had been mixed together; they could not be retrieved. Reif himself, who had bought his own high school class ring back in 1932, would never sell his; "I'm too sentimental. To me it means my high school days—the songs, the girls. . . . What a story every one of those rings could tell. But I guess if you need the money . . ."

She walked out of the Holiday Inn. It was a hot summer afternoon. In her car, she tuned the radio to a country and western station. "Oh, I really liked what I was," she thought, and then she didn't think anymore.

Fifteen

"This would be excellent, to go in the ocean with this thing," says Dave Gembutis, fifteen.

He is looking at a $170 Sea Cruiser raft.

"Great," says his companion, Dan Holmes, also fifteen.

This is at Herman's World of Sporting Goods, in the middle of the Woodfield Mall in Schaumburg, Illinois.

The two of them keep staring at the raft. It is unlikely that they will purchase it. For one thing, Dan has only twenty dollars in his pocket, Dave five dollars. For another thing—ocean voyages aside—neither of them is even old enough to drive. Dave's older sister, Kim, has dropped them off at the mall. They will be taking the bus home.

Fifteen. What a weird age to be male. Most of us have forgotten about it, or have idealized it. But when you are fifteen . . . well, things tend to be less than perfect.

You can't drive. You are only a freshman in high school. The girls your age look older than you and go out with upperclassmen who have cars. You probably don't shave. You have nothing to do on the weekends.

So how do you spend your time? In the 1980s, most likely at a mall. Woodfield is an enclosed shopping center sprawling over 2.25 million square feet in northern Illinois. There are 230 stores at Woodfield, and on a given Saturday those stores are cruised in and out by thousands of teenagers killing time. Today two of those teenagers are Dave Gembutis and Dan Holmes.

Dave is wearing a purple Rolling Meadows High School Mustangs windbreaker over a gray M*A*S*H T-shirt, jeans, and Nike running shoes. He has a red plastic spoon in his mouth, and will keep it there for most of the afternoon. Dan is wearing a white Ohio State Buckeyes T-shirt, jeans, and Nike running shoes.

We are in the Video Forum store. Paul Simon and Art Garfunkel are singing "Wake Up Little Susie" from their Central Park concert on four television screens. Dave and Dan have already been wandering around Woodfield for an hour.

"There's not too much to do at my house," Dan says to me.

"Here we can at least look around," Dave says. "At home I don't know what we'd do."

"Play catch or something," Dan says. "Here there's lots of things to see."

"See some girls or something, start talking," Dave says.

I ask them how they would start a conversation with girls they had never met.

"Ask them what school they're from," Dan says. "Then if they say Arlington Heights High School or something, you can say, 'Oh, I know somebody from there.'"

I ask them how important meeting girls is to their lives.

"About forty-five percent," Dan says.

"About half your life," Dave says.

"Half is girls," Dan says. "Half is going out for sports."

* * *

An hour later, Dave and Dan have yet to meet any girls. They have seen a girl from their own class at Rolling Meadows High, but she is walking with an older boy, holding his hand. Now we are in the Woodfield McDonald's. Dave is eating a McRib sandwich, a small fries, and a small Coke. Dan is eating a cheeseburger, a small fries, and a medium root beer.

In here, the dilemma is obvious. The McDonald's is filled with girls who are precisely as old as Dave and Dan. The girls are wearing eye shadow, are fully developed, and generally look as if they could be dating the Green Bay Packers. Dave and Dan, on the other hand . . . well, when you're a fifteen-year-old boy, you look like a fifteen-year-old boy.

"They go with the older guys who have the cars," Dan says.

"It makes them more popular," Dave says.

"My ex-girlfriend is seeing a junior," Dan says.

I ask him what happened.

"Well, I was in Florida over spring vacation," he says. "And when I got back I heard that she was at Cinderella Rockefella one night, and she was dancing with this guy, and she liked him, and he drove her home and stuff."

"She two-timed him," Dave says.

"The guy's on the basketball team," Dan says.

I ask Dan what he did about it.

"I broke up with her," he says, as if I had asked the stupidest question in the world.

I ask him how he did it.

"Well, she was at her locker," he says. "She was working the combination. And I said, 'Hey, Linda, I want to break up.' And she was opening her locker door and she just nodded her head yes. And I said, 'I hear you had a good time while I was gone, but I had a better time in Florida.'"

I ask him if he feels bad about it.

"Well, I feel bad," he says. "But a lot of guys told me, 'I heard you broke up with her. Way to be.'"

"It's too bad the Puppy Palace isn't open," Dan says.

"They're remodeling," Dave says.

We are walking around the upper level of Woodfield. I ask them why they would want to go to the Puppy Palace.

"The dogs are real cute and you feel sorry for them," Dan says.

＊　＊　＊

We are in a fast-food restaurant called the Orange Bowl. Dave is eating a frozen concoction called an O-Joy. They still have not met any girls.

"I feel like I'd be wasting my time if I sat at home," Dan says. "If it's Friday or Saturday and you sit home, it's considered . . . low."

"Coming to the mall is about all there is," Dave says. "Until we can drive."

"Then I'll cruise," Dan says. "Look for action a little farther away from my house, instead of just riding my bike around."

"When you're sixteen, you can do anything," Dave says. "You can go all the way across town."

"When you have to ride your bike . . ." Dan says. "When it rains, it ruins everything."

In the J. C. Penney store, the Penney Fashion Carnival is under way. Wally the Clown is handing out favors to children, but Dave and Dan are watching the young female models parade onto a stage in bathing suits.

"Just looking is enough for me," Dan says.

Dave suggests that they head out back into the mall and pick out some girls to wave to. I ask why.

"Well, see, even if they don't wave back, you might see them later in the day," Dan says. "And then they might remember that you waved at them, and you can meet them."

We are at the Cookie Factory. These guys eat approximately every twenty minutes.

It is clear that Dan is attracted to the girl behind the counter. He walks up, and his voice is slower and about half an octave lower than before.

The tone of voice is going to have to carry the day, because the words are not all that romantic:

"Can I have a chocolate-chip cookie?"

The girl does not even look up as she wraps the cookie in tissue paper.

Dan persists. The voice might be Clark Gable's:

"What do they cost?"

The girl is still looking down.

"Forty-seven," she says and takes his money, still looking away, and we move on.

* * *

Dave and Dan tell me that there are lots of girls at Woodfield's indoor ice-skating rink. It costs money to get inside, but they lead me to an exit door, and when a woman walks out we slip into the rink. It is chilly in here, but only three people are on the ice.

"It's not time for open skating yet," Dan says. "This is all private lessons."

"Not much in here," Dave says.

We sit on benches. I ask them if they wish they were older.

"Well," Dan says, "when you get there, you look back and you remember. Like I'm glad that I'm not in the fourth or fifth grade now. But I'm glad I'm not twenty-five, either."

"Once in a while I'm sorry I'm not twenty-one," Dave says. "There's not much you can do when you're fifteen. This summer I'm going to caddy and try to save some money."

"Yeah," Dan says. "I want to save up for a dirt bike."

"Right now, being fifteen is starting to bother me a little bit," Dave says. "Like when you have to get your parents to drive you to Homecoming with a girl."

I ask him how that works.

"Well, your mom is in the front seat driving," he says. "And you're in the back seat with your date."

I ask him how he feels about that.

"It's embarrassing," he says. "Your date understands that there's nothing you can do about it, but it's still embarrassing."

Dave says he wants to go to Pet World.

"I think they closed it down," Dan says, but we head in that direction anyway.

I ask them what the difference is between Pet World and the Puppy Palace.

"They've got snakes and fish and another assortment of dogs," Dan says. "But not as much as the Puppy Palace."

When we arrive, Pet World is, indeed, boarded up.

We are on the upper level of the mall. Dave and Dan have spotted two girls sitting on a bench directly below them, on the mall's main level.

"Whistle," Dan says. Dave whistles, but the girls keep talking.

"Dave, wave to them and see if they look," Dan says.

"They aren't looking," Dave says.

"There's another one over there," Dan says.

"Where?" Dave says.

"Oh, that's a mother," Dan says. "She's got her kid with her."

They return their attention to the two downstairs.

Dan calls to them: "Would you girls get the dollar I just dropped?"

The girls look up

"Just kidding," Dan says.

The girls resume their conversation.

"I think they're laughing," Dan says.

"What are you going to do when the dumb girls won't respond," Dave says.

"At least we tried," Dan says.

I ask him what response would have satisfied him.

"The way we would have known that we succeeded," he says, "they'd have looked up here and started laughing."

The boys keep staring at the two girls.

"Ask her to look up," Dan says. "Ask her what school they go to."

"I did," Dave says. "I did."

The two boys lean over the railing.

"Bye, girls," Dave yells.

"See you later," Dan yells.

The girls do not look up.

"Too hard," Dan says. "Some girls are stuck on themselves, if you know what I mean by that."

We go to a store called the Foot Locker, where all the salespeople are dressed in striped referee's shirts.

"Dave!" Dan says. "Look at this! Seventy bucks!" He holds up a pair of New Balance running shoes. Both boys shake their heads.

We move on to a store called Passage to China. A huge stuffed tiger is placed by the doorway. There is a PLEASE DO NOT TOUCH sign attached to it. Dan rubs his hand over the tiger's back. "This would look so great in my room," he says.

We head over to Alan's TV and Stereo. Two salesmen ask the boys if they are interested in buying anything, so they go back outside and look at the store's window. A color television set is tuned to a baseball game between the Chicago Cubs and the Pittsburgh Pirates.

They watch for five minutes. The sound is muted, so they cannot hear the announcers.

"I wish they'd show the score," Dave says.

They watch for five minutes more.

"Hey, Dave," Dan says. "You want to go home?"

"I guess so," Dave says.

They do. We wave goodbye. I watch them walk out of the mall toward the bus stop. I wish them girls, dirt bikes, puppies, and happiness.

Jesus on a Tortilla

It was a hot New Mexico morning. Mrs. Maria Rubio was making burritos for her husband's lunch. The husband, Eduardo, was still in bed.

Mrs. Rubio was working with the tortillas, rolling them around the ingredients. She had rolled two of the tortillas into burritos, and was preparing to roll the third, when she looked down at the tortilla. She gasped and spoke aloud.

"It is Jesus Christ!" she said.

She was referring to a pattern on the tortilla, made by a series of skillet burns. She was convinced that the skillet burns formed a picture of Jesus. She determined that this was a miracle.

She ran to her daughter, Rosie. Rosie looked at the tortilla and said, "It is Jesus."

Mrs. Rubio took the tortilla to her sister, Margarita Porras. Mrs. Porras said, "I think it's Jesus, too."

She took the tortilla to the bedroom. Her husband examined the tortilla and said, "It's Jesus, all right."

Mrs. Rubio called a family friend, Mike Salmon.

"She was crying," Salmon recalls. "She said that there was the image of Jesus on her tortilla, and she thought that perhaps God was punishing her. I had her sister get on the phone, and her sister said, 'I have seen it, and it looks like Jesus.' "

By now the group knew they would have to do something.

They decided to have the tortilla blessed.

Carrying the tortilla very carefully, they walked to the Our Lady of Guadalupe Church, across the street from the Rubios' home. The Rubios live in the small New Mexico town of Lake Arthur, two hundred miles south of Albuquerque. When they got to the church, they found that the pastor was not there; he serves three churches in the area, and alternates among them.

So, still guarding the tortilla, they got into the Rubios' 1968 Chevrolet and drove the seventeen miles to the city of Dexter. There, at the Church of the Immaculate Conception, was the Reverend Joyle Finnigan.

Mrs. Rubio explained about the image of Jesus appearing in the tortilla.

Father Finnigan examined it.

"I think this is just a coincidence," he said.

"It is not a coincidence," Mrs. Rubio said. "I have been rolling burritos for twenty-one years, and this is the first time the face of Jesus ever appeared in a tortilla."

So, reluctantly, Father Finnigan blessed the tortilla. He warned Mrs. Rubio that if she tried to save it, it would undoubtedly get moldy, even if she kept it in the refrigerator.

But Mrs. Rubio had different plans for the tortilla. She drove back to her home, and placed it in a plastic frame, covered with glass. Beneath the tortilla she placed a mass of cotton, giving the appearance that Jesus was floating on a cloud.

She built a small shrine to the tortilla, placing it on a table and erecting a makeshift chapel around it.

"This is a miracle," she announced to her friends. "It is meant to change my life."

She resigned her job as a maid, and said that she would be tending to the tortilla full-time. Her husband kept his job as a farm worker.

Soon the word spread about the tortilla with the face of Jesus. People began to come to Mrs. Rubio's front door. She let them in and led them to the tortilla shrine.

According to witnesses, many of the visitors dropped to their knees as soon as they saw the tortilla. Some prayed aloud. Many cried, the tears streaming down their cheeks.

Local newspapers heard about the tortilla, and sent reporters and photographers to take a look. More and more people came to the Rubio house, and became convinced that it was, indeed, the image of Jesus in the tortilla. (In fairness, it must be mentioned that reporter Ken Walston of the *Albuquerque Journal* said, "It looks more like Leon Spinks to me.")

Mrs. Rubio put a sign on the outside of her green stucco house, inviting anyone who wished to see the tortilla to come in, free of charge. The tortilla shrine rapidly became a phenomenon; Mrs. Rubio purchased guest books, and so far more than eight thousand persons have signed the registers.

"They have come from New Mexico, Texas, Arizona, Colorado, California, New York—everywhere," she said.

The visitors began to light candles in front of the tortilla, and place flowers around it. They placed photographs of members of their families who were ill in front of the tortilla, and left the photos there, hoping for a healing power.

"The tortilla has not become moldy," Mrs Rubio said. "It is just like on the day I first saw the image of Jesus on it.

"I used to be an impatient woman. I used to have troubles. Since this miracle happened, I am no longer impatient. I do not know why this has happened to me, but God has come into my life through this tortilla.

"I see happiness come into the faces of the people who visit the tortilla. That is enough for me."

So still the visitors come, and every night Mrs. Rubio kneels down and prays in front of the tortilla. Some people have offered to buy it from her, but she has refused.

"It is my own miracle," she said. "I will keep the tortilla forever."

A Man and His Music

On a Tuesday evening, at a nightclub called the Blue Max, in Rosemont, Illinois, a comedian named Jerry Dye told his last joke of the night and walked offstage. Simultaneously the house orchestra began to play and the featured singer, Frank Sinatra, Jr., came forward holding a hand microphone.

Sinatra, thirty-seven, wore a neatly pressed tuxedo with a red handkerchief showing from the breast pocket. "Good evening, everyone, and welcome to the show," he said, and then began a number called "Singin' the Blues."

The house was perhaps sixty percent full. Sinatra finished the song and, almost without taking a breath, segued into the next one, "Too Close for Comfort." When he had completed it, he said, "I'll bet it's been a while since you've heard that number."

For the next hour, Sinatra worked his way through a list of middle-of-the-road standards. The members of the Blue Max's orchestra were young men, many in their early twenties; they were paid by the evening to back up whoever was booked into the room. But Sinatra turned to them as if they were the Nelson Riddle Orchestra and said, "Ladies and gentlemen, the wonder of the large band is that it possesses many colors."

During his first break for patter, Sinatra motioned toward the rear of the room and said, "All you nice folks in the back from International Harvester, we thank you for coming tonight," and the International Harvester group applauded themselves. For the first thirty minutes, Sinatra made no references to his father, but then the orchestra hit the opening chords of "That's Life," and he said, "As they say on Madison Avenue, let's put up the flag and see who salutes."

He did a fine job with the song, standing with his legs apart and jabbing at the air with his right arm, and when he had finished it the audience was cheering as they had not cheered his previous efforts. And with the smallest of smiles, Sinatra said, "Every night we do that number, and every night I know wherein your loyalty lies."

He did not perform any more songs associated with his father, although factors he could not control—his face, the timbre of his voice —were a constant reminder to the audience, and would have been even if he had had another name. Certain mannerisms were almost haunting in their familiarity; the way he lit his cigarette so that the action was a part of the song's percussion, the way he credited a songwriter with "A marvelous song—Johnny Mandel." But when a man in the audience, perhaps emboldened by the drinks the waitresses kept delivering, called out for "My Way," the singer said, "No, I only sing one Sinatra song per show."

At the end, he said, "This is the curtain call. Except we don't have a curtain, and you didn't give us a call." He sang two more songs, a ballad and an up-tempo number backed with lots of brass, and then he said, "We are delighted that you are here. This nightclub gets very, very lonely when no one is here." And then he walked off.

I had arranged to meet Sinatra in a hotel coffee shop half an hour after the show. He walked in precisely on time; he had replaced the tuxedo coat with a dark-blue poplin jacket. We shook hands and took a table.

He had told me on the telephone that he was reluctant to get together with me; not because he didn't want to talk, but because he could not figure out why anyone would be interested in anything he had to say. We were handed menus, and he immediately started up on the same theme; he said he was afraid he was wasting my time, because he could think of nothing of importance he might offer on any subject.

"All I've ever been is a traveling singer," he said. "For seventeen years I lived on the road, and that's all I know about."

Up close his face looked even more jarringly like the face on a 1955 Frank Sinatra album cover; the eyes, though, were deep brown. In the front, his dark hair had begun to turn gray. Although the publicity photos I had seen of him made him look like a young boy, the man sitting across from me was fully grown, at the beginning of middle age.

"I only travel fifteen weeks a year or so now," he said. "For one thing, it isn't easy to find clubs that want to feature my kind of music. But the main problem is paying for musicians. I used to have a full band travel with me, but I can't afford it anymore. The airline prices are just too high. So I have a guitar player and a pianist who work for me, and then I hire musicians in each city.

"No one gets rich doing this. You don't make forty thousand dollars a night, like you would if you were a rock group. This week I have to pay four trumpet players, four trombone players, and five saxophone players. I'll be lucky if I walk out of here with a hundred dollars."

I asked him if he ever considered any other way of making money. He shrugged.

"This is what I have always done," he said. "I have to work. I don't own stocks. I have a house with a mortgage.

"I know I don't sing the kind of music that appeals to this generation. A rock concert . . . I do not understand that kind of commerce. I won't call it music. I would have no more chance of succeeding at that than landing the space shuttle. I know that rock bands play to tens of thousands of people every night, but to me the number of people in the audience is immaterial. I've worked clubs where the capacity was sixty; the incentive is not in the number of people you sing to, but singing right for the people who are there."

I asked him if he didn't envy the entertainers who could, indeed, pack a football stadium with fans.

"I travel with two people," Sinatra said. "Jeff Morrison is my conductor and pianist. Dan McIntyre is my guitarist. None of us gets famous. None of us gets rich. I've never sold a million records, never had a hit movie, never had a hit TV show. I've worked in joints all my life.

"What you have to understand is that, in this business, I'm a struggling little guy. I'm one of many singers who are trying and not quite making it. I do not have a recording contract, for example. Would I like to have one? Of course. I'm a singer. Of course I'd like one. But all during my career I've been singing the music of the forties, and they have wanted rock stars. In all these years I have made a total of four albums, and none of them sold.

"I'm going to be forty years old soon, and I'm too damn stubborn to change. All I can do is go out there whenever someone will hire me, and sing, and hope someone in the audience sees me and likes me. If people like me, then perhaps there will be more offers, and if that happens, perhaps the price will rise."

We had been talking for an hour when I finally brought up his father. He had not mentioned it, but I could not avoid it any longer. So I asked him: How did he deal with being Frank Sinatra's son, and with being a singer who had trouble finding work?

"Even if I didn't have the name, it would be a problem," he said.

"People see me, and they say, 'This guy looks like Frank Sinatra, this guy sounds like Frank Sinatra.'

"That will always be with me. So you ask me how I deal with it? I don't dwell on it. What would you do? If I dwell on it, I will be in a straitjacket in an institution. If I dwell on it, it will kill me."

If he were not Frank Sinatra's son, of course, I would not have come to see him. That fact was so obvious that it did not need to be verbalized. He knew it and I knew it, and to say it out loud would have seemed to serve no purpose.

And if I had not thought to come see him, neither would the people in his audiences. For all his life he must have been living with that knowledge, and if he is ever tempted to forget it, there will always be a man like the one in the audience this night, who, at the end of a song, said in an audible voice: "Well, he's not his old man."

Of course he isn't. We are a nation of men who spend most of our lives trying to escape the shadow of our fathers, whether they are famous or obscure. With most of us, it is simply a matter of growing older, of building our own lives and our own identities until, one day, we wake up as our own men.

For some, though, it is destined never to happen, and I sought out Frank Sinatra, Jr. because he seems faced with a curse few of us will ever know. He told me that he did not, in fact, go into the music business at the urging of his father, or in an attempt to imitate: "When I was five years old, my mother arranged for me to take piano lessons.

I wanted to go out and play ball with the other boys, but she insisted, and soon I couldn't get Rachmaninoff and Chopin out of my head."

And if there was ever any doubt about how he would spend his life, it disappeared one night when, as a high school boy, he went to see Leopold Stokowski conduct a 124-piece orchestra in New York's Carnegie Hall: "I stared at that old man, and I listened to the music coming from that orchestra, and I sat in my seat and I just trembled."

That will never matter to the men and women who come to see him in a lounge somewhere. They will pay the cover charge and buy the drinks because of the name, and because by some twist of their own fortunes they find themselves not in Las Vegas or Atlantic City, but in Rosemont, Illinois, on a Tuesday night with nothing to do. They will demand something that the singer cannot provide, but he will do his best to come close; because for him, too, it is a Tuesday night in the middle of his life, and he, too, by a configuration of the fates, has found himself in Rosemont.

We were the last people in the coffee shop. Sinatra was in no particular hurry to leave; although it was late, his next shift did not start until nine o'clock the following night, and all that lay ahead was a day in his hotel room.

He said he didn't feel like going to sleep yet; back home in California, he said, he could kill time during the day by auditioning for television shows, but here there was really nothing for him to do in the afternoon. If he went to bed now, that would only mean he would wake up that much earlier. I asked him if he really walked into Los Angeles casting sessions cold, reading from scripts with the other hopeful actors.

"Oh, yes," he said. "I'm not at the point where I won't read for a part. And once in a while I get a small part in a show . . ." He let his voice trail off.

He said again that he didn't feel like going to his room just yet.

So we talked into the night. I asked him about the tuxedo. It seemed, in a way, part of another age; entertainers for the last twenty years or so have been dressing a bit more casually, and especially for members of his generation, the tuxedo seemed an oddity.

"That's the way I was raised," he said. "It's the idea of bringing a little class to the nightclub and showing a little respect for the audience. I know some people might not understand that, but I wouldn't feel comfortable dressing any other way."

He said after his week's engagement at the Blue Max had ended, he would return to his home in Los Angeles and continue looking for work. He does not have a manager; he books his own appearances and arranges his own travel. He has never married, and he said, "I live the kind of life that most single men lead. I do my laundry, and take my dry cleaning in, and go to the market."

The waitress came by and said that she was about to unplug the coffeepot, so if he wanted another cup, now was the time to say so. She left the check and walked away.

Sinatra got up to leave. "The thing that keeps me going is that I like my life," he said. "It's not the greatest, but I can get by doing the thing I like the best, and that's nice. I have my pianist and I have my guitar player, and very shortly, if everything goes okay, I'll have my own drummer again. If it doesn't take much to make you happy, then your chances of being happy are pretty good."

Backing onto the Unemployment Rolls

As soon as the new photocopying machine appeared in the office, Jodie Stutz knew what she had to do. Eventually she would lose her job over it, but she was a woman obsessed.

Miss Stutz, twenty-one, was a secretary for Deere & Co., the giant farm machinery manufacturing firm in Moline, Illinois. All day long she looked at that photocopier, and all day long the same desire danced through her mind.

"I had to make a Xerox copy of my butt," Miss Stutz said.

In her younger days, Miss Stutz had made Xerox copies of her face. She would open up the lid of the machine, smash her face against the glass—always keeping her eyes closed to protect them—and grope for the "Print" button. Then the machine would whir, and the photocopy would come out, all grainy and neat-looking.

But this new machine was so beautiful. She knew it called for something special.

So she waited for closing time. After everyone else had left the office, Miss Stutz recruited another secretary to stand lookout for her.
Then she closed herself in the Xerox room. She yanked her pants down,
leaped up on the machine, sat on it, and pressed the button.

In a few moments she had the finished photocopy of her posterior.

"It looked great," she said with no false modesty.

She stashed the copy in her purse, and she and her friend left the
office without being noticed.

But her vanity got the best of her. Within a few days, she showed
the photocopy to some friends in the office, and the word began to
spread.

"People were begging me to see it," Miss Stutz said. "That's when
my troubles began."

The following events are Miss Stutz's version of what happened next.
Deere & Co. officials will not comment on their version.

A few weeks after the furtive evening in the Xerox room, Miss Stutz
was summoned to the Deere & Co. personnel office, where a woman
named Joyce Kuehl waited for her.

"She said that there were rumors that I had taken a Xerox copy of
my rear end, and wanted to know if it was true," Miss Stutz said.

Miss Stutz, who was carrying the photocopy in her purse, said it was
completely untrue.

"Hey, I lied," Miss Stutz said.

Next she was called in by Jack Fritts, administrative manager of the
advertising office where she worked. He asked her if she had made a
photocopy of her posterior.

"Just a rumor," Miss Stutz said.

Fritts reportedly said to her: "You go back to your office and you
think about it, and if you decide that the rumor is true, and if we find
out it's true, you will be fired."

Miss Stutz was determined to keep lying, but next Fritts and Jim
Coogan, Deere's director of advertising, reportedly called in the other
secretary who had watched the door during the photocopying session.

"They really gave her the third degree," Miss Stutz said. "They
threatened to fire her if she didn't tell the truth, so she started crying
and admitted it."

So Coogan and Fritts called Miss Stutz back in.

"They said that making a Xerox copy of my butt was not in the best
interests of the company," Miss Stutz said. "I said that I was real sorry,
and I would never do anything like that again, but they said I had a
choice. Either they would fire me or I could quit. So I didn't want be-

ing fired on my record, so I quit."

Miss Stutz said that various rumors—all of them false—had made their way to the management of Deere & Co.:

1. That she had thrown a big party in the Xerox room on the night of the incident.

2. That she had put a routing slip on the photocopy of her posterior, and had sent it to all the Deere & Co. branches and factories in the United States.

3. That she had autographed copies and given them away.

4. That she was completely naked in the Xerox room, taking shots of various parts of her body.

5. That three men had helped her get undressed and then guarded the door for her.

6. That she had sent out copies as an invitation to a birthday party.

Deere officials do not deny Miss Stutz's story, but neither will they confirm it. "On individual personnel, we do not discuss company matters publicly," a company spokesman said.

Miss Stutz is annoyed that she had to resign, and lost a good job. "It was just a silly mistake," she said. "Deere & Co. creates a routine that everyone follows. The corporation breeds mediocrity and dullness. If you don't conform, you are simply eliminated. The company can tolerate sloppy work and lazy employees, but it can't tolerate humanistic mistakes."

Miss Stutz is now working as a waitress in a Mexican restaurant. Her career at Deere & Co. is over, but she has her memories.

"It was such a great picture," she said.

A Matter of Time

Probably every man has fantasized about it. That didn't make it any easier to do. I held the telephone to my ear, but I couldn't make myself punch the buttons.

During Vietnam, when I was breaking in as a newspaper reporter, I would often be ordered to call the families of casualties and get information on the sons they had just learned they'd lost. I found it easy; it was part of being professional. I have had to make calls like that all my working life, and they don't bother me at all. But now my hands were shaking.

I hit the number, area code first. It rang twice, with that peculiar sound long-distance calls give you. She answered.

"Hello?"

My throat was dry.

"Hello?" she said again.

"Lindy?" I said.

In the summer of 1963, when it dawned on me that I was in love, and for the first time, it didn't occur to me that there would ever be any women in my life other than Lindy Lemmon. I was sixteen; she was thirteen. The whole world was Columbus, Ohio, that summer. We would sit all day on the corner of Bexley Park and Gould, hidden by big shrubs, listening to a transistor radio and watching while the DDT truck went by, and we would calmly discuss what things were going to be like when we were married.

"Little Deuce Coupe" would come out of the radio, and we would hold hands, and when she ended it four months later it was the saddest I ever felt in my life. Within two years I was out of high school and out of Columbus, and suddenly there were all these other people in my world, and with everything I learned I felt myself becoming a little less innocent. I wasn't trying to be that way; it just happens and you can't help it, and sometimes, when I was on the road in some strange hotel room, or typing a story on deadline on a borrowed portable Olivetti set up on an airplane tray table, it would strike me that the boy I had been during the summer of '63 would be worth looking for, if I could ever find the time.

That's when I would think of Lindy. If I had become a little too jaded to suit myself when it came to matters in general, I was probably jaded most of all when it came to women. I would think back to the feeling I'd had in the autumn of our breakup—when all my friends were concerned only with how our football team would do in the Central Buckeye League, and I was concerned only with the fact that I would apparently never get over Lindy—and the memory that I could hurt so intensely left me with a sense of wonder.

All of us have doubtless wanted to go back and see the first girl we loved; we think about it, but we don't consider doing it because we're not supposed to do things like that once we're grown-ups. And yet, the more I thought about trying to find the boy I'd been, the more I thought that I would have to find Lindy, too. I was married now—in love with someone else—but that didn't seem to have anything to do with it.

So I did some checking around back in Columbus. Lindy was married, too. Her husband was an executive with a steel company; they had three children and were living in Toledo, Ohio. Once I had the information, I delayed for days before going any further. But when I did I found that their number in Toledo was listed with directory assistance. And I was still shaking when she said "Hello?" for the second time, and I said, "Lindy?" and, across the miles, she said, "Who is this?"

I don't usually drink on airplanes, but during the flight from Chicago to Toledo I kept calling the stewardess back to my seat.

The phone call hadn't been what I had expected. I thought I was going to have to do a lot of explaining about who I was, but the first thing she had said after "Where are you calling from?" was "I saw you on 'Phil Donahue.'" It didn't make me smile; it made me kind of sad, because the boy I was looking for had nothing to do with anything like that.

But now it was a week later, and the plane came through a low cloud bank, and then we were on the ground in Toledo. I could feel my heart. I walked off the plane; no one was at the gate. So I took the escalator down to the baggage-claim area; there were Lindy and her three children.

I was thirty-two. She was twenty-nine. She wore a sweater and a skirt and boots that reached her knees. She had been beautiful when she was thirteen, and had the same face now, but she was undeniably an Ohio housewife waiting in an airport.

We stood there. She spoke first.

"This is Joey, and this is Matthew, and this is Megan," she said.

We rode through Toledo in her station wagon. The back section was folded down; the children were playing there.

"Who's Bob Greene?" asked the boy named Matthew.

"A friend of Mommy's," Lindy said.

We pulled into her driveway. There were five bikes in the garage, and a snowplow. Her husband was at work. Inside, the house held the artifacts of any American family: a Sears food processor and a copy of *Sports Illustrated* with her husband's name on the address label and an Elton John greatest hits album. I had seen these things in so many other places, but this was Lindy's house, and I looked at the album cover and thought about Elton John's having arrived on the scene and flourished and started to fade away, all in the time since I had seen her.

She made grilled cheese sandwiches for the children and me; they drank red-colored pop with it. I knew that I should be thinking important thoughts, but it was happening too fast. It had seemed like such a good idea to come here, but now . . . Lindy was clearly puzzled about what I was doing in her house. When I had asked if I could come she had said yes, but I could tell she was not entirely comfortable with it, and I couldn't blame her. If I couldn't explain to myself exactly why I was here, I certainly couldn't explain it to her.

After lunch she sent the children upstairs, and we put some albums on and sat in the living room. We started to talk; it was all too polite, and I found myself listening to the sound of my own voice in the big room. It sounded as odd as I felt.

She pulled out an old high school yearbook and turned to the back. Someone had signed: TO LINDY—I'LL NEVER FORGET THE TIMES WE HAD. YOU'LL GO FAR. I'LL NEVER FORGET YOU. STEVE.

"I wonder who Steve was," Lindy said.

There was a pounding above us, and for a moment it was like back in Columbus, when we used to think her parents were coming downstairs, but Lindy said, "That's just Megan trying on my shoes."

When I fell silent she asked me if there was something wrong, and I said I'd like to go to my motel.

She dropped me at the Sheraton Westgate, saying she would come back later to have dinner with me. I spent the next few hours in the first-floor barroom of the motel, chuting quarters into the jukebox and talking with one of the waitresses. It was much easier than talking to Lindy; it occurred to me that I had done this so often in so many different cities that it was far more real to me than the idea of Lindy and her family.

As I waited for her, I realized that I had no right to be doing this; I was so used to intruding into people's lives for my professional purposes that I had blithely intruded into Lindy's for my own personal ones. But I wasn't going to find that boy from 1963—at least not here; all I was going to do was confuse Lindy and make her wonder what it was I wanted.

When she arrived we went to the motel dining room. She had white wine with her dinner; I had never thought of Lindy having a drink. I pretended it was a newspaper interview and asked questions by rote. I learned that she had converted to Catholicism, that she taught a

Sunday-school class, and that she took aerobic dance lessons. I was already thinking of flight schedules back to Chicago.

After dinner she said she wanted to call her husband because her nine-year-old had been sick. We went up to my room.

I sat on the bed and watched her as she called, and she said: "The medicine for him is on top of the refrigerator. The instructions are with it." She listened for a few moments and then said, "I'll talk to you about it when I get home." I could imagine his questions; I didn't blame him for asking. When she hung up, neither of us had to say anything; we both got up and headed for the door at the same time.

We sat in the car in the parking lot of the Sheraton. She had left the station wagon at home and brought her husband's sedan to the motel; there were sales-promotion pamphlets scattered on the front seat.

It was raining. She had turned the ignition on and switched on the radio. The drops splattered on the front windshield and then dripped slowly to the hood. She was behind the wheel, turned toward me.

"Bobby, you've been so quiet," she said.

I said I knew it; I tried to explain the things I had been thinking in the bar, about intruding on her life and looking for something I had no right to expect to find.

"I thought it was my fault," she said. "I thought you thought I was boring."

I didn't think I was hearing her right.

"Look," Lindy said. "You have this life that's all worldly and full of experiences. And I'm living in Toledo, Ohio, and I don't see how you can expect to just fly in here and for me to fit into that."

There was no way for me to tell her. The best I could come up with was, "Jesus, Lindy, you don't have to be anything. The only reason I'm here is because you're Lindy."

A song from the radio filled the car. We looked at each other; for a moment it seemed as if we might hold hands, but we both had people at home wondering about us, and so we just kept staring.

The minutes passed, and cars pulled in and out of the parking lot, and on the street the stoplights turned from green to yellow to red and back again. There was nothing much to say; we were two grown-ups in search of something we were probably better off not thinking about. The rain kept falling, and we looked out the windshield at the cold Ohio night.

Grif

The first time I ever saw a copy of the *Chicago Sun-Times* was in September of 1965, when I came to Evanston from Ohio to go to college. It couldn't have been more than a few weeks before I tore a Jack Griffin column out of the paper, folded it up, and stuffed it into my wallet for keeping.

Since that day, there has never been a time when I have walked around without a Griffin column. I ripped that first one out of the paper because I was so stunned that a columnist could capture feeling and emotion and life with the precision that Jack did; I forget what the subject of the column was, but I remember thinking that seeing such a marvelous piece of writing in a newspaper was a rare thing indeed, and that I had better hold onto it.

Later, of course, I found out that with Jack, it wasn't so rare at all. He did it all the time. So it began: I would carry a Griffin column around for a couple of months, and then one morning I would pick up the paper and, damn, he'd done it again. So I would replace the yellowing column with the new one. I used to force the columns on people, make them read what Jack had written, not leave them alone until they had shared the same thing that had touched me.

Later, when I was hired by the *Sun-Times*, I looked forward with almost giddy anticipation to meeting Griffin. But when I first came to the city room, and saw him over in the sports department, banging away at his typewriter, I became nervous and couldn't bring myself to do it. So even though we were working in the same room, I remained a fan from afar.

I kept tearing his columns out, though. I remember one, about a man Jack met in the Cleveland airport. The man was waiting for his son's remains to be shipped home from Vietnam. The column was so moving, so alive with emotion without resorting to maudlin sentimentality . . . when I read that one, I made myself approach Griffin to tell him what I thought. He was in the middle of· writing the next day's piece. He looked up and said, "Oh. Thanks." That was it.

I used to see him in Riccardo's. He would never sit with the rest of the crowd. Instead he would stand way on the other side, over by the wall, by himself. He would drink his beers and look down at the surface of the bar, thinking his thoughts. Most of the time he kept his trench coat on. And he never got rid of that crewcut. I idolized him.

When the editors of the paper first gave me a column, I found out quickly that all of my self-assuredness might be pure sham. I didn't know the city well enough, and for all my desire to make the thing work, I felt lost. There weren't many people who were too anxious to go out of their way to help me, either.

One day—it must have been during the first or second week I was writing the column—Jack appeared at my desk. "Come on, kid," he said. "We're going to take a little drive." I didn't know he knew who I was.

He took me down to a grimy, ancient gymnasium on 63rd Street, under the L tracks, and we walked up a dark flight of wooden stairs. There, alone in the dimly lit room, was Muhammad Ali, then still in exile from boxing because of his anti-Vietnam views, working out on a heavy bag.

"Hey, Champ, come here for a second," Jack said. Ali came over. We spent the afternoon there—Jack and Ali did almost all of the talking, and I just listened—and on the way home, Jack said, "It's your column." I said that he had done all the work, I hadn't even known what questions to ask—and Jack interrupted and said, "Forget it. Write the column."

We stopped for a drink on the way back. It was the first of many times. Griffin up close was the same as Griffin in the newspaper—tough and soft at the same time, full of knowledge about the harshest sides of life, but just as full of hope that the harshness can be beaten by the good. No one could put anything over on Jack. He was always a sucker for a pretty woman, but that was by his own choice.

He began to invite me down to his solitary end of the bar. It was as high an honor as I ever hope to receive. God, he could laugh. When the cancer infested him last year, he stopped coming around. The space at the end of the bar was empty. It was no fun to be there anymore.

Jack died Wednesday night. I'm trying to figure out a way to end this piece, and even as I'm typing, I know that I'll steal my last paragraph from Jack. He wrote it when Ray Brennan died in 1972, and like most things Jack ever did, there is no way to do it better:

I know he wouldn't want it this way, but I can't help it. I'm going to stay out late tonight and cry for my friend.

Kathy's Abortion

"Oh, Jesus," she moaned softly. She squeezed my hand.

The vacuum machine purred steadily and the fetus that was her unborn child was sucked through a clear plastic hose and into a large glass bottle.

"Oh," she said again, and scratched my forearm.

"We're almost done," the doctor said. "I just have to check and make sure you're all clean and empty."

She squeezed my hand harder.

"I didn't tell anybody about this," she said. This was the afternoon before.

"My girl friend and I were talking, and she started talking about having babies. This person is a person I grew up with; we grew up in the same parish, and we always had the same ideas about everything. She has this idea about abortions, that they're morally wrong.

"And I started feeling guilty about not feeling guilty. Because I really don't. It's just something I have to do."

In the morning she would be having her abortion. Her name is Kathy; she is a twenty-seven-year-old executive with a marketing firm. She is single. She was one of the thousands of women who have legal abortions in Chicago each week. She was different in one way: the public would be going along with her, through the eyes of a newspaperman who would be with her every step of the way.

"I knew I was pregnant all along," Kathy said. "I knew it before I got the test. The nurse told me. She sounded concerned, like she knew I was single. 'You're . . . uh . . . pregnant.' Not like she was talking to a married woman. 'You're pregnant!' Not like that.

"It's not a baby. I just refuse to think of it as a baby. I mean, I don't think, count up the months, and in October you'll have a baby. I know

I'm pregnant, that's true. But I don't think there's a baby growing inside of me. I can't be thinking about that. I just want to go there in the morning and get it done."

That night Kathy went to see a play at the Goodman Theatre. The production was *Much Ado About Nothing*.

At 8:03 A.M., Kathy walked through the front door of the Concord Medical Center, 17 West Grand. She was wearing green Levi's, a down jacket, and Adidas running shoes. Her boyfriend, the man who had made her pregnant, had dropped her off outside. The other women who would be having their abortions during Concord's first shift had already started to arrive.

They came in breathlessly, each of them looking around for the desk where they would check in. If you didn't know where you were, you might think they were college women on the first day of registration for classes. They were handed manila folders stuffed with pieces of paper.

Rock music from WBBM-FM came out of a speaker in the ceiling. A man was singing, "Never gonna fall in love again, / No I never want to feel the pain, / Or remember how it used to be. . . ." The music seemed overly loud.

"I was upset outside," Kathy said. "I guess I'm kind of scared." She flipped through the forms. There were nineteen chairs in the waiting room, most of them a bright yellow. Over the receptionist's desk was a sign saying that the Concord Medical Center accepted Master Charge.

Kathy filled out an informational sheet. "Age?" "Twenty-seven." "Religion?" "Catholic."

The love songs continued to come from the ceiling. Kathy scanned a legal consent form: "I hereby authorize Dr. (Name to Be Filled In by Counselor), and such assistants as may be selected by him, to terminate my pregnancy. . . ."

At 8:37 A.M. Kathy's name was called. She was directed to the cashier's office. She gave the cashier a check for $175.

The room where the women wait before going in for their abortions is called the auditorium.

On the canvas chairs, many women from days and weeks past have written with ball-point pen. They have written their last thoughts before the operation. On one chair, there was a heart drawn. Inside the heart were the words, "Connie and James forever."

The writing on the other chairs was much the same. "Rich and Elaine." "Mike and Michelle." "Shelly and Rich." The love songs from the radio played in here, too.

"Now I know you're going to be tense," said Lydia Dershewitz, the counselor assigned to Kathy. "The best thing you can do if you feel yourself tensing up is to just tense everything up as much as you can, and then let it go. The letting go helps."

Mrs. Dershewitz and Kathy were in a small room going through the counseling session, the last thing a woman does before she has her abortion. The counselors are attuned to the women's emotions; if there is any hesitation about having the operation, the counselors are instructed to advise the women to go back home.

"I don't want to have a baby," Kathy said.

From the ceiling, the radio. A commercial jingle for a clothing store: "Look to the Limited. . . ."

Mrs. Dershewitz picked up a plastic model of the female pelvic area and explained to Kathy, step by step, what the operation would be like. Mrs. Dershewitz pulled the plastic model apart, and said, "First the doctor will examine you to see the size and position of your uterus. This takes about thirty seconds. . . ."

Kathy lay on the operating table.

There were three other people in the room: the doctor, the nurse, and the newspaperman. All three were dressed in surgical scrub suits and masks.

Kathy was on her back. Surprisingly, the radio was playing even in the operating room. As she waited for the abortion to begin, the Bee Gees sang "Stayin' Alive" from the movie *Saturday Night Fever*.

The doctor looked at Kathy's chart so that he could call her by her first name.

"I'm going to examine your uterus now," he said. "This will be a little uncomfortable."

Kathy looked over at me.

"Come here," she said.

I stepped closer to the operating table.

"Hold my hand," she said.

I did.

"I don't even like going to the doctor's office," she said.

The doctor pushed a lever, and the table rose.

"Lift up your hips," he said. "Now this is going to feel a little wet and cold."

He swabbed an orange-colored antiseptic agent known as Betadine between Kathy's legs.

"Now I'm going to insert the speculum," the doctor said.

She gasped and pulled my hand down to her chest. She began scratching my arm.

"Are you all right?" the nurse asked.

"Fine," Kathy said.

The doctor swabbed more of the astringent inside of Kathy. By now she was shaking softly and gripping me with a great deal of strength.

"I'm going to give you a shot now," the doctor said. "It's a pain-numbing agent."

He passed an enormous needle into Kathy, and injected the drug into her cervix. She couldn't see the needle, and didn't seem to feel the shot.

"Now this is going to feel really weird," the doctor said. "These instruments are dilators. They're to stretch the opening of your cervix." The nurse handed him the instruments and he inserted them.

"Okay," the doctor said. "You're halfway home. You're going to feel a cramping or tugging sensation next." As he spoke, the nurse handed him a long, clear plastic tube. The doctor guided the tube into Kathy's womb.

Without notice, the doctor turned on the vacuum aspirator. It began to hum.

"Oh, Jesus," Kathy said, squeezing my hand. She kept talking as the fetus was sucked from her.

It looked like a mixture of blood and mucus. It was pulled through the tube and into a glass bottle sitting on a table. The red fluid kept flowing from Kathy and into the bottle. The entire process took perhaps two and a half minutes.

"We're almost done," the doctor said. "I just have to check and make sure you're all clean and empty in there."

He reached inside Kathy with a curette and scraped some remaining tissue from the lining of her uterus. Then he turned the vacuum machine on again. More material was sucked from her body and into the bottle.

"You're done," the doctor said.

The nurse lifted the bottle and carried it to another table, out of Kathy's line of vision.

Kathy sat up. She was still holding my hand. Perspiration covered her face. The nurse helped her off the operating table and led her toward the recovery room.

The recovery room was long and bright. Kathy lay on a cot. Other women, fresh from their own abortions, lay next to her on other cots. Kathy lay in silence for forty-five minutes.

At 10:15 A.M. Kathy and I walked out of the Concord Medical Center and into the sunlight. The counselor had told her to eat some lunch and then to rest for the remainder of the day.

"I don't want to think about it now," Kathy said. "I was on the bed in the recovery room . . . and all of a sudden I wanted to burst out and cry a whole lot. I looked at the ceiling and . . . I tried to think about Miami. I didn't want to think about what had happened. I looked up at the ceiling and I tried to pretend I was in Miami."

Thirty-five Years

We were always going somewhere. That was part of the deal. Growing up meant getting away. So one of us set off for Chicago, and one of us set off for Florida, and one of us set off for Colorado.

Debby came home, but Timmy and I never did. He has climbed mountains in Peru and now he's a bartender in Boulder, waiting for the next thing. I do whatever it is that I do. We don't get home very often, and when we do it is just to hit and run. We are brothers and sisters, and we call each other once in a while.

My parents are still at home, of course. They didn't leave. We never thought much about that, Debby and Timmy and I; we didn't consider that maybe they might want to go away, too, that maybe the wanderlust wasn't ours exclusively. We assumed that we would always have a hometown, and that meant that our parents would always be there. Somehow they weren't allowed to leave. That was how the rules were.

They seemed to understand it. Not once, during all the years of our wanderings, did our mother and father express any envy of our freedom, any questioning of our reluctance to stay put. Timmy would head for South America in search of a mountain, or I would go to Europe on a business trip—looking at my watch the whole time—and never once did our parents say that maybe they would have liked some of that, too.

We were rootless enough. There was nothing to hold us down. I don't know where we got it; certainly it didn't come from our parents, who taught us stability. Timmy is just as likely to be in Maine tomorrow morning as he is in Colorado, if he feels the whim; I've lived in so many hotel rooms these last ten years that they don't even feel strange anymore.

Why did we become that way? Probably because we knew that home would always be there. That if we needed a place to go, we could head back for that most familiar destination of all, the one we set off from in the first place. Everything else in the hometown might change, but as long as our mother and father were there, we had a place to call our own. That kind of knowledge gives you the courage to move around.

It is an age of divorce and infidelity and the death of the family. Marriages break up more easily than they are formed, and those who do stay married wait a long time before having children, hedging their bets. Staying together is such a burden. Raising a family is such a responsibility. So limiting. No wonder divorce is becoming one of our most sacred institutions.

My parents have stayed married for thirty-five years. While we, their children, have been free to roam and explore every possibility in life, they have lived in the same town this whole time. We children went out to get lost or get away or get famous—whatever we wanted—and they stayed, having given us that freedom. I don't know what it is that we are trying to accomplish in our disordered lives, but they have accomplished what they set out to do. They raised a family.

Thirty-five years and a family raised. The three of us children never once doubted that they were there to turn to if we needed help, and I don't recall that we ever said thanks. I have been the worst offender. I have become so proficient at putting words on paper for consumption by large numbers of people that I have lost the ability to communicate privately with the two people who have meant the most to me. I can't write a letter; I learned long ago that writing a letter to one person is a skill I have given up in exchange for the other.

Worse, I don't even talk to my parents very well. I am much better with strangers. Put me in an airport bar in an unfamiliar city, and I am quite glib. Stop me on the street and I may even be charming. Any number of waitresses will tell you how easy I am to get to know. It is only with the people I love that I become silent.

Perhaps they understand that; I know I don't. I accept it, though, and live with it, just as Debby and Timmy and I live with the knowledge that of all the things we may accomplish in our scattered lives, nothing can possibly be as impressive as the memory of the house we grew up in and what it represented. That is what my parents have accomplished in this life; they have given us that house, and the memories of the years we were a family in it.

So they have been married thirty-five years now. That is a monument of sorts, and Debby and Timmy and I have decided that finally it is their turn. They spent thirty-five years in the same town, making sure that we would always have a home if, in the course of our moving about, we felt we needed it. Now we are trying to assure them of the same thing. We have asked them to go to Europe, as a gift from us. They have never been there. Now they are ready to depart.

I don't know what they'll find there—in France and Italy and England—but I'm pretty sure it won't measure up to what they have known in our hometown. That's the secret we want them to know: No matter how fine a time they may have in the fabled lands where they will travel, it will never measure up to what they have created in the town of our growing up.

Debby and Timmy and I have known that for years. Now our parents will find it out. Thank you if you have read this far, but today's column is not for you. It is for them.

The Four of Us

The man sitting across the dinner table said, "I can never make you understand. There's only four of us who will ever understand exactly how it was, and that's John, Paul, George, and myself."

The man, whose name is Ringo Starr, said, "You can talk about it and talk about it until the cows come home. I don't know why it happened to us. Well, actually I do know, or I think I know. I think I was born for it to happen to me. How else can you explain it? There were four of us in the band, and then there was a fifth person, and that fifth person was just . . . a kind of magic, you know? Magic.

"And now some sort of myth has developed around us. A lot of the people who talk about us are kids; they weren't even born when we were still together. I don't know. Every time I talk about it . . . I don't know."

His companion asked him: What about all of the money offers for the four of them to do one more show together? There had been an item in the newspaper the other day reporting that one promoter was willing to pay $45 million for the four of them to sing on one stage for just one night.

"I think it was fifty million," Starr said, toying with his lamb chops and potatoes. "But the thing is, we don't want to do it. We don't want to get together. And if we did want to get together, we could do it ourselves; we wouldn't need anybody from the outside offering us any money. I think these promoters keep coming up with these big money offers just to get their names in the paper. It makes them little heroes for a day.

"Why does everyone want us to sing together again? It's like something they can't have, I suppose. We're all in our thirties now. I'm thirty-seven. A lot of people say, 'I never saw them, and I want to see them just once.' Well, I never saw the Beatles, either. I really wish I could have, but unfortunately I was onstage. I would have loved to have been out in the audience and have seen the Beatles. I would have liked to see what all the excitement was about.

"We would get the same response every night. The people would cheer and applaud and scream whether we were good or we were bad. And then John and Paul and George and I would go backstage and we would tell each other how we thought we'd done. Because we were the only people who could really judge. We were the only people who were taking an honest look at us.

"Maybe in five years no one will want us to join together again, and then we can forget about it. Someday they'll forget about it. I mean, in forty years, when I'm seventy-seven, I hope there still aren't people saying that the Beatles ought to get together for one more show. There really wouldn't be much point in that, would there?"

Starr, who now works on his own, said that he knows he can never accomplish more than he did as a younger man.

"You have to stop talking to yourself about that or it will drive you crazy," he said. "I'll never top what the Beatles did. But there's the satisfaction of working. I try to get better at what I do. I mean, you'll always be famous as a name. I know I'll never be anonymous. When I'm eighty-five, they'll be calling me 'ex-Beatle Ringo Starr.' But just for yourself, you've got to work and try to do better.

"I'm like anybody else. You get up, you go out, you sit in the sun, you go to the office, you watch the TV, you play records—I mean, I live my life. Just like you."

That couldn't be precisely true, his companion said.

"Well, there are differences," Starr said. "I like to make friends, for example, but people tend to come at me too fast. If you come on straight with me, I'll come on straight with you, but people come at me with some preconceived notions about me. I mean, they've heard of me. And you can't just"—he snapped his fingers—"make a new friend like that."

His companion said that millions of people all over the world now play old Beatles albums as part of a true nostalgia, as an attempt to bring back memories.

"Well I do it, too," Starr said. "I play records by the Beatles. Not a lot, but I do it. It brings back a certain period in my life, too, you know."

His companion asked if he considered himself a part of history.

"I am," Starr said. "I can't help it. I'm being pompous answering that way, but I can't choose it. We changed everything, and I know it.

"And it was . . . fantastic. There were some bad times, but it's like the old saying, even the bad times are good. I'm glad I went through it. Am I making any sense? It's like I told you. There are only four of us who will ever understand it. Just the four of us."

Speck

STATEVILLE PRISON, Illinois—"Parents ought to be careful about their kids," said mass murderer Richard Speck. "Because any kid can end up to be like me. I don't know why it happened to me. But any kid can end up just like me."

Thus spoke the man convicted of slashing and choking eight nurses to death in 1966 in one of the most savage crimes of the century. He had just told me that he receives letters in his prison cell every week from women who want to correspond with him, visit him, meet him, and develop romantic relationships with him.

"A lot of them send pictures," Speck said. "A lot of them women are pretty. Some of them women's gotta be nuts. Here's half the country down on a person, they call him all kinds of names—and these women are trying to get to meet him. It sure gets way out. I give their addresses to my cellmates. I don't want nothing to do with them women."

Why do the women want to meet Speck? Perhaps it is a particularly strange permutation of the same reason you are reading this story, and the same reason I was talking to Speck at the Stateville Penitentiary. There is something about a Richard Speck—some abhorrent evil incarnate in the mass murderer—that defies people to accept the fact that a savage killer is also, undeniably, a human being.

For almost two hours I talked with Speck. He spoke with a slow drawl. He looked like a somewhat sinister, pockmarked John Unitas, in a blue prison suit over a purple T-shirt. Prison officials were startled when Speck agreed to talk to me—he loathes the press, and has consistently refused to grant interviews—and the only reason Speck gave me when I asked was, "I read your column, man."

He shocked me by readily admitting that he had indeed killed the nurses—the first time he had confessed his guilt. But almost as surprising, in a more subdued but equally dramatic way, was the manner in which he talked about his life. It was the paradox again—the mass murderer as a human being.

Speck, wearing handcuffs and chains, said he had just come to the main prison building from his cell in a solitary confinement unit, where he was being kept as punishment.

"They got me in solitary because I turned a job down," Speck said. "They wanted me to work in the vegetable room. I wouldn't do it."

"What's wrong with the vegetable room?" I asked.

"A man's got to get up at four-thirty in the morning to work in the vegetable room," Speck said.

"I don't like to get up that early. Chow starts at about fifteen minutes after six, and that's early enough for me. They got me in the labor pool, which means I'm locked in my cell all day after chow. There's three of us to a cell. We watch TV. We got a color TV in our cell.

"I like Clint Eastwood, Charles Bronson. I watched *Magnum Force* the other night. It was all right. Clint Eastwood, he always plays good.

I watch '60 Minutes,' the news, keep up on the outside world. And Carol Burnett. I watch her comedy show.

"What's that dude who played in *Shaft*? Richard Roundtree? I like him. Him and Eastwood and Bronson. They're violent players. I'm not a violent man."

"Then why do you like violent movies?" I asked.

"Same reason you pay and watch 'em," Speck said. "What would you rather see, Walt Disney or a Charles Bronson flick? But I do watch 'Wild Kingdom.'

"I read *Newsweeks*, *Times*, *Hustlers*, *Playboys*. I was buying hardcore pornography through the mail, but it got too expensive. It wasn't worth it."

I asked Speck if he ever expected to get out of prison.

"Between now and the year 2000, yeah," Speck said. "I do my time day by day. In due time, I'll get out. I want to go into the grocery store business. I want to own one. I used to work at Jerry's Food Market in Dallas, Texas. I put up stock and kept the place clean. I worked from three in the afternoon until seven in the morning."

Speck said that one of his pleasures in prison was "getting high."

"I like hooch [moonshine] and I like speed," Speck said. "I don't like marijuana. I used to stay high on reds [barbiturates], but no more. It's all right to get high on that stuff when you're young, but I'm thirty-six now. That's too old for reds.

"We had some good hooch in our cell. We have a two-hundred-dollar stereo in there, too, and I turned over two gallons of the hooch and it messed the stereo up. I had borrowed eight tapes from one of the brothers, a black dude, and the hooch just ate the tapes up.

"I like that hooch, though. I stay up at night as long as it takes me to fall asleep or pass out from the hooch or from whatever we have at the time."

I asked him if he wasn't afraid of getting in trouble for talking about contraband kept in his cell. Speck laughed.

"How am I gonna get in trouble?" he said. "I'm in here for twelve hundred years."

I told Speck that, in their day, men like John Dillinger had been national celebrities even though they were vicious killers. I asked Speck if he felt the same way.

"You're talking about two different categories of people," Speck said. "Dillinger and them guys, that was the Depression, they were robbing banks because that was their only way to survive. Me, I'm not like Dillinger or anybody else. I'm freakish."

I asked him if he ever thought about Charles Manson, America's other famed mass murderer.

"What do I want to think about that fool for?" Speck said.

"Why do you think he's a fool?" I said.

"He's doing life in prison, I wouldn't call him too damn intelligent," Speck said.

"You're doing life in prison," I said.

"I'm another damn fool," Speck said.

"Nah, I'm not a celebrity," he said. "That's all propaganda. Here. Look at this."

He pushed up his left sleeve—and there, where his notorious "Born to Raise Hell" tattoo had been, were a number of ugly scars.

"I burned that tattoo off with a cigarette," Speck said. "I had that put on me when I was fourteen or fifteen. By the time I was sixteen or seventeen I knew it was nasty and cheap. I wanted to get rid of it. My mother had an appointment for me at Parkland Hospital, the same place where Kennedy ended up dying. I was gonna get the tattoo removed. But I ended up in jail before I could keep the appointment. I wasn't born to raise hell."

"Then what were you born for?" I asked.

"Same thing as you or anybody else," Speck said.

"What's that?" I said.

"You're making a living, ain't you?" Speck said. "You was on one road. I was on another road. What happened to me was nobody's fault but my own."

Speck said that he paints in his cell—oil paintings of animals, still lifes, African scenes. He said that he does not dream while sleeping.

"Ain't nothing to dream of," he said. "Twelve years behind bars, what's there to dream of. Only ones keeping me going is my mother and my five sisters.

"If I could get out of here for one night, I'd get on a plane, go to Texas, and see my mother. The only women I care about is my mother and my five sisters. And if I was out for two nights, I'd go to a nightclub. I always wanted to own a nightclub. Just a regular nightclub, like Jack Ruby's."

He said that he is not considered a celebrity inside the walls of Stateville, "except by the fools.

"Them's your young dudes. The old-timers, they treat me the same as anybody else. We're all in here doing time.

"I don't get no jobs here in prison. The only ones who gets good jobs is stool pigeons, people who'll tell on another inmate to an officer.

I'm not a stool pigeon. You could kill a man in front of me, and I didn't see it. My back was turned."

He talked about the letters he received from women. I asked if he perceived himself as a romantic figure.

"Hell, no," Speck said. "Do you think you're a romantic figure?"

"Well . . . yes," I said.

"Well, you're conceited, man," Speck said, and laughed.

"Do you laugh a lot in here?" I said.

"What am I supposed to do, cry for twelve hundred years?" Speck said.

He said that most of his friends in prison had been black—"guys like Jeff Fort and Bull Harris, guys from the Blackstone Rangers. My hero is Clay, the boxer. In music, I like Clyde McPhatter, Bo Diddley, Little Richard, Fats Domino, Chuck Berry. I never did like Elvis. They called him the king of rock and roll, but if Chuck Berry had been white, he'd have been the king of rock and roll."

Speck said that although at the time he killed the nurses "I had no feelings," he is sorry now.

"I had no feelings at all that night," he said. "They said there was blood all over the place. I can't remember. It felt like nothing.

"I'm sorry as hell. For those girls, and for their families, and for me. If I had to do it over again, it would be a simple house burglary."

Speck said that if he ever gets out of prison, he plans to change his name and try to live anonymously.

"I'd like to be just plain Richard Speck, but that's impossible," he said.

"If anybody messes with me though, they'll be a fool. Because if they do, I'll be back in prison."

Why?

"They'll never mess with nobody else."

What's that supposed to mean?

"That speaks for itself."

Speck got up to go back to solitary confinement. He said he had a final thought for the American people.

"Just tell 'em to keep up their hatred for me," Speck said. "I know it keeps up their morale. And I don't know what I'd do without it."

Baseball and the Facts of Life

He is nine years old; his name is Brett. For three years he has been asking his parents if he could play in the Little League. This summer they said yes.

He is small for his age, with curly brown hair and bright blue eyes. The girls think he is cute, but he tells his mother he doesn't care about that. When his mother and father said he could play in the league this year, he just about exploded with joy. In other summers, he watched baseball on television; this year he was going to play.

His parents took him to the first practice, and they could see it in his eyes: he idolized the man who was coaching the team. The other boys had played in years before—Little Leaguers start young—but Brett didn't care. At last he was going to be one of them.

After the first few games, he would come home from practice, and his parents could sense that something was wrong. It is best not to pry into the secrets of little boys, but they were concerned. So one night, after dinner, they walked over to see his team play.

They watched as the game started, and their son did not get in. There were fifteen boys on the team, some of them very good. But most of them were bigger than Brett, and stronger; they were the ones who played the whole game. The coach let Brett in for one inning; when the inning was over, the coach took him out.

At home, after the game, Brett's parents asked him what had been bothering him.

He said that at the beginning of the season, the coach had said that every boy would play. But for Brett, that meant only the bare minimum—one inning each game. The coach was afraid that if Brett stayed in for too long, the team might lose the game. As it was, he was put in right field, the place that boys who are not good enough are traditionally sent.

His mother started going to every game. She would watch as Brett stood on the sidelines, his eyes alive, everything in his face almost begging to get in. And every game she watched as the coach reluctantly let her son play for one inning, and not a moment more.

At home, Brett would put his uniform on four hours before he was supposed to go to the game. He would walk around the house in it, look at himself in the mirror, check the clock every few minutes; the games were scheduled to start at six P.M., but Brett would get there at quarter to five, just to be sure. Every game was going to be the one when he would really get to play.

And his mother kept going to the games. Even from a distance she could see those eyes lighting up every time it seemed he might get to go in. She would see those eyes, and then she would see the coach not even knowing her son was there. The coach looking at the more skillful boys out on the field, and her son looking at the coach; it made her feel sick to see it.

One day, after the game, when no one was looking, she approached the coach. She asked him why.

"I have to keep the best ones in," the coach said. "We're in a league, you know. We're trying to win. I have five boys on the team who only play one inning. Your son is one of them."

At home, Brett would ask his father to practice with him in the driveway. The father is not an athletically inclined man, but of course he said yes; Brett said he was "working on his arm," as if that would help change things at the next game.

And every game, he would get into his uniform early; every game, he would be the first one at the field.

His mother watched one game as he got in. The boys who got to play regularly—the skillful ones—horsed around between innings, did tricks on their bikes and made jokes with each other. Brett, though, looked only at the game. He never even got a drink of water. This night, when he got to bat, he kept in mind the coach's admonitions about not backing away from the ball. The pitch came in hard and close, and it hit him hard enough to make him cry. When the inning was over he stood expectantly on the sidelines, hoping to get back in. But the coach only called to the regulars: "Double the limit at the Dairy Queen if you win." Brett did not play again that night.

One evening it happened: for some reason a lot of the boys had other things to do, and there were only nine present when it was time for the game to begin. His mother was there again, and she saw the coach tell Brett that he was going to get to start the game in right field. She saw him begin to smile, and then to suppress it; he ran out to right field, part of the starting team.

In the middle of the first inning, one of the regulars rode up on his bike. The coach was clearly glad to see him. When Brett trotted off the field, he saw that the other boy had arrived. The coach took Brett out; his evening was over.

The season is almost finished now. Brett does not put his uniform on four hours early anymore; he does not watch the clock. He still goes to the games, but he has learned his lesson. He doesn't talk about base-ball around the house.

His parents are trying to find a moral in all of this. They know it happens to many boys in thousands of cities around the country every summer. His parents tell themselves that maybe it will turn out to be a good experience; maybe it will teach their son something about life, and about dreams, and about putting too much faith in those dreams.

That's what they tell themselves, but they don't believe it. All they know is that their son, at the age of nine, has been shown that he isn't good enough. We all learn that sometime in this life; some find it out earlier than others. The other night, Brett told his parents that he wasn't going to play baseball next summer. The eyes weren't as bright; that's what hurt his parents the most. The eyes weren't as bright.

An Unmentionable Occasion

To understand this, we must set the scene precisely. We are in the living room of Kristine Costello, in Methuen, Massachu-setts, a suburb of Boston. Color photographs of her two children, Lea and Michael, adorn the walls. Fourteen other women, all invited here by Mrs. Costello, sit in chairs, on couches, and on the floor, drinking rosé wine.

With the exception of the reporter, there are no men in the house. Mrs. Costello's husband, Michael, had run a sweeper over the carpet-ing before the guests arrived, but he understood that once the party began he was expected to depart.

The women here range in age from their twenties to their fifties. Some of them are housewives; some of them hold outside jobs. The suburb is essentially mainstream American middle class, and so, by appearances, are the women.

Up a short step in the dining room, directly next to Mrs. Costello's supper table, is a metal clothing rack. Right now the rack is covered with a white satin drape, but soon, when unveiled, it will reveal the garments that have apparently drawn the women to the party. There will be filmy, see-through negligees; there will be nightgowns with names like French Connection and Flowing Passion, all gauzy and cut low in the chest and high up the legs; there will be crotchless panties; there will be lacy brassieres with the nipples snipped out.

At the moment, though, Tiffany James is addressing the group. Mrs. James is running the party tonight, and she invites the women to have another glass of wine. She thanks them for coming and assures them that their husbands won't be disappointed when they get home.

"Relax, sit back, and have the time of your life," Mrs. James says. She hands each woman in the room a scorecard and a pencil, and begins to deliver something called the Sensuality Test:

"If you're wearing a bra and panties of the same color, give yourself ten points.

"If you've ever finger-painted with a member of the opposite sex, give yourself ten points.

"If I say 'whipped cream' and anybody blushes, give yourself twenty points."

When the test is over, Mrs. James has everyone in the room read off her score. There is much giggling. She says she is just about ready to show the clothing, but first she wants the women to be even more comfortable. Once more, wine is poured.

"I want us all to know each other," Mrs. James says, "so I'm going to go around the room, and I'd like each of you to say your first name, and then to say something sensuous about yourself that begins with the first letter of your first name. I'll start: My name is Tiffany, and I like touching."

There is a momentary silence. These women would look at home in a Betty Crocker ad or in a corporate secretarial pool. But within thirty seconds, they have begun.

"My name is Carol, and I like caressing."

"My name is Linda, and I like luscious lip service."

"My name is Karen, and I like kinky men."

What we have here is a phenomenon so startling and yet so obvious that, had one pondered the factors that led to it, one could have almost predicted it. This is the natural outgrowth of free and open sexuality reaching into the heartland; it is the place where the sexual revolution and the Tupperware party meet.

Tiffany James, the woman directing tonight's party, is executive vice-president of UndercoverWear Inc.; along with her husband, Walter, she runs the company. Since this party is so close to the firm's head-quarters, in Woburn, Massachusetts, she is acting as the party agent. But there are more than eight hundred UndercoverWear agents in thirty-five states; virtually every weeknight of the year, there is an UndercoverWear party going on somewhere in the country.

The premise of these parties is a simple one: American housewives have been titillated and aroused by the sexual openness that has spread across the nation. Most of them are not swingers or cheaters; they may feel a few twinges of raciness, but basically they love their husbands, their children, and their homes. They want to sample some of the exotic new pleasures they know are out there, but they do not want to feel dirty about it, and they certainly do not want to feel guilty.

Enter UndercoverWear Inc. By 1977 Walter and Tiffany James had realized that there was money to be made if they could find a way to offer these women tame, unthreatening thrills; to let them feel vaguely naughty without being unfaithful; to give them some quiet sin for a few hours, and then to deliver them safely home to their families again.

So UndercoverWear built up a line of bedroom attire that ranged from the risqué to the lewd. Instead of advertising it in the backs of true-confessions magazines like the old Frederick's of Hollywood mer-chandise, however, they arranged to bring it right into the women's own living rooms. There was to be none of the furtiveness of ordering from a magazine coupon. The Tupperware imitation was calculated and intentional; Mr. and Mrs. James realized that a great many women would find it more exciting to purchase nighties that bared their breasts than to watch demonstrations of burping bowls. And yet this was all to be done in the name of pleasing their husbands. This was to be done out in the open with friends; this was to be done with a sense of humor; this was to be a party.

"The party plan eliminates any feeling of embarrassment about pur-chasing these kinds of products," Mrs. James says. "If a woman wants to wear a garter belt and nylons for her husband, she might hesitate before going into a store. The feeling is, "This salesclerk is going to think there's something wrong with me; I'm not as sweet and demure as I look, and what's she going to think of me?'"

At an UndercoverWear party, however, the emphasis is on making the women feel they're all in it together. Although, as Mrs. James says,

"It's our firm belief that what happens between a husband and a wife in the bedroom is private," the UndercoverWear parties are designed to assure the women that they are not having their bedroom fantasies alone.

The UndercoverWear theory of success is based on the assumption that these are not women who usually purchase revealing lingerie—"Maybe the husband would buy the wife one black nightie a year, at Christmas," Mrs. James says—and the whole idea of the parties is to persuade the women that what they are doing is socially acceptable. "We want the women to tell themselves: 'Just because I choose to wear something sensuous in my bedroom, that's no negative reflection on me.' Women today have a desire to be feminine and still think they're normal.

"We're not just selling them a piece of lingerie. We're selling them an UndercoverWear night. Not the night of the party, but the night they get to show the garments to their husbands. That's what the agents tell them at the parties: 'When you get your UndercoverWear, schedule your UndercoverWear night.'"

So, as darkness falls, the parties begin. No men are allowed. As each piece of lingerie is removed from the rack for display, the women are encouraged to talk about it. There is more a tingle of teenage romance in the room than a feeling of lust; the women *ooooh* at the items as if what they are looking at are tiny puppies instead of fringe-covered bras. The phrase most commonly spoken in the room is, "Isn't that pretty?"

The UndercoverWear agent realizes, though, that her commission depends on getting the partygoers to order the products, and that the most effective sales pitch is not based on aesthetics. So when a woman across the room asks, "Does that one come with pants, Tiffany?" Mrs. James looks her in the eye and says, "Yes, but we can't guarantee how long they stay on."

There is an odd combination of forces in play as the party progresses into the evening. On the one hand, the women are indulging their fantasies, feverishly marking down the names of the garments they hope to purchase at the end of the night. On the other hand . . . there is no real flavor of wickedness or raw sexuality here. This is definitely not a female version of a stag party. Times may have changed, and the items the women order may be of the variety that must be hidden from the children, but this *does* feel the way a Tupperware party must feel. The attraction for the women seems to be social; the party is like a gathering of sorority sisters, and the merchandise is, in a way, incidental. Sexy clothing may be the excuse that has brought them here, but simply being together away from men is clearly as important to them as the nightgowns they are buying.

"It's nice to be in someone else's home shopping," says Chris Canto, a social worker, who will purchase $50 worth of merchandise at the end of the evening. "I don't think there's anything dirty in the show; it's all very pretty." And Kristine Costello, in whose home the party is taking place—and who will receive free merchandise for being the hostess—says, "I like shopping at home with my friends. It's like a night out with the girls."

The reasons the women give for being in the room are traditional and almost wholesome. "I'm not one to order from a catalog," says one. "You can't really be sure of the quality and sizes in a catalog." And the youngest woman at the party—Carol Medeiros, eighteen, a salesclerk who plans to be married within the next year and who will spend $150 tonight—says she is planning to save the garments for her marriage. "They're for my hope chest," she says.

It is as if the whole world has changed, yet nothing has changed at all. Twenty years ago many of the fashions being sold here would have been too revealing to be featured in a girlie magazine; but here the women are, writing down their choices, talking quietly with one another, making new friends even as they select Fringe Benefits or Jungle Fever.

Perhaps it is best that the men are not allowed to see this; it would deflate the very fantasies that the UndercoverWear phenomenon is designed to inspire. In the male imagination, the idea of a party like this probably conjures up the dark emotional muskiness of a gang bang. But that's not it; if the truth be told, this is one part orgy, nine parts sewing circle, and the amazing thing about the women here is that they seem able to juggle both elements yet somehow keep them separate.

And now Tiffany James has finished the presentation. The last nightgown and pair of panties have been displayed; now the women are descending on the metal rack, grabbing Softly Sensuous and Double Trouble and the rest.

It is time to try them on. The women take their favorites and head for Mr. and Mrs. Costello's bedroom, for the children's rooms, for the bathrooms. Three or four of them go into each room at the same time, taking their own clothes off, putting the UndercoverWear fashions on.

In a matter of minutes, they are back in the living room. The effect is stunning. Earlier they had been in housedresses or slacks and sweaters. Now they are standing around together like so many hookers, all cleavage and belly and leg, telling one another how cute they look and how pleased their husbands will be. The voices are a jumble:

"Tiffany, does this one have bottoms?"

"Tiffany, does this one come with snaps?"

Tiffany James is busy accepting orders, telling each buyer that the items will be delivered in approximately three weeks. Some of the women are standing in front of a mirror staring at themselves. "Well, Eddie," says one, "you'd better be prepared."

"That looks so pretty on you," Mrs. James says to one customer, even as she is moving to the next and asking, "Did you want to try on Little Bo Peep?" It is 9:45 on a Wednesday evening in northern Massachusetts. In an hour these women will be back at home, ready to tuck the children in and turn on the coffeepot for the morning and drift to sleep. Perchance to dream.

Partying with the Prince

I went to a party with Prince Charles Tuesday night. It was pretty much fun.

His Royal Highness did fling gin and tonic in my eye at one point, but other than that he was a perfect gentleman, and it was well worth taking the time to pal around with him.

I almost blew the whole thing before it even started. A couple of weeks ago, one of my bosses said to me, "How would you like to go to a party with the Prince of Wales?"

I thought that Wales was a fairly insignificant country, and a scribe can't be accepting every invitation that comes his way, so I said, "Well, I just did a story about a race car driver from Wales who got his money stolen at O'Hare, so I think I've done enough Wales stories for one year."

Then, some time later, I was relating this set of events to a friend, and he said, "You idiot, the Prince of Wales is Prince Charles! The next King of England!"

"Are you sure?" I said. "I think Prince Charles is the Prince of England."

"He is the Prince of Wales," my friend said. "And this is probably the only chance you will ever have in your life to meet the next King of England."

I'll admit that I was impressed. I have never known a member of royalty, although I did once meet Fats Domino.

I informed my original source that I would, indeed, like to go to the party. I called out for my secretary to pencil Prince Charles in on my calendar. Then, remembering that I did not have a secretary, much less a calendar, I wrote the date and time down on the surface of my desk.

Soon after, I received a letter from the British consulate general. The man who wrote the letter had dropped his customary English reserve. He even stooped to using an exclamation point:

> I think that you already know that this reception is NOT a press conference and that there should be no attempt to interview His Royal Highness in the course of any conversation, nor should any remarks made at the reception be regarded as for publication. Needless to say, no cameras, microphones, tape recorders, notebooks, or any professional paraphernalia!

Needless to say, indeed. I don't even go to bed without a pen and paper. I was properly chastised. However, no Bic, no Bic. So there was nothing for me to do but run a washrag over my sport coat, dust off my shoes, and head for the Drake Hotel.

I presented my letter of invitation and was directed to a dining room, where drinks were being served for the prince, the British ambassador, the consul general, and a number of us media studs.

Waiters fed us some food. Prince Charles was a little late in showing up at the party, but then his plane had just arrived at O'Hare an hour earlier, and you know how long it can take waiting around that lower level for your bags to come moving by on the conveyors.

When the prince did come into the room, he looked swell. Apparently he is one of those fellows who can wear a suit right off the rack, for his clothes did not look as if they needed any alterations at all. He made his way around the room, saying howdy to each guest in turn, and when he came to me I calmly uttered the line I had been rehearsing all afternoon:

"Charmed, I'm sure."

I would like to tell you what His Royal Highness had to say to me. I truly would. What the hell, you're family. But the constrictions placed upon me by the letter from the consulate general prohibit me from revealing the details. Let me just assure you that the information passed on to me by Prince Charles was quite explosive, to say the least.

Upon rereading the letter, however, I find that while it does forbid me from telling you what the prince said, there are no restrictions about telling you how he said it. His voice, in other words.

It is rather deep. More like John's than like Ringo's.

After Prince Charles had finished introducing himself to all us revelers, he called for a drink and began to make idle conversation with small groups. It was at this point that he threw the gin in my face. He was talking about the Concorde, and how it made too much noise when it was taking off over his castle. He gestured wildly with his left hand, which happened to have been resting on top of his drink. The gin and tonic flew directly into my right eye. I think I'm allowed to report that.

Oh, I'm going to break protocol. It can't hurt if I tell you one little thing that he said to me, and besides, how often am I going to be in this position, anyway?

The next King of England said, "Are they paying you money to be here?"

He carried himself quite well, and in fact had the second most regal bearing of anyone in the whole room. The person with the first most regal bearing was Maxwell McCrohon, managing editor of the *Chicago Tribune*, but then Charles is only twenty-eight. He has time.

Actually, Prince Charles seemed relieved that everyone in Chicago was being so nice to him. He may have been thinking back to his ancestor, the late King George V. Early in this century the old-time mayor of Chicago, William Hale (Big Bill) Thompson, said he would "punch King George in the snoot" if the king ever came to Chicago.

No one punched Prince Charles in the snoot. The party continued. It was quite uproarious, but all good times must come to an end, and before long it was time to go home. I waved goodbye to His Royal Highness. I am not allowed to tell you what he said in return.

Reflections in a Wary Eye

Waiting to see Nixon, I killed time in the cafeteria. I watched a woman eat an egg-and-muffin sandwich and wash it down with a root beer. It was eight o'clock in the morning, in a federal office building in lower Manhattan.

I was early. Nixon's letter had said to come at nine, but I wasn't going to risk being late for this one. I made notes, as if this would be a regular interview, but that wasn't my reason for being there at all. I didn't care if I never wrote about it.

Spending time with Richard Nixon . . . for people of my generation, the people who had been in college during his election and his years as President, the very idea was like a tingling promise. We were the people who had professed to hate him most passionately. Despising Nixon, for a time, was a required course. And yet in the years since he had left office, it had become clear that he was the one political figure of our age who was bigger than life. There was no player in the national drama who came close to Nixon; the *idea* of Nixon was somehow central to the experience of being an American in the second half of this century.

I wanted to meet him the way an eight-year-old wants to go to Disney World. I couldn't imagine anything more tantalizing. In a can't-buy-a-thrill age, the notion of sitting alone with Nixon—just listening to him talk—had an appeal that, for me, went way beyond the idea of journalism. We had exchanged letters. I tried to express some of those sentiments to him, in more formal language. I couldn't believe it when his second letter said he would "welcome a visit."

His office phone number was unlisted; I had been given a floor number and told to look for a certain number on a door. At quarter to nine, I rode the elevator up. There were Spanish-speaking people looking for an immigration-processing office. Thirty feet away, I found the door. There were no words on it. I tried the knob; it was locked.

A woman let me in. There, on the walls, were huge color blowups of the Nixon presidency: Nixon riding in a motorcade, smiling and waving; Nixon with his arm around a young Chinese boy; Nixon with Brezhnev. A lone secret service agent, wearing a brown suit and reading a copy of *National Geographic*, sat visibly bored in a chair facing the door I had just come through. The telephones did not ring.

It looked like the office of a middle-level civil service functionary. The secretary and the secret service man spoke neither to each other nor to me. I figured Nixon would make me cool my heels for a while, let the anticipation build. But at nine o'clock straight up, the secretary said, "Would you like to come with me?"

We walked through a door, and there, sitting next to an illuminated globe at the end of a long room, was Richard Nixon, sixty-seven.

"Mr. President, you have a visitor," the secretary said.

When he rose and said, "So . . . did you just fly in?" the first thought to come to my mind was: Dan Aykroyd.

I couldn't shake it. It occurred to me that in these years since he left office, he has been invisible so much of the time that we have come to know him mainly as caricature. Often it was as if he really *were* just an idea, not even alive. And yet here he was, grayer than I had expected, wearing a blue suit and hunched over ever so slightly. On his desk was a small pile of letters; behind the desk were an American flag and a flag bearing the seal of the President of the United States.

We sat facing each other in armchairs near the globe. He was talking, but I was just staring at him. He was the one who seemed nervous; he was making small talk, trying to be friendly, filling the air with words so there wouldn't be the chance of even the most momentary uncomfortable silence. He was asking questions about where I had stayed the night before and how much it had cost, and when I finally made myself pay attention to his words, he seemed to be saying something about some friends of his who had gone out for a milkshake in New York.

" . . . And they said they had gone to Rumpelmayer's," Nixon said. "And they asked me how much I thought a milkshake cost. I thought to myself: McDonald's. Eighty cents? Ninety cents?"

He looked at me as if he expected me to say something. When I didn't, he said:

"Do you know how much that milkshake cost?"

"No, sir," I said, "I don't."

"That milkshake cost three dollars and forty cents," Nixon said.

We began to chat. I had promised myself that I would ask him only the things I was truly curious about. That wasn't Watergate, and that wasn't politics; I figured that if this would be the one time in my life I was alone with Nixon, I'd rather just try to get him to talk about himself.

So fairly quickly we came around to the subject of his stiff and bloodless public image. He said he was well aware of it; he realized that it hurt him in the eyes of some, but that he could never change. "I wear a coat and tie all the time," he said. "It isn't a case of trying to be formal, but I'm more comfortable that way. I've done it all my life. I don't mind people around here in the office, particularly younger people—they usually take their coats off. But I just never have. It's just the way I am. I work in a coat and tie; believe it or not, it's hard for people to realize, but when I'm writing a speech or working on a book or dictating or so forth, I'm always wearing a coat and tie. Even when I'm alone."

I was calling him "Mr. President." I wasn't sure why; before I had arrived I had thought about how I would address him, and I had decided on "Mr. Nixon." But now I wasn't doing it. It didn't seem to be because of his own formality, or even out of intimidation; rather, in a strange kind of way, I sensed I might bruise his feelings by demonstrating that I could skip the title he obviously loved so much. So "Mr. President" it was, but it felt so awkward on my tongue that I decided to ask him about it. When he had been in office, had he allowed even his closest aides to relax a little and call him anything less austere?

"Never. And none did."

When I said that his best personal friends must have had the luxury of calling him Dick or Richard, he shook his head. He told me that even Bebe Rebozo had followed this protocol.

"So when you were out on a fishing boat," I said, "and you were trying to relax, and Rebozo wanted to offer you a beer—he said, 'Would you like a beer, Mr. President?' "

"Yep," Nixon said. "That's right. That's the way."

I had told him in my first letter that I had been among his legions of young critics. He seemed to be intrigued by this, welcoming questions that sprang from that experience, and when I saw that he was warming to them, I asked how it had affected him when he heard the two famous phrases: "Tricky Dick" and "Would you buy a used car from this man?" I said that when people of my generation and political persuasion had tossed off those words, it had never occurred to us that there was really anyone on the receiving end. Nixon had always seemed so much bigger than we were, so far removed, that at the time it had not seemed possible that he could have his feelings hurt.

"If I had feelings, I probably wouldn't have even survived," he said. "I remember very clearly something. I was speaking down in Williamsburg, Virginia, and this was right after I had become President. And I think we had made the first announcement about our first withdrawal of twenty-five thousand. And this very pretty girl, she was I guess sixteen, seventeen, came up and spit full in my face and said, 'You murderer.'

"I borrowed a handkerchief from a secret service man and wiped it off, and then I went in and made my speech. It was tough."

In a way, telling that story seemed to bring him to life. It struck me that to anyone else, the key part of the tale would have been the girl's spitting. But Nixon's voice rose and the set of his jaw became firm precisely when he said, "It was tough"; that's what he wanted me to understand—that no matter how badly people treated him, he could not be touched.

Our conversation was running well past the hour I had hoped for. I had always heard that Nixon hated anything close to psychological questioning, and as we talked about personal matters, I was watching closely to see if he would recoil. But for some reason he didn't; rather, he seemed to be almost relishing the course the discussion was taking. Twice his secretary buzzed him to give him the opportunity to end the appointment; twice he told her that it was all right, he wanted to keep going. I found myself wondering: Is it possible that he's lonely up here? Is it possible that he really needs the company?

I couldn't think of any other explanation for what was happening. Maybe it was as simple as the fact that when you're the most famous national catchphrase of them all, people stop treating you as if you're flesh and bones. The more I made it clear that I liked hearing these stories, the looser Nixon got; he seemed delighted to have an audience that was treating him neither as a criminal nor as a face from a history book. It occurred to me that maybe, in light of the way it had all turned out for him, he didn't get the chance to do this very much.

He began to ramble a bit, telling brief stories, throwing off quick opinions—about thirteen-year-old girls he had seen smoking marijuana on the street near his home, about Lyndon Johnson's inviting him to the presidential bedroom and greeting him from beneath the covers, about his fears concerning young people's watching television instead of reading books. He was smiling more, and looking me in the eye, and asking me questions. I told him I was noticing this; I asked him why, he thought, this side of him seemed so foreign to people.

"I never wanted to be buddy-buddy," he said. "Not only with the press. Even with close friends. I don't believe in letting your hair down, confiding this and that and the other thing—saying, 'Gee, I couldn't sleep because I was worrying. . . .'

"I believe you should keep your troubles to yourself. That's just the way I am. Some people think it's good therapy to sit with a close friend and, you know, just spill your guts. Not me. No way."

I said that on the surface such an attitude might promise a person self-protection, but that in the end it would probably result in his being so isolated and so remote that no one truly knew him.

"Yeah," Nixon said. "It's true. And it's not necessary for them to know."

We had been talking for nearly two hours. Nixon appeared to be growing tired. His sentences were drifting off; he was looking out the window more often. With no warning, he put his hands on his knees and said, "Well, anyway, I have to knock this off."

We stood up. I was feeling curiously emotional. Nixon did not seem to have the old vigor that had inspired such passions in the land. At one point he had said to me, "Frankly, the sense of your mortality grows as you get older. I mean, after all, you read the obituary page, and you read of people sixty-nine, seventy, sixty-five . . . all of my generation. They cut off. They die. Heart attacks, cancer, what have you."

I suddenly felt a little like a kid who had grown up and moved away and was having a meeting with a father he'd never gotten along with, but who he now finally realized would not be around forever. I tried to say something; Nixon seemed to sense the direction in which I was heading, and moved to cut me off. If I was going to get sentimental, he wanted to avoid it, and so before I could even start he was steering us back to harmless small talk. He asked me if I had seen the World Series game the night before.

"George Brett's hemorrhoids," Nixon said. "They put that in the paper. Damn. They shouldn't do that. That's private. Who the hell wants to read about hemorrhoids?"

All the while he was moving me toward the door. I started to thank him for seeing me, but he wasn't listening.

"Carter had them," Nixon said. "Remember, he had them early on? It's probably the tension that creates them."

And then he was opening the door and shaking my hand, and I was walking out.

He called out to me, and I turned around. He was framed in the doorway.

"How old are you?" Nixon asked.

"Thirty-three," I said.

Nixon smiled. "Thirty-three," he said. "Let's see. I was thirty-three years old when I was first elected to the House. It's a good time to be alive."

He nodded almost imperceptibly. Then the door closed. I had a real desire to say something to someone, but the secretary was typing a letter, and the secret service agent was still reading his magazine, and there was nobody else around.

Business Lunch

I am never going to make it in the world of big-time business and grown-up behavior. It's not that I can't balance a checkbook (which I can't) or that I'm not sure how to read the stock tables (which I'm not). Those are obstacles which, I have found, can be overcome.

My shortcoming is far worse, and it dooms me to failure in the world of commerce forever.

I do not know how to have lunch.

Oh, I know how to eat a sandwich or go to McDonald's. I know how to put food down my gullet in the middle of the day. If I can do it by myself, I'm fine.

What I can't do is have a business lunch. "Let's have lunch" has become the most common phrase in white-collar workaday America, and I don't know how to do it. I have tried and I am terrible at it.

Most people, it seems, are perfectly capable of making a lunch date with a business associate, breaking bread, having pleasant conversation, and then going back to work.

I can't do it. Dozens of times every week a telephone caller or letter writer will suggest, "Let's have lunch and discuss it," and I will panic and tell a lie. I will say that I already have a luncheon engagement that day. Which is not true. I never have a luncheon engagement.

But to lie is better than to have to go through with it. Others may sparkle and charm at lunch. I sit at the table and twitch. I look at my watch. I stare dumbly over my companion's shoulder. I yawn. I take my handkerchief out and make a ball of it. I kick the floor. People ask me, "Are you feeling well?"

I do not mean to be doing these things. It is just that I feel very awkward and uncomfortable having lunch with a person who has anything in mind but eating. I realize that I am alone in this, but I feel that the place to conduct business is the office. Business at lunch makes me nervous. Business should not be discussed over food. It makes the food bad and the business bad.

I am not just talking about my specific business, which is writing newspaper columns. I gave up on luncheon interviews long ago, when I kept dropping my notepaper in the gravy and losing my pen in the lettuce. Every time my interview subject would say something worth writing down, I would have a fork in one hand and a knife in the other. It became disconcerting for everyone, with me throwing the silverware to the table and grabbing for my writing utensils. And every time I thought of the perfect question, it would be garbled through a mouthful of cheeseburger.

But even when people understand that no interview is going to be conducted, they still want to have lunch. To "try out an idea," or "tell you about something you might want to consider," or "discuss an interesting opportunity with you." When I tell them to tell me right now, on the phone, they are shocked. To most people involved in business in this country, if it doesn't happen at lunch it doesn't happen.

I guess the reason I am so bad at having a business lunch is that I am never sure which part is the business and which part is the lunch. We sit down at the table and the other person starts making small talk and I just slump there and don't say anything. I know that this person does not really want to talk about the Cubs or what he saw on TV last night. He is just filling the air until the business part. Which is a perfectly fine concept, except that something inside me tells me that I'm not allowed to talk until the official part starts. I mean, somebody's writing this off, and I don't want to cheat.

I also get the impression that we're supposed to be laughing all the time. Not hilarious laughter, but the laughter of good fellowship, to let each other know that although this is business, it is also still lunch. I am not a very good laugher, and often I sound to myself as if I am gagging when I try to make an appropriate response to my luncheon partner's good-natured storytelling. All around the dining room there is pleasant laughter filling the air, and then there is me, smiling broadly and making a heaving sound.

When someone I can't say no to suggests having lunch, it ruins my day. There are so many decisions involved in having lunch, and from the time I get up until the time it is over, my day is totally devoted to the lunch. Where should we go? Should he suggest a place or should I? Is the place too impressive or too shabby? When should I get there? Should I risk being too early and have to stand around, or take a chance on getting there too late and making him impatient? When the waiter asks if we would like a drink, should I have one and seem like a daytime drunk, or say no and seem like a prissy great aunt? And if I say yes and he says no, what will he think? Or if I say no and he says yes? It goes on and on, until the time the check comes and we both hesitate, then both grab for it, then both pull back, then both reach again.

What it does is make me exhausted. I get up from the lunch and go back to the office and collapse on the typewriter. I feel as if I have just been to dancing school.

So what I do, when the rest of the world is at lunch, is to sit at my desk. It does no good. I call people, and their secretaries tell me they are out to lunch. I wait for the phone to ring, but it never does, because everyone is out to lunch. I look for someone in the next office to talk to, but there is no one, because they are out to lunch.

I have two pieces of white bread and a glass of ice water. I put it on my expense account as steak Diane for two. Then I stare at the wall and wait for everyone to come back. It's pretty interesting. We should talk about it. Let's have breakfast sometime.

The Country's Going Through a Rough Spell

I'm in love with a wonderful girl. She's thirteen years old, she lives in El Paso, Texas, and her name is Paige Pipkin. In an age of glamour girls and disco queens and Playmates of the Month, Miss Pipkin has the rarest of qualities. She can spell.

Last week Miss Pipkin correctly spelled the word *sarcophagus* and thus won the 54th National Spelling Bee in Washington, D.C. She triumphed over a young man who misspelled the word *philippic*, and thus she finished first in the competition, which is sponsored each year by the Scripps-Howard Newspapers.

The idea of a National Spelling Bee seems somehow out of date, but I think it's great. If you deal with the written word and you receive a lot of mail, then you know that people simply can't spell anymore. It is a skill that is becoming extinct in America—people apparently feel that they don't need to know how to do it, or that it is too hard to bother with.

When I go through the mail each day, I am constantly dismayed by this trend. It is getting to the point where a letter with no misspelled words is the exception. The problem goes across the board—letters from students, letters from businessmen, letters from people in public life. Even the most prosperous executives have secretaries who can't spell. And—worst of all—I sometimes get letters from teachers, and even their letters are full of misspellings.

This may seem like a minor thing, but I don't think it is. If I know that a person can't spell, then I have trouble trusting anything else about him. If he can't even get the spelling of a word right, then why should I put any faith in his version of events, or his opinions? Obviously he is sloppy in his thinking if he can't even take the trouble to make certain of the spelling of the words he uses.

I fear I am in a minority here. I don't know if there have been any official studies done on the problem, but just from personal observation I know that, in the last decade, the ability of people to spell has diminished rapidly. And yet you hardly ever hear it discussed.

I identify with Alexander Portnoy, the fictional protagonist of Philip Roth's *Portnoy's Complaint*, on this issue. In the book, Portnoy meets a beautiful, loving, affectionate woman and immediately falls for her. But he soon makes a terrible discovery about her. He finds notes she has left for the cleaning lady, and sees that each note contains five or six misspellings. It dismays him. He wants to love her, but he knows that this awful flaw rules such a thing out. He could never truly be in love with a woman who can't even spell.

Say what you will about my writing. You may think it's lousy, it may annoy you, it may even make you sick. But believe me on one thing. I am a hell of a speller. Ask any copy editor I've ever worked with. They will tell you. In the ten years I have been writing a news-paper column, I have misspelled no more than three words. And that's an outside estimate; to be truthful, I don't think I have misspelled any.

It's not such a great feat—all you have to do is look up the words you aren't sure of. Today, for example, before I turn this column in to the copy desk, I will look up *protagonist*, which was used two paragraphs above this one. A simple enough step.

But most people aren't willing to take it. That's the worst thing about the new inability of Americans to spell. If it just had to do with misspelled words, it would be one thing. But it is symbolic of an overall lack of discipline, a readiness not to care, a willingness to be second-rate. I know it may seem like a small thing to you, but it's really not. All the talk lately about the U.S. auto industry suffering because workmanship allegedly is inferior to workmanship in Japan—that's precisely the sort of thing that starts with a nation of people who can't even spell correctly.

And it's destined to get worse. In the television age, all print skills are going to suffer, and spelling is going to be the first one to go. People are going to decide that knowing how to spell is an archaic discipline, and they are going to decide they can get along without it. And the worst thing is, they'll be able to—if enough people just can't spell, then businesses, by default, are going to have to employ them anyway, and try to look past this fault.

Which takes us back to Paige Pipkin, the thirteen-year-old spelling champ from El Paso. For some reason, she has grown up believing that she must have enough pride in herself to be a perfect speller. It is difficult to imagine that she will ever fail in any important area of her life; you know instinctively that she is the kind of young woman who will succeed, because she cares about doing things right.

So congratulations to Miss Pipkin for winning the National Spelling Bee. If there were any justice in this world, they would have crowned her Miss America.

We Came for the Killing

POINT OF THE MOUNTAIN, Utah—We came for the killing. There was no other reason for us to be waiting outside the fence at the Utah State Prison, so early in the morning, with chill darkness still shrouding the hillsides.

We came for the killing. That is not what we told ourselves, of course; we are in the news business, and it was easy to say that we were only here because our jobs demanded it. Leave that for the Ethics of Journalism textbooks. The fact is, we came for the killing, and we could hardly wait for the killing to begin.

We came for the killing because we, just like our fellow citizens, are caught up in the bizarre morbidity and eerie attraction of death rites, and the thought of a firing squad bringing the death penalty back to our lives was a magnet we could not resist.

We came for the killing, and because we carry press cards, we were allowed on the killing site. And you, fellow citizen—you would have been on the killing site, too, given the opportunity. And if you say that this is not true, if you say that you want no part of the sickness that drew us toward the house of death—well, if not you, then your neighbor. We got the message a long time ago. You want to hear about the death rites, and you want to hear it all. You have read every word of the firing squad stories, and you will read every word of this. There is no escaping it.

It is the strangest of paradoxes. Here, in this early week of 1977, two stories dominate the news, and the national consciousness is homed in on them both. Let us take the second one first: the inauguration of a President who spoke during his campaign of love, and goodness, and the spirit of life. It worked, his words of love and life; we elected him, and now he will be our leader.

But that is the second story of the week. The first one, the story at the Utah State Prison, the Gary Gilmore story, may tell us more about America than the happy story in Washington. The story in Utah was about hatred and evil and the tingly drama of violent death, and if the relative fevers of American interest in the two stories were somehow to be measured, which do you think would win out? In your heart of hearts, which story would you rather hear a teller of stories unfold?

We told you everything we could about the house of death in Utah. We told you what the condemned man ate for breakfast. We told you what color were his clothes. We told you how the shed for the riflemen was constructed. We told you about how the man's body shook and trembled as the bullets bored into his chest. We told you how the blood poured from beneath his shirt, and how it covered his pants. We told you where the blood remained, a sign of the killing ritual even after the killing was done, and the dead man driven away.

We told you everything, but we didn't tell you everything. We told you what you expected to hear; we told you everything we knew about the killing and the killed.

But there is something we left out, something we didn't tell you. We didn't tell you about ourselves. We didn't tell you what we did up on Point of the Mountain. We, your representatives in the free press, your guardians of the First Amendment—we didn't tell you about us.

We didn't tell you how we rushed to the death shed the moment we knew we could get away with it. We didn't tell you how we crawled around the sandbags in front of the dead man's chair, the sandbags still fresh with his blood. We didn't tell you how we hurried into the firing squad's canvas booth, and how we squinted out of the vertical slits where the rifles had been, squinted out at the chair and made ourselves a gift of the same view the executioners had viewed.

We didn't tell you how we touched everything, touched every possible surface in the death shed. We didn't tell you of the looks on the faces of the prison guards, who watched in amazement as we went about our doings with such eagerness, such lust. We didn't tell you what we did to the death chair itself—the chair with the bullet holes in its leather back. We didn't tell you that, did we? Didn't tell you how we inserted our fingers into the holes, and rubbed our fingers around, feeling for ourselves how deep and wide those death holes were. Feeling it all.

Why didn't we tell you that? Why didn't we tell you about ourselves? Probably because we understand the basic truth of it all. We understand that we are you, and you are us, and there are some things that we don't want to admit out loud about ourselves. Don't even want to think about. If we were monstrous, we were monstrous in a small way; probably better if we just forget about it, we and you both.

And besides, the killing at Point of the Mountain was only the beginning. There will be others; there will be more. And we will be there, too, and you will be right along with us. Oh yes you will. We will always come for the killing.

Fade to Silence

He was a big man on the radio then. Cruising in our cars, we would hear him every night. He was the first person to play the Beatles for us. We knew his name.

He had a professional voice, I think. It was hard to tell. This was the era of the AM shouters, and he was one of them. We never heard him talk in a regular voice, except once.

We were driving around. It was the night of the day Kennedy got killed. There wasn't much traffic. Most people were home watching TV. A lot of the radio stations were giving news, or playing symphony music without ads. Not his. His station kept playing rock and roll.

Someone got the idea to go down and see him. We didn't think it was odd that we had never thought of it before. The station was right off the main street, the call letters shining in vertical neon on the side road. On the way to the station we listened to him shout. Downtown was empty.

We drove up to the front door of the station. It was locked. The building was dark, except for one window on the second floor. He was talking on our radio. Then he read an ad. A song came on, and we got out of the car.

We tossed pebbles at the lighted window. A man appeared. Then he went away. The car door was open in the November night. His voice came back on again. He talked some more. We threw some more pebbles. On the air he said something about somebody being at the window. We looked at one another. We were kind of thrilled.

When the next song came on, he walked to the upstairs window again. He looked down at us, and then he yanked it open. He asked us what we wanted. He didn't sound friendly. He didn't sound like him. He wasn't shouting.

We didn't say anything for a moment. Then one of us said that we had just wanted to come down and see him. He acted as if he were surprised; he asked us if we were kidding. We yelled up that we weren't. The song was ending. He said to wait a minute.

He was gone and his voice was back on the radio. He said that he had some visitors. He read another commercial. We talked to each other. We said that he didn't look like his voice. He was short and he wasn't young. Some of us said that was wrong; we said it just seemed that way, looking at him up through the window.

When the song came on he was back again. Now his voice was welcoming. He had a piece of paper. He asked us our names, and he asked us where we went to school. We were wearing our letter jackets, stomping our feet against the sidewalk to keep warm. We asked him if we could come in. He said no. He said he could get fired.

We stayed outside for about an hour. He talked to us between each song. He seemed happy to have the company. I think it was our idea to leave.

The rest of the night he talked about us about once every half hour. It was unusual. We were cruising the same streets, listening to the same station, and there were our names. We thought the whole world must have been listening; we felt very famous. Five minutes before each hour there would be news from Dallas. They had a man in custody.

The next weekend there was a dance. We heard that he was going to be the emcee. We paid our fifty cents to get in. He was at a microphone. He was shouting. We waited on the floor next to the stage. When there was a break we motioned for him. He came over. We told him who we were. He remembered us.

He went back to the microphone and said our names. After that we would listen to see where he would be appearing each weekend, and then we would go to the dance. He seemed to like us. He seemed to like the idea of having someone to talk to. Once one of us asked him how much money he made. He said fifty dollars a week. But he said the big money was in the weekend dance appearances.

It didn't occur to us that there were thousands of him, in every city and small town in the country. Voices in the night, narrating the lives of the people growing up in the miles of the station's reception. To us he was a star; he was like the famous singers whose records he played. It didn't make much sense that he would want to have us around, but clearly he did. The more we saw of him, the less of a star he became. We must have followed him around to weekend dances for about six months before we stopped. I don't remember why.

We all went away to college, and when we came back he was not on the radio anymore. He was still in town, though. The last time I saw him he was selling men's shoes in a department store about three blocks from the radio station. I saw him, kneeling on the floor, putting someone's socked foot onto one of those hard metal measuring devices. I was sure it was him. I was going to go over and say hello, but then I didn't. Sometimes it's better not to say anything at all.

Boy at His Best

Today, magazine reading is a part of your life that you take for granted—one of the predictable pleasures of your adult years. Chances are, though, that you were already a magazine reader back when you were nine and ten and eleven. You probably don't remember it right offhand, but every month there was a magazine you waited for the mailman to deliver.

That was an important event in your life. And if you think about it, maybe it will be the advertisements that bring the name of the magazine back to you: the coupon allowing you to become a salesman for the American Youth Sales Club's all-occasion greeting cards (if you sold enough, you could win a Daisy air rifle). The picture of second baseman Johnny Temple urging you to buy a MacGregor baseball mitt.

And the stories: "We Canoed the Arctic Ocean." "Batboy for the Braves." "Here's How They Make Rope." "Lucky 13" ("In one terrific week we met President Eisenhower, breakfasted with Congressmen, and toured Washington and New York. We knew for sure we were the Lucky 13 Explorer Scouts").

The magazine, of course, was *Boys' Life*. At its peak, it had 2.65 million subscribers and a phenomenal hand-to-hand pass-on rate. *Boys' Life* was what American boyhood was all about; you read it because you were a young male, and it entertained you and made you feel as if you were part of something bigger than yourself.

You probably haven't seen *Boys' Life* in years; for all you know, it doesn't even exist anymore. It would seem difficult to believe that today such a publication could still be sold to American males who are approaching the brink of adulthood. You've seen so many twelve-year-olds leafing through *High Times* and *Hustler* on the newsstands; come to think of it, you've never seen *Boys' Life* for sale anywhere.

And you may wonder: Is the magazine still alive? Or did it die with so many of the now-moldering dreams and delusions about boyhood in America?

On the third floor of a modern glass-and-brick building in a secluded industrial park outside Dallas, in Irving, Texas, the editorial office of *Boys' Life* sits quiet as a computer-operations room. The floors are thickly carpeted; the staff of twenty-three work in sound-absorbent red-and-white cubicles.

Boys' Life is owned and published by the Boy Scouts of America; although its motto is "For All Boys," about eighty-five percent of its readers come from Boy Scout and Cub Scout troops. Fifty-two percent of all Scouts subscribe to *Boys' Life*. A subscription is not included in the membership fee, but troop leaders sell it to Scouts or their parents. Over the years there have been several attempts to offer *Boys' Life* on the nation's newsstands, but all have failed. Circulation is down to 1.5 million these days, and the magazine has been reduced in size, too, from the one in the memories of generations of American men. Gone are the old *Life*-size pages, replaced now by ones the size of *Time*'s— a change necessitated by escalating production and postal costs.

Pinned to the wall of the executive editor's cubicle is a list of proposed stories for an upcoming issue. The rundown could have been written in 1953: "How to Hit a Softball." "Repair a Dripping Faucet." "Pets: Rabies Is a Killer."

Recent editions are stacked on a table. The graphics are sharp, the color photographs of excellent quality. The articles are about junior golf champions and learning how to water-ski and building plastic models. The Think & Grin joke pages, featuring contributions from readers, are filled with little-boy humor. From Alan Smith, of Bedford, Texas: "*Smart:* 'What do you call an elephant that lives in Los Angeles?' *Alec:* 'An L. A. Phant.'"

There is little laughter in the *Boys' Life* office, though; it is spacious and sterile, and the editors, writers, and graphic designers toil away in their own work spaces. Chatter is at a minimum; as the staffers pass one another they will say hello, but mainly they stay at their desks and efficiently put together their monthly message to the boys of America.

Robert E. Hood, fifty-five, the editor of *Boys' Life*, joined the magazine in 1953. Since then, he has worked nowhere else; he has watched America change and has seen the number of names on his subscription list slip by more than one million.

"I've done what I can to keep up with the times," Hood says. "The look of the magazine has changed. Because of television, we had to go to big color pictures, since boys were used to the TV screen. And boys' attention spans have shortened. We used to publish articles that ran up to thirty-five hundred words. Now, though, if we go over fifteen hundred words, they won't stay with it."

Hood knows, however, that the reason for the magazine's decreasing readership has nothing to do with any editorial failings on his part. American boys in the 1980s are not the same as American boys in 1955, and yet Hood feels his responsibility is to put out a magazine that reflects the values of a quarter-century ago.

"You have to come back to the word *wholesome*," he says. "The parent is buying the magazine for the boy, and the parent has a certain idea of what he wants the boy to be like, even if he isn't really like that.

"So what do we write about? There is a heavy slant toward sports, adventure, hobbies, and Scouting. And the kid will still save his magazine, will still keep it in his room the same way boys did back in the Fifties.

"Remember," Hood says, *"Boys' Life* is probably the one piece of mail that boy will receive all month. It's very important to him."

When *Boys' Life* was founded in 1911, there were four other magazines aimed at the same young-male market, all of them successful: *St. Nicholas, Youth's Companion, American Boy*, and *Open Road*.

"Now we're the only one left," Hood says. "And if it wasn't for the Boy Scouts of America, *we* wouldn't survive."

His point is an obvious one. *Boys' Life* subscriptions are sold for $4.20 a year through Scout troops. And since the magazine is not considered an attractive sales medium by many national advertisers, it relies on those subscriptions for its continued existence. "Think about it," Hood says. "They can't advertise tobacco in our magazine. They can't advertise alcohol. They can't advertise cosmetics, the way they can in a magaizne like *Seventeen.* They can't even advertise clothes very well. We never could attract the clothing business. Boys are just not fashion plates."

Indeed, Hood is convinced that in many such ways, American boys today are not all that different from the boys of twenty-five and fifty years ago. "If you're asking me whether the basic nature of the boy has changed, I'd have to say that the answer is no," he says. "They are still interested in collecting stamps, the same way they were in 1955. Why? I don't know, but it's consistent. Why do they continue to read that corny joke page, Think & Grin? I don't know, but they do. What is the most popular feature in the magazine? A True Story of Scouts in Action, just as it has always been."

Hood is not certain, but he feels that the remaining *Boys' Life* readers are the American boys who are managing to resist the salacious temptations of the present-day United States, and who desperately want something to cling to. "I can't promise you that none of our readers are also flipping through *Playboy* and smoking pot," he says. "But I know those things aren't as prevalent as among boys who don't read *Boys' Life*.

"The subject of sex I haven't dealt with at all. It's too big to handle. With our readers, we'd get hit with all kinds of hell if we started writing about sex or sex education. The repercussions from the churches and the parents . . . look, the editor of this magazine has an implied contract with the mother or the father of the boy who reads it. And to publish certain kinds of stories in the magazine would be to violate that contract, no matter how the boys would respond to them."

The staff members of *Boys' Life* agree. They feel that regardless of the negative influences in American society, there is a part of a boy that remains unchanged—a "pocket of innocence," as one editor puts it.

Dick Pryce, a fifty-five-year-old senior writer for the magazine, thinks that the mothers and fathers who subscribe to *Boys' Life* for their sons are yearning for an America that reminds them of the days when they were growing up.

"Many, many parents out there want that kind of life for their boys," Pryce says. "They want a childhood that is good and nonsexual and non-drug-related, and we've got it in this magazine. We provide it for them."

So *Boys' Life* publishes stories about magic tricks and camping trips and circus clowns. Its letters to the editor are addressed to a mythical burro named Pedro; its regular columns are about bicycling and fishing and nature and coin collecting. Its editors look around them and wonder about the magazine's—and their own—future.

Are the men and women who put out *Boys' Life* shouting optimistic messages into an empty canyon? It is not that easy simply to dismiss the magazine and its editorial philosophy as anachronisms; for one thing, the Reagan years promise to be a period during which Americans grasp for earlier values, and for another, *Boys' Life*'s circulation figures, while drastically reduced from what they were twenty years ago, are nevertheless far from unimpressive.

So even if the magazine is doomed to slide even further from its status as an American institution, a visitor to its offices can't help but be affected by the people who put it together. To use a corny phrase, they are doing good work; they may be unsure how much of an audience remains for their philosophy, but the very fact that they are attempting to provide a clean, upbeat, general-interest magazine for young boys—during a time when such a thing seems unwanted and out of date—should count for something.

It is also heartening to see what the magazine seems to have done for its staff members. They may be living in a time warp, but working at *Boys' Life* has kept the children in them alive, too. That's probably inevitable when your morning mail brings you a letter from a ten-year-old boy in Tacoma, Washington, who just wants to let you know that his favorite fish is the trout.

"There is no such thing as a mature man," one editor said to me, and the sentiment was offered without a trace of cynicism. His voice sounded almost hopeful as he said it.

Robert Hood gazes out his window. The Texas plains beyond are like a moonscape; Dallas is somewhat off in the distance, but from the offices of *Boys' Life* the rest of America seems very far away.

"The whole world is changing," he says. "A generation ago, when a boy was growing up, Mommy was home in the daytime, so she could be a den mother. But today? Mommy works. She's never home. So the Scouts can't get leaders."

He flips through some galley proofs for an upcoming edition. The proofs are piled neatly on his desk, and he seems preoccupied as he glances at them.

"Sometimes I'll get together with friends at night," Hood says. "And often there will be people there who I don't know, and I'll be introduced, and they'll ask me what I do. And I'll tell them that I'm the editor of *Boys' Life*. And they'll be amazed. They'll wonder how it can survive. They'll ask me, 'How can you continue to do this in the teeth of what goes on in the world these days?' "

Hood looks out his window once more.

"I ask myself the same questions," he says. "Are we coddling these boys? Are we spinning cotton webs of fantasy with an idealistic view of a life that just doesn't exist anymore?

"I don't know. I wish I knew what the answer was, but I just don't know."

Retirement Dinner

The event was a retirement dinner for a man who had spent forty years with the same company. A private dining room had been rented for the evening, and the man's colleagues from his office were in attendance. Speeches and toasts were planned, and a gift was to be presented. It was probably like a thousand other retirement dinners that were being held around the country that night, but this one felt a little different because the man who was retiring was my father.

I flew in for the dinner, but I was really not a part of it; a man's work is quite separate from his family, and the people in the room were as foreign to me as I was to them. To me most of them were names, overheard at the dinner table all my life as my father sat down to his meal after a day (one day in forty years) at the office; to them I was the kid in the framed photograph on my father's desk.

Names from a lifetime at the same job; it occurred to me, looking at the men and women in the room, that my father had worked for that same company since the time that Franklin Delano Roosevelt was president. Now my father was sixty-five, and the rules said that he must retire; looking at the faces of the men and women, I tried to recall the images of each of them that I had built up over the years at our family dinners.

My father was seated at a different table from me on this night; he appeared to be vaguely uncomfortable, and I could understand why. My mother was in the room, and my sister and brother; it was virtually the first time in my father's life that there had been any mix at all between his family and his work. The people at his office knew he had a family, and we at home knew he had a job, but that is as close as it ever came. And now we were all together.

A man's work, if he is any good at it, is as important to him as his family. That is a fact that the family must, of necessity, ignore, and if the man were ever confronted with it he would have to deny it. Such a delicate balance; the attention that must be paid to each detail of the job, and then the attention that must be paid to each detail of the family, with never the luxury of an overlap.

The speeches began, and, as I had expected, much of their content meant nothing to me. They were filled with referencs and in-jokes about things with which I was not familiar; I saw my father laughing and nodding his head in recognition as every speaker took his turn, and often the people in the room would roar with glee at something that drew a complete blank with me. And again it occurred to me: a man spends a life with you, but it is really only half a life; the other half belongs to a world you know nothing about.

The speeches were specific and not general; the men and women spoke of little matters that had happened over the course of the years, and each remembrance was like a small gift to my father, sitting and listening. None of us really change the world in our lifetimes, but we touch the people around us in ways that may last, and that is the real purpose of a retirement dinner like this one—to tell a man that those memories will remain, even though the rules say that he has to go away.

I found myself thinking about that—about how my father was going to feel the next morning, knowing that for the first time in his adult life he would not be driving to the building where the rest of these people would be reporting for work. The separation pains have to be just as strong as to the loss of a family member, and yet in the world of the American work force, a man is supposed to accept it and even embrace it. I tried not to think about it too hard.

When it was my father's turn to speak, his tone of voice had a different sound to me than the one I knew from around the house of my growing up; at first I thought that it came from the emotion of the evening, but then it struck me that this probably was not true; the voice I was hearing probably was the one he always used at the office, the one I had never heard.

During my father's speech a waiter came into the room with a message for another man from the company; the man went to a phone just outside the room. From my table, I could hear him talking. There was a problem at the plant, something about a malfunction in some water pipes. The man gave some hurried instructions into the phone, saying which levers to shut off and which plumbing company to call for night emergency service.

It was a call my father might have had to deal with on other nights, but on this night the unspoken rule was that he was no longer part of all that. The man put down the phone and came back into the dining room, and my father was still standing up, talking about things unfamiliar to me.

I thought about how little I really know about him. And I realized that it was not just me; we are a whole nation of sons who think they know their fathers, but who come to understand on a night like this that they are really only half of their fathers' lives. Work is a mysterious thing; many of us claim to hate it, but it takes a grip on us that is so fierce that it captures emotions and loyalties we never knew were there. The gift was presented, and then, his forty years of work at an end, my father went back to his home, and I went back to mine.

Voices in the Night

On the night she finally knew she was in trouble, Alix Lacy was near the end of her shift. It was almost two A.M.; she had been on the air for four hours. As usual, she was alone in the studios of KBCO-FM, in Boulder, Colorado. She worked without an engineer; there was no one else in the building.

The light on her telephone was blinking again; like the phones in most sound studios, hers was wired to flash a light rather than to ring. She knew it was him. By this time, she thought she could feel it when he called.

She spoke into the microphone. In her soft, unthreatening voice—perfect for Boulder—she announced the next record. For all the listeners who were waiting, she put an album on one of the two studio turntables. The music played, and the telephone light kept blinking, and with the microphone turned off she started to sob.

It is a phenomenon of American late-night radio: the female voice wafting over the airwaves, comforting and stirring at the same time, offering a promise of companionship for listeners who are lonelier than they might want to admit. For women disc jockeys with the right kind of voice, the night shift offers professional opportunity; men want to hear women play them music when it is dark outside, and station managers all across the United States are aware of this.

Alix Lacy is one of the women who sought a career doing this kind of work. Lacy, twenty-seven, worked the ten P.M.–two A.M. shift at KBCO. Her voice was not overtly sexual; in the words of one of her bosses, she came across on the air "like the typical Boulder lady—beautiful, yet simple and wholesome."

Ray Skibitsky, who is the KBCO station manager, said, "I think some listeners have a fantasy in the back of their minds that the female late-night disc jockey is sitting there talking to them, and them alone."

There are no surveys that measure that type of attitude. But one thing Skibitsky and Dennis Constantine, KBCO's program director, were sure of: when they walked the streets of their town and stopped in at bars and restaurants, people would find out what they did for a living, and one of the first questions was always, "What does Alix Lacy look like?"

When the calls started, Alix Lacy barely noticed them. As a matter of routine, she gave out the station's telephone number during her show. The purpose was to allow listeners to call with requests.

At some point—she does not remember precisely when—she realized that someone was calling and hanging up on her, and that a pattern was beginning to emerge. Right when she would start her shift, the phone would blink, she would answer it—and the caller would hang up. This would occur several times. Nothing would happen until the middle of her shift. Then the caller would do it again; a flurry of calls. Things would get quiet. Then, near the end of the shift, another flurry. She would answer; the caller would hang up.

The KBCO studio is in an office complex that is deserted at night. Alix Lacy worked alone in a room on the second floor, up a flight of stairs. The only entrance or exit for her was the glass door at the top of the stairs. As the hang-up calls continued, night after night, she found herself, for the first time, thinking about that.

One night, after her shift, she left a note on the bulletin board: HEY, EVERYBODY, IS ANYONE ELSE GETTING HANG-UP CALLS A LOT? She asked the other on-air performers to initial the note if they were receiving similar harassment. No one else was.

The caller never said anything. Lacy told herself that "he'll burn out pretty soon. At least he'll say something." She realized she had already decided the caller was a man.

Station employees went on vacation, and Lacy was shifted to fill in for some of them. One week she was on the air from six A.M. until ten A.M. Just after six, the phone flashed. She answered it. The caller hung up. Then again in the middle of the shift. Then just before ten. Another week she was assigned to the two P.M.–six P.M. shift. The caller did it again.

She felt something funny happening inside of her. The caller was beginning to become a person to her—a man—and she was frightened of him. She asked her superiors to authorize a phone trace on the calls, which they did; but the telephone company said that, because of technical limitations, they were unable to isolate the calls.

Against her will, she began to feel her stomach knot every time she arrived at the studio for her show. The caller had never threatened her, had never said a word. Yet he was reaching her. She began to refuse to answer the phone during the first hour of her shift. She would see the phone blink, and she would know it was the caller, and she would not pick it up. She would talk on the air and play the records, and all the time she would be looking at the light on the phone. Finally, she would make herself pick it up. Then the caller would hang up. Sometimes the caller would let the phone ring for an hour and a half before she picked it up; when he heard her voice, he would replace the receiver.

There were other callers, too, of course; KBCO listeners who wanted her to play records for them. When she looked at the lights blinking, she thought she could tell which callers were normal, and which was the one. "I kind of know what his calls feel like," she said. She realized that such a thing sounded absurd. "I know that something like this can run away with you, but once it's happening, knowing that doesn't help." She had become obsessed with the blinking light: "Every time it blinks, it's like a knife going into me again and again."

Her bosses knew that something was wrong. "I listened to her tapes, and it was clear that she was distracted," said Dennis Constantine. "It's fairly easy to tell when a disc jockey isn't paying attention to what she is doing."

To Alix Lacy's great consternation, the presence of the caller was taking over the hours she spent at the studio. "I feel as if he is trying to touch me," she said. "He's not touching me by saying anything; he's touching me by getting me to react to his consistency." Ray Skibitsky told her that by refusing to answer the phone when she thought it was the caller, she was only encouraging him; she was verifying to him that he was getting to her. She knew this was true; still, when she felt it was the caller on the other end, she could not pick up the receiver. She could only stare at the light and try to get through her show.

Her conviction grew stronger. She was fearful that the caller was going to come to the studio with a gun, shoot his way through the door, and come up the stairs to where she sat before the microphone.

One afternoon she called Peter Rodman, a KBCO host and Boulder journalist. She told him about her fear about the gun; Rodman said, "Alix, the door is glass. If anyone wants to do anything, all he has to do is kick the door in. Why are you thinking about a gun?" Rodman's talk persuaded her to ask the station management to have a man answer her phone for one night; maybe if the caller heard a man's voice, he would stop.

Ray Skibitsky agreed to do it. He came to work with Lacy one evening; when the phone began to blink, he picked it up. Whoever was on the other end hung up. He sat with Lacy throughout her shift. Near the end, the caller hesitated before hanging up. The caller let out an exasperated sigh. It was definitely the sigh of a male. Then the line went dead.

The next two nights, he did not call. Alix Lacy was ecstatic. She thought she had been silly in the extreme for worrying about it. At the end of the week she worked an earlier shift than usual and her voice on KBCO was replaced that night by fellow disc jockey Rick Lofgren. Lofgren worked his shift. When he finished and walked out to his car in the parking lot, one tire had been slashed and all the air let out of another.

Both Lacy and her bosses knew they had a problem. It was not so much a horror story as something even more disturbing: the idea that someone with access to a medium of mass communication could become mentally trapped by one person in the audience with a will to disrupt her life. When Lacy had gone into radio work, she had liked the idea that, sitting behind a microphone in an isolated room, she could reach thousands upon thousands of strangers. Now one of the strangers was reaching her.

"I sensed there was a guy out there doing this," Ray Skibitsky said. "But what was there to do? He obviously gets his gratification and his kicks by doing this to her. But there have been no overt threats. When you look at it objectively, it's just an annoyance. If she could just ignore it, she would see that. But she can't."

When Lacy arrived at work one day, there was a letter addressed to her from Bob Greenlee, the owner of the station.

"I am not unaware of your concern over the belief you are being harassed by a telephone caller," the letter began.

Ray mentioned that he came in this week to answer the phones while you were here and he too senses that there may be someone on the phone who, for whatever reason, gets off on having you answer the phone and then hang up.

As you know, we have little control over sick minds who would do this to someone. Try as we might, it is impossible for us to do anything to trace or catch up with the person calling you. And even though you are upset by having to put up with this situation, I believe it is a continuing disruption of your work at this station and must now step into the matter. I have authorized Dennis Constantine to find a person to answer the phone for you during your shift for the next week. If, at the end of that time, you cannot pull yourself together and live in peace with yourself, the situation is not correctable by any further actions from us. I will need to address the matter of finding another person to do your work. . . . You are an excellent employee, we all like you very much, and hope you can find the inner strength it will require to get over the fear you have.

Alix Lacy decided to take a vacation. As of this writing, that is where she was.

She was sick at heart. She knew that when she returned to work, the caller would be waiting for her; and she knew she could not continue to live her life thinking about him. To her, the only logical solution seemed to be to leave Boulder, or to get out of radio work. It almost made her shake to think about it; the best thing about the vacation was that she did not have to see the phone blink at her every night. She had talked to Constantine and Skibitsky about a possible leave of absence, but she knew that was only delaying her final decision.

She had gotten some jobs around Boulder playing records at parties; it was a big step down from talking to the listeners of KBCO, but at least she could see her audience. She was also studying jazz piano; something was telling her that she had to come up with an alternative way to make a living.

"My voice . . ." she said. "I've always had a voice that people commented on. I just think it's a pleasant and conversational voice. I've never felt it necessary to project my sexuality through my voice. The last thing I ever wanted to do was provoke someone with it.

"I know that if I don't quit, I'm going to get fired. It's funny, isn't it. . . . I know how foolish all of this sounds, and I know that everyone thinks I should just ignore it. I feel like a fool for letting it get to me."

But it has. All over America, there are voices being sent out into the night; all the voices entering all the bedrooms and automobiles and bars. Implicit in the voices is a sense of power; the power to reach people, to touch their minds and change them, if only in small ways. Seldom do you hear about someone touching the voices back.

"There is this movie, *Forbidden Planet*," Lacy said. "It's about this invisible monster that attacks a spaceship. They try to find the monster, but it turns out that there's really nothing there. See, the monster was the subconscious mind of the scientist himself. I've been thinking about that a lot. Why am I creating this invisible monster in my life? And then I realize how far it's gone. I'm even questioning myself."

One thing bothers Lacy most of all, she said. It is a belief she holds —a belief that goes beyond all the rationalizing and all the intellectual understanding of what has happened.

"I'm not afraid, but I know I will meet him someday," she said, "I know how that sounds, but I've thought about it and I know it's true and there's nothing I can do about it. He's created this thing between us, and he's out there, and someday we'll meet."

What a Man, Part One

All little boys have idols when they are growing up: John Wayne, Roy Rogers, Mickey Mantle.

I was no different. I had a boyhood hero. But he wasn't a movie star, a cowboy, or a baseball player.

My hero was Ellsworth (Sonny) "What a Man" Wisecarver.

Ellsworth (Sonny) "What a Man" Wisecarver became a headline figure in the news during the 1940s when—starting at the age of fourteen—he eloped with two married women. Both women already had children. The newspapers tagged Wisecarver with the nickname "What a Man," and called him the "Boy Lothario." For a while every move he made was a national event.

The Sonny Wisecarver story began in 1944 when Sonny, fourteen, eloped with Mrs. Elaine Monfredi, twenty-one, of Compton, California, the mother of two.

The couple met as Sonny walked by Mrs. Monfredi's house after school one day.

"He whistled at me as I opened the door to look in the mailbox," Mrs. Monfredi recalled.

After that day, Sonny and Mrs. Monfredi saw each other after school and holidays. Her husband was a metal worker in a war plant.

In May of 1944, Sonny and Mrs. Monfredi eloped to Colorado and were married.

"Sonny is an ideal husband," Mrs. Monfredi said then. "He doesn't believe in hitting women."

Sonny said:

"Elaine's the kind of wife I want because she likes to have a good time without getting drunk."

Mrs. Monfredi's husband, James, when informed of the incident said, "She can choose between me and this boy. She can stay away or come back."

However, Sonny's mother, Mrs. Mildred Wisecarver, called the police and reported that Sonny had run off with Mrs. Monfredi. The mother said that "Sonny is a good boy but large for his age."

The couple was apprehended in Denver, and Mrs. Monfredi was charged with child stealing. The marriage was annulled.

But a year later—in November of 1945—Sonny eloped again, this time with Mrs. Eleanor Deveny, twenty-five, of Los Angeles, whose husband was serving in the Army in Japan. Mrs. Deveny had two children whom she left behind. Sonny was now sixteen years old.

"I thought I could be as happy with my husband as anyone could be," said Mrs. Deveny. "Then I met Sonny. It was love at first sight. I couldn't resist him. He's a perfect lover. I love him more than I do my own husband. He's the kind of guy every girl dreams about but very seldom finds."

It was at this point that the press gave Wisecarver the name Ellsworth (Sonny) "What a Man" Wisecarver—although some papers referred to the boy as "Woo Woo" Wisecarver. In headlines, where there was not room for the full name, Wisecarver was usually referred to simply as the "Boy Lothario."

Mrs. Deveny said that she had met Sonny when she had gone to visit an ailing friend at a house where Sonny was boarding. Sonny and Mrs. Deveny said that they were going out for a sandwich, and then fled the state together.

"I knew how old he was," Mrs. Deveny said, "but it didn't make any difference. He's more of a man at sixteen than a lot of men are at thirty-five."

She said that she was not concerned about her husband in the Army.

"I don't know if my husband knows, but I still love Sonny," she said. She cashed one of her husband's Army paychecks and gave the money to Sonny.

Police apprehended the two before they could get married, and Sonny was taken to an Oroville, California, jail cell.

Mrs. Deveny said that she would like to join Sonny in his cell. "If Sonny still wants me, I'd like to divorce my husband," she said.

Sonny, however, told jail guards that he "didn't give a hoot" if he ever saw Mrs. Deveny again.

Judge A. A. Scott of the California Superior Court—who had presided over the Sonny Wisecarver case at the time of his first elopement at fourteen—said, "He's done this before and he'll do it again."

Sonny's mother said that the first time her son had run away with a married woman she had thought that he had been seduced, but now she was convinced that Sonny was the aggressor in his romantic adventures.

The judge asked Sonny's mother to sign a complaint against Mrs. Deveny for contributing to the delinquency of a minor.

In court, Sonny's mother said, "I can't go through life signing complaints against girls who run away with my son."

"Don't do it, Mother," Sonny whispered.

But she signed the complaint anyway. Sonny was charged with "leading or in danger of leading an idle, dissolute, lewd, or immoral life," and of being "persistently and habitually beyond the control of his parents." He was sentenced to a term in a youth detention camp.

The judge said, "If Ellsworth gets into any more of these jams, he will be the most sought-after man in the United States, especially if these floozies keep making lurid statements to the press."

"Why can't I live my own life, without people always telling me what to do?" Sonny said.

He went to the youth detention camp, but escaped in 1948 because he wasn't allowed to smoke.

When news of his escape was reported, the Los Angeles Police Department was besieged with telephone calls from women wanting to know if Sonny was still at large.

He found work as a busboy and a baby-sitter, and sold magazines door-to-door in the Northwest, using the name "Johnny Donovan." At one point he tried to join the Army, but was rejected because of his juvenile delinquency record.

Meanwhile, Mrs. Deveny's husband, Corporal John Deveny, read the news about his wife and Sonny in the Japan edition of *Stars and Stripes*, the Armed Forces newspaper. He said he was "shocked." He came back to the United States and said, "It's a husband's duty to stand by his wife. I'm going to stand by her."

Mrs. Deveny said that she would probably resume her marriage, "because John has been sport enough to forgive me."

In 1947, at the age of seventeen, Sonny Wisecarver married Betty Zoe Roeber, also seventeen, of Las Vegas, Nevada. Miss Roeber had been an usherette in a Las Vegas movie theater, and had met Sonny while showing him to a seat.

"I've been through a lot, and I don't want my wife to suffer any embarrassment from my past," Sonny said. "If folks will only forget the mistakes I made as a kid, now that I'm really and honestly married, I'll prove that all this talk about me is untrue. I just want to live a normal married life with Betty."

The two set up housekeeping in a trailer home. But a year later, Betty left Sonny, saying that he "couldn't make a home for me."

Ellsworth (Sonny) "What a Man" Wisecarver hopped a freight train for Salt Lake City to look for a job.

What a Man, Part Two

Ellsworth (Sonny) "What a Man" Wisecarver, the fourteen-year-old Boy Lothario of the 1940s who became a national headline figure by eloping with two married women, today is a bus driver in Las Vegas, and describes himself as "just an average forty-eight-year-old man with a little potbelly."

Wisecarver—who as a teenager became a heartthrob for the women of America because of his reputed prowess as a lover—says that women do not even give him a second glance today.

"That whole thing was just a crock," Wisecarver says. "Just a crock."

Wisecarver—who says that he always detested the "What a Man" and "Woo Woo" nicknames given to him by the press—said that when he began eloping with married women at the age of fourteen, he was merely a victim of circumstances.

"Opportunity just presents itself, and you answer it," he said. "It was World War Two. All the husbands were gone. The women wanted attention. I gave it to them. Wouldn't you take advantage of the same circumstances?"

He said that his enormous fame in the Forties was more a result of the newspapers' needing bright feature stories to write than of any real power over women held by him.

"The papers were full of stories about the war," Wisecarver said. "They needed to write something different. So the newspaper writers heard about me, and they wrote a lot of crap."

Of the two married women he eloped with—Mrs. Elaine Monfredi, twenty-one, whom he wed when he was fourteen, and Mrs. Eleanor Deveny, twenty-five, whom he ran away with when he was sixteen—Wisecarver said:

"I never hear from them anymore. I don't know what happened to either of them."

Wisecarver's name dropped out of the news in the late 1940s, after he, at age seventeen, had married a seventeen-year-old usherette in Las Vegas. The papers reported the marriage, and then a year and a half later, reported that the girl had left Sonny, and that Sonny had hopped a freight train heading for Salt Lake City.

"We got back together after that, but by that time the newspapers had forgotten about me," Wisecarver said. "Our marriage lasted for twenty-three years. Then we were divorced."

Wisecarver is married again. He and his wife, Elaine, thirty, have a nineteen-month-old son, Michael.

"I drive a tour bus for Transportation Unlimited here in Las Vegas," Wisecarver said. "I met my present wife on the job. She was a hostess on the bus company's nightclub tour. She used to ride with me."

Asked to explain his reputation as a young Romeo, Wisecarver said:

"I have no idea. All it was was luck, that's all. Women ride my bus every day now and don't even give me a second glance.

"I think the women fell for Sonny because he is a very nice person," his wife said. "Other than being a very nice person, I don't think there's anything. I mean, I don't think he has any special magnetism or anything like that. Women do like a very nice person with an honest and open personality. That's an admirable quality in any person."

Wisecarver is devoted to his seventy-seven-year-old mother—who, during the days when he was eloping with older married women, pleaded in tears to a judge, "I can't go through life signing complaints against girls who run away with my son."

"My mother still lives in California," Wisecarver said. "She's forgiven me. She loves me. That's a woman's place in life, isn't it?"

Reminded that a judge once warned, "If Ellsworth gets into any more of these jams, he will be the most sought-after man in America," Wisecarver said:

"It never happened. I wear a bus driver's uniform with the company emblem, but my name's not on display in the bus, so no one ever notices me. I drive tours to Hoover Dam, to Death Valley, to the Grand Canyon, sometimes to Disneyland.

"I'm just an average run-of-the-mill bus driver who goes home to his family. We live in Las Vegas, but we never go to the Strip. This town is only a swinging town for the little old ladies with nickels. An old people's Disneyland is all it is. People who live here don't go out. I try to raise my little boy, make my house payments, and just get by."

Asked why he decided to run away with married women when he was such a young boy, Wisecarver said:

"Oh, every boy does that."

Asked if he had a good time back when he was the Boy Lothario, he said:

"I suppose I had a good time. Wouldn't you?"

And then Ellsworth (Sonny) "What a Man" Wisecarver laughed out loud.

Classroom Lesson

PHOENIX, Arizona—It was a drizzly Monday morning, and Don Stanley, thirty-five, was teaching his class of twenty-seven fifth-graders in Room 30 of the Hopi Elementary School on Lafayette Boulevard.

The day was not extraordinary; just another March morning in Arizona. I was sitting in the back of the classroom, at a desk designed for the ten-year-olds who filled Room 30. Just watching; a normal day in a normal American school.

Stanley, wearing casual slacks and a sweater, was running the boys and girls through math exercises. He would call them to the blackboard one by one; he would set up a multiplication problem, and then have the children work out the solution.

"Why did you place the decimal point there?" Stanley would ask, and a little girl would reply, "Because it belongs there."

Most adults—if they aren't teachers or school administrators—never see the inside of an elementary school classroom while it is in session. We are used to getting our news of schools from the papers: teachers' strikes, and vandalism, and problems with reading scores. Life in an elementary school becomes blurred together with other topical things that pass in and out of our consciousness.

Which is why this morning spent in Room 30 was proving so interesting to me. There would be no news made here today; no conflict, no passion, no violence. And yet what was going on was so important; here in Room 30, as in hundreds of thousands of other classrooms around the United States, these children were being formed into what they will be when they suddenly turn into the next generation of fully grown American citizens.

I watched Don Stanley with the children. Teachers are paid absurdly low salaries, compared with what people in business and industry receive as compensation. But as I watched Stanley going from desk to desk, I was reminded that his job—and the jobs of other elementary school teachers around the nation—are so much more important than the things the rest of us do in the name of commerce.

He stopped to help a girl with a word she was stumbling over in a textbook. He explained to a boy why the multiplication sum he had just completed was wrong. He bent over a desk to answer a question another girl had for him.

It must be easy not to care. For a teacher, usually there is no one looking over your shoulder, and especially in an elementary school, the people you're in contact with every day are too young to really know whether you're doing a good job or a bad one. If you're not putting out, they won't know; they have no frame of reference.

And that is the awesome thing about the American educational system. As easy as it is to say that children's characters are shaped at home and not at school, that's probably incorrect. Certainly children spend so many hours at school that the classroom experience becomes the central one in their lives. A bad home environment can damage a child forever, but an indifferent school environment can bring results that are every bit as ominous.

What can a child pick up if the classroom environment is good? That it's important to be curious. That making an effort to be correct is better than being sloppy and letting yourself be wrong. That progress is one of life's most important elements, and that if you let yourself stay in the same place you were yesterday, your vistas will never change.

Those attitudes are almost as important as the specific information a teacher imparts. When you're ten years old, if your teacher lets you know that he or she cares that you're learning, cares that your reading is becoming more sophisticated, cares that you are trying to master complicated mathematical concepts—if those things happen—then you're going to be a ten-year-old who stands a much better chance of being a successful and happy twenty-five-year-old and thirty-year-old and forty-year-old.

That's what I was thinking about in Room 30—how parents blithely turn their boys and girls over to strangers who will have such a monumental effect on their lives. Even the most concerned parent can have very little control over what goes on in his child's classroom—and yet that is where much of what the man or woman that child grows up to be is determined.

It's such a moving responsibility that teachers have—and it's made all the more so when you realize that they are among the least-honored groups of Americans. We expect them to be there, and we give our children to them, and then we go about our own daily lives—seldom thinking about what they mean in regard to what the people of this country, and ultimately the country itself, will become.

So I sat in Room 30 of the Hopi Elementary School. Don Stanley announced that it was "free reading time," and the boys and girls reached into their desks to pull out the books they wanted to spend time with.

They sat silently in their chairs and opened the books to the pages where they'd stopped last time around. Don Stanley stood at the front of the class, next to the blackboard, and he looked out at the twenty-seven children. I think there was pride in his eyes. That's what I think.

We Interrupt This Program . . .

If you are too young to remember it, or too old to have been a part of it, there is no explaining. Cruising the streets of the hometown in 1964, accompanied by the voices of the Beatles coming from the car radio, it was a time when anything seemed possible. This was during the days when a new Beatles record would be released every six weeks or so; each one was like a gift, a new chorus for the sound track of our lives.

We were all indestructible. I remember speeding down a highway through a snowstorm with some friends, late at night; the car skidded and swerved, and suddenly we were crashing through a guardrail and the car was tumbling down a gulley. When it came to a rest, we looked around at one another; there we were, in our high school letter jackets, unhurt, and the radio was still blaring and there were the Beatles singing "I Want to Hold Your Hand." And we stood in the snow, laughing; young and new and invincible, laughing.

They made us happy. That's a simple thought, and it's hard to conceive of in these times when everyone is so sophisticated about the machinations of the music industry. But we didn't know about the music industry then. We weren't even buying albums yet. Those voices coming from the car radio, though, didn't need any translating. They were narrating the happiest times of our lives.

If you ever drove by a lake on a warm summer night, with the sounds of "Things We Said Today" filling the car; if you ever parked with your high school date as "Please, Please Me" came out of the radio; if you ever headed home from your part-time job to the strains of "A Hard Day's Night"; then all the words that are being written and spoken about John Lennon's death are superfluous. You don't need to hear. You know.

That's what struck me Monday night. The television was on, and the newsmen were trying to explain the murder in stiff and mundane words. A few feet away, in the kitchen, a radio was playing; the station had already started to broadcast Lennon's songs, and so as the TV newsmen announced the details of the shooting, there was John Lennon's voice, singing "A Day in the Life" and "I Am the Walrus."

And the Beatles music coming from the kitchen made the words on the news seem . . . stupid. Made them seem stupid in the way that Beatles music always made more traditional forms of communication seem naive and incomplete and uncomprehending. Part of that had to be illusion, of course, but magic is always largely illusion.

The impressive thing is that the magic never went away. Within an hour of the news of Lennon's death, my phone at home started ringing; I was hearing from friends I hadn't spoken to in years. And when I started to make my own calls, I discovered that everyone was having the same thing happen: All over the country, men and women were reaching out to hear familiar voices, to touch friends in the aftermath of the news.

Maybe the men and women hadn't given more than a passing thought to Lennon in years. That's not what mattered. The important thing is that, grown-ups now, living in condominiums and town houses, raising families, surviving busted marriages, seeking corporate successes, realizing career failures, they were finding themselves drawn together again by the idea of the Beatles.

We are a generation that has never been very enthusiastic about the idea of growing up, anyway; we hang onto the memory of our younger years with a ferocity that surprises people older than us, and puzzles people younger than us. And it is hard to explain; certainly the experiences we had during the years in which we came to maturity are no more or less deserving of preservation than similar time periods lived through by those who came before us.

One of the manifestations of this attitude has been a recurrent cry that the Beatles reunite, as if by appearing onstage together again, they could somehow give us back the time that we have lost forever. The Beatles themselves—especially John Lennon—realized the folly of this; perhaps one of the most valuable things they did was to refuse to be a part of that. For by attempting to recapture something that belonged to the past, they would have run the very real risk of ruining even the memory.

No, it is good that when we think of the Beatles now, it will be in terms not of some multimillion-dollar reunion concert in the Eighties, but of four young men who were as fresh, as cocky, as exuberant, and as innocent to life's darker moments as we were when we and they were fortunate enough to share the planet.

Our thoughts should not be of a December night in 1980, when voices on the news told us of a shooting in New York. We have been through similar nights before, when the voices were telling us of the loss of other men who were important to us, and our memories are filled to overflowing with the details of such tragedies.

Besides, those are the thoughts of grown-ups, and there are enough of those to last us a lifetime. Better to think of summer nights with "Sgt. Pepper" coming out of the car radio, and life stretching out ahead like the most perfect and level two-lane highway ever built.

Those nights are what John Lennon and his friends gave us. It was something very simple, and yet something that no politician, no author, no artist was ever quite able to do. The Beatles made us happy. God, it was something.

Captain of His Ship

Sometimes, when you're not looking for anything, something comes up and strikes you as clear as daybreak. I had been traveling by bus through corn-and-soybean country for several days; my reasons were personal ones, and I had found what I was looking for, and now I was on my way back to Chicago.

I seldom ride interstate buses, but these few days had been enough to convince me that there is little romance to them. As a traveler who usually finds himself in airports, I had become numbed by this week's endless hours in dank, musty buses, heading slowly between places that no other form of public transportation serves.

My fellow passengers were not inflation-fighters; they were on the buses because buses are the lowest common denominator of American transportation. There is nothing cheaper; the low price was the only reason that the people were aboard. They were the bottom social stratum of the country's travelers; they needed to get someplace, and the bus was all they could afford.

Now I was on the last leg of my journey; the Trailways bus I was on had started the trip in St. Louis, and was on a nine-hour run through Missouri and Illinois. Several hours into the ride, I began to notice something.

It was the driver. He was a young man with a mustache and sideburns; I would have to guess he was in his early thirties. What struck me was the manner of crispness and precision he brought to his job. He was dressed neatly, and he addressed his passengers politely, and at the rest stops he timed his schedule exactly with his wristwatch.

When a passenger approached him with a question along the way, the driver did not act as if he were annoyed; he took time to answer in a friendly, informed way. It was, frankly, a lousy route; instead of heading directly to Chicago, the schedule called for him to stop at any number of tiny towns along the way: Clinton, Fullerton, Farmer City, Gibson.

Usually there was no bus station in these cities; the driver would pull the coach into a gas station parking lot, or stop in front of a restaurant. One person might get off, or two might get on. It hardly seemed worth his time to be making the detours to serve so few passengers.

And yet he carried out his job with class. He welcomed each passenger to the bus; hurried out the door to assist with baggage; made a fresh count of travelers for his logbook at every stop. I got the impression that he was memorizing all of our faces; we might be with him only for one gray autumn day, but we were his passengers and he seemed to be making an effort to take a personal interest in that.

He was just a long-haul bus driver heading up some forgotten route in the middle of the country, but for his attitude, this might have been a Boeing 747 on its way to Paris. I found myself wondering what struck me so oddly about this man, and in a second the realization came. This attitude of his—this pride in the work he was doing—was the very thing we have for so long been told has vanished from the American work force.

Had the driver taken a lazy and slovenly approach, no one would have ever known; the passengers on an interstate bus aren't the kind of people who have the pull to make trouble. They have no alternative; if they don't like the bus, there's no cheaper way for them to go. Certainly there was no prestige built into the driver's work. Trailways isn't even the big name in long-haul buses; Greyhound is.

But on this ride, it was as if the idea of not doing his job well had never crossed the driver's mind. And a funny thing was happening; because the driver found dignity in his own work, he instilled his load of passengers with a small feeling of dignity, too. Oh, they knew they were riding on an uncomfortable bus with men and women who probably couldn't afford any other means of transportation; but because the driver had pride, the passengers seemed to feel a little better, too.

At one toll booth the driver paid the attendant, then leaned out the window to say something. I listened. The driver had seen a car stalled on the side of the highway several miles back, and was advising the toll-booth man to telephone the state police to inform them that there was a traveler in trouble. I hadn't noticed the stalled car, but the driver had, and he obviously considered this part of his job.

When we pulled into the station in Chicago's Loop, the driver stood at the bottom of the steps leading out of the bus, helping each passenger depart, saying goodbye to each of us. He stayed there until the bus was empty.

It was something to see. Most of the passengers had no one to greet them; they wandered out of the station one by one. In a bus station there is none of that sense of drama you're always getting at a big airport; here the feeling was not of an adventure beginning, but of dreary, uneventful life continuing.

And yet, because of his attitude—the way he feels about his work—the driver had, for a few hours, made things different. When I arrived home, I realized something inexcusable: for all the driver's impressiveness, I hadn't even bothered to learn his name. So I called the Trailways dispatcher and found out. It is Ted Litt.

Paper Boy

When I was twelve, maybe thirteen, I would ride the bus downtown with my best friend, Jack Roth, and we would kill the day just walking around the stores.

When darkness came we would wait for the bus to take us home. Standing on Broad Street just east of High, we would look over at the big building across the street from the Statehouse. It was the building that was the home of the *Columbus Dispatch*. Atop the building was a red neon sign that spelled the paper's name out in Old English script, and beneath the logo was the slogan: OHIO'S GREATEST HOME NEWSPAPER.

We would stand there, Saturday dusk after Saturday dusk, and we would stare up at the sign, blazing red in the sky, and it would seem that there was nothing more powerful in all this world than the *Columbus Dispatch*.

I've been thinking about that lately because, with the seemingly endless stories of great newspapers wheezing and dying, I figure it is unlikely that young boys and girls stand on corners in awe of newspaper buildings anymore.

Which is probably not all that unhealthy; there was a time when newspapers were thought of as so all-potent that nothing on earth could stand in their way. They were burly and arrogant and at times despotic; they ruled their cities, and to cross the publisher or editor of the town's leading newspaper was akin to political suicide. Newspapers were in fact what governments were supposed to be in theory: the rulers of their constituents, the monarchs of their municipalities.

So it is probably good, in a way, that such a thing is disappearing. But I find it mostly melancholy; I am a newspaperman, I have been a newspaperman since I was sixteen years old, and I sense the passing of an era. Newspapers will surely survive, in one form or another. But many newspapers will die—many already have—and even the ones that live are unlikely to cause young boys to stand on the street corner in reverie.

When the *Washington Star* was going down, Mary McGrory, the paper's superlative columnist, complained that people often stopped her as she went about her rounds and said, "And how is the *Star* doing?" It made her feel awful; the question was asked as one might ask about a relative with a terrible and incurable disease. More than anything else, that question made her understand how things were changing. In a past that seems shockingly recent, such a question might have sounded absurd. Newspapers occasionally died before, yes; but never did they seem so generically weak, so fragile; never did they seem worthy of the public's worried concern.

Newspapers have been hated, and they have survived that; newspapers have been idealized, and they have survived that. But never before have newspapers been patronized, and even pitied. It is happening now, in each town where a great newspaper faces death. Speeches are made on city-council floors, and statements are read by concerned mayors, and eulogies are delivered by television anchormen to audiences the newspapers would love to have. It used to be the newspapers that told the councilmen and the mayors and the television reporters what the agenda was. Everything seems to be turning around.

There is a temptation to go overboard in telling what it feels like to walk into a newspaper's city room. The fact of the matter is, there is no way to go overboard. When I first entered a city room it was the most intoxicating feeling I had ever experienced, and that feeling stays with me to this day.

Much of the sensory onslaught has changed in this electronic age; but twenty years ago, to hear the clatter of a floorful of typewriters, and smell the musk from the pastepots, and hear the reporters yelling "Boy!" as they summoned the copykids to pick up their stories—to wander into that atmosphere for the first time was to know, instantly, what you wanted to do for the rest of your life.

Forget literature; immortality lay in a front-page by-line about a four-car fatal on I-70. In the city room, suddenly nothing seemed small-town anymore; if you went out and saw something, and then came back and wrote it up, everyone you knew—all of your neighbors, all of your family, all of your friends—would know about it in the morning, too. If you hadn't seen it, no one would know it had happened; because you were there, everyone would know.

There was no feeling in the world like finishing your last paragraph on deadline and seeing the sheet of yellow paper move from city editor to copy editor to slot man to pneumatic tube—and then, forty-five minutes later, while the rest of the city slept, to see the first papers come up with that story on Page One, and your name riding atop it.

It was a guarantee of eternal adolescence; the world was reinvented each day, each morning you were going to see something you had never seen before . . . and then you were going to get paid to tell people about it. And the people were out there; that was a given, they needed you, they had always needed their newspaper, they were waiting for that paper boy to show up with their daily news. You sat in the city room and you could almost sense those people waiting for that thump on the front stoop, the sound that announced that you and your newspaper had arrived again.

There was no real hint that the audience was not always going to be there. Television was a presence, true, but it seemed not to threaten the local morning and afternoon papers. In the city room, you sensed that over at the TV stations they were waiting for that thump at their front door, too, to learn what the news really was. All through the decade of the 1960s, that was the case; television was everywhere, but it was taking its cues from the papers.

It was during the 1970s that this changed. Working in the city room, you did not notice it right away. You were too busy fashioning the day's facts into newspaper stories; that consumed so much of your time that it did not occur to you that, just maybe, people weren't reading the front page the same way they used to. They didn't particularly like to read, and now they didn't have to. Television had become the front page, and if you were candid with yourself, you had to admit that television was pretty good at it. This skill you were so proud of—this boiling of accidents and local disasters into swallowable stories—was easily transferable to the television screen. And those people who were waiting for that thump at the front door . . . now they were waiting for the anchormen whose names they knew instantly. A by-line suddenly seemed like something out of the Gay Nineties.

If you were lucky, your publishers and editors were anticipating what was going on, and were changing your newspaper into something it had never been before. They were conceding the front page to television, and concentrating on special sections and features and columns. If you were unlucky, your publishers and editors were pretending that nothing had changed, and the product you were putting out every day was being delivered to an audience that, maybe without even knowing it, felt that it was somehow quaint in the 1980s. The delivery process itself—the printing of thousands of papers, each to be hand-delivered or peddled individually—seemed ominous in an age of electronic efficiency and economic peril. In any event, the newspaper you dreamed of as a kid—the newspaper that was your town's major way of finding out what happened yesterday—was gone forever. You could pretend it was still the same, but there were days when you noticed that even you didn't read most of the front-page stories past the first two paragraphs. And you were a newspaperman.

When newspaper reporters gather these days, it is this kind of thing they talk about. They have all had the experience: they have run around on a story all day, hurried back to the office, gone over their notes, crafted the information into a smooth and concise report. And they have gone to bed knowing that, by the time the readers reach out the front door for their papers in the morning, all of the information will seem very old. The readers will have heard all about it on the late-night TV news before going to sleep. As often as not, the newspaper reporters will have watched the same broadcasts.

The common response among most of us is to try to do what we do better or in a different way than the television reporters. Give the story a different twist, or a literary flair that can't be carried off on TV. Sometimes this works; many newspapers prosper. But they aren't what they were before. They aren't their communities' principal source for news—and that is what made us go into newspaper work in the first place. If someone had told us that we were going to be working for a sort of daily magazine published on newsprint, we probably would have said no thanks.

I have hedged my bets. I work for this magazine, and I also work for "ABC News Nightline," a television program whose technological reach astounds me each time I come in touch with it.

But I am different from the other people who work for *Esquire*, and I am different from the other people who work for ABC. I am different because I am a newspaperman; not a former newspaperman, but a newspaperman who walks into a city room every morning of his life. My home base is the *Chicago Tribune*, and I am a little embarrassed to admit that the feeling I get in that city room is the same I got so many years ago, when I was first allowed to feel whatever it is in the air of a newspaper office.

In many ways I am afraid to leave it; all the signs tell all of us that newspaper work is like manufacturing buggies in the days when automobiles first took to the streets, but when you are in love with something, you cannot walk away. My magazine colleagues deal with proofs for glossy pages as part of their daily routine; my television colleagues watch the news being fed to New York from satellite points around the world. I wait for the first edition to come up, just as I did when I was sixteen years old.

Some people dream of writing great works of literature; some people dream of stirring people's imaginations with the beauty and flow of their prose.

For some of us, though, for some reason, the goal was considerably less grand. All we wanted to do was go out every day and see something new, and then write what we saw into stories that people would read in their newspapers the next morning. Everything else was extra.

And the funny thing is, the dream goes on. In today's mail I received a letter from a young man with whose work I am familiar. He has a job in a fairly secure part of the publishing industry. In his letter, though, he told me that he wanted desperately to be a newspaperman. He named the paper to which he is applying; it is a newspaper that— if I know anything about this business—will be dead within two years.

But I wrote him the letter of recommendation; I said that he is a fine young talent, and that he will do good work if only he is given a chance. He is not an obtuse person; he must realize that there is no certain future in what he is pursuing. But something inside him makes him want to do it, and I did not feel like talking him out of it. I just wrote the letter and mailed it off, and I hope he gets the job.

So it is not the best feeling when we see what is happening in the newspaper community. We are supposed to be fairly glib when it comes to any other subject—newspapermen, it is said, can write about cats or kings—but we stumble around when we try to explain what all of this is doing to us.

For me it's fairly simple. I have my limitations, but I have the ability to do something that I doubt Saul Bellow or John Updike can do. Sitting on the rewrite bank, I can give you fifteen inches about a four-alarm fire on a twenty-minute deadline. It may not count for anything, but I can do it.

Michael Testifies

It begins with a boy running downstairs to buy ice cream on a muggy August night. This is how it ends:

Early afternoon Monday. Michael McCullough, sixteen, is wheeled into a second-floor dayroom on Ward B-23, Oak Forest Hospital. The orderlies are quick as they steer Michael's bed; within seconds, the boy is attached to a blue-and-white Bennett Respiration Unit, Model A-1. A long white tube is stretched from the machine over toward Michael's neck. A green nozzle is inserted into Michael's trachea. The machine, replacing a portable device Michael has worn in the hallway, is switched on; the noise begins. A steady pounding, once every four seconds. The oxygen, stored in a large green tank behind the respirator, is being pumped into Michael's system. It is the only way he can breathe.

The judge, Wayne W. Olson of the Cook County Circuit Court, looks briefly at Michael. Michael cannot look back; his head rests on a white pillow, and his eyes are directed toward the ceiling. He is paralyzed from the neck down.

"All right," Judge Olson says. "Please bring the jury in."

The jurors, who have come by bus from Chicago's Criminal Courts building, begin to file in and to find their places in plastic chairs that have been set up in the hospital room. When they have settled, a gavel sounds; court is in session. There is silence in the room, save for the ceaseless, once-every-four-second thump of the machine that is keeping Michael McCullough alive.

He is not expected to live very much longer. Dr. Joseph Woo, who has treated Michael at the hospital, has told Judge Olson that the chances are "very slim" that Michael will ever move his limbs again; that the prognosis for Michael's life expectancy is "very poor"; that in all likelihood Michael will "very slowly waste away."

But on Monday, Michael is not wasting away. On Monday, even though he cannot speak and he cannot move, Michael is trying to find justice for the horrible thing that happened to him last summer. Which is why the extraordinary courtroom session is being held inside the walls of Oak Forest Hospital.

Briefly, this is the background:

Michael, who lived in one of the high-rise Robert Taylor Homes public housing buildings at 4946 South State, was watching television around 8:30 P.M. last August 17. He told his mother that he wanted to go downstairs and buy some ice cream from the Good Humor man. He decided not to take the elevator; instead, he began to run down one of the building's staircases.

When he got to the ninth floor, he was stopped by two young men. They tried to rob Michael. He resisted. One of the boys pulled a gun and shot Michael in the face. The bullet lodged in one of his vertebrae, paralyzing him below the neck. Since that evening, Michael has not been able to move, has not been able to breathe without the respirator, has not been able to speak a word above the level of a hissing, barely audible whisper.

But on Monday Michael was going to talk.

The two young men accused of shooting Michael—David Bracey, eighteen, and Tony Gathings, also known as Tony Jackson, seventeen— both of whom live in Michael's building, sit at a makeshift defense table in the hospital room. They stare at Michael curiously, as if they are watching a TV program. Their faces show no other expression. Michael's face is propped at an angle where he cannot look back at them.

Judge Olson swears in Dr. Patricia Scherer, an associate professor at Northwestern University who specializes in speech disorders. Judge Olson explains that Dr. Scherer will act as Michael's interpreter. Dr. Scherer walks over to Michael's bed, and leans close to his face. A team of doctors and nurses stands nearby, ready to come to Michael's assistance if he needs them.

George Pappas, an assistant state's attorney who is prosecuting the two young men charged with the attempted murder of Michael, stands across the room and says in a very loud voice, "Michael, I want you to tell the ladies and gentlemen of the jury and everyone here your first and last name."

Michael moves his lips. No words come out.

Dr. Scherer, hovering over him, watches. She turns to the jury and says, "Michael McCullough."

"Michael, how old are you?" Pappas asks.

The lips move again. Dr. Scherer watches again.

"Sixteen," Dr. Scherer says.

Pappas asks, "Is your address 4947 South State?"

Michael's lips move rapidly. Dr. Scherer looks at the motion, and then responds:

"He says no. He says that he lives at 4946 South State."

Pappas and his co-prosecutor, George Lynch, exchange short smiles. Michael has just let the jury know that his mind is still sharp enough to allow him to be a credible witness. Now Pappas begins to get into the meat of the testimony.

Pappas leads into the night of the shooting. He establishes that Michael was on his way to the Good Humor man.

"After you left your apartment on the twelfth floor, how did you begin to go downstairs?" Pappas asks.

Michael's lips move.

"I walked," Dr. Scherer answers for him.

Pappas: "What happened on the ninth-floor landing?"

Michael: "Two boys stopped me."

Pappas: "Two boys you knew from before?"

Michael: "Yes."

Pappas: "Can you identify those two boys?"

Michael: "David Bracey and Tony Jackson."

Pappas: "What did they say to you?"

Michael: "I don't remember exactly."

Pappas: "Well, what happened next?"

Michael: "David Bracey grabbed me around the neck."

Pappas: "Where was David Bracey standing?"

Michael: "Behind me."

Pappas: "And where was Tony Jackson standing?"

Michael: "In front of me."

It is becoming very difficult for Michael to do even this much moving of his mouth. The discomfort shows in his eyes. The doctors and nurses bend over him to see if he wants to stop. But he is not finished with what he has to say. The two defendants stare over at the hospital bed.

"What happened next?" Pappas asks.

"Tony Jackson tried to get in my pockets," Michael's lips say.

Pappas: "And what were you doing?"

Michael: "Holding my pockets."

Pappas: "Did you see a gun?"

Michael: "Yes."

Pappas: "Who had the gun?"

Michael: "Tony Jackson."

Pappas: "What did he do with the gun?"

Michael: "He shot me."

The respirator thumps away. There is no other sound. Pappas hesitates before asking his next question, then manages to continue.

"Before he shot you, did he say anything?" Pappas asks.

Michael's mouth begins to move uncontrollably, wildly. Dr. Scherer attempts to comfort him.

"Just relax, Michael," she says.

Pappas repeats his question. Dr. Scherer moves her face closer to Michael's.

"He says that Tony said, 'I ought to shoot you,' " Dr. Scherer says.

Pappas: "After that did he pull the trigger?"

Michael: "It was already cocked."

Pappas: "Where did he shoot you?"

Michael: "In the jaw."

Pappas: "What happened next?"

Michael: "I fell to the ground."

Pappas: "What did Tony Jackson and David Bracey do then?"

Michael: "They ran."

Pappas: "No further questions."

Outside the windows of the hospital room, the February wind blows the empty limbs of trees. A brightly painted red fire escape and a green delivery truck are the only flashes of color in the area.

Sherwood L. Levin, the attorney for the two defendants, begins to question Michael in detail, making him go over the story one more time, in greater length. Michael is exhausted; at one point he has to stop and rest for fifteen minutes, but he goes on. He does not waver in his testimony.

Levin says, "To the best of your knowledge, Michael, did you know that the gun was loaded?"

The respirator pounds away. Michael moves his lips.

"I was shot," Dr. Scherer says for him.

More pounding. More moving of Michael's lips.

"It must have been loaded," Dr. Scherer says for him.

Michael's mother, Bernice, watches her son, motionless beneath his white hospital sheet. She has other children; she knows that Michael probably will not live; she also knows that, because of Michael's testimony, her other children may be threatened, may be in danger. She has said that Michael is the quietest of her children, and that he has few friends; before the shooting, his greatest joys had been to play solitary games of basketball, and to watch television alone. This is a proud moment for her, watching her paralyzed son stand up for himself.

There is more cross-examination, more questions from both sides.

"He is very tired," Dr. Scherer pleads.

But Michael goes on.

Defense attorney Levin asks Michael if David Bracey has come to see him in the hospital.

"Yes," Michael's lips say.

But prosecutor Pappas has another question.

Pappas: "Did David say that you should testify that you shot yourself?"

Michael: "Yes."

The two defendants glare at Michael, whose eyes cannot focus back at them. He has not testified the way they wanted; his testimony has been that the two boys tried to murder him. There are no further questions.

Judge Olson dismisses the jury. They leave by way of Michael's bed, looking at him as they pass. The defendants walk by, also, but Michael will not look back. The day's testimony is ended; the jury is expected to retire for a decision later in the week.

Soon Michael is alone in the room with his doctors and nurses. His lips have stopped moving. He is so tired. But his eyes shine. The nurses nod at him in approval. His day in court is over. The respirator drones on. When he had set out to get the ice cream last August, he had been carrying two dollars in his pocket. . . .

Putt-Putt à Go-Go

It was a nasty day in the city. The headlines told of murders and warfare. The people on the street were full of meanness and sarcasm. Even the traffic lights seemed to be staring insolently. I needed solace.

Some guys turn to rotgut whiskey. Some guys turn to cheap women. Some guys will even have a cigarette.

Me, I'm different.

I go to Putt-Putt.

I pulled up to the Putt-Putt on Devon Avenue in Elk Grove Village, Illinois.

I sauntered in. The fellow at the desk knew not to fool with me. He handed me a putter and a blue ball.

"Red," I said, not looking at him.

He quickly replaced the blue one with a red one.

I hit the course. The Elk Grove Village Putt-Putt is a triplex; you get your choice of Course No. 1, Course No. 2, or Course No. 3. My luck was still rotten. It was a Wednesday night, and Course No. 1 was being used for the weekly tournament. I always like to try Course No. 1 when I hit a new Putt-Putt. But tonight I didn't feel like company.

So Course No. 2 it was. No sooner had I teed up than the strains of "Hurt So Good" were replaced on the Putt-Putt loudspeaker by the voice of the course manager:

"Ladies and gentlemen, the discount bonus has been won on Course No. 2 by Carol, with a red golf ball. We will now be switching back to the blue or the green. First person scoring a hole in one after the conclusion of this announcement with a blue or green golf ball, please bring the golf ball to the clubhouse and claim your discount prize."

That did it for me. My red ball was out of the running for a while. No free game in the offing. I didn't care. I stroked it toward the cup. Naturally it missed.

I could tell you about Putt-Putt. I could tell you that there are more than one thousand Putt-Putt courses around the world. I could tell you that Putt-Putt is to miniature golf what Wheaties is to the generic grain cereal at your local discount grocery store: the genuine article. I could tell you that Putt-Putt courses are generally found in smaller towns and medium-sized cities; there are no Putt-Putts in New York or Los Angeles or Chicago. I could tell you that there are no windmills or trick holes on a Putt-Putt course; the game is all skill.

I could tell you that Putt-Putt was founded in Fayetteville, North Carolina, by a fellow named Don Clayton in 1954. I could tell you that one of the main reasons he built his first course was as therapy to prevent a nervous breakdown. I could tell you that there is a Professional Putters Association that sponsors a full-scale national tour, with prize money all the way. I could tell you that in cities like Albany, Georgia, and El Paso, Texas, and Grand Rapids, Michigan, the professional Putt-Putt tournaments are seen weekly during the summer on a syndicated television show.

I could tell you a lot, as a matter of fact. But I didn't come to the Elk Grove Village Putt-Putt for you. I came for me.

You can spot the hotshots a mile away. I spotted one.

He had that glazed look in his eye: the look that says he plays six or seven hundred rounds of Putt-Putt every summer. I tossed my ball in front of his and introduced myself. He said that his name was Steve Baumgartner.

"Sounds familiar," I said.

He nodded in the direction of one of the Court No. 2 light poles. His name was posted near the top. He held the course record. Twenty-five.

"Ever played this course before?" he said.

"Not this one," I said.

He offered to show me around. Putt-Putts always look simple; the holes are short, and they're each par two. The bumpers are orange, and the carpets are green. But each hole has its own personality, and if you don't know the breaks, you aren't going to get your aces.

"This one breaks very lightly to the right," Baumgartner said as he knocked the ball toward the first hole. It did. He put it in the cup.

We began to walk the course. Putt-Putt isn't as time-consuming as, say, medical school. Twenty minutes is a long time for a round.

"You can play this hole thirty times and never get the ball to roll the same," Baumgartner said as we walked to the tee mat on the fifth hole. "The secret is to play the ball off the back wall."

He said he was twenty years old; he spent virtually every night from spring to autumn at the Elk Grove Village Putt-Putt.

"I came here for the grand opening seven years ago," he said. "I saw the spotlights and my ma drove me over. I shot about a forty—a couple over par—and that hooked me right away."

He was a gangly fellow with the beginnings of a moustache. He said it was hard to explain to other people his addiction.

"They say, 'What's Putt-Putt?'" he said. "Even the ones who know it's miniature golf think of those courses with the elephants and the windmills. They don't realize how special Putt-Putt is.

"When you're playing well, there's nothing else in the world. You want to play fast. You want to play the course in ten minutes. You know what all the course records are, and breaking them is all that matters to you."

"Crimson and Clover" was on the loudspeaker. I asked him if the constant music broke his concentration.

"No, not at all," he said. "When you're putting well, the music seems to be turned off. There are no other sounds than the ball banking toward the hole. Here on sixteen, you never want to bank the ball with the break." Three seconds later it was in the cup.

On Devon Avenue the trucks and cars roared by just feet from the Putt-Putt course. Next door was VFW Post No. 9284. The VFW signboard said that Friday was fish-fry night; Saturday was prime-rib night; Wednesday and Sunday were bingo nights. Bingo didn't interest me. I wanted to talk about Putt-Putt.

I walked to the clubhouse. The owner of the course, Shirley Swiglo, was passing out scorecards and pencils to customers. I motioned with my head for her to join me at the picnic bench by the Coke machine when she had a chance.

She looked like she expected trouble from me. She seemed relieved when she saw that I only wanted to know about her Putt-Putt course.

"We open every year in mid-April, and we stay open as long as the weather lets us," she said. "Sometimes we're still open in mid-November, but usually it's mid-October.

"We're open seven days a week. We open the gates at ten in the morning, and we stay open at night until the last person is off the course. As long as they want to play, we'll stay here. The latest that's ever been is three-twenty in the morning. Some nurses from the Alexian Brothers hospital came over after the night shift. They said they would rather play Putt-Putt than drink after work, so we accommodated them."

Mrs. Swiglo's husband, Bob, joined us at the picnic bench. As gentle as she was, he was that tough. He said he had to be that way. When you own a Putt-Putt, it's an invitation for the wrong elements to try to take over.

"Why do you think we keep the lights turned on so brightly out on the courses?" he said.

I said I didn't know.

"You turn the lights down, you get your undesirables," he said. "It's a fact. Bright lights is family-oriented. Dim lights isn't."

"If people are proud to be seen," Shirley Swiglo said, "they have no reason to object to bright lights."

"There's no loitering here," Bob Swiglo said. "No hanging around. I won't have it. In seven seasons, we've only had to call the police three times."

I asked him about those three occasions.

"The first time was for a hopped-up kid. Marijuana. The second was when a ten-speed bike was stolen; the owner forgot to lock it, out in the parking lot. The third was when our neighbors over there were having a cocktail party, and they started hitting golf balls at us from their back yard."

He said that the marijuana problem posed the greatest potential threat to the tranquility of the Putt-Putt.

"I know when they're hopped up," he said. "You can see it in their eyes. I tell them, 'Sorry, boys. You can do it. But you can't do it at the Putt-Putt.'"

As much as I liked talking to the Swiglos, I hadn't come to Elk Grove Village to jawbone. I had come to putt.

I went out onto Course No. 3. Playing directly ahead of me was a twenty-four-year-old truck driver named Jim Daniels. His putting partner was Cathy Benjamin, eighteen, a cook at the local Burger King. They invited me to play along. They told me this was their first date.

Jim stroked the ball toward the hole.

"Nope," he said as the ball missed.

"No can do," Cathy said.

He said he had asked her out planning to go to the movies: "I was going to go to *Conan* or *Foxfire*." But they had mutually decided that Putt-Putt was a better idea.

"You can talk while you play, and get to know each other," Cathy said.

"The sport is important too, but not that important," Jim said. "If you cheat, the only person you're cheating is yourself."

They were having a good time. Too good a time for me; I was itchy to hit the ball and keep moving. I played through, but in a couple of holes I ran into a foursome. The players were Tom Polak, a thirty-six-year-old program analyst for United Airlines; his daughter Lisa, twelve; his other daughter, Lauri, eight; and Lisa's friend Julie De-Prado, twelve.

"The wife brings them here more often than I do," Polak said to me. "But I have the night off, and they wanted to play."

Lauri tugged at his pants.

"Oh, Lauri, we're in trouble on this hole again," he said.

They were obviously playing best-ball; the father and the eight-year-old against the two twelve-year-olds. Lauri putted and missed.

"Bravo! Bravo!" Lisa yelled.

I moved on.

At the clubhouse, Shirley Swiglo was giving an orange ball—the symbol of a hole in one, the replacement ball a winner is given along with his discount coupon prize—to a girl who had just claimed an ace. After the girl walked away, I asked Shirley how she could be so sure that all the holes in one really were holes in one.

"I have to be honest with you," Mrs. Swiglo said. "Some of the kids cheat. But when we catch them, we just tell them to go back out on the course and try again. We don't actually call them cheaters. They get the message. And we make a friend."

On the wall were dozens of snapshots of birthday-party groups that had come to the Putt-Putt. Bob Swiglo was inspecting the snapshots, and making sure that nothing unruly was taking place on the Putt-Putt premises.

By this time about a hundred people were on the three Putt-Putt courses. A crescent moon hovered above. I sat back down at the picnic bench. My new *Esquire* had just arrived; it was the issue celebrating the glories of New York City.

I read silently from a story on New York night life:

At night, Manhattan island is speckled with the light of a thousand campfires. From downtown to up, from East Side to West, illuminated signs and soft-glowing rooms mark the spots. Elaine's. Studio 54. P.J. Clarke's. The Red Parrot. Rúelles. The Odeon. Le Cirque. One Fifth. Café Central. Joe Allen. Raoul's. Central Falls. Bathed in the glow are the people of New York who like, who crave, the social whoop-de-do. No other place in America has, in variety or number, so many incandescent gatherings.

I wasn't so sure. It seemed to me that if they built a Putt-Putt in Times Square, New York might instantly be rid of about half its problems. But I wasn't here to solve New York's troubles. I was here to play Putt-Putt. I was going to stay late. Who knew? I might even finish my night with some Alexian Brothers nurses. Stranger things had happened.

Ira

Ira is twenty-nine and lives with his parents. He has never spoken a word.

When he was born on September 12, 1953, he seemed to be a normal baby. After a few months, though, his mother and father began to worry. Ira seemed unable to hold up his head properly.

His parents took Ira to a number of doctors. When the baby was eighteen months old, the diagnosis seemed certain. Ira was suffering from severe brain damage. The physicians warned that he would probably never be able to function as anything but an infant.

The parents are middle-class Jewish people; they live on Chicago's Far North Side. They made a determination early on: They would not put Ira in an institution. He would live with them. If he remained a baby forever, so be it. He was theirs.

And now he is twenty-nine. When friends call his parents' home, they hear an almost constant low, rumbling sound in the background. The sound is made by Ira. Because of the problem in his mind, he cannot help himself from making the noise. It fills the house all day, every day.

He must be watched constantly; he is in danger of hurting himself by damaging his head with his fists. His mother, who is fifty-two, bathes him and helps him go to the bathroom. His father shaves him.

Ira seldom goes outside. In addition to the brain damage, he developed curvature of the spine when he was a teenager, and because of this, he is forced into a stooped posture. He feels pain when he walks. Sometimes his mother will take him into the back yard, but that is about all.

He has never been to a barber shop, never been to a dentist. Friends of his parents who work in those fields visit the house. Other old friends, though, don't visit the way they used to. When Ira was small, they seemed to be able to deal with his handicaps better than they do now.

"It's hard to blame those people," Ira's mother says. "When their children were growing up, they could identify with what we were going through with Ira. Because Ira was a child just like their boys and girls. But their children went to school, and graduated, and went to college, and got married. Ira remained a child. And they don't know how to respond to that."

Ira's parents do not know how much he is aware of them. He is their son, though, and they do what they can to make his life more serene. They play music for him—classical works and operas. The music seems to soothe Ira. He will kneel by the record player, and he will appear to be content.

At night Ira will become restless. His mother has not slept through until the morning since Ira was born. She will hear him in his room, and she will go to him and turn him over and cover him with blankets. She will stay with him until he has fallen back asleep.

She does not think about what might have been. "I made the decision a long time ago," she says. "He is with us, and that's the way it will be. Certainly our life is not like most people's. We can't really go out, and it's awkward to invite people in.

"But that's all right. Ira has given my life a purpose. He has taught me about love. By trying to give him a good life, I feel there's a reason for me to be on Earth. When you think about it, what am I giving up? I don't go to the movies, and I don't go out to see people as much as I might. But isn't all of that sort of minor, compared with providing a life for my son?"

Once each year, on a Jewish holiday, Ira's parents take him to their synagogue. It is a holiday filled with songs, so they do not have to worry about his noises bothering the other worshipers. The mother and the father sit on either side of Ira, each of them holding one of his hands, so he does not start hurting himself.

The rest of the time, though, they are at home together. Once in a while his mother will wonder about whether he truly knows who she is. Twenty-nine years have passed without any definite sign. "I do think he knows that he is loved," she says. "I can't guarantee much beyond that. There's no definite way that he responds to me. It's just a sense I have, that he knows.

"Sometimes he will look at me straight in the face. He will look me in the eye, and I will think that it's a sign of recognition. Maybe I'm fooling myself, though."

She has one great fear. She has lived all these years with him in the house. She wonders what would happen to Ira if she and her husband were to die before Ira did.

"My hope for him is that his parents will be alive all of his lifetime to take care of him," she says. "I don't know what else to do but to hope, because if I think too much about it, it makes me too uncomfortable."

She is resolved to the life she has chosen. Her days begin and end with Ira. She has learned to limit the things she yearns for.

But she does allow herself to have one dream.

"I know it will never happen," she says. "But I would give almost anything to hear him talk before I'm gone.

"Not a sentence or anything. I know that will never happen. But if he would say a word one day . . . I know it sounds selfish. I think about what it would be like if I was sitting with him one day and he looked at me and said 'Mama.'"

O'Hare Ballet

It is almost midnight. Here it comes again, off in the distance. A small light; if you hadn't been doing this for hours already, you would think it was a star. But the light grows; it enlarges and comes closer, and then it picks up speed and in the final seconds you can see the silver metal hurtling toward the ground, and then it hits and rolls, and back where it started, almost precisely in the same place, another light has appeared and started to grow, started to come toward you.

You are sitting in the window, as you have been all evening. You have touched a button, and all the curtains all around the suite have pulled back. Beneath you and directly in front of you is O'Hare International Airport. This suite is meant for serious business, but that is not your purpose; you are at play here, and you are hypnotized.

The complex is called the Mayor's Suite; built by the management of the O'Hare Hilton—the hotel that is located directly on the grounds of O'Hare—the suite is designed to be offered for use to the mayor of Chicago during an emergency or weather crisis at the airport. It wraps around one entire end of the top floor of the hotel; there are speaker-equipped telephones and telescopes mounted next to the floor-to-ceiling windows, and every amenity that could be needed in a command post.

You are staying in the suite tonight; not to judge its efficiency as an emergency center, but to watch O'Hare from this vantage point, and to think about this miraculous combination of steel and glass and concrete out on the midwestern plains. O'Hare has become such an integral part of modern American culture that it is taken pretty much for granted; unless there is a crash or a hijacking, it is seldom in the news.

But O'Hare, perhaps more than any similar piece of real estate in the United States, has an importance that was unknown in earlier decades, and will probably only be fully appreciated in decades to come. We know that we are the "mobile society"; the phrase has become a cliché, so much so that we accept it and do not think about it. O'Hare is the epicenter of that mobile society—perhaps the greatest single symbol of American life today.

If you think of O'Hare as a city in itself, it is the largest municipality in the world—50 million people a year pass through its concourses. It is the world's busiest airport; if you are an American and you do any traveling at all, you are likely to spend time in O'Hare. Because of its position between the coasts, it is the one point where travelers venturing from one spot to another inevitably end up.

And yet it is easy not to think about it, other than to know it is there to use. Which is why, sitting in the window on this autumn night, you have been so transfixed by what you are seeing. The Mayor's Suite gives you a view of O'Hare you have never been privy to before—stretching out below you are all of the individual terminals, all of the massive jets. When you hurry to O'Hare on business you think only of Flight 224 or Gate G-7; tonight you are in no rush, and all the flights, all the gates lie beneath you, with those jets moving in and away with a rapidity and tempo that is dizzying. It never stops, not for a minute, and the geometric beauty of it is such that you sometimes have to remind yourself that it is not a liquid piece of art you are watching, it is basic transportation, human beings meeting schedules to move from one American city to another.

Those dots of light off in the distance are the baubles that draw your eye the most. Hours ago, at smaller airports all across the land, men and women and children said goodbye to their loved ones, and climbed on board the jets that—right now—are approaching O'Hare. Important trips to every one of those families, nagging worries in the minds of every one of those husbands and wives and mothers and fathers, waiting at home for a telephone call to say that, yes, we have arrived safely.

You sit in the window, though, and all of those lives are a series of the bright dots, each forming in the same piece of the blackness out there, each moving toward you at the exact rate of one every thirty seconds. Turn your head to the right, and you can see the men up in the control tower, bringing those dots in. It is a hard bit of magic to put on paper; but there are two color television sets in the Mayor's Suite, and not once in all these hours have you been tempted to turn one of them on. You have taken advantage of the stereo, though; music is coursing through each of the speakers mounted in the walls of the Mayor's Suite, and all of those dots—all of those planes filled with human hope and trust—are dancing for you to that music as they move in toward you, and their appointment with the ground.

And down to your left, the other facet of O'Hare: illuminated silver cylinders thundering down a runway and up into the air, these leaving O'Hare, these, too, at the rate of one every thirty seconds. Lining up and waiting and then disappearing into that same blackness.

The pioneer days seem longer ago than you can imagine—the days of spending months crossing from one end of America to the other. Perhaps some of those early Americans passed over this very piece of midwestern ground on their way west, not knowing what time would bring about.

You fall asleep in the window; when dawn opens your eyes, the music is still playing. Now, in the early light, the jets are breathing puffs of exhaust into the cold morning air, pulling away from their gates one by one, lining up still to greet the sky. And off in the distance here they come, screaming silver players in a drama that never ends.

Railroad Man

He was a railroad man, and there was no grandeur at the end of the line.

He was a railroad man for forty-two years, but that ended last week. His name is Charles Ford. Back in 1936, when he was a youngster of twenty-three, being a waiter on the railroad was one of the best jobs a black man could hope for.

"If you worked for the railroad, you were decent," he will remember now. "It was good for the neighborhood to have a railroad man. Stores would give you credit."

So he went to a training school for railroad waiters, run by the Pennsylvania Railroad. The waiters would learn their trade in abandoned dining cars. The railroads ruled the nation then, and for Charles Ford it was a prestigious life he was setting out on. He graduated from the training school and got his first job. The pay was $47.50 a month.

He was good at his job. He liked to serve people. It was almost an outmoded calling in the twentieth century, but it is what he did. He yearned to work for the railroad he thought was best, the Atchison, Topeka and Santa Fe, and before long he did. He was hired to be a waiter on the Super Chief, the queen of the Santa Fe line, the luxury train that traveled between Chicago and Los Angeles.

"Oh, it was a beautiful job," he will remember now. "You had to know you were sharp. You had to know what you were doing."

He waited tables on that train, and his superiors recognized his skill. He was promoted from waiter to valet, and then to bartender. He wore a white jacket and white bow tie, hand-tied, and he was proud about what he did.

Maybe he was invisible to most of his passengers; he was just the man with the friendly and helpful face, the man who mixed the drinks and passed the hors d'oeuvres and made the passengers feel special as they rode the train in pampered comfort. Soon he was promoted again, this time to serve in the first-class section of the train; it was the epitome of accomplishment for a man like Charles Ford.

Yes, he may have been just the man behind the bar to his passengers, but he remembered them. There was Walt Disney, traveling to Hollywood and telling the bartender about someone called Mickey Mouse; there was Elizabeth Taylor, sitting up at the bar most of the night after she had left Nicky Hilton; there was a skinny young woman named Diana Ross and her two partners, the Supremes, heading off for Hollywood to seek their fortune. Sometimes Charles Ford would serve drinks in the Turquoise Room, the elegant private dining room of the Super Chief; always he would try to make the trip memorable for those on board.

That railroad run became his life. He had a family, but he missed birthday parties, graduations, funerals, Christmases, anniversaries, because he was on his run. Air travel became dominant in the United States, and the railroads diminished in their importance, but Charles Ford stayed on the job.

Then Amtrak was born; the railroads were nationalized, and his beloved Super Chief was no more. He had been a waiter and bartender on the railroad for so long that his seniority outdistanced almost everyone else, and he accepted a job with Amtrak; he put in for runs from Chicago to New York and back, so he could be with his family on weekends.

It was not the same, of course. With the government running the railroad, there was not the same pride and special feeling he had known as a young man.

"The other men who worked on Amtrak, they would look up to those of us who had been on the Santa Fe," he will remember now. "They wanted to do things the way we had done it on the Santa Fe."

And all of a sudden it was 1978; Charles Ford would be sixty-five. It was time to retire.

For a railroad man like Charles Ford—a waiter, a bartender—there is no glory at the end. No gold watch. No banquet. No word of thanks. When a railroad man's final run ends, he leaves the station. Someone else bids for his run, and the man with the next highest seniority gets it, and everyone moves up a notch in the pecking order. For a faithful worker, there is not much of a "Well done" given.

The scenario for a man like Charles Ford is to come into the station, turn in his money, sign his report, pick up his bag, and say, "So long"— to men who do not even look up from their paperwork to know, care, or acknowledge the final farewell to the work of a lifetime. And it is no surprise—many of the men in the station were not even born when the Charles Fords of this world started working on the railroads.

In August a private club made up of retired railroad waiters, bartenders, cooks, and Pullman porters gave a dinner in recognition of retirees. Charles Ford bought a new suit and new shoes for the occasion; he took his family to the dinner. But somehow his name was forgotten, it was left off the list; when the names of the railroad men were read, Charles Ford was not mentioned. It would only have been thirty seconds of recognition, but he missed it.

So last week Charles Ford turned sixty-five, and he rode his last run from New York into Chicago's Union Station.

On the train, he changed from his bartender's uniform to his street clothes. He turned in his equipment and his receipts. He walked into the station. He stopped at the bar and had a drink. Then, his life as a railroad man over, Charles Ford went home.

1964

There's an old question: If you found your home on fire, what's the one item you would carry out to safety?

I wouldn't have to think twice. At the bottom of my shirt drawer—buried safely beneath the shirts that don't get worn in either summer or winter—is a spiral-bound book with a cover of imitation black leather. Embossed on the cover, in faded gold ink, is "1964."

Down near the bottom, the cover informs me that the notebook was a gift from "Archer, Meek, Weiler Agency, Inc.—All forms of Insurance—175 So. High St.," in Columbus, Ohio. And inside the book is the most precious commodity I own. It is the year I turned seventeen years old, recorded day by day, in pencil and in ball-point pen. It is the thing we all wish for and are seldom granted: time preserved.

I suppose there are millions of teenage girls who keep diaries, but I would guess that the number of boys who do it is tiny. I know it is a secret that I kept to myself. What happened was, at a convention of high school journalism students from around the state of Ohio, a teacher advised us that the best way to discipline oneself as a conscientious reporter was to keep a daily journal—to make oneself record the minutiae of each day, whether one felt like writing or not. So, for the year 1964, I did it.

I wrote late at night, just before bed. That year, cruising the streets with my friends, questions would often come up about when a specific major event—meeting certain girls, getting into a fight—took place. My friends would mention a day, and I would know they were wrong; I had it recorded in the Archer, Meek, Weiler diary. But I never said anything. To admit that I was keeping a diary would be—to use the only appropriate term of the era—queer.

I did it for just that one year. And now, when memories of time escaped are the most valuable currency I can imagine, I have 1964 available to me any time I want it. And I am finding that I want it quite often.

❖   ❖   ❖

The notations are nothing if not cryptic. Day by day, in a style reminiscent of the late Walter Winchell, they recorded concerns long forgotten but at the moment of writing so current they needed no elaboration:

> Did OK in Algy—Got unknown in Chemo—I wish Dianne would ask me to Sadie Hawkins—Pariser said I could have his STP date—Senior—but Marje said Roth should take it—I might get some Dayton girl—We're doubling with Gary Robbins—I hope this girl (if she comes) is cool—Reserve match after school—Got 80 and C+ in French—damn!—I tried so hard—that's getting me down—got poorboy and Towncraft shirt after dinner—played ball at White's house—she's cool—like to get her—did a lot of Chemo—hope I go up!—Didn't think too much about L.

And that was what Tuesday, April 21, 1964, was like in my life. The value of the book is that, unlike most men of my generation, it makes it impossible for me to bathe my teenage years in a warm, unfocused glow of nostalgia. For some reason, those of us now in our thirties take great pleasure in looking back on those years as if they were some pleasant, seamless movie backed by a sound track of Top 40 songs. I have no such luxury; I know specifically what it was like. So my friends from those years like to joke about the time we went through the guardrail. They tell the story as if it were a prank. Here is what the diary says for the day of February 15:

> I'm awful lucky to be around to write this tonight—Today Chuck, Dan, Gi, Jack, + me went to Dayton—Chuck, Jack, + me didn't have permission—messed around in Dayton—got chased by a guy in a 409—scared—saw Bart, Gary Snyder, Joyce Burick—Jack kissed Joyce—on the way home, all went well until about 10 miles out of Columbus—we hit an ice patch, swerved four times—each time we slid farther—finally Gi yelled "Here we go"—we crashed into the guardrail, flew over an embankment—hit 3 times—I was sure I was going to die—but everyone was all right—2 ambulances came, towtruck, cops—We were so scared—Gi drove home—parents don't know yet—We went to Candy's and Robyne's at night.

There it is. Early in the evening we almost died. By the end of the night we were trying to romance Candy and Robyne. We were invincible; life was going to go on forever. Death, when it did show up, was a passing notation. November 27:

Up at noon—Took mom to beauty parlor—went downtown with Jack at 3—got "Gone, Gone, Gone"—cool girl waited on Jack—Uncle Abe died—went with Katz, Dan, Chuck at night—talked about stealing liquor—went to Jackson's party—took ½ pint of vodka—Gingold party in Eastmoor—went to Dan Goldberg's—I took ⅞ bottle of 151 proof rum—didn't like doing it, but had to prove I had balls.

"Uncle Abe died." A man's full life had ended; in my priorities, it fit in between buying an Everly Brothers record from a good-looking salesclerk and stealing a bottle of liquor from the parents of a friend. It's not the way one would choose to remember the time, but apparently that was the reality.

The combination of naiveté and sophistication is startling. We were all virgins at the beginning of 1964; on the night the first of us made love to a girl, the rest of us—unbeknown to him—locked ourselves in a bathroom next to the bedroom where it was going on. From June 6, 1964:

Scott got Carla—screwed her—Cruised with Dan in morning—went to Excelsior Club with Jack, Dan, Scott—played ball, got friendly with Sue Young—she's a good girl—can't decide whether I'd like to go with her or not—went to dinner with Scott—after dinner went to the apartment—fixed stuff up, locked ourselves in bathroom—they came in—started to talk—quiet for about 20 minutes—then he said "I can't get this damn package open"—but he did—and he got her good—she was breathing real hard and crying a lot—we told him later—had some beer—talked to Bill Shenk for a real long time—Boy, I have to get a screw—It sounded like hell, but it's just something I have to do—that's my goal for this summer—got home after 2.

And yet, later that summer, when—in a gift from the fates I am still thankful for—I had a brief affair with a twenty-seven-year-old married woman, the notations in the diary do not read like the thoughts of an inexperienced high school boy who is being seduced by a bored housewife. If I were to recreate it only from memory, I would tell it as if it were something out of *Summer of '42*, with the woman plotting to take me to bed even as I dreamed of fishing trips and bike rides. But reading the diary now, it is apparent that I was the instigator.

From the moment my friends and I met the girls for whom this woman was acting as a summer-outing chaperone, the diary makes it clear that I was falling for her. And not doing it silently; trying to make her notice me, to make her think of me not as some seventeen-year-old kid hanging around with his buddies, but as a person so special that she had to let me into her life. At one point she urged me to take out one of the teenage girls she was in charge of; she said that the girl liked me, so, almost on command, I spent a few hours with the girl. But afterwards, I was back again, too shy to ask the woman myself, but putting myself in place, waiting for her to ask me.

In the diary, it is in shorthand:

. . . she kept touching me—talk got to love—I said I'd get her later—she said "talker"—I said "wait and see"—she said "I've been waiting all week"—she put her arm over me—I was going nuts—she said "What are you thinking about?"—then she put her hand on my chest—She said "It's about your heart"—we started. . . .

And later:

. . . all night long I kept touching her. . . .

I feel funny committing this to print now; but there seems no other way to convey how much this book labeled "1964" means to a man now thirty-four. It was half my life ago, and yet because of the book I am there again. When you are seventeen you are too new at things to edit yourself; you put it down as it happened, and let it go at that. Some nights I feel the book is burning itself up in that dresser drawer.

My guess is that a grown man could not keep a journal like the one kept by a seventeen-year-old boy. By the time we are adults, we censor ourselves even in our thought processes. In the diary, if something bad happened in my life, I could write, "And the all-time loser loses again," and I would mean it. The next day I would write of cruising with my friends, and there would not be a hint of despair.

And the longing . . . that spring I was named an editor of my high school newspaper. At the same time, I was a returning letterman on the varsity tennis team. To be an athlete at my high school was far greater in prestige than to be on the paper, but I knew I wanted to be a writer, and it was important for me to do the job. So I skipped practices so that I could get my page in the paper prepared for the printers. Slowly and steadily I began to drop in position on the tennis team; by May it was apparent that I was not going to earn a letter again that year.

It doesn't sound so bad now; as a matter of fact, in light of the way things turned out, I seem to have made a fairly wise decision. But the diary tells me what the specter of failure meant to me:

> . . . Coach Weis said that I'm down to fifth doubles—I pray so much that I can get back to my old position—I need that letter— without it, I'm just nothing again—Please, God, help me. . . .

"Without it, I'm just nothing again." How many of us have felt that way in the business world, or in our personal lives? But it is an emotion that you can never express when you're supposed to be mature and responsible. You swallow hard and put on a good face for the world and let your insides churn. And you lie; you tell everyone how well things are going, while all the while something inside you is crying, "Please, God, help me. . . ."

Maybe that is the thing the book marked "1964" gives me above all else. Reading the book now, I see—raging and uncontrolled—the emotions that, as a man who is a reporter, I try to chronicle in others every day. They are buried so deep in most of us that they will never surface; but when you are seventeen, writing for an audience that, at the time, you are sure will never be anyone but yourself, they lie there at the level of your skin. You will never see them more clearly.

When I take the 1964 diary out, it is usually to look up a specific incident. What prompted it this last time was a phone call I got from my brother. He just had his tenth high school reunion. At the party, a woman told him that, back when she was a little girl, she had once had a tantrum and had tried to beat me up.

I knew it was in the diary. And I found it. June 19, 1964:

> . . . Went to Sue Dworkin's—Crummy—watched *King Creole* with Bill and Kenny at Gi's—then back to Dworkin's—this little kid beat the hell out of me—went to White Castle with Ed and Ken. . . .

As usual, once I had the diary in my hands, I couldn't put it back. I turned to January 1, and closed the door, and for the next few hours, I was seventeen again.

There is a place in the diary—August 9—where I write about the first words by me ever to appear in a newspaper. I was working as a copyboy on the night shift at the *Columbus Citizen-Journal*. I was doing the fire runs—the little agate lists of emergency calls—and I saw something unusual, about a man who had been hospitalized by a golf ball with a liquid center that exploded.

. . . I phoned the man's house and talked to his wife—Got the story and wrote it up—Keesee changed it slightly and said good—at first I was scared he'd throw it away—Stine headed it "Golf Ball Fights Back"—I saw it on the galley—it was a thrill to see it in print—My first printed work. . . .

There are days when 1964 seems a thousand years away. But it is always right there when I need it; why I should need it is another question, but I can't seem to find the answer to that one anywhere in the diary.

Normal

This is really getting perverted. When the letters began to arrive, I ignored them.

That wasn't hard to do. A lot of mail comes into this office, much of it nuts. If you want to read about degradation, evil, degeneracy, larceny, and madness, it's all there. For some reason a cross-section of the worst aspects of humanity shows up in each of my mail deliveries.

So I was a little surprised to read the message contained in the first letter:

Hi! I'm writing to you neither to complain nor to be very interesting or important, but because you ought to get some mail from some normal people. I assert that I am normal.

The writer was a woman from the south suburbs. She wrote:

Before backing my claim to normalcy, please let me state that today is every bit as sunny and lovely as yesterday! I am normal because I like America, good steaks, soda pop, my nice husband, our little rented house, multivariate calculus and "Tucson," a fur-bearing dog.

I had to admit, the letter was different from what I am used to. The woman wasn't asking me to intercede in a child-custody case; she wasn't telling me how her husband was beating her or how she had been abused as a child; she wasn't complaining that a lawyer or a doctor was defrauding her; she wasn't, in short, writing about any of the things that the people who write me usually concentrate on.

"As a normal person I feel that I have a certain obligation to correspond with you," she wrote. "So this is my first in a series of letters."

Like I say, I ignored it. But soon there was another message from her:

Did you watch the Indy 500 race on the TV? What a great race! The cars were incredible and the drivers superb! I am happy that Gordon Johncock won the race because he is an Indy veteran, he had won an unhappy victory in 1973 and because he was Mario Andretti's team partner. My husband and I drove to Indianapolis to see the final day of time trials and so had the opportunity to watch Andretti practice. His car was excellent, he suffered a great loss when his car was ruined before the race ever began.

I went about my business. The news of the world was the usual: murders, wars, meanness. And there was a letter from the woman:

We enjoyed a pleasant Memorial Day holiday. We began the morning by driving our bicycles down to Crown Point for the annual Dunes Century bike ride. We followed the arrows that are painted on the street to the "Y," and golly, I guess the ride was on Sunday, so we drove the bikes back home. Boy, those hills outside of "Crowntown" went smooth that morning!

After work I hit the places I usually hit. I heard the usual ration of complaints and groaning. When I got to work the next day, I realized that I was subconsciously anticipating the morning's first mail delivery. When it arrived I quickly flipped through all the envelopes. I figured out that I was hunting for something from my "normal" correspondent. She didn't disappoint me:

My dad came over with his electric lawn mower. Remember how it rained last week? This is the time of year that grass sends up its stalks of seed. My husband scythed down the lawn with the ol' push-mower. I got to mow most of the lawn, instead of my dad doing it, because he would have, but he did do the dog yard and he followed me, holding the cord and pointing to spots.

A man called up yelling about some dispute he was having with a government agency; a woman told me that she had hired a private eye to follow her cheating husband around, and would I expose the husband in print? I waited for the next letter.

Here is what the "normal" woman said:

My mom had a barbecue with salads (green, Jello-O and potato), steaks charred on the gas grill, baked beans, the choice of two homemade salad dressings, garlic bread, hot dogs and hamburgers, cottage cheese and tomato slices and then watermelon and chocolate cake. My sister and her new husband brought the center irises from their lovely garden, and his grandparents brought two of the salads. Afterwards we went home. My husband drank some beer and we watched television.

I went out to do an interview that night; some public relations people from California were trying to sell me on their client. They were quite persuasive, but I found myself wondering if I would hear from the "normal" woman again.

The next day I did.

My mother and I went to my sister's new husband's grandparents' house to pick peonies. My mother loves peonies! After we had lunch, we took a walk.

As I mentioned, this is getting perverted. But I can't help it; with all the terrible news the world has to offer, I find myself looking forward to hearing the details of this "normal" woman's life. For example —you might not know it, but she and her husband are thinking about renting another house:

It's an old-fashioned house. It's a block away from the commuter bus stop. It has a washer and dryer in the basement, a large kitchen, porches, an attic, a yard for Tucson the fur-bearing dog, and a garden. And what a garden it is! The owner keeps the garden as a relaxing hobby. He's a barber. He's also quite friendly, a silver-haired man. He doesn't sell the vegetables, so we can eat all we want.

I don't know where this is leading. All I know is that when I arrive at work each day, I have my choice of the two Chicago newspapers, the *New York Times*, the *Wall Street Journal*, and a stack of mail. I can read any of it. But these days, all I want to do is read about the "normal" woman and what she's up to. Perverted. But nice.

Handled with Care

The day the lady took her clothes off on Michigan Avenue, people were leaving downtown as usual. The workday had come to an end; men and women were heading for bus and train stations, in a hurry to get home.

She walked south on Michigan; she was wearing a white robe, as if she had been to the beach. She was blond and in her thirties.

As she passed the Radisson Hotel, Roosevelt Williams, a doorman, was opening the door of a cab for one of the hotel's guests. The woman did not really pause while she walked; she merely shrugged the robe off, and it fell to the sidewalk.

She was wearing what appeared to be the bottom of a blue bikini bathing suit, although one woman who was directly next to her said it was just underwear. She wore nothing else.

Williams at first did not believe what he was seeing. If you hang around long enough, you will see everything: robberies, muggings, street fights, murders. But a naked woman on North Michigan Avenue? Williams had not seen that before and neither, apparently, had the other people on the street.

It was strange; her white robe lay on the sidewalk, and by all accounts she was smiling. But no one spoke to her. A report in the newspaper the next day quoted someone: "The cars were stopping, the people on the buses were staring, people were shouting, and people were taking pictures." But that is not what other people who were there that afternoon said.

The atmosphere was not carnival-like, they said. Rather, they said, it was as if something very sad was taking place. It took only a moment for people to realize that this was not some stunt designed to promote a product or a movie. Without anyone telling them, they understood that the woman was troubled, and that what she was doing had nothing to do with sexual titillation; it was more of a cry for help.

The cry for help came in a way that such cries often come. The woman was violating one of the basic premises of the social fabric.

She was doing something that is not done. She was not shooting any-one, or breaking a window, or shouting in anger. Rather, in a way that everyone understood, she was signaling that things were not right.

The line is so thin between matters being manageable and being out of hand. One day a person may be barely all right; the next the same person may have crossed over. Here is something from the author John Barth:

> She paused amid the kitchen to drink a glass of water; at that instant, losing a grip of 50 years, the next-room-ceiling plaster crashed. Or he merely sat in an empty study, in March-day glare, listening to the universe rustle in his head, when suddenly a five-foot shelf let go. For ages the fault creeps secret through the rock; in a second, ledge and railings, tourists and turbines all thunder over Niagara. Which snowflake triggers the avalanche? A house explodes; a star. In your spouse, so apparently resigned, murder twitches like a fetus. At some trifling new assessment, all the colonies rebel.

The woman continued to walk past Tribune Tower. People who saw her said that the look on her face was almost peaceful. She did not seem to think she was doing anything unusual; she was described as appearing "blissful." Whatever the reaction on the street was, she seemed calm, as if she believed herself to be in control.

She walked over the Michigan Avenue bridge. Again, people who were there report that no one harassed her; no one jeered at her or attempted to touch her. At some point on the bridge, she removed her bikini bottom. Now she was completely undressed, and still she walked.

"It was as if people knew not to bother her," said one woman who was there. "To tell it, it sounds like something very lewd and sensa-tional was going on. But it wasn't like that at all. It was as if people knew that something very . . . fragile . . . was taking place. I was im-pressed with the maturity with which people were handling it. No one spoke to her, but you could tell that they wished someone would help her."

Back in front of the Radisson, a police officer had picked up the woman's robe. He was on his portable radio, advising his colleagues that the woman was walking over the bridge.

When the police caught up with the woman, she was just standing there, naked in downtown Chicago, still smiling. The first thing the police did was hand her some covering and ask her to put it on; the show was over.

People who were there said that there was no reaction from the peo-

ple who were watching. They said that the juvenile behavior you
might expect in such a situation just didn't happen. After all, when a
man walks out on a ledge in a suicide attempt, there are always people down below who call for him to jump. But this day, by all accounts, nothing like that took place. No one called for her to stay
undressed; no one cursed the police officers for stopping her.

"It was as if everyone was relieved," said a woman who saw it. "They
were embarrassed by it; it made them feel bad. They were glad that
someone had stopped her. And she was still smiling. She seemed to be
off somewhere."

The police charged her with no crime; they took her to Read Mental
Health Center, where she was reported to have signed herself in vol-
untarily. Within minutes things were back to as they always are on
Michigan Avenue; there was no reminder of the naked lady who had
reminded people how fragile is the everyday world in which we live.

One in 100 Million

Soon it will be summer. Baseball games will dominate
the television screen, and millions of men and women will be sunning
themselves at poolside, prancing around tennis courts, slamming golf
balls into the distance.

And I will still be trying to explain why I did not go to the Super
Bowl.

I arrived in Detroit on Monday of Super Bowl week. I had every
intention of going to the game the following Sunday. I did what any
tourist could be expected to do: I checked into the Westin Hotel,
nodded hello to the robot standing sentry in the lobby, went to the
magazine rack and picked up copies of *Industry Week* and *Easyriders*
to read in my room, and accepted with gratitude one of the John Weitz
designer briefcases that were being given free by the National Football
League to all reporters covering the game.

I went to the Silverdome in Pontiac. Both teams were scheduled for
workouts, and reporters were being allowed to visit.

Since I do not regularly cover sports, my attitude toward professional athletes has always been the same as that of most media consumers: these are huge, wealthy men. But as I walked among the San Francisco 49ers, all I could think about was that these people were *babies*. I mean, we are used to seeing them in uniform, with those bar-fronted helmets covering their faces; and anyone you see on television becomes sort of ageless, anyway.

Here, though, in the flesh, it was striking to notice just how young they were. If they weren't playing in the NFL, they would have looked at home pumping gas in a service station. They were clearly awed by all the attention they were receiving on this morning. It was close to zero outside, but inside the Silverdome it was seventy and some of the star players had up to two hundred reporters swarming around them.

I approached Milt McColl, a twenty-two-year-old rookie linebacker. On Sunday, he would be playing in front of 100 million people. He was wearing his jersey with the number 53 on the front. He was looking over at the mobs surrounding Joe Montana, the famous quarterback, and Bill Walsh, the famous coach.

"I hope they can get out of there safely," he said.

Like a few of the other nonstars, McColl was in the awkward position of waiting around on the forty-yard line to see if anyone wanted to talk to him. No one seemed interested. Another 49er in the same situation was Rick Gervais, a twenty-two-year-old safety. As I watched him glancing at the reporters who kept passing him by, I felt that the dynamic reminded me of something. I walked up to say hello, and right away he got it exactly.

"This is sort of like my first high school dance," he said.

I asked him which was more fun.

He glanced up at the girdered dome of the stadium. "Oh, probably my first high school dance," he said.

There was a party for visiting press at the Henry Ford Museum in Dearborn. Much laughter and music filled the room; people were drinking and a band was playing, and the atmosphere was clearly one of fellowship and good fun.

I stood in a group that surrounded an automobile that was part of the museum's exhibit. The men and women in the group were telling each other dirty jokes. By this time the Up With People singers were performing, and an old Beach Boys number was being amplified on the public-address system.

I kept looking at the car. It seemed familiar. Someone spilled a drink, and a waiter went to fetch a fresh one, and then a woman came around carrying a tray of champagne. I couldn't quit staring at the car. It was an old black Lincoln, a kind I have never owned, but still, I was having the distinct feeling that I knew it.

So I broke off from the group. With their voices behind me and the music in the air, I looked at the plaque that was mounted on the wall above the car. The plaque informed me that it was the car in which John F. Kennedy was riding on the day he was assassinated.

In the Super Bowl press room, a sportswriter was morosely drinking a beer. He had just received a message from his editor. The editor was dissatisfied with the writer's coverage of pre-game week. The editor had said that the reports were "not trivial enough."

I rode out to the Silverdome again. It was a weird sight, just off the highway in an isolated part of southern Michigan. For miles it seemed like there was nothing but freeway and franchise fast-food restaurants, and then, rising off the ice and snow, there it was.

It was completely wired by now. CBS trucks were parked in the lot outside the stadium, and there was nowhere you could walk without being physically reminded of the fact that on Sunday half of America would be looking at this structure. In person, the Silverdome seemed more a mirage than a real place; it didn't truly have to exist—its actual presence here in Michigan seemed almost unnecessary. CBS had paid $6 million for the right to telecast pictures of it during Sunday's broadcast; but the eighty thousand or so people who would be here in the seats were so insignificant next to the hundred million who would watch the television show. The morning after the game, the network images of the Silverdome would have disappeared. It would seem odd to find the structure itself still here.

Everyone involved in the Super Bowl knew that they were basically taking part in a television program. Which was only right; the young men on the playing field were children of the television age. Ricky Patton, the 49ers' running back, had the given name of Ricky Riccardo Patton. When his mother had been pregnant with him, she had been a fan of *I Love Lucy*.

The parties at night began to seem bizarre. At one, a striking blond woman in a low-cut black dress was stationed at the front door to welcome guests. An ABC camera crew turned its lights on her to get a shot, and the effect was to make the dress disappear. She stood there smiling, and in the lights you could see her entire body. She wore no underwear.

About an hour later she circulated from group to group. A reporter who had had too much to drink looked at her and said, "You really have nice tits."

She smiled at him and said, "Thank you."

Later I talked to her; her name was Barbara Nichols, she was thirty-one, she was a model, and she was volunteering her time to the Michigan Host Committee. I asked her if she had been offended by what the man had said.

"No," she said. "It happens wherever I go. I have the best body in the city, and men are always saying things like that. It's no different than if he had told me I had nice legs."

I asked her if she had trouble dealing with moments like that.

"You just learn that men are little boys," she said. "The funny thing is, though, that little boys are beginning to act the same way. I was modeling at a show at Cobo Hall, and this twelve- or thirteen-year-old boy kept hanging around and looking at me. About the fifth time he came up, I said, 'You're so cute, I'd like to have you for my son.' And he said, 'Are you kidding? I want you for my wife.'"

She said that she had two daughters. She said that the most common reaction she got from men was for them to make some excuse to touch her. "I'm used to being the center of attention, and I have a very good sense of humor," she said.

The truest moment of the week for me came one afternoon at the Silverdome. The Cincinnati Bengals had just come onto the field. They had been through their rounds of interviews, and now it was almost time for practice to begin.

A group of about ten of them walked down to the far end of the field. They had a plastic baseball bat and a hollow plastic baseball. Almost as if by instinct, they divided into sides and started playing ball.

I stood among them and watched. They clearly didn't think it was anything special; there was some time to kill, and they were going to kill it this way. Here we were at the site of the Super Bowl, and these young men were playing baseball on the football field. They pitched and swung and caught and ran the imaginary bases, and I thought: This is it. For all the publicity and all the false enthusiasm about the Super Bowl, this is what it comes down to. These men have been remarkable athletes since they were small boys, and what they do when they have a few minutes is revert to whatever it was that brought them onto playing fields in the first place.

Forget the hundred million viewers; forget the network cameras; forget the parties. Of all the young boys who dream of being athletes, these had made it to the Super Bowl. But certain things had not changed; as I watched them laughing and swinging at the ball and arguing over plays, I realized that what I was seeing probably was a more genuine story of sports in America than what would be telecast Sunday.

The winner of the contest for the official drink of Super Bowl week was an alcohol-and-ice-cream concoction called "Referee's Revenge." In the top-floor bar of the Westin it would cost you over six dollars, but you got to keep the glass.

I kept my glass one night, and in the morning I saw it on my hotel-room dresser. Next to it was a pile of press releases from the NFL. My coat was draped over a chair; my official NFL pin, complete with its own number, was attached to the lapel. The pin was my badge of admission to all Super Bowl–week activities in Detroit.

I rode out to Pontiac again. I had obtained permission to enter the Silverdome even though interviews were not being allowed this day. Practice had ended; I walked out to the fifty-yard line and stood on the emblem that had been painted with the NFL's official design.

I looked up to the top deck. I realized that the Super Bowl had become an American secular holiday; people all across the country were covetous of tickets to Sunday's game. And yet, as I stood on the field, I realized that I really didn't want to see it. The holiday was the television show, not the athletic contest on this field. I knew that I would feel closer to the game if I was back home watching it on TV than if I was here. To be here on Sunday . . . somehow it would be essentially false. I would not be one of the hundred million.

I sat down on the fifty. No one came by and told me not to. I just sat there in the center of the field and looked around the Silverdome, and I knew that I was going to go home.

I made my goodbyes to the people I knew in Detroit, and I headed out of the city. I thought of a quotation from Duane Thomas, the former star running back of the Dallas Cowboys: "If this is the ultimate game, then why are they playing it next year?"

On Sunday, I slept late. I took a shower, had a sandwich for lunch, and turned on the pre-game show.

Like the rest of America, I sat and watched for the entire afternoon and early evening. It was sort of strange; every time the teams moved across the fifty-yard line, I saw that painted emblem and thought about how I had sat on it and had decided that I ought to leave.

There was one play—a kicking play for which the 49ers' special team was in—and there was a scramble for the ball down by the goal line, and I heard the announcer say the names of Milt McColl and Rick Gervais. I watched them get up from the pile of players, and they looked like noble and battered gladiators. I tried to put that image together in my mind with the memory of talking to them as they stood like wallflowers at a high school dance, waiting for someone to come up to them.

I went in to work the next day. Someone approached me and said, "I heard you went to the Super Bowl." I didn't know quite how to answer. The person said, "How was it?" and I thought about it, and that's when I said for the first time that, no, I didn't go. Which was true enough, and even if it weren't, it would have to do.

Heads You Lose,
Tails You Lose

Nothing fascinates Americans like a loser, and if the loser is one of monumental proportions, so much the better.

On July 2, 1979, amid much hoopla, a new coin was introduced to the public. It was the Susan B. Anthony dollar—slightly larger than a quarter, 8.1 grams in weight, featuring a portrait of the famous suffragist on one side and an image of an eagle landing on the moon on the other.

Treasury officials expected the coin to be a hit. They were hoping, in fact, that people would like it so much that it would eventually replace the one-dollar bill completely. The reasons for their optimism were economic and practical ones. It costs three cents to mint a Susan B. Anthony coin and only 1.8 cents to print a paper dollar. But the dollar coin will last approximately fifteen years; the paper dollar will last only eighteen months or so. Government officials figured that if

Americans used Anthony coins instead of paper dollars, the Treasury would save up to $50 million a year in printing and processing alone.

Nothing of the kind has happened, of course. The Anthony dollar has become one of the most miserable busts in the history of U.S. currency. Most Americans refuse to carry the coins. Bank tellers and cashiers in stores have learned not to even try to give them out as change; people won't take them. The most common complaint is that the coin is hard to differentiate from a quarter when you're reaching into your pocket, but the dislike seems to be more visceral than practical. People aren't sure why, but they hate the Anthony dollars; they don't even like to touch them.

When panicky Treasury officials turned to opinion leaders in search of support, they got only ridicule. In Congress, Representative Frank Annunzio, a Democrat from Illinois, said, "If we do eliminate the dollar bill and instead use the dollar coin, the Treasury would be required to issue every American a pair of suspenders." Frustrated by the reluctance of its customers to accept the coins, the Skokie Federal Savings and Loan Association in Skokie, Illinois, sold them for fifty cents apiece one Friday. In Dallas, something called the Bonehead Club singled out the Anthony dollar as the "most monumental goof" of the year.

Meanwhile, the Bureau of the Mint was churning out millions of coins that no one would go near. By the spring of 1980, when production was halted, the Mint had issued 840 million Susan B. Anthony dollars; of those 840 million, 525 million were sitting stacked in federal vaults, in deep storage, untouched.

Without Frank Gasparro, there would be no Susan B. Anthony dollar. Gasparro, seventy-one, is chief designer for the Mint. When his superiors told him that he was supposed to draw a woman for the face of a new dollar coin, he said fine—he would draw Miss Liberty.

"But they told me they didn't want Miss Liberty," Gasparro said. "It had to be Susan B. Anthony."

Gasparro had no idea what Susan B. Anthony looked like. He lives in Philadelphia, so he went down to the offices of the Philadelphia *Bulletin* and asked permission to look in the newspaper's photographic morgue. He found two photographs of Susan B. Anthony. In one, she was twenty-eight; in the other, eighty-four.

"I chose the younger one," Gasparro said. "She was a very attractive woman at twenty-eight."

So he designed the coin with a twenty-eight-year-old Susan B. Anthony on the face. Feminist groups began to complain that Anthony was too "pretty." A fine arts commission objected to it. Even Gasparro's wife said the drawing stank.

"I'll tell you how I feel about my work," Gasparro said. "People look over my shoulder and always criticize everything I make. Every coin is criticized. It hurts my feelings. I have to watch my step and not lose my composure."

He started over. He drew a new face of Susan B. Anthony, trying to approximate what she looked like in middle age. This new drawing featured a square jaw, a hooked nose, a drooping right eye, and a heavy browline. Gasparro had misgivings about it, but the people at the Treasury seemed to like it fine. So the coin was released to the public and immediately became one of the most amazing flops in the history of U.S. coinage.

"I was listening to a radio talk show one night," Gasparro said. "One caller said the coin looked like it was designed by an Arab. The moderator said it was the most hideous thing he'd ever seen. I called up to defend my coin. I said I drew the picture. But the moderator hung up on me."

The director of the Mint at the time the Anthony dollar was introduced was Stella B. Hackel. She became the chief supporter of the coin. She still doesn't understand what happened.

"It's so practical," she said. "It's easy to use. I do it all the time. I always carry the coins with me, in my purse."

Unfortunately, whenever she pays for something with an Anthony dollar, she has to say, "This is a dollar, not a quarter." She has traveled the country talking about the coin and is flabbergasted that most Americans have never even held one, much less carried one around. From what she can tell, the prejudice against the coin is overwhelming. She went to New Orleans to talk to a convention of bankers about promoting the Anthony dollar more vigorously. Of nine thousand delegates at the convention, fewer than one hundred showed up to listen to her.

"It hasn't worked *yet*," Hackel said. "For over a century people have been used to the idea of a dollar bill, and they're slow to change. But a medium of exchange is a medium of exchange. People can learn."

She knows that all signs indicate they don't want to. With half a billion of the coins in storage, there is no appropriation to mint more of them this year. When Hackel goes to her own bank in Virginia, she knows not to ask for Anthony dollars. The bank doesn't carry them.

"I just don't understand it," she said. "These coins are very nice and convenient and easy to use. They are very clean. A dollar bill gets dirty and messy. Toward the end of its life, it becomes very unpleasant to handle.

"But this coin is shiny and clean. I just don't understand the resistance."

Like private corporations, the Bureau of the Mint has a marketing division. Its function is to smooth the way for its "product" with the people who will help merchandise it—in the case of the Anthony dollar, merchants, vendors, retailers, pinball machine operators, and other significant purveyors of coins.

"Naturally, like all Americans, we like success," said Frank De Leo. "The marketing group can't roll over and play dead. We have to try to figure out what went wrong, and correct it."

De Leo is the Mint's liaison officer to the Federal Reserve, and when he tries to persuade people to use the Anthony dollar in their change drawers, his message is simple: "You carry a dollar bill in your wallet with a ten-dollar bill, and there's no confusion. So if you can tell a dollar bill from a ten-dollar bill, and they're the same size and color, why should it be a problem with this new coin?"

De Leo is getting weary of hearing himself talk. "There is an extraordinary amount of resistance to this coin out there," he said. "The public just doesn't seem to go for it. As far as I can tell, this coin isn't being accepted anywhere."

One of the things that is whispered around the Mint is that some of the negative feelings have to do not with the size of the coin, but with the fact that it has Susan B. Anthony on its face. Some Mint people think the public, perhaps subliminally, associates Miss Anthony with the women's movement, and even with the Equal Rights Amendment—and that the public dislikes the coin for this reason.

"Let's just say that marketing studies have told us not to put too much emphasis on the feminist angle," De Leo said.

In show business, when a performer's reputation is in trouble, his managers often hire a public relations firm. In what is believed to be a first in the annals of government currency, the Federal Reserve hired a PR agency for the Susan B. Anthony dollar: DWJ Associates, located in Manhattan. The fee was $150,000.

"Our job was to get the good story out about the coin," said Michael Friedman, executive vice-president of the PR firm. "But we made a false assumption. We assumed that there would be good stories to get out. There weren't. The negative thing got rolling, and it never stopped.

"We were looking for any little piece of good news about the coin, so we could feed it to the networks and the wire services. The stories didn't have to come from big cities; we were looking for the little town that decided to pay everyone in Susan B. Anthony coins—that kind of thing. We'd take *anything*. Spokane, San Luis Obispo, Dover-Foxcroft, Mobile . . . our feeling was that as soon as something good happened, we could start to build a success. But nothing good ever happened. Anywhere."

Friedman has his own theory of why the coin failed. He feels that, especially in a time of inflation, the Anthony dollar didn't *look* like a dollar; it was so small that people refused to take it seriously.

"Look, I used it, but I stopped after six months," Friedman said. "I got sick of it. I got sick of walking into the bank and having the tellers say 'Here comes that nut.' I got sick of fighting with cab drivers."

DWJ Associates has scrapbooks filled with news stories about the Anthony dollar. Getting space in the papers wasn't the problem. The problem was that people had already made up their minds that they wanted nothing to do with it.

"All the publicity in the world can't sell something that people don't want," Friedman said.

"You want to know what hurt the coin? The coin hurt the coin."

While everyone else can reflect on the disastrous past of the Susan B. Anthony dollar, one man has been charged with the responsibility of planning its future—if, indeed, it is to have one. He is Dr. Alan J. Goldman, assistant director of technology for the Mint. Goldman is a sour sort of fellow to talk to, as well he might be; he seems exasperated and annoyed that he has to fool with this matter.

"I can change the color of the coin," he said. "But I'm not sure that anything will happen."

And that is what Goldman is doing. He has transformed the metallurgic makeup of the Anthony dollar and has determined that he can give it a bronze tint by using a combination of aluminum, silicon, and copper. That will make it look different from a quarter.

"I don't believe it will work, though," Goldman said. "To make this coin fly, you've got to force it into use."

What he means is, you've got to withdraw dollar bills from circulation. Goldman's theory is that if paper dollars aren't available to people, they will have to use the Anthony dollar. That, he thinks, is the true answer to this dilemma. "As long as people are given a free choice," he said, "they will not use this coin."

Making policy decisions is not his job, though; his job is to change the color of the coin. So he is doing it, even though he knows that, somewhere down the line, more complaints await him.

"You see, when the bronze Susan B. Anthony coin tarnishes, it will tarnish to a greenish color," Goldman said.

When he talks to you about his work for even a few minutes, he begins to sigh; you get the impression that discussing the merits of the Susan B. Anthony dollar is not his favorite activity.

"Frankly," he said, "you are wasting my time."

Best not to leave the Anthony dollar on that note, however. The last word should go to Frank Gasparro, the septuagenarian designer who created the coin.

"Sometimes I'll go home at night," Gasparro said. "I'll pull the coin out, and I'll look at Susan B. Anthony. And I'll say, 'Well, you're not Marilyn Monroe, but you're mine.'"

Life of a Salesman

For a while there, before we knew any better, we spoke of them with the deepest disdain. "I suppose I might be a *salesman* when I get out of school," we would say, kidding. Sometimes, in bars, we would continue the joke. A stranger would initiate a conversation and ask what we did; "I'm an insurance salesman," we would say, breaking our friends up.

To a whole generation the very word—"salesman"—conjured up the worst possibilities that life could offer. To be on the street day after day, making business calls trying to peddle a product one did not necessarily believe in—that was the depth of hypocrisy, or so we told ourselves. That was the ultimate in selling out—and boring besides. We were a generation that was going to be creative and alive and free of spirit. We may have been a lot of things, we thought, but we were not going to be a generation of salesmen.

Well . . . I am on the road a lot. One of the staples of my life is the moment when I get off a plane, or arrive at an airport to catch a flight, and spend my spare minutes at a pay telephone. The phones are generally in a line, close together; you are able to hear what your neighbors are saying, to your left and to your right.

And what I overhear, time after time, is one of the melancholy stories of our modern age: the salesman checking in with his home office to confess he has not been able to make the sale he was sent out to consummate.

There is a pattern; I have seen the drama acted out enough times that I can almost tell when it is coming. The man moves the receiver away from the wall, then hesitates before making his call. He is figuratively, if not literally, taking a breath. When his superior back home answers, he begins the conversation in a hearty tone of voice. But soon enough he is required to give the news—it usually comes in some variation of "They think they're going to have to pass on it for now"—and it is not long before the party on the other end terminates the call.

I see these same men at tables for one in hotel dining rooms, on stools in hotel bars. I see them heading out into a city not their own at eight A.M., dressed as if they are expected at a fancy dinner; I see them coming back late in the afternoon, their ties loosened, their eyes distracted.

I see them everywhere, and I have come to understand that they are among the bravest of us. They face on a daily basis what we all dread the most: flat, cold rejection. Even the best of them hears "No" more than he hears "Yes"; the unlucky ones hardly hear "Yes" at all. Yet all of them get up each morning and go out to do it again—move through a world where they usually are not welcome, usually are considered a nuisance. And they dare not ever let their fear show on their faces; once they do, they are dead.

Especially in the current economic climate, their task seems brutal. No one has extra money to spend; individuals don't have it, and corporations don't have it, and everyone has been advised to ride the bad times out and wait for a turnaround. But the salesmen can't do that. If they don't sell, their families don't eat; if they don't sell, they don't live. Before they walk out the door in the morning they know they are probably going to fail. But they have no choice other than to try.

The rest of us can ease through our bad days without being stuck in the ribs. If things are not going well, the signs are usually subliminal. The salesman, though—there is no subtlety in the way he is told the bad news. There are a million ways to paraphrase it, but the basic message never changes: We don't want what you're selling. Go away.

Even on the good days, it is hard to imagine that the salesman's sleep comes easily. Even on the days when someone has said the magic word—"Yes"—the salesman goes to bed knowing that he's got to do it all over again in the morning. Can he feel glory? Doubtful. The product is never his own. If he is able to sell it, the producer assumes that the product is so good it sells itself. When he is unable to sell it, the producer assumes that the salesman is lousy. Lousy, or getting old and tired.

So I see them everywhere—so will you, if you look. And it occurs to me that the salesmen are no longer only the older men so scorned by a generation. As I hear their tales on the pay telephones to either side of me, I glance over and see that more and more of them are a part of that generation. That generation is aging like every generation before it, and many of its dreamers are now salesmen, dreaming different dreams.

If there is something heroic about them—and I think that there is—it is a heroism that is destined to be felt only in their own hearts, or perhaps in the hearts of their families. They have learned to smile when they feel like cringing; they have learned to hit the streets when they feel like locking the door. Most of them may not have ever imagined they would end up doing precisely this. But as long as there is life and as long as there are businesses, there will be salesmen. When this generation is long forgotten, another generation's salesmen will be knocking on doors and taking a breath before phoning the home office. Trying to find a palatable explanation for that ugliest, most familiar word in their lexicon—"No."

Meeting Them More Than Halfway

There is absolutely no news in this story. But if you are getting a little tired of reading about warfare, crime, and meanness, you might want to give it a try anyway.

George and Thelma Washburn, of suburban Hinsdale, met a couple named Von and Lois Cook, of Mishawaka, Indiana, some years ago. Although they live a fairly long way from each other, the Washburns and the Cooks like to get together a couple of times a year, just to say hello.

This summer they decided it might be nice if they had dinner together. The Washburns didn't want to ask the Cooks to drive all the way to the Chicago area, and the Cooks didn't want to ask the Washburns to drive all the way to Mishawaka. So they compromised. They selected a town midway between—the town of Valparaiso, Indiana—and they agreed to meet there for a Sunday dinner.

They asked around, and someone recommended a Valparaiso restaurant called the White House. The food was supposed to be good.

The Washburns and the Cooks—all of them are in their sixties, by the way—decided to make a dinner reservation for five P.M. that Sunday. One of them called to make the reservation. Then they made arrangements to meet in the restaurant's cocktail lounge at three P.M., talk for a few hours, and then eat.

On the appointed day, George and Thelma Washburn drove from Hinsdale to Valparaiso. They found the restaurant, on the corner of Jefferson Street and Route 49. The restaurant was a beautiful old house. The Cooks were waiting for them in the parking lot.

The Washburns were so happy to see their friends that it didn't even strike them as odd that the Cooks' car was the only one in the lot.

"You're not going to believe what happened," Von Cook said as the Washburns got out of their own car.

The Cooks had gone into the restaurant, only to be told that it was closed for the day. Usually the White House is open Sundays and closed Mondays—but this particular week, it was closed on Sunday because the owners were having a private family party. The party was due to start in a few hours, and the guests would be arriving.

"The owners told us to come in when you arrived, and they would recommend someplace else around here," Von Cook said.

So the Washburns and the Cooks went into the restaurant. The owners—twin brothers, Harry and John Pappas, both fifty-eight—led them to the cocktail lounge and insisted that they have a complimentary drink. The brothers were apologetic; they explained that the woman who took the reservation over the phone must have forgotten that the restaurant was due to be closed that Sunday.

The Washburns and the Cooks drank their cocktails and talked. And then the brothers appeared again.

"We feel so bad," Harry Pappas said, "we want you to stay for the party. We want you to be our guests. We insist."

The Washburns and the Cooks didn't know what to make of this. But they didn't have time to decide. Soon the guests started to arrive. There were seventy-five people in all; they had come to the restaurant to honor the high school graduation of the Pappas's niece, a young woman named Cathy Poulas.

Harry Pappas pulled the Washburns and the Cooks aside.

"I know you probably don't feel comfortable with a bunch of strangers," he said. "Nobody does. So just mingle if you wish—but I'm going to set you up your own table out on the terrace, where you can visit with each other like you planned in the first place."

The Pappas brothers moved a table out onto the back terrace. There were plants out there, and a big back yard, and a fish pond. The Pappas brothers said that the buffet was inside, in one of the big rooms; the Washburns and the Cooks were to eat as much as they wanted. There would be no charge.

And so the party started. The Washburns and the Cooks were overwhelmed; they knew no one here, and all of a sudden they were joining people at the lavish buffet table. There was roast beef, and ham with pineapple, and a stew, and salads, and desserts. They helped themselves and went to their private table on the terrace.

They relived old times together, but they were interrupted as guests from the party came out to introduce themselves and welcome them. The Pappas brothers came out, too; they told the story of the White House restaurant—how it had been the family house for years, and how four years ago the brothers had decided to make it into a restaurant. The Pappas brothers explained all about the history of the house, and the significance of each room.

When the Washburns and the Cooks had finished with their meal and their conversation, they walked back into the house. The party was still in progress.

Mrs. Washburn didn't know what to say; she couldn't believe that they had been taken in just as if they had been invited. So she stood in the middle of the room full of strangers and said: "Thank you all. I just hope you had as nice a time today as we did."

The people in the room started to say goodbye to them, and the Pappas brothers got up to show them to the front door.

"Get home safe," Harry Pappas said.

So the Washburns drove toward Hinsdale, and the Cooks drove toward Mishawaka. Mrs. Washburn thought to herself: All you hear about is unfriendliness and nastiness; people are supposed to distrust each other and keep to themselves in a cocoon of self-protection. Once in a while, in a small restaurant off the main highway, you see another side.

Miss McNichol Will See You Now

Kristy McNichol, a cigarette dangling from her lips, fumed in the lobby of Los Angeles's Century Plaza hotel. America's preeminent cinematic symbol of youthful wholesomeness was clearly miffed.

"I look in my closet at home," she said. "The clothes are on the floor. I look for my Louis Vuitton bag. The Louis Vuitton bag is missing. I look for my two Sony Walkmans. The Sony Walkmans are gone. My videotape recorder—gone. My alarm clock—gone."

"Have you called the police?" I asked.

"No," Kristy said. "I called my accountant."

"You're going to have to call the police if you want to get insurance money," I said. "There has to be a police report."

"My accountant said I didn't have to call the police," Kristy said.

Her grandfather interjected: "If she calls the police it'll be in the papers." Her grandfather's name was Don Corey. A gentleman of sixty-four, he wore brown-and-white-striped pants, a yellow shirt that he had not tucked in, and running shoes.

Kristy took another drag from the cigarette. Her diamond earrings glistened in the artificial light. "I don't have to call the police," she said. "I'm just never going to talk to the person who did it again."

"You know who did it?" I asked.

"Maybe," Kristy said.

"Who?" I asked.

"Maybe an ex-boyfriend," Kristy said.

"Someone you went out with would do something like that to you?" I asked.

"You never know," Kristy said. She ground out the cigarette in a glass ashtray. She was clearly in no mood to chitchat.

Kristy decided that a remedy for last night's burglary of her condominium would be a shopping trip. A baby-blue limousine waited for her outside the hotel. She walked briskly to the car. Her grandfather and I followed.

The driver, a young blond-haired man named Jimmy, said, "Where to?"

"Century City Shopping Centre," Kristy said.

Her grandfather started to tell a story.

"I was a winner on the Arthur Godfrey 'Talent Scouts' program," he said. "It was 1947."

He had to stop his story because we were at the shopping center. It was directly across the street from the hotel. We could have walked to it in less than a minute.

"Pull into the garage," Kristy said.

The chauffeur did.

In the Broadway department store, we rode the escalator. Kristy seemed to know where she was going. Her grandfather and I hurried to catch up.

In the electronic-entertainment department, she walked up to a salesman.

"Miss McNichol," he said. "How nice to see you."

"I'd like another VHS videotape machine just like my other one," she said.

"The big one?" the salesman said.

"The 250, like I had before," Kristy said. "Is it available?"

"For the next few days we have a special on the 450," the salesman said.

Kristy's grandfather said, "Does it have remote control?"

"That doesn't matter," Kristy said. "Bring me one."

The salesman went into a back room. When he came out he was carrying a videotape machine in a box. Kristy had not asked the price. She handed him her American Express Gold Card.

"Also I have to get another thing," she said. "You know the Sony Walkman with the case on it?"

"I don't believe we carry cases for the Walkman," the salesman said.

Kristy's grandfather said, "Not a Walkman case. The whole Walkman."

"It's nice that you keep us in business during these times of economic stress," the salesman said with a laugh.

Kristy lit another cigarette. "Jimmy?" she called.

The chauffeur appeared.

"I want you to carry this videotape recorder to the car," Kristy said.

"Joey is the person who is closest to me," Kristy said. She referred to Joe Corsaro, a Beverly Hills hairdresser who was twenty-six. Kristy was nineteen.

"Joey knows that I can't be tied to one person, though," she said. "For instance, I just got back from a trip to Hawaii with Tim Hutton."

"What did Joey say?" I asked.

"He didn't say anything," Kristy said. "He knows it's my business. I'm free to be with other people. To meet, and talk, and exchange ideas."

"A trip to Hawaii sounds like quite a way to exchange ideas," I said.

"Yeah," Kristy said. She smiled. "I know."

We were walking through the shopping center. Kristy entered a store called Leather Bound. She walked directly to a large suitcase.

Her grandfather said, "Where do you kill the cow for this?"

"These are almost all calf," the salesman said.

"I love leather," Kristy said. "Don't you have anything bigger than this?"

"That's the largest one we have," the salesman said. "It is three hundred ninety dollars."

"I wish you had a bigger one," Kristy said, and left the store.

She walked into a shoe store. She gazed around for a second or two. "Nope," she said.

"What didn't you see?" I asked.

"I didn't see quality shoes," she said.

In a clothing store called Judy's, she led her grandfather to a display showing a skimpy garment made of leather, festooned with metal zippers.

"Can you see me in this, Grandpa?" she said.

"Good," her grandfather said.

"It's not good, it's disgusting," Kristy said.

"I was just thinking of your great-looking legs," her grandfather said.

She reached toward her grandfather's mouth. She took the cigarette he had been smoking. She put it in her mouth and inhaled. She handed it back to her grandfather. She also handed him her purse. "Carry this for me," she said.

She wandered around the store. She saw a woman's tuxedo suit.

"Let me have this," she said to a saleswoman. She handed the woman her Gold Card.

"Aren't you even going to try it on?" I asked. "How do you know it fits?"

"It probably fits," Kristy said.

"But what if it doesn't?" I said.

"Usually I can tell," Kristy said.

Kristy was hungry. So the three of us went to Lindberg's, a health-food restaurant in the shopping center. There was a brief wait for a table. A young man who was also waiting, not quite able to believe that he was standing next to Kristy McNichol, got up the courage to talk to her. He asked her what her next movie project would be.

"It's about a handicapped girl," Kristy said.

The boy said, "Do you become handicapped during the movie?"

Kristy's grandfather said, "No, before the movie I break her legs."

The young man blushed. "The only reason I asked is that I work with handicapped people. I work with blind people."

"Is that right," Kristy said.

"Have you ever worked with handicapped people?" the young man asked.

Kristy looked to see if our table was ready. "I've thought about working in an orphanage," she said.

"Do you know places?" the young man said. "Because if you don't, I could suggest some places."

Kristy's grandfather said, "Give us your name, maybe we'll call you."

For lunch Kristy ordered a dish called the Health Nut. Kristy said that she would like to be with regular people more, but that she rarely got the chance.

"I was on a cruise with Joey once, and I wanted to get a little lunch, so I went down to the dining room without him, and some people recognized me," she said. "They asked me if I wanted to join them. They said, 'Sit with us.' That was nice."

"Did you do it?" I asked.

"No," Kristy said.

"Why not?" I asked.

"I was in a hurry," Kristy said.

I asked her why she thought so many people felt such warmth toward her when they saw her on the screen.

She ate. "I don't know," she said. "People say I invite people into my eyes. That's what I've been told. Maybe that's it."

I asked her how she met young men.

"It isn't hard," she said.

I asked her to give me an example.

"All right," she said, "I was at this club called the Lingerie. I saw this guy wearing black leather pants and an Elvis rockabilly shirt. I thought he was hot. I danced with him."

"Did he call you after that?" I asked.

"I called him," she said. "I don't give out my number."

"Was he surprised to hear from you?" I asked.

"I don't know," she said. "I just said, 'Hey, this is Kristy.' We got together."

"So what happened?" I said.

"I think he was trying to get me in the palm of his hand," Kristy said. "I think he thought maybe I would be weak. I'm not."

She said that she almost never read any of her fan mail. I asked her why not.

"I get a lot of feedback just walking around," she said. "I hear so much from people on the street, from my family. I don't need to go home and read letters saying how great I am."

"She doesn't have the time," her grandfather said.

"I just don't feel like reading them," she said.

" 'I adore you,' 'I love you,' 'I want to marry you,' " her grandfather said.

" 'I'll jump out of a window for you,' " Kristy said. "I don't need that."

We were in the parking lot that was constructed beneath the shopping center. Kristy had forgotten on which level the limousine was parked; we had not seen the driver since he had been dispatched to carry the videotape recorder.

All around us people moved toward their cars or toward the passageways into the shopping center. I suggested that we go down another level to look for the car.

Kristy just stopped walking. She stood in the garage and put her hands on her hips. She began to shout:

"Jimmy!"

There was no answer. She shouted again:

"Jimmy!" "Jimmy!" "Jimmy!"

Still no response. She shot a stare at her grandfather, who had been standing silently. He caught the look. In a second he was shouting, too:

"Jimmy! Jimmy! Jimmy!"

* * *

The next day Kristy had a lunch date with Joey Corsaro at Benihana of Tokyo, on La Cienega Boulevard. When I arrived they were already eating.

Joey wore a white sleeveless T-shirt. He was brown and lean and quite handsome. Between bites of food he reached over to rub Kristy's leg, or caress her arm. He said nothing.

I asked her if she ever had trouble with people envying her.

"Not women," she said. "Just the guys. I can see it in their eyes. It's males."

I asked her why she thought they felt that way.

"Probably because I've done more in nineteen years than they'll do in their lifetimes," she said.

She reached over to run her hand up Joey's forearm.

I asked her what she thought the greatest public misconception about her was.

"That I'm the all-American girl," she said. "Perfect and cute and good and level-headed."

I noticed that Joey was wearing a clear jeweled earring in the lobe of his left ear. I asked him if it was a diamond.

"What, do you think Kristy would give me a piece of glass?" he said.

The Jimmie Soules Suite

DECATUR, Illinois—The person taking my reservation at the Holiday Inn suggested that I try staying in the Executive Suite. I figured that as long as I was in Decatur, the Executive Suite sounded fine.

But then she discovered that the Executive Suite was already booked for the night.

"We could put you in the Jimmie Soules Suite," she said.

"The Jimmie Soules Suite?" I said.

"Yes," she said.

I wasn't going to argue. When I arrived I took my key and went to the second floor, and there, where Room 227 would normally be, was a door with a big brass plaque mounted on it, and inscribed on the big brass plaque was "Mr. and Mrs. Jimmie Soules Suite."

Now, as you know if you read this column regularly, there is nothing I like better than hotel rooms. They bring me inner peace and grant me sustenance; I prefer being in a hotel room to being in my own home. I am a person who pays close attention to hotel rooms.

But in all my travels, I had never come across anything like the Jimmie Soules Suite. I don't mean the room itself; it was very nice, with a canopied bed and an AM-FM radio and a new couch. But the name of the room—I have heard of Monarch Suites and Presidential Suites and Royal Suites and Regal Suites. But a Mr. and Mrs. Jimmie Soules Suite?

Another traveler might have shrugged and let the matter go. But I lay awake and pondered the perplexing question: Who was Jimmie Soules? Did he own this Holiday Inn? Was he a famous entertainer in Decatur? Was he a former governor of Illinois I had never heard of?

My sleep was fitful. In the morning, as I was checking out, I said to the desk clerk:

"I don't mean to be ignorant, but who is Jimmie Soules?"

The young woman returned a blank stare.

"Hasn't anyone ever asked you that question before?" I said.

"Not that I can recall," she said.

I couldn't continue my life without knowing. Jimmie Soules. Jimmie Soules. I sought out the manager of the hotel—at Holiday Inns they are called "innkeepers"—and requested an audience. The innkeeper's name was Dieter Schultz.

"Who is Jimmie Soules?" I said.

"You don't know who Jimmie Soules is?" Schultz said.

"You mean I ought to know?" I said.

Schultz laughed. "I'm only kidding you," he said. "Jimmie Soules is just a man who hangs around the hotel."

"What do you mean?" I said.

"He's a good fellow who hangs around the hotel, so the innkeeper who was here before I took over named a suite after him," Schultz said. "He's like a fixture here. When I arrived six years ago to take over, this man walked up to me and said 'I'm Jimmie Soules.' His name was already on the suite by then, of course."

I felt a sense of awe. Having a hotel room named after you . . . to me, that is the greatest honor a man could ever achieve. And this man Jimmie Soules had done it just by hanging around the Holiday Inn.

I knew I must find Jimmie Soules.

In Decatur, it wasn't that hard. Jimmie Soules turned out to be an eighty-one-year-old man who was delighted to learn that I had slept in his suite the night before.

"Hope you liked it," he said.

I couldn't believe I was really talking to Jimmie Soules. Stammering and struggling to make conversation, I asked him what he did for a living.

"I'm in the bird-repellent business," he said. "I control pigeons, starlings, and sparrows. I can get rid of them without killing a single bird."

I couldn't think of a follow-up question, but luckily for me, Jimmie Soules was still rolling.

"I can walk out on any ledge at two o'clock in the morning, even if it's only twelve inches wide, and check out the birds," he said. "Some people say I even think like a bird. When a pigeon flies, I can tell where he's going."

I said that sounded great, but my main interest was the hotel suite. Had he really had it named after him just by hanging around the Holiday Inn?

"I'm in there quite a bit," he said.

I said that it must be quite a thrill to sleep in a hotel room with your name on the door.

"To tell you the truth, I have never slept in that suite," Jimmy Soules said. "I used to ask my wife to go stay there with me, but she always said that we had a beautiful home and she preferred to sleep here. She passed away in February, and we had never slept there. But when my grandson was married, I let him sleep in the suite on his wedding night."

I was a little flabbergasted. I said goodbye to Jimmie Soules, and repeated how much I had enjoyed sleeping in his suite.

"Thank you," he said.

In the days since, I have reflected on the experience. Some men want to be president. Some men yearn to win the Nobel Prize. Some men lust to sit in the anchor chair on the "CBS Evening News."

But Jimmie Soules, eighty-one, of Decatur, Illinois, has achieved the only dream that I find thrilling. To have your name on the door of some Holiday Inn somewhere, marking your presence in the hotel even on the nights you are unavoidably detained at home . . . that, to me, is what the promise and possibility of America are all about.

Rush Week

This is a story that happened ten years ago. It bears retelling today.

The story should be repeated because, all of a sudden, fraternities are very big on the college campuses once again. A movie called *Animal House* has a lot to do with it. For a few years fraternities suffered a lull in popularity, but now they are back. National magazines are devoting feature stories to fraternity pranks, and television news shows are filming fraternity parties. The country is being told about the fun and craziness of the college fraternity system.

But there is another side. As long as the fraternities exist, there will be another side.

The boy's name was Jon. He was a bright kid. He came to Northwestern in that autumn of 1968 for his freshman year, and he signed up for fraternity rush.

He had something wrong with the way his body was formed. It made him look unusual. Maybe he didn't know what lay in store for him during rush week; maybe he did know, but had determined that he would do his best anyway.

His best wasn't very good. At the first house where he showed up for a rush date, one of the rush chairmen saw Jon and grinned. Jon didn't look like all of the other freshmen who were going through rush, so he made an easy target.

He was placed in a corner, by himself, and he was allowed to sit there for two hours. No one greeted him, no one talked to him. When the others went downstairs to the dining room for their meal, Jon was left to stay by himself in the living room.

He waited the whole time, and when the meal was over and all of the other freshmen were leaving the house, Jon got up and walked out with the rest. He went on to the next house on his schedule, and again he was sized up at the door, and again he was shunted aside.

At some of the houses it was more subtle than at others. Some fraternities had entire rooms where young men like Jon were placed, so as not to disturb the other freshmen who were judged to be fraternity material. Not all of them had physical disabilities such as Jon's, of course; most were simply not handsome, or were awkward, or were dressed poorly. They were extraneous; they got in the way of rush week.

At one house, Jon was led out onto a fire escape and made to stand there for over an hour. It was an astonishing kind of cruelty; maybe things are different in fraternity rush now. Maybe things have changed.

And then, one night, two active members of one of the fraternities were assigned to make a rush call on a good prospect in a freshman dorm. The two were seniors; they were becoming disillusioned with the fraternity system, but they were going through with rush week this last time. They looked through the dorm for the boy they wanted, and somehow they went to the wrong room, and there was Jon, crying on his bed.

The two seniors could have turned and walked out, but for some reason they didn't. They sat down and they asked Jon what was wrong. He was reluctant to discuss it, but then he told them; told them what had happened to him during rush week, and how it was breaking his heart.

He told them about how he hadn't been given even a sliver of a chance, even by one house. He told them how desperately afraid he was of college. They listened to him and they understood that Jon's story was the story of so many boys who signed up for fraternity rush, and were then casually humiliated because, for various small reasons, they were not judged suitable. It was a hurt that would stay for years, and they knew it.

The two seniors listened, and they talked quietly to Jon, and after they had left him in his dorm they knew they would have to do something about it. Jon was determined to continue with rush week, and they knew they could not let him go through it alone.

So they went to the central rush office, and they got a copy of Jon's rush schedule for the rest of the week. And that night they started to visit the houses where Jon would be going in the days to come.

At every house, the two of them asked to talk to the fraternity members. They explained what they had come for. They told the fraternity men about Jon, and the way he looked. And they said: We are not asking you to take him into your fraternity. We are just asking you not to hurt him anymore.

Surprisingly, the fraternity men listened. There were a few snickers, but not many, and by the time the two of them were through they had talked to every house where Jon was scheduled to go. The two of them didn't talk much to each other about it; they didn't know exactly why they were doing this. But it was the first grown-up thing they had ever done, and it felt right.

Jon went through the rest of rush week. He was not asked to join a house, but he was treated with decency. The fraternities he visited assigned members to talk to him, to eat with him, and to make him feel welcome. Perhaps the pain was lessened a little.

The two seniors ended up quitting their fraternity. Part of it had to do with Jon, and part of it had to do with other aspects of the fraternity system. They just wanted no part of it anymore.

They lived in an apartment off campus. As far as they knew, Jon didn't know about what they had done. They completed their senior year, and in the spring they prepared to graduate.

And then, one day, a congratulatory graduation card came addressed to them in the mail. They opened it. It was from Jon. "Thank you," it said. . . .

Targets

I arrived in Atlanta on a Monday evening. The number of murdered and missing children stood at twenty-three. There had been no arrests.

I did not want to talk to police officials. I did not want to talk to psychiatrists. I did not want to talk to social workers. I had read enough of what they had to say about the case.

I wanted to talk to children. Every time I heard about the Atlanta killings, all I could think about was how they must be affecting the children who were living in the middle of them.

But children do not have press conferences, and children do not have public relations spokesmen. Until they were dead, the children of Atlanta had no way to get people's attention. And it was not the dead children of Atlanta I was curious about. It was the children who were still alive. So I got on a plane.

❖   ❖   ❖

"I don't go outside," said Denise Durr. She was a tiny girl, seven years old. "He might kill me or my friends."

School had just let out for the afternoon. I had been waiting across the street for half an hour. It was a strange way to be conducting business, but I was finding it was the only way.

The city of Atlanta and the public schools had decided that no one from news organizations would be allowed to talk to children on school property. It was a policy that probably made sense. It ensured that the corridors would not be overrun with camera crews.

But if I wanted to talk to children, I certainly couldn't stop them on the streets individually. Not in the terrified atmosphere in 1981 Atlanta. I had to go to a place where the children would feel safe in numbers, and where they might talk to me without running away.

So that meant spending time standing across the street from elementary schools in black neighborhoods, looking at my watch and waiting for the final bell of the day to sound. A number of motorists slowed down and gave me quizzical glances. It was hard to blame them.

It was working, though. The children, buoyed by the courage that comes from being together in large groups, stopped to talk to me. We talked one at a time; they all stood around and watched. I seemed as much a curiosity to them as they were to me. I got the impression that they didn't see many white men spending time in their neighborhoods.

The worst thing was how normal the idea of random murder had become to such little children. They talked about it easily, the way children in other cities might talk about a favorite television show. If, in the rest of the country, the story of the Atlanta killings was a horrible abstraction, here it was a tumorous part of everyday life.

So my wonder grew as child after child told me of an obsession with the idea of death. "He may get me next," said Roderick Hednut, ten. Troy Lee, twelve, said, "I can't get to sleep. I keep thinking the man may come and get me." Larcquo Sharpe, eleven, put it as a question: "The children haven't done anything to him. So if we haven't, why doesn't he stop?"

It all seemed so out-of-sync. The week was warm in Atlanta, and these children should have been on their way to play. But they weren't; they had orders to be home within fifteen minutes after the end of the school day. If a visitor from another country, or another year, had overheard our conversations, he would have been startled. The boys and girls were healthy-looking and handsome. Nickie Marshall, nine, smiled shyly. She might have been telling me about her first sweetheart. But what she said was: "I think I'm going to get kidnapped or something. I've been having dreams about it. One night I dreamt this man, he was following me, and I ran and he caught me and I was kicking and screaming and he killed me."

Law enforcement officials were speculating that the Atlanta murders might not be the work of one killer, but of several. To the children, though, there was only one person at work. He was a man, and they called him "the Snatcher."

And as the children told me the words their parents were using to warn and discipline them, I had to wonder what future scars these months will leave on their souls. "If you're not in by dark, the Snatcher's going to get you." "You be good, or you're the next one the Snatcher's going to snatch."

Some of the children were full of braggadocio, and it was not hard to understand. In the face of the killings, it was an outlet, a mask. So when a seven-year-old boy named Richie Kraft said to me, "If he tries to get me, I'll cut his nose off," the other children watching us talk started to giggle. And Frederick Williams, seven, seemed to be addressing the killer himself when he said in a defiant voice, "What if someone came up to you and had a gun in *your* face? What would you do then?"

With others, though, it was different. I spoke with a sixteen-year-old boy named Anthony Zachary. "I'm not worried," he said, although his eyes betrayed his words.

I asked him how he could say he was calm, with all the children dying.

"I've got protection," he said, and at the same time he reached into his back pocket, pulled out a switchblade knife, and flashed its six-inch blade in front of me.

In another setting it might have been an ominous moment. But as he postured here, waving the knife before my mouth, he seemed very alone, and very vulnerable.

One of the unexpected things about spending time in Atlanta was the fact that every person on the street did not seem to be the murderer; every face did not seem to conceal the secret of the child killer.

I had expected to presume malice everywhere I turned. In a city where the child killings had been going on for so long, it seemed natural to assume that every stranger encountered would stand at least a chance of appearing to be the one.

But it wasn't like that. If I had believed, from afar, that everyone was going to seem like the killer, I was finding that precisely the opposite was true. The bodies had been turning up for so long, and the person or persons responsible had been evading capture for so long, that now, in Atlanta, it almost seemed as if no one was the killer.

Because the victims had all been black, I had been spending my time only in black neighborhoods.

One afternoon, across the street from a school out of which the children emerged minutes earlier, I stood and talked to the black boys and girls for a long time. I was getting used to hearing their fears and unhappy fantasies; by now the pervasive terror that had at first stunned me was becoming commonplace.

As usual, all the children waited while I asked my questions; they did not break off one by one, but left as a group. And I was getting ready to depart when I noticed that three boys had stayed behind.

They were white. For some reason they went to this nearby all-black school; they were the only white children I had seen in days. Hesitantly, they asked if I would talk to them, too.

Their names were David Stewart, Philip Bailey, and James Koenig. We started to speak, and it immediately became evident that they were every bit as frightened as the black children with whom I had talked. Their fear seemed almost more intense, if that is possible, because they were supposedly safe.

David Stewart was twelve. "The man may change from black to white," he said. "He might come to get me." James Koenig, ten, said, "He might come and kidnap me. I have dreams every night that I might get killed like the other kids got killed." Philip Bailey, also twelve, was too bashful to say much of anything.

I stood there, not knowing what to say to them. It was clear that they just wanted someone to talk to. After a few moments of awkward silence, they left, together.

The fear kept the children virtually locked inside after school hours. The months of this particular kind of house arrest were beginning to wear on them.

Rodrigues Martin, eleven, was an athletic-looking boy who appeared as if he belonged on a playing field. "I can't shoot basketball, I can't play football, I can't do anything," he told me. I heard this from child after child. They were at the age when they should have been unleashing all of their young energy, and yet it, too, was a victim of the murders. Some of the boys and girls spoke with a kind of depressed listlessness that I had come across before—in prisoners at maximum-security penitentiaries.

One evening during my stay in Atlanta, I went over to the Omni complex. I had learned that I was not likely to see many children after dark; a seven P.M. curfew kept most of them inside, and the reality of the murders was a persuader for those who might not respect mere statute.

On this night, though, I saw a young boy in a sport coat walking along with his father. I introduced myself to the man; I explained what I was doing, and asked if I might talk to his son. He said yes.

The father told the boy it was all right to go with me. We walked about twenty feet away; the boy was still within eyeshot of his father, and shoppers were strolling past us, but we were in effect alone. It was one of the few times during the week when there had not been other children around as I talked to someone.

The boy's name was Tony Smith. He was nine, and quite small. As I talked to him, his voice quavered, and I thought I saw his eyes filling with tears. And then he said it: "Do not kill me."

His voice was so soft that I thought I might have misunderstood. I asked him to repeat what he had said.

"I want to have a family," he said. "Do not kill me."

I had talked with more than one hundred children since I had arrived in Atlanta. Virtually all of them I had met through the random method of waiting for the various black schools to empty out. But there was one child I specifically wanted to meet.

He was Johnathan Bell, twelve years old, whose younger brother, Yusef, had been the fourth child to disappear. Yusef had been missing for seventeen days when he was found strangled.

Many of the children I had spoken with had given me grisly details of what they would like to see done to the murderer if he was eventually caught. Most of the boys and girls wanted him to die, some in gruesome ways. It did not seem particularly bloodthirsty to me; these were little children, after all, and their imaginations had been fueled by dark reality.

So I accepted their judgments, but I wanted to know what Johnathan Bell would say when I asked him the same question. Did he want his brother's killer to die? I went to his home one evening, chatted aimlessly with him for about fifteen minutes, and then asked him. Say the killer was found. What would he like to see done to him?

His answer, when it came, was delivered in a calm voice. Johnathan Bell looked me straight in the eye. It was clear he had thought about it before.

"I think he should be put in a room," he said. "With white all over it. A white room.

"And then they should put pictures of all the children he killed up on the wall. All of those pictures.

"And then they should leave him in there. For life."

When I left it was on a morning flight. I was back in the town where I live by midafternoon.

On the way to my home from the airport, I saw children playing and running in city parks; children walking along the sidewalks together; children talking casually on street corners. Atlanta seemed very far away; like a vivid scene out of a book you only half-remember. Like a flash from a terrible time out of your past. Like a moment from a child's dream.

Bachelor of the Month

On page 114 of the March 1981 issue of *Cosmopolitan* magazine, in the Cosmo Tells All section, there appeared the magazine's Bachelor of the Month. The feature is a mainstay of each edition; when a woman purchases the magazine, she knows she will find a capsule description of a real-life eligible male.

The small black-and-white photograph in the March issue showed a handsome, smiling man with dark hair and a moustache. He was wearing a short-sleeved polo shirt and a pair of faded blue jeans, and was gripping a racket with his right hand.

The sketch read:

Chicago's Jeff Kaiser, 30, owns Lakeshore Centre, a "total athletic environment" where 11,000(!) members can swim, sun, play tennis, even indoor ski. Jeff, whose *other* passions include opera and sailboat racing, wants a "warm-spirited woman who's not always crying 'me, me, me.'" Big-hearted girls may write 1320 W. Fullerton Ave., Chicago 60614.

Men who happen to glance occasionally at *Cosmopolitan* may have fantasized about being stopped on the street by a *Cosmo* editor and offered the Bachelor-of-the-Month slot, and the chance to be displayed before all those *Cosmo* women. In the case of Jeff Kaiser, it did not happen precisely that way.

Howard Bragman, twenty-five, is a publicist with the Richardson & McElveen public relations firm in Chicago. Late last year, he was talking on the telephone with Jane Makley, an editor at *Cosmo*. He was pitching a story idea about one of his firm's clients. Makley was not responding well to the pitch, but she and Bragman were having a pleasant conversation. At one point Makley asked Bragman how old he was—they had never met face-to-face—and when he told her, she said, "Maybe you should be a Bachelor of the Month."

For the briefest instant, Bragman's brain buzzed with the possibilities. Not for nothing is he an ambitious young publicist, though. Immediately all lustful thoughts disappeared from his head, and were replaced by two words: *ink* and *client*.

So it was that the phone rang at the Lakeshore Centre club—a client of Richardson & McElveen—and Jeff Kaiser, who had never heard of the *Cosmo* Bachelor of the Month, took the call and learned that Howard Bragman thought he could get him into the magazine.

Six months later Jeff Kaiser sat in his apartment on the fourteenth floor of a high-rise on the North Side of Chicago. In his hand was a drink; on the table, on the couch, and on the floor were more than seven hundred letters from women.

Howard Bragman had submitted Kaiser's photograph to *Cosmopolitan*; the publicist had also given the magazine some facts about Kaiser's background, and within a month of the first conversation between Bragman and Jane Makley, Jeff Kaiser had been selected for the March issue.

Now Kaiser—a divorced father of two—picked up a stack of the letters, allowed the envelopes to tumble through his hands and back to the floor, and tried to explain the feeling.

"My PR man told me it would be good for business," Kaiser said. "So I told him to do what he had to do. I had no idea they put your address in until some writer from the magazine called to interview me. When I found out that they actually printed a place where women could write, I almost pulled out, but it did seem like it would be good publicity for the club.

"And then it started. Thirty, forty, fifty letters a day, every day. Phone calls from all over the country at the club. Women would lie, would make up business excuses to talk to me. And I would come to the phone—and here would be some woman calling from South Carolina, and she would say, 'Oh, my God, I didn't believe you were real.'"

Kaiser has been physically attractive all his life, but now, because his photograph had appeared in the magazine, he was learning for the first time what it is to be a celebrity. "It's all a matter of levels of fantasy," he said. "The women who are writing are one level below me. I'm one level up, because I'm in the magazine. And then above me is someone like a movie star. At least that's how I'm starting to think about it; I'm new at this, you know.

"This is what I think it is: the magazine makes you famous, but unlike most famous people, you're accessible. They print your address. See, that's the fantasy: they're telling the woman that here's this attractive man, or this rich man, or this talented man—and here's where you can write him, and he'll get your letter.

"It's like they made me a Playmate of the Month, but they changed the rules. It's like they printed the Playmate's address next to her picture. They could never do that in the case of a woman. But their whole gimmick is that with a man, they can do it."

From Iowa:

Dear Jeff:

Here goes. This is a first. I've never responded to anything such as this before. But I decided that since you were so nice-looking in *Cosmo,* I would let you know. Probably along with hundreds of other women! I am 5′11″, 130 lbs. and 27. I work for the U.S. Postal Service as a clerk-carrier. . . .

From Florida:

Dear Jeff:

I was just sitting here on the beach reading a *Cosmopolitan* magazine when your beautiful smile caught my attention. And since the article read "Big-hearted girls may write," I decided that I would. . . .

From Wisconsin:

Dear Jeff:

I have never written a letter like this and I don't know why I'm starting now. I guess because Chicago is relatively near where I live. I'll only be 18 on June 26, but I feel older than that because I feel so stifled in my life the way I'm living. . . . I am waiting to find a two-sided relationship that will remain two-sided and not become one-sided for either side after any amount of time. I have an intense need for hugging and being hugged. . . .

Many of the women enclosed photographs with their letters. The great majority of them were quite attractive; the women writing to Jeff Kaiser did not appear to be people who would have any trouble finding a man. They were professional women and salesclerks; credit managers and students. "I never thought I would answer an ad in a magazine," wrote a fashion model from northern Illinois. "I hope to God you don't know any of the same people I do." And there was the woman dentist from Georgia; the letter was on her office stationery, and above her signature there was only one sentence: "Why not make your next dental appointment in Atlanta?"

Almost all of the women said that this was the first time they had written to a stranger from a magazine; almost all of them made at least one reference to being "big-hearted" or not being interested in crying "me, me, me." There were the predictable letters from both ends of the spectrum: a few women who included lewd photos of themselves, and a few lost and solitary women whose cries of loneliness were almost heartbreaking.

But all of the others were from women who seemed bright or pretty or both. If one tried to read all the letters—and trying to do so was an endeavor that took many hours—one ended up deciding that these women did, indeed, have ample opportunities to meet men in their hometowns. But their demands were high; they indicated that the men they knew bored them, were dreary. They knew nothing about Jeff Kaiser. Maybe if they met him at their own offices, they would never have thought to approach him. But his picture had been in *Cosmo;* in all America, he had been selected as Bachelor of the Month; thus he was interesting. His appeal had been officially validated.

None of the women mentioned sex in the letters. Not one. Few even hinted at it. At least on paper, they were not lusting for Jeff Kaiser. They were idealizing him.

Brenda Groendyk, twenty-seven, is a receptionist at the Steelcase office-furniture manufacturing plant in Grand Rapids, Michigan. Her letter began: "Dearest Jeff: I saw your picture and description in the latest *Cosmopolitan* magazine and was immediately intrigued. Can we meet?" She signed it "Amour." Stapled to her letter was a color snapshot of herself in a blue bikini, squinting in the sun next to a chain-link fence. Her blond hair curled over her shoulders. On the back of the photo, in blue ink, she had written: "I do not bleach my hair! I have not had a silicone job!"

I called her and explained why I had seen her letter. I said I would like to talk to her. She agreed, and we met for dinner.

"I mainly wrote it to see what would happen," she said. "Most of the men I meet are either boring or married. Grand Rapids is kind of a conservative city, and I'm a little more progressive with my ideas."

She has never been married, but said that the possibility of matrimony was not included in the reasons she wrote to Jeff Kaiser: "When you get married, you think in terms of a normal man. Not someone who's had his picture in a national magazine. That's too unbelievable. I just wanted to meet him and see if we liked each other."

Most of the women I spoke to echoed that. Some were embarrassed, and even angry, that someone other than Kaiser had seen the letters. But when we talked, the recurrent theme had to do with their inability to find someone they considered "good enough" in their own towns. There were plenty of men to sleep with, if that's what the women wanted; but they didn't necessarily want that. What did they want? An "interesting" man. And how were they so sure that this man in Chicago—this man they had never met—would please them where others hadn't? The answer: He had been in *Cosmo*, hadn't he? Out of all the bachelors in America, he had been chosen that month. When I told them about Howard Bragman and his public relations firm, there was often a moment of vague confusion. It had not occurred to them that the Bachelor of the Month might require a middleman, a business partner.

They put that out of their minds, though. The *Cosmo* profile of Jeff Kaiser had been only fifty-four words long, but that was enough to convince the women. Paula Grecco, twenty-eight, of Cuyahoga Falls, Ohio, told me: "If I'm going to go out with a guy, I don't want him to be some factory worker who's making eight dollars an hour at General Tire." When I asked her what was so wrong with her town, she said, "Sucks." She said, "Some days I get asked out five times, but I haven't had a date in a month. I just don't choose to be with these men."

Many of the women used harsh words to describe the men they knew: "hillbillies," "wimps," "losers." The women had put themselves on the line to the man from *Cosmo* because they thought he might be able to rescue them from all that. Every woman I talked to said to me: "Do you know if he's going to call me?" Some of them said it at the beginning of our conversations, and some of them said it at the end, but they all said it.

Three months after he had first appeared in *Cosmopolitan,* Jeff Kaiser had failed to contact a single one of the seven hundred women who had written him. He had not made one call; he had not written one note.

"I don't know how to say this without it sounding arrogant," Kaiser said. "I have a very full life with women as it is. I don't need to meet these women who have been writing. I'm glad that I did this. It was good for the club. And it was great for my ego to get the mail. But I don't have to actually meet the women for my ego to feel good. There's a fantasy here, but meeting the women has nothing to do with it. Just getting the letters takes care of that.

"If one woman lets you know she thinks you're attractive, you might think about it. But when you're getting fifty letters a day, all saying the same thing? Even if you do start to think about one of them, you've forgotten her by the time you open the next envelope.

"This was an interesting experience. But I didn't do it to meet any new women. Maybe someday I'll call one, or write one.

"But I doubt it."

Woody in Exile

COLUMBUS, Ohio—Darkness had just given way to dawn. The visitor waited on the sidewalk outside the hotel. Across Third Street, the sign on the Ohio State Federal Savings and Loan Building flashed that it was thirty-five degrees.

A gray pickup truck pulled to a stop. The visitor walked around to the passenger side and climbed inside.

"Thanks for picking me up, Coach," the visitor said.

"Well, that's all right," said Woody Hayes. "I'm glad to have the company."

Hayes was behind the wheel of the truck. It has been almost a year since his career as head football coach at Ohio State University was brought to an end when he slugged a Clemson University player during the Gator Bowl. Hayes is a national catchphrase; the words "Woody Hayes" bring nods and knowing smiles whenever they are mentioned. Now there is a new football era in Columbus; a new coach, Earle Bruce, has an undefeated team, and Woody Hayes's twenty-eight-year reign is past tense.

Now the new coach is preparing his team for the season's climactic game with Michigan, and that is the talk all around Columbus; but Woody Hayes still lives. He gets up every morning at his house at 1711 Cardiff Road, and he goes through the day. He is sixty-six years old; behind the wheel of his truck he wore a dark blue business suit and a brown felt hat pulled down hard over his white hair.

"We're going to Westerville, Ohio," Hayes said. "I'm supposed to talk to some high school students. It's . . . what do you call it? When you tell them what they're supposed to do in life?"

"Careers Day?" the visitor said.

"Right," Hayes said. "Careers Day. I'm supposed to tell them about the coaching profession."

A woman in a station wagon backed out of a parking space, causing Hayes to stop. In the front seat the woman's son, a teenager, dozed, his head resting on his chest.

"Look at that kid," Hayes said. "Now there you have a drug victim."

"Oh, come on, Coach," the visitor said. "That kid's not on drugs."

"Well, he's either a drug victim or a lazy son of a bitch," Hayes said. "Yessir. Lazy. I know about these things. Too many people like that out there today."

Hayes headed onto Interstate Highway 71, on his way to Westerville. He talked nonstop; he seemed happy to have a listener. His subjects shifted quickly from international politics to literature to history to women's rights, sometimes with no interconnective phrases. It was cold in the truck, but he did not turn the heater on. He talked all the way to Westerville.

"Now where is this place?" he said to himself as he drove down Main Street. "It's Westerville North High School, but we're heading south. Doesn't make any sense. I don't know why they build these schools so far out into the country. The kids can't walk, and it makes them soft. Wastes gasoline. People don't . . . people don't think."

He found the high school and pulled into the parking lot. He left the truck next to the students' cars; on the way into the school he passed a man, perhaps a teacher, who did not say hello. "Good morning," Hayes said.

When the man had passed from earshot, Hayes said, "They don't even say hello. That stupid. . . . He didn't even say hello. People are so unfriendly these days. Back in Newcomerstown when I was growing up, everyone said hello to everyone. Things have changed. People act stupid."

The speech was in the high school gymnasium. There were several hundred students present; when Hayes talked about coaching, it was in the present tense ("On our team we tell our players". . . . "When we're getting ready for a game. . . ."). Suddenly, though, for some reason not readily apparent, Hayes shifted his talk to United States intervention in Japan following World War II. He was shouting, combative, and he stepped from the microphone, as if it was not loud enough for him. He approached the students in the bleachers, and he bellowed:

"Do you know who that man was? No, you don't want to say his name because you think he was too much a chauvinist! Well that man's name was . . . Five-Star General Douglas MacArthur!"

The students sat in silence, bewildered. Hayes seemed to realize something, and returned to the microphone, where he quickly finished up his talk about coaching.

In the truck on the way back to Columbus, he talked about his pain for the first time. He said that after having Ohio State football be his whole life, he could not bring himself to attend a game this year. Most Saturdays, he said, he spent in a cabin he had built down in Noble County.

"Sometimes I listen to the games on the radio," he said. "But I can't go.

"You know, the worst thing in the world is feeling sorry for yourself. Self-pity will kill you. I can't have it.

"You can't dwell on what used to be. You can't . . . bring it back. The football. . . . I've got to separate myself from it."

For a few minutes Hayes and the visitor rode in silence. Then Hayes cleared his throat, as if to cut off the thoughts that had filled the truck, and he said:

"Do you know what President of the United States I feel the least use for?"

"Who's that, Coach?" the visitor said.

"Woodrow Wilson," Hayes said.

"Why's that?" the visitor said.

"Come on, you know," Hayes said.

"No, I don't," the visitor said.

"Because Wilson wasn't a man's man," Hayes said. "Yessir, he wasn't a man's man."

And on he drove, a legend in exile, heading down I-71 in pursuit of the rest of his life.

"Ever See Your Old Man Cry?"

I told the man I wasn't a social worker. That usually works. With him it didn't. He was back the next day.

"Look, sir . . ." I began.

"I know," he said. "I know. But honest to God, you got to do it."

"I can't," I said. "I'm not the person you want."

"I wouldn't be here if I wasn't begging you," the man said. "You got to talk to him."

He was a worried-looking little man in a rumpled brown suit. Everything about him said defeat.

"I don't know why you're coming to me," I said. "I just write stories and put them in newspapers. You need somebody with some training in this."

"I tried," he said. "Please. I trust you."

"Well you shouldn't," I said.

"Please," he said.

I said okay. The next afternoon he brought the kid down.

The three of us went into a little office with a long table and some chairs. The kid stared at the floor. The father fidgeted. We could hear people walking around out in the hallway.

"Maybe you'd better wait outside," I said to the man. He left the room, almost apologetically.

The kid and I sat in silence for maybe a minute.

"This is stupid," the kid said.

"Agreed," I said.

"What do you think you are, a shrink?" the kid said.

"I don't want to be here any more than you do," I said.

"Then what are you doing it for?" the kid said.

"Your father," I said.

"What's he to you?" the kid said.

"Nothing," I said.

The kid had bad skin and he picked at his fingernails. I would guess he was seventeen. He was bigger than his father.

"What did he tell you?" the kid said.

"That you're on pills a lot," I said. "That he thinks you're stealing. That he thinks you and your friends are stealing."

"He's lying," the kid said.

"He doesn't think so," I said.

"So he drags me down here," the kid said.

"He couldn't drag you anywhere," I said. "I figured you wouldn't show."

The kid lit a cigarette.

"So why did you?" I said.

"You ever see your old man cry?" the kid said.

We looked at each other some more.

"What are you supposed to tell me?" the kid said.

"I don't know," I said. "I guess I'm supposed to tell you to straighten out."

"You never liked to get high and run around?" the kid said.

"I never stole anything," I said.

"I can't believe it," the kid said. "He takes me to a newspaper."

"Would you have preferred the cops?" I said.

He played with his cigarette.

"I don't even read the newspaper," the kid said.

"Some days neither do I," I said.

"So why does my old man have me here?" the kid said.

"Some people believe in magic," I said.

"Well, tell me whatever you're supposed to tell me," the kid said.

"I'm not going to tell you anything," I said.

"What am I supposed to do?" the kid said.

"You're supposed to sit here for awhile and then you're supposed to go out there and pretend that you're going to try to make your old man happy," I said.

He shook his head.

"Why should I try to make him happy?" the kid said.

"Because he cared enough to come down here," I said.

"Yeah, and you don't even have anything to tell me," the kid said.

"I hate this worse than you do," I said. "I got better things to do."

"Then why aren't you doing them?" the kid said.

"Because I thought your father was going to cry when he was talking to me, too," I said. "I don't see a whole lot of people who care that much anymore."

We wasted about fifteen minutes more. Mostly he smoked and I looked at the wallpaper.

"All right," I said. "Let's go."

The father was waiting on a couch in the hallway. He was up and shaking my hand before we could even get out the door. He looked at me like he expected me to nod or something. I just motioned to the kid. The two of them, father and son, walked together toward the elevators. They didn't appear to be talking.

I stopped for a drink on the way home. Sometimes it helps me sleep.

Direct Male

THE AD: It is probably one of the most famous advertisements in modern American merchandising history. For ten years, it has been appearing regularly in 109 magazines and newspapers, ranging from *Psychology Today* to *National Lampoon* to *Man's Action*. You would be hard pressed to find a male in the United States who has never seen it.

The ad varies slightly: sometimes it features photographs of several attractive young women, sometimes only one. The copy has been refined over the years. But the one constant in all the ads is that the main element on the page, in the biggest type, is the title of the book being marketed: *How to Pick Up Girls!*, by Eric Weber.

And the promise is explicit: "Starting today, you'll be able to walk up to just about any woman who catches your eye, start a conversation, a relationship, maybe even a love affair right then and there. . . . It costs less than a tankful of gas—yet it's so much more of a help when it comes to meeting the kind of beautiful women you've always dreamed about."

THE BOOKS: There are a number of them. *How to Pick Up Girls!* is the bestseller, the flagship; but they all address the same theme. There are *How to Make Love to a Single Woman, 100 Best Opening Lines!, Picking Up Girls Made Easy* . . . inexpensively bound, not sold in bookstores, available only via direct mail from Symphony Press, of Tenafly, New Jersey.

If *How to Pick Up Girls!* has become part of the national mythology through the magazine advertisements, you would still have a difficult time finding an American man who will admit that he has bought a copy. There seems to be a certain shame associated with being an owner.

And yet, someone out there is buying the books. During an economically difficult time for the book publishing business, Symphony Press generates an estimated two million dollars in revenues a year selling *How to Pick Up Girls!* and its brethren. The books' average price is $11.50 a copy; there is no retailer, no wholesaler, no middleman. Symphony Press is Eric Weber, one assistant, and two secretaries. It has developed into a productive and thriving loneliness industry, apparently impervious to the inflationary and recessionary factors that influence the rest of the country's business environment. Symphony Press has tapped a market that seems as if it will never go away.

THE MESSAGE: The Symphony Press books provide a combination pep talk and battle plan. The reader is assured that women really do want to meet him—are sitting home alone at this very moment, in fact, just wishing that a man had picked them up during the day. On the other hand, it is made clear to the reader that women have to be tricked into saying yes—that only the cleverest of men will be quick and wily enough to trap a woman.

The most striking thing about *How to Pick Up Girls!* is its elementary tone. Far from dropping his reader off in the middle of an exotic secret world, Eric Weber almost leads the fellow by the hand and asks him not to be afraid. One chapter, for example, is called "Sure, I'd Get Picked Up!" and features such testimonials as the quote from a woman named "Linda," who says: "Of course I get picked up. How else am I going to meet guys?"

Other chapters include "Women Get Horny" ("Janet" tells Weber: "Sure, women get horny. Sometimes I go home and read a sexy book because I don't have a sexy man around"); "Beauty and the Beast" (Weber's friend "Tom" has a face that is a cross between a gorilla's and a toad's, but he managed to marry "Laura—one of the prettiest brunettes I've ever seen"); and "Relax" (Weber advises: "Do not, if at all possible, get uptight. You are not on a bombing mission over enemy territory. You're not hunting bull elephants. You are simply going to talk to a woman. That is all").

But if at one moment Weber is persuading his reader that women are not dangerous and threatening, at the next he is cautioning that same fellow to be as devious as possible, lest they get away. Nothing Weber prescribes is straightforward; everything is intended to reel in a girl before she feels the hook. Weber even has advice for his readers about the richest streams to fish. "Pretend you're shopping for a gift for your mother or sister in a fashionable women's clothing store," he writes. "These places can be real gold mines because they're simply crawling with thousands of young, good-looking girls." And, in a passage apparently not revised since the book came out during Vietnam days:"March in a peace demonstration, even if you're secretly for war. I've heard countless stories of guys who've picked up fantastic broads at peace demonstrations."

None of this shows any signs that the author is smirking. Indeed, Weber's "Fifty Great Opening Lines" seem to be offered almost gently to his reader, as if Weber understands that the man has often agonized over what he might possibly say to a woman. The lines read humorously at first, then become almost unbearably sad with the realization that every night there are men memorizing them: "Do you have an aspirin?" "How long do you cook a leg of lamb?" "Is there a post office near here?" "Wow! What a beautiful day!"

Weber seems to understand that many men are sensitive about the way they look; he knows they spend so much time staring at beautiful women that they become self-conscious about what they see in their own mirrors every morning. So he spends an inordinate amount of space trying to convince his readers that their looks don't matter.

A woman named "Connie" is quoted as saying: "I've come to find men attractive who at first gave me the chills I thought they were so ugly. It's amazing how many times this has happened to me."

And Weber advises: "Just what do women find sexually stimulating about men? You'd be amazed!

"Women are nuts. They really are. They're totally unpredictable.

"If a group of guys standing on the corner spots a girl with huge breasts and a deliciously curvy behind, they all go crazy and elbow each other in the ribs.

"Women don't work that way at all. . . . So don't get all neurotic and insecure because you're not the spitting image of Paul Newman. Without realizing it, you may have some incredible feature that will literally drive women wild. . . ."

If the contents—and success—of the Symphony Press books seem to speak unhappily of the state of the American man's psyche, the same assumption cannot automatically be made about the American woman's. Eric Weber has tried for years to market a similar line of books aimed at females (*How to Pick Up Men!*); the books have been dismal failures. The women don't order.

THE MAN: Eric Weber, thirty-eight, has been married for twelve years. He and his wife have four children. He looks like a slightly older version of Joe Rossi, the reporter on the "Lou Grant" television series;

he speaks with the hurried authority of a progressive-rock disc jockey who has suddenly found himself on an easy-listening station and has been instructed to tone it down.

Weber was a trainee at an advertising agency when he got the idea to write *How to Pick Up Girls!* from his own history of insecurity with women. Having assembled and marketed the book in his free time, he rose to become vice-president and associate creative director of Young & Rubicam before he decided to run Symphony Press full-time.

"I know what the American male is like," Weber said. "Like him or not, I understand him. He thinks he's looking for instant sex. But that's not really what he's looking for. He's looking for a woman to like him. That's all he wants. Just a companion. Nothing would make him feel happier than for a woman to like him. I understand that. Actually, I feel for him.

"Ninety-five percent of my message is trying to get the man to calm down, to not be so afraid at the idea of meeting a woman.

"I know what men need to hear. They need to be told that women aren't that critical of them. That women aren't that booked up. That women don't mind it if you're a bit of a bumbler; they find it endearing. That the way a man looks isn't as important to women as it seems to men. That the pretty girl in the office isn't having four orgies tonight; she's at home wishing there was a little romance in her life."

Weber is convinced that the average buyer of his books probably doesn't even realize his true reason for making the purchase.

"He probably sees the ad and says to himself, 'I'll meet a girl on a plane and screw her standing up in the bathroom,'" Weber said. "Or, 'I'll meet a girl on the street and take her to a hotel room and then never see her again.' It's acceptable for a man to want that. But the real reason he's buying the book is the one he's afraid to admit. That he just wants to have a woman to be around.

"The so-called sexual revolution is a kind of myth," Weber claimed. "I don't think this alleged sexual sophistication has filtered down to the population as a whole. What the 'revolution' probably means is that boys and girls who are going together are sleeping together a year earlier than they used to. But the typical man is still saying to himself, 'I have five bucks to go to a movie, but I don't have a girlfriend to take.'"

Weber recognizes that the true theme of his books seems to be loneliness—but he prefers a different phrase. "I like the word *fear* over *loneliness*. Because what the men who buy the books are dealing with is a terrible fear of rejection. They are so afraid of women. I pride my-self on knowing what's in men's minds and hearts, and that fear is what it is."

Although he realizes he is open to charges that he exploits this fear, Weber denies it. "I happen to be a painfully cynical person about a lot of things," he said, "but not in this area. In this area I am a virtual innocent, a virgin. It is one of the great wounds in a person's life to be shy and fearful of women. I don't take advantage of that. I try to help."

THE MEANING: The men who purchase Eric Weber's books will never have to make eye contact with a clerk in a bookstore. Which is important. As much as the mail-order arrangement is an economic boon to Weber, it is also a psychological necessity to the men who want to read *How to Pick Up Girls!*. Weber realizes that if men had to buy the books over the counter, many probably wouldn't; in our society it is all right to go to a newsstand and purchase a magazine filled with color photographs of wide-open genitals, but it is too embarrassing to purchase a book that is a tacit admission of your solitary despair.

We happily admit our lust; we desperately hide our loneliness. That is the key to the success of the Symphony Press books and the genius of the advertising campaign. Even as a man is slipping his check into the envelope, he can tell himself that he wants a beautiful pickup, while the truth is that he wants only the courage to say "Hello."

We are supposed to be living in an era of unprecedented openness and candor between men and women; but behind the smiling, inviting woman on the cover of *How to Pick Up Girls!* is the story of a society in which making friendly contact with a woman is still considered an almost unreachable victory for a man—a conquest in the most unsexual meaning of that term.

Better not to talk about that; Eric Weber understands that to address the desperation directly would be to unmask the whole charade. No wonder Weber never writes about loneliness. Listen to his code lan-guage:

"Do you know that women get just as horny as you do? Well, it's true. They sit home, all by themselves, and think how terrific it would feel to hop in bed with someone. Anyone . . ."

Rock of Ages

In the vast and echoing emptiness of Detroit's Cobo Arena, Bob Seger walked to the front of the stage. With his guitar in his hands, he began to sing the first words of "Main Street": "I remember standing on the corner at midnight, trying to get my courage up. . . ."

His voice did not carry. This was late on a Saturday afternoon, at a technical sound check, and something was wrong with the microphone. In a few hours the arena would be filled with more than twelve thousand people, but now the doors to the hall were locked, and Seger had no audience.

With his voice reaching only a few feet beyond the stage, he sang a couple more verses, then stopped. He looked out at the thousands of empty chairs. Tonight he was coming home. After fifteen years of struggling to make a name for himself outside small pockets of the Midwest, Seger had the number-one-selling record album in the country. For six consecutive concerts, Cobo was sold out: nearly seventy-five thousand fans were paying ten-dollar top to hear this thirty-five-year-old rock and roll musician from southern Michigan sing his songs.

Seger gazed up at the top balcony. Behind him, his Silver Bullet Band continued to play the chords of "Main Street," but Seger did not resume the lyrics. He kept staring at those faraway seats, and after a moment a smile of the purest joy spread across his face.

We all grew up with the dream. If in the 1940s and early 1950s American boys yearned to become baseball stars, by the end of the Fifties the dream had turned to rock and roll. New generations wanted only to be Elvis Presley or the Beatles or the Rolling Stones. Some even pursued the dream, forming local bands, playing at school dances, maybe doing some club work around the hometown. But then, inevitably, they gave it up. It was a child's dream; if you weren't a rock and roll star by the time you were twenty or twenty-two, you went out and found legitimate work. You couldn't stay a kid forever.

Bob Seger never figured that out. All the signals told him that he was never going to make it; the signals told him to join his contemporaries who had quit believing in Peter Pan, who had invested in the idea of real work, who had to admit that they often didn't even know the names of the new bands who were making it big. Seger was on the rock and roll road when he was twenty and was still on it when he was twenty-five and when he was thirty. Traveling by car, he sometimes played as many as 265 one-nighters a year, and no one outside the Michigan-Illinois-Ohio circuit cared who he was. In a good year he might walk away with $6,600.

He played bars and he played nightclubs and he opened for touring big-name bands who, it suddenly seemed, were younger than he was. His singing voice developed a whiskey-and-cigarettes rasp; the members of his band changed; his record companies had no idea what to do with him; and still he stayed on the road. The boys he'd gone to high school with were making something of themselves, laboring in the real world, their futures laid clearly and neatly out ahead. And Bob Seger, of Ann Arbor, Michigan, was a grown man singing rock and roll songs.

Maybe they wondered—those boys who had known him when they were all teenagers—wondered what Seger thought about when he realized the audience for rock and roll music was now up to twenty years younger than he was. Wondered what it would take before he would learn that nothing was going to happen. Wondered how it would feel when Bob Seger, nearly forty, had to admit the worst and fill out a job application.

Then, in 1980, something changed. Seger finally—almost magically—caught on. The record-buying public seemed weary of New York alienation and Los Angeles slickness. But Bob Seger had never become a part of either coast; he remained, instead, quintessentially midwestern—singing of summer nights in the back seats of cars, and of feeling alone in a small town, and of words spoken to him by girls who had probably long ago forgotten his face and his touch.

By the beginning of last summer his album *Against the Wind* had led the *Billboard* charts for six weeks; it had sold 2.5 million copies at a total retail price of more than $20 million. Virtually every concert on his nationwide tour was a sellout; fifteen-year-old children were clapping their hands above their heads as he sang the hymns of his Michigan boyhood.

The dream had come true, but it had come late. And was it as lovely as he had hoped? Was it worth the wait? Seger is a man sensitive to the slights and small hurts of the world; yet for fifteen years, while no one paid attention, he had refused to compromise. Now, finally, they were listening. What thoughts raced through his mind as, at last, he saw the crowds coming to be near him?

"I always felt I had something to offer," Seger said. "There were times when I was fed up, and I'd find myself playing in a club somewhere, and other bands were making it big . . . and I'd say to myself, 'Well, if you have to play in clubs five nights a week, big deal.' I knew I could always at least do that. I sing pretty good. I could always play a bar gig."

Seger was drinking beer with a lone visitor backstage at Cobo; the third concert of the six-night stand had ended an hour earlier, and now he was barefoot in a small room. His brown hair hung to his shoulders; streaks of gray had begun to come to it. He was stocky, with thick arms in a short-sleeved shirt; he could have been a worker on the General Motors assembly line. He talked with the same constant burr in his voice that was coming out of radios all across the country.

He seemed as bashful as the awkward boy in "Main Street" and "Night Moves," his breakthrough hits about growing up in the Midwest. Yes, he said, the sight of a beautiful woman he's never met before still leaves him speechless, unable to say anything that makes sense. In a crowded room where people want to make him the center of attention, he admitted, he'll grow uncomfortable and "want to move away." But he never moved away from Michigan, he said, because he was afraid that Los Angeles or New York would eat him up. "I never was that good at hyping people or putting myself across. All I could do was write and play, and I figured that if I kept playing away, sooner or later they'd realize I was out here."

The dream had, indeed, started for him the way it had started for the rest of us: listening to songs on the radio and standing in front of the mirror, pretending to be a star. "I'd only do it when my mom wasn't home. I'd be too embarrassed when someone else was in the house."

But why, then, had it stuck with him? When the others with the same dream had long ago given it up, why had he held on?

"I had this rebellion, and I felt very much alone," Seger said. "Maybe I had a larger need for affection than the other people. I don't think it was that I had more ambition. I think it was that need to be liked, to be known. I'm thirty-five years old, and I ache a lot after being on the road so long, and I weigh ten pounds more than I should. But when I go on the stage and I see the people out there and I hear them, all the aches and pains go away. They're saying, 'We accept you.' That's what I hear when they cheer.

"For such a long time, everyone around kept trying to convince me I was going to make it. For all those years, all those people were saying, 'It's going to happen, it's going to happen, it's going to happen.' It got to be so frustrating, because nothing *was* happening. Finally the only thing I could do was to stop listening to them. It got to the point where I didn't think I could believe anybody. I knew it wasn't going to happen, and I lived with it, and now . . . this."

Seger said that he dreads but understands the fate of people who work jobs that bring no satisfaction: "Maybe they decided one day, 'This is as far as I'm going to get, and I'd better dig in for the long, slow fade.'" The specter of the slow fade is something that is constantly on his mind—the image of reaching as far as he can reach and not being able to produce, not being able to deliver any longer.

"I say to myself, 'You're thirty-five and you're rich, can you still rock and roll anymore?' On the real cold dark nights, it goes through my mind: the idea of a grown man in a children's game; the money thing—making a career out of something that was once natural for me. When and how do I gracefully leave off?

"I see the kids out there, and they seem to be enjoying it, but then I think maybe it's just the visceral excitement of hearing a monster guitar riff. As a writer, I'm thinking about the words, but maybe that kid's just thinking of the drum beat. What I'm trying to do is make someone out there feel, 'I'm not alone. Someone else feels the same way.' But sometimes I think that maybe a lot of people can't have the insights or don't really care.

"How long can you maintain? You've got to do what Al Kaline did, I think: he knew he could have played ball for three or four more seasons, but he said, 'Nope, I'm not going to do it.'

"I can't see a fifteen-year-old kid wanting to see me when I'm forty-five. I tell myself to give it two more years and then look at it. But I've been saying that since I was thirty-two. When I decide that I'm not going to do it anymore, though, at least I'll be able to say to myself: 'I liked what I was doing, and I think I was pretty good at it, and I never felt embarrassed by it.'"

The night passed as Seger and his visitor talked. The conversation eventually turned to small things; Seger said that for all the songs

he has written, he is unable to write personal letters, even to someone he feels very close to. "I don't want them lying around to haunt
me," he said, and laughed.

He said that he never wants to go on television; whatever it is he
has to offer, he thinks the camera would kill it. "If I were to go on
a talk show, I wouldn't know what to say." he said. "I don't know
how I would explain my life in eight minutes. I remember once I
heard that Lennon and McCartney were going to be on the 'Tonight'
show. I got real excited, and I stayed up to watch it . . . and Johnny
Carson wasn't even there that night. He was off, and Joe Garagiola
was the guest host, and here were John Lennon and Paul McCartney
trying to make jokes with Garagiola. It made me sad to watch it.
I don't think I could do that. It would seem to trivialize everything
that I think I am."

Gradually, as they were heading home, members of the Silver
Bullet Band drifted into the room to say goodnight. Seger waved
to them. It was getting very late, and soon only the janitors remained
in the arena. Still Seger didn't budge. He was tired, but the memory
of the twelve thousand voices in Cobo was still with him. It was as
if by staying and talking in this back room, he could make the night
go on endlessly.

"I have a cabin up in northern Michigan," he said. "Sometimes
I'll tie my hair back and walk down to the bar and sit around in
front of the TV set with the old guys there, yelling for the Tigers.
They don't know who I am, and that's fine, because that's how it
always was before. I'm just some guy."

Finally Seger and his visitor got up to leave. As they headed for
the door, Seger had another beer in his hand, and the visitor had
one more question:

Now that he had made it big—fifteen years later—did the dream
still hold? After wanting the success so fiercely for so long, did he
find it as sweet as it was supposed to be?

"Oh, yeah," Seger said. "Absolutely. Terrific."

They walked through the empty corridor, toward the door to the
arena, and then Seger stopped.

"Nah," he said. "I didn't give you the right answer. It isn't as good
as I thought it would be. I don't guess it ever is, is it?"

He headed for his car, his steps sounding in the deserted parking lot, a Michigan boy come home from the road.

The Truth About 1968

A college student came to see me the other day. The purpose of her visit was official; she was a reporter for her school newspaper, and she had been assigned to seek out certain information.

"Here we are, into the Eighties," she said. "And yet many college students today are still preoccupied with the idea of 1968. We know that 1968 really happened, but from what we hear, it's hard to believe. From everything we've heard, a lot of us would rather be going to school in 1968 than right now. I am working on a story about whether 1968 ever actually existed—and if it did, what it was like."

She explained that hers was a mission searching out history. She had been told to locate relics such as myself, men and women who had actually been college students in 1968, and to ask them questions about what had gone on. Whether the legends were true. Hers was sort of an archaeological expedition into the hazy past.

Well . . . I helped her all I could, providing her with exhaustive information about what the world of the college student had been like in 1968. And after she left, it occurred to me that she probably was not the only person wondering such questions. There are doubtless millions of people out there who were not around in 1968, and who would benefit by a truthful, sober, and frank recall of what happened in those college days.

Thus, just as I helped the student reporter, I will help all of you youngsters who want to know. I will tell you the same things I told her. Here, broken down into specific areas, is the truth about what college was like in that wonderful year of 1968.

HOUSING—There were no dormitories, fraternities, or sororities. Instead, upon arrival on campus each fall, students were assigned to various communes and crash pads with names such as "Peace Farm" and "Hanoi Heaven." Regular meals were forbidden; our diets consisted solely of granola and nuts. Money was outlawed; instead, we lived off the land, sharing all material goods for the benefit of the people. For four years we slept on the floor, because we felt it was more natural, and a symbol of solidarity with our brothers and sisters in the Third World. We often lived fifteen or sixteen to a room; there were no keys or locks, because we were all beautiful and we trusted each other.

VIOLENCE—We all carried guns, provided by the university at the time of registration for classes. Hand-to-hand combat with police officers was a daily occurrence, with the students invariably winning. We received classroom credit for learning to make bombs. Instead of Homecoming, we tore down historic campus buildings brick by brick. Aside from this, we were generally very loving.

SEX—All students had sex in public several times per day. This was often done outside, in the mud. It was not uncommon for a student to have had more than one thousand sexual partners by the time he or she graduated. Birth-control pills were provided free in big barrels placed at strategic locations around the campus. During warm months both men and women usually went naked, including to class.

PARENTS—We all killed our parents.

ATTIRE—Clothing stores as we know them today did not exist. We wore only Army fatigues, available at various trading posts around the campus. Students were required to paint their faces with warpaint. Shoes, of course, were forbidden; we went barefoot on campus at all times.

RACE—It was far more socially acceptable to be black than white. Many students were black during the academic year, becoming white only to go home for Christmas and summer vacations. I, for instance, was black from my sophomore year until the time I graduated and began looking for a job.

DRUGS—All students were heavily drugged all the time. LSD was routinely pumped into the campus drinking water supply, and student assistants handed out marijuana on our way into classes. Vending machines around campus offered mescaline, barbiturates, and amphetamines. Drinking fountains spurted sweet wine for the purpose of washing the pills down. Beer was outlawed; any student convicted of drinking beer was automatically expelled.

POLITICS—We were all, of course, Communists.

MUSIC—Loudspeakers constructed all over campus blasted rock music into every corner of the college, including classrooms. This was constant and at an ear-piercing volume, day and night. When we arrived on campus we were given the home telephone numbers of all four Beatles, whom we were encouraged to call any time we felt like talking.

ACADEMICS—There were no classes as such. Instead we all gathered outside every day and said bad things about Lyndon Johnson while our professors congratulated us for being so young and wonderful. We were all given automatic "A's" just for living in such an exciting and dramatic time.

It does seem like a long time ago. Just talking about it to the college reporter made me nostalgic. She took notes while I filled her in, and then said she had to go back to campus.

"Goodbye," she said.

"Peace," I said.

By Any Other Name

In 1971, the first year I was writing a newspaper column, a fourteen-year-old girl made an appointment to see me. She came to my apartment on a Saturday afternoon.

She was in the ninth grade and had started using drugs two years earlier. Now, she said, she had stopped; her parents had found out and had gone with her to have a talk with their family doctor. But just as she was giving up marijuana, stimulants, and depressants, her classmates were starting. She felt ostracized. She was thinking of taking up the drugs again just so she wouldn't feel left out.

It was a winter afternoon when we talked; she said she hadn't eaten lunch, and I went to the refrigerator and made her a sandwich. My strongest memory of our encounter is of her overcoat lying on the couch; as she told me of the pills she had been taking, I looked at the coat and saw that her mittens were attached to the sleeves with metal-and-elastic clamps.

We spoke for several hours, and at the end I said that I did, indeed, want to write a column about her experience. I asked her if she wanted me to use her name. She thought about it for a moment, and then she said she would be more comfortable if I just used her initials. Her initials were J. C.

Two days later the column appeared. The headline was AT 14, J. C. IS OFF DRUGS. And two days after that I received a telephone call. It was from the girl's mother.

"I don't know if you'll ever have the experience of having a daughter who is so traumatized that she can't get out of bed," the woman said. "She's been sobbing for twenty-four straight hours."

The girl had gone to school on the morning the column appeared, and immediately discovered that virtually everyone she knew had read it and had easily identified her. They were livid; she had, in effect, told all of their parents about the drugs they were taking. The girl's mother asked me if I understood what this was going to do to the rest of her daughter's high school life, and I said I understood. But I didn't, really; I was brand-new at writing about people's personal experiences for large audiences. I had been given a regular column in a major newspaper in one of America's biggest cities, and the column was being distributed to more than one hundred other papers. I was twenty-three years old.

I've been thinking about that 1971 story because now, a decade later, people are questioning the credibility of reporters, especially young reporters, especially young reporters who write about ordinary citizens, especially young reporters who write about ordinary citizens and do not publish the real names of those citizens. For reasons that have become famous by now, some readers and many editors are beginning to question the practice of writing about people without identifying them precisely; it is occurring to readers and editors both that it is uncommonly easy for a writer to present a a word picture of a person who does not, in fact, exist.

The hard thing about dealing with the question is that the skeptical readers and editors are right; it would be easy to fabricate characters. In the case of the fourteen-year-old girl, if I had changed her initials, or merely referred to her as "she," no one would ever have been able to trace her. And I wish I had; I do not know what happened to that girl in the months and years after I published her story, but I do know that I caused her pain when I didn't have to, and that the story wasn't worth it. I have written two thousand newspaper columns since the one about J. C.; I am not twenty-three anymore, and one of the things I have learned is that filling up one's allotted space for a day is almost never worth bringing pain to a person who has done nothing to deserve it.

I am not talking about the kind of work that a Jack Anderson does; I do not deal with politicians who have abused the public trust. In my newspaper work, it is more likely that I will be discussing a man who has just been fired and is feeling the tormenting self-doubt that comes with being told that, in effect, he has no worth; or a woman who has decided, after great debate, to have an abortion and has allowed me to accompany her into the operating room; or a middle-aged wife whose husband has just hired a young female sales associate to travel with him, and whose marriage is being threatened by the pressures that the new situation brings.

Of course, not all of my stories are like that. When I talk to a Richard Speck or a Patricia Hearst, the reader comes into the story with certain images and expectations about the subject; what I try to remember, though, is that famous people share a common humanity with obscure ones, and that no matter whom I am interviewing, the best service I can provide the reader is to let him know what it was like to be there. To the extent I am successful at that, I succeed at my job; to the extent I am not, I fail. And more often than not, the episodes I am relating have to do with people who have never been in the public light before, and whose deeds are private.

For ten years I have been writing stories like those, and it has never occurred to me to discuss in print the decisions I have to make in doing them. But my editors at *Esquire* have asked me to address the question, on the theory that because of recent history, readers might be curious. So, as you may have surmised by now, this month's American Beat is a little different from most. It is not a story; it is about stories.

Almost no one ever asks me not to print their names.

It's not that they are brave; it's just that the experience of talking to a reporter who is taking notes is so foreign to them that they are unable to project forward to the morning when they will see their words in print. They are too busy thinking about what is going on in the reporting process.

But it is not unusual for me to write a newspaper column in which a person's name does not appear. I will not make up a name or use a pseudonym; I will simply use the third-person pronoun, so that the question of the proper name ever comes up.

What generally happens is that, at the end of an interview, if I think the topic discussed is especially sensitive or potentially embarrassing, I will say: "Look. I'm glad we talked, but I don't think you want your name connected with this." Often the person will be surprised; there are tricks to the business I am in, and one of the tricks is to make an interview subject feel so comfortable and so warm that he cannot conceive of being betrayed by this nice fellow who is asking the questions and making the notes.

As often as not, though, the person I'm with has never been interviewed before. He is wary at first; it takes a while to make him understand that this is not a surgical procedure. There are tricks to that, too; I will stumble around in my conversation, I will make my questions sound exceedingly dumb, if he is having a few too many drinks I will drink right along with him. I may or may not be a likable person in real life, but I can be a likable person in an interview situation; it's just another trick I have learned.

So at the end of our talk, if I said to my new acquaintance, "You are a fascinating person and people are really going to like and admire you when they read about you," chances are he would willingly give the okay to use his name. What he doesn't know is that the sight of his words and his world in cold print, in front of hundreds of thousands of strangers, is going to jar him; is going to jar him and confuse him and make him wonder why he opened himself up.

I decided a long time ago that in situations like those, I had the obligation to help protect a person even if he didn't know enough to protect himself. In the case of the man who has been fired, or of the woman who is holding my hand as the abortion is completed, or of the wife who is losing trust in her traveling husband, it is not the names and addresses that are important; it is the stories.

Is a reader going to be any more moved by a fired man's anguish if that reader knows how to find him and call him on the telephone? Not if I'm doing my job well. If I can move the reader without subjecting the man to any further personal humiliation, then everyone is served better. If I can't, then I'm better advised to look for another story.

I don't mean to give the impression that these decisions have to be made every day; the great majority of newspaper stories, mine included, feature the names of people who will not be damaged by the reading public's knowing who they are.

But when questions do come up, I think a writer has the responsibility to give them more than a fleeting thought. In one issue of *Esquire*, I wrote about going back to find my first girlfriend, with whom I had fallen in love when I was sixteen and she was thirteen. I learned that she was living in Toledo, Ohio, and I flew there to see her. That month's column was about seeing Lindy Lemmon again, all that time later, now that we were both grown-ups.

The question I was most often asked about the column was: What was Lindy Lemmon's real name? Readers assumed that because the column touched on such a personal subject, I must have used a pseudonym. Well, her real name was Lindy Lemmon, but I didn't just throw it into print. I discussed it with her, and she discussed it with her husband, and then with her parents, and we decided together that it would do her no harm for our story to appear in the magazine.

But in another *Esquire*—in the column about the *Cosmopolitan* magazine Bachelor of the Month—there appeared a list of letters written to the bachelor from women around the country. The letters were real, but at the last minute—after going into galley proofs— we decided to omit the women's hometowns. It was the opinion of *Esquire*'s attorney—and I agreed with it—that to publish the names of the smaller towns might make the women too easily identifiable by people in those towns.

Maybe it was the memory of fourteen-year-old J. C. in 1971, but I didn't think it was worth the chance of having those women's friends and families know that they had written to a man whose photograph had appeared in a magazine, and had offered him their company. The letters were real; it wasn't necessary to identify the writers to make them seem more real.

The business I am in is a strange one. I intrude into people's lives for an hour or a day or a week, and I scrape their lives for what I can, and then I display the scrapings to strangers. I get paid for this; whether it is a moral calling or not, I do not know, but I have no other craft.

When you write about people in a personal way, they react strongly. It is as if you have been to bed with them; the experience stays with them, and often you will hear from them years later. Sometimes at first you will not even remember their names; the encounter you shared that put their names in print was singular to them, but on the next day, while they were still thinking about it, you were having a new encounter with someone else.

The one thing I have not dealt with here is why the people choose to share their lives with a reporter in the first place. I have never known the answer to that, and I don't suppose I ever really will. It probably has something to do with the need to feel special and important, if only for a moment; to validate one's own individuality and uniqueness.

So what do you owe them? Maybe nothing; probably a little kindness. No more or no less than you owe anyone else in this life.

Looking back over this column, I fear it hasn't addressed the specific issues it set out to address. But *Esquire* has a feature called Why I Live Where I Live, and this is probably the closest I'll come to answering that question. I live on the printed page as much as I live somewhere on a map, and maybe that's what this exercise has been all about. I'll be back next month, and with a real story.

Elvis: Visitation

MEMPHIS—For twenty years they called him an idol, but that was just a show-business hyperbole. On Wednesday, in an incredible, frightening, unforgettable way, the term turned literal. The embalmed body of Elvis Presley, displayed in a casket in the foyer of his Graceland mansion, became a frozen idol for thousands upon thousands of hysterical men, women, and children who crushed their way to worship it.

At first the idea seemed impossible: the suggestion by Presley's father, Vernon, that his son's body be made available for a public viewing. No one outside of Presley's inner circle had ever been on the grounds of Graceland before, and the idea of laying the body out there, with any and all fans welcome to attend, brought to mind visions of uncontrollable crowds battling each other and storming the gates.

It happened.

The white gates of Graceland, adorned with green metal guitars and musical notes, were scheduled to swing open at three P.M. The massive grouping began the night before. Three hours before the gates opened, it had become a mob.

When the people finally were let in, single file, this is what they saw:

Elvis Presley, his face puffy and pale, dressed in a white suit, a light-blue shirt, and a white tie. His black hair was brushed back off his forehead. His eyes were closed. The casket was placed just inside the front door of Presley's home, and was open from the top of his head to the middle of his chest. White sheets covered the foyer's red carpeting.

Some wept. Many gasped. Some prayed aloud. Mourners left the casket in tears, unsteady on their feet; some staggered the several hundred yards back to the front gate.

Meanwhile, outside, the thousands who still were waiting charged against that same gate, trying to force their way in every time it would open to let mourners depart. There was shouting and screaming, and scores of people had to be carried away by medics. It was a scene of hysteria that matched the wildest Presley concert.

The setting was unlikely, especially for those who had never visited the site of Graceland before. The estate is on Elvis Presley Boulevard in a section called Whitehaven in the southern part of Memphis. With the exception of Graceland, Elvis Presley Boulevard is a commercial street; the Tuffy Muffler and Brake Shop is one block away, the Mr. Tax income-tax preparation service is across the street. On Wednesday, several blocks down the boulevard, the Bellevue Drive-In Theater was showing a movie called *Autopsy*.

But Graceland sits alone. It is surrounded by a flagstone-and-brick wall, with a red brick guardhouse at the front gate. The temperature in Memphis neared ninety Wednesday afternoon, and the thousands waiting on the street outside began to feel it early. They were crushed behind police lines, with virtually no space between each other, and by noon there were screams of panic every few minutes, as medics rushed to rescue persons who had passed out standing up, and who had no room to fall.

Cars crept by the front of the Presley estate in both directions, slowed by people spilling out onto the street. At one point a woman weaved out of the crowd, seemingly in a daze. A police officer called to a nearby man, "Hey, are you her husband? Better come take care of her before she faints." With that the woman collapsed into the side of a moving Germantown Flowers truck, and then tumbled to the ground.

She, like the others who could not withstand the long hours, close quarters, and intense heat, was carried inside of the gates to Graceland, placed on the grass, and tended to by first-aid workers. Most of the affected persons were women and children. Some were in convulsions.

But the convulsions were minor compared with the reaction that would come when the crowd was allowed inside to glimpse Presley's body—the body of a former truck driver from Tupelo, Mississippi, who was once so poor that he had to sell his own blood, and soon after became one of the most influential figures in the history of popular culture.

Just before three P.M., security officers began to allow small groups from the crowd of eighty thousand onto the property.

The mourners—virtually all of whom were dressed casually, in some cases even sloppily—walked silently up one leg of a long, loop-shaped driveway.

As they approached the main house, the line slowed. There was absolute silence.

Officers from three police forces—the Memphis city police, the Shelby County sheriff's office, and the Presley private security squad—stood at several-yard intervals, making sure that no one broke out of line. Three police helicopters hovered over the mansion. Purses and packages were searched to assure that no cameras were taken into the presence of the body.

A guard driving a baby-blue golf cart with the word "Lisa"—the name of Presley's daughter—painted on the side and a half-peeled "I'm Just Crazy About Elvis Presley" sticker on the back cruised along the side of the line.

The house was made of sand-colored stone, with a white colonnade in front. It sat in the midst of acres of tree-lined grounds. There was a swimming pool off to the right.

Seven steps into the house and there was Elvis Presley, dead.

The mourners were allowed to stare for only a few seconds, but those seconds had their effect. Men, women, and children left the casket as if they had been punched in the stomach. They sucked in air. They cried aloud. They shook with grief. They shook on their feet. In death, as in life, Presley could reduce a crowd to animal emotions.

At the same time, more trouble was developing at the front gate. Those not yet allowed on the grounds were storming the gate every time it would open a few inches. Again and again, a sheriff's deputy made the announcement on a bullhorn:

"Ladies and gentlemen, if you do not cooperate with the officers, we will have to discontinue. If you do not quit pushing and shoving at the front gate, we will shut the gate and discontinue. We will have no alternative but to close the gates."

But the people were allowed to continue coming in. The mourners arriving, giddy with anticipation, marched past the mourners departing, broken with grief. Original plans had called for the viewing to terminate at 5:00 P.M.; the time was extended until 5:30 P.M. when it became apparent that only a small portion of the crowd could be accommodated by that hour.

It was a scene to remain indelible in the memory. The house, with the body of a rock-and-roll singer, dead at forty-two. The grass, filled with weak and unconscious victims of the heat. The driveway, alive with continually moving mourners. The gates, with a riot growing closer by the minute.

It was Wednesday, August 17, 1977, at 3674 Elvis Presley Boulevard, Memphis, Tennessee.

Elvis:
"He Would Have Laughed"

MEMPHIS—They entombed Elvis Presley in his family crypt Thursday, and even as his body was being sealed away for eternity, show-business stars, politicians, business leaders, and newspaper editorialists were somberly praising, eulogizing, acclaiming, and sanctifying him.

Elvis would have laughed.

He would have laughed because he remembered how it started— how it was a flood of outrage, negative publicity, and even downright hatred on the part of mainstream America that began his startling rise to a prominence unheard of in the history of popular culture. He would have laughed because he would have known how curious it is, twenty years later, that he had stayed the same while the whole world came around to accept and embrace him.

"We lost a good friend today," Frank Sinatra said on the day that Presley died.

Twenty years ago, asked to comment on Presley, Sinatra said, "Rock and roll is phony and false. It is sung, played, and written for the most part by cretinous goons, and by means of imbecilic reiteration and sly, lewd, in plain fact dirty, lyrics. . . . It manages to be the martial music of every sideburned delinquent on the face of the Earth."

Yes, Elvis would have laughed. He would have laughed because in the beginning it was only the kids who would have him. Now the President of the United States, Jimmy Carter, says, "Elvis Presley's death deprives our country of a part of itself. He was a symbol to the people the world over of the vitality, rebelliousness, and good humor of this country." Elvis would have gotten a kick out of that one. Twenty years ago, if Dwight D. Eisenhower was having any thoughts about young Elvis Presley, he was keeping them to himself.

Newspaper editorials and columns written by music critics this week have placed Presley on a level with fallen Popes. Here in Memphis, the *Commercial Appeal* said, "He came out of a mold that the youth of the 1950s comprehended. He communicated, he gave dignity and respect to the pubescent girl or boy who was frightened of growing up, unsure of being loved, afraid of acting natural."

Twenty years ago newspaper editorials were calling for the banning of Presley shows and phonograph records, were warning parents that Elvis would pervert and damage their youngsters. And the entertainment writers—who since Presley's death have strained their superlatives in an effort to top each other in praise—were even rougher on him back then than were the editorialists.

Jack Gould of the *New York Times*, twenty years ago:

Mr. Presley has no discernable singing ability. His specialty is rhythm songs which he renders in an undistinguished whine; his phrasing, if it can be called that, consists of the stereotyped variations that go with a beginner's aria in a bathtub.

Dick Williams, entertainment editor of a Los Angeles newspaper, twenty years ago:

If any further proof were needed that what Elvis offers is not basically music, but a sex show, it was provided last night. The Presley show resembled one of those screeching, uninhibited party rallies which the Nazis used to hold for Hitler.

Columnist Hedda Hopper, twenty years ago:

I applaud the parents of teenagers who work to get the blood-and-horror gangster stories off TV. They should work harder against the new alleged singer, Elvis Presley.

English music critic Tom Richardson, twenty years ago:

I have never met Elvis Presley, but already I dislike him. I know that this man is dangerous.

And if the writers back then were hard on him, his fellow entertainers were harder still. Most of their comments echoed Sinatra. They resented Presley's being a part of their business; they considered him an anomaly who would go away in a few months, and they would denounce Presley in the most sniggering, patronizing terms to any interviewer who would listen.

On the day of Presley's funeral, many of those same entertainers were giving solemn, mournful quotes about how close they had always been to Elvis, what a dear friend he had been, how they felt as if they had lost a brother.

The whole world was behaving that way Thursday. It was a world that Presley had changed forever, while refusing to change one bit himself. And with all the comments being made after his death, it was sort of a shame that he couldn't be around to hear the sober extolling and glorification. He would have had a comment of his own.

It wouldn't have taken him even one word to deliver it.

Elvis would have laughed.

And then sneered that sneer.

Elvis: Bidness As Usual

ACAPULCO—The correspondent lay in the sun, putting in a hard day's labor. The correspondent's eyes were closed. Next to the correspondent was a portable radio. The voices were all in Spanish. The correspondent did not understand a word of it.

Then a commercial came on the air. The Spanish-speaking announcer said a number of words that the correspondent could not comprehend, and then gave the name of the product: "La Piña Colada Elvis."

The correspondent stirred. He almost opened his eyes. But then he told himself that the heat was getting to him, and that it had been an aural illusion.

But five minutes later, the same commercial appeared: "La Piña Colada Elvis." And five minutes after that. And five minutes after that. And five minutes after that.

"La Piña Colada Elvis" was the most heavily advertised product on Mexican radio. And even though the correspondent was not bilingual, he began to catch on. La Piña Colada Elvis was a soft drink. A soft drink made out of pineapple juice and coconut juice.

A soft drink named after the late Elvis Presley.

"Oh, no," the correspondent said aloud. "Harry Geissler has struck again."

And so the correspondent arose, walked inside to a telephone, and had the international operator place a call to the United States. Within minutes, the correspondent was talking to Harry Geissler.

"Of course I know about the Mexican Elvis soft drink," Harry Geissler said. "What do you think, I'm not paying attention to my bidness? I'm a responsible bidnessman. I know what's going on."

Harry Geissler is a huge, bearlike, street-tough, gravel-voiced East Coast businessman who is a former steelworker and a third-grade dropout. He also happens to be the man who has the exclusive worldwide concession on cashing in on all Elvis Presley memorabilia. In the months since Presley's death, Geissler has brought in some $14 million selling Elvis Presley products.

While millions of Americans were mourning Presley's death last summer, Harry Geissler was doing something else. He was flying down to Memphis, where he impatiently waited until the funeral was over and then opened negotiations with Colonel Tom Parker, Presley's manager.

"They didn't want to do nothing until after the funeral," Geissler said. "So I waited around. Then I bargained with the colonel. Me and the colonel, we play the same circuit, you know what I mean? He's a hyper and I'm a hyper. We're both in the hypin' bidness."

The result of the bargaining was that Geissler and his company—Factors Etc. Inc.—signed a contract taking over all rights to market the Elvis Presley name and likeness.

And in the time since, the worldwide marketplace has been glutted with Elvis Presley T-shirts, Elvis Presley coffee mugs, Elvis Presley Christmas tree ornaments, Elvis Presley costume jewelry, Elvis Presley bubble gum, Elvis Presley wristwatches, Elvis Presley belt buckles . . . the list goes on and on, and only Harry Geissler knows where it will end.

And now . . . "La Piña Colada Elvis"?

"Nothin' I can do about it," Geissler said. "They're just using the name 'Elvis.' They're not using his likeness, and they're not using the name 'Presley.' I've looked into it. They can claim that their soda pop is named after an Elvis somebody else. As soon as they use 'Presley' or put his picture on the bottle, that's when I sue."

Geissler is, indeed, quite a suer. So far he has launched more than five hundred lawsuits against persons trying to sell Elvis Presley products without going through Geissler. The lawsuits vary in damages claimed, going up to $50 million. Most businessmen stop trying to sell their products as soon as Geissler sues them. The other suits, Geissler wins.

"I know my bidness," Geissler said. "I get the others off the market." Geissler himself is not an Elvis Presley fan.

"I never seen him perform," Geissler said. "Maybe I seen him once, on TV. Look, I'm not a fan. I'm a bidnessman. I used to sell Davy Crockett hats and Hula Hoops. I am a street man. I'm very crude, very tough, very pushy. This is the key to my bidness. That's why Colonel Parker respects me. He knows I'm only in this for the money. He needs me to protect his boy."

Crudeness aside, though, there are some products that Geissler has refused to let use the Elvis Presley imprimatur.

"I veto products in bad taste," Geissler said.

Such as what?, the correspondent asked.

"Let me see," Geissler said. "I said no to an Elvis Presley air freshener, and I said no to an Elvis Presley pornographic statuette."

The correspondent asked Geissler what new Elvis Presley products had been adjudged to be in good enough taste to market.

"The big ones this year are gonna be Elvis Presley jump suits, Love Me Tender cosmetics, Hound Dog soap, and Elvis Presley bedspreads," Geissler said.

The correspondent said goodbye and hung up. Then, prior to going back into the sun, he called room service.

"One Piña Colada Elvis," the correspondent said.

Elvis: Imitation Blues

The mania over Elvis Presley continues, a year and a half after his death. Sometimes the craziness becomes literal. The following pair of conversations may sound like fiction, but they are real.

"He looked just like Elvis. That's what drew me to him."

Yes, ma'am, but what's your complaint?

"He was an Elvis imitator, one of the ones who perform in the nightclubs."

But why are you so upset, ma'am?

"He took my money."

The Elvis imitator?

"Yes, he tricked me into giving him my money."

How much money?

"Thirty-two thousand dollars."

You gave thirty-two thousand dollars to a guy who looks like Elvis Presley?

"It took me twenty years to save it."

May I ask how old you are, ma'am?

"Forty-one."

Why did you do it?

"It started the first day I met him. I was walking down the street to work, and he was sitting in his car. He said, 'Don't I know you?' and I said I didn't know him. But he looked so much like Elvis, we sat in his car and went for a ride."

And then what happened?

"We went up to his apartment. There were pictures of him and pictures of Elvis all over the walls."

What did you do?

"Talked. He had Elvis's habits, his complete habits. He talked just like him."

Did you notice anything else about the Elvis imitator?

"He was a filthy, dirty man. The shower stall was filthy dirty. He would walk around the apartment in his underwear. After a while, when I started doing domestic work for him, I would clean up the shower stall."

And what happened next?

"He tricked me in. He knew he was going to do it. He's done it to other girls, too. He was just like Elvis. He would spend time with me and take me places and make me fall for him. Then, a little bit at a time, he would start taking my money."

What do you mean, taking your money?

"He would drive me to the bank, and he would send me in to get the money. Then he would take it. He would always say he would pay me back. But he knew he was never going to pay me back."

If you really just handed your money over to him, like you say you did—why did you do it?

"I guess I kind of started to dig him. I really did dig him."

Even though you say he was taking your money?

"Yes. I still have pictures of him. I took pictures of him when he was singing, and I took pictures from his apartment."

What would you do when you were together?

"He'd stand in front of the mirror wearing Elvis clothes. He'd talk just like Elvis. And sometimes he'd sing Elvis's songs to me, like 'Blue Suede Shoes.' I know he was only singing them to me because he knew I'd go get money for him."

When did you first sense something was bad?

"He had other girlfriends. He just used me to clean his apartment and pay his rent and give him money."

Did anything make you especially angry at him?

"One day he wanted me to get him money, and I told him that I had to go have mouth surgery, and he said, 'Okay, no money, I don't see you.'"

And what were you thinking this whole time?

"I was trying to win him for the Lord. But I realized that he was just trying to take advantage of me because I liked him so much, and the way he was taking advantage of me was to take my money."

What else could you have been doing with your money?

"I have a ten-year-old son who is living with my parents. I never gave any money for the support of my own son."

Doesn't that bother you?

"I would like to be like Elvis's mother."

So what is it you want?

"My money back. Elvis was always giving money to people. This man is always taking money away. He isn't very much like Elvis after all."

The Elvis imitator was contacted. He was, indeed, a performer who has imitated Presley onstage. He was asked if he had ever heard of the woman.

"Yeah, I heard of her," he drawled. "Why?"

He was told what the woman had said.

"This is one of the fans I've had trouble with over the years," the Elvis imitator said. "Elvis had them, and I've had them."

The Elvis imitator was asked to respond to what the woman said.

"She's got something wrong with her mind," he said. "I didn't take any money from her. I took pity on her, but I shouldn't have. She called me three and four times a day until I had to get my number changed. Elvis had girls threatening to commit suicide. I've had some too, although not as many as Elvis did."

"It's not worth discussing or writing about," he said. "Things like this happen to a performer. It happened to Elvis, too."

Pray for us all . . .

The Voices of Fear

We were on the elevator. This was at the Northwestern University Medical Associates Building in Chicago.

We rode in silence, and then the other passenger—a young black man, perhaps twenty—said my name. That happens sometimes when they put your picture in the newspaper. At first you think it's flattering, and then you come to realize that it has nothing to do with you. If the delivery truck drivers went on strike, or if your bosses decided to take your face out of the paper, people would forget in two weeks.

I asked him how he was doing, just trying to be polite, and he looked embarrassed. In a moment I found out why.

"I . . . can't . . . talk . . . very . . . well," he said. He was apologizing. There was a pause of several seconds between words, and I could see his mouth working, trying to make the sounds.

He said some nice things about what I did for a living, and it seemed to be getting harder for him. I asked him his name, and by that time we had reached the ground floor, and as he struggled to tell me, the elevator door opened. I didn't want to walk out on him, so we stood in the elevator together and the door closed and finally he was able to tell me.

I had some time to kill. I took a seat in the lobby of the building, and looked at my watch. A woman came out of the elevator, and walked to a pay phone. She wore a housedress and moved slowly.

I listened to her conversation. "I'm calling from the clinic," she said into the phone. "They found out what it was. The tube had come out." Her voice was shaking. "They put a new tube in, and they put a bag on it."

There was a silence as she listened to the person on the other end. Then:

"The doctor wasn't as nice as the last one. He did it very quickly. Do you think the tube could come out again?"

Then:

"I told him I rode the bus down here." Her voice was wavering badly now. "He said it was okay to ride the bus. I wonder if I should take a cab home."

Across the way I saw the young man from the elevator. He was looking at me.

The woman hung up the phone. Instead of leaving, though, she put some more coins in and made another call.

"I just saw the doctor," she said. She sounded worse. "He told me the tube had come out. He put a new tube in."

The young man was walking across the lobby, and then sat down next to me.

"I . . . have . . . a . . . speech . . . impediment," he said.

He was wearing nice clothing. The trip to the clinic must have been a big event for him. He had traveled halfway across the city to seek this assistance.

"I'm . . . trying . . . to . . . get . . . help," he said, moving his head jerkily and trying to get the words out. "I . . . want . . . to . . . learn . . . how . . . to . . . talk . . . better.

"I . . . didn't . . . know . . . it . . . cost . . . anything," he said. "They . . . told . . . me . . . I . . . should . . . get a card . . .

from . . . Public . . . Aid."

It was very bad with him. This terrible thing that had gone wrong with his ability to speak should have been treated when he was a small child. Now he was an adult. He told me that he lived on the South Side, and that he had come to the clinic because he had heard the doctors could cure people like him.

He was just finding out that it was more complicated than he had thought. He was a stranger in this part of the city, east of North Michigan Avenue. He knew that his odds of competing in the world without being able to communicate were zero, and he seemed near desperation.

"Will . . . you . . . help . . . me?" he said.

I felt lost. Because he had read some of my stories in the paper, he thought I might be able to make some magic for him. I told him that if he had any trouble with Public Aid, he should give me a call and maybe I could clear a way for him.

He looked down at the floor, and I realized why.

"Do you have trouble with the telephone?" I said.

"I . . . can't . . . talk . . . on . . . the . . . telephone," he said. "If . . . I . . . pick . . . up . . . the . . . phone, . . . my . . . voice won't . . . work."

The woman at the pay phone had dialed again.

"Hello, it's me, I'm kind of scared," she said.

I told the young man to take down a phone number. I told him that if I picked up the phone and there was no voice, I wouldn't hang up, and that I would know it was him. I told him not to panic; I would wait until he was able to speak.

The woman was dialing again. "Hello?" she said. "I'm at the clinic. I rode the bus down here. The tube had come out. A new doctor put a new one in, but he was so quick with me that I didn't have a chance to ask him any questions. Do you think I should go back up there?"

The young man said to me, "I . . . have . . . to . . . have . . . an . . . appointment . . . with . . . the . . . clinic . . . social worker . . . now. Maybe . . . she . . . can . . . help . . . me . . . with . . . the card. I . . . want . . . to . . . thank . . . you . . . very . . . much."

He walked over to the elevator. The woman was still on the phone. She hung up, and hesitated with a coin in her hand, deciding on whether to make another call.

So much fear. The woman turning to familiar voices in hopes that someone will tell her everything was all right. The young man with no voice trying to find one for his own. The elevator door closed and the young man disappeared. The woman put the coin back in her purse and headed back out to the street. So much fear. . . .

Hefner at Home

HOLMBY HILLS, California—It is the dinner hour. The man of the house sits at the head of the long table. There is no wife. The children are grown. The man reaches over to a small brown box that has been placed a few inches from his napkin. He depresses a button atop the box, and within seconds a butler is beside him.

It is a night for celebration. It is the birthday of the man's girlfriend. She has turned twenty-two today. He is fifty-two. There have been gifts; now the butler has brought the birthday cake, candles aglow.

The man smiles at his girlfriend, and then his voice begins to echo in the massive room.

"Happy birthday to you . . ." sings Hugh Hefner.

It is another night at home. The girl's birthday is not really the one that is on Hefner's mind. After all, she is only twenty-two; his magazine, *Playboy*, has just turned twenty-five. The girl, whose name is Sondra Theodore, was not born when Hefner crafted the famous first issue of *Playboy*, with the Marilyn Monroe nude. There have been many beautiful young women, perhaps thousands of them, in Hugh Hefner's life before this young woman; there will be many more after she is gone.

"But I do fail," Hefner had been saying a few hours earlier. A visitor had asked Hefner about his legendary success with women, and about the popular notion that, at least for Hugh Hefner, there is never a moment of rejection from a female.

"I need the failure," Hefner said. "There are going to be women who say no. The possibility of failure adds something to it. After all, this isn't some fiefdom where I can have any beautiful woman I want."

But, the visitor said, that is precisely what the Hefner legend is about.

"If every woman found you desirable, that would be pathetic," Hefner said. "If every woman desired the exact same thing in a man, then one or two people would be getting all the action. Believe me, women turn me down."

And, when that happens, does it dismay him?

"Depends on the circumstances," Hefner said. "I'm realistic. Everyone talks about the sex symbols created by *Playboy*. Well, the major sex object created by *Playboy* over the last twenty-five years happens to be me."

Indeed. The person most often pictured in the pages of *Playboy* is not a particular beautiful nude woman; it is Hefner. In the current issue, Hefner's photograph appears seventeen times. For a quarter of a century, his personal fantasies have become the fantasies of millions of men around the world, and those men have never been given the chance to forget who Hugh Hefner is.

"It's been a personal adventure, and I've taken people along with me," Hefner said. "Everything that has happened to me has been a product of my own adolescent dreams and aspirations. I have lived out my dreams as a kind of surrogate for a large part of the population."

And his dreams have not changed. Then and now, he has surrounded himself with nineteen- and twenty-year-old girls; the fantasies of the teenaged Hefner have held up. Some ridicule him for this, but he cares not at all. Even though he is a big part of the Southern California celebrity scene now, there remains something about him that is basically midwestern and basically adolescent.

"I've managed to hold onto my childhood," Hefner said. "I may be fifty-two years old, but inside me there is a little boy. I love that little boy. I love him and I keep in contact with him.

"And I'm not sorry about not becoming jaded. Out here, especially in show business, you find people who have spent their entire lives, all their energies, trying to become stars, and then they tell you what a bore being famous is. Punching photographers. Well, fame is wonderful. I love it.

"I suppose I could get tired of what I have, but I'm not tired of it. I have built here what could be viewed as a perpetual woman machine. I don't go night after night looking for a new woman, but the women are here. And one of the things I am finding out is that age doesn't mean anything to women."

That is probably easy for the fifty-two-year-old editor and publisher of *Playboy* to say, the visitor said. But what if he were a fifty-two-year-old shoe salesman?

"If I were a fifty-two-year-old shoe salesman, then I would probably think that girls thought about age," Hefner said. "But I have learned something very interesting. And that is that women, although they say they like a faithful and monogamous man, are very attracted to a man who has . . . had a lot of romantic experiences. The more experienced you are, the more desirable you are to a woman. If a woman knows you have been with a great many beautiful women, she somehow finds that a very attractive thing.

"I think the next ten or fifteen years are going to be the best of my life. My life has never been sweeter than it is right now."

And now it is after midnight. Hefner is in the game house of his mansion. With all the women who have passed through his homes during these past twenty-five years, it is not a woman to whom Hefner has been loyal. The person who has lived with him the longest is a man, a man named John Dante. Dante is Hefner's best friend; they met in Chicago, and Dante has lived with Hefner for thirteen years.

Tonight Hefner and Dante play pinball. Six past and future Playmates, uniformly gorgeous, sit on a couch and watch the endless games. Hefner is in his pajamas. It is two o'clock in the morning, and some of the women are stifling yawns, but they will wait. This is Hugh Hefner's world. The boy survives.

Lines from the Heart

I was working on a newspaper story about a person who had reached the heights, whose life had taken a sudden negative turn, and who now had to start over again from the bottom.

I vaguely remembered a line of poetry that applied to the circumstance; I believed it was by William Butler Yeats. I checked several poetry anthologies, with no luck.

I telephoned Northwestern University's English Department. I said that I was looking for a line of Yeats; did they have any suggestions where I could turn?

"Why don't I connect you with Professor Torchiana," the secretary said.

The name jarred my memory. I recalled sitting in a vast lecture hall at Northwestern, fourteen or fifteen years earlier, listening to Professor Donald Torchiana talk about classic poets long dead. It was a required class; I had no real interest in poetry then, and I don't now, and Torchiana's name had not occurred to me in all the years since. I was vaguely surprised to find that he was still at Northwestern.

My musing stopped as he picked up the call. I introduced myself.

"There's this line I'm looking for, I think it's from Yeats," I said. "It has something to do with a ladder and starting over . . ."

Torchiana interrupted, in a deep, rhythmic voice. He said:

" 'Now that my ladder's gone, I must lie down where all the ladders start, in the foul rag-and-bone shop of the heart.' "

"I think that sounds right," I said.

There was silence on the other end.

"I want it to be exact," I said. "Do you want to look it up or something?"

"It's correct the way I gave it to you," Torchiana said.

"Well . . . thanks," I said.

He hung up.

I don't know why, but in the months following our brief conversation, I found myself thinking about Torchiana.

Most of us who go to college check in one September day and check out four years later. College is a phase, a holding area between childhood and adulthood, a place to learn to live outside the constrictions of one's family. When we remember college, it is generally in terms of our contemporaries, the young men and women who shared classes and dormitories with us. In our minds, the colleges we attended did not truly exist before we arrived, and ceased to exist after we left.

The thought of Torchiana stayed with me. It seemed so unusual to consider that for all the years my classmates and I had been out of college he had remained at Northwestern, discussing Yeats and Joyce and Eliot and the other poets with ensuing classes of students who stayed forever young. We who had sat in the lecture halls with him had left the poets behind; we had gone out to pursue money or fame or happiness or any combination of those things.

Torchiana, though . . . he was still at the university. In an age of electronic images flashing across video screens, he apparently was still discussing the merits of dead poets. The life he was leading seemed so far removed from the lives of the students he spoke to, who then moved on into the world of American commerce and industry.

I had never had a private conversation with Torchiana while I was at Northwestern. He had no reason to remember me, or even to recall that I was in his class; I probably got a C, just another young man out in the seats.

But now I wanted to talk to him. I checked the schedule of classes; on a Wednesday evening, I headed for Northwestern and Professor Torchiana's poetry lecture.

I heard the voice before I got to the room. Torchiana was reading aloud from W. H. Auden; the words carried out into the second-floor hallway of Anderson Hall.

There were ten students in the class: nine women, one man. Torchiana, fifty-eight, of course looked older than I had remembered him. He was a handsome, bald man with the countenance of a dignified bulldog. He was wearing a yellow corduroy coat, a blue shirt, a dark-blue turtleneck. He seemed to have a cold; he was coughing and sniffling.

I took a seat. He held a paperback book open in front of him. Now he was quoting from Wallace Stevens. Each word was pronounced with precision, with care; for all these years since I had seen him last, he had been reading these same words aloud for new groups of students. The people in the class did not take their eyes off him. There had always been something in Torchiana's manner, a ferocity, an intensity, that demanded attention.

He glanced at the ten students through black-rimmed glasses. "In a funny way, Stevens is telling us that we love living in a world of illusion," Torchiana said. "It is an illusion that we were ever alive."

I sat in the room while he talked of poetry with this handful of people. I knew that, out in the city, hundreds of thousands of others were staring at movie or television screens.

Torchiana read another line from Stevens, and then said to the class: "Now, what does he mean by 'the barrenness of the fertile thing'?" There was silence.

Torchiana spoke softly:

"Ultimately our world is barren."

*   *   *

Class ended just after nine P.M. I waited until the students had left. I approached Torchiana. I didn't quite know how to explain my presence, so I just told him that I was revisiting Northwestern. Did he have time to talk?

He was putting on a heavy overcoat. He nodded. I asked if I could buy him a drink.

"Do you have a car?" he said.

I said that I didn't.

"Well, neither do I," he said. "But we can go to the Orrington Hotel."

We walked along Sheridan Road. It was a frigid, snowy night; we seemed to be the only two people on the street. His cough worsened.

"I'm so broke all the time, I have to teach these night classes," he said. "Night classes and summer school."

On the mezzanine of the Orrington, we found a bar of the kind favored by college students. There were video games and a jukebox playing an old Janis Joplin record. The room was overheated; we were the only people present out of our twenties. We took a table in the corner.

I didn't know where to start; didn't really know exactly what I was doing here. So I asked him about the energy he had put into reading the poetry to the students this night. Surely he had read the poems thousands of times before. Where did he find the will to give each word meaning?

"It's a performance," he said. "It doesn't matter if it's the thousandth time or the tenth time. The kids are out there. They've paid their money."

He told me that teaching poetry and literature at Northwestern was the only job he had ever had. He had come to the school in 1953 and never sought work elsewhere. He had been a B-17 pilot in World War II, flying twenty-four missions over Germany and Austria. Then he had returned to college, and then he had been hired at Northwestern, and here he was.

I asked him what made him do it. His students just drifted through; listened to him read them poetry for a term, then graduated and went out to pursue wealth. But Torchiana . . . he stayed on, with his poets inside of books.

"When you decide that this is how you're going to spend your life, you settle on this early on," he said. "I told myself a long time ago that I'm going to teach and I'm never going to make any money. You deal with that fact at the beginning.

"When I was an instructor, I worked at the Railway Express office at Christmastime. I sold my blood at the hospital on occasion."

He let it drop. He seemed vaguely uncomfortable to be addressing the subject; after a lifetime of doing this, here was a stranger demanding to know why.

He told me that he was divorced and that his children were grown and gone. He rented out rooms in his home to graduate students, for the income.

"I don't go to the movies," he said. "I don't own a TV or a radio. They don't interest me."

I asked him if—with his love of poetry—it ever frustrated him to dwell on the words of others. Didn't he write his own poems?

"Yes," he said. "Right now I'm working on three poems."

Who got to read them?

"Nobody."

I asked him why.

"I don't know," he said. "They're not very good. I just write them, I don't send them out. I never leave them alone. I'm always working on them."

Did he never feel the urge to at least read his own poems to his classes?

"No," he said. "They're not paying for that. They're there for Joyce and Auden and Yeats and Stevens . . . they're there for the curriculum."

I asked him if it was hard, in this world of mass communication, to put out for a room of ten people. When he thought of all the performers with audiences in the millions, did he ever have trouble delivering to so few?

"They're there in good faith," he said. "They've showed up. I do what I can to fulfill that faith."

The jukebox was playing "Every Little Thing She Does Is Magic," by the Police. We each ordered another drink. Torchiana said that if he could afford it, he might consider retiring. But the money was not there.

"You think what you might do," he said. "Give yourself over to reading and writing, without having to worry about grading papers. Perhaps travel more, meet a more varied set of people. But I'm here for the duration."

I asked him if Northwestern had a mandatory retirement age of sixty-five.

"You can stay on until you're seventy, but I don't think I'll last that long," he said. "Frankly, my health is not very good, and I don't think I'll live to see seventy. But I probably have ten more years in me, and I'll spend them teaching here."

There was a line I had heard him quote in the class just completed; he had been reading from Auden, and he had said:

" '. . . for poetry makes nothing happen.' "

I asked him if he thought that was true.

"Auden was going out of his way to play down himself and the importance of what he did," Torchiana said.

But what about the truth of the sentiment? After all these years of teaching the poetry of others, could he candidly proclaim that poetry does, indeed, make things happen?

"If it doesn't make anything happen, then at least it teaches man how to praise," he said. "Maybe that's enough."

The jukebox kept playing hits old and new, and the beeping from the computer games became constant, and outside the storm grew worse. Maybe some of the students in the barroom had had Torchiana in a class, but they didn't come over; we drank by ourselves, and we decided before long that it was time to go home.

We walked down a long hallway toward the front of the hotel. He said that he had papers to grade at home; I still hadn't really explained the instinct that had brought me to see him, and so he told me that he hoped I had enjoyed my trip to the university, and hoped that the memories had been pleasant.

He had his books of Auden and Stevens in his hand. Both of us were supposed to be pretty good with words; and yet there was no way of letting him know that I had come back to Northwestern not to look at the campus, but to find out about him—and that what I had found had moved me, in ways that I had not quite expected. So I didn't say anything. He was going to walk to his house; I was going to call a cab.

I asked him again if he had never considered letting his friends and students see his own poetry, instead of the poetry of others he had been teaching for twenty-eight years.

He didn't answer. He just shook his head no, and before I could make a proper goodbye he walked out into the snow. I watched him pass beneath a streetlamp. You could still hear the jukebox playing down the corridor.

Love Story

TRUE ROMANCES:

John and Mary (names have been changed to protect my health) have been man and wife for twelve years. John is an ironworker. Mary, who stands five foot two and weighs 180 pounds, is a typist. John works days. Mary works nights.

Mary is proud of her family life. "My family has no derelicts in it," she said. "I know karate."

But love, as it will, winked at Mary. It winked in the person of Elroy, a thrice-divorced clerk for the county. He met Mary one night after work, at an informal gathering in a tavern. He asked her to dance. She accepted. When the song ended, she said to him:

"You're a jerk."

Several months passed. Then, one night at work, Mary received a telephone call from Elroy. Elroy wanted to know if Mary would like to go out on a date.

For all the years since her marriage to John, Mary had been faithful. But by this point, according to Mary, "You get aggravated and disgusted and stuff. I was super-bored and not taking part in activities or hobbies." So when Elroy called, Mary was receptive.

"Are you still a jerk?" she inquired.

"No," Elroy said.

"Okay," Mary said. "Pick me up after work."

And thus Mary, a mother of four daughters, began her tempestuous affair.

At first, she thought it would be merely a lark:

"I thought, hey, I'll go out with this dope and spend his money."

But the fling turned into romance:

"He treated me real gentle and all that crap."

Soon they were meeting on the sly three and four times a week.

"We'd drink or eat or hit a motel," Mary said.

Love was not blind; Mary knew that Elroy had a few minor character flaws.

"I knew he was a nut," she said. "He'd been married three times, and he mentioned something about being in an alcoholic drying-out ward once, and I knew that he was a home invader. He burglarized apartments. But he told me he was through with all that. Still, sometimes when we were drinking, his pupils would dilate, and he would talk about crazy things, like doing more home invasions to support his habit. He never mentioned what his habit was and I never asked. I was very attracted to him physically."

For a year, Mary and Elroy met in the shadows. Then, on a recent Sunday, Mary borrowed her husband's car and she and Elroy went for a ride. Mary's husband John, who had borrowed another car, saw them cruising, and cut them off on a side street.

"John was going to punch Elroy's face in," Mary said.

But Elroy ran away.

That evening, John took his four daughters to a shopping center. While they were inside a store, Elroy came to the parking lot, stuck a rag in the gas tank of John's car, lit it, and tried to blow the car up.

Luckily the wind blew the flame out. But later that night, John and Mary looked out their front window and noticed that John's car had exploded.

After the fire department had doused the flames and the charred hulk of the car remained on the street, Mary went to Elroy's house to confront him.

"Did you go and torch my husband's car?" Mary said.

"Oh, no," said Elroy. "I have been sleeping."

"I do not want to see you again," Mary said.

Several days later, the apartment of Mary's cousin Bertha was burglarized and set on fire.

"I found Elroy with some of Bertha's possessions," Mary said. "He had taken seven bottles of liquor, a pair of handcuffs, and a gold badge that a police officer had given Bertha as a memento. Bertha works in the Cook County's sheriff's department, in the field of locking up prostitutes."

Mary again confronted Elroy with the evidence.

"I cannot remember," said Elroy. "I must have had an alcoholic blackout."

Mary said to Elroy, "I am giving you the brush-off."

She said to Elroy's brother, "Tell him if he ever comes near me again, I will blow his brains out."

John, for his part, said, "I was going to tear Elroy apart limb by limb. I'm a pretty big boy. But I decided not to, because I might get arrested for it."

Now John and Mary's marriage is on solid ground again.

"We never used to shop together," Mary said. "That has changed."

"There's one thing you can say about my wife," John said. "She is not the worst woman in the world."

The Real News

DELAFIELD, Wisconsin—In the city where I live, there are four million people. When I woke up on a Saturday morning, much of the news of those people was unhappy. In the criminal courts building, a man was on trial for allegedly murdering thirty-three boys and young men, the most killings charged to one person in United States history. The city's schoolteachers were fighting with the Board of Education; children had not been to classes in two weeks. The firefighters were angry, too; they talked of walking out on their jobs. An arson-for-profit ring was being investigated, in which human lives were traded for insurance dollars.

The choice I had was the choice a newspaper reporter makes every day: which of those big-city crises to think about before the end of the shift, and the deadline for the next column.

But on this Saturday, I chose none. Instead I borrowed a ride just two hours to the north, and here I sit in another world.

The temperature here in Wisconsin is below freezing. I am in the living room of a house where I have never been. Out the window, Lake Nagawicka is frozen solid. There is a small island out in the middle of the lake. In the summer, the townspeople approach it by boat. This afternoon, though, children are walking out over the frozen surface of the lake, their black rubber boots flopping against their ankles, heading for that island on foot.

On a map, I am not far from the big city in which I make my living;

indeed, the sounds of the big city's radio stations stayed clear most of the way up here. It was only in the last twenty minutes or so of the ride that the city voices disappeared, and were replaced by the voices of the smaller Wisconsin broadcast outlets.

It is quiet here. I feel like an intruder; I am a stranger in the house, and as I walk around the first floor I realize that this place has nothing to do with the seemingly frantic life I have left fleetingly behind. If I were to talk about the important news stories of the city, the people here would be puzzled, as well they should. Up here, those stories seem to have no true importance, no relation to life as real people live it.

I look at the framed photographs on the wall of this house. Generations of a family I know nothing about, the faces smiling proudly for photographers going back to almost a century ago. The history in this house has nothing to do with stories that once appeared on the front pages of newspapers; the history here is a personal history, and walking in the midst of it I sense a significance that could never be matched by news stories that appear one Monday and are forgotten two weeks hence.

Around the edge of the lake, a number of bait shops that double as taverns peek out over the ice. The Leprechaun, the Light House; to a visitor they look the same, but each has its own clientele, its own personality. There are pool tables, and racks of potato chips and pretzels for sale. The faces, it is easy to sense, are here every Saturday afternoon.

Some of the people of Delafield talk over their beer; some play a hand of cards. A few read the region's daily paper, the *Waukesha Freeman*. There are wire-service stories about the White House and the Kremlin and the FBI, but those are not the ones that have caught the fancy of this afternoon's readers.

Instead, the men and women in the Leprechaun read that Waukesha North High School lost in overtime, 61-55, to West Allis Hale last night. This was not the only important basketball game up here; West Bend East beat Oconomowoc, 67-65, and Kettle Moraine defeated Slinger, 59-56.

And there is other news. Anne Dennis, daughter of Mr. and Mrs. Daren Dennis of Waukesha, is engaged to be married to Richard Jonas, son of Mr. and Mrs. William Jonas of Pewaukee. The prospective bridegroom works at the Quality Aluminum Casting Co.; the wedding will be on July 26 at St. Mary Catholic Church.

Ruth Heinzen of Waukesha has been named the No. 1 Sales Associate of the year by Relocation Realty. James Burmeister will present an organ recital at the North Shore Presbyterian Church in Shorewood. The town's Choral Union will hold auditions in Carroll College's Shattuck Auditorium; the auditions are open to any interested singer.

Surely there is heartache and crime and unhappiness here in Delafield; these are the 1980s, and the plagues of the real world cannot be kept at bay, not anywhere.

But from where I sit on a freezing afternoon, all is quiet. I watch those children tromping out toward the island, over the ice; one pulls a sled behind him. It is silent here in the house; only the sound of the dog pacing around on the wooden floor upstairs provides an occasional interruption.

It is nearing dusk; soon those children will return from the island. Their parents will be waiting. It will be time to go to dinner at Karl and Gretchen's, the restaurant which has served the families of Delafield on Saturday nights for generations.

Dusk; time for me to return, also. In a few hours I will be back in the city of deadlines and crises and news that never stops. For now, though, the only news that matters is right out that window, over the frozen lake. It is news of another kind; news that there is more than one way to live a life. That is today's news from Delafield.

The Fortunate

In Private Dining Room No. 9 of Chicago's Palmer House hotel, twenty men and women are playing a game. They are playing with a certain degree of passion; the room is filled with shouts and groans and shrieks.

On the surface, this is surprising. Nothing exceptional seems to be going on here. There is an old green chalkboard at the front of the room, with letters of the alphabet taped across its top. There is a portable wheel, which, when spun, rotates and then stops at various points denoting dollar denominations. There are three casually dressed people who appear to be in charge.

The atmosphere in the room is unusually tense. And perhaps it should be. For the men and women who are playing, this will be—by their own admission—one of the most important half hours of their lives.

By the time the weekend is over, more than six hundred contestants will have passed through the room. "Wheel of Fortune," an NBC television daytime game show, has decided that its pool of available players has just about worn out in the southern California area. So the show's producers have come here to recruit prospective contestants from the Midwest.

The game, as seen on television, is fairly simple. Three people at a time compete in an electronic version of the old children's game "hangman," in which one attempts to spell words by guessing letters one by one. The winner of each televised round gets to select from an array of mechandise displayed onstage.

"I decided that our viewers had seen enough tanned faces from Los Angeles," says Nancy Jones, the show's producer. "There is a certain California look and attitude we're trying to get away from. So here we are."

Jones has heard all the theories about the greed and money-lust that drives people to try to appear on game shows. She thinks such theories are wrong; according to her, there is a simpler dynamic at work.

"The motivating factor is not money, and the motivating factor is not merchandise," she says. "The motivating factor is that people want to be on television. To be on television is, to most people, the ultimate American experience. Our contestants know that they are unlikely to walk away from the show with very much in terms of merchandise.

"We don't even pay our contestants' way to California. They don't care. They're happy to pay their own expenses. All they want to do is to be on national television once in their lives."

In Private Dining Room No. 9, the three "Wheel of Fortune" staff members who are running the tryouts—Paul Gilbert, Tony Pandolfo, and Reva Solomon—are explaining to the contestants what will happen next.

"In a moment we're going to leave the room," Pandolfo says. "We're going to talk about how you did, and then we're going to come back in and read off a list of names. If you hear your name called, we would like you to stay in the room a little longer. If you don't . . . well, we'd like you to sort of not stay in the room."

A man calls out: "I notice that when someone wins the jewelry, you always say that they get a gift certificate. Does that mean it's not the exact piece of jewelry we see on the show?"

"That's right," Pandolfo says. "You can select your own jewelry. And we deliver our prizes anywhere in the United States. Right to the house. Actually in the house, not out on the curb. The only thing we ask is that all the prizes be sent to one address. You can't have the washing machine sent to your house, and the microwave oven to your Aunt Millie in Cleveland."

The man nods. He does not know it, but he has already lost. During the tryout game, Gilbert, Pandolfo, and Solomon have made notes about which contestants seem best to them: the most enthusiastic, brightest, and liveliest. The man with the question is not one of them.

Mary Farris, twenty-five, wife of a carpenter, mother of two, has paid $118 for a round-trip TWA ticket from Kansas City so she could be here this afternoon.

"I saw them announce that they would be in Chicago," she says. "I always play along with the game on TV, and at home I always win. With the two babies I never get out, but I had to come here to try."

Many of the prospective contestants echo her sentiment. In the main, they are women, the majority of whom spend most of their time inside their houses. This is to be expected; to be a "Wheel of Fortune" fan, you must be home during the day.

"I know I'm going to be picked," says Sandy Burnell, twenty-seven, of Elgin, Illinois. She has three children, and she stays home with them. "When I came down here to play the game, I knew that I would have to smile a lot and look excited.

"My husband can't afford to leave the city, but I have relatives in California, and so I told him that if I have to leave him and the kids for a few days—hey, I have to go for it."

Mike Maty, a twenty-eight-year-old sales representative from Evergreen Park, Illinois, says, "You have to smile a lot when you're playing the game, but a lot of smiles is something I've got. When I was playing, I made sure I was making a lot of eyeball contact.

"I know the odds are against me getting on, and even if I do get on I know the odds are against me winning. But I'm a media fan, and I'd like to say that I was on TV once."

The Nancy Jones theory of why people try out for "Wheel of Fortune" seems to be holding; virtually all of the people who are asked say that, to them, the prizes are secondary to the chance of appearing in front of a network camera. One man has just found out this morning that he has lost his job. But he has kept his "Wheel of Fortune" appointment anyway.

"You try to be outgoing when you're playing," he says. "You show a lot of teeth. I have nine grandchildren—I'm fifty-three—and if they could see me on a game show, it would make their granddad seem important to them."

Elaine Kloth-Goodman, a thirty-four-year-old flight attendant for United Airlines, says, "My ultimate dream was to be a stewardess, which I achieved. So I'm here because you always have to have a new ultimate goal." And Wendy Jurs, twenty-nine, says, "A person has to have some gratification and achievement and satisfaction in their life. If someone says to me now, 'What do you do?' all I can say is that I'm a bartender.

"But if I do well enough here today, then for the rest of my life I can say that I was on a game show."

Pat Sajak, the sandy-haired thirty-five-year-old man who is host of "Wheel of Fortune," is not taking part in the tryouts. But he is in town with the show's hostess, Susan Stafford, to tape some midwestern-scenery shots for the program's opening and closing segments.

"All of the people who are trying out are trying to show that they are enthusiastic, warm people," he says as he sits in a room of the Palmer House. "It's all great fun for them here. But sometimes it goes away when they step out there in front of five cameras and two hundred people in the studio audience. Their confidence wanes. This is real. This is television.

"Why are they here? I've tried to come up with philosophical answers—you know, looking into the heart of America. But I don't think there are any big answers.

"It's a simple target if you want to make fun: middle-class Americans jumping up and down. But I don't think this has anything to do with people's desire to see other people feel foolish. We're not doing *Macbeth*. We're not trying to be uplifting. This is just a case of people trying to prove they can be as smart as people on television. People like the idea of having a moment in the sun; there's nothing so terrible about that."

Back in Private Dining Room No. 9, a new batch of contestants is getting acquainted with Paul Gilbert, Tony Pandolfo, and Reva Solomon.

"I'm scared that if I get on, you'll have a hard puzzle," a woman says. "Remember when the answer was 'Massachusetts Institute of Technology'?"

"Yes," Gilbert says. "But most of our answers are much shorter."

"One thing you should remember," Pandolfo says, "is that when you are actually on the show, you can get nervous and make mistakes on even the obvious answers."

"I remember that one show," a contestant says. "I'll never forget it. There were only two letters left, and the person said she was ready to solve it, and she said, 'A bird in the hand is worth two in the dish.'"

In the hallway outside Private Dining Room No. 9, Susan Stafford has arrived. A roomful of contestants is inside trying out, but here in the corridor the next group is waiting, and the sudden appearance of the hostess of "Wheel of Fortune" takes them by surprise.

Most stare in silence. But one—a woman who has attempted twice to qualify for the show, and who has been told that she will not be allowed in the room a third time—moves toward Stafford almost involuntarily.

"Susan . . ." she says, and begins to cry.

Through her sobs she says, "I'm so embarrassed to be like this. But it's been such a terrible year. I lost my mother—she was seventy-eight years old, but she was so youthful, she looked like sixty—and nothing seems to be going right, and now I can't even get in and try again."

The tears well out of her eyes. "I'm sorry, Susan, I know there's nothing you can do," she says.

Stafford puts her arms around the woman. "I can hug you," she says, and in the middle of the crowd they embrace.

In an anteroom down the hall from Private Dining Room No. 9, Gilbert, Pandolfo, and Solomon are deciding which members of the latest group will get to make it to the next round. They are referring to a seating chart filled in with the first names of the people in the game room.

"I like three of them," Pandolfo says.

"What did you think of Pam?" Solomon says.

"I don't know," Pandolfo says. "She started out strong, but she got kind of quiet in the end."

"Anyone else?" Solomon says.

"Karen I didn't like at all," Pandolfo says.

"Is that the one with her foot up on the chair in front of her?" Gilbert says.

They are running late. Pandolfo is clearly in charge. He begins to read names from up and down the rows on the chart:

"Dan, yes. Joel, no. Leslie, no. Karen, no. Alice, no. Janet, no. Vickie, yes."

They have been in the anteroom for less than five minutes when they leave to give the news to the contestants.

The wheel is spinning. Outside the Palmer House, darkness has come to Chicago. The losers are already on the way back to their homes around the Midwest. But here in the room the day's last group of contestants is playing the game.

"Spin, spin, spin!" shouts Debora Adrian. Her fellow players cheer her on. In the questionnaire she filled out, she noted that she is twenty-seven; that she lives in Fairfield, Iowa; that she is married with two children; that she works as a dental assistant; and that her hobbies are "making jewelry, traveling, and raising hogs."

Now Paul Gilbert calls on her to pick a consonant. "I'll take a W," she yells.

But there is no W in the correct answer. Another contestant is selected to make a choice of letters; he does well, and comes up with the solution: "Liver and onions."

The three "Wheel of Fortune" producers leave the room. Debora Adrian—who has driven five hours from Iowa to Chicago for this tryout—waits for their decision.

"The day they announced on the show they were coming to Chicago, I asked my husband's permission to call long-distance to make a reservation to try out," she says. "He said he didn't care. I called straight from eleven-thirty in the morning till four-thirty in the afternoon before there wasn't a busy signal, and I finally got through.

"What an experience this has been. If I get to be on the show, it's great. But even if I don't, I'll have this day to remember for the rest of my life."

King of the Wild Frontier

In the middle of the 1950s, when television was just passing the stage of being a novelty in American homes, something important happened.

People had already become used to the idea of the TV set introducing strangers to them. What had been inconceivable only a few years before—the concept of moving pictures appearing in one's own home, inside an electronic box—was on its way to becoming commonplace.

So people were adapting to the idea of men and women dancing into their living rooms. What they weren't prepared for—because it had never happened before, there was nothing in history to prepare them for it—was the phenomenon that occurred when the TV camera and a specific performer mutually discovered an almost perversely magical chemistry.

When that happened, the result was instant folk-hero status for the performer. In a moment's time, he was part of tens of millions of lives. He became something that had no antecedent in the world.

In its most extreme sense, this phenomenon happened to only two people. One we all remember with no prodding. Elvis Presley, because of the jarring way his physical presence carried over the airwaves, changed the country's social history. Because of the publicity given Presley's sad end, we tend to think of him as the only man with this visceral power. When we recall television during those days, it seems that Presley was the one male figure who affected Americans—especially American children and teenagers—so strongly.

But there was another. If you think back, you may recall a television show know as "Davy Crockett, King of the Wild Frontier."

Finding Fess Parker in the 1980s is not an easy task. Unlike Presley, Parker did not remain an American institution; following his portrayal of Davy Crockett, he reverted to his status as a journeyman actor and then seemingly disappeared.

But when Walt Disney's "Davy Crockett" shows were being broadcast, the response to Parker was astounding. In its fury and its scope, it was every bit the equal of what was happening with Presley. In his portrayal of Crockett, Parker brought to the small screen a presence that was palpable; people looked at him, and they listened to him, and they tingled.

The face and the voice combined to represent everything that was ideally male in the United States. Davy Crockett coonskin caps were seen in every elementary school in the country; there were trading cards and lunch boxes and dolls. "The Ballad of Davy Crockett" was the number-one-selling record in the United States for sixteen consecutive weeks. Columnist Hedda Hopper wrote that Parker was "the greatest he-man find since Gary Cooper and Clark Gable."

But twenty-five years later, Fess Parker seemed impossible to locate. The standard Hollywood reference points—agencies, studios, celebrity services—said they had not heard of him in at least a decade. Some ventured that he might be dead.

So it was intriguing when I was put in contact with an attorney in Santa Barbara, California, who acknowledged that he represented Parker. Not as an actor; Parker didn't do that anymore. Now, I was told, Parker dealt in real estate, including mobile-home parks. He was just another American businessman trying to make it.

I waited in room 640 of the Beverly Hilton hotel. Parker had agreed to meet me; he had said he would call as soon as he arrived in the lobby.

When the phone rang and he said he was there, the voice was startling. All this time later, it was that voice of Davy Crockett at the Alamo. I sat there with my *Los Angeles Times* and the remains of my room-service breakfast, and I felt like I was nine years old.

The room had a balcony overlooking the Hollywood Hills; Parker had driven two hours to meet me, so I asked him if he felt like riding the elevator up and just relaxing out on that terrace, instead of going to a restaurant. He said that sounded good.

Several minutes later he knocked on the door, and when I opened it Parker stood in the hallway, six feet six, fifty-seven years old, wearing a brown suit and carrying a briefcase. His hair had gone completely gray, but he wore it long, as in the Crockett days. Most of all, he had that unforgettable squint that had mesmerized and haunted so many million living rooms.

We shook hands and I led him to the balcony. We sat out in the warm morning air; he looked like nothing if not a successful executive in the first-class cabin of a jet. And yet he had known a part of the American dream that few others will ever know. I asked him about it.

"Well . . ." he said. He spoke slowly. "It's an interesting thing to live with."

He told me the story: how he had been a young actor with sixteen or seventeen movies to his credit when, at the age of twenty-nine, he had been offered the part of Crockett in the Disney productions. How he had shot all three segments—"Davy Crockett, Indian Fighter," "Davy Crockett Goes to Congress," and "Davy Crockett at the Alamo"—in 1954. And how he had no idea of what effect the programs were going to have on the country, or on his life.

"The first episode showed at the end of 1954," Parker said. "And the first idea I had of the impact it was having was when I went to a little town in Texas to visit an old friend of mine and he asked me to go to a dance class his wife was teaching to say hello to the children. And when I walked in that room . . . it was as if every child was gravitating toward me. I still remember them automatically moving toward me."

He said the fame, when it started, was impossible to contain. All it was was three television shows, and yet television was so powerful that nothing more was needed.

"There was a dinner in Washington honoring a retiring assistant secretary of defense," Parker said. "I was invited. I walked in wearing that coonskin cap and buckskin outfit—Mr. Disney required that I wear it everywhere I went in public. This was a formal dinner. Everyone was in tuxedoes or evening dresses.

"So there I was at the head table. Some of the most important people in the government were there. Senators, generals, admirals. And I sat at that head table with that getup on, and people tried to make speeches. And suddenly this line began to form in front of me. People just stood there staring. They weren't listening to the speeches. They were just looking at me."

"Mr. Disney sent us on a tour of forty-five cities to promote the shows. I remember arriving at the airport in New Orleans. For twenty-five miles the route was lined with cars, people waiting to see me. They said it was a bigger reception than Eisenhower got when he was there. I grew accustomed to things like that. In Scotland, people pushed through the glass in a department-store window. In Holland, they chased me down the street. There is nothing that prepares a man for something like that."

Parker said that the experience began to affect him. "When I started to do that job, I had never had a filling in any of my teeth," he said. "Within three years, I had thirteen. I think it must have been the tension. I was pulled off the set once, because it was some sort of Walt Disney Night at the Hollywood Bowl. They drove me to the Bowl, and they put me onstage in my Davy Crockett cap and uniform, and they handed me a guitar. The Los Angeles Symphony Orchestra was behind me, and the Roger Wagner Chorale, and I was supposed to sing 'Farewell to the Mountain.' There were twenty-five thousand people in the audience.

"It wasn't fun. It was awesome, but it wasn't fun. It had gone beyond the dream. I wasn't allowed to go out and eat. I was kept practically like an animal in my room."

Unexpectedly, that was all going to end soon. At the height of the success of Davy Crockett, Walt Disney grew bored with it. He had determined that he would film no more Davy Crockett adventures, even though he had created the most popular character in America.

"I don't claim to have known Mr. Disney that well," Parker said. "I was never even in his home. From what I could tell, he was like an artist who didn't want to paint the same picture over and over again. All he was interested in at that point was Disneyland. He was pressured into making a two-part show that second year—'Davy Crockett and the River Pirates'—but that was it.

"He was always very polite to me. If I wanted to see him, the secretaries let me walk right into his office. I would ask him about various opportunities, and he would hear me out. But I got the impression that by this time he was thinking about other things. People I knew pointed out to me that the attention span of the American public is very short, and I tried to make Mr. Disney understand that I was concerned about how that applied to me.

"I was under personal contract to him. I still harbored some illusion that I was going to have a well-rounded film career. But it wasn't to be. I remember I went out and bought a copy of the play *Bus Stop*. I thought if I could appear in that movie with Marilyn Monroe, it might give me a new career. I asked Mr. Disney if I could do it. I think I still have my copy of the play in my library at home, with his note in it: 'I don't think this is a picture you ought to do. Walt.' "

Parker said that he finally got out of his contract with Disney, then became involved in other television and movie projects, including a Crockett-like portrayal of Daniel Boone. None of it approached what had happened to him with the Davy Crockett programs. His counterpart, Presley, had become an American icon; Parker was finding that he was just another actor again.

"I never met Presley until years later," he said. "Our images were vastly different, but with what was happening to us so suddenly, I suppose the same possibilities for self-destruction were there. When I did meet him, it was after all of this was over. He was appearing in Las Vegas, and I went to the show and I was led back to his dressing room to meet him afterward. I was in a business suit and he was in the white jump suit. I shook hands with Elvis and his father, and that was about all there was to it."

By that time Parker had decided that if there was any future for him, it was in the field of business. He tried out a few theme parks, then settled on the mobile-home-park idea. He said it has worked well for him.

"In my community I'm thought of as a controversial character," he said. "A rich man who isn't against hurting the environment because I'm a developer. I suppose some people there think that I'm greed personified."

I looked over at Parker. He was staring out at the Hollywood Hills.

"It's different, trying to be a successful businessman," he said. "Even after Davy Crockett, when I would meet people—merchants, executives—I could tell that they thought what I did wasn't worth much. They knew that what I had done was transitory, fading, momentary. They didn't sense any accomplishment.

"But whatever I do now, I will make it or not make it as a businessman. I had something very unusual, but that was a long time ago. It's over. Out is out."

We sat for a while in the sun. Parker said that it was rare for him to be in Beverly Hills; he had once lived there, but now preferred to remain in Santa Barbara, away from the entertainment community.

"There probably isn't a day when I don't get some reminder of what happened to me," he said. "When people find out who I am, they tell me how much I meant to them when they were children.

"But then there's the other side of it. I'll call some businessman, and I'll try to leave a message with his twenty-one-year-old secretary, and she'll say, 'Wes Parker? How do you spell that?' "

I told him that, whatever becomes of the rest of his life, he is doubtless destined for an obituary that begins, "Fess Parker, who in the

1950s achieved superstardom as the frontier character Davy Crockett . . ."

Parker squinted again as he looked out at those hills.

"That's fine," he said. "That's fine."

The Prettiest Girl in Kanawha County

Sam Hindman, the executive editor of the Charleston, West Virginia, *Daily Mail,* was on the phone.

"How would you like to come down here and pick the prettiest girl in Kanawha County?" he asked.

"Yes," I said.

"This is the thirty-sixth year for the Miss Kanawha County Majorette Festival," Hindman said. "I know you're busy, but I really think . . ."

"Sam, I said yes," I said.

"Our paper sponsors it, and if you would just think about it for a couple of days . . ."

"Sam," I said. "Yes."

An official of the Miss Kanawha County Majorette Festival called me several days later. He stressed that my only function was to select the prettiest majorette in the county. High school marching bands and majorette corps would be competing in skill categories, too; I was to ignore those. All I was required to do was catch a Piedmont flight to Charleston, show up at the proper time, and decide who was prettiest.

Just to make sure I was not missing the point, a letter soon arrived from Mel Verost, who handled promotion for the festival. He outlined where I was supposed to be and whom I was supposed to meet. Then he emphasized my duties:

"The selection is based purely on your ideas of beauty, stature, poise, and personality.

"It's best to ask contenders to say something so you can see their teeth."

I arrived at Laidley Field just after dark. The temperature was in the forties, but that was not stopping some seven thousand residents of Kanawha County from showing up and selecting seats in the grandstand.

I was wearing a coat and tie; a young man stopped me and asked me if I was the judge. I confirmed that I was.

He introduced himself. He said that he was Ivan Fraser, seventeen, a senior at South Charleston High School.

"We have a pool to see who's going to win," he said. "I bet two dollars."

I asked him who he had his money riding on.

"Two long shots," he said. "Lisa Barker and Lisa Bianconi. They have short hair, so the odds are against them."

The marching bands and majorette corps were arriving. The young men and women represented eleven high schools: East Bank, Stonewall Jackson, Dunbar, Sissonville, George Washington, South Charleston, Herbert Hoover, Saint Albans, Nitro, DuPont, and Charleston. They took preassigned seats in the bleachers on the opposite side of the football field.

My official judging duties were not scheduled to start for another fifteen minutes, so I talked to some of the majorettes. "My whole family is here," said Kim Canterbury, sixteen, of Charleston High. "The rules are really rough. You're not allowed to use curling irons or blow dryers. Last year they blew a fuse in the locker room."

Vanessa Jones, seventeen, of DuPont, said, "Every girl in Kanawha County sets her goal on being Miss Majorette from the time we're in Little League. That's when we start cheering for the peewee football teams. I was Little Miss Majorette when I was five years old. You're well aware even back then how important it is. All the little boys say 'hi' when you're a majorette."

Terri Busby, seventeen, of Stonewall Jackson, said, "Being Miss Majorette is the best thing that can happen to a girl. It's the biggest thing you can be."

But Beth Bruney, seventeen, of Nitro, said, "A lot of the time Miss Majorette becomes disliked because people say she thinks she's the queen of everything. Every girl wants to become Miss Majorette, but

I hear it's not so easy once you get the title."

Our idle gossip had to stop because a voice on the stadium's public address system announced that the majorettes were supposed to take to the field. A pageant official was impatiently motioning to me; I walked over to him, and he handed me a clipboard with a score sheet on it.

"Walk slowly past them and examine them," he said. "Narrow them down. You'll make your final selection later."

The majorettes—ninety-nine of them—were lined up in a giant U-shape on the football field. The stands were filled to capacity. I waited for someone to tell me to start, but no one did. So, under the lights, I began to march past them, like a general reviewing his troops.

As I reached the beginning of each high school's corps, the young women snapped to attention. All wore short skirts, tall hats, and knee-high white boots. As I walked past, some raised their legs in a kicking motion.

It had rained in the afternoon, and the dampness of the field, combined with the rapidly falling temperatures, caused a number of the majorettes to chatter their teeth as they flashed wide, glistening smiles. Traffic whizzed by on I-77 behind the stadium. In the distance I could see a RED ROOF INNS—SLEEP CHEAP! sign and the dome of the West Virginia state capitol.

Each young woman wore a big number pinned to her chest, so that I could identify all of them easily. I jotted down the numbers of the ones I found the most strikingly attractive; I noticed that all of the majorettes were looking at me as I walked, so I pretended to be writing something down on the clipboard even when I wasn't. I didn't want to hurt anyone's feelings. Also, I was worried about snipers among the family members up in the stands.

When I had reached the end of the line, pageant officials looked at the clipboard and remarked that I had not done a very good job of narrowing the contestants down. I apparently had been taken with too many of the young women; my list was well into double figures. So I was directed to make another swing past them and to work on winnowing the list. I was informed that this was the first time in the history of the pageant that a judge had been required to walk by the majorettes twice.

The Reverend Ross Harrison of the Good Shepherd Southern Baptist Church, in Scott Depot, gave the invocation. "Lord, these young people here on this field represent the happiness of Your creation," he said. "Smile upon them tonight." Then the combined bands of the eleven high schools played the national anthem.

The marching and twirling competition began. I was seated at a table on the fifty-yard line; police officers stood between me and the crowd. I leaned back to watch the precision routines, but I was quickly handed a pair of binoculars. I was instructed to single out the young women who still remained on my list; by the time the competition was over, I was to have examined them through the high-powered lenses and to have finished with just one majorette from each high school.

The bands' routines were intriguing. The majorettes from East Bank appeared dressed as rabbits in front of a wood-and-cardboard representation of the Playboy mansion. Then, as the band played "The Stripper," they removed their rabbit suits to reveal homemade Playboy Bunny costumes. As the band played "Centerfold" in the cold West Virginia night, they danced around with champagne glasses balanced on waitresses' trays.

This routine had barely ended when master of ceremonies John Barker intoned, "The Sissonville majorettes will appear as the Fruit of the Loom gang dancing to 'Tutti Fruitti.' Then they will peel off their fruit skins and dance on top of boxer shorts to the music of 'Short Shorts.'"

Robin Toner, a reporter for the *Daily Mail*, was sitting next to me. I sneaked a look at her notes. She had written: "George Washington High—Mixed tribute to Walt Disney and world peace."

I fixed my binoculars on the undulating numbers.

There are probably many parts of America where something like the Miss Kanawha County Majorette Festival would not fit in. Certainly the routines that were going on out on the field were lacking in what some people would describe as world-weary sophistication.

But I couldn't help thinking, as I watched the Charleston High School majorettes pretend to drive a cardboard eighteen-wheeler while their band played "On the Road Again," that this probably was not the worst way in the world to grow up. Forget about the rightness or wrongness of selecting a bona fide beauty queen this far into the Eighties; the real point was, for whatever reasons, all of these West Virginia teenagers had decided to opt for the discipline it took to participate in this exercise. Put aside the grand meaning of it all; they were fifteen and sixteen and seventeen years old and, instead of swallowing Quaaludes behind the school or trying to slip backstage at the Civic Center to hook up with the lead singer of AC/DC, they spent their time practicing and getting ready for this.

That may not be such a bad thing. I had to quit my musing, though; the last band number of the night, "Ease On Down the Road," was concluding, and the majorettes were scurrying off the field. It was time for me to make my choices.

I walked back ten feet to the pageant officials' area. I handed my selections to the chief official; he gave me a somber look and offered his hand, which I shook.

John Barker announced: "Here are the semifinalists for the Miss Kanawha County Majorette title." The stadium grew silent.

"We will call the young ladies by number first, and ask them to come forward and line up on the west side of the platform. Then we will introduce them by name."

He called the numbers. Each school exploded into cheers as the numbers were announced. The majorettes came running to the center of the field.

"For a closer look at these beauties," Barker said into the microphone, "we will now ask each one to walk onto the platform . . . go to the center for a brief pause . . . then return to her corps."

I was led to a spot next to the platform. Each majorette walked up a flight of steps to the platform, struck a pose, smiled, stared at me, then walked down the stairs. Behind me the stands were in turmoil. Once in a while you pause and reflect on what factors have led you to this precise point in your life.

One of the majorettes looked at me directly and winked at me. I felt quite old. I may be easy, but not that easy. She wasn't going to seduce this geezer with a bat of her eye. I smiled back at her and she pranced down the stairs.

I handed my final selections to the pageant committee.

The trophies for marching and twirling excellence were handed out. Then John Baker announced, "Now we will see who is the fairest of them all." I felt someone standing next to me; it was Kelly Ellis, last year's Miss Kanawha County Majorette, who was returning to help crown her successor.

Barker spoke: "The second runner-up is . . . from George Washington High, Blaire Bartrug!

"The first runner-up is . . . from Nitro High, April Lawhorn!"

I looked behind me. Seven thousand people were on their feet. Someone handed me a bouquet of roses from Dudley's Flowers. "And now, ladies and gentlemen," Barker announced, "the new Miss Kanawha County Majorette, who will hold the title for the next year . . . I give you . . . from DuPont High School . . ."

The stadium erupted.

" . . . Karen Persinger!"

She came running across the field toward me. I walked out to meet her. From the stands, her parents were running, too. The bands were playing; the drums and horns were sounding.

"This isn't happening!" Karen Persinger screamed at me. "This isn't happening! This is not happening!"

"I think I know what you mean," I said. I looked for the majorette who had winked at me, but she was lost in the crowd.

Blue Eyes and Cancer

I meet people when I'm on the road. It's one way to keep travel schedules and airports from driving you crazy; if you allow strangers into your life, even if for only a few hours, then your trip is never wasted.

In Dallas I met a woman named Tressa Hawkins. She was twenty-two; we were having a drink in the barroom of the Amfac Hotel, out by the airport. We were telling each other the things that strangers generally do, and I guess it was during our second round of drinks that she told me she had cancer.

I was startled; she was an exceedingly attractive young woman, bright and vital and the picture of health. She pulled her collar back and showed me a three-inch scar at the line of her collarbone. It had been left there after a biopsy.

When she was sixteen, she found out that she had Hodgkin's disease—cancer of the lymph system. Now she was in remission, but she knew that the cancer could become active again at any time, without warning.

"The subject will generally come up without my bringing it up," she said. "I'll say that I have a doctor's appointment, or that I'll be at the doctor's all day, and people will ask me what's wrong.

"I used to just say I was sick. It was like I was protecting them, and I didn't really like that. So then I would say that I had Hodgkin's disease. A lot of people don't know what that is. So I guess I shock them now, but I just say that I have cancer."

Because she would seem to be just any pretty young woman in any office building, people are often confused when they find out she has cancer. They have cancer-ward stereotypes, and Tressa certainly doesn't fit those images. The only thing different about her is her matter-of-fact attitude about the chance she may die younger than most people.

"It'll be seven years in July since I found out," she said. "I pass each year. I'm always aware when one more year has gone by and I'm okay."

She said that one thing having cancer has taught her is not to be afraid to take chances, to go after things that she otherwise might be too shy to attempt. And she realizes that one of her biggest potential problems is that some people aren't sure about how to react to her.

"I don't whisper that I have cancer," she said. "I just say it: 'I have cancer.' I have blue eyes and I have cancer . . . it's just another thing about me.

"If people can't handle that, that's their problem, not mine. If you like someone and they like you back, then it's not a problem. I just find myself a lot quicker to let someone know that I like them than if I weren't in this situation. I find myself not wanting to pass up opportunities."

She told me a couple of stories that illustrated how afraid people who don't have cancer can be of people who do.

"People wrongly think that it's contagious," she said "I know one woman who has cancer, and she went to another woman's house. The hostess served them coffee. She served herself in a regular cup. She gave my friend a paper cup. The message wasn't very subtle.

"And one night I was at a bar called Friday's. I walked past a group of men, and they started talking to me. This one man kept asking me what the scar on my throat was. I guess he was just trying to make conversation. I'm not ashamed of what's happened to me, and I'm always ready to acknowledge it, but standing up in a bar full of people didn't seem like the place. He kept asking me and he kept asking me, and finally I said, 'Look, will you just shut up? I have cancer. I had a biopsy.'

"And do you know what he did? He moved about three feet away from me. I'm sure he didn't even realize he was doing it. But the word 'cancer' made him back away."

She told me that she was not afraid to begin relationships with people, but then she told me a story that contradicted what she was saying. It was about a man named Jerry she had known; a man who, it so happened, also had cancer.

Theirs was mainly a long-distance relationship. She lived in Dallas, he lived in Houston. They talked on the telephone and wrote often. She called him one day, and there was no answer at his apartment. She called his parents' house.

"I'm so sorry," the man's mother told Tressa. "His funeral is Tuesday."

Tressa was able to finish the telephone conversation before breaking down. She was surprised; mixed with her grief was an unexpected kind of anger.

"It was a case of 'How dare you,' " she said. "I was thinking, 'How dare you die without telling me. Couldn't you have at least picked up the phone and said, "Tressa, I'm dying"?' "

It has been almost a year since I met Tressa Hawkins. The reason I am telling you her story now is that I called her apartment in Dallas the other day, to wish her a happy new year. The phone rang twice, and then a recorded voice said the number had been disconnected.

I called her mother's house. I was expecting the news. But her mother said that Tressa had just had her phone number changed; she gave me the new number, and when I called, Tressa answered.

She laughed when I told her what I had been afraid of. So I reminded her of the story she had told me about her friend who had died, and who had not let her know.

"Hey, I'm okay," she said. "I'm sorry to laugh. I just don't think of people thinking of me dying. *I* don't think of me dying."

She laughed again.

"Very much," she said, and then she changed the subject.

Dance Card

I was nursing a late-evening drink in the top floor barroom of a hotel called the Red Lion Inn in downtown Omaha when a local woman made a terrible mistake.

She came up and asked me to dance.

I looked her in the eye. I smiled. I slid from my chair and rolled underneath the table. I curled up into a ball and began to sob and chew on the leg of the table.

Other than that, everything was okay.

I'm sure there are many men out there who share this problem. Dancing is just something that never worked for us. We could play baseball, we could do pullups, we could run around a track, and no one noticed anything wrong. But when we stepped onto a dance floor, it was as if we were in Portugal. That is, something was vaguely out of place.

It's not that we were aggressively bad dancers. It's just that we felt stupid even trying to do it. The legs and arms might have been going in the proper direction, but we couldn't stop asking ourselves what business our legs and arms had doing that in the first place.

My dancing history is not a happy one. It started when, as a mere lad, I was enrolled in something called Mrs. Potts' Dancing School against my will.

Every Friday afternoon I was put in a tiny suit, a tie was jerked up against my little neck, and I was dropped off at the YWCA, where other children of my age were waiting.

The enterprise was conducted by Mrs. Potts herself. Mrs. Potts was a dead ringer for Queen Elizabeth, and she always wore an evening gown. Her assistant, a fellow named Doc Hyatt, was clad in a tuxedo. The boys and girls were taken into an anteroom where they were directed to pair up. Then—under orders from Doc Hyatt—we were led into the main ballroom, where the boys were ordered to present their "dates" to Mrs. Potts and say, "Good evening, Mrs. Potts. May I present to you my companion for the evening, Susie Snowflake."

(By the way, "Susie Snowflake" is not some pathetic literary device I have chosen to use here. "Susie Snowflake" is the precise example that Doc Hyatt used every week when instructing us on the proper comportment in front of Mrs. Potts.)

Elvis Presley had burst upon the national scene by this time, and Mrs. Potts realized that she was risking a revolt if she confined us to the waltzes being played on the record player at the far end of the YWCA ballroom. So, to keep in step with the times, once each evening she would allow us to attempt a dance referred to by her as the "Chicago Rock and Roll."

I remember it still. It went toe-heel, toe-heel, back-forward; toe-heel, toe-heel, back-forward. Little suburban rebels without causes, that's what we were; and had I not been apprehended attempting to kiss Betsy Cook on the dance floor one night and watched very closely thereafter by Doc Hyatt, I might have been relaxed enough to improvise my own steps to the Chicago Rock and Roll.

As it was, I was a miserable failure.

Soon enough I was a teenager. On weekend evenings we would drive to a place called the Whitehall Recreation Center, in the next town over from ours. We told ourselves that the girls in this town were of looser morals than the girls in our own; thus, for some reason that escapes me right now, we made certain to use false names when we introduced ourselves to them. (The name I always used—I swear this is true—was Mike Holiday.)

The biggest hit record that winter was "Louie, Louie." But at the Whitehall Recreation Center, it was felt that a better dance song was the number on the other side of "Louie, Louie"—if memory serves, it was called "Haunted Castle."

The biggest studs at the Whitehall Recreation Center knew how to do a dance called the Skip. We thought we were pretty cool, but we hadn't a clue about how to do the Skip. We would hang around the periphery of the dance floor, trying to look sullen, dark, brooding, and sensitive. Then we would spend the rest of the weekend in front of a mirror, trying to perfect the Skip.

When your self-image is sullen, dark, brooding, and sensitive, it is difficult to reconcile three hours of jumping in the air in front of a mirror, flailing your arm to the right, jumping in the air again, flailing your other arm to the left, all the while trying to keep a bored, worldly look on your face. By the time we had mastered the Skip and had returned to the Whitehall Recreation Center, the Skip was obsolete; now the other people were doing a dance called the Pony, and we couldn't have seemed to be bigger fools if we had come in the door doing the minuet.

Things only got worse. Gradually, as we grew older, we could pretend that we didn't dance because we had disdain for the whole process. When *Saturday Night Fever* came along, we could sneer at its followers and say that disco made us sick; the truth was, we knew that if we had been unable even to master the Skip when we had been in much better physical condition, we had no chance of duplicating what John Travolta was doing on the screen.

Once in a while a symbolic gift from heaven came along. Crosby, Stills, and Nash were on a tour of the United States; it was reported that, in a Washington club, a woman asked Graham Nash to join her on the dance floor, and Nash coolly replied, "Musicians don't dance."

I guess when you're Graham Nash you can get away with that. I could have used him in Omaha. Good evening, Mrs. Potts.

Twenty-seven-twenty-two

BEXLEY, Ohio—It was a vacation of sorts, perhaps the strangest I have ever taken. And, although it had none of the glamour of a flight to Mexico or Europe, it turned out to be one of the most satisfying few days I have had in years.

Of all the places I have dreamed of visiting, I have been lucky enough to visit most. And yet the place that is always most on my mind always seemed an impossible destination. Not because it is remote; it is not that far a journey from Chicago to central Ohio. Not because it is expensive, either; money is not even a factor.

But it remained unlikely because people just don't do things like this. What I wanted to do was go back to the house in which I grew up; not just look at it from a car driving by, but spend time there, visit it, remember it as it was. Several families have lived there since my own family moved away; often I have thought about what the reaction would be if I just showed up unannounced someday, but I always rejected that as a fantasy.

This time, though, I did it. I hadn't the nerve to simply knock on the door. But I found out the names of the people who now live in the house—Stanley and Elaine Shayne and their children—and I wrote them a letter asking if they'd mind. Mrs. Shayne called me and said it would be fine with them.

So I found myself on Bryden Road in Bexley, Ohio, again. The street is still made of red bricks, and when I walked up to the front door, I had a feeling of anticipation that couldn't be equalled at Buckingham Palace or the Ritz Hotel in Paris. To be granted leisurely time again in the most important place in one's memory—that is a true luxury, and I was prepared to savor it.

The Shayne family couldn't have been more understanding; they let me know that it was okay for me to be there (they even put a "Welcome Home" sign on the big tree in the front yard), and yet they realized that it was not them I had come to visit, but the house. They went about their daily business and let me wander. For the better part of three days, I lived at 2722 Bryden Road again.

It was jarring, moving, weird. Think about what it would be like if you were turned loose in the house where you grew up. You would find that it had been redecorated several times as families had moved in and out; you would find strangers living in the rooms you always associated with your parents and brothers and sisters. Everything would be different, yet everything would be the same. One moment you would feel a thousand miles away, the next you would feel as if you had never left. It would be confusing and exhilarating and happy and sad, all at the same time.

My visit was all of those things. I found myself climbing the front stairs countless times, looking into bedrooms, sitting on the front stoop waiting for the paper boy to arrive. The Shaynes got used to me soon enough; they had their meals, and talked in the living room or the back yard, and just allowed me to have the run of the place.

It was like being in a movie you half-remember; it was like you had seen it a long time ago, and now you weren't really seeing it, you were inside of it. You recognized the set precisely, but you didn't know the actors, and even as you moved among them they couldn't really see you.

So I went to my old room, and the boy who lives there now was lying on his bed listening to music. What a feeling. That might have been me in there when I was his age, but now I was standing in the doorway, an observer, almost afraid to step inside.

In the upstairs hallway was a little cranny built into the wall to hold a telephone. I had forgotten about it completely, but seeing it again took me back to all the nights I had pulled the cord into my own room and locked the door for privacy. And sure enough, on this evening the phone had been pulled away, and was locked in one of the children's bedrooms.

The interior of the house looked completely different, but every few minutes I would come across a touch that almost made me shiver. The front door, for example; it had been painted and refinished, but when I went to open it, the knob and latch felt so familiar in my hand; I looked at them, and although I hadn't thought about them in years, I knew immediately that they were the same ones. When you spend all of your growing-up years coming through the same door, you don't forget something like that so quickly.

And the wooden bannister that runs up the stairway and then curves around next to the bedrooms—as I walked I found myself letting my hand glide across the top of it, and I realized that this was a habit I had ever since I was a child. Everywhere I turned there was something like that; the bathrooms had been refurbished and decorated, but in the children's bathroom the old-fashioned heater was still built into the wall beneath the window; you wouldn't imagine that something like that would affect you, but believe me, it does.

The house seemed very small to me. Which is inevitable, I guess; when you are growing up, your house is your whole world, and once your world becomes the real world itself, one building can never seem quite so imposing again. As I stood at the top of the stairs I realized that, of course, there was nothing inherently romantic in this structure; it was just one house on one block in one small city.

Still, when the three days were over, I had a feeling of satisfaction that is hard to describe. I hope, someday, the people in the Shayne family will look back on their years at 2722 Bryden Road with the same warmth and joy that I do; and I hope, if they ever get the urge to come back, they won't be too shy to ask, and that the people who live there in that future summer will not be too protective of their privacy to say yes.

Because I can promise them this: it may not be the most lavish vacation they will ever spend, but it will surely be one of the best.

Arnold Zenker
and "The Way It Is"

In the period of one week, Dan Rather did three things. He got Walter Cronkite's job; he was given a contract for $8 million; and he appeared on the cover of *Time* magazine. In the United States, those are probably the three nicest things that can happen to a person.

And of the three, the most impressive is getting Cronkite's job. By now it has been said so many times that Cronkite is the most trusted man in America that you don't even listen to the words as someone says them. Since the 1950s he has sat in that "CBS Evening News" anchor chair; there has been no one else as the official nightly voice of CBS than Cronkite.

Well, that's not precisely true.

There was Arnold Zenker.

You probably have forgotten his name, but for thirteen days in 1967, Arnold Zenker found himself in the unusual position of having to be the most trusted man in America.

What happened was, the American Federation of Television and Radio Artists—Cronkite's union—went out on strike. Cronkite would not go on the air; neither would the other big-name CBS correspondents. Frantically, the CBS bosses looked around their headquarters in Manhattan. They needed someone to broadcast the news.

They found Arnold Zenker, a bespectacled middle-management executive who had once done a little radio work. He had never appeared on television.

For thirteen nights, Arnold Zenker became Walter Cronkite. His face and voice were beamed into every town and hamlet in the nation. He received thousands of fan letters. And then the strike ended and Cronkite came back to work and the "CBS Evening News" with Arnold Zenker became kind of a dim memory.

Listening to all the talk about Cronkite and Rather, I found myself wondering how Arnold Zenker was reacting to it. After all, it could have been him with the $8 million and the cover of *Time*. I decided to track him down.

"I've gone on with my own life," Zenker said to me. "I live in Boston; I haven't worked for CBS in years. I own a company that trains business executives how to communicate better. I have absolutely no desire to be on television again."

Zenker said that when he was recruited to sit in Cronkite's chair, events moved too quickly for him to panic.

"First they told me that because I had done radio before, I should do the radio news, so I did," he said. "Then they told me that I might as well do the morning news on television. I said that I had never been on television, but they said to go ahead and do it anyway. Then I stayed around and did the noon news on television. Then I went home and went to bed.

"But the telephone rang. They said they wanted me to come back and do the evening news, Cronkite's news. So I took the bus back to work and I did it. I guess I was too dumb to be nervous, because I just wasn't nervous. I had never been the focus of that kind of publicity and attention before, but I just sat in that chair and read the news every night.

"The funny thing is, I was appearing in all those millions of homes all over the country every night. And yet I walked the streets and rode the buses during those thirteen days, and no one recognized me. People think that if you're on television one time or even three times, you're famous. But from my experience, you have to be like a chewing gum ad, on there over and over and over again, before people start to remember your face."

When the strike ended, Zenker went back to his middle-management job. He said that he passed Cronkite in the hallways of CBS several times, but Cronkite never spoke to him. And his own co-workers seemed a little wary of him; they didn't know how to treat him now that he had become a nationwide star—and now that the stardom was over.

"A very unusual thing happens to people who have been on television," Zenker said. "When you go off television and people see you, they act as if you had died. It's as if when you're not on television, you're dead. You go on living your life, but it doesn't count because you're not on TV anymore."

With all the news of Rather's ascension to Cronkite's job, Arnold

Zenker said that he has been feeling no remorse about what could have been.

"I don't think about it at all," he said. "It's as if the star of a Broadway play got sick, and an understudy had to go on for thirteen days. You don't think you're Laurence Olivier because of it. It's just something interesting that happened to you.

"I suppose my story is a vicarious thrill for a lot of people in America, because we seem to like stories about the underdog, the kid who's thrown in when the star is sick and who does all right.

"But honestly, I don't think about it. Walter Cronkite and Dan Rather have nothing to do with my life. I'm just Arnold Zenker, and that was just something that happened to me for thirteen days in my life thirteen years ago."

Date

A few blocks from Rush Street in Chicago there is a video dating service known as Sneak Previews Inc. Its purpose is simple: single men and women pay its owners a fee; they are interviewed on-camera, and their tape cassettes are kept on file. Then, as members of Sneak Previews, they have the right to examine other people's tapes, and decide if they would like a date with any of those people.

It is an enterprise for the modern age. Men and women are able to decide on a person's attractiveness within seconds of when the person appears on the screen. As the owner of Sneak Previews, Joseph De Bartolo, says, "Our members generally have very high self-esteem. You're usually an attractive person or you wouldn't come in here."

And indeed that seems to be true. When you join Sneak Previews, you are putting yourself on the line. You know that other people will be looking at you, judging your appearance and the visible aspects of your personality. Those people will be making a decision about you.

And so a visitor to the offices of Sneak Previews is struck by the self-confidence, the smoothness, of the members. On videotape, an attractive blond woman says that she works out with bodybuilding equipment in her spare time; she describes herself as "spunky; I'm crazy." She says she is looking for a "successful" man with "charm, charisma, and class." A handsome young sales executive says, "I don't have much trouble meeting people," and it is easy to believe him. The people on the Sneak Previews tapes, in the main, seem to be young, attractive, and well-off.

So it is somewhat of a shock to browse along the shelves in the Sneak Previews offices, and to select a cassette marked simply, "Nancy." That's how all of the cassettes are marked; first names only.

With most of the cassettes it is a matter of slipping them into the playback machine and waiting for a new youthful, attractive image to appear on the screen. With Nancy's cassette, though, something different happens.

Nancy is an elderly woman; the off-camera interviewer asks her her age, and she replies that she is seventy.

The interviewer asks her why she has come to Sneak Previews.

"Why?" she says. "Because I'm very lonely. No other reason."

She is wearing a simple green dress; her hair is close-cropped. The interviewer asks her what she hopes to do on a Sneak Previews date. Most of the respondents on the other tapes have mentioned nights on the town, racquetball, Sunday brunches.

"I just want to meet someone to share dinner with," Nancy says. "To talk with on the phone. To pass the time."

It is clear, from the tone of the off-camera interviewer's voice, that he is vaguely uncomfortable. With most of the other Sneak Previews members, it is almost a lark for everyone involved, a little adventure. This Nancy, though . . . she has come here to pay her money because she really is hoping for something.

"If I just had someone to sit and watch TV with," she says. "I don't go out to shows anymore. But I do enjoy the TV. I like that doctor who comes on at nine o'clock. What's his name? Quincy."

The interviewer continues with his questions; they come from a prepared list, and each person hears the same ones. Nancy begins to talk as if she has forgotten she is on-camera, though.

"My husband died seven years ago," she says. "You get so lonely when that happens. Every year you get lonelier."

She says that she has a grandson who is a Chicago police officer; she says that she has come to Sneak Previews because her daughter told her that she had to start getting out of the house. The interviewer finishes up his list of questions, and then the tape ends.

A visitor to Sneak Previews, after coming across Nancy's tape, asked Joseph De Bartolo how it had happened to be in his files.

"She called up and made an appointment," he said. "She lives in Berwyn. She took the train down here and paid her money. I tried to be gentle with her. I said, 'You know, ma'am, we really don't have a lot of people who it might be appropriate for you to choose.' "

"And she said, 'That's okay. I don't expect to walk out with a date today.'

"I didn't want to just take her money and give her nothing in return. But she said she was lonely, and she wanted to try. So I keep her tape on file just in case an older gentleman comes in here some day. I don't know what else to do."

The visitor left Sneak Previews. A few hours later, though, he found that he was still thinking about Nancy, and what it must have taken for her to bring herself downtown to the video dating service on the periphery of Rush Street. De Bartolo had given the visitor her address and phone number; the visitor called her and explained that he wrote a newspaper column, and that he wondered how she was doing since she had been to Sneak Previews.

"They were very nice to me down there," Nancy said. "But I haven't received an offer for a date as a result of it. They were honest; they explained that they don't have many older people on file."

She said that she used to go to the Melody Mill Ballroom, near her home, but that now she just stays around the house. She said she knew that going to the video service was a long shot; she said she realized it probably wasn't designed for people like her. But it is so hard for her to meet people; she felt it was worth a try.

"Companionship is a very important thing for anybody," she said. "Not just people my age. But if it doesn't work out, that's all right, too. I'll just do without."

The Sky's the Limit

At gate D-11 of Chicago's O'Hare International Airport, a voice was sounding on the public-address system: "Outbound passenger Clarence Waldron, will you please return to the gate and see an agent. Outbound passenger Clarence Waldron."

The announcement was going largely unnoticed, because directly next to gate D-11 was Ella Fitzgerald, who was singing "Give Me the Simple Life." Miss Fitzgerald was backed by a three-man combo.

An elderly woman was being pushed through the gate area in a wheelchair. She glanced over at Miss Fitzgerald. Someone handed the woman a plastic cup filled with champagne. The woman's companion continued to push her. The woman stared at Miss Fitzgerald, then at the cup of champagne, then at Miss Fitzgerald again, evidently bewildered.

The idea was this: Continental Airlines was reintroducing the Pub compartment on all of its wide-body aircraft. The Pub was a bar-and-lounge compartment located between the first-class section and coach. The flight that was about to leave from gate D-11—a DC-10 bound for Denver, and then for Los Angeles—was going to be the official inaugural flight for the Pub compartments. To introduce the new service, Continental had hired Miss Fitzgerald and her combo to perform aloft, in the Pub, all the way west. For her day's work, Miss Fitzgerald was to be paid fifty thousand dollars.

Some sixty-seven members of the news media had been invited to be passengers on Flight 17. Added to the regular passengers on the flight, this placed the load on board at well over two hundred.

Some of those regular passengers were annoyed by the commotion at the gate. Flight 17 was already almost an hour late leaving Chicago, and Miss Fitzgerald was still performing at O'Hare. When the passengers had bought their tickets, they had not been informed that this would be a special flight.

"I have a connection to make in Denver," said Gene Collerd, a clarinet player. "I have an audition to get to in San Francisco.

"I like Ella, but I really have to make my plane in Denver. I'm shelling out my own money for this audition."

As the day grew later and Miss Fitzgerald continued to perform, a truck rolled up to the DC-10. It was a snowy, frigid day in Chicago. Men from the truck began to de-ice the airplane's wings.

Leroy Neiman, the artist, had been commissioned by Continental to do a painting of Miss Fitzgerald in performance. A Continental press release said that Neiman "was on hand to capture the one-of-a-kind performance with initial sketches which he will use to complete a painting in his unusual and colorful style."

But as the passengers finally were allowed to walk through the jetway and onto the plane, Leroy Neiman came rushing off the plane. There was no explanation; he did not reboard, and was not seen again for the rest of the flight.

Once in the air, virtually all of the reporters and cameramen on board left their seats and pushed their way up the aisles toward the Pub compartment, which had seating for only ten persons.

Denis Quinlan, a publicist working for Continental, got on the plane's public-address system. "Please," he said. "Please . . . bear with us for just a few minutes."

The rush to the Pub continued, though, and soon flight attendants were ordered to draw curtains so that it would be blocked off.

"Please," Denis Quinlan said over the PA system. "We've got a little bit of weather here. The captain would like you to remain seated until he turns the seat-belt sign off."

Miss Fitzgerald, sixty-four, began to sing "You're Driving Me Crazy" in the Pub compartment. She stood in front of her combo—a drummer, a bass player, and an electric-piano player—who in turn stood in front of one of the DC-10's exit doors. She wore a dark-blue dress with gold jewelry.

Reporters, photographers, and TV camera crews jostled to try to enter the Pub.

"Please," Denis Quinlan said. "Everyone will get a chance."

Miss Fitzgerald sang "Blue Moon." As she surveyed the scene in front of her, her face showed confusion.

❖   ❖   ❖

In the back of the plane, the regular passengers were also confused. Slowly word was spreading among them about what was going on. There would not be room in the Pub for them to see Miss Fitzgerald singing; flight attendants passed out Ella Fitzgerald albums to them instead.

A voice on the public-address system told these passengers that if they looked at the screen at the front of their cabin, they could see Miss Fitzgerald's performance. If they put their headsets on, they could hear her on channel one.

They looked at the screen. There was a glimpse of Miss Fitzgerald in the Pub, but then Barry Bernson of WMAQ television in Chicago walked in front of the lens. When Bernson eventually wandered away, Miss Fitzgerald appeared again momentarily. Within seconds, though, the shot of her was blocked by *Time* magazine photographer Arthur Shay.

Channel one was broken; the passengers in the back of the plane attempting to hear Miss Fitzgerald sing got only static.

Stephen Wolf, the president of Continental Airlines, was on board, sitting in the first-class cabin. I slipped into the seat next to him.

"Are you a nervous flier?" I said.

"A nervous flier?" he said. "Not really. Are you?"

I confessed that I was.

"To tell you the truth," Wolf said, "I was on this small airplane out in California the other week, and we hit some turbulence, and the wings started shaking, and I thought my goddamn stomach was going to . . . but you don't want to hear about that, do you?"

"Well, I guess it's reassuring that you're not a nervous flier," I said. "I mean, you fly all the time, and you're the president of a whole airline."

"I've only been president for six weeks," he said.

Miss Fitzgerald was singing "All of Me." In the back of the plane, the paying passengers searched through the dial to try to find a sound track on their headsets to match the performance on the screen. They could not. On the screen, Miss Fitzgerald was a dull shade of green.

The plane rocked slightly. Flight attendants tried to edge past reporters in the aisles to serve a meal. The Pub was filled past capacity, and the curtains had been drawn again to keep people away. Back in the cabin, all that could be heard was the sound of cymbals.

"I'm going to go out on a limb," said Paul Galloway of the *Chicago Sun-Times*. "I don't think airplanes are ever going to make it as an entertainment medium."

A young public-relations aide walked up to Denis Quinlan.

"The NBC crew has requested that they be upgraded to first class on the way back," the aide said.

Quinlan looked around the cabin, as if seeking a doorway.

Miss Fitzgerald and her combo took a break. She returned to her seat in first class. I followed her.

"So," I said. "I imagine this is a lot of fun for you."

She looked up. She seemed not quite to believe where she was. "Yes it is," she said.

She turned to her companion in the next seat and said, "My stockings are starting to fall down."

"So," I said. "I guess you probably haven't done anything like this before."

"There's a first time for everything," Miss Fitzgerald said.

"I imagine the acoustics on an airplane aren't as good as the acoustics in a concert hall," I said.

"We are trying the best we can," Miss Fitzgerald said.

Back in the coach section, Kimberly Mayer, a business reporter for the *Rocky Mountain News*, was hunched over a legal pad. She was writing out her story in longhand.

It began with a dateline that was the stuff of newsmen's dreams: "SOMEWHERE OVER NEBRASKA—. . . ."

The airplane landed in Denver. Passengers got off; passengers got on. Miss Fitzgerald was led out to the concourse in Stapleton International Airport. In front of gate C-11, a temporary stage had been set up for her.

Passersby in the airport stopped to see what was going on. Miss Fitzgerald seemed not to want to think about it. She simply stepped up to the microphone and began to sing "The Lady Is a Tramp."

The airplane took off for Los Angeles. Miss Fitzgerald sang "Blue Moon" again.

* * *

A paying passenger managed to get into the Pub section. Somebody handed him a glass of champagne. He looked around. He stared at Miss Fitzgerald. He stared at the videotape crew from "Entertainment Tonight" that was photographing her. He stared at the reporters who were crouched in every nook of the Pub.

The passenger stared at Miss Fitzgerald's drummer, Bobby Durham.

"Did anybody ever tell you that you look like that guy on 'The Jeffersons'?" the passenger said to Durham.

The captain of the flight, Bud Kootz, fifty-two, turned the controls over to his first officer and wandered through the cabin.

"Do you feel nervous flying with the president of the airline looking over your shoulder?" I asked.

"Nah," Kootz said.

"When you're taking off, you don't think about the president of Continental sitting in the first row of first class?" I said.

"Nah," he said. "One takeoff's pretty much like another. I just get her up there."

"Did they tell you about this flight way in advance?" I asked.

"I didn't know about it until yesterday," he said. "Someone told me that Ella Fitzgerald was going to be singing on board. I didn't know what they meant."

"But one flight is just like any other flight to you?" I said.

"Oh, I guess when we get to the hotel tonight I may call my wife and say, 'Honey, guess what?' " Kootz said.

Miss Fitzgerald sang "They Can't Take That Away from Me." She seemingly had decided to put out of her mind where she was and how she had gotten there. With a handkerchief in her left hand, she began to scat-sing. She closed her eyes and tilted her head toward the ceiling of the airplane, and did about thirty seconds of the most magical jazz singing one could imagine. Then someone dropped a bottle of beer, and a flight attendant knelt down to wipe it up. Miss Fitzgerald scrutinized the scene in front of her and returned to the traditional lyrics of the song.

"Ladies and gentlemen," came a voice over the public-address system, "as you can tell by the angle of the plane, we are in our descent to Los Angeles International Airport."

The floor of the DC-10 was, indeed, beginning to point in the direction of the ground.

"Please return to your seats," the voice said. "Please make sure your seat belts are fastened, your seats are in the full upright position, and all carry-on luggage is stored safely beneath your seats."

Miss Fitzgerald was singing: "You can take the 'A' train, if you want to get to Harlem in a hurry. . . ."

Outside the windows were the night lights of southern California.

Fatal

This is how it happens.

On a recent Sunday afternoon, a brother and sister named Robert and Wendy Muchman drove out to suburban Flossmoor, Illinois, to visit their parents. Robert Muchman, who was twenty-four, was a law student at De Paul; Wendy, who was two years older, was an attorney in Chicago.

Their parents, Irwin and Beatrice Muchman, had just returned from a vacation trip to Italy. So the children welcomed them home. Because their parents were tired from the trip, Robert and Wendy left for the drive back downtown early, around dinnertime.

Robert was driving. In his car, a 1980 Toyota, he pushed the buttons to the radio. There was a new song by Supertramp he wanted his sister to hear; he thought she would like it. But no station was playing it as he looked.

They were on I-57, heading toward the city. They talked easily; unlike some brothers and sisters, they were very close and were comfortable in the company of one another. Robert worked full-time at the Harris Bank; Wendy was proud that he was able to be earning a living at the same time he was completing law school. Robert was engaged to be married in January; the money he was earning at the bank was being put away to start his new life.

So Robert drove, and the two of them talked, and the radio played. It was a normal Sunday, dusk in Chicago, and Robert said, "Oh, my

God," and Wendy saw the other car jumping the median from the other side of the highway.

Just before the car hit, Wendy could see the driver. He appeared to be unconscious as he slumped over the wheel. His car slammed into Robert's, and when Wendy opened her eyes she saw that her brother was probably dead.

He was bleeding from a severe head wound, and blood was coming from his mouth. Almost without thinking what she was doing, Wendy reached inside her brother's mouth to pull his tongue out; if there was any chance he was still alive, she wanted to make sure he could breathe.

"Robbie," she called. She said his name again and again. He did not answer.

A Chicago police officer named Ron McAuley arrived at the scene of the accident and radioed for an ambulance. Wendy ran up to a nearby house and said, "We've been in a car accident." The owner of the house let her come inside to use his phone.

She called her parents. She couldn't allow herself to tell them that she thought Robert was dead; so she said, "There's been an accident. Please meet us at Roseland Hospital."

"Are you all right?" her parents asked.

"I hope so," she said.

"Is Robbie all right?" they asked.

"I don't know," she said.

Down on the highway, a nurse had stopped to try to help. One of those terrible city scenarios was taking place; for some reason no ambulance had responded to the officer's call, and he was trying again to get some help.

"What time is it?" Wendy kept asking. She looked at her brother, who had not moved. She was wearing a watch, but she was not aware of it. "What time is it?"

An ambulance finally arrived. Wendy said to the nurse who had been helping, "Please . . . please ride with us to the hospital." The police officer told the nurse he would take care of her car if she rode with Robert, so she said that she would.

At the hospital, Wendy saw her mother waiting by the emergency entrance. She hurried to move her mother out of the way so she would not see Robert when he was carried out of the ambulance. But Wendy's father was right there when they carried his son into the emergency room. He saw his son's face and he slumped down.

The hospital personnel carried Robert into a treatment room. Wendy wandered around the emergency area; she looked into a room and saw the driver of the other car. His name was Ronnell Reynolds, of Calumet Park; later, the police would charge him with reckless homicide and driving under the influence of alcohol.

Wendy Muchman looked at the man. She had read dozens of articles about drunken driving, seen dozens of television reports. She could think of only one thing: she wanted to kill the man. She wished she had a gun so she could kill him. For twenty-four years her brother had built a life; now, with his impending marriage, the most important part of that life was about to begin. Had Robert and Wendy left their parents' house five minutes earlier, or five minutes later, their car would not have been in the path of Ronnell Reynolds's car when it jumped the median. She wanted to kill him, but instead she walked away from the room.

A woman came to the area where the Muchmans were waiting. The woman didn't have to say much. Just two words: "I'm sorry."

The Muchman family went to look for a telephone. Ever since Robert's engagement, his mother had been keeping a scrapbook and filling it with news of the wedding plans. Now they had to call his fiancée and let the phone ring and explain that Robert was dead.

These things happen every day. Cars collide, and drivers are charged with being drunk behind the wheel, and lives are changed forever. It's so common that no one considers it to be a big deal. Usually it doesn't even make the paper; this one didn't. Robert Muchman's parents went back to their home, the son they had raised now gone; Wendy Muchman went back to her apartment. This is how it happens.

Rejection

This is my favorite story of the year. Maybe of any year. Chuck Ross is a young free-lance writer who is anxious to get his first novel published. Like many aspiring authors, he has sent his work around to different New York publishing houses, hoping that an editor will see it, like it, and decide to bring it out in hardcover. And like many aspiring authors, he has received nothing but rejection slips.

After a while, though, Ross began to wonder if his writing really was unpublishable—or if publishers are just prejudiced against unknown authors who have yet to have a book in print.

So he decided to conduct an experiment. He sat down at the typewriter, and copied the entire text of *Steps*, by Jerzy Kosinski, onto white paper. *Steps* won the National Book Award for Kosinski in 1969; since its publication in 1968, the novel has sold more than 400,000 copies. Not only has it proved itself to be a work of high quality, but it has established itself as a big seller in the marketplace.

Ross then decided to submit the manuscript to a number of publishers—but not to call it *Steps*, and not to say it was by the well-known Kosinski. In other words, he wanted to see if the publishing houses would accept the award-winning *Steps* if they did not know that it had been written by a prominent, proven author.

He thought he would probably get caught. And well he should have. Four of the publishers he sent the manuscript to—Random House, Houghton Mifflin, Doubleday, and Harcourt Brace Jovanovich —have published books by Kosinski, and Random House was even the original publisher of *Steps*.

In addition to those four publishers, he also sent the manuscript to The Atlantic Monthly Press; Farrar, Straus & Giroux; Harper & Row; Alfred A. Knopf; Seymour Lawrence; David McKay; Macmillan; William Morrow; Prentice-Hall; and Viking.

Then he sat back to wait and see what would happen.

And what did happen?

All fourteen distinguished publishing houses rejected the manuscript—including the four that had published works by Jerzy Kosinski. None of the houses thought that the book was worth publishing.

Harcourt Brace Jovanovich—which had published Kosinski's *Being There* and *The Devil Tree*—wrote:

> While your prose style is very lucid, the content of the book didn't inspire the level of enthusiasm here that a publisher should have for any book on their list in order to do well by it.

Random House—the original publisher of *Steps*—sent a form rejection notice.

Houghton Mifflin—which had published Kosinski's *The Painted Bird*, *Cockpit*, and *Blind Date*—sent a letter that said:

> Several of us read your untitled novel here with admiration for

writing and style. Jerzy Kosinski comes to mind as a point of com-
parison when reading the stark, chilly, episodic incidents you have
set down. The drawback to the manuscript, as it stands, is that
it doesn't add up to a satisfactory whole. It has some very impressive moments, but gives the impression of sketchiness and incom-
pleteness. . . . We do not see our way to publishing this particular
work as it is, but if you should ever have other manuscripts in
progress now or in the future, we would be happy to consider
them.

In other words, Kosinski's book sounded like Kosinski, but wasn't as
good as Kosinski.

After all fourteen publishers had turned the book down, Ross did
some thinking. He knew that most publishers will give a book serious
consideration only if the author has a literary agent, and Ross didn't
have an agent.

So Ross sent the manuscript to thirteen prestigious literary agents,
with a letter asking the agents to represent him in selling the book
to a publisher.

All thirteen agents turned him down.

Julian Bach wrote:

Thanks for having sent me your untitled novel. You write clearly
and well, but I felt that the novel jumped around so much that
it did not hold interest, and I would not be the right agent for it.

Lurton Blassingame wrote:

From the section I read of your untitled novel, it seems too frag-
mented and dreamlike to be a good commercial bet. Of course,
I may be wrong. Good luck with it.

Helen Brandt Literary Agency said they were not "sufficiently enthusiastic" to try to place it.

An agent at Curtis Brown wrote:

I'm afraid the novel's episodic nature and the lack of strong characterization would not allow this book to compete in a very tough
fiction market.

Candida Donadio & Associates wrote:

We have read your novel with great interest, and although we
found the style quite intriguing, we have decided to return it.
When all is said and done, we felt the manuscript lacked that all-

important dramatic tension for us to consider taking it on.

Ross knew he had discovered something important about the publishing industry, and the chances that an unknown writer has of breaking in. He wrote an article about his experiment for *New West* magazine, and went on the "Tomorrow" show to talk about it. He thought the publishers might learn something from his experience.

"But I guess not," he said the other day. "I went to the American Booksellers Association convention to talk to the publishers about what I did. They all thought that it was very amusing or silly. They agreed that it probably could happen again tomorrow. But the attitude was, 'So what.' They didn't think it proved anything."

So Ross is back at his typewriter again, working on his own novel. He still thinks it's worth trying.

"If you're a writer, you have to hope," he said.

Scot's Tap

We were driving around the North Side, looking for a place to eat. I don't know what me think of Scot's Tap.

"I never heard of it," my companion said.

"On Clark Street," I said. "Just south of Howard."

There was a time when Scot's Tap represented everything that was Chicago to me. I was in college, and every night my friends and I—fraternity brothers, co-workers on the student newspaper—would go to Scot's Tap for dinner. True, it was only about 300 feet inside Chicago, just over the Evanston line, but as soon as we walked into Scot's, we knew that we were in the big town.

No college kids eating wheat germ in Scot's Tap. At Scot's, the lights were dim and the decor was red and the patrons were served steaks. Sinatra was on the jukebox, and Sinatra's pictures were on the wall. The waitresses brought us cocktails—at the time, you couldn't even get a beer in Evanston. For college seniors anxious to get out, Scot's Tap offered a welcome preview of a world beyond milk shakes and marijuana.

The real draw at Scot's Tap though—the real clue to us that this was, indeed, Chicago—was Scot himself. Not that we ever met him; we were too intimidated. Scot was a savvy-looking guy with a pencil-thin black moustache, a sharp dresser, a man who looked like he would be at home making trips to Las Vegas. He would hang out at the end of the bar, talking business with men in expensive suits. To us, he seemed to be glamorously notorious—we didn't know what his past was, but it had to be full of intrigue. He was Chicago, all right. Scot didn't seem to be a man you would want to cross.

On the wall, Scot kept a framed black-and-white photographic portrait of himself, looking dapper in a dark suit. Next to it was another framed portrait, this one of a beautiful blond woman in a low-cut dress. We always assumed this was Scot's wife or mistress. We were afraid to ask anyone.

Once, one of us got a little drunk, and got up the courage to approach Scot. Scot was at the bar, and our friend walked up to him, waited until Scot turned around, and then said, "Cash a check for me?"

Scot looked him in the eye.

"No," he said.

The food and drink were always good, Sinatra's voice always filled the room, and soon enough I was, indeed, living in Chicago, which on a good night sometimes lived up to the smoky, unspoken promises of Scot's Tap. I had not been back in years, and so it was that I told my companion to take me there.

But when we arrived, Scot's Tap was gone—replaced, in 1979, by a Greek family-style restaurant. We went inside. There was no sign that this had ever been Scot's. It was bright and bustling and full of people with children. Scot wouldn't have been caught dead in the place. We ate our dinner there, and then drove away.

I was lamenting the loss of yesterday's dreams. We were driving through a residential neighborhood in Rogers Park, on our way back downtown, when, like a mirage, a recently constructed building appeared on our right. On its front was a sign that said, "Scot's Restaurant."

"Quick," I said. "Pull in there."

We got out of the car and walked through the front door. The voice of Frank Sinatra sounded throughout the room. The carpets were red. The lights were low. On the wall were framed black-and-white photographic portraits, all in a row—Sinatra, Richard J. Daley, Maurice Chevalier, George Raft. And, at the very end of the row, the portrait of Scot, looking every bit as cunning and worldly wise as the rest.

I went to the bar and ordered a drink.

"Scot here?" I said.

"You just missed him," the woman bartender said. "He's back in his office."

"Could you get him for me?" I said.

She pointed to a telephone, with two buttons lit. "You see those lights?" she said. "He's on the phone. No one interrupts Scot when he's talking business."

"He's talking on two lines at once?" I said.

"Sometimes he talks on four lines at once," the woman said. "Scot talks a lot of business."

So I waited. Thirty minutes passed. I ordered more drinks. Finally, a pleasant-looking man wearing a green golf shirt and a pencil-thin moustache walked up to the bar. It was Scot.

I was confused. He looked like any of a hundred men I had met over the years in Chicago. He smiled and introduced himself. A pleasant man who happened to own a restaurant. I started to jabber about the college days at Scot's Tap, and the mystique we had built up, and the amazing circumstances of finding Scot in this new place on this different street.

He looked at me as if I were a little crazy.

"Yeah?" he said.

I wanted to tell him what we had thought of him, and what he had represented to us, and how to us he had embodied so much of the Chicago legend that we had built him into an ominous icon. He was smiling at me, puzzled, and I pointed at the picture by the front door, the picture of the beautiful blond woman in the low-cut dress.

"Scot," I said. "We always wondered . . . is that your wife?"

He looked over at the picture.

"Nah," he said. "That's Julie London."

I paid for the drinks and motioned for my companion to leave with me. Sinatra was still on the jukebox. Scot said to come back soon, but sometimes there's no going back.

Island of the Lost Boys

All you have to do is walk in the door to know that something is wrong.

The men in the office are dressed in business suits. If you extend your hand, they will shake it and say hello. Once they have been introduced to you, some of them will even fall into casual chatter.

But something stays amiss. There is the undeniable feeling that the men in this suite of rooms have been harmed. They are wary; they are not young men, and yet they seem to be lacking a certain self-assurance that typically comes with age. There is something in their eyes that advises you to be careful in here; these people are more fragile than most you will meet. They seem to have been wounded.

The office is the headquarters of the Chicago chapter of an organization called Forty Plus. The qualifications for membership are simple. You must be at least forty years old. You must have earned a salary of at least $25,000 a year. You must be unemployed.

The office is in the basement of the Illinois Athletic Club, on South Michigan Avenue. The Athletic Club leases Forty Plus the space; up one floor, executives of Chicago business and industry gather for lunch, for drinks, for a workout or a massage. Down here the members of Forty Plus keep to themselves. They are not considered a part of the Athletic Club; they are merely tenants.

Most of them have been let go by the businesses for which they worked. The problem of unemployment in America has become stereotyped; our quick reaction is to think of auto workers or factory laborers standing in line at a government office building, waiting for a check. As unpleasant as that is, it is an image that the country has learned to live with.

There are others, though. There are these men. They have been executives and managers for most of their working lives; now they have been fired. Each of the men here has heard about Forty Plus and has gravitated to it.

The purpose of Forty Plus is to help these men find employment. Notices of openings are posted, mailings extolling the members' strengths are sent out, job-counseling sessions are held. But those don't seem to be the real reasons the men keep coming to this basement every day.

They come because, after all these years, they need a place to go when the working day begins. They have been going to the office for all their adult lives; now they can't stop. They never expected to be put out on the street; as often as not, they were the men who did the firing. Now, out of work, they sit in the basement and talk with one another. Their old colleagues might not understand, but the other men here surely do. In an eerie way, you feel as if you have found yourself on some sort of island of lost boys. They are all waiting to go back home.

One afternoon I sat and talked with them. I took notes and wrote down all of their names; I think I will not identify them, though. One day soon, perhaps, some of them will be back at work, and they do not need an announcement in a national magazine that they were once here.

Here is what some of them said.

A sixty-year-old engineering executive: "I think we all go through different stages when this happens to us. We get up in the morning and get ready for the day, but there is really no day to get ready for.

"It calls on every resource you have. All your life you have been a productive man; you have done your best. And when this happens, a certain unreality sets in. Every morning you tell yourself you have to keep going. Somehow or other you are going to make it.

"The predominant feeling is that you have let your family down. Your wife and your children have depended on you and taken you for granted. And now you aren't bringing anything home. You feel very guilty for putting them through this."

A forty-six-year-old financial manager: "It's very difficult to leave the business that fired you. When you are an executive, the place really begins to feel like your own; you take a personal pride in the company, and you feel a personal identification with it. It just doesn't occur to you that they are going to fire you.

"Twenty years ago, if you had told me this was going to happen someday, I probably wouldn't have believed you. Managers were just not let out of work. It happened to lower-echelon people, but not to the managers. Today, because of the economy, there is no longer quite the stigma to being unemployed. At least that's what I tell myself.

"But when the boss calls you in and informs you that you will be leaving, it's still a terrible shock. You try not to take it personally; you tell yourself it's because of what the economy has done to the country. But your self-esteem can't be unaffected by it."

A forty-seven-year-old vice-president of a chemical company: "The day it happened I came home early and called my wife and two daughters together, and I told them that I was now unemployed.

"Looking back on that day, I guess I was in total shock. It probably took me an hour after I was fired for it to sink in. I live in a suburban area; on the days that I come downtown, I ride the train, and I see everybody else carrying their briefcases, and here are all these folks going to their executive positions. It gives me a lot to think about.

"You are used to running your own life, and suddenly you have no control. You go through moments of real self-doubt. You can't predict when things will happen, and you're used to making things happen. You sit at home, and you get filled up with hope every time the phone rings. And then it turns out to be for your wife or for one of your daughters."

A forty-six-year-old general manager of a manufacturing firm: "When I go to work again, I'm going to be a little different than I was the last time around. That's one good thing that will come out of this. I'm going to have a little more compassion for people, because I'm finding out that compassion is sometimes in short supply.

"I never needed compassion before. Because I was never unemployed. But next time I will answer my own phone. Since I've been out of work I have heard too many secretaries say that a man is in a meeting, when it would have meant a great deal to me if he would just have taken the call. And I will see as many people as I can who are looking for work, even if I have no specific job open at that moment. I'm learning that it doesn't cost anything to show people a little kindness. I'm not sure I ever would have learned that if this hadn't happened."

Forty Plus is open to both men and women. But on the days I was in the office, there were no females present.

That's probably not surprising. We live in an age in which the idea of working women has become normal. Women in positions of responsibility are no longer uncommon; women compete with men for jobs at virtually every level of the marketplace.

But somehow there is a difference. Somehow there is no shame for a woman to be unemployed; if a woman, especially a married woman, finds that she is going to be staying home full-time, she can be safe in knowing that no one will be whispering about her or avoiding her gaze on the sidewalk.

That is not the case with men. I got the impression that one big reason they came to Forty Plus was that they didn't want to be at home when the mail carrier or the dry cleaner showed up at the door. One of the men told me that a neighbor of his, who had been fired by his company, never told his children about it. He got up every morning as usual, shaved, put on a suit and tie, rode the train downtown, and just killed the hours until it was time to take the train home. This was less painful for him than admitting he was unemployed. He did it until he found a job again.

One morning, after one of the men from Forty Plus had gone downtown to look for a job, I rode out to his house to talk with his wife.

She led me to their back yard; we sat on a terrace and she brought out coffee and cups. "It's been a very painful thing to watch," she said. "He is a very ambitious, creative man, and when a man like that is denied work, it kills him. He wants to go to work in the morning, and this is the first time in his life he hasn't been able to do it."

She said the day it happened, he had called her and said he had to talk to her right away. "I knew something was wrong," she said. "But he wouldn't tell me over the phone. He said, 'It's not the kids,' and that set my mind at ease a little bit. But I couldn't imagine what it might be.

"It slices right through your life. Suddenly your world is completely different than it was the day before. Six weeks after he was fired, and there was still no sign of work, I think his ego hit rock bottom. For a man who has always been an achiever, something like this is literally devastating."

I asked her what the most noticeable change in him was. "The sleep pattern is different," she said. "When he's awake, he can put on a brave front. But now he'll wake up in the middle of the night and just stare at the ceiling. I can tell that he's close to panic, thinking about what he's going to do.

"I'd like to roll over and tell him, 'I understand; I'm here; I care for you.' But I don't let him know that I know he's awake. I just lie there and pretend to be asleep.

"When he comes home from a job interview, I know how it went before he's even in the house. I can tell by the way he's walking from the car. By the way he's holding his shoulders, and the look on his face.

"I don't ask him questions. I don't want to put that kind of pressure on him. I just try to make him feel that he's welcome at home. It's the best I can do."

At Forty Plus there is no paid staff. The members run the organization themselves; when and if they find work, they graduate from "active" to "corporate" status and are invited to continue to help out.

On a normal day, though, it is only the active members who are present. The ones who are lucky enough to have secured employment are at their offices. The Forty Plus members in the basement divide up responsibilities: a man with a background in publishing helps put together the brochure that promotes the virtues of the brethren to prospective employers. A man with experience chairing meetings plans formal get-togethers for the membership. A man with a deep, resonant, confident voice answers the telephone.

The men of Forty Plus are constantly checking the phone-message center. This is their business number now, and they know that at any time the message may be waiting that will set them free. In most offices, if you are visiting and there is a phone call, your host will have his secretary take a message so that he can call the person back. Not at Forty Plus. When it is announced that a man is wanted on the phone, he breaks off his conversation to take it immediately.

Sometimes there is good news. One day while I was there, a bell clanged. I was informed that this was the signal that one of the members had found work.

It was one of the men I had spoken with on a previous visit. He had come downtown to announce his new job; he had brought a box of doughnuts for the others. He had literally changed in physical appearance since I had seen him last; his face looked more alive, he carried himself with a new sense of strength, he somehow even seemed larger.

I congratulated him and asked him how it had happened.

"I had my fifth interview with this company, and they offered me a job," he said.

I asked him when he would be starting work.

He smiled and looked me in the eye. "Tomorrow," he said.

The others in Forty Plus lined up to shake his hand; he told them that they, too, would soon be back at work. What he did not say, of course, was that this was goodbye; he was no longer one of them.

The change I saw in that man was startling; it seemed to symbolize the unparalleled importance that work has in a man's life. Family, friends, and home may have their niches; but without work, a man loses an irreplaceable part of himself.

One of the Forty Plus members, trying to explain it to me, said, "Self-confidence is about as easy to lose as a dollar bill, I guess." It is a lesson that these men learned late; sitting with them in their basement office, I doubted that they would soon forget it.

Gangs of Princes

Once upon a time, twelve years ago, there was a world that had never been seen before, and may never be seen again.

At the beginning of the 1970s, the executives who ran the popular-music business were discovering something intriguing. Rock and roll, which had been a steady money-maker for them ever since its inception in the 1950s, suddenly had become a growth industry that knew virtually no bounds. Rock and roll was bringing $2 billion a year into the national economy. Young entrepreneurs with no show-business credentials at all were instantly transformed into the elite of New York and California entertainment society.

There was a curious aspect to all of this. Even though the financial rewards available through the rock and roll business had no discernible limits, the general-circulation press had been slow to pick up on the news. This bothered the music entrepreneurs; the surest way to place a band into the public consciousness was through publicity, and yet there were no established conduits into the mainstream media. Opportunities were being lost.

Coincidentally, a new generation of reporters was coming along at precisely this time. We were just out of school; we had not gained the seniority to cover national politics or global crises, yet we had potential access to great numbers of readers.

So much money was available in the rock and roll industry that it became common practice for the managers of prominent bands to invite various young reporters to accompany the groups on national tours. As often as not, much of the expenses would be picked up by the bands. This worked out for everybody. The reporters got into print, bringing to their publications news of a social phenomenon that had gone all but unnoticed by older editors. The bands got widespread publicity, and made more money. And—most interesting of all—we outside observers gained regular access into a netherworld that we had scarcely imagined to exist. We wrote stories filled with quotes and impressions from arenas; but we often failed to tell how affected we were by what we had become a part of.

Now, all this time later, we are different, and so is the entertainment world. The era of the all-aboard rock and roll show is over; the unlimited money has dried up, and the same blockbuster philosophy that rules the literary world applies to the rock world, too. A decade ago, any number of bands, both established and brand-new, traveled first-class with room for any journalistic stowaways they could induce to join up. Now such a luxury is only for the few groups at the very top of the music business; for the rest, the road is a no-frills highway delineated by ledger sheets and absolute budgets. The music world, like the rest of the world, has turned cautious. And with the caution has come the end of that bizarre landscape we were allowed to glimpse—and which, often enough, we did not even recognize for the improbable, previously unobserved American territory that it was.

It was simplicity itself. On a Friday morning, if you were bored, you could place a long-distance call to one of the rock and roll public-relations firms that had blossomed to meet the needs of the booming business. You might call Gibson and Stromberg, a California agency with billings all over the music community (their slogan was "Six Flacks; No Waiting").

"What's going on?" Gary Stromberg would say.

"What have you got this weekend?" you would ask.

And he would check his list of itineraries, and by dinnertime you would be in the front cabin of a jet bound for some medium-sized city in the Northern Hemisphere, where a chauffeured limousine would be waiting for your flight, and a room on the band's floor of the town's best hotel would be waiting for your presence. By the end of the

night you would be drinking champagne with the members of the
group, consorting with the most beautiful women in the state, and
recovering from the screams of thousands of teenagers and the voltage
of towering banks of speakers. Remember, the night before you had
slept in your own bed; that morning you had reported to work in
your regular news office; and on Monday you would be back in that
same office. For the weekend, though—any weekend you wanted—you
would live like a twentieth-century prince.

In Montreal late one evening, I sat in a hotel restaurant with members of the Guess Who, a band that had scored a hit with the song
"American Woman." Tom Jones, the Welsh torch singer, was in town
also, and the restaurant had been kept open for our entourage and his.
The people in the Guess Who party and the people in the Tom Jones
party had little in common, other than that they were used to this
kind of deference. We sat on opposite sides of the dining room, while
waiters three decades older than us stayed up all night to do our
bidding. Late in the meal, an elderly couple appeared at the maître d's
desk; they wondered if they could get a cup of soup before bed. They
were summarily turned away; for them, the restaurant was closed.

The amazing thing was, no one seemed to resent this. The presumed
story on rock and roll was that adult America despised it; but in all
the hotels and all the airports and all the restaurants I passed through,
I saw nothing but envy and curiosity in the eyes of the citizens. The
bands would walk into an airport drunk at eight in the morning,
making rude noises and cursing aloud; the men and women on the
way to their breakfast flights would often come up for autographs,
even though they had no specific idea who these young men were. It
was as if they were immeasurably pleased to see that someone was
allowed to live totally free of constrictions; if it couldn't be them, it
might as well be us.

The availability of women was beyond normal comprehension. Teenage girls, college co-eds, married women—they were all there. In an
era when young people were reputed not to respect anything, they
were in awe of the traveling bands. The bands represented money,
fame, freedom, an escape from the hometown—everything young
America wanted. The women were part of the reward.

It was the time when the feminist movement was making its most
important inroads in the United States, but you couldn't tell it on
the rock and roll tours. Women willingly were treated as currency.
Girls who had slept only with their boyfriends eagerly teamed up and

went to bed in pairs with anyone from the tour party who beckoned them. Young wives lied to their husbands and sneaked out to cruise the bands' hotels. In other parts of American society, maybe, young men had trouble finding female companionship; not in this world. In Norfolk, Virginia, one night after a concert, there were so many women in the hallways of our hotel that the police had to come in with dogs to drive them out.

The attitude of the bands was the same as if the women had been room-service food. There was always plenty, and you could get it at any time, so why give it any thought? At the Clemson, South Carolina, Holiday Inn one warm spring night, I was in a room with Rod Stewart's band of the time, Faces. A young woman had been hanging around the group all evening, making it apparent that she was willing to go off with anyone who would have her. But that was too conventional for the men in the band. Instead of making love to her, they gathered around her, stripped her of her clothes, and placed her on the floor of the room. Then, methodically, they began to take objects and insert them into her. Bars of soap from the bathroom, room keys, a banana, the banana peel—they laughed as they gorged her. And the woman laughed, too. She lay spreadeagled and talked to the band as they did their work. Faces was one of the biggest draws in the world; the woman was clearly honored.

With another band, en route to a concert date, we sat on the plane near a young woman of extraordinary beauty. Almost always, women on the commercial flights would come over to talk to the groups, if only to find out who they were. But this woman was reticent. So the musicians approached her. It turned out that she was going to her father's funeral; he was to be buried that afternoon. One of the guitarists slipped her a piece of paper. Early that evening I saw the young woman arrive at our hotel, the piece of paper in her hand. She had come straight from the cemetery. She went to the room of the lead guitarist and the drummer, and she stayed locked up with them for two days.

With the Alice Cooper group in Sacramento, California, one evening, we returned to the hotel to find dozens of the town's teenage girls waiting. They were decked out in glitzy finery, and they obediently went to the rooms of whoever motioned to them. I never discovered how so many young girls managed to stay away from home overnight so often, but they always did. In the morning the members of the tour party went to the waiting cars for the trip to the airport. The girls from the night before lined up in the parking lot. In the early daylight, they looked far less exotic than they had the previous evening; their makeup was rubbed off, their faces were pale, and their clothes were wrinkled. Who knew what they thought they had gained from the night? They stood several feet from the cars, wanting only a goodbye. And the members of the band, on cue—they had done this many times before—looked at the girls and, Bob Hope-style, began to sing: "Thanks, for the memories. . . ." The girls still stood in the concrete lot, watching the laughing musicians drive away.

There were chartered airliners with built-in bedrooms and showers, and butlers aboard to serve multicourse meals. There were Hawaiian luaus in the dressing rooms of the arenas after the shows, with grass-skirted dancing girls to hand-feed us our supper. There were employees of the record companies to go out day or night to procure any amusement.

The ironic thing was, most of the fans who paid for the records and the concert tickets were unaware of the scope all this had taken. It was a time when a so-called social revolution was in vogue; the rock and roll stars were supposed to be the ultimate people's people. They dressed in jeans and T-shirts and boots, as if they were one with the audience; the boys and girls out in the seats did not comprehend that their money was going toward the bands' oil tax shelters and shopping-center investments.

The clearest example I saw of the attitude of the bands toward their fans came one night in Madison Square Garden, when Jethro Tull was performing before a packed house. Ian Anderson, the band's lead singer, was into the encore, and the audience was surging toward the stage. Some managed to reach the bottom of the wall that led up to the stage itself; by standing on one another's shoulders, they could boost each other up so that they were close to their heroes.

I stood by an amplifier on the stage and watched. Ian Anderson kept singing, and you could see the young fans getting nearer. You couldn't see their faces; but you could see their fingers reaching up over the front edge of the stage as they prepared to pull themselves up.

Terry Ellis, the manager of the band, was watching, too. Very calmly he picked up a hammer and walked over toward Ian Anderson and the microphone. Ellis knelt down. Coolly, every time he saw a set of fingers reach up onto the stage, he brought the hammer sharply down on those fingers. A youngster would reach up blindly to the stage; Ellis would smash his hands with the hammer. The effect was the same as touching a match to a tick; as soon as the hammer came down, the fans would drop back down into the audience. We would never see a whole person; the fingers kept inching onto the stage, and Ellis kept cracking the fingers with his hammer, and eventually the concert ended.

It was a way of life I do not expect to see again. Parts of it I will always remember; parts I am unable to forget. I am not sure if it is something I will tell my grandchildren about.

Bar Child

WASHINGTON—The first time you saw him, you wondered what he was doing there. The tavern was south on Pennsylvania Avenue, in a dying neighborhood where the tourists never come. He was perhaps eight years old, no older, a little kid in cut-off pants and sneakers and a T-shirt.

It was one of those nights that have been plaguing Washington, with the temperatures staying in the nineties, the air full of moisture and filth. You had been wandering, and you had ended up in this part of town and you had decided to look inside.

The television set over the bar was turned on. A few men sat staring at it. The booths were full of people out to slake their thirst on a cruel summer night.

And there was the bar child, sitting by himself at a table too tall for him, looking across the pale Formica top, talking to no one.

The one waitress moved past him, and he didn't look up. You figured that he had wandered in off the street, and that no one had had the time to tell him that he shouldn't be here, that bars were for grown-ups. You chuted a fistful of quarters into the juke, and when the songs had run themselves out you left. It was ten o'clock at night, and the bar child was still there.

In the nights to come, you found yourself returning. Maybe it was because you couldn't stomach the happy bars of Georgetown, and maybe it was because this place didn't seem like Washington at all;

maybe it was for no reason, just a habit that you were falling into quickly. The pattern fit: you were most comfortable in a place where you knew nobody and nobody knew you.

The bar child was there every night. He always seemed to be wearing the same clothes, and sitting at the same table. Now you saw that the waitress would stop and smile at the boy once in a while, but the boy did not smile back. One night he had a comic book; mostly, when the TV wasn't on, he played with a tattered menu.

You make your living intruding into other people's lives, so for a while you didn't ask. You figured that you did enough of that kind of thing during the working day, and that at night you should leave alone something that was none of your business. But one night you walked toward the tavern, and the bar child was outside, almost as if he was waiting for you.

He had a crushed beer can, and he kicked it along the sidewalk, metal scraping concrete. He was careful not to wander far. The neighborhood is bad; he knew not to kick the can past the boundaries of the building housing the bar. The street was raucous, but the sounds were not joyful. Up to the north, shimmering in the dirty haze, bright through the distance and the hot grime, was the dome of the Capitol of the United States.

You walked in, and the bar child followed. He walked to his table. He had his crushed beer can in his hand. You got some quarters at the bar and played your music, and when the waitress came to get your order you hesitated, and then you asked her.

"Oh, it's such a shame," she told you. "His father is the cook here. The mother ran away. There's no one to take care of him. So he comes to work with his father every night, and he sits out here while his father is back in the kitchen. This is no place for a little boy, but there's no one else to look after him. He just sits here in the bar until eleven o'clock every night."

The drinkers were loud this night, but the bar child did not seem to mind. Nothing that happened in the tavern affected him; laughter or shouting, they were all the same. The waitress would stop to talk to him, but if he said anything back, he didn't bother to lift his head.

You looked over at him, and thought of saying something, and just then he turned and looked at you and his eyes had nothing in them. The bar child didn't want to be bothered, not by a stranger, not by another face that came into his world uninvited every night. You had been fooling yourself outside; he had not been waiting for you. He knew better than to wait for anyone.

So you kept quiet, and you finished your drink and you let your music play out and when you left, he was still there. He was there when you went back the next time, and he has been there every time since. And you found yourself wondering: How long until the bar child leaves? How long until he grows old enough to walk away from his father and become a part of the streets that will swallow him up? How long until he is a little boy no longer?

One night you stayed late, and as you left you took one last look at the bar child. His head was down on the table, and the noise wasn't touching him. He was sleeping. . . .

Getting to the Heart of a Man Named Veeck

By now it's old news that Bill Veeck has lost the Chicago White Sox; it happened last Friday, and already the papers have been filled with tributes written about Veeck by sportswriters who know him well.

I have never met Bill Veeck. Like everyone else, I was aware of his impeccable reputation for decency and class, but I have never had a chance to shake his hand. Last May, though, something happend. I didn't write about it at the time, because Veeck didn't want me to.

But now—because it looks as if Veeck will be disappearing from the Chicago scene—I want to do it.

It was May 27, a Tuesday. I had written a column about a thirty-five-year-old man who had four children—boys fifteen, fourteen, and ten, and a girl seven. His wife had left him, and eight months earlier he had lost his job.

Every day since then, he had looked for work. There were no jobs. The gas had been shut off in his apartment; he and his children had no hot water, and could not bathe.

The man told me, in the flattest and saddest of voices, that he had decided to start committing crimes to feed his family.

"I never committed a criminal act in my life," he said. "I never even thought about it. But now I'm starting to see it in a different light. I'm starting to think that most people out there robbing are probably people just like you and me. They just can't see any other way out.

"God knows that I don't want to hurt anyone. I wouldn't take money from an innocent person on the street, like those thugs and bums. But now I can understand what goes through a man's mind when he goes into a grocery store or a bank and says, 'This is a stick-up.' That person knows that he doesn't have anything to look forward to. He's doing it because he has to."

It was a story that belonged in another country, in another century. But it was happening in the economic environment of the United States in the 1980s.

That morning, the phone didn't stop ringing. People had read the column, and wanted to help.

Every caller offered to send money. And to every caller, I explained that the man was not looking for a handout. The gift would be gone in a few weeks. What he wanted was a job. Could the caller ask around and see if there was a job for the man?

That took the callers by surprise. There were no jobs. I became resigned to it as I answered the phone all morning: this was another case of a newspaper column that would stir people's emotions for a few hours, and result in absolutely no change in the life of a man in trouble.

Around noon, the phone rang again.

"This is Bill Veeck," the caller said.

We had never spoken before. Veeck got to the point immediately.

"Is this fellow willing to work?" he said.

I said I believed he was.

"Well, I've got a big old ballpark out here," Veeck said. "I could probably use another hand to help keep things up. It's just manual labor, but if he wants work why don't you send him out here and let us talk to him."

I said I would call the man right away. But I wondered something. All the other callers had been full of sympathy, but no one had been willing to give the man a chance at a job. Why was Veeck doing it?

"Oh, I went through the Depression," Veeck said. "I've seen this before. Sometimes when a fellow is in trouble you want to go out on a limb for him."

I called the man; I told him not to get his hopes up, but that if he went out to Comiskey Park, there might be the possibility of a job for him.

The rest of the week went by; I work every Sunday, and so on the following Sunday I was in my office, writing a column.

I got a call from the security desk. The man was downstairs; he wanted to see me.

He came up. He was nervous and apologetic about taking my time. He was a big man with the softest of voices.

"I just wanted to thank you," he said. "I wanted to do it in person. I would have been here sooner, but when I got to Comiskey Park they hired me right away, and I've been working there ever since."

I said that I was glad to hear the news, but that I wasn't the person to thank. I write newspaper columns all the time and nothing happens. The person who mattered was Bill Veeck.

The man began to cry. "I'm sorry to be like this," he said. "But I was just out of hope, and it looked like nobody in the world cared, and then this happened. It's saved my life and the life of my family. I'll never forget that somebody was willing to give me a chance. I didn't know that people like Mr. Veeck really existed anymore."

Neither did I, I said. Neither did I.

He Was No Bum

A bum died. That's what it seemed like. They found his body in a flophouse on West Madison Street, Chicago's Skid Row. White male, approximately fifty-five years old. A bum died.

They didn't know.

He was no bum. And his story . . . well, let his story tell itself.

The man's name was Arthur Joseph Kelly. Growing up, he wanted to be a fireman. When he was a child he would go to the firehouse at Aberdeen and Washington, the home of Engine 34. His two sisters would go with him sometimes. The firemen were nice to the kids. This was back in the days when the neighborhood was all right.

Arthur Joseph Kelly became a teenager, and then a man, and he never quite had what it takes to be a fireman. He didn't make it. He did make it into the Army. He was a private in World War II, serving in the European Theater of Operations. He didn't make out too well. He suffered from shell shock. It messed him up pretty badly.

He was placed in a series of military hospitals, and then, when the war was over, in veterans hospitals. Whatever had happened to him in the service wasn't getting any better. He would be released from a hospital, and he would go back to the old neighborhood in Chicago, and suddenly the L train would come rumbling overhead and Arthur Joseph Kelly would dive to the ground. Some people laughed at him. He didn't want to do it. A loud noise and he would drop.

He walked away from a veterans' hospital in 1954. He decided that he had to live in the real world. But he was in no condition to do that. He tried for a while, and then he went back to the only place that he remembered as being a place of happiness.

He went back to the fire station at Aberdeen and Washington.

Some of the men of Engine 34 remembered Arthur Joseph Kelly from when he was a boy. They remembered him as a bright-eyed child wanting to be a fireman. And now they saw him as a shell-shocked war veteran.

They took him in.

They fed and clothed him and gave him a place to sleep and let him be one of them. He wasn't a fireman, of course, but he lived in the firehouse, and he had the firemen as his friends. The military people didn't know what to do with his veterans benefits, so some of the firemen went to the Exchange National Bank and arranged for the benefit money to be paid to a special account. The firemen of Engine 34 took it upon themselves to become Arthur Joseph Kelly's conservator and guardian.

The years went by. Some of the firemen were transferred, and some retired, and some died. But there was always at least one fireman at the station who would take responsibility for Arthur Joseph Kelly. The firemen didn't ask for anything in return, but Kelly would stoke the furnace and clean up and help out as much as he could. There were maybe a dozen firemen over the years who became his special guardians—the ones who would deal with the bank and the military, and who would make sure that no harm came to Kelly. For a long time it was the Sullivan brothers; when they left Engine 34, another fireman willingly took over, and then another.

Once Arthur Joseph Kelly went to a Cubs game. A car backfired. He hit the ground. There was some snickering. But an older man, who had been in the service himself and was familiar with shell shock, helped Kelly up and said, "That's all right, fellow. You'll be all right." After that, Kelly stayed close to the firehouse.

His mind and his nerves were not good. The firemen had to remind him to bathe, and to change clothes, and to eat properly. They did it, for twenty years and more, without anyone asking. "He's an easygoing fellow," one of them said. "He doesn't harm anybody. It's not so hard for us to take care of him."

Then the firehouse closed down. The firemen were transferred to another station house, at Laflin and Madison. Arthur Joseph Kelly went with them, but it wasn't the same. It wasn't the firehouse he had loved as a child. He didn't want to live there.

So the last fireman to take care of him—George Grant, a fifty-one-year-old father of eight—found Arthur Joseph Kelly a place to live. It wasn't much—it was the room on Madison Street—but every month Grant would take care of the financial arrangements with the bank, and would go to Madison Street to give money to a lady who ran a tavern near Kelly's room. The understanding was that she would give Kelly his meals at the tavern. No liquor. The firemen didn't want Kelly to end up as a Madison Street wino.

"The firemen had started taking care of Art way before I even got on the force," Grant said. "I just happened to be the last in a long line of men who took care of him. I didn't mind."

When Arthur Joseph Kelly was found dead in his room, they thought he was a bum. But they should have been at the funeral.

Arthur Joseph Kelly was buried with dignity. He was carried to his grave by uniformed firemen. They were his pallbearers. Most of them were not even born when, as a boy, Kelly had started hanging around the firehouse. But they were there at the end. The firemen never let Kelly live like a bum. They didn't let him die like one, either.

Bait

We were driving along the Northwest Tollway, just outside the Chicago city limits. Darkness had replaced daylight.

"All these people worrying about Tylenol," said Tony De Lorenzo.

He was driving. "It doesn't have to be Tylenol next time. Whoever is doing it could put the poison anywhere. He could inject it into a pickle."

De Lorenzo was an FBI agent. We had just met.

Earlier in the day I had received a call at home from Jim Squires, the editor of the *Chicago Tribune*. The *Tribune* is where I work. Squires said he had something important we had to discuss, and he asked me to come in right away.

When I got to his office, he said he had had two surprising visitors. One was Edward Hegarty, the head of the FBI's Chicago office. The other was Richard Brzeczek, the superintendent of the Chicago police department. They had arrived together.

Hegarty and Brzeczek had an unusual request. The search for the Tylenol killer was getting nowhere. Seven people were dead. The Chicago area was in a panic; the rest of the nation was also frightened. The FBI had sent in one of its top criminal-behavior analysts from Quantico, Virginia. He was convinced that if the killer was made to feel some sort of human identification with his victims, the killer might surface.

Hegarty and Brzeczek wondered if I would be willing to write a column that might elicit that response. They realized they were treading on uncertain ground; they made it clear to Squires that they were not attempting to dictate what I would write, or even to suggest what form the column might take. But they thought we should know what their man from Quantico was saying.

Squires and I sat and talked about it. We are both part of the reporting generation that was taught to get queasy at the idea of journalists working hand in hand with law enforcement agencies. We both remembered stories of police units trying to infiltrate antiwar groups during Vietnam days. This, though . . .

"God, I'd like for that guy to be caught," Squires said.

"I know," I said.

We agreed that I should at least talk to the agent from Quantico. Then I would decide what to do.

Tony De Lorenzo pulled into the parking lot of the Mount Prospect Holiday Inn. John Douglas, the FBI criminal analyst from Quantico, was registered in room 215.

We rode the elevator upstairs. John Douglas was a dark-haired FBI man in suit pants and a vest; he had taken off his jacket. He motioned us into the room. There were a few uncomfortable moments of silence, and then he began.

"We've got an attorney general out here who's going on television every night calling this guy a 'madman,' " Douglas said. "That may be true, but calling him that isn't helping anybody."

He said that his specialty was studying the criminal personalities of multiple-murderers. He said that it was closer to an exact science than many people might believe; men who killed more than one person had certain things in common, and one of those things was that they became intensely curious about their victims in human terms.

"If this guy with the Tylenol considers his victims to be only numbers, then he'll never show himself," Douglas said. "But if he starts thinking of them as people . . . then we've got a chance."

He explained that he had followed my newspaper column in his hometown paper, the Fredericksburg, Virginia, *Free Lance-Star*. He said he felt funny proposing that I help him; but had I considered writing about the Tylenol case?

I told him that there was one story I thought was potentially a great one. A twelve-year-old girl named Mary Kellerman had been the youngest victim of the Tylenol killer; she had had a cold, and she had taken a Tylenol capsule from a bottle her mother had bought at the grocery store the night before, and she had collapsed in her bathroom and died. The Kellerman family had talked to no reporters; nothing was known of what they were going through.

"That's a story I would want to write even if I had never heard of you," I said to Douglas. "If you can get me into that house, I'd like to talk to her parents."

He said he thought it could be arranged.

"They have refused to talk to anybody," I said.

"If you knew how much they want the person who killed their daughter to be caught . . ." Tony De Lorenzo said.

We talked for about an hour. Douglas said he knew it was a long shot; but if I decided to write about Mary Kellerman, the FBI would place the Kellerman house under surveillance and would place Mary Kellerman's grave, in a nearby cemetery, under twenty-four-hour surveillance, too.

"Stranger things have happened," Douglas said. "You'd be surprised how many times these guys go to look at the grave or to look at the house."

Tony De Lorenzo picked me up at home the next morning. We

drove out to the Colony Square shopping center in Mount Prospect; there we were met by another FBI agent, LeRoy Himebauch, who had been in contact with the Kellerman family. Himebauch was to take me to their house. De Lorenzo would wait for me in the shopping-center lot.

The Kellerman house was about a fifteen-minute drive away. Dennis Kellerman answered our ring. His wife, Jeanna, was waiting in the living room.

I invited Himebauch to listen in on the interview. Normally I like to do them alone. But I wasn't fooling myself; the Kellermans had allowed me in here because the FBI had told them it might help to find their daughter's killer. I thought they would be more comfortable with the agent in sight.

It was about as difficult as these kinds of conversations get. Mrs. Kellerman wept as we spoke; she kept blaming herself for purchasing the bottle of Tylenol. She said she had reached for a smaller bottle in the grocery store; but then, because she had thought she might need a Tylenol even after Mary's cold was better, she selected the bigger bottle. The bottle with the cyanide in it.

Dennis Kellerman's voice faltered as he recalled the morning Mary died:

"I heard her go into the bathroom. I heard the door close. Then I heard something drop. I went to the bathroom door. I called, 'Mary, are you okay?' There was no answer. I called again, 'Mary, are you okay?' There was still no answer. So I opened the bathroom door and my little girl was on the floor unconscious. She was still in her pajamas."

Mrs. Kellerman told me that Mary had been their only child; she was unable to have any more children. Mary had been born one month premature; as she entered the world she did not cry, and Mrs. Kellerman had been afraid. But the doctor had smiled and had said, "It's all right; she's only sleeping." And she had been; from then on she had always been a quiet child.

I finished with the interview in about an hour. I thanked the Kellermans. I told Dennis Kellerman that I was curious about one thing.

"I think if this had happened to me, I wouldn't want to help with the investigation at all," I said. "I think I would just want everyone to go away and leave me alone. I wouldn't care if the guy was ever caught. I would just want to hide and be by myself."

"No," he said. "It's not like that. I can't even tell you. I can't even tell you what I would give for that guy to walk in my front door right now. Because once he walks in that door, he's mine."

LeRoy Himebauch and I walked out to his car. He unlocked the door on the passenger side for me. Then he walked back up to the house.

I saw him talking with Dennis and Jeanna Kellerman. They were listening intently.

When he returned to the car I asked him what that had been all about.

"When I was listening to you doing your interview, I kept thinking that they're going to crack up if they just stay in the house looking at each other," he said.

"So what did you do?" I said.

"I told them about groups that help out the parents of young children who have died," he said. "I told them if they contacted any church, they would probably be put in touch with one of the groups."

"But I saw you give them a piece of paper," I said.

Himebauch hesitated for a second.

"I gave them my number," he said. "I told them that if they couldn't find a group to help them, then I'd find one for them."

We rode toward the shopping center.

"I had to make them understand that I wasn't trying to help them as an FBI agent," he said. "They had to understand that it wasn't part of my official duties. It's just that . . . I don't know. Sometimes if you let your business define everything you do, you end up not doing the things you ought to do as a person."

When I got to the paper, the column came quickly.

It began:

If you are the Tylenol killer, some of this may matter to you. Or it may make no difference at all.

If you are the Tylenol killer, your whole murderous exercise may have seemed beautiful in the flawlessness of its execution. You doctored the capsules, and the people died, and you put fear in hearts all over the nation. If you are the killer, the success of your mission may be sustaining you.

If you are the Tylenol killer, though, you may be harboring just the vaguest curiosity about the people on the other end of your plan: the people who were unfortunate enough to purchase the bottles you had touched.

If you are curious, come to a small house on a quiet, winding street in Elk Grove Village. Come to 1425 Armstrong Lane. The people who live there, Dennis and Jeanna Kellerman, feel you have already been inside anyway. . . .

Every copy editor who handled the column questioned me about whether I really wanted to include the address. They pointed out that printing the address would make it simple for anyone to find the house.

I couldn't tell them that that was precisely the point. I simply asked them to leave it in.

The column ran and was widely reprinted around the nation. Squires and I did not discuss with anyone the details of how it had come to be written; we decided that if the word got out about the FBI's interest in the story, then whatever we were trying to accomplish would be undermined.

I have my own questions about the propriety of all this. As journalists, we are supposed to be independent agents. If this episode were to appear in an ethics of journalism textbook, I do not know how I might react to it. It is one thing to say that a reporter should never cooperate with a law enforcement agency; it is quite another, when seven people have been poisoned to death in the area where you live, to say that no, you will not help.

As I write this, the Kellermans' house is under FBI surveillance; so is Mary's grave at the cemetery. The killer has not shown himself. With each passing day it seems that he will not. It is far from certain whether the Tylenol killer will be apprehended. If he is, there is no guarantee that the arrest will have anything to do with what you have read here.

Because of the time between my *Esquire* deadline and the publication of the magazine, this story will not appear until the February issue. By then the case may be resolved. If it isn't, at least enough months will have passed that I will be sure the original newspaper column will have outlived its usefulness in luring the killer. And I don't want to keep this whole thing to myself any longer.

You get up every morning and you go to work and you try to do your job. Sometimes you wonder if you're doing it right. In the end, as always, here we are. You put words on paper and you hope they reach somebody.

His Name Is Sam Brooks

I give up. Sam Brooks wins.

Sam Brooks is a lumbering, annoying sixty-seven-year-old man from Brooklyn whose entire life is devoted to getting his name in the newspaper. I met him two years ago in New York.

"Put my name in your newspaper," Sam said.

I politely told him that a person had to do something newsworthy to get his name in the newspaper. It was as if I were talking to a wall.

"Put my name in your newspaper," Sam said.

I explained again why I could not do it. I went out to dinner with some friends. I went back to my hotel room and got in bed. There was a knock at the door. I opened it.

"Put my name in your newspaper," Sam said.

I slammed the door. I went to sleep. Several hours later, the telephone rang.

"Put my name in your newspaper," Sam said.

Most people are nicer to Sam than I have been. So far, he has gotten his name into 149 newspapers. You have to understand that this is a fairly estimable feat, seeing as how Sam doesn't even pretend to have anything going for him other than wanting to get his name in the newspaper. He has a personality reminiscent of the old Jackie Gleason character the Poor Soul, or maybe Duane Doberman on "Sergeant Bilko." A lot of people feel sorry for Sam just looking at him. He kind of mopes into the room, and says, "Put my name in your newspaper."

He travels the country by bus, carrying his moldy old clippings in a sack. Several times since I met him two years ago, he has taken the bus all the way from Brooklyn to Chicago in order to ask me to put his name in the newspaper. A couple of those times Sam was thrown out of the newspaper building by security guards. When he finally did get to me, I said, "Sam, I'm not going to put your name in the newspaper. If you wanted to talk to me, why didn't you just call me from Brooklyn? Why did you take the bus all the way out here?"

"I don't have a phone," Sam said. "Put my name in your newspaper."

Some newspapers give in to Sam quite easily. The *Houston Chronicle*, for example, ran a story on its weather page last month with the simple headline, THIS IS 148TH TIME SAM BROOKS HAS GOTTEN STORY IN A NEWSPAPER. Others are less kind. At the *New York Times, New York Daily News, and Chicago Tribune,* security guards have standing orders to throw Sam out whenever they see him.

And Dick Hitt, a columnist for the *Dallas Times Herald,* did a whole column about Sam—but didn't mention Sam's name. Now that's pretty mean. Sam bent over backwards for Hitt. "What I gotta do," Sam said to Hitt, "say something newsworthy? Okay, Joe DiMaggio's a moron."

A newspaperman in Buffalo shoved Sam out the door of his office. Sam yelled back at him, "I meet lots of young runaway girls on the buses. I hope one of 'em is your daughter on her way to join the Manson gang!"

Sam has developed a certain strategy. He tries to find cub reporters or interns who are eager to get bylines. Or he goes into newspaper offices on Sundays, when there aren't so many security guards around and the news is generally slow.

Sam is a retired mailman and he lives on his pension. He spends virtually all of his time riding the buses and asking people to put his name in the newspaper. The other day a fellow reporter came up to me and said, "There's some crazy guy out there who's getting thrown out. Definitely crazy."

At first I didn't think of Sam. After all, one never knows when he's in town. But about three hours later, as I was leaving the building, I got on the elevator and there, clutching onto the sleeve of one of the newspaper corporation's vice-presidents, was Sam.

"Put my name in your newspaper," he said.

I looked at him.

"Remember me?" Sam said. "We met in New York . . ."

"Yes, I remember," I said.

"I rode all the way from Brooklyn to see you again," Sam said. "All the way from Brooklyn to Chicago."

"Well, you'd better go back," I said.

"Put my name in your newspaper," Sam said.

"Go home, Sam," I said.

"Put my name in your newspaper," Sam said.

I ran away. Sam ran after me.

"Put my name in your newspaper," he yelled.

I escaped. He is gone now. I have just arrived at work. There was a letter from Atlanta waiting. It was from Sam.

"Put my name in your newspaper," the letter said.

I give up.

Damn it.

Audition

He came into the theater out of the rain, and he waited. He was carrying a bag in his right hand, the kind of bag that you might take to a gymnasium.

Auditions had been called for ten A.M. The musical was casting for actors and actresses, and the word had gone out among the theatrical community. By the time the doors to the theater opened, there was a line.

The young actors and actresses waited in the lobby. The man with the bag did not fit in; most of the other men and women were in their twenties, and he was at least twenty years older than that. There were curtains that led into the theater itself; one at a time, the applicants were called.

Once they got inside, they found a stage set like a bedroom suite. Placed rudely near the bed was a piano; here the audition pianist would lead each one through the two-minute tryout. Each had been instructed to bring a ballad and an uptempo song; if he or she were lucky, another two minutes would be allotted and the second song would be heard.

The director and his associates sat in the second row of plush red seats, clipboards on their laps. It was a beautiful theater; each man and woman seemed to hesitate for a moment upon entering.

The routine was simple. "Good morning," the director would say. "Good morning," the actor or actress would say. "What do you have for us?" the director would say. And the man or woman would hand the sheet music to the piano player.

There was no conversation. The person auditioning would sing

a song. The director would say "Thank you, that was nice." The singer would say "Thank you," and leave. The stage manager would bring
the next one in.

The fear of rejection was everywhere, you could almost smell it,
but it was lost behind the smiles. The ones with a chance would be
telephoned that evening and asked to return; this was never mentioned. It was all very polite. No one revealed that he had a dream.

This had gone on for hours, when the stage manager said to the
director, "Watch out for this next one. He's got bells."

It was the man with the bag. He came into the room, and he was
jingling. He had bells in the bag.

The first thing he did was to fall down. It happened right by the
edge of the steps. He meant for it to happen. He crawled over the
stage, hand over hand. Some of the director's associates were stifling
laughter, but it was not funny.

The man brought the bells out of his bag. He began to shake them.
He handed his music to the piano player, and then, to the tune, began to prance in slow motion around the stage.

No one knew what to make of it. All of the others had stood in place
and let the director judge their voices. The man with the bag spotted
the bed on the stage; he slithered onto it, tried to crawl between the
sheets. There was silence from the director and the others.

The man with the bag started to sing the words to "Brother, Can
You Spare a Dime." Without a warning he began to strip; he un-
buttoned his shirt, very slowly, bottom to top. His voice began to shake
as he sang the song. It was getting uncomfortable in the room.

"Thank you, that was nice," the director said.

The man with the bag, his chest bare, stopped in his tracks. It was
as if he had been electrified.

There was no motion in the theater. The director and his associates stared at the man. The piano player paused with his fingers
over the keys.

"May I at least ask you something?" the man said.

The director said yes.

"What did you think of me?" the man said.

Of all the people who had come to try out that day, he was the
only one to ask. He, the strangest and most puzzling of them all, was
the only one to verbalize the question that was in all of their hearts.
At first glance he was so different from all the others because his
actions seemed to indicate something wrong with him, a certain
madness; but really he was just a permutation of the rest, all of their

dreams stretched beyond the breaking point and laid bare and quivering for the world to see.

The director hesitated.

"Well . . ." he said, "to be honest with you, we were looking for more of a traditional audition than something . . . ah . . . improvisational."

The man with the bag stood in place.

"Oh," he said.

Then:

"I guess that's what it's all about, isn't it? I mean, doing it in front of people. I can only do it in the basement in front of the mirror so many times." His voice was shaking terribly.

He buttoned his shirt. The piano player handed him his bag, and he put the bells back in.

"Maybe someday someone will want me," he said.

And then, on the way out:

"It's always easier in the basement."

And then he was gone. For the rest of the afternoon the actors and actresses came and went, but somehow there was a chill in the theater that would not go away.

After the Last Knockout

The last white heavyweight boxing champion of the world finished making his final bed of the morning. He swept up in front of the motel, then waited to see if any more guests would be checking in.

It was a balmy day in Pompano Beach, Florida. The motel was not one of the fancier ones in the area; called the Sea Cay, it had only fourteen rooms, each of which could be rented for as little as twenty-five dollars a night. This was in part due to the modest nature of the accommodations, in part due to the location of the structure— not on the beach itself, but over on a commercial throughway, Ocean Boulevard.

The motel had no office. Persons who wished to check in merely looked around for someone to give them a key. The owner/manager/ maid/desk clerk—the last white heavyweight boxing champion of the world—went to the room closest to the street and picked up a magazine.

The floor was covered with a worn orange carpet. The room was dominated by a large bed; this one had not been made. A half-full plate of doughnuts, left over from breakfast, sat on a shelf. Sunlight streamed through the window.

Ingemar Johansson read his magazine. At fifty he weighed more than he would have liked: 250 pounds. His close-cropped hair was gray. Today he wore a red T-shirt, a pair of madras Bermuda shorts, red socks, and frayed blue running shoes. There was a small swimming pool outside the door; only one guest reclined by its edge, his face turned up toward the sun. Johansson preferred to be indoors. He sat with his back to the window, flipping the pages.

"Ingo," they called him back in 1959. On the evening of June 26 that year they chanted the name: "Ingo, Ingo, Ingo." In Yankee Stadium he knocked Floyd Patterson to the canvas seven times in the third round. When the night was over he was heavyweight champ.

He had never lost a professional fight. Before the match with Patterson he had been mainly a curiosity: a challenger from Sweden, a handsome, barrel-chested young man with an easy smile and piercing blue eyes. After the fight his picture was seen in magazines and newspapers virtually every week. He appeared on television variety shows. He signed movie contracts. He was on his way to becoming a matinee idol.

It lasted one week short of a year. On June 20, 1960, in the rematch at New York's Polo Grounds, Patterson knocked him out in the fifth round. They fought one more time, in Miami Beach on March 13, 1961. Patterson again won by a knockout, this time in the sixth round.

Johansson went back to Europe then. Sonny Liston took the heavyweight title from Patterson, and then Cassius Clay took it from Liston. The boxing world was changing. Clay became Muhammad Ali. Within five years after that night in Yankee Stadium, Ingemar Johansson was virtually forgotten.

Johansson opened the door of the motel room to let a visitor in. The visitor had heard that Johansson was running the Sea Cay; he had called the motel (the number is that of a pay phone next to the pool) and had asked if he could come by. Johansson had said yes.

Johansson walked to his chair. The mail carrier had just arrived;

Johansson flipped through some bills. He was cordial, if not friendly; if the visitor wanted to talk, that was fine, but it was clear that Johansson would just as soon be working around the motel.

"The only boxing I follow anymore is on TV," he said in response to a question. "I don't go to matches."

His accent was still thick. He said that he had owned the motel for three years, and that it provided him with a living income.

"In my life I like to move around," he said. "Three, four, five years in one place, and then move to the next place. It's a good way to live. You can choose exactly the kind of weather you want."

He said that after he had been champion he had lived in Switzerland, in Majorca, and on the Spanish mainland before coming to the United States. He said he liked south Florida about as well as anyplace else.

"Pompano is nice," he said. "There aren't many people here, which I like. If I want to see people I drive over to Fort Lauderdale. There are older people here, and in a business like mine, the kind of people who come to the motel determines everything. Here if I rent a room to a person, I know who will be sleeping in the room. In Fort Lauderdale, with all the young kids, you rent to one person and you can be sure that ten will be sleeping in the room."

The visitor started to ask about the title fights with Patterson. Johannson shrugged and looked away, as if he had heard the questions too many times before.

"A championship fight is not much different from a regular fight," he said. "If fighting is your business all the fights are the same, whether there are one thousand people watching or fifty thousand. Maybe there's a difference to the public. But to a fighter it's always the same thing. There's another guy in the other corner, and you have to knock him down.

"Boxing is not like any other sport. You train just as hard, but you risk everything every time you go into the ring. If you lose once, you're on the way out. If you lose again, you're considered out of the running. It's not like football, where you can lose one Sunday, and then win the next Sunday and be a hero again."

There were no trophies, photographs, or other memorabilia visible in the room. Johansson said that he preferred it that way: "Everything I won is stored in bags in Sweden." He said he used to have a big blowup of a picture of him hovering over Patterson, but he had not really liked it; he got rid of it long ago.

The visitor asked when it had occurred to Johansson that he might be the best boxer in the world.

"I never thought about it," he said. "You don't think about being the best in the world. You just think you have a chance of winning the next fight. I never thought I was going to lose, and I kept winning, and after I fought enough fights I was the champion. And then I lost and I wasn't the champion.

"That was okay, too. Just because I had become the champion didn't mean I was going to be the champion forever. About thirty guys in the whole world have ever been heavyweight champion, so if you are one of them then it's pretty good. It's not going to go on forever."

Johansson seemed vaguely uncomfortable talking about boxing. The visitor asked him if this was so, and Johansson said yes.

"The boxing has never been the main thing with me," he said. "I've never thought of my boxing career as my life. My life right now is living in Pompano and running my motel. I get up in the morning and I go for a run—that is part of my life. Everybody has something in their life that suits them. I'm fifty and I'm still looking for mine."

The door opened. A strikingly handsome blond man in swimming trunks came in. He talked to Johansson briefly in Swedish; then he went back outside, where he was applying a new coat of white paint to the Sea Cay's sign.

"That was my son, Thomas," Johansson said. "He's twenty-seven; he lives in Sweden, but he is here helping me this month." Johansson himself had been divorced twice; he was currently unmarried.

The visitor asked Johansson if he thought he would finally settle for good in Pompano Beach.

"No," he said. "As much as I like it, I always have to look for new places to stay. Small things make you feel good about a place. I was in California recently, and I went fishing. Here in Florida you catch tropical fish. But in California they had the same kind of fish we had in Sweden when I was growing up—mackerel, flounder, cod. I went out on a pier and bought a pole for one dollar. I threw the line in, and right away I caught three or four mackerel.

"It reminded me of home, fish-wise."

He said that some people recognize him, some don't. Usually they feel they have seen him someplace, but can't figure out where. "The more kilos I take off, the more they know who I am," he said.

Most of his evenings, he said, are spent watching television. "But there are no shows in the last two or three years that I'm really interested in. I don't like the family stuff. The show I really liked was

'The Untouchables.'

"Now even the detective shows are half detective and half funny. I don't like that. I like funny things, but either you're a tough show or you're a funny show. You shouldn't be both. This 'Magnum, P.I.' . . . it's for kids. He's not tough. He's more like a joke. Shit, let's face it."

He said that he thought Americans are brought up differently from people in other countries. "You always hear Americans say that America is the best country in the world. In Sweden children don't learn that in school. It just isn't something you are taught. I think it is a good thing about America; it makes American people try harder.

"But the kids today in this country are different. When I was growing up, a kid did what he was told. If you did something wrong, then the teacher was allowed to beat you up a little. Today, the kids wait outside the school and beat the teacher up. I could have done that, but I never would have."

The visitor asked Johansson if he recalled what it felt like to hit someone in the ring.

For the first time in the conversation, Johansson smiled widely. "Oh, that's the best feeling in the world," he said. He stood up. He clenched his right fist, and he slammed it into his left palm.

"When you hit someone the right way, the feeling runs right up your arm," he said. "It's . . . it's the best."

Johansson had some things to do around the motel. So the visitor walked out to the pool, where Thomas was fixing one of the chairs.

The visitor asked Thomas if he thought his dad had any bad feelings about having to run this place every day after having once had all the perquisites that come with being champion of the world.

"No, he really kind of likes it," Thomas said. "He doesn't want to live in the past. He knows that's over. He's a guy who wants to do everything by himself. If he sees a piece of furniture he likes in a store, he doesn't think about buying it. He says, 'I think I'll go home and make one like it.' "

Thomas said that one reason his father liked living in the United States was that, as time has gone by, he has stopped being constantly reminded of who he used to be.

"In Sweden, that would never happen," Thomas said. "I can't even explain to you what it is like to be Ingemar Johansson in Sweden. The night my father won the championship is the only thing in people's lives that they remember exactly where they were. It is like when President Kennedy died in America. In Sweden, every person who is old enough can tell you what he was doing when he heard my father had become the champion.

"Here . . . he doesn't have to live with that so much."

Johansson had talked with one of the motel's guests and had returned to the room next to the street.

The visitor stopped in to say goodbye and to wish him well.

"If I can be in good shape and stay away from sickness, that's all I want," Johansson said. "That's a lot."

The visitor asked him what a good day for him was.

"A good day?" he said. "When the motel is filled up, when I've been out running in the morning, when I've paid my bills. That makes me feel good."

And he really felt that he was still looking for a way to spend his life?

"It's true," Johansson said. "I'm sure if people will have anything to remember about me, they will see in a book what happened in nineteen-hundred-fifty-nine.

"That's for them, though, not for me. It doesn't matter so much to me if they remember me as champion. It doesn't mean so much to me if they remember me at all."

The Pleasure of Your Company

BOSTON—It's one of those nights. I've just come back from the bar on the first floor of the hotel, and now I'm in my room. The local eleven o'clock news is on the television set; strangers are telling me about the world. My plane tomorrow leaves at noon.

I like this work, but by definition it's solitary in nature; the reporting business has undergone rapid modernizing changes in the last century, but in a lot of very important ways it's still the same as when all you needed for a story were a man, a pencil, and a train ticket. Which is fine; there's a lot of romanticism to that, and in fact it's one of the main draws of the job.

Sometimes, though—it usually happens to me during the Christmas season—you ask yourself what the wisdom is in doing something that sends you off on your own so often, putting you in towns where you know no one, with the express purpose of delving into people's lives to extract a story, and then fleeing like the wind before a real human connection can be made. Most people wouldn't live like this.

The feeling goes away soon enough, but when it's there we all deal with it the best way we can. So tonight—back at the hotel from the story, having a final drink in the barroom before trying for sleep—I reached into my briefcase and pulled out the envelope I've been carrying around.

It had arrived back in my office, bearing a Tampa, Florida, postmark. When I opened it I had found another envelope inside; it was clearly a wedding invitation.

The invitation said that Kathryn Riley and Stephen Mark Smith were requesting my presence at their wedding. The location was the First Baptist Church in Tampa; a reception was to follow at the Holiday Inn Downtown.

I was puzzled; I didn't recall knowing anyone in that part of Florida. And then a handwritten note dropped out of the envelope, over the signature of Kathy Riley.

"I know it's a trifle unusual for you to receive a wedding invitation from two total strangers," the note said. "In attempting to explain myself, let me begin by saying that while we are strangers to you, you are not a stranger to us."

She went on to explain that she and her fiancé had been reading the column for the last several years in the *Tampa Tribune*. She said some very flattering things, the details of which are not necessary to go into here; the point was, some of the things I had been trying to say and do in the column had reached her, and had stayed with her. She seemed almost apologetic about sending the invitation; she assumed I would consider it an odd thing for her to do.

I guess she would consider it even odder if she knew that her invitation was now sitting on top of a hotel bar table in Boston, while I reread her note as the jukebox played. I hadn't realized why I had been carrying the invitation around, but I suppose it had something to do with instinctively knowing that it might come in handy at a moment like this—the inevitable moment when you find yourself wondering whether what you're doing has any value to anyone but yourself.

There's an unwritten contract when you do this kind of work. You go out and see things and put yourself in situations you probably have no business being in—all aimed at coming up with a story you can tell.

The unwritten contract says that there's someone at the other end. You always assume that; your various bosses can show you surveys and studies that can approximate just how many people you are reaching every day. But somehow none of the numbers ever seem real; they're too big, you can't think in terms of figures like that, and often it takes a voice on the phone or a letter in the mail—a letter like this wedding invitation—to remind you of why you do what you do.

I read through Kathy Riley's note again. Near the end, it said: "And so while making out our guest list, we quickly realized there were people we felt close to even though we had never met them."

Her list made me smile; it was a short one, and I found myself in the company of Walter Cronkite, Bob Seger, Captain Kangaroo— "each of you," Kathy Riley wrote, "during the course of our lives, has in your own way meant something special to us."

I listened to the music in the barroom, and thought about what an unusual thing it is to be a part of someone's life because you are somehow included in their media mix. Cronkite, Seger, the Captain . . . we had all ended up there because of twentieth-century communications, which seems a cold and bloodless thing.

And yet what can be less cold than the idea of a young man and woman, half a continent away, wanting you to be present on the afternoon they become man and wife? It's funny; when you do a job like this one it is with you all the time, day and night, weekends, too. It obsesses you, and yet you know that when you enter the lives of the people on the other end, you'll be lucky if they give you a couple of minutes a day.

Best not to ponder that, though; sometimes, apparently, those few minutes are enough. It is nearing midnight in Boston; in the next room, I can hear people talking. Time for sleep; there are places to go in the morning.

Cheeseburgers

For A. S. G.

Contents

308 *Contents*

Contents 309

Introduction

When I first became a newpaperman, there was a city room cliché. The reporter would come back to the office after a day of chasing a story. He would sit down, go over his notes, and craft his piece on deadline. A copyboy would take it to the city editor, who would pass it on to the copy desk, who would send it downstairs to be set in type.

And then the reporter would head for the bar closest to the newspaper building, and his colleagues would begin to come in at the end of their shifts, and they would say to him: "What really happened?" And he would tell them. The story he would relate in the bar often would bear little resemblance to the story he had just written for the newspaper; in almost every case it would be better, truer, livelier.

When I started writing a column, I made one resolution: I would try to tell the same story in the newspaper that I would want to tell my friends later on in the bar. My rule of thumb was that if I succeeded in doing that, I was succeeding as a reporter. That rule still seems to hold up pretty well.

I think of the prototypical national columnist, and I envision six hundred Washington pundits sitting back in six hundred easy chairs, sucking on six hundred pipes and spewing out six hundred great thoughts about the MX missile debate in Congress or the latest Supreme Court decision. It often seems that if a story didn't first appear on the front page of the *New York Times* or the *Washington Post,* then it just doesn't qualify as news.

I'm after something a little different. I like to think of my stories as snapshots of life in America in the Eighties—snapshots taken as I wander around the country seeing what turns up. My guiding principle is that if something interests me viscerally—as a person, not necessarily as a "journalist"—then I'll try to write about it. The nicest compliment I ever get is that my stories sound not so much like someone who is sitting down at a typewriter with something he has been assigned, but like someone who is calling his best friend at the end of the day and saying, "You'll never guess what I saw today. . . . You'll never guess who I met today."

So most of the stories in this book probably don't fit the classic definition of "news." I was curious about what the Alamo was like in the middle of the Eighties, so I went to take a look. I wanted to know what went on at the factory that manufactures Trojans, so I paid a visit. I wondered what it must be like for Frank Gifford to have walked into rooms all of his life and always to have been considered the coolest guy in every one of those rooms, so I sought him out and asked him. Stories like that. The stories come from two places: my monthly "American Beat" column in *Esquire* magazine, and my syndicated newspaper column based in the *Chicago Tribune*.

There is one story in the book that bears some amplification. In my last collection, *American Beat,* there was a story called "Reflections in a Wary Eye"—an essay about a meeting I had with Richard Nixon after he had given up the Presidency. The story consisted mostly of my reactions to spending the time with Nixon. I received many letters from people saying that they would enjoy reading, in detail, exactly what Nixon had said during the meeting. "Reflections in a Wary Eye" had originally been an *Esquire* column; I had also written a five-part newspaper series that was basically the raw transcript of my conversation with Nixon. Because so many people have expressed curiosity about it, I have put those newspaper stories together for this book; the entry is called "Nixon on Nixon." It's not a very stylish writing job, but it provides a view of the man a little different from most.

A word of explanation about the title of this book: Someone once told me that the name of a book like this—a collection—should convey the fact that it's "a bunch of things that you like a lot." That's cheeseburgers.

BOB GREENE

Remember the Alamo?

I wanted to see something real. I had had enough of the Eighties; enough of the disposable and the modern. I wanted to go somewhere that felt . . . different.

I thought about it. In all of the United States, where could I go that promised a change? Where could I go that was unspoiled by the rush of time?

It took me several days to figure it out, but when the answer came it was as clear as daybreak. The Alamo. Of course. The Alamo.

I had never been there, but it had to be perfect. I envisioned the big, legendary old mission standing out by itself on the high desert, the wind whistling over the empty miles, sagebrush bouncing along the plains. The Alamo—where for thirteen days in 1836 Jim Bowie, Davy Crockett, Colonel William Travis, and their brave companions fought off the attack of Santa Anna's Mexican troops. The Alamo—that was it. Everything else in America might be geared to let a fellow down, but the Alamo remained. I closed my eyes. I could almost see it, standing lonely sentry in the desolate heat.

I caught a midday flight to San Antonio. The trip was smooth; riding to my hotel from the airport, I thought about getting into the south Texas mood. Maybe I'd stop somewhere and have a long-neck bottle of Pearl beer. Honest, full-bodied, robust Pearl.

I looked out the window of the cab. The billboard on the right said TASTES GOOD—ONLY 68 CALORIES—PEARL LIGHT.

At the Hyatt my room overlooked the lobby atrium. It occurred to me that I had no idea how to get to the Alamo. I picked up the telephone book to see if it could give me any guidance.

From the San Antonio telephone directory:

Alamo Accessories Filter Division. Alamo Advertising Specialties Company. Alamo Aligning Service. Alamo AMC Jeep Renault Inc. Alamo Answering Service. Alamo Auto Parts. Alamo Awning. Alamo Bail Bonds. Alamo Barber & Beauty Supply. Alamo Belt & Screw Inc. Alamo Bone & Joint Clinic. Alamo Catering. Alamo Childbirth Training Association. Alamo Continuous Guttering. Alamo Dog & Cat Hospital. Alamo Fitness & Leisure Company Inc. Alamo Hearing Aid Service. Alamo Ice Cream & Delicatessen. Alamo Legal Clinic. Alamo Limousine Service Inc. Alamo Maid Service. Alamo Pawn Shop. Alamo Pecan Co. Alamo Ready Mix Concrete Inc. Alamo Rent A Car. Alamo Spring Co. Alamo Toyota. Alamo Uniforms. Alamo Welding & Boiler Works Inc. Alamo Wheel Aligning.

I went downstairs and asked the doorman how I would get out to the Alamo, and if he could arrange transportation for me. I said I'd need a way to get back, too; I didn't want to be stranded out on the desert.

He smiled a curious smile at me.

"Just walk over to the next block," he said. "It's right across from Woolworth's."

"What's right across from Woolworth's?" I said.

"The Alamo," he said.

I walked a block. There, across from Woolworth's, was the Alamo.

It was right downtown. In addition to Woolworth's, the edifices that surrounded the Alamo included the H. L. Green Variety Store, the G/M Steak House, the Big Apple unisex jeans store, Maldonado Jewelers, and Texas State Optical.

In front of the Alamo itself was Vasquez's Snow-Kone stand.

Next to Vasquez's Snow-Kone stand was a vending box for *USA Today*.

I entered the Alamo. It was tiny. It felt like a one-room schoolhouse. It was dwarfed by the rest of downtown San Antonio.

My fellow tourists included young women wearing Walkman headsets, and young men carrying tape players the size of suitcases. Most of the visitors wore T-shirts; the printing on the front of the shirts featured promotional slogans for the Incredible Hulk, for "M*A*S*H," for Nike running shoes, for the Men at Work '83 North American Tour.

A woman from the Daughters of the Republic of Texas handed out Alamo pamphlets. There was a sign advising GENTLEMEN REMOVE HATS, but the sign was widely ignored; males inside the Alamo favored baseball-style caps bearing the trademarks of Caterpillar tractors and International Harvester farm machinery, and the logo of the Johnson Space Center.

There was a courtyard outside the Alamo. I ran into a family in the midst of an argument. The son was blasting a song called "Ride Like the Wind" from his tape box; his mother, carrying a camera with faces of Mickey Mouse on the strap, and wearing a T-shirt bearing Elvis's face and the words THE KING LIVES ON, was telling him that he had to keep the tape turned off.

"Didn't you see the sign that said 'Quiet, please'?" she said.

"That was for the library, dummy," he said.

In the courtyard of the Alamo were two soft-drink machines—one Pepsi, one Coke. I walked toward them, passing on the way three babies in blue canvas Aprica strollers.

Apparently not even the Alamo is safe from jitters about crime. On the Pepsi machine, a red-and-white sign advised: NOTICE—ALL MONEY REMOVED FROM THIS MACHINE DAILY.

Back inside the Alamo I walked over the flagstone floor and stopped in front of a case that held some of Davy Crockett's personal effects. There was Crockett's beaded buckskin vest with onyx buttons; a lock of his hair; his fork; his bear-hunting knife; his razor; his powder case and shot pouch; and his rifle, "Old Betsy."

I heard a mother saying to her son: "Doesn't look like John Wayne, does it?"

I followed her eyes. She was looking up at a portrait of Crockett, painted from life in 1834 by an artist named John C. Chapman. I found it hard to fault the woman standing next to me; if the truth be told, Davy Crockett—at least based on the evidence of the Chapman painting—looked like a cross between Bob Hope and Abbie Hoffman.

I asked Mrs. Boyd (she was wearing a name tag) of the Daughters of the Republic of Texas if I might speak to someone in charge. Mrs. Boyd had sort of a stunned look on her face; I got the impression that she spent many days inside the Alamo. She directed me to a man named Charles Long, who she said was the Alamo's curator.

Charles Long sat in a private office; above his desk was a portrait of Jim Bowie.

There was a digital clock beside Long, and an AM/FM radio. A Radio Shack pocket calculator rested on his desk, as did a Kodak Disc 4000 camera. He leaned against an IBM Selectric typewriter.

I asked him what it felt like, coming to work at the Alamo every day.

Before he could answer, there was the sound of an electronic beeping. "Just a second," Long said.

He picked up a beige-and-brown Freedom Phone 1550—one of those wireless telephones, manufactured in Japan. A metal antenna protruded from the phone.

"Alamo," Long said.

I waited while he completed his conversation. When he had, he told me that it had been a lengthy fight to keep the Alamo as a shrine.

"For a long time, it was used for commercial purposes," he said. "When motion pictures first came along, the first place in San Antonio they were shown was right on the side wall of the Alamo. The promoters sold tickets."

I asked him if that was the most blatant example of the Alamo's commercial use.

"Oh, no," Long said. "Years ago, there used to be a liquor store and a hardware store in the long barracks. And at one time the Alamo was a police station, and then a bank."

I excused myself and walked over to the Alamo's gift shop. A woman in an I'M WITH A STUPID T-shirt asked her husband, wearing a CHARLIE DANIELS BAND T-shirt, to buy her a book of Texas recipes.

A sign said that a movie telling the story of the Alamo would start in five minutes. I followed the directions, and ended up in a long, bench-filled room.

The film was not projected on a movie screen, however. At the front of the room was a 105-channel, cable-ready, large-screen Quasar Compu-Matic television set with a sign that said it featured electronic remote tuning. The set was of the type commonly used by bars and taverns to show sporting events. In the ancient room, the battle of the Alamo was reenacted on the screen all day long; when the videotape was over, it repeated itself.

If the woman who had seen Davy Crockett's portrait had been disappointed by the way he looked, I hoped she had continued her tour of the

Alamo. There were two other exhibits that, judging by the size of the crowds, were the most popular on the grounds—and that probably would have pleased her more than the Crockett painting.

One of these exhibits was a picture of Davy Crockett, Jim Bowie, and Colonel Travis fighting off the Mexican hordes. In this picture, Davy Crockett looked much more like John Wayne. This was because Davy Crockett *was* John Wayne; the painting was of Wayne's 1960 movie *The Alamo.* Jim Bowie looked like Richard Widmark (who he in fact was); Colonel Travis looked like Laurence Harvey (likewise). The painting was far more satisfying to the visitors than the actual portrait of Crockett.

But as a crowd pleaser, the painting was nothing compared to an artifact that was displayed inside a glass case. At first the object was puzzling; it looked like a gold director's chair.

Which, in fact, it was. It was John Wayne's Screen Directors Guild Award, which officials of the Alamo displayed along with the genuine Crockett-Bowie-Travis memorabilia.

I walked out of the Alamo. Downtown was bustling; the street in front of the Alamo was busy. A city transit bus passed by. On the side was a painting of San Antonio's skyline. Superimposed on the buildings were the faces of the Newswatch 12 television news team—male anchor, female anchor, sportscaster, weatherman.

I followed the wall surrounding the Alamo around to the back, to see what I might find if approaching from the rear. But it was more of the same; more downtown buildings and, overlooking Bonham Street, two billboards for RonRico rum and Merit cigarettes.

I decided to take a stroll rather than go directly back to my hotel. I thought I might pick up some more authentic frontier color if I didn't make such a big thing of looking for it.

I passed a restaurant and glanced up at its sign. It was called Lone Star Yogurt.

Back at the Hyatt I went for a drink to the Regency Club, a top-floor hospitality room constructed to give guests the best view of San Antonio. Directly out the window, sixteen floors below, was the Alamo itself; I was surprised the management of the Hyatt hadn't decided to build an enclosed skywalk to it.

Late at night, alone in my hotel room, I couldn't sleep. I got up and got dressed; I walked back over to the Alamo.

Now I was the only person on the grounds. The building itself was locked, but bright lights illuminated its limestone front. In the artificial light, something showed up that hadn't been quite so noticeable in the daylight: names—names carved by visitors on the facade of the Alamo. Lil Garrett, J. D. Thomas, Billy Waters; I stood there and moved slowly from one edge of the Alamo to the other, reading the names.

I looked back the other way. There was the Hyatt; there was Woolworth's; there was Texas State Optical. A chill wind had come up; now it seemed very cold at the Alamo. I had a Pocket Flight Guide in my suitcase in my room; I could be out of town by ten the next morning.

The Goods

Out past the railroad tracks in a crumbling industrial section of Trenton, New Jersey, is a long, low-slung, mustard-yellow building. This is the building where they manufacture Trojans.

They manufacture Trojans twenty-four hours a day. More than 1.1 million Trojans on a good day, 170 million Trojans a year. There are other brands of condoms for sale, but in the United States the word "Trojans" has become almost generic. The Trojans brand—which was launched more than fifty years ago—accounts for 57 percent of the condoms sold in drugstores in the U.S.; all of the other manufacturers split the rest of the market.

Nowhere on the outside of the building is the word "Trojans" apparent. Just the name of the parent company: Youngs Rubber Corporation.

The manager of operations and planning at the Trojans plant is Daryl Kress, thirty-seven, a former lieutenant commander in the navy. A trim, serious man in a dark-blue suit and crisp white shirt, he sits behind a tidy desk; in front of him is a coffee cup painted with the legend LIEUTENANT COMMANDER.

At no time does Kress use the term "condom," or "prophylactic," or "rubber" when mentioning the product that is manufactured in this building. Instead he refers to what is made here as "the goods."

"The goods come in seven different varieties," Kress says. "Regular, nipple-end, nipple-end lubricated, ribbed . . ." Or he says, "When the goods are shipped from our plant . . ."

When he is explaining the tensile strength of the product, he reaches into a top desk drawer and comes out with a foil-wrapped Trojan. He opens the package and—still unsmiling—lifts the condom to his mouth. He blows into it and inflates it, then hands it to me for inspection.

Kress says he is married, with two sons, ages fourteen and twelve. He says the world in which his boys are growing up is far more relaxed about Trojans than the world in which previous generations of American males grew up.

"With us, we always hoped we'd get the druggist instead of that gal who worked behind the counter," he says. "Now most of the time they aren't sold behind the counter. They're hung up right next to the cash register. Heck, you just pull as many packages as you need off the rack and go right to the check-out counter."

Kress leads me into the manufacturing area of the Trojans plant. The heat is overwhelming; in some parts of the building the temperatures approach 180 degrees. And the smell—the intense, hot, oppressive smell of liquefied latex—is enough to knock you to your knees.

When it first hits us, I stop in my tracks. I have never smelled anything like it before.

"What is that smell?" I say to Kress.

"I don't smell anything," he says.

The interior of the Trojans plant looks like some woodcut used to illustrate the Iron Age in an old encyclopedia. There is absolutely nothing high-tech about what is done here; the four main manufacturing machines, each as long as a city block, creak and groan and rumble as they do their ceaseless task.

Inside the machine we are standing in front of, 3,412 glass forms in the shape of penises move, pointing downward, along a conveyor belt. The forms are dipped into liquefied latex. They are pulled out of the latex, with a thin rubber coating now formed on the glass. They are heat-dried. They are dipped a second time. A ring is mechanically formed around the top of each new condom. Talc is applied to prevent the condoms from sticking to themselves. The condoms are mechanically rolled off the glass forms in preparation for the next step of the process.

Kress raises his voice to be heard above the sound of the machines. "The goods are tumbled dry to remove the excess talc," he says. "Follow me."

"I guess this puts to rest the joke we all used to tell each other," I say to Kress.

"What joke is that?" he says.

"Well, you know," I say. "When a kid buys a rubber, his friends ask him what size he got. But it's obvious from looking at these things being made that they're all the same size."

"Actually, that's not true," Kress says. "There are two standard sizes in the world for these goods. An American size and a Japanese size."

"What's the difference?" I say.

"The Japanese size is smaller," Kress says. "When you lay one of these goods flat and measure its width, it is fifty-two millimeters wide. It is 7.1 inches long. The Japanese standard is forty-nine millimeters wide and 6.3 inches long."

As we walk through the factory, we pass some of the more than two hundred laborers who divide the three daily shifts at the Trojans plant. They are members of the United Rubber, Cork, Linoleum and Plastic Workers of America.

I ask Kress if the workers are allowed to take samples of the project home.

"There's no official policy on it," he says. "But we wouldn't say anything if they did. We make so many each day, it wouldn't make any real difference."

He says that, despite the recent rugged economy, there have been no layoffs in the Trojans plant.

"In a recession, our business actually goes up a little bit," he says. "People tend to stay home instead of going out."

Each of the million-plus Trojans that are manufactured daily is individually tested for holes or other flaws.

Each Trojan that comes off the line goes to the testing rooms. Here, women sitting at long tables slip the Trojans over more forms—called mandrels—that move by on another conveyor belt. These mandrels, also long and erect, are made of metal; they point upward. After the women place Trojans over them, the mandrels are dipped into an electrolytic solution; if any of the charged solution gets through a condom and makes contact with a steel mandrel, a mechanical alarm is tripped and that Trojan is rejected.

The steel mandrels move past the women in rapid, unrelenting succession. In front of each woman is a bin full of new Trojans; all day long she reaches into the bin, comes out with a Trojan, slips it over the top of a mandrel, then reaches back into the bin for another Trojan before the next mandrel moves past her.

Some of the women use their right hands to apply the Trojans to the mandrels. Some use their left hands. Some use both hands. There is no music in the room; there is no visual diversion. Just the mandrels moving by. When you first catch sight of the testers doing their job, you are struck by two immediate impressions: first, this has to be one of the most deadening, monotonous, dreary forms of human endeavor; and second, these women would really make great dates.

As the mandrels pass by the women and the Trojans are slipped over the tops, I approach several of the testers and talk to them. The conveyor belt does not stop; the women continue to work with the Trojans and the mandrels while we speak.

A fifty-three-year-old grandmother named Wilber Holloway tells me she has been doing this for seventeen years. "It took me about six weeks to learn," she says. "The trick is in how you pick them up."

I ask her what she thinks about all day while she is doing this.

"Money and men," Mrs. Holloway says. "I dream of winning the lottery, and I dream of young men."

Cindy Gerner, thirty-three and married, says, "It takes patience at first. You get nervous that you're going to break them when you put them on, and because you're nervous you do break them. You get your system down before long, though."

She says she thinks about different things to get her through the day. "I'm a Baptist," she says. "While I'm doing this I either go over Bible verses in my head, or I think of songs I heard in church."

Terry Scott, twenty-four, says that sometimes at night she dreams of the mandrels moving past her. I ask her what she tells strangers when she meets them and they ask her what she does for a living.

"I tell them, 'Flip rubbers,'" she says.

Daryl Kress leads me through the room where the Trojans are sealed inside foil packets, and then he takes me back to his office.

"The mail is very interesting," he says. "We think we have the best quality-control operation in the business, but when you sell as many goods as we do, you're bound to get some complaints."

He searches through his desk, and finds some correspondence. He flips through the letters and begins to sort them out.

"We had one man write us to complain that his Trojan was all dried out—he said that the lubricant had dried up. He sent us the package, so we took a look at the date on it. The guy had been carrying the thing around for eleven years."

I ask him what the most common complaint is.

"People write us to say that their Trojan won't unroll. Nine out of ten times, they're doing it backwards. They're doing it in the dark, and instead of unrolling it, they're trying to roll it up tighter."

I ask him if people really take the time to write letters about something like that.

"Oh, yes," he says. "They can get pretty eloquent. One man wrote us to accuse a Trojan of 'complete prophylactic recalcitrance.'"

Kress is busy; he is due in another part of the plant, used to test the strength and resilience of the Trojans. Here the condoms are placed on a machine that inflates them automatically.

"You'd be amazed at how big these things can get," Kress says.

And indeed the machine does blow the Trojans up until they are approximately the size of shopping bags.

We walk through the shipping area. Charles Reed, forty-four, who has been working in the Trojans plant for twenty-two years, is packing the individual cartons of Trojans into big brown boxes; the boxes will be loaded onto trucks and distributed around the nation. Reed hardly looks up as he scoops the small packages from the end of the conveyor belt and arranges them in the larger crates.

"When you first come to work here, I guess you think it's going to be a pretty sexy job," Reed says. "I mean, this is an awfully famous product. But before long you quit telling people where you work.

"The reason is that they're going to react one of two ways. Either they're going to think it's tremendously interesting, and they're going to ask you questions all night about it. Or they're going to think it's funny, and make a lot of jokes.

"Now I just say that I'm a machine operator, or a shipping clerk. It makes things easier."

Like the Trojans factory itself, the large brown crates in which the individual packages of condoms are packed for shipping do not have the word "Trojans" printed anywhere on their exteriors.

"That was a conscious decision," Kress says. "These things sit around a lot of docks on their way to their destinations. We feel that if we were to print the name of the product on the outside of the shipping box, it would become a fairly pilferable item in transit."

As I leave the Trojans factory, I pass through the reception area. A secretary is on the telephone; a security camera is sending a black-and-white picture of the parking lot onto a TV monitor; a copy of *Reader's Digest* is placed on a coffee table.

Behind me, behind a series of doors, are the machines and mandrels and pallets and workers. Ahead of me, the real world waits again. On a table, someone has left a package of Trojans. On its front, the design is soft pastel; a young couple is shown in profile, strolling on a deserted beach. The printed slogan is brief and to the point: FOR FEELING IN LOVE.

Behind Closed Doors

GRAND RAPIDS, Mich.—I finished shaving in the bathroom of my room at the Amway Grand Plaza Hotel, and turned the knob to return to the bedroom. The door stuck. It stuck for only a moment; one good shove opened it up. But in that moment my life flashed before my eyes, and I was transported back through time to a day in the distant past, a day that was one of those breakthrough experiences in a man's walk through this world.

Some people remember when a bullet intended for someone else whizzed past their ear. Some remember when a car on the highway swerved threateningly toward their own. Some remember when a snake on a forest path struck out at them.

My brush with the hereafter was not quite so dramatic. But it has stuck with me all these years.

It was the summer of 1968. I was a college kid from Ohio, assigned by my hometown newspaper to work as a copyboy at the 1968 Democratic National Convention in Chicago, doing errands for the Scripps-Howard newspaper chain.

I was very excited. This was my first out-of-town trip as a newspaper-man—all right, a copyboy—and Chicago promised to be a thrilling place.

I received my assignment only a few days before the convention was to begin; much too late to get a room reservation. I was told, though, that a veteran Scripps-Howard reporter named Jim G. Lucas was ill, and that I could have his room. All I had to do was show up at the Palmer House, tell the desk clerk that I was Lucas, and take his room.

This I did. I checked in at the hotel on the afternoon before the convention was to begin. The city was packed; every room in the hotel was taken. In the morning I was supposed to report to press headquarters and meet my Scripps-Howard bosses.

So I had some dinner by myself, and decided to get a good night's sleep. I went back to my room, put the "Do Not Disturb" sign on the outside door-knob, then locked the door and fastened the chain lock.

In the morning I was up early. I wanted to get started on time and im-press my bosses. I went into the bathroom, took a shower, shaved, and headed back into the room.

But it was not to be. The door had stuck in the closed position. It was jammed solid. The knob would not even turn.

This struck me as unusual—even as a naive twenty-year-old I realized that hotel doors were supposed to open when you wished them to. Still, I did not see any reason to panic. There would be some way to open the door, and I would be on my way.

Alas, no. The door was stuck and stuck good. I was in that bathroom, like it or not.

As the minutes passed, the situation became progressively less humor-ous. I tried the door, I pushed at the knob, I hit my knee against the wood. Not only did it not open—it didn't budge.

That is when the facts of the situation struck me. I was in a jam-packed hotel where all the employees, this particular week, were overworked and harried. I had the "Do Not Disturb" sign on the outside of the room's main door. That door was double-locked and chained. No one from the Scripps-Howard papers realized I had even arrived in Chicago. My family back in Columbus knew I had set out for my trip—but did not realize that Bob Greene was registered not as "Bob Greene," but as "Jim G. Lucas."

No one in Chicago would come looking for me; the hotel staff would be too busy to investigate a "Do Not Disturb" sign that remained on a door for days on end, and the Scripps-Howard people would assume that I had sim-ply never arrived. Anyone back home who phoned the Palmer House would be told that there was no Bob Greene registered.

I sat on the floor of the bathroom and reached a calm, rational conclusion: I was going to slowly starve in this bathroom. This bathroom would be where I died.

I began to scream and shout. I began to bang on the walls. My voice soon grew hoarse, but I heard only echoes. The Palmer House is built as solidly as any great old hotel can be built; no one was going to hear me.

I tried to pace, but there was nowhere to go; this was a small bathroom. I was naked, of course; for some reason my nose had started to bleed, and when I looked in the steamed-up mirror what I saw did not please me: a nude, bedraggled youth from the American heartland, with terror in his eyes and blood running down to his chin, trapped like a hamster.

An hour passed; it seemed like a day. I sat on the edge of the sink. I knew I was a goner. And what a way to die—slowly feeling the life seep out of me while, only a few feet away, in the Palmer House corridor, other men and women walked blithely to the elevators.

I began to use my only weapon—my frail but willing body. I stood at one end of the bathroom, picked up as much speed as I could in five or six feet, leaped into the air, and slammed myself against the door, like a human battering-ram. Every time I did this I picked myself up from the cold tile and made myself do it again. It hurt, and the vision in the mirror was ridiculous. But it was my sole chance.

For at least nineteen times I flew through the air and hit the floor. On what seemed to be the twentieth try, though, the miracle happened. I hit the door—and went sailing into the bedroom. I had unjammed it. I felt as if I had escaped from Alcatraz.

When I got to work, the Scripps-Howard editor asked why I was so late; I thought about explaining, but then thought better of it. "I got locked in my bathroom" didn't seem like the proper response for a fledgling tough-guy reporter. And now, fifteen years later, here I am in Grand Rapids, still gun-shy at the first hint of a sticky bathroom door. You can be in my nightmare if I can be in yours.

Party Line

On a recent Sunday afternoon, just after lunch, Vic Larson picked up the telephone in his house, which is in Park Ridge, Illinois. Larson's intention was to call a friend. But when he held the receiver to his ear, he did not hear a dial tone.

What he heard instead were voices. Maybe a dozen voices, talking intermittently, sometimes talking all at once. Larson thought about hanging up, but for some reason he did not. He stayed on the line.

It did not take him long to figure out what was going on. Because of some kind of glitch in the telephone company's computer system, people from all over the area were picking up their phones and dialing into this one circuit. They found themselves talking not with the people they had intended to call—but with this random group of strangers.

Vic Larson joined in the conversation. He is twenty-eight years old, a senior medical technologist at Lutheran General Hospital. He recognized almost immediately that most of the people on the telephone circuit were a decade or so younger than he was; older people would find themselves part of the party line and hang up, but teenagers would stay on.

Larson listened, and he talked. "Anyone from Park Ridge?" a voice would say. "Yeah, I'm from Park Ridge," another voice would answer. "Anyone go to Maine South?" "Yeah, I go to Maine South." Larson found himself smiling as he stayed on the phone.

For three hours he held the receiver to his ear. He wasn't sure quite why he was doing it, but he was having a great time. The makeup of the group on the phone kept changing; some people would hang up, but then more would get patched into the circuit. Vic Larson kept talking to the other people.

It was kind of like he was back in high school. That's what appealed to him about it; staying on the phone and talking with these strangers made absolutely no sense at all, but for a few hours on a Sunday afternoon, he wasn't sitting around his suburban house; he was acting like a high school kid.

Around 2:30 P.M.—he had been on the phone for better than two hours—some of the people on the line began shouting out their phone numbers. Larson wrote one of the numbers down on a piece of paper. The boys and girls on the line said they should all get together at four o'clock; they should meet at River Road and Higgins, over in Rosemont. One of the boys said he would be in a red Dodge van; the van would be the place where everyone should congregate. Boys' voices said they would be there; girls' voices said they would be there.

Just after 3:00 P.M. a dial tone came onto Larson's phone line. He clicked the receiver a few times, trying to get the party line back; he couldn't. Apparently whatever had gone wrong in the telephone computer had been fixed; the party line was no more.

Larson sat around the house for a while. He kept thinking about what he had just been a part of. He wasn't sure why he had liked it so much; maybe it was because, last summer, he had gone to his high school graduating class's ten-year reunion and had been so disappointed. He couldn't really put his finger on what it was about the reunion. It had just seemed to him that everyone had . . . averaged out. The jocks were in the same businesses that the nerds were. Everyone had grown up.

On the phone today, though . . . no one had grown up yet. Larson had felt, for a few strange hours, that he wasn't a working man taking his two days off between shifts; this was the *weekend,* just like in high school, and he was like everyone else—looking for action, looking for something to do.

On an impulse, he called the number he had written down—the number someone had shouted out over the party line. A young man answered; when Larson asked if the young man had been a part of the conversation, the young man acted defensive, as if he would get in trouble if he admitted it. But finally he said yes, he had been on the line; Larson asked if the gathering at River Road and Higgins was still on, and the boy said he thought it was.

Just before four o'clock, Larson decided to do it. He thought to himself: I'm going to look foolish. I'm older than these kids, and I've got a receding hairline, and I'm starting to get a spare tire around my middle. But I have to go meet them.

He got in his car. He headed toward Rosemont. His feeling of foolishness was mixed with a twinge of excitement. He wasn't sure what he would do when he got there. Maybe not even get out of the car. But he knew he had to go. He was envisioning something out of a movie. Maybe thirty people or so, all strangers just a few hours before, now having a picnic together next to the red van. He hoped he would have the nerve to join in. He promised himself: If the kids weren't old enough to drink, and they asked him to buy them beer, he wouldn't do it.

He approached the intersection. There was a gas station, and a car wash. He looked for a red van. He didn't see one.

He cruised around the streets bordering the intersection for the next twenty minutes. He looked in the parking lots. No red van. No group of people. He drove until he was certain that no one else would be coming.

So he drove back home and parked his car. He went back into his house and walked around for a while. Then he sat down in front of the television set. He waited for "60 Minutes" to start. It was Sunday night, after all.

The Most Famous Man
in the World

It was the voice that was shocking.

"How much you going to pay me?"

The voice was slurry, blurred, almost a whisper. Coming over the long-distance line, the words seemed to be filled with effort.

I said that as far as I knew, *Esquire* did not pay people who were written about in the magazine. In any event, this was a special sort of issue; fifty men and women from the past fifty years had been selected as the most influential of their time. He was one of them. The magazine wanted to include him in the issue.

"You're just using me to sell magazines," Muhammad Ali said. The voice was fading. "You just want to put me on the cover."

No, I said, Ali would not be on the cover. But he would be in very good company.

"I'm the most famous man in the world," the voice said.

I said that there would be other famous people in the issue; people, perhaps, as famous as he.

"Who?" Ali said.

I said that some of the others were John F. Kennedy, Franklin D. Roosevelt, Martin Luther King.

"They're all dead," Ali said.

I waited for American Airlines Flight 184 from Los Angeles to arrive at Chicago's O'Hare International Airport. Ali's manager, Herbert Muhammad, had told me that Ali would be on board, and then would be switching to another flight to Washington, D.C. Ali would be addressing a rally of Muslims in Washington.

Herbert Muhammad had said he could not guarantee that Ali would speak with me; it would be up to him. He said that if I wanted to take a chance I should pack a bag, buy a ticket to Washington, and be at the gate when Ali's plane arrived.

So I sat on a chair directly next to where the jetway opened into the terminal. The plane was a few minutes early. About a dozen passengers disembarked, and then came Ali. He was wearing a gray suit; he wore no belt with the pants. The suit was expensive, but his brown shoes were worn and scuffed.

I walked up to him and introduced myself. He did not look at me, but he said: "Where's Herbert?" The voice was as soft and fuzzy as it had been on the phone.

I said I didn't know; I said the Washington flight would be leaving in forty-five minutes from a gate just down the corridor.

Ali removed his suit jacket. Even though it was a frigid winter day, he was wearing a short-sleeve blue shirt. He began to walk toward the next gate.

The scene in the airport was like one of those brokerage commercials in which everyone freezes in place. I have traveled with celebrities before; I had never seen anything like this. Everyone—everyone—stopped in their tracks when they caught sight of Ali. He was considerably heavier than in the days when he had been fighting; now he had just turned forty-one, and his hair was flecked with gray. But there was no question about his recognition factor; each pair of eyes stared at him, each mouth silently formed the word "Ali."

"Champ, you're the greatest there ever was," a man cried. Ali walked past him, not looking.

"Where's Herbert?" his voice said again.

I said again that I didn't know. A woman—she was middle-aged, well dressed, not eccentric looking in the least—caught sight of Ali and dropped to her knees in front of him, as if praying. He stepped around her.

I led him to the proper gate. We took seats in the boarding area. He was carrying a briefcase; actually, it was bigger than that, more like a salesman's sample case. He opened it and took out a book called *The Spectre of Death, Including Glimpses of Life Beyond the Grave.*

He opened the book. He leaned over to me and began reading aloud from it, but so softly that I could barely make out the words:

"Life will soon come to an end, and we will part with the comforts. Whenever you see a dead man being led to the grave, remind yourself that one day you will also meet your end. . . ."

I asked him what else he had in the salesman's case. He began to rummage through it; the contents looked like something in a bag lady's sack. Pamphlets, old photographs, receipts, scraps of paper—the case was chock-full. He pulled out a copy of the Bible and opened the cover. There was an autograph I could not quite make out.

"Oral Roberts," he whispered.

A woman was standing in front of us. Her young daughter—she said that the girl's name was Clarice, and that she was six—was with her. The woman shoved the girl gently in Ali's direction. The girl kissed Ali on the cheek.

"She's not real, real friendly," the mother said. Ali, saying nothing, stood up and kissed the mother on the cheek, too.

"See," the mother said to her daughter, "now you met somebody great."

A man named Joseph Loughry, manager of international banking programs for General Electric Information Services in Rockville, Maryland, stopped in front of Ali. "I have a little guy named James," Loughry said. Ali, not looking up, not saying anything, accepted a piece of paper from Loughry, and wrote on it: "To James from Muhammad Ali."

Loughry said some words of thanks to Ali, but Ali neither spoke to him nor looked at him. When he had walked away, Ali said to me: "The least little thing we do, God marks it down. Each little atom, He sees. On the day of judgment, all the good and all the bad will be weighed. Every leaf that falls from a tree, God sees. Think of all the trees."

A man was sitting behind us, in a chair facing the other way. "Watch me do this," Ali said. He rubbed his thumb and first two fingers together in a way that resulted in a cricket sound. He turned around, placed his fingers next to the man's ear, rubbed the fingers together, and made the sound.

By the time the man turned around, Ali was looking away, as if nothing had happened. But then he did it to the man again. The man jerked his head to the side. He rubbed his ear. When he had gone back to his newspaper, Ali reached back again, made the cricket sound with his fingers again.

The man stood up and looked around. But Ali was talking to me again, as if nothing had happened. I said something about him being treated as a "super figure."

"Super nigger?" Ali said.

"Figure," I said. "Super figure."

"I know," he said. "I heard you the first time. I was just joking. I don't know about 'super figures.' But I do know that I am the most famous person in the world."

"Are you sure?" I said.

"Who's more famous?" Ali said.

"What about Reagan?" I said.

"Be serious," Ali said. "If Reagan were to go to Morocco or Persia, he could walk down the street and no one would bother him. If I go there, they have to call out soldiers to guard me. I can't go outside."

"Why?" I said.

"What do you mean 'why'?" Ali said.

"Why you?" I said. "You were a great boxer. But all of this other stuff . . . why you?"

"I don't know," he said. "I'm not smart. I'm dumber than you are. I can't spell as good as you. I can't read as good as you. But people don't care. Because that shows I'm a common person, just like they are."

At that moment a woman named Pam Lontos interrupted us. She handed Ali a business card; the card indicated that she was the president of a sales motivation firm based in Dallas, and that she made motivational speeches.

"Have you ever done any motivational talks about how to believe in yourself?" she said to Ali.

He did not speak, did not look at her.

"I'd like to talk to you about making public speeches," she said. "Are you with any booking agency? I think you'd be amazed at how much money you can make for just forty-five minutes' work. You can make just a ton of money."

Ali still did not look up at her.

"The booking agency I'm with handles David Brinkley and Norman Vincent Peale," she said. "Wouldn't you like to make a lot of money just by getting up and talking?"

"I talk for free," Ali said. "For God."

Just then Herbert Muhammad arrived. Ali's manager was a rotund man wearing a fur cap. "Ali, where have you been?" he said. "I've been looking all over the terminal for you."

The gate agent announced that the flight was boarding; Pam Lontos walked away, and we got in line to get on the plane. There was a businessman in front of us. Ali reached forward, put his fingers next to the man's ears, and made the cricket noise. When the man turned around, Ali was looking in another direction.

We sat in the first row of first class on the right side of the plane. Ali was by the window; I was on the aisle. Other passengers were filing on. Ali didn't seem to be paying any attention to them, but then he said to me, "I have to do something."

He climbed over me. He reached for a man who was heading back into the coach section. He tapped the man on the shoulder.

"*Psst*," Ali said.

The man turned around. His face froze at the sight of Ali. Ali pointed to the floor of the plane, where a ticket envelope lay.

"You dropped something," Ali said.

"Why . . . why, thank you," the man said.

But Ali had already turned away. He walked up to the cockpit. He bent over slightly and ducked inside. He tapped the pilot on the shoulder.

The pilot and the first officer and the flight engineer looked up in wonder. Ali nodded at them. Then he turned and came back toward his seat by the window. Before he could get there, though, a flight attendant who was struggling to lift a carton onto the overhead rack said to him: "Would you like to put that up there? You have more muscles than me."

Silently Ali put the box away. He slid past me. Another flight attendant leaned over and said: "Would you like a cocktail or a soft drink after we take off?"

"Milk," Ali said, so softly that the woman could not hear.

"I beg your pardon?" she said.

"Milk," Ali said, looking straight forward.

We taxied out onto the runway. As we picked up speed and then lifted off, Ali said to me: "You never know when your time to die will come."

About five minutes into the flight, he turned to me and said, "I'm not going to say anything to you for a while. It's time for me to pray." He held up his wrist; he was wearing a fancy watch with a floating arrow inside.

"This is a Muslim prayer watch," Ali said. "We have to pray at different times during the day. An alarm goes off every time I have to pray. The arrow is always pointing towards Mecca."

"Where'd you get it?" I asked.

"The king of Saudi Arabia gave it to me," he said. "He was wearing it on his arm and he took it off and gave it to me. I was wearing a Timex before." He closed his eyes, as if in prayer.

When he opened his eyes, he said to me: "My desire, my main goal now, is to prepare myself for the hereafter. That should be all men's goal."

"But what about life right now?" I said.

"This life is not real," Ali said. "I conquered the world, and it didn't give me satisfaction. The boxing, the fame, the publicity, the attention—it didn't satisfy my soul.

"Who could be more popular? Who could achieve greater heights? It's all nothing unless you go to heaven. You can have pleasure, but it means nothing unless you please God."

A man who had been sitting across the aisle unbuckled his seat belt and came over to us. He was William Doré, the president of Global Divers & Contractors, Inc., in Lafayette, Louisiana.

"Ali," he said, "I want to shake your hand. I made twelve dollars on you when you fought against Sonny Liston."

"Is that all?" Ali said.

"I only bet three," Doré said.

Ali was looking away by now.

"It's been a pleasure to watch you over the years," Doré said. "You've done a lot for the game."

When Doré had returned to his seat, Ali said to me: "Boxing was nothing. It wasn't important at all. Boxing was just meant as a way to introduce me to the world."

But he was interrupted in mid-thought. Pam Lontos, the motivational speaker, had come up from the coach section; she was kneeling in the aisle, and she was pushing a brochure at Ali. The brochure began: "The basics of broadcast selling help you find your true potential, to turn that potential into profit . . ."

A flight attendant put both hands on Lontos's shoulders. "Ma'am," the flight attendant said, "if you want an autograph, we'll be happy to bring you one back."

"But I don't want an autograph," Lontos said as she was led back into coach.

Ali was sniffling. He seemed to be getting the beginnings of a cold. He took the small pillow from behind my head, tore a piece from its paper casing, and blew his nose. In a moment he was sleeping.

We were approaching Washington. Ali tapped me on the shoulder. He pointed out the window. The lights of the monuments and government buildings were below.

"What do you think of that?" he said.

"It's pretty," I said.

"Look at all those lights on all those houses," he said. "Those are all my fans. Do you know I could walk up to any one of those houses, and knock on the door, and they would know me?

"It's a funny feeling to look down on the world and know that every person knows me. Sometimes I think about hitchhiking around the world, with no money, and just knocking on a different door every time I needed a meal or a place to sleep. I could do it."

We walked into Washington's National Airport. A group of Muslims were waiting in the concourse for Ali; they were sponsoring the rally he had come to address.

We walked toward the baggage claim area. There was an immediate difference in Ali. On the airplane, even though his voice had still been slurred and vague, his mind and his attention had appeared to be fairly sharp. In here, though—with every person calling to him and stopping to gaze at him—he seemed to put himself back into the same sort of trance he had apparently been under back at O'Hare. His eyes glazed over; he looked at no one; his face took on a blank, numb expression. As the voices spoke his name, this grew more marked.

All I could think of was: He's not punch-drunk in the traditional sense. He's not woozy from being hit too many times. Rather, he is suffering from a different kind of continual beating. For twenty years and more, he has been assaulted with constant attention, constant badgering, constant touching, every time he has ventured out in public. That is what he has had too much of—not the fists, but the nonstop contact from strangers. Clearly it had done something to him; and what it had done was most noticeable when he was in the midst of more onslaughts.

He moved through the crowds. His eyes stayed unfocused. Only once did he speak. A man stepped right in front of him. The man talked not to Ali, but me. He said: "Hey, ask Ali if he can still fly like a butterfly and sting like a bee."

"Float," Ali whispered, not looking at the man. "Float like a butter-fly."

There was screaming and shouting as Ali was led to a car waiting outside. We were driven by one of the Muslims to a Holiday Inn downtown. It was not one of Washington's fancier hotels. Ali's suite was on the far end of the seventh floor.

The manager of the hotel, Thomas Buckley, was waiting for Ali in the living room of the suite. "Is there anything I can do for you?" Buckley said.

Ali's cold seemed to be getting worse. "How do you make it hotter in here?" Ali said.

Buckley went to the thermostat and adjusted its lever. "I'm in the service business," Buckley said.

Ali's eyes still seemed to be somewhere else. His voice was barely decipherable.

"Service to others is the rent you pay for your room in heaven," he said.

In the morning, Ali sat in the hotel's coffee shop with Herbert Muhammad and several of the Washington-based Muslims. He wore the same suit he had been wearing the day before. His address at the Muslim rally was not for another day; today he had been scheduled to appear at several inner-city schools.

"Herbert," Ali said, his voice as soft as it had been the day before, "what does Allah give you credit for?"

"What do you mean?" Herbert Muhammad said.

"Well," Ali said, "if you help an old lady across the street, does Allah give you credit for that?"

"I'm sure He does," Herbert said. Ali nodded; Herbert turned to me and said, "Ali has a good heart."

Ali had ordered some wheat toast; it was slow in arriving. He reached across the table and took a piece of toast from one of the Muslims' plates. When Ali's toast came, he took the top piece and handed it back to the Muslim.

The woman at the coffee shop's cash register picked up the ringing telephone. She listened for a second, and then came over. "Mr. Ali," she said, "it's for you."

"Who is it?" Ali said, looking at his wheat toast.

"The person said he was Eddie Cantor," the woman said.

Ali stood up and walked to the phone.

"Ali," Herbert called to him before he got there, "who are you going to talk to?"

"Eddie Cantor," Ali said in an emotionless tone.

"Ali," said Herbert, laughing, "Eddie Cantor's dead. If he's calling you I want to hear about it."

Ali picked up the telephone and started talking. As he did, he used his fingers to make the cricket sound next to the ear of the cashier. She looked around, then rubbed her ear furiously. Ali did it again. She rubbed her ear again.

He came back to the table. I asked him who had been on the phone.

"Eddie Kendricks," he said. "He used to sing with the Temptations."

"How did he know to find you here?" I said.

Ali shrugged. He looked at his Muslim prayer watch, then gave me a signal to be silent. As the others in the coffee shop worked on their breakfasts, he closed his eyes and prayed.

We drove through the streets. At the Sister Clara Muhammad Elementary School, up a flight of stairs in a run-down section of town, Ali stood in front of a class of seventy-five students. He crossed his arms while the children sang to him. Once in a while he motioned back and forth with a finger, as if conducting an orchestra.

"I'm so happy to see all you children," he whispered to them. They were very young; it was obvious that they knew he was an important man, but unclear if they knew precisely who he was.

At Shaw Junior High School, in a modern, low-slung building, faculty members and students ran toward him and pawed at him as he was led to the school auditorium. Lipstick smeared his cheeks from where the female teachers had kissed him.

We were shoved back and forth in a sea of bodies as we tried to get to the stage. The school band was playing; the auditorium was alive with shrieks and shouts.

"This is the whole world," he said to me. "This is what my whole life is like."

He made it to the stage. While the band played the theme from *Rocky*, he took a blue comb from his pocket and ran it through his hair.

"Boys and girls," the principal said into the microphone, "being here on this stage with this man is probably the greatest moment of my life. And it should be the greatest moment of your life."

Ali, whose cold had seemed worse all morning, took out a handkerchief. A cook from the school's kitchen yelled, "Muhammad Ali, I love you." Ali blew his nose.

The principal called Ali to the lectern. He said that he wanted the students to ask questions of Ali, but that he wanted to ask the first one himself.

"Muhammad," he said, "would you say your toughest fight was with Frazier?"

"My toughest fight was with my first wife," Ali said.

He talked with the students for about fifteen minutes. On the way out he stopped in front of a couple of boys. Ali began to shadowbox with them, moving his feet back and forth in the famous "Ali Shuffle." The boys held up their hands and backed off. A woman teacher who had not been at the assembly caught sight of him and began to tremble. "Oh, Lord," she said, her eyes wide.

At Cardozo High School, in one of Washington's toughest neighborhoods, police officers stood guard at the front door. The students were gathered in an assembly, but had not been told that Ali was scheduled to come.

So they were listening to another speaker when, unannounced, Ali walked in a back door of the auditorium. First a few of them caught sight of him, then a few more. A buzz moved through the room as he walked, sniffling, down the aisle toward the stage.

By the time he was halfway there the chants had begun: "Ali! Ali! Ali! Ali!"

When he started to speak, though, his voice was so soft and slurred that no one could hear him. They began to call out for him to speak louder; but he didn't seem to notice, he just kept calling them "boys and girls" in that whispered tone.

He asked if there were any questions. A pretty young woman in the front row, who had been visibly puzzled by his slow, quiet, faltering speech pattern, raised her hand, and he pointed at her.

"Are you really Muhammad Ali?" she said.

Ali stared at her. "I'll see you after school," he said. "And tell your boyfriend that if he don't like it, I'll see him after school, too."

A fellow who apparently was her boyfriend stood up. "Fool," Ali said, "I'll see you after school." But beyond the first five or six rows, no one could hear him.

Ali turned to the principal and, with his fists raised, again went into the boxing routine and the Ali Shuffle. The principal shook his head and backed away.

Ali was coughing badly as we arrived at Dunbar High School. He followed wherever the local Muslims led him; in this case, into an administration office.

Ali stood there coughing and wiping his nose, waiting to be instructed where to go next. A female administrator looked up at him and said, "This man is sick. Has anyone called a doctor for him?"

But he was already being taken to a classroom. In the hallway a young mother who was visiting the school ran up to him and handed her baby to him. Ali reached out for the child, but Herbert Muhammad said, "Ali, you have too bad a cold to be handling that baby." Ali handed the infant back.

We moved through the corridors. Children moved to the doors of their classrooms. Ali leaned close to me and said, "They're all mine. This is what Allah has given me. This is heaven in the world." We moved past an elderly man who for some reason was at the school. Ali made the cricket sound with his fingers next to the old man's ear, but the man, apparently hard of hearing, did not react.

We went into the school library. Everyone in the room stopped what they were doing. One boy, though, had his back to us; he was reading at a table, and was immersed in his book.

Ali approached him. He put his hand on the boy's shoulder. The boy looked up and his mouth fell open. He started to say something, but Ali held a finger up to his own mouth, as if to silence the boy.

On the way out of the room, Ali passed by a tall, muscular young man. Ali stopped.

They looked at each other. Then Ali held up his fists. He went into the Ali Shuffle and began to leap about in front of the young man.

The young man did not back off. He held up his own fists. He did not attempt to strike Ali, but neither did he give an inch. He moved with Ali, making it clear that he was not afraid. Ali began to perspire. The young man moved closer. The young man had a confident smile on his face. He started to push Ali, establishing command of the situation.

No one in the room stirred. Ali coughed. The young man brought his punches closer and closer to Ali's face. Their arms began to make contact. The sound of their forearms slapping against each other echoed off the walls, and suddenly there was a clattering sound, and everything stopped.

There, on the yellow carpeting, was Ali's Muslim prayer watch. Ali slowly leaned over. He picked up the watch and fastened it back onto his wrist.

"Come on, Ali," Herbert Muhammad said. "We're running late." They moved toward the door of the school library. Ali's eyes met the eyes of the tall young man for just a moment. Then they clouded over, and once again he seemed to be somewhere else.

Born Too Late

It had been a lousy week all around, but then I met Mary Jackson and things immediately got better.

Mary Jackson—she has the perfect American name, right?—is sixteen. She wanted to talk to me for a very specific reason.

"You were around when the Beatles were around," she said. "I want to know what it was really like."

I thought she was kidding, but she soon made it clear that she wasn't.

"I wish I had been a kid when you were a kid," she said. "No one my age understands how much I love the Beatles."

She said that any time she sees pictures and movies of the Beatles, or hears their music, her reaction is the same.

"Rebellious, free-spirited, happy, confused," she said. "I just wish I lived during a time when everyone was walking around like that all the time."

She was wearing a Beatles T-shirt with a Beatles button on it. She reached into her purse and pulled out her Beatles wallet and her Beatles key chain.

"I look like any girl my age and I talk like any girl my age," she said. "But I'm different because of the Beatles. If you believe in the Beatles, you're different."

She said that she worked part time selling jeans at a Gap store.

"These girls come in wearing AC/DC T-shirts," she said. "I hate the music they listen to. AC/DC, Rush . . . those guys sing songs about 'TNT' and 'Dirty Deeds Done Dirt Cheap.' Real deep, huh?

"And if I hear Michael Jackson sing 'Billie Jean' or 'Beat It' one more time, I think I'm going to throw up. If you listen to the Beatles, you get a feeling about life that other people don't have. Even on a song like 'Long Tall Sally,' you can hear them beating it out and you can imagine them smiling and moving around. . . .

"Other kids my age listen to the Beatles once in a while and they dig 'em, but not to the extreme like I do. I'll get up at three o'clock in the morning to see *Yellow Submarine* on TV, and when the movie's over I'll get dressed and go right to school."

She said one of the things she feels especially bad about is her year of birth, which was 1967.

"I've thought about it, and I wish I had been born in 1952," she said. "That way, in 1964, when the Beatles came over to America, I would have been twelve, and I would have been fourteen in 1966, and they still would have been touring."

As it is, she said, she was in the sixth grade when she realized she loved the Beatles.

"There was this physical attraction to doe-eyed, baby-faced Paul McCartney," she said.

Even now, she feels that way.

"Paul makes me melt," she said. "I go to Beatlefest every year, and I see guys who look like Paul, and even that makes me start shakin'."

If she is totally infatuated with McCartney, she feels even more deeply about the late John Lennon.

"Paul McCartney is the perfect male image," she said. "But John Lennon is my hero.

"People say that John was 'slain,' but I never use that word, because John was not defeated.

"All the things the Beatles make me feel, John makes me feel the strongest. If I'm feeling real nervous I'll go into my room and turn up 'Helter Skelter' as loud as I can, and even if my mom is mad at me for doing it I think, 'Yeah, you don't bug me, Mom,' because I'm thinking about John Lennon."

She said that the Beatles are the most important thing in her life.

"The Beatles have been the answer to every misery I have had in my teenage years," she said. "Even in the eighth grade, I'd sit in school during the last hour of the day and think about what Beatles albums I'd play when I got home.

"People say the Beatles hit it big because they came along right after Kennedy died. People say that youth lost a hero in Kennedy, and the Beatles took his place. But that can't be the reason, because I wasn't around when Kennedy died, and I still love the Beatles."

She said she baby-sits for the children of parents in their thirties, and that she envies the parents.

"Right now, nothing's going on in the world," she said. "But when those people were teenagers, they could go to the record store and say, 'When's the new Beatles album coming in?' Or they could drive around and change all the stations on the car radio, trying to find Beatles songs."

Her pleasures, she said, are simple.

"After school I'll go to the 7-Eleven, buy a bag of Taco Doritos and two liters of Pepsi, go home, put on my headphones, play 'A Day in the Life,' turn off my mind and relax and float downstream."

She is ready for the new school year to begin.

"Last year I dated a football player," she said. "But this year I know that God will bring me a Paul McCartney look-alike."

Johnny Appleseed in the Eighties

Johnny Appleseed roamed the countryside in the early 1800s. Some people think Johnny Appleseed was a myth, but he wasn't. His real name was John Chapman; he was born in Massachusetts in 1774, and he devoted his life to sowing seeds so that there would be fruit for the pioneers as they headed west.

He often traveled barefoot, and sometimes he wore a coffee sack for clothing. He planted his seeds in Pennsylvania, Ohio, and Indiana. He was extremely kind to animals, sometimes purchasing sick livestock from farmers and then nurturing them back to health.

Because of this, the story of Johnny Appleseed was passed down from generation to generation; he became a genuine American folk hero, and he is remembered fondly after all these many years.

But you have to wonder: What would the story of Johnny Appleseed have been like if he had lived in the 1980s?

He might start off in relative anonymity, but a reporter from the "P.M.

Magazine" television show in Pittsburgh would hear about him by the time he reached the western border of Pennsylvania. The reporter would video-tape a cute feature on Appleseed, including cutaway shots of the reporter, in his blazer and gray pants, strolling and talking to Appleseed, in his cof-fee sack, as they walked down the road.

Soon enough Charles Kuralt would pick up on the story; Appleseed would appear on the entire CBS network, and by the next day he would be the talk of every office lunchroom in the country.

Within a week, *USA Today* would give Appleseed its ultimate accolade—a small color picture on top of Page One with a teaser headline referring to a story about him in the Life section.

Phil Donahue would invite Appleseed on his show as a representative of a coming trend—men who dress in coffee sacks and walk barefoot drop-ping seeds on the ground.

By the end of the first month, Appleseed would sign on with the Inter-national Creative Management talent agency in New York. From that point on, all decisions about his career would go through the agency. The first thing that the agents would demand is that anyone wishing to deal with Appleseed would have to fly him first class and provide him with a chauf-feured limousine for ground transportation.

After the initial flurry of stories in the press, Appleseed's new managers would hire the bicoastal Rogers and Cowan public relations agency to handle all future media inquiries. Reporters wishing to speak with Appleseed would now have to get prepared statements from his publicist.

Appleseed would sign a book contract to tell the story of his life. The book would be ghostwritten by a former newspaperman, who would be paid a straight fee; all royalties would go directly to Appleseed.

When the book was in galley proofs, it would be sold to NBC for a miniseries.

Appleseed's managers would license designer versions of his coffee-sack clothing, complete with his signature across the front. They would fret over a way to license the rights to his bare feet, but would give up in frustration.

A chain of "Johnny's Apple Shops" would be franchised in malls nation-wide. The stores would sell apples, apple pies, apple turnovers, apple candy, apple cake, etc. The visual trademark would be an apple tree planted next to the front door of each store; the apple trees would be made out of plas-tic, for longer wear. Appleseed himself, accompanied by managers, publi-cists, and security guards, would make a national promotional tour, visiting the stores and signing autographs. This effort would be buttressed by a series of television commercials, in which Appleseed would smile and say, "Hi! I'm Johnny Appleseed, and I'd like to invite you to my Apple Shops. . . ."

Appleseed would retain a team of investment counselors to advise him on his growing wealth. He would move to Beverly Hills, California, and buy a house with a pool, a sauna, a hot tub, a Jacuzzi, and a tennis court. He would be spotted at a disco in the company of Cathy Lee Crosby; within a week their picture would appear on the "Star Tracks" page of *People* magazine.

Appleseed would appear as the featured guest on "Lifestyles of the Rich and Famous," offering host Robin Leach a tour of his home, and granting an interview about the pleasures and headaches of being a worldwide celebrity.

In the fall, Westinghouse Broadcasting would offer Appleseed his own talk show. The company would cite surveys showing that Appleseed was the most trustworthy celebrity in the country, in the eyes of the American people. For his hosting duties Appleseed would give up the coffee sack, instead wearing clothes made especially for him by Ralph Lauren. On the wall directly behind the talk-show chairs, though, a logo showing Appleseed in his old coffee-sack garb would be prominently displayed, to act as a nostalgic reminder for viewers.

The book, the miniseries, the designer coffee sacks, the Johnny's Apple Shops, and the talk show would be enormous hits for two years.

In the third year, all of them would begin to decline in popularity.

By the fifth year the book would be out of print, the miniseries would be off the air, the designer coffee sacks would be out of production, the Johnny's Apple Shops would be in Chapter 11 bankruptcy, and the talk show would be canceled.

In the sixth year Johnny Appleseed would be arrested for possession of cocaine. His picture would appear in the paper; his head would be hanging, his posture would be slumped. His managers would issue a statement saying that he was "struggling with personal problems." A judge would release him on probation, with the stipulation that he seek counseling.

Cut

I remember vividly the last time I cried. I was twelve years old, in the seventh grade, and I had tried out for the junior high school basketball team. I walked into the gymnasium; there was a piece of paper tacked to the bulletin board.

It was a cut list. The seventh-grade coach had put it up on the board. The boys whose names were on the list were still on the team; they were welcome to keep coming to practices. The boys whose names were not on the list had been cut; their presence was no longer desired. My name was not on the list.

I had not known the cut was coming that day. I stood and I stared at the list. The coach had not composed it with a great deal of subtlety; the names of the very best athletes were at the top of the sheet of paper, and the other members of the squad were listed in what appeared to be a descending order of talent. I kept looking at the bottom of the list, hoping against hope that my name would miraculously appear there if I looked hard enough.

I held myself together as I walked out of the gym and out of the school, but when I got home I began to sob. I couldn't stop. For the first time in my life, I had been told officially that I wasn't good enough. Athletics meant everything to boys that age; if you were on the team, even as a substitute, it put you in the desirable group. If you weren't on the team, you might as well not be alive.

I had tried desperately in practice, but the coach never seemed to notice. It didn't matter how hard I was willing to work; he didn't want me there. I knew that when I went to school the next morning I would have to face the boys who had not been cut—the boys whose names were on the list, who were still on the team, who had been judged worthy while I had been judged unworthy.

All these years later, I remember it as if I were still standing right there in the gym. And a curious thing has happened: in traveling around the country, I have found that an inordinately large proportion of successful men share that same memory—the memory of being cut from a sports team as a boy.

I don't know how the mind works in matters like this; I don't know what went on in my head following that day when I was cut. But I know that my ambition has been enormous ever since then; I know that for all of my life since that day, I have done more work than I had to be doing, taken more assignments than I had to be taking, put in more hours than I had to be spending. I don't know if all of that came from a determination never to allow myself to be cut again—never to allow someone to tell me that I'm not good enough again—but I know it's there. And apparently it's there in a lot of other men, too.

Bob Graham, thirty-six, is a partner with the Jenner & Block law firm in Chicago. "When I was sixteen, baseball was my whole life," he said. "I had gone to a relatively small high school, and I had been on the team. But then my family moved, and I was going to a much bigger high school. All during the winter months I told everyone that I was a ballplayer. When spring came, of course I went out for the team.

"The cut list went up. I did not make the team. Reading that cut list is one of the clearest things I have in my memory. I wanted not to believe it, but there it was.

"I went home and told my father about it. He suggested that maybe I should talk to the coach. So I did. I pleaded to be put back on the team. He said there was nothing he could do; he said he didn't have enough room.

"I know for a fact that it altered my perception of myself. My view of myself was knocked down; my self-esteem was lowered. I felt so embarrassed; my whole life up to that point had revolved around sports, and particularly around playing baseball. That was the group I wanted to be in—the guys on the baseball team. And I was told that I wasn't good enough to be one of them.

"I know now that it changed me. I found out, even though I couldn't articulate it at the time, that there would be times in my life when certain people would be in a position to say 'You're not good enough' to me. I did not want that to happen ever again.

"It seems obvious to me now that being cut was what started me in determining that my success would always be based on my own abilities, and not on someone else's perceptions. Since then I've always been something of an overachiever; when I came to the law firm I was very aggressive in trying to run my own cases right away, to be the lead lawyer in the cases with which I was involved. I made partner at thirty-one; I never wanted to be left behind.

"Looking back, maybe it shouldn't have been that important. It was only baseball. You pass that by. Here I am. That coach is probably still there, still a high school baseball coach, still cutting boys off the baseball team every year. I wonder how many hundreds of boys he's cut in his life?"

Maurice McGrath is senior vice-president of Genstar Mortgage Corporation, a mortgage banking firm in Glendale, California. "I'm forty-seven years old, and I was fourteen when it happened to me, and I still feel something when I think about it," he said.

"I was in the eighth grade. I went to St. Philip's School in Pasadena. I went out for the baseball team, and one day at practice the coach came over to me. He was an Occidental College student who had been hired as the eighth-grade coach.

"He said, 'You're no good.' Those were his words. I asked him why he was saying that. He said, 'You can't hit the ball. I don't want you here.' I didn't know what to do, so I went over and sat off to the side, watching the others practice. The coach said I should leave the practice field. He said that I wasn't on the team, and that I didn't belong there anymore.

"I was outwardly stoic about it. I didn't want anyone to see how I felt. I didn't want to show that it hurt. But oh, did it hurt. All my friends played baseball after school every day. My best friend was the pitcher on the team. After I got whittled down by the coach, I would hear the other boys talking in class about what they were going to do at practice after school. I knew that I'd just have to go home.

"I guess you make your mind up never to allow yourself to be hurt like that again. In some way I must have been saying to myself, 'I'll play the game better.' Not the sports game, but anything I tried. I must have been saying, 'If I have to, I'll sit on the bench, but I'll be part of the team.'

"I try to make my own kids believe that, too. I try to tell them that they should show that they're a little bit better than the rest. I tell them to think of themselves as better. Who cares what anyone else thinks? You know, I can almost hear that coach saying the words. 'You're no good.'"

Author Malcolm MacPherson (*The Blood of His Servants*), forty, lives in New York. "It happened to me in the ninth grade, at the Yalesville School in Yalesville, Connecticut," he said. "Both of my parents had just been killed in a car crash, and as you can imagine, it was a very difficult time in my life. I went out for the baseball team, and I did pretty well in practice.

"But in the first game I clutched. I was playing second base; the batter hit a popup, and I moved back to catch it. I can see it now. I felt dizzy as I looked up at the ball. It was like I was moving in slow motion, but the ball was going at regular speed. I couldn't get out of the way of my own feet. The ball dropped to the ground. I didn't catch it.

"The next day at practice, the coach read off the lineup. I wasn't on it. I was off the squad.

"I remember what I did: I walked. It was a cold spring afternoon, and the ground was wet, and I just walked. I was living with an aunt and uncle, and I didn't want to go home. I just wanted to walk forever.

"It drove my opinion of myself right into a tunnel. Right into a cave. And when I came out of that cave, something inside of me wanted to make sure in one manner or another that I would never again be told I wasn't good enough.

"I will confess that my ambition, to this day, is out of control. It's like a fire. I think the fire would have pretty much stayed in control if I hadn't been cut from that team. But that got it going. You don't slice ambition two ways; it's either there or it isn't. Those of us who went through something like that always know that we have to catch the ball. We'd rather die than have the ball fall at our feet.

"Once that fire is started in us, it never gets extinguished, until we die or have heart attacks or something. Sometimes I wonder about the home-run hitters; the guys who never even had to worry about being cut. They may have gotten the applause and the attention back then, but I wonder if they ever got the fire. I doubt it. I think maybe you have to get kicked in the teeth to get the fire started.

"You can tell the effect of something like that by examining the trail you've left in your life, and tracing it backward. It's almost like being a junkie with a need for success. You get attention and applause and you like it, but you never quite trust it. Because you know that back then you were good enough if only they would have given you a chance. You don't trust what you achieve, because you're afraid that someone will take it away from you. You know that it can happen; it already did.

"So you try to show people how good you are. Maybe you don't go out and become Dan Rather; maybe you just end up owning the Pontiac dealership in your town. But it's your dealership, and you're the top man, and every day you're showing people that you're good enough."

Dan Rather, fifty-two, is anchor of the "CBS Evening News." "When I was thirteen, I had rheumatic fever," he said. "I became extremely skinny and extremely weak, but I still went out for the seventh-grade baseball team at Alexander Hamilton Junior High School in Houston.

"The school was small enough that there was no cut as such; you were supposed to figure out that you weren't good enough, and quit. Game after game I sat at the end of the bench, hoping that maybe this was the time I would get in. The coach never even looked at me; I might as well have been invisible.

"I told my mother about it. Her advice was not to quit. So I went to practice every day, and I tried to do well so that the coach would be impressed. He never even knew I was there. At home in my room I would fantasize that there was a big game, and the three guys in front of me would all get hurt, and the coach would turn to me and put me in, and I would make the winning hit. But then there'd be another game, and the late innings would come, and if we were way ahead I'd keep hoping that this was the game when the coach would put me in. He never did.

"When you're that age, you're looking for someone to tell you you're okay. Your sense of self-esteem is just being formed. And what that experience that baseball season did was make me think that perhaps I wasn't okay.

"In the last game of the season something terrible happened. It was the last of the ninth inning, there were two outs, and there were two strikes on the batter. And the coach turned to me and told me to go out to right field.

"It was a totally humiliating thing for him to do. For him to put me in for one pitch, the last pitch of the season, in front of all the other guys on the team . . . I stood out there for that one pitch, and I just wanted to sink into the ground and disappear. Looking back on it, it was an extremely unkind thing for him to have done. That was nearly forty years ago, and I don't know why the memory should be so vivid now; I've never known if the coach was purposely making fun of me—and if he was, why a grown man would do that to a thirteen-year-old boy.

"I'm not a psychologist. I don't know if a man can point to one event in his life and say that that's the thing that made him the way he is. But when you're that age, and you're searching for your own identity, and all you want is to be told that you're all right . . . I wish I understood it better, but I know the feeling is still there."

The Mugging of
Howdy Doody

It's not the major headline stories that tell us the most about what is happening to our world; sometimes the smaller news items speak much more eloquently of what is going on.

And so it is that the most telling and symbolic story of the year is the mugging of Howdy Doody.

If you saw the story at all, it was probably in one of those "people" columns that boil news of "personalities" down to one paragraph. The news was that the original Howdy Doody marionette had been assaulted and damaged in a New York suburb.

It seemed to me that there was more there than could be reported in a brief item. So I got in touch with Howdy Doody's owner—E. Roger Muir, the former executive producer of the old Howdy Doody television show.

"It happened, all right," Muir said. "It's enough to make you sick."

Muir oversaw the production of "The Howdy Doody Show" during its legendary years on NBC television from 1947 to 1960. During those years, Howdy—the grinning, freckle-faced marionette—became beloved to a generation of American children, and an unwitting symbol of what this country was like during simpler and perhaps happier times.

Muir now is a partner in a video production firm in Larchmont, N.Y. When he came to work one morning, he saw immediately that burglars had broken into his offices.

"Whoever did it completely ransacked the place," he said. "They came in during the night, and they uprooted potted plants, they destroyed three television sets, they threw everything around."

On the floor, amid the debris, Muir found Howdy Doody.

"They had assaulted him and torn him apart," Muir said. "Howdy's head was in one room. They had ripped his right arm off, and that was in another room. And the rest of his body was thrown in a third room. His clothes were all torn."

Muir picked up Howdy Doody's smiling head, and all he could think about was how twisted things had become in our modern society. He knew that the crime rate was high; he even knew that some criminals routinely vandalized and destroyed the homes and offices that they burglarized. But casually destroying Howdy Doody?

"Howdy had been displayed in a trophy case in my office," Muir said. "He was one of the three original Howdys that still remain. The children who watched the show thought there was only one, but we used three Howdys for different purposes at different times.

"Seeing Howdy torn into pieces . . . it made me just sick to my stomach. He had this big gash on his face; it looked like they had stomped on him. I don't know why it affected me so strongly, but it did. There was just no reason for anyone to do this.

"Some witnesses saw three men running away from the office. They appeared to be between eighteen and twenty-two; they probably didn't even know who Howdy Doody was. In a way, that's fortunate; if they had known how valuable Howdy was, they would have taken him instead of ripping him apart, and then we'd never have seen him again."

One of the first things that Muir did after notifying the police was to call Buffalo Bob Smith, the genial human host who appeared on TV with Howdy for all those years.

"Buffalo Bob was just sick about it, too," Muir said. "He was almost in a state of shock. He kept saying, 'Why would anyone do such a thing?'"

Muir got in touch with Pady Blackwood, a New York puppet master who specializes in the repair of dolls and marionettes. Blackwood said he would attempt to repair Howdy.

"When Howdy was brought to me, I couldn't believe what I was seeing," Blackwood said. "It was as if he was the victim of an ax-murderer.

"They brought me a suitcase full of parts, basically. Luckily, Howdy's body is made of wood, so it was pretty sturdy. But his face is more brittle; there was a lot of damage."

Blackwood worked for more than a week putting Howdy back together. "I felt very emotional when I was doing it," he said. "I grew up in Kansas City; our family didn't have a television in the late Forties and early Fifties, and I would go down to the local furniture store after school every day. There was a TV set there, and I would watch 'Howdy Doody.' It was

the thing that first got me interested in puppets and marionettes. And now
. . . this."

The surgery was a qualified success. Howdy's arm was sewn back on, and
so was his head. There are suture marks where the neck and head are joined,
but Howdy's famous bandanna covers the scars.

E. Roger Muir has tightened security precautions in his offices; there
are new locks, and Howdy has been stored in a new case. But Muir realizes that all the precautions in the world can't change the basic message of
what has happened.

"We now live in a world where someone would do something like this to
Howdy Doody," he said. "There's no getting around that."

All Stars

One of the great side benefits of the reporting business is
that you get to meet people you'd otherwise never have a chance to be near.
But you get spoiled; you meet those folks on such a regular basis that before
long they become just sources of quotes for you—you lose sight of the fact
that most people would kill for the opportunity to spend time with them.

It's too bad. I've had a chance to sit down with a couple of men who
were President of the United States, and I met Prince Charles once; after
each of those encounters I felt like kicking myself for not feeling more like
a little kid about it.

Last week, though, I felt like a little kid.

As part of the festivities surrounding the All-Star game, dozens of members of baseball's Hall of Fame came to Chicago for an old-timers' game
the day before the main event. I went out to Comiskey Park; by the time I
got home I had stars in my eyes, and I was calling friends all over the country
to tell them what had happened.

It was simple; in the space of one hour, I talked with Joe DiMaggio,
Stan Musial, Willie Mays, Duke Snider, Roger Maris, Bob Feller, Bobby
Thomson, and Pee Wee Reese.

I suppose I had forgotten how much I had idolized them. We go nuts over baseball stars when we are little boys; by the time we are teenagers our allegiance has switched to other folks—rock stars and the like—and we forget how much the baseball players meant to us. When I say "we" and "us," I'm referring to my own generation; I really don't know if little boys today feel quite the same way about the millionaire ballplayers with agents and financial advisers as we did about the men whose faces appeared on our Topps baseball cards.

That's what it was like last week—like being a wide-eyed boy again, collecting baseball cards that had suddenly, in a fantasy, come true, sprung to life. It was sort of like having someone say, "Come with me," and then walking with that person into a private room and finding out that all of the Beatles were waiting to say hello.

Except this was even better. Of all the good things that have happened to me, I don't think any will surpass the moment last week when I realized Duke Snider was being nice to me.

Duke Snider. I had sat in my bedroom as an eight-year-old, writing letters to him in care of the Dodgers in far-off Brooklyn, begging for an autographed picture. He was more glamorous to me than any movie star— because he wasn't acting; he was a real-life hero whose luster didn't fade when the film ended. If someone had told me back then that one day Duke Snider would actually sit down and speak with me as if we both lived in the same universe, I would have thought that person was engaging in a cruel taunt.

And yet here we were, on a summer afternoon in the 1980s, and as the other old-timers took batting practice and Duke Snider and I sat watching, he gently tried to give me some perspective on what was real and what was myth.

"I went to the car wash last year," Snider said. I had just blathered some embarrassing version of the emotions contained two paragraphs above this one.

"I went to the car wash last year," Snider said. "And when my car came out, the fellow said that I owed him $2.50. And I said, 'I thought it cost $4.' And the fellow said, 'Yes, sir, but we give a discount to senior citizens.'"

I knew the anecdote wasn't an apocryphal one; Snider isn't the firm-jawed stud of those 1955 baseball cards now, he is a white-haired man who might, indeed, pass you unnoticed on the street. But the great thing about this gathering was that it didn't matter; it was so marvelous to be able to spend time with these men who had meant so much to so many of us that nothing else counted.

So Pee Wee Reese told me that his leg was bad, and that in the old-timers' dressing room Snider and Willie Mays had helped him put his uniform on. The Comiskey Park organist played "When I'm Sixty-four" as we talked, and when I told Reese the name of the song, he said, "Do they have one called 'When I'm Sixty-five'?"—and said that he would, indeed, turn sixty-five later this year.

Joe DiMaggio said that he wants to look the truth "right in the eye—I am an old-timer now, and I know it." Roger Maris said that although he remains unhappy that he never got what he felt was the proper recognition for hitting sixty-one home runs in a single season and breaking Babe Ruth's record, "baseball basically meant everything to me"—and that holding a bat during warm-ups on this day, he had been surprised and a little saddened to realize how awkward it felt. Willie Mays was unexpectedly unpleasant—combative and defensive and sensitive to slights that just weren't there. But even that was interesting; who ever thought that the chance would come to find out anything at all about Willie Mays, except batting averages and historical anecdotes?

And it was fine to discover that some legends and stereotypes are based on truth. At the beginning of this day, while the rest of the old-timers waited leisurely in the locker room, getting dressed and renewing old friendships, one man hurried onto the field alone and, in full uniform, paced back and forth, impatiently waiting for the others to come out and play baseball with him. Ernie Banks.

When I headed home from Comiskey Park, I realized that those men could never understand what meeting them had meant. I am one of millions of American males who grew up almost dizzy with reverence for them. We were the dreamers; they were the dreams. And it was gloriously good news on a hot July afternoon to discover that, after all these years, the dreams are still there.

Bathroom Humor

The village of Schaumburg, Illinois, is buzzing over a controversy involving bathroom humor.

At the Hyatt Regency Woodfield hotel, there is a disco called the Playground. Several weeks ago, workmen installed video screens above each of the three urinals in the Playground's men's room.

When a man walks up to a urinal, he trips an electronic eye that causes a film to be projected onto the video screen above that urinal. The films feature attractive, scantily clad young women saying naughty things.

"The idea was for it to be funny," said Larry Sode, technical director for the Playground. "It was supposed to make people laugh; it was supposed to be one more reason for them to come to the Playground."

Each film lasts between ten and thirty seconds. The women are dressed in negligees, in bikinis, in low-cut gowns, in leotards. The screens are positioned so that the women seem to be looking into the eyes of the men in front of them.

There are about twenty-five different things they say. Some of the milder samples:

"Aren't you the Lincoln Park flasher?"

"Nice try."

"Do you know what a woman says when she's sexually satisfied? [Pause] I didn't think so."

Larry Sode said that response from the Playground's customers has been overwhelmingly enthusiastic.

"They love it," he said. "Everyone out here is talking about it. People are lined up trying to get into the men's room. We haven't advertised it or anything, but people are coming to the Playground just to go to the men's room.

"We've even caught women trying to sneak in so they can see the films."

Unfortunately, some other Schaumburg residents have also dropped by to see the films—Mayor Herb Aigner and police officers dispatched by him. They are not amused.

"Look, I like a good joke as well as anyone else," Mayor Aigner said. "But a lot of this stuff isn't funny. It's just dirty.

"Yes, I paid an inspection call on the Playground's men's room last week. Frankly, I find the whole thing sleazy. A lot of this isn't good-natured humor; it's sleazy humor. I asked our police chief to have a look, too.

"I must confess, I do not find this kind of thing in keeping with the image of a Hyatt hotel. We look for certain institutions to maintain a level of taste above the average, and Hyatt hotels are one of those institutions.

"We in Schaumburg have worked very hard to keep certain elements out of our village. You won't find pinball machines or video parlors out here. You won't find adult bookstores out here. And now we have the Playground doing this kind of thing. I find it upsetting."

The mayor said that he has determined there is nothing legally he can do to make the Playground stop featuring the risqué jokes on the video screens above the urinals.

"It's not a case of forcing them to stop," he said. "There's nothing we can do. This is America, and in America we have something called freedom of speech. There is no Schaumburg ordinance they are violating.

"But are you asking me if I would prefer that they took those screens down? Yes, I would. I wish they would get the message and stop doing it. I would feel better if those screens weren't there.

"It lowers the prestige of the hotel, and more importantly, it lowers the prestige of Schaumburg. If a man goes into the men's room and sees a woman on a screen above the urinal saying sleazy things, what does he do next? Maybe he goes back out into the bar and starts looking around to see if he can find any hookers."

At the Hyatt Regency Woodfield, general manager Helmut Brenzinger said the purpose of the video screens was not to offend anyone.

"There is no nudity on the part of the women in the films," he said. "And there is no profanity. It is more double meanings, not profane words.

"I was born in Germany, so I probably do not understand all of the phrases. But the customers seem to like it very much. They realize it is strictly fun. Maybe they're a little shocked at first, but they end up realizing it is all in good fun."

Brenzinger said he did not mind if the Village of Schaumburg wanted to keep sending police officers to monitor the video screens.

"I have no problem with that," he said. "I like having the police here. It helps to keep the rowdies out.

"I know that Schaumburg is a very conservative city; the city administration is very strict about what can happen here and what cannot happen. Believe me, I support them one hundred percent. I want what they want. But this is just good fun."

In the meantime, Larry Sode—as technical director of the disco—is responsible for the maintenance and operation of the video screens in the bathroom. He has no interest in the political ramifications of the controversy.

"That's between the village and the hotel," he said. "I just happen to be very proud of the job we've done in setting this up. Do you realize that we have a JBL speaker over each urinal? When the women on the films speak, the sound quality is excellent. This is a very high-class operation."

A Testing Time

For a couple of years, I had been having a nagging feeling. The feeling was that I was dumber than I had been in high school.

This feeling hit me at all kinds of times, but usually when I was trying to add up a column of figures without using a calculator, or attempting to do some elementary long division or multiplication in my head. Something had definitely happened to me, and I suspected that it had happened to a lot of men and women like me who had been out of the high school classroom for twenty years. The mental exercises that used to be so simple now loomed as almost impossible; there were plenty of social moves that I had learned in the real world, but a lot of cerebral skills that I had owned as a high school junior seemed to have gone with the wind.

Rather than brood on this, I decided to do the only logical thing:

I would take the SATs again.

The SATs—it stands for Scholastic Aptitude Test, but the shortened version is always used in the plural—are administered by the Educational Testing Service and, of course, are the most intimidating thing that happens to a boy or girl during his or her high school career. The SATs measure verbal and mathematical abilities; the results of the tests, figured against a scale of eight hundred points, are sent to university admissions offices, and play a significant role in determining whether a high school student will get into a particular college.

I was a pretty smart kid in high school; I did well on my SATs, scoring a 724 on the verbal part and a 706 on the math part. That, though, was in 1964; as I have mentioned, I was convinced that I had become considerably dumber during the ensuing years.

So I decided that I would be one of the 1.6 million people a year—virtually all of them high school juniors and seniors—to take the SATs. I had only vague memories of the test; the memories involved pain, clocks, and lead-point pencils. I was not especially looking forward to going through with it again, but it seemed like something that had to be done.

I applied for the SATs. It turned out that there wasn't any age limit; as long as I sent in my eleven dollars, I could take the test.

I filled out my application form. There were spaces to list the colleges to which I wished my test results sent. I thought about it for a minute, then wrote in Harvard, Princeton, Yale, and Ohio State.

I received my admission ticket in the mail, along with an orientation booklet. The ticket informed me that I would be taking the test at Evanston Township High School in Evanston, Illinois, on a Saturday morning.

The orientation booklet was sixty-two pages long, and I didn't open it until the night before the test. Just trying to read it made me dizzy. I got only to page 6; there was a section headed "The Day Before the Tests," and it said, "You'll accomplish little by worrying about the next day. Read a book, watch a television program you enjoy, or do anything you find relaxing."

I took the booklet to a bar that I like and laid it on the wood surface in front of me. I halfheartedly attempted to read the section called "Test-Taking Tips," but the music and the conversation around me were too loud and soon enough I gave up.

Shortly after 8:00 on a crisp Saturday morning, I walked into the lobby of Evanston Township High School. There is something about a high school on a Saturday morning that feels the same after all these years. I went to the school office and was directed to a study hall on the first floor. About twenty boys and girls were already there, lined up. They were not being allowed inside yet. I joined the line.

The two girls in front of me were showing each other snapshots from the previous spring's prom. One of the girls displayed her two pencils—the orientation booklet had instructed each of us to bring "Two No. 2 pencils with erasers." The girl said, "My mother is so bogus. She told me, 'You'd better bring more than two. What if one of them breaks?' I said, 'Mom, did you ever hear of pencil sharpeners?'"

I sheepishly looked down at the front pocket of my shirt, where I had stashed six sharpened pencils, just in case five of them broke.

We were allowed into the room. There were three adult proctors there, all women. One of them sat at a desk and made each of us present ID cards with photos on them; the cards had to verify that we were the same people whose names were on our admission tickets. This was new; I did not recall having to do it twenty years ago. Apparently it was to discourage students from taking the tests for their friends.

We were instructed to sit in vertical rows, leaving an empty row between each row of us. I found a seat; it was one of those desks that are attached to the chair, and as I slipped into it my mind flooded with high school memories.

I looked around the room. There were approximately fifty-five of us taking the test. I had expected to be the object of curiosity—after all, these kids were seventeen, and I was thirty-seven—but no one was paying a bit of attention to me. These boys and girls were scared to death. I could have been Kareem Abdul-Jabbar and they wouldn't have noticed.

The chief proctor said something else that was new: "Calculators or wristwatches with calculator functions may not be used."

Then, reading from a manual, she said a series of sentences that began with the phrase "Do not worry": "Do not worry if you do not complete a section by the end of the allotted time." "Do not worry if you do not know the answer to every question."

Ha. Easy for her to say.

Another one of the proctors began handing out the answer forms. I looked around the room.

There was total silence. Whatever wise-guy poses these students might affect during the school week were gone; these were the SATs that were heading their way, and nothing in the world was more serious than that.

The boy sitting closest to me had on a white jersey that said LAS VEGAS on the front and featured colorful drawings of playing cards and dice on the back. Another boy, sitting a couple of aisles to my left, made a steering-wheel motion to a friend of his over by the window; the friend nodded yes. He had driven to school; he would give the other boy a ride home.

The tests were handed to us. They were in booklet form. The chief proctor said that there were six sections; we were to have thirty minutes to complete each of them. If we completed a section early, we were to sit quietly at our desks with the test booklets closed.

It was just after 9:00. The proctor looked at her watch. Apparently she was waiting for the second hand to hit the twelve. After what seemed to be an interminable wait, she said:

"You may begin."

The covers of fifty-five booklets were pulled open; fifty-five of us leaned over our answer sheets.

It became evident right away that, for me, the verbal part was going to be pretty easy. I had assumed that I would have to identify sentence structures that I had long forgotten the terms for; but the test wasn't like that at all. Most of the verbal questions were commonsense things; I have been writing every day for a lot of years now, talking to copy editors as a matter of course, and I wasn't having any problems with the verbal stuff.

The math was another story. With the math, much of the time I didn't even understand the questions. There was a long line drawn; the farthest point to the left was marked P, the midpoint was marked Q, the farthest point to the right was marked R. The space between P and Q was marked $x + y$. The space between Q and R was marked $2x - y$. The question was, "Segment PR is divided into two segments with lengths as shown above. If Q is the midpoint of PR, which of the following statements must be true?" We were asked to choose any one of five: "$x = 0$," "$x = \frac{1}{2}y$," "$x = \frac{2}{3}y$," "$x = y$," "$x = 2y$."

I developed a terrible headache doing the math questions. There was some pretty simple stuff that you could figure out using basic logic; but a lot of it was truly impossible for me to deal with. I kept thinking that, twenty years ago, I had come very close to totally mastering questions just like these; now I was stumped. I forged on, with very little enthusiasm, and even less hope.

At the end of the first two test sections—one hour into the morning—the chief proctor said that we would have precisely five minutes to go out into the hallway and relax. We marched out there. All of us looked dazed, unhappy, and disoriented, although I believe that I was the only student to go to the water fountain and take an Inderal for his blood pressure.

We went back into the room. There was something vaguely comforting about being there. Maybe it was the clear, definite tone of the instructions in the test booklet. In the real, grown-up world, so much is left up to individual interpretation. Here, at the end of every page, there was a bold arrow marked with the words GO ON TO THE NEXT PAGE. And at the end of every test section, a spaced-out, capitalized S T O P. And the flat-out message: IF YOU FINISH BEFORE TIME IS CALLED, YOU MAY CHECK YOUR WORK ON THIS SECTION ONLY. DO NOT WORK ON ANY OTHER SECTION OF THE TEST.

The chief proctor was just as definite about what she was doing. At the end of the fourth section of the test—the second hour—she said, "We will now have a one-minute stretching period. You may stand and stretch by your desks." When one boy started out into the hallway, the proctor said, "The stretching period is to be conducted by your desk only. You may not leave the room."

The rules, the feeling of sitting in that combination deskchair, the sounds I was hearing—the girl behind me popping her gum, the fluorescent lights above me humming softly, the hiss from the pipes—I don't know why, but I liked it a lot.

We finished the test a little after noon. Many of the boys and girls knew each other from school; they talked about the questions on the way out of the building. As I left, the chief proctor said to me, "Do you mind if I ask you a question?" I thought she was going to ask the obvious one: What was I doing there? But she said, "Why did you choose to wear a tie this morning?" I was so startled that I could only answer, "If you don't look sharp, you're not going to feel sharp."

Weeks went by. I was aware of a vague sense of apprehension; occasionally I lost sight of what it might be about, and then I remembered: my SAT scores were going to be coming.

One day there the envelope was, in the morning mail. The return address said it was from the College Board. I knew it was ridiculous to feel nervous; these results weren't going to have any effect on my life. I was already a college graduate; these scores weren't going to get me in or keep me out of anywhere.

But my hands were undeniably shaking as I ripped open the envelope. And there they were: my scores. Verbal—780. Math—500.

My instincts while I had been taking the test had been correct. In the verbal sections, I had actually gone up more than fifty points since high school. But in the math sections, I had dropped more than two hundred points.

That was sort of depressing to me—being two hundred points dumber in math than when I was seventeen years old. I kept it to myself, though. How could I burden people with my problem? My contemporaries were walking around worried about making partner at their law firms, about getting a mortgage for a new house, about deciding whether to accept a transfer that would move their families halfway across the country. When they asked me why I was so down in the mouth, I just couldn't say it:

"I screwed up on my SATs."

Scene of the Crime

You walk into the small, neat, neighborhood clothing store at 5408 West North Avenue, Chicago, and you realize that this is the awful news that never makes the paper. The news of what happens afterward.

You walk into the clothing store—it is called The Spot—and you see the owner standing near the cash register. His name is Kwang Nam Kim; he is forty-four years old, a true believer in the American dream. He came to the United States from Korea ten years ago, accompanied by his wife and two sons. Kim had been a tailor in Korea. But he wanted more for his family.

So he brought them to Chicago. He got a job at Hart Schaffner & Marx; his wife, Kyung Soon Kim, worked there too, as a seamstress. When he had saved enough money, he opened up The Spot in this West Side neighborhood, and he and his wife went into business for themselves.

On January 18, 1982, Mr. and Mrs. Kim were working alone in The Spot right after the store had opened for the morning. Two young men came into the store. They casually tried on some jeans and jackets. Then they announced that they were going to rob the Kims.

Mr. and Mrs. Kim did exactly what the men told them to do. They did not resist, they did not try to call the police. The men ordered them into a back room and told them to lie on the floor, face down. They did. The men went back out front to steal whatever they wanted.

Before the men left the store, they went to the back room again. The Kims were still face down, still following orders. One of the men pointed a gun at the back of Mrs. Kim's head. He pulled the trigger. The bullet bored through her head and exited through her mouth. Then the men left the store with $100 and some clothing.

The murder of Mrs. Kim was handled in crisp, professional style by all the police and law agencies involved. Chicago police arrested two men— LeRoy Carter, Jr., nineteen, the gunman, and Earvin Newsome, twenty-one, his accomplice. Carter pleaded guilty and was sentenced to forty years in prison; Newsome was vigorously prosecuted by assistant state's attorneys Michael Spivack and Joan Corboy. He was found guilty and sentenced to thirty-three years in prison.

This time the criminal justice system worked precisely the way it is supposed to.

And on a summer night a year and a half later, Kwang Nam Kim stands alone in his store, his wife dead for no reason. A handsome, immaculately dressed man, he waits for seven P.M., closing time.

You enter the store and introduce yourself. Kim is polite and quiet. He locks up the store; he invites you to visit with him in his apartment above the store. You walk up a flight of wooden stairs.

You sit with him in his living room. Kim speaks halting English; he is more comfortable speaking Korean. His son John, fifteen, a student at Weber High School, joins you to act as translator. The other son, Sam, nineteen, is away at summer school at Harvard—paid for by the work his father and mother put in downstairs.

There is a classical music album—*Swan Lake*—resting next to the stereo. The apartment is small but well tended. Kwang Nam Kim sits on the edge of a chair and tries to tell you what it is like to live, after having lain next to his wife in their store while she was casually executed.

"We came to America to have a better life," he says. John translates. "I wanted to live better, so I would be able to send my sons to college. I never knew this would happen, of course."

You ask him if he is satisfied with the results of the court cases against the two men. He seems not very interested. The court cases seem to have nothing to do with him.

"It's a little hard on me, yes," he says. "But at least I can hope to see my sons grow up."

He says that his life is simple now. He opens the store each morning, he stays until early evening, he goes out to dinner, he goes to bed. He has not been out with a woman since the death of his wife, and has not even thought of the prospect of marrying again.

He says the worst time of day for him is in the morning. "I go down to open the store," he says. "I play some Korean music on a tape player. It is the music my wife and I used to listen to. When I hear that music, I think of being with her in the store, and I miss her very much."

John, listening to the words about his mother, continues to translate for his father.

Kim says that he tries not to think of the past, but of the future. But he says that sometimes he cannot help thinking about his wife, and what his life might have been like had the men not chosen to come into his store that morning.

"She was the best wife a man could ever have," he says. "She was the best . . ." He has to stop, because all this time later his eyes are welling over with tears, and he is crying.

"She took care of us," he says, and the tears roll down his face.

You sit with him and you wonder what you can possibly say. You think of what you had asked Michael Spivack, the assistant state's attorney who successfully prosecuted the case. Forty years for one defendant, thirty-three years for the other. Relatively stiff sentences. You had asked Spivack if he felt justice had been done.

"I don't know," Spivack had said quietly. "What's justice?"

Teen Idol

Several odd things have happened to me in my life, but perhaps none was ever as odd as the one I never talk about—the time I appeared in *Dig* magazine.

Dig magazine is long dead. But when it was around, in the late 1950s, it had a loyal audience of young boys and girls who were hooked on the movie stars, TV actors, and rock singers of the day. It was basically a fan magazine; it's probably safe to say that the same youngsters who read *Dig* went on to read *Rolling Stone* a decade or so later.

Dig had a section—it was a two-page center spread—that featured pictures and brief comments from readers. They printed thirty or forty of the pictures every month; the readers signed their names and addresses, and other readers, if they so chose, could write letters to them.

One day in 1959, without telling anyone in my family or any of my friends, I wrote a letter to *Dig*. It was brief:

My name is Bobby Greene. I am only 12, but I dig *Dig*.
I dig Elvis, Kookie, and Ricky. My address is 2722 Bryden Rd., Columbus 9, Ohio.

I enclosed a sixth-grade school photograph in which I let my eyes half-close in what I hoped resembled a come-hither bedroom look, and in which I attempted a sultry Presley sneer.

I never expected anything to happen. The school year ended, and I went off to Camp Arrowhead, in Jackson, Ohio. I spent the summer hunting frogs and playing baseball and doing other boylike things; on the last day of camp my father drove down to pick up my friend Allen Schulman and me and take us home.

When my father arrived, he didn't say anything. He merely handed me a large box that had been in the back seat of the car.

In the box were approximately four hundred letters. All were addressed to "Bobby Greene."

For a second, I didn't know what had happened. But I only had to open the first letter to find out.

It went something like:

> Dear Bobby—
> I loved the way you looked in *Dig,* and I just had to write you. I live in Louisville, Kentucky. . . .

The letters were all from young girls. *Dig* had printed my picture and note. Some of the girls had enclosed the clipping from *Dig*; the editors, for some reason, had added a year to my age, so the text under my picture said, "I am only 13, but I dig *Dig.*"

Apparently the motivation of the editors was to make me seem like an older man. It had worked; the whole ride back to Columbus I opened the letters, and I was shocked by what I read.

There was no getting around it. At twelve, I was a national sex symbol for young girls. They couldn't have Elvis or Kookie or Ricky—if you need to be told who Ricky was, by the way, you are of the wrong generation to be reading this—but they had my home address and my sneering, leering picture right in front of them.

Most of the letters were pretty tame; the girls said that they wanted to "meet" me, and let it go at that. But the message was clear; because I had been in *Dig,* I had become a celebrity to them. The only specific letter I remember came from a girl who said, "My father drives a dumptruck and my measurements are 33-23-33."

This all presented a dilemma for me. Yes, I had sent the letter; and yes, I had sent the now-notorious photograph. But basically I was a pretty sheltered, innocent, suburban kid; what was I supposed to *do* with all these girls?

When I got home I asked my parents what they thought. "You wrote to the magazine, so you have the obligation to answer each of those girls," my mother said. I went to my room with the box of four hundred letters and I started to try to answer them.

Within a day, though, I knew it was going to be impossible. The mailman showed up, and he had dozens of more letters. The onslaught had just begun. Every day I would get a bundle of letters. I became jaded by them, inured to them; I would go out into the back yard and sit under a tree and casually open the letters up. Always the contents would be the same: a letter from a girl who also dug Elvis, Kookie, and Ricky; a photograph of the girl; and an invitation to write or visit her.

This went on for months, every single day. I answered some of the letters; most I just kept under my bed in my room. I didn't know what I was supposed to do with them once I had finished reading them, but I knew it would be wrong to throw them away.

Even after the letters stopped arriving regularly, they continued to trickle in once in a while. Two or three years later, at least once a month, I would get a letter that began: "I don't know if you still live at this address, but I found an old copy of *Dig* magazine . . ." One letter came five years later; it began, "I figure you must be 18 by now . . ." [They were still operating under the assumption that I had been thirteen, not twelve, when *Dig* had ordained me.]

I grew up and moved away, and went to college and got on with my life. But the experience of being in *Dig* had affected me in ways I was not quite able to define; I always knew that other boys might have certain advantages over me—but that they had never been made a teen idol by *Dig*. Somehow it had changed my life.

Even now, when each day's mail arrives at my newspaper office, I flip through it, half-expecting a letter to begin:

> Dear Bobby—
> I just came across an old copy of *Dig* magazine. You must be 37 by now. . . .

And I always know I can answer: "Thirty-six. The editors of *Dig* added a year."

Dog Days on Publishers Row

So you say you want to be a published author. You're looking for advice.

You've sat under a bare sixty-watt light bulb for years. You've cranked reams of white bond paper into your ancient manual typewriter. You've poured your heart, your soul, and your very guts onto those pages. You've come up with your idea of a masterwork.

But you can't get anyone interested. Publishers send your book back with form rejection notices. Agents tell you they can't help. You're confused. You know your stuff is good; why won't anyone print it? What can you do?

All right, you asked for a straight answer, and a straight answer you'll get. You want to get your book published? You want to see your work in the stores? You want enthusiasm from the Manhattan literary community?

Be a dog.

One of the major titles on the spring list of Doubleday and Company, one of New York's oldest and most respected publishers, is *C. Fred's Story.* The byline on the book belongs to C. Fred Bush.

C. Fred Bush is a dog. Specifically, he is a golden cocker spaniel; he is owned by Vice-President George Bush. Although the words in the book were actually written by Bush's wife, Barbara, the narrative is told from the dog's point of view, purportedly in the dog's own voice.

Doubleday is not taking C. Fred Bush's book as a joke. Interest in the book reaches to the very top of the Doubleday corporation, and that interest has filtered down to employees all through the publishing house. Doubleday is poised to commit its full resources to the literary debut of George Bush's dog.

The editor at Doubleday assigned to handle *C. Fred's Story* is Lisa Drew, who has been with the house for twenty-two years.

"The idea came to me directly from Nelson Doubleday, the president of the corporation," Drew said. "It's very unusual for Mr. Doubleday to get directly involved with bringing a book into the house, but Mr. Doubleday is a friend of the Bushes', and a neighbor, I think, of the Vice-President's mother in Florida. Mr. Doubleday asked me if I was aware of the Bushes' dog. He told me that the dog was really kind of a character, and that he thought there was a book there."

Drew wrote a letter to Mrs. Bush. "Mrs. Bush told me that C. Fred got a lot of fan mail," Drew said. "Apparently whenever there was a picture in the paper of the Bushes and the dog, people would write to the dog. Mrs. Bush would write letters of reply over the dog's name. One day Mrs. Bush's chief of staff said, 'Why waste it in a letter? Why not put it in a book?'"

Drew conferred with Mrs. Bush; they decided that the book should contain both text and photos and should describe the dog's life in Washington and on his travels around the world.

"As far as point of view goes, we decided early on that it had to be by the dog," Drew said. "He talks about his views of the world and how proud he is to be the Bushes' dog. This is a dog who has taken trips to China, New York, Maine, back to Texas. It wouldn't have worked in the third person. It had to be first person, in the dog's voice."

Drew said that Mrs. Bush's manuscript went through the editing processes largely unchanged.

"The major suggestion I made was for Mrs. Bush to get rid of all the exclamation points," Drew said. "She had a tendency to include four or five exclamation points after each sentence. And I asked her to use another typewriter. The one she was using was the kind used for typing speeches, with the big letters."

At any publishing house, one of the key executives who will determine the financial success of a book is the subsidiary rights director. The subsidiary rights director is in charge of selling a book to paperback houses, to magazines that will excerpt it, to book clubs.

"At our first meeting, when this book by the Bushes' dog was presented to us, our first reaction was, 'Gee, is Lisa serious?'" said Jackie Everly, Doubleday's director of subsidiary rights. "When we found out that she was, we got right into it. We're not exactly a bunch of pushovers. We have to be hard-nosed. We have to consider what the book will mean to us in the sense of business."

The ground rule was that Mrs. Bush would donate the dog's personal royalties to two charities. Doubleday's revenues from sales of the book, though, would remain with the publishing house; Everly was to handle subsidiary arrangements as she would with any other Doubleday title.

Everly said she thought she could help make *C. Fred's Story* a winner for Doubleday. "We lunch with people from the magazines, the book clubs, and the reprinters," she said. "This is a perfect kind of book to talk about at lunch. We like to whet these people's appetites for the book, and this dog's book is very upbeat. We have more than five hundred books a year on our list, and frankly, we just don't have the time to have a separate lunch for each book. But this is a book that is coming up all the time at lunch."

Everly said that, based on her experience, "I think rights-wise it will be a very successful book. I don't see how it can miss, to tell you the truth. Especially if it goes on the bestseller list in hardcover, the reprinters are really going to stand up and take notice. The fact that the book is written by a dog will not hurt us at all. I think this is something we can run with."

Alex Gotfryd is Doubleday's art director. To him fell the task of supervising the design of the Bushes' dog's book's jacket. "A book jacket is a tool of promotion and advertising," Gotfryd said. "When a person carries a book on a bus or on the subway, or walks down the street carrying it in his hand, that's free advertising. A jacket can be thought of as a little poster. And the poster should emphasize the content of the book."

In this case, Gotfryd said, "I knew right away that the main element on the front of the jacket had to be C. Fred Bush himself. After all, it's his book. So when people look at the jacket we've come up with, they'll see a dog. Actually, they'll see a dog and Mrs. Bush; she's holding him."

He said he had attempted to make the jacket "attractive and appropriate"; the color scheme he accepted was red, ivory, and dark blue. "A great deal of thought and effort and logic and intelligence go into these decisions," he said. "The whole idea is to come up with a jacket that is imprinted in the memory. If a potential customer does not buy it the first time he sees it, perhaps he will remember it and buy it the second time."

His goal with the jacket for *C. Fred's Story,* he said, was "to capsulize the essence of the book, but not to give away the book entirely. There should be a little mystery in the cover, a little drama—we should make the reader discover something special about the book, but not make him work too hard.

"I'm an artist, but I'm also a businessman. I'm hired to produce a very fine commercial package. I try to seduce the customer to pick that book up in a bookstore and to purchase it. I think that in the case of this dog's book, we should do very well in those terms."

For Dick Heffernan, Doubleday's sales manager for trade books, the problem is always the same. Doubleday's thirty-two trade sales representatives present the house's list of books to booksellers twice a year. That means that on each client call, a sales representative has approximately 250 books to pitch.

"We don't require our salespeople to actually read any of the books they are selling," Heffernan said. "A good reader is not necessarily a good salesman, and vice versa."

Instead, Doubleday prepares a "T.I. (title information) sheet" for each book, summarizing what the book is about. Included on the T.I. sheet is a "keynote"—a phrase that describes the book in twenty-five words or less.

That way, even if a sales representative has never seen a particular book, he can describe it to a bookstore owner in precisely the way Doubleday's executives would like to have it described.

"You have to understand, on some books we have only five to eight seconds to talk about it with a bookstore owner," Heffernan said. "On a major title, we might take up to a minute."

C. Fred's Story Heffernan said, will probably fall somewhere in between. "It won't be a one-minute presentation, because it's not the biggest book on our list," he said. "But it won't be an eight-second presentation either, because we consider it to be an important book.

"The keynote we give the sales reps will probably be something like: 'A cute little story told by the Bushes' dog and all about the dog's travels around the country and the world.'"

When a sales representative is presenting the book titles to a bookstore owner, Heffernan said, it is not difficult to tell how the bookseller is reacting to each pitch. "You get a pretty good feeling for it," he said.

"You can see the response in the other person's face. He usually places his order right there, before you go on to the next title, so it's important that you make your sale the first time around."

Heffernan said that, compared with other books on the Doubleday list, *C. Fred's Story* should be a relatively simple sell. "No questions about it. No matter how good a first novel might be, for example, this dog's book is much easier for us to sell. You've got the fact that the author is a dog, you've got the fact that in addition to being a dog he's the Vice-President's dog, you've got guaranteed advertising and promotion and publicity, you've got a possible Phil Donahue . . . this book has all the elements."

Elizabeth St. John, Doubleday's publicity manager, said she has seldom encountered a title that promised to make her job easier than *C. Fred's Story.*

"Barbara Bush has promised us to help as much as she can in the promotion of the book," St. John said. "She is an enormously well-known political figure, the wife of the Vice-President—and, at least in Washington and New York, the dog will be made available to the media, also. We can't really ask the dog to make the entire tour—a publicity tour is grueling enough as it is for a human being."

Mrs. Bush is scheduled to make appearances on behalf of the book in New York, Chicago, Washington, Los Angeles, and San Francisco, St. John said. "With someone like her, who has been on all the shows, we'll ask her what her preference is. Normally it can be hard to book someone on a show—the network morning shows in particular. But of course in this case, that will be no problem. Mrs. Bush can talk about this book on virtually any show she chooses."

The publicity drive has begun even before the release of the book. "We sent out a release about C. Fred Bush," St. John said. "We showed a picture of him riding aboard—what is it called, the plane where the Vice-President rides? Air Force One? Air Force Two? In any event, we sent out a very nice photo of the dog on board that plane. The book has everything going for it. It's brief. It has sixty-two photographs of C. Fred. It has a message, and the message is that celebrities are just like us. They have dogs that they spoil and they love just like we do. In that sense, *C. Fred's Story* is a very intimate book."

Although St. John was uncertain whether George Bush would take part in the publicity campaign, "the important thing is not so much Vice-President Bush's participation, or even Mrs. Bush's participation. The important thing is that we get the word out that the Bushes' dog has written a book, and that the book is in the stores. I think we can do that. And I think we have one of the big books of the spring."

And for you who still say you want to be a published author; for you who say you're still slaving away under that light bulb, still cranking that paper into your typewriter; for you who say that you've become discouraged by reading this, and that you want to know what the moral is:

Quit whining. Just shut up and eat your Alpo.

Underpass

The first few times, I didn't realize why I was feeling that way.

I had arrived in Dallas the week before for the Republican National Convention; each morning I would get in a cab and head for the convention center, where our temporary newsroom was set up. All the way down the freeway nothing would seem amiss. Then we would ride through an underpass, and I would get this uncomfortable sensation. Thirty or forty seconds later it would go away.

This happened for three or four days, and then I figured it out. It wasn't just any underpass we were riding through; it was the triple underpass from November 22, 1963. And the parks and buildings around it; they weren't just any landmarks in any city. There they were: Dealey Plaza. The grassy knoll. The Texas School Book Depository.

There is a syndrome; maybe you share it with me. Whenever I see something that's supposed to be dramatic and historic and important, it never quite feels that way. We are fed so much instant history these days, I always fail to feel the impact of the places I have been taught are historic.

But it was so curious; every time another cab would drive through that underpass, and I would look over at the red brick building, I experienced a wave of nausea. To tell the truth, I felt a little as if I wanted to cry. I'm a little embarrassed to admit something like that; but the fact is, I don't think I've ever been as affected by being in a particular place.

My generation has been accused of acting as if history did not exist before we came along; we have been accused of being shortsighted and naive when it comes to events that truly matter. And I know that there are events that must be just as affecting to older Americans: the start of the Great Depression, the bombing of Pearl Harbor, the death of Franklin Delano Roosevelt.

For millions of us, though, there was one day that divided the hemispheres of our lives. The world seemed innocent and tranquil and full of trust, and then on that November 22, it didn't seem that way any longer. We couldn't have told you that at the time. Only as the years passed did we realize what had happened.

There is a tendency to overanalyze the legacy of that November 22. Historians and political scientists and sociologists have debated the subject for more than twenty years. In the end, though, it has less to do with history, less to do with politics, less to do with sociology, than it has to do with real life. I know that when I think of that day, it is not in broad, monumental terms. My thoughts are quite basic; quite simple.

Sixth-period English class, Bexley High School. A bright fall day in Ohio. Mrs. Amos is at the blackboard, and then the loudspeaker on the east wall of the room crackles to life. An unusual occurrence; announcements from the principal's office were generally made in the morning.

A disc jockey's voice over the loudspeaker: "This is your country music station . . ." Laughter in the classroom; someone must be fooling around down in Jones's office.

Then the sound of other stations blipping in and out, as an unseen hand twists the radio's knob, moves the tuner. And finally the words from Dallas—words of the gunshots. In a few minutes we will know that the President is dead; now we are merely told that shots have been fired at him, and that he is presumed to be injured. None of us could have told you that he was even taking a trip that day.

I remember walking home. I sat on the front stoop until the paperboy arrived with the evening *Columbus Dispatch.* I had never seen a headline that big; a newspaper had never seemed so important. When my parents had finished reading it, I took it and put it on the top shelf of my closet. For some reason it seemed important that I not throw it away.

I remember going out that night and walking the streets. I had never felt any interest in politics; I had not been one of the young Americans who were fanatical followers of the man who had been President. But inside it seemed that something had been cut out of me; nothing that had happened in my life had ever made me feel this way, and I was scared about it. It was cold that night; later I would meet up with my friends and we would drive around and the radio—WCOL—would tell us that a man had been arrested in Dallas. But what I recall most clearly is walking all by myself, and never having felt so alone.

In later years we would learn things about that President and that administration that would have surprised all of us on that November night; as a matter of fact, a recent nonfiction best-seller was a family history of that

President and his parents and his brothers and sisters and their children, and the information in that book was of a nature that we weren't reading about in 1963. But that doesn't really matter; what matters is that there was a time when things felt different, and that that time ended in an instant, and that a lot of us still haven't been able to shake it. When we try to figure out when everything changed in the world, we always come back to that day.

Which is why, riding through that underpass, seeing that red brick building and those plots of grass, I didn't feel like a grown man on his way to work. I felt like a sixteen-year-old kid sitting out on a cement stoop, reading a front-page story that somehow didn't seem real. It was cold in Ohio that November afternoon; in Dallas last week, with the temperatures exceeding one hundred degrees, I rode through that underpass each morning and the chill came back from over all the years.

The ABC's of Courage

It is nearing dusk. The man has finished his day's labor; he is a plumber, and today he was working at a construction site, and his shift has ended.

Now he is sitting in the dining room of Mrs. Patricia Lord, in Cicero, Illinois. Mrs. Lord and the man are bending over a list of words.

"Can you try these now?" Mrs. Lord says.

"Yes," the man says.

He looks at the top word on the list. The word is *is*.

"Is," the man says.

"Yes," Mrs. Lord says.

The next word on the list is *brown*.

The man looks at it for a moment. Then he says: "Brown."

"Yes," Mrs. Lord says.

The next word is *the*.

"The," the man says, touching the word with his hand.

"Yes," Mrs. Lord says.

The next word is *sleep*.

The man hesitates. Seconds pass. He is having trouble with this one. Finally he says: "Play?"

"No," Mrs. Lord says. "Look at it again."

The man stares. He says nothing. Then he says, "I don't know what it is."

"All right," Mrs. Lord says softly. "Skip it and come back to it later."

The man is fifty-five years old. He is trying to learn how to read. He is a large man, balding and wearing thick glasses; he bears a resemblance to the actor Ernest Borgnine. His plumber's work clothes—denim overalls, a flannel shirt—are still on. Today, as he does twice a week, he has driven straight from work to Mrs. Lord's house. His hands are dirty from his day's labor; as he points to the words on the spelling list you can see that he has not had time to stop and clean up. He has been coming to Mrs. Lord's house for just over a year.

The next word on the list is *down*.

"Down," the man says with confidence in his voice.

"That's right," Mrs. Lord says "Very good."

The man—we will not name him here, because he has asked us not to— never learned to read as a child. His mother was sick and his father was an alcoholic; the boy did not do well in school, and at the age of twelve he dropped out and began to work. Sometimes his mother would try to teach him something; his father, if he had been drinking, would say, "What the hell are you bothering to teach him for? He don't know nothing."

The man went through most of his life hiding his secret. He learned to be a plumber; he married and started a family. He concealed his inability to read even from his wife and children; his wife did all the paperwork around the house, read all the mail, handled all the correspondence.

A year and a half ago, the man lost a job because he could not read. The company he was working for required each employee to take a written test about safety procedures. The man knew the rules, but could not read the questions. The company allowed him to take the test over, but he didn't have a chance. He couldn't admit the real problem.

Out of work, he felt panic. He heard that a local community college was offering a nighttime course in reading improvement. He enrolled. But as early as the first evening he realized that the course was meant for people who at least knew the basics of reading. After a few sessions he approached the teacher after class.

"I know you can't read," the teacher said to him. "If you'd like to keep coming just to see what you can pick up, it's all right."

Instead, the man went to a dime store and bought a book called *Reading Fun* for ninety-three cents. The book was designed for pre-school-aged children. On the pages of the book were simple, colorful pictures of ambulances and taxis and trucks, followed by the proper word for each picture. He looked at the pages and tried to teach himself. He couldn't.

Finally, he sat down with his wife. "You know when I lost my job?" he said. And he told her he couldn't read.

Time went by. On television, he heard a public service announcement about private tutoring offered by the Literacy Volunteers of Chicago. He called up and explained about himself. The person on the other end of the line said that there were no suitable volunteers available at the moment. The man left his name.

Four months later, while he was out of the house, the literacy organization called. When the man arrived back at home, his wife said she had some news for him.

"There's a teacher for you," his wife said. "Her name is Pat."

Patricia Lord, fifty-nine, remembers the first time he showed up at her door.

"He was such a nice man," she said. "At first I didn't realize how deep his problem was. But it soon became clear—he didn't even know the alphabet."

So, twice a week, they started to work together. "He was so grateful," Mrs. Lord said. "I do this for free, but he kept saying that if I ever needed any plumbing done, even if it was an emergency in the middle of the night, he would do it for nothing."

She taught him the alphabet. She taught him how to print letters. She taught him the first words other than his own name that he had ever known how to read or write.

"We work with reading cards," she said. "He picks out words that look interesting to him, and I'll teach him. One of the words he wanted to learn, for instance, was *chocolate*. He was fascinated by it because it was longer than most of the other words on the cards. So we learned it."

There are books scattered all over Mrs. Lord's home—*The Fate of the Earth,* by Jonathan Schell; *Findings*, by Leonard Bernstein; *Schindler's List*, by Thomas Keneally.

"I tried to explain to him about the pleasures of reading," she said. "It's something he's never known. I've always gotten so much information and so much joy from reading, but when I try to explain that to him, it's almost beyond what he can imagine. When I was young I had a friend, and we'd go sit together in the park and just read for hours, and talk about what we were reading. The idea of something like that seems to intrigue him.

"I tell him that one of these days he'll be able to read a book," Mrs. Lord said. "That's far off in the future, though. I have a second-grade spelling puzzle book, and even that's way too advanced for him right now.

"But he's making progress. There's a list of about forty words that he knows now. When a lesson goes well, he is definitely elated. He'll smile at the end of the session, and he'll get more talkative than usual, and he'll just seem . . . lighter. I can tell that he's feeling good about it."

In the time since he started studying with Mrs. Lord, the man has found a new job. His employers do not know that he cannot read; he is deathly afraid that they will find out and that he will be fired again.

"I never liked to hear anyone called a dummy," he said. "Even when I was a kid, I didn't like it. In fact I once beat up another kid for calling a boy a dummy.

"Let's face it, though, when you work construction, the others would be embarrassed to work with you if they knew you couldn't read—wouldn't they? If they found out about me, I think they'd make it hard on me. Some people get their kicks like that."

He said it was losing the other job that convinced him he had to learn how to read. That, and something else.

"I've got a little granddaughter," he said. "I never want her to come up to me and say, 'Grandpa, read this,' and I can't do it. I already went through life not being able to read to my own children. I want to be able to read to my granddaughter."

He said he was proud of how far he had come in his life without knowing how to read. "I can take a blueprint and figure out how a whole building works," he said. "I built my own house. I think that's a pretty good accomplishment for a man who can't read. That, and going this far in my trade."

Still, he has always known how large the gap in his life was.

"All my life, I've wanted so badly to be able to read something," he said. "I've had to pretend, all my life. When I would go into a restaurant with people from the job, I would hold the menu up and pretend to be reading it. But I didn't understand a word. I'd always ask the waitress what the specials were, and when she'd say them I'd choose one of them. Or I'd order something that I knew every restaurant had.

"It was something I thought about all the time, but who could you go talk to? Many's the time that I wished I could read something. But I knew there couldn't be too many people willing to help a person like me, so I just did my best to keep it a secret.

"I've never written a letter in my life. When the holidays came, it was very hard for me to pick out a card for my wife. I'd look at the cards, but I'd have no idea what they said. So I'd buy her a flower instead."

Now that he is studying with Mrs. Lord, he said, he can at least hope that things will change.

"I dream that before long I can really read something," he said. "It doesn't have to be a lot, but just to be able to read something from start to finish would be enough. Mrs. Lord tells me that once you start to read, it comes easier all the time.

"It scares me that there's a possibility I can't do it. I'm fifty-five years old, after all. I get disgusted with myself if I have a bad day here, and I miss a lot of words.

"But when there's been a good day I'll feel great at the end of our lesson. I'll go home and tell my wife, 'I learned this word.' Or I'll say, 'Teacher says I have good handwriting.' And then my wife and I will work on the spelling cards."

He said that, because he is working again, sometimes he will have to skip tutoring sessions. "It kills me when that happens," he said. "But the construction business is pretty good right now, and sometimes in the afternoon the boss will tell me that he needs me to work overtime. I can't tell him why I have to be here. So I'll go off to a pay phone and call Mrs. Lord and give her the bad news.

"I think about reading even when I'm at work, though. I'll be working, but I'll be reciting the alphabet in my head. I keep the spelling cards in my truck, and if it's time for a coffee break I'll go out there and work on my words."

He said that, before he started trying to learn to read, he never picked up a newspaper or a magazine. "Now I like to pick them up and look at them," he said. "I think to myself that maybe someday I can read them.

"And I'll go into a store now and pick up books. I'll pick up the ones that have covers that look interesting. And then I'll flip through them until I see some words that I know. Most of the pages are filled with words that I don't know. But then I'll see some words that Mrs. Lord taught me—*an* or *is* or *the*—and I'll stare at them. It feels so good to know them."

It is getting darker outside. The man has been up since before dawn. His truck is parked outside Mrs. Lord's house; motorists pass by on their way home.

At the dining room table, Mrs. Lord is helping him to write a sentence. "Let's try 'The cow is brown,'" she says. "First word *the*."

The man checks his list of words. Then, on a clean sheet of paper, he writes: *The*.

"Good," Mrs. Lord says. "Next word, *cow*."

He checks his list and writes the word.

"Very good," Mrs. Lord says. "Now *is*."

That word he knows easily. He writes it.

"Now *brown*," Mrs. Lord says.

He thinks for a second, then writes *brown* at the end of the sentence he has built.

"Right!" Mrs. Lord says. "End of sentence!"

The man looks up. There is something very close to pride in his eyes.

"I can't wait until I can write a letter," he says. "The first letter I write is going to be to my wife. I'm going to tell her how much I love her."

On the cover of *Esquire* every month there is a slogan: "Man At His Best." Once in a while, when you really aren't expecting it, you find out what that means.

One Night with You

The only socialite I know in Chicago, Sugar Rautbord, was in the newspaper building where I work, having her photograph taken for a fashion layout. She stopped by my office.

She asked me what I was up to, and I said that I was about to embark on a trip to various cities. I said that I wasn't especially looking forward to the trip; in many of the cities where I'd be stopping, I didn't know anyone.

"What cities?" she said.

"Oh, Houston . . ." I began.

"Houston?" she said, her eyes brightening. She reached for my telephone. "May I?" she said.

She dialed a long-distance number. "Carolyn?" she said. "I'm sending you a man." They had a brief conversation. Sugar handed me the telephone; across the miles I spoke with Carolyn, whoever she was. She invited me to call her when I got to Houston.

After I had hung up, I asked Sugar who it was that I had been talking to.

"Her name is Carolyn Farb," Sugar said.

"And who's that?" I said.

"You may have read about her," Sugar said. "She's the woman who got the twenty-million-dollar divorce settlement in Houston."

I thought about that for a moment.

"Not the woman with the closet?" I said.

"Well . . . yes," Sugar said.

"My God," I said.

There are very few magazine stories I remember precisely, but there was no forgetting the story in *People* magazine about Carolyn Farb's closet. Actually, the *People* story was about rich people's closets in general; but the story had referred to Carolyn Farb as the "queen of closets."

The story had said that Mrs. Farb's closet took up two thousand square feet—"more than some three-bedroom homes," according to *People*. Her closet consisted of six rooms, including one equipped with a sofa, a telephone, and a table, presumably to give Mrs. Farb a chance to stop and rest should she become tired while walking through the closet's other rooms. The closet, according to the story, accommodated fifty evening bags, ninety pairs of shoes, sixty hats, twenty pairs of boots, seventy-five gowns—"easily over one thousand pieces," by Mrs. Farb's own estimate.

The really stunning thing about the *People* article, though, was the picture. The picture showed Mrs. Farb, in a beautiful black outfit, smiling and sitting on the couch in her six-room closet, with her clothes arrayed in the background.

After the article appeared, Mrs. Farb was divorced from her husband, Houston developer Harold Farb. They had been married six years; the twenty-million-dollar figure for the settlement was widely publicized. Commenting on the size of the settlement to a Texas reporter, Mrs. Farb said: "Even though we had a house full of servants, I always looked after him myself. I saw to it that he was very pampered. I banished chicken from the house because he hates chicken. I personally went to the bakery and bought his favorite pineapple pies. And when he went on trips, I always packed his bags myself."

My plane arrived in Houston early in the evening. I always feel lonely when I walk into a strange airport.

I walked over to the bank of pay phones. I dialed the number that Sugar Rautbord had given me.

"Mrs. Farb, this is Bob Greene," I said. "We talked on the phone when Sugar called you."

I asked her if she would like to have a drink. She said that might be all right.

"Maybe you could swing by my hotel after I check in, and we could just go down to the lobby and have a drink in the hotel bar," I said.

"Where are you staying?" she said.

I told her the name of the hotel. There was a pause.

"That is definitely not a place for me," she said. "And I would hope it is not a place for you."

I told her I'd call her when I arrived at the hotel and checked in, and she said that would be fine.

I arrived at the hotel. It was lovely and modern. I got to my room and I dialed Carolyn Farb's number again. I planned on telling her that the hotel was clean and in a nice neighborhood and really quite acceptable for a quick drink.

But before I could tell her anything, she said, "I've sent my security man to pick you up."

"Your security man?" I said.

"Yes," she said. "He should be pulling up to the hotel any minute. But I didn't know what to tell him to look for. I have no idea what you look like."

"I'm just kind of average," I said.

"Well, his name is Warren," she said. "He'll be driving either a Jeep Wagoneer or a Silver Shadow Rolls-Royce."

"Okay," I said.

Warren Hill was a rangy-looking Texan in his early sixties. He wore a blue police-style uniform and a large gun in a black holster. He was waiting for me in the Wagoneer.

"I prefer to drive this over the Rolls," he said.

We pulled into traffic. A thunderstorm was on its way; the sky was black, and bolts of lightning cracked across the towering Houston skyline.

I asked him how he happened to be Mrs. Farb's private security detail.

"Well, I used to work for a security firm that Mr. Farb owned," he said. "I was assigned to the house. But when Mr. and Mrs. Farb separated, he pulled all security from the house. Mrs. Farb asked me to stay on and work for her, and I have ever since."

We were on a side street in a decidedly unprosperous area of Houston. Hill stopped the car.

"Mr. Smith, I think we're lost," he said to me.

We drove around the block a few times, and he regained his bearings. Within fifteen minutes we were entering the exclusive River Oaks section of Houston.

"Have you ever met Mrs. Farb, Mr. Smith?" Hill said.

"Not yet," I said. "What's she like?"

"Just like Cinderella," he said.

"How do you mean?" I said.

"She expects people to treat her like a princess," he said. "And in return, she treats you like a real gentleman. She really does."

We drove along River Oaks Boulevard. As we approached the country club, we swung into a driveway that curved up to a house fronted by white columns.

"We're here," Warren Hill said.

I climbed out of the car and headed for the front door. Down by my feet, a creature leaped out of the grass. I halted in my tracks.

"What was that?" I asked.

"Just a frog," Hill said. "Mrs. Farb keeps frogs. She thinks they're good luck."

He took a key from his pocket and unlocked the front door. We walked into the black-and-white foyer.

"Mrs. Farb," Hill called out. "Mrs. Farb. Mrs. Farb."

There was no answer.

"Mrs. Farb," he called again.

"Warren?" came a female voice. "Is that you?"

"Your guest has arrived, Mrs. Farb," he called.

"I'm in here," the voice said.

I walked into a den. Sitting on a couch, holding a TV channel changer, was Carolyn Farb, in a perfectly tailored jacket and pants.

"Hi, I'm Bob Greene," I said.

She was staring at the television set. "The Burning Bed," starring Farrah Fawcett, was on.

"This is really quite good," Mrs. Farb said. "Do you mind if we have a drink here so we can see the show?"

"That would be fine," I said. She stood up and led the way to a small room that contained her bar.

"What would you like?" she said.

"Well, if you have any lime juice, I'd like a vodka gimlet," I said.

She poured herself a glass of white wine. She reached into a refrigerator and pulled out a bottle of chilled Stolichnaya vodka. "Now what was it you said you needed to make a gimlet?" she said.

"Just some Rose's lime juice, if you've got any around," I said.

She rummaged through a low cabinet and came out with a bottle of Rose's. As I poured it into my vodka, though, I noticed that apparently the lime juice had been sitting around for years. It had turned deep red in color. My gimlet was approximately the color of a beet.

"I think we have a problem with the lime juice," I said.

"Why?" Mrs. Farb said. "What's the trouble?"

"Well, I think it died," I said. "Look at the color."

"What color is lime juice supposed to be?" she said.

"Well, sort of the color of a lime," I said.

She sighed. "That Ricky," she said.

"Who's Ricky?" I said.

"My houseman," she said. "He's supposed to be in charge of stocking the bar. Ricky is a little light in the loafers."

I poured myself a whiskey and Coke, and we went back to the den. Mrs. Farb kept one eye on Farrah Fawcett and did her best to make conversation while still keeping track of the movie.

"Right now I'm making preparations for the Noche de las Américas Ball," she said. "I'm going as Queen Isabella, and I'll be escorted by Jon Lindsay, who is a county judge here. He's going as King Ferdinand."

I tried to make idle chitchat, but I felt like a high school boy who had finally gotten a date with the most buxom girl in the class, and who was doing his best to look anywhere but at the girl's sweater. Only it wasn't Carolyn Farb's chest I was preoccupied with. It was her closet. All I wanted to do was get one look at the famous closet. But how to ask? I couldn't just come out and say it. Should I say, "Would you give me a tour of the house?"

Should I say, "So . . . where do you keep all your clothes?" I didn't have a clue.

We talked of minor matters, and finally she said, "Are you getting hungry?"

"Sure," I said. "Where's your icebox? I'll just make myself a sandwich."

"Don't be silly," she said. "We'll go to the River Oaks Grille."

We walked out to the Wagoneer. "Will Warren be driving us?" I asked.

"No," she said. "I will drive."

We sat in the front seat. She searched for something. She seemed to be annoyed. Finally she called out: "Warren!"

Warren Hill, still in full police uniform, appeared. He walked to the driver's side of the car.

"Help me find the headlights," Mrs. Farb said.

Hill reached in and pulled the headlights on. He returned to the house. It was oppressively hot in Houston; I reached for the car's air-conditioning unit to try to turn it on.

"What are you doing?" Mrs. Farb said.

"Trying to start the air conditioner," I said.

"Don't fool with it," she said. "I can tell you're not very mechanical."

We rolled forward, but before we had gone five feet Warren Hill came running in front of the car. Mrs. Farb slammed on the brakes.

"What is it, Warren?" she said.

"It looks like rain, Mrs. Farb," he said. "I wanted to show you where the windshield wipers are. And I brought you this." He handed her a black umbrella.

"Thank you, Warren," she said. "When you get back inside, will you leave a note for Ricky? Tell him we need some new lime juice."

The River Oaks Grille is a popular gathering spot for residents of the neighborhood. Detracting from its high-toned name and clientele, though, is the fact that it is located in a shopping center.

Mrs. Farb and I pulled up in the Wagoneer. There were dozens of spaces all over the parking lot—the shopping center looked like any small shopping strip in Ohio or Kansas or Missouri—but the River Oaks Grille had a parking attendant stationed outside the front door. Rather than just pull into a vacant space, Mrs. Farb left the car with the attendant.

We walked into the restaurant. "Carolyn!" a voice called out. "Hello, Carolyn!" came another voice. "Wonderful luncheon today, Carolyn," came another.

"We had a luncheon for Jack Lousma, the former astronaut who's running for the Senate in Michigan," Mrs. Farb explained to me. "It was a lovely affair; I think people enjoyed it. There were a lot of astronauts there. Walt Cunningham. Alan Shepard. Alan Bean."

We were led to a table for two. Bob Mosbacher, a Houston oilman, came by and said hello to Mrs. Farb. So did several other patrons.

She looked over at me. "You have a rather abstract expression on your face," she said. "Are you all right?"

"I'm fine," I said.

I asked her what the most important thing in her life was.

"Being constructive," she said. "Doing something with my life. When I was growing up, people took me as a pretty girl. But it was more important to me to be intelligent and constructive. That's why I don't like to be known only as a socialite. I am social, but the term is so frivolous, don't you think?"

I asked her if people treated her differently than they had before her divorce; had all of the publicity about the financial terms affected their attitudes?

"I was a person before my twenty-million-dollar settlement and I'm a person now," she said. "But to answer your question—yes. Sometimes when you're in my financial position things are difficult. I'd like to be the host of a television talk show, for instance. But I sense some resistance to that, and I really can't put it into words, but I think it has something to do with the divorce publicity. You can be discussed for a job like that, but because you're a wealthy person, some people can't believe that the desire for the American Dream is still there."

I said that in spite of that, she seemed to lead a fairly jampacked life.

"I think it's fun," she said. "I'm an Aquarian, and we're energetic. I like to have a good time, but there are many times when I just like to stay home. I like my house. It's like a flower. When I first walked into the entrance hall of that house, I felt its spirit."

It was warm in the restaurant. "Do you mind if I take my jacket off?" I said.

"Go right ahead," she said. "I can't take mine off. I'm not wearing anything underneath."

After dinner we returned to the almost empty parking lot. The Wagoneer was approximately twelve feet from the front door.

"It's that one over there," Mrs. Farb said to the attendant, who walked the eight steps to the car and drove it up to us.

We drove through River Oaks and pulled into the driveway of Mrs. Farb's house. Warren Hill was marching back and forth across the front lawn, on patrol.

Mrs. Farb shut off the motor. We walked to the front door.

"I'm getting a little tired," she said. "I think I'm going to turn in. Would you like Warren to drive you back to your hotel?"

What could I say? The same thing was on my mind that had been consuming me all night, but how could I put it? That if she didn't mind, I'd prefer to just borrow a pillow and sleep in her closet? I extended my hand and she shook it.

She disappeared into the house. I opened the passenger door of the Wagoneer.

"Ready?" Warren Hill said.

"Ready," I said.

ABCDJ

It was one of those things that wasn't supposed to happen, but did. I was on the road, and I passed through my hometown; I was staying not with my family, but in a Hyatt Hotel.

In the lobby I heard a voice call my name. I looked over.

"Allen," I said when I saw him. I said the name calmly, as if seeing him was the most natural thing in the world.

He was staying in the hotel, too. He said he was in town on business; like me, he had long ago moved away.

In high school there were five of us; best friends. We were known as ABCDJ—Allen, Bob, Chuck, Dan, and Jack. ABCDJ is what it said in our senior sketches in the high school yearbook; ABCDJ is what had been engraved on the pewter beer mugs we gave each other when we went off to college. I don't know if they kept theirs; mine is still on top of my dresser. It's where I keep old pennies.

We couldn't believe it. Back in the old town, here we were staying at the Hyatt, purely by chance. The other three—Chuck, Dan, and Jack—had not moved away. Allen and I found ourselves talking about them, and before we knew it we were making phone calls.

Within an hour and a half, a miraculous thing—at least miraculous in the context of our personal universe—had happened. The five of us were sitting around a table in the barroom of the Hyatt. For the first time in eighteen years, ABCDJ were together again.

You'd think it might be difficult at first, or awkward. But it wasn't; it was as if no time at all had passed, and within moments we were telling stories and finishing each others' sentences and laughing as if high school had been yesterday, not two decades distant. Our stories probably would have been boring to anyone else; probably they were boring to anyone in the bar who was overhearing us. But I cannot recall the last time I was so excited about something. I have met so many people in the years since ABCDJ disbanded, and still I feel more comfortable with these people than with anyone else in the world.

We were talking about first girlfriends and first fights and first beers; it was true—the five of us had had our first beers in each others' company. If someone had come into the bar and looked at us, he would have seen five men who are not young anymore; we are each thirty-six, and there's no getting around the fact that much time—half our lives—has passed since the stories we were telling had been present-day reality. That's what people coming into the bar were seeing—five guys who are pretty old, and getting older.

But we sure didn't feel that way, at least not this night. We have been through the same personal crises and social changes that have affected much of our generation; things have not always turned out the way we had in mind. Among the five of us there have been eight marriages, eight children. Someone at the table said that his own child had just had Miss Barbara as a substitute kindergarten teacher; Miss Barbara, the woman who had taught us in kindergarten in 1952.

The hour grew later, and the other people in the bar were leaving, but we stayed on. No one was saying it out loud, but this piece of happenstance—this surprise coming together of ABCDJ—was the best thing that had happened to us in years. We kept looking at each others' faces; we kept remembering what those faces had looked like when we were teenagers.

I said something stupid, and the others laughed. Dan shook his head and said: "String . . ."

It was what I had been called in high school. I was a skinny kid; "String" was short for "stringbean," and here in the Hyatt, Dan kept laughing and saying "String," and none of us thought it was remarkable at all.

Just before two A.M. the bartender said that last call was coming up. The reactions among us to the closing of the bar were so interesting; we fit right back into the late-night patterns that we had fit into in 1964. One of us said he had to get home to his wife. One of us said he wanted to get a bottle and go to Allen's room or my room and stay up talking until dawn. One of us said he was hungry; was that all-night rib place out on the east side still open twenty-four hours? One of us quietly tried to get the telephone number of the cocktail waitress. One of us looked dreamily off into space.

But it was time to go. We didn't take our leave dramatically; we were all thinking about how special these hours had been, but none of us tried to put it into words. Someone said something about doing it again the next night, but we knew that would not happen; this was magic, it had happened because it had been destined to, and there would be no repeating it. If we had not been awkward when we had come together earlier in the evening, now we were, at least a little bit; we simply didn't know how to say what we were thinking.

So we stood in the bar of the Hyatt and we said goodbye. We shook hands, like businessmen cementing a deal. We walked out, Allen and I on the way to our hotel rooms, Chuck, Dan, and Jack on the way to their homes. There was something in the air; something fragile and precious. I know that men aren't supposed to confess that they love each other, but I don't know what else you'd call it.

R.I.P. Blinky

Jeffrey Vallance, a twenty-eight-year-old artist who lives in Canoga Park, California, was vaguely troubled about society's attitude toward animals.

"We categorize animals," Vallance said. "We call some animals 'pets,' and we keep them around the house. We call other animals 'food,' and we eat them."

Vallance thought this was odd: "In other cultures, the animals we call 'pets' are regarded as food. In Indochina, for example, people eat dogs all the time. I consider all animals to be the same. I don't think in terms of 'pets' and 'food.'"

Vallance tried to think of a way to dramatize his theory. After a while, the right idea hit him.

He went to a Ralph's Supermarket in his area, and headed for the meat section. His intention had been to take a piece of meat home and make it his pet. But when he saw all the portions of beef, they just didn't seem like pets to him.

So he went to the poultry section. There he found an array of frozen chickens in plastic bags. This was more like it. Although the chickens did not have heads or feet, they still seemed like chickens to him.

He carefully sifted through the chickens. He found one with good coloration. He picked it up. He knew he liked it.

"I named it Blinky," he said. "I decided on its name right then and there."

He took Blinky to the checkout counter and paid for it. He gave the checkout clerk a ten-dollar bill and got change back.

"I didn't get any other groceries," Vallance said. "If I had bought a box of cereal, for example, at the same time I bought Blinky, it would not have been as pure an experience."

Vallance took Blinky home. He took it out of the plastic wrapper. He looked at it for a while. Soon, though, it began to thaw.

"I knew I'd have to do something," he said.

He drove to the Los Angeles Pet Cemetery, which is located in Calabasas. He left Blinky inside a shoebox in his car. He went inside and said to the clerk, "I have a dead bird I'd like to bury."

"What kind of bird is it?" the clerk said.

"A hen," Vallance said.

Vallance filled out a number of forms and paid the fee for pet burial. He went out to his car and brought the shoebox inside. Some attendants took the shoebox into a back room to prepare Blinky for burial.

After a few minutes, one of the attendants came back out.

"Exactly how did your pet die?" the attendant said.

"I don't know exactly how it died," Vallance said. "It just died one day." [He chose those words because he wanted to tell the truth.]

Vallance picked out a headstone. On it he ordered inscribed: "Blinky. The Friendly Hen."

Soon Vallance was informed that Blinky was laid out in the viewing room. Blinky was resting in a small, satin-lined casket. Blinky was thawing quite severely by this time, so the pet cemetery attendants had placed a paper towel beneath it. A spotlight was shining on Blinky; taped organ music played in the background.

Vallance went out to the gravesite. Pet cemetery workers lowered Blinky's casket into the ground by using ropes. Then they filled in the dirt.

The next week the headstone arrived. The pet cemetery called Vallance; he returned to see the headstone installed in place.

Vallance had taken photographs of Blinky at the grocery store, at his home, and in the casket. He is a conceptual artist—his idea of art is more wide-ranging than the traditional idea of art—so he combined the photographs and a little text into a booklet he titled "Blinky." The booklet was included with his other artwork, as a sort of project.

But an interesting thing happened. Vallance could not think of Blinky as an art project. Blinky was his pet who was gone.

"I found myself going back to the pet cemetery to visit Blinky's gravesite quite often," he said. "I still go regularly. I keep the area around Blinky's grave neat and well tended. I leave flowers."

Vallance's friends who know the story inquire about the dead chicken. "How's Blinky?" they will ask, and Vallance will say that he has just visited the gravesite over the weekend, or whatever.

Vallance says that he does not consider this whole story to be a joke.

"My feelings about Blinky are quite complicated, and quite serious," he said. "I have a very sentimental attitude toward Blinky. I think of Blinky as being my pet. Blinky is much more than a frozen chicken to me. Blinky is very special.

"I feel as if I rescued Blinky from all the millions of chickens who are slaughtered and sold as food. In a sense, Blinky is sort of the Unknown Chicken. Maybe Blinky was supposed to end up as food on somebody's table, but as long as that chicken is buried beneath the headstone I bought, Blinky's soul lives on."

Ford Under Glass

I looked at Gerald Ford's christening gown and booties, which were protected inside a glass case.

On this blustery Wednesday I was one of 527 visitors to the Gerald Ford Presidential Museum, located on the banks of the Grand River in Grand Rapids, Michigan. On some days there are more visitors than that; on some less.

The museum is a starkly modern, three-sided, forty-thousand-square-foot structure that was built with private funds and is maintained at U.S. Government expense. There are other museums in the world that feature more extensive collections of artwork, photography, or historical artifacts; but this is the only place inside whose walls you will find in excess of ten thousand individual pieces of Gerald Ford memorabilia.

The curator of the Gerald Ford Presidential Museum is Will Jones, forty-two. His office is on the second floor of the museum, just off a private elevator; standing on the carpet by his door is a small stone statue of Gerald Ford, made of Pennsylvania rock. The stone has been painted so that Ford appears to be wearing a black suit.

"Our goal here is to commemorate the life and career of Gerald Ford and the period of American life in which he lived and operated," Jones said.

He said that the museum staff is always on the lookout for potential new Gerald Ford exhibits.

"Let me give you a recent example," he said. "Back when he was a congressman, Mr. Ford presided over the 1960 Republican National Convention. He used two gavels at the convention—one to open it, one to close it.

"Now, we had the gavel he used to close the convention. The one he used to open the convention, we did not. But we've located it, and now we have both gavels at the museum."

I asked him how he could be sure the gavel was genuine.

"I'm afraid I don't understand," Jones said.

I asked if there wasn't a chance this was not the authentic gavel that Ford had used to open the convention.

"Oh, no, we're sure," Jones said. "This is the one."

I asked if people from across the country planned their vacations around coming to Grand Rapids and touring the Gerald Ford museum.

"I don't honestly believe that we're many people's final destination," Jones said. "I have no illusions about that.

"People tend to come here if they're on their way to somewhere else. A lot of people come through western Michigan in the course of a year, and once they hear that we're here, they come on over. We get a lot of bus tours."

I asked him if it was a wearying job: thinking full-time about the political career of Gerald Ford.

"I love this job," he said. "It's a great job. I was curator for ten years at the Eisenhower museum in Abilene, Kansas, and I didn't get Eisenhowered out. So I'm certainly not Jerry Forded out."

The exhibit hall, arranged over two levels of the Gerald Ford museum, is a sprawling, well-lighted place. Its purview of life in the White House is somewhat limited, because Ford served only two years and was never elected to the Presidency by the general population. But what it lacks in scope, it makes up for in detail; it is perhaps the only location in North America, for example, where you can get a minute-by-minute account of the *Mayaguez* crisis. ("On May 12, 1975, Gerald Ford's customary workday began with a jolt," a wall plaque reads.)

The exhibit hall is divided into subject areas, each featuring a particular motif. In "The Navy Years," for example, Ford's actual sea uniform can be viewed, as well as his footlocker. In most display cases there are relevant quotations from Ford concerning that time in his life; in "The Navy Years" display case, Ford is quoted as recalling: "My wartime experiences had given me an entirely new perspective. The U.S., I was convinced, could no longer stick its head in the sand like an ostrich."

For those who do not wish merely to read Ford's words, however, his tape-recorded voice can be heard all over the exhibit hall. There are various videotape and film presentations, each of these also centering on specific moments from Ford's life ("Congressional Leadership"; "A New Vice President"; "'76 Campaign"). Sometimes, as you walk from display case to display case, you are beset by a confusing and overlapping cacophony of Ford voices.

All is not politics at the museum, though; one display case features three dresses worn by Betty Ford, with a plaque noting that Mrs. Ford had been awarded an honorary citation from the Parsons School of Design for her "high standard of taste and excellence." But most exhibits are more somber; at "The Pardon of Nixon" area, there is a letter that had been sent to Ford by Walter Hoving, chairman of Tiffany & Co.: "Dear Mr. President: You did the right thing. Let the hyenas howl."

I was perusing an exhibit titled "Romance and Marriage." The plaque informed me that in 1947 the future Mrs. Ford had given Ford a Christmas stocking filled with gifts, including a pair of knitted argyle socks and a pipe lighter engraved "To the Light of My Life."

Standing next to me was Anna DeGraaf, eighty-one, of Denver; she told me that she was in Grand Rapids visiting her grandson, Ken Terpstra, who was with her at the museum.

"President Ford was always a favorite of mine," Mrs. DeGraaf said. "So this is something I was anxious to see. Of course, I doubt if I would have made a special trip."

Ken Terpstra said, "I live in Grand Rapids, and until Grandma came to visit, I had never even come over to the museum. Isn't that something?"

"Well, I'm glad you're with me now," Mrs. DeGraaf said to him. "This is a grand opportunity."

The other tourists with whom I spoke were in a similarly upbeat mood.

Harold Christy, a retired schoolteacher from Indianapolis, said he had learned of the Gerald Ford museum only when he had gone to his local auto club to pick up a map for his vacation.

"At the Triple-A they give you a magazine, and there was a story about the museum," he said. "I've been a member of the auto club for twenty-six years, and I've learned that you can get some pretty good ideas through that magazine.

"My wife and I looked at the map, and we noticed that this was right on the highway. So we decided, 'Why not?' We stayed over an extra night; we're in a motel out on Route Eleven.

"I'm a lifelong Republican; Ford was a Navy man, and I was an Air Force man; we're of the same generation; so this seemed like an ideal place for us to spend a day."

Over by the red, white, and blue "Jerry Ford for Congress" Quonset hut, Ernestine Allen and Bev Janeway, of Jasper, Indiana, said that they had come to the museum as part of a bus tour.

"This was a package deal," Mrs. Allen said. "The museum was on the itinerary for the tour, so here we are."

"Yesterday we went to the tulip farms and the wooden-shoe factory over in Holland," Miss Janeway said. "The shoe factory was okay, but the tulip farm was spectacular."

"Next we're going to the 'fish ladder,' but I don't know what that is," Mrs. Allen said.

The centerpiece of the museum is a full-scale reproduction of the Oval Office. The Office is decorated exactly as it was during the Ford years in the White House; the furniture is precisely in place, and there are more plaques explaining various tidbits and sidelights. (The plaque for the replica of the antique Presidential desk reads, "In August, 1974, embedded microphones were removed on Ford's instructions.")

Although visitors are kept off the carpeting by ropes, you can stand and look at the Oval Office for as long as you want; more tape recordings of Ford play intermittently as you watch the room. There is a pen-and-pencil set with a football in the middle; there is a set of pipes that were actually smoked by Ford; there is the ship's wheel from the S.S. *Mayaguez*; there is the AMVETS Golden Helmet Award.

At the gift shop of the Ford museum, an array of souvenirs is offered for sale to visitors.

"Our little seventy-five-cent Gerald Ford commemorative coins are probably our most popular items," said Judy Lovejoy, a cashier at the shop. "But we just started getting Gerald Ford pencils in stock; they're only thirty-five cents, and we can't get enough of them. People seem to want anything that says 'Gerald Ford' on it."

Indeed, the variety of items available for purchase is impressive. There is a Gerald Ford museum booklet ($5); a Gerald Ford museum poster ($10); a Gerald Ford commemorative envelope ($3); a Gerald Ford bronze medal ($12); Gerald Ford campaign buttons (50 cents to $2); a Gerald Ford portrait folder ($3); Gerald Ford photos ($2 to $2.50); a postcard featuring a color photograph of Gerald Ford's golden retriever, Liberty, posing on the White House lawn (15 cents); a cookbook containing recipes submitted by Betty Ford ($9.95); matchbooks embossed with the Presidential seal (six for $2); a Gerald Ford glass mug ($2); a Gerald Ford napkin ($2); and a Gerald Ford crystal candy dish ($20).

"People really want to buy," Mrs. Lovejoy said. "It's not uncommon for one person to spend forty, fifty, or sixty dollars. That happens at least a couple of times a week."

I took a break from my tour, and went back to my hotel for lunch. Sitting in my room, I decided to call Gerald Ford at his home in Rancho Mirage, California. He was not in when I phoned. But later he returned my call.

"I am very, very proud of the job that was done in the presentation of my life," Ford said. I asked him what pleased him most about the museum.

"I would have to say the full reproduction of the Oval Office," he said. "We made a decision to make it full size. At the Truman museum, the Oval Office is only three-quarter size. At the Johnson museum, the Oval Office is only seven-eighths size. But when you walk into the Oval Office at our museum, it's the exact same size of the Oval Office where I worked. My attitude was: If you're going to do it, do it right."

A female voice came onto the line: "Hello?"

"I'm on this line," Ford said.

"Hello?" the voice said. "Hello?"

"I said, I'm on this line," Ford said, and there was a clicking.

"That was Betty," Ford said.

I asked Ford how often he got to visit the museum.

"We get back to western Michigan several times a year," he said. "We were just there, as a matter of fact, for the Tulip Time Parade. I've never gone in for being romantic about things, but when I walk through the museum I get goose bumps.

"Naturally I'm proud. I feel damn lucky for myself to have a museum like that. But more than for myself, it's an illustration of what can happen to a person in this country. It can happen to anybody."

I walked back over to the Gerald Ford museum. Lines of schoolchildren were waiting to go through the front door.

Off on the far side of the museum, unmarked by plaques or signs, were two cement crypts built into a grassy slope. These crypts, I had been told, will be the final resting places for Gerald and Betty Ford; they have informed the museum staff that they wish to be buried right here, in Grand Rapids, on the museum grounds.

I stood next to the crypts and looked around. Off to one side was the museum building, rising into the gray, cloudy afternoon. Directly in front was the Grand River, rolling gently by. And off to the other side was Sullivan's Riverview Furniture store, and beyond that Interstate Highway 96, heading ever eastward, toward Lansing.

Mrs. Hybl and the International Loveline

Mrs. Charlotte Hybl, a sixty-year-old grandmother who lives in Berwyn, Illinois, answered her ringing telephone one day. Whoever was on the other end seemed to be in great pain.

"He was breathing heavily, taking very deep breaths," she said. "He seemed to be seriously ill.

"I said, 'May I help you?' But he just kept breathing hard, and then he hung up."

Mrs. Hybl was perplexed, but she put the call out of her mind. She couldn't keep it out of her mind for long, though. Because that phone call was the first of many. Men started calling the Hybl home at all hours of the day and night. Usually the men moaned, groaned, or simply breathed in and out.

"I was very puzzled," Mrs. Hybl said. "But then a man called, and he said, 'I'm calling about the ad.' My husband and I had placed several ads in the *Tradin' Times* newspaper, trying to get rid of some old furniture. So I said, 'Which ad?'

"And the man said, 'The ad for telephone sex.'"

Mrs. Hybl asked the man what he was talking about. He said he had seen an advertisement for something called International Loveline in a men's magazine. International Loveline was a telephone sex company. Men were supposed to call a certain number, give their credit card number, and then a woman would get on the line and talk filthy to them.

"I asked him to read to me the phone number from the ad," Mrs. Hybl said. "He did—it was my phone number, but it had the 213 area code in front of it. He had dialed the 312 area code by mistake, and got my home. Apparently all of the other men had made the same mistake."

Mrs. Hybl asked the man what magazines carried the International Loveline ads. He said the ads appeared in the scuzzy, hard-core magazines; he had seen this one in *Hustler*. Mrs. Hybl and the man said goodbye to one another.

The next day Mrs. Hybl drove down to the nearest newsstand to check out the ads.

"I went in, and there were *Oui* and *Penthouse* and *Hustler*," she said. "I opened them up, but I had to close them. As much as I wanted to know what the ad said, I couldn't stand to look at the pictures. So one of the men who owned the newsstand said he would find the ad, and would call me at home.

"He called that same day. He'd found the ad in *Hustler*. It was for the International Loveline, all right, and it had my phone number, except with a 213 area code in front of it. He told me that ad was for 'phone sex . . . the ultimate in phone fantasy.'"

During the ensuing weeks, the calls did not let up. Mrs. Hybl and her husband—Charles Hybl, also sixty, a vending-machine serviceman—got used to picking up their telephone and hearing men in the throes of passion.

"One Spanish-speaking man called seven times the same night," Mrs. Hybl said. "I couldn't make him understand that he should have been calling 213, not 312. Another man called and asked me to talk sexy to him. I said, 'I'm a sixty-year-old grandmother.' He said, 'Could you talk sexy to me anyway?'

"Another man called and said, 'Let's get hot.' I told him that if he wanted to get hot, he should take a hot shower."

Mrs. Hybl was losing her patience. She tried to call the 213 number, but got nowhere with the people on the other end. She did determine that the International Loveline was headquartered in Los Angeles, which did not surprise her.

"I don't know what I should do," she said. "Apparently these men are so worked up that they can't tell the difference between 213 and 312. But I've had this phone number for thirty years. I can't just change it."

At this point I volunteered to call the International Loveline for Mrs. Hybl. I dialed the number. A sultry-sounding woman answered by saying: "International Loveline, do you have a major credit card?"

I said that I certainly did, but that I did not want to talk just then. I identified myself, and asked to speak to the manager.

Several seconds later, a man's voice came onto the line. The man declined to identify himself, but said he was the owner of International Loveline.

I explained Mrs. Hybl's problem to him. He listened.

"That's too bad, but I don't know what I can do about it," he said. He said that when men from around the country called International Loveline, they gave the Loveline operator their credit card numbers. After the numbers were verified, the operator contacted the dirty-talking Loveline women at their homes—and those women called the men back, and said nasty things to them.

"It's like having sex on the phone," the owner said. "The women who work for me are college students and housewives. The college girls can do the phone calls during study breaks, and the housewives can do the calls while they're working around the house. It's easy work for them, it's a good way to make a little extra money, and they can do it without leaving home."

I asked him if he would consider changing his number, so that Mrs. Hybl would not be bothered anymore.

"I can't do it," he said. "I have nine telephone lines, and my advertisements are running in magazines all over the country. It would cost me thousands of dollars to change the number. Tell her to change her number."

I called Mrs. Hybl hack and gave her the bad news. She said that she didn't want to change her number. She asked me if I had any other ideas.

"Well, have you considered talking dirty to the men when they phone?" I said.

"I called one of them an S.O.B.," Mrs. Hybl said. "But that's about as dirty as I'm willing to get."

Permanent Record

There are thousands of theories about what's gone wrong with the world, but I think it comes down to one simple thing: The death of the Permanent Record.

You remember the Permanent Record. When you were in elementary school, junior high school, and high school, you were constantly being told that if you screwed up, news of that screw-up would be sent down to the principal's office, and would be placed in your Permanent Record.

Nothing more needed to be said. No one had ever seen a Permanent Record; that didn't matter. We knew they were there. We all imagined a steel filing cabinet, crammed full of Permanent Records—one for each kid in the school. I think we always assumed that when we graduated our Permanent Record was sent on to college with us, and then when we got out of college our Permanent Record was sent to our employer—probably with a duplicate copy sent to the U.S. Government.

I don't know if students are still threatened with the promise of unpleasant things included in their Permanent Record, but I doubt it. I have a terrible feeling that mine was the last generation to know what a Permanent Record was—and that not only has it disappeared from the schools of the land, but it has disappeared as a concept in society as a whole.

There once was a time when people really stopped before they did something they knew was deceitful, immoral, or unethical—no matter how much fun it might sound. They didn't stop because they were such holy folks. They stopped because—no matter how old they were—they had a nagging fear that if they did it, it would end up on their Permanent Record.

At some point in the last few decades, I'm afraid, people wised up to something that amazed them: There is no Permanent Record. There probably never was.

They discovered that regardless of how badly you fouled up your life or the lives of others, there was nothing permanent about it on your record. You would always be forgiven, no matter what; no matter what you did, other people would shrug it off.

So pretty soon men and women—instead of fearing the Permanent Record—started laughing at the idea of the Permanent Record. The kinds of things that they used to be ashamed of—the kinds of things that they used to secretly cringe at when they thought about them—now became "interesting" aspects of their personalities.

If those "interesting" aspects were weird enough—if they were the kinds of things that would have really jazzed up the Permanent Record—the people sometimes wrote books confessing those things, and the books became best-sellers. And the people found out that other people—far from scorning them—would line up in the bookstores to get their autographs on the inside covers of the books.

The people started going on talk shows to discuss the things that, in decades past, would have been included in their Permanent Records. The talk-show hosts would say, "Thank you for being so honest with us; I'm sure the people in our audience can understand how much guts it must take for you to tell us these things." The Permanent Records were being opened up for the whole world to see—and the sky did not fall in.

If celebrities had dips in their careers, all they had to do to guarantee a new injection of fame was to admit the worst things about themselves—the Permanent Record things—and the celebrity magazines would print those things, and the celebrities would be applauded for their candor and courage. And they would become even bigger celebrities.

As Americans began to realize that there was no Permanent Record, and probably never had been, they deduced for themselves that any kind of behavior was permissible. After all, it wasn't as if anyone was keeping track; all you would have to do—just like the men and women with best-sellers and on the talk shows and in the celebrity magazines—was to say, "That was a real crazy period in my life." All would be forgiven; all would be erased from the Permanent Record, which, of course, was no longer permanent.

And that is where we are today. Without really thinking about it, we have accepted the notion that no one is, indeed, keeping track. No one is even *allowed* to keep track. I doubt that you can scare a school kid today by telling him the principal is going to inscribe something on his Permanent Record; the kid would probably file a suit under the Freedom of Information Act, and gain possession of his Permanent Record by recess. Either that, or the kid would call up his Permanent Record on his computer terminal, and purge any information he didn't want to be there.

As for us adults—it has been so long since we have believed in the Permanent Record that the very mention of it today probably brings a nostalgic smile to our faces. We feel naive for ever having believed that a Permanent Record was really down there in the principal's office, anyway.

And who really knows if our smiles may freeze on some distant day—the day it is our turn to check out of this earthly world, and we are confronted with a heavenly presence greeting us at the gates of our new eternal home—a heavenly presence sitting there casually leafing through a dusty, battered volume of our Permanent Record as we come jauntily into view.

Wimp's Funeral

By now there can't be too many people in Chicago who haven't heard about the funeral of Willie M. ("Wimp") Stokes, Jr., the South Side professional gambler who was buried in a casket that had been custom-designed to look like a Cadillac Seville automobile.

Stokes, twenty-eight, appeared at his own visitation propped up in the coffin, his hands on its steering wheel. The casket was equipped with blinking headlights and taillights, a windshield, whitewall tires, a Cadillac grille, and a vanity license plate featuring his "Wimp" nickname.

Stokes was dressed for the occasion in a flaming red suit, a rakish gray hat, and diamond rings. During the visitation he had several thousand-dollar bills sticking out from between his fingers.

More than five thousand people came to the A. R. Leak Funeral Home to pay their respects and view the casket. The *Chicago Defender,* a newspaper serving the black community, covered the proceedings for two days, on the second day devoting a full page of pictures to the funeral; the *Defender,* which referred to the coffin as a "casketmobile," completely sold out copies of the editions featuring the funeral coverage. The newspaper, which normally sells for twenty-five cents, reportedly was going for up to five dollars in the Loop.

Stokes passed away after being shot in the head by gunmen as he stood on the steps of Roberts Motel, 79th Street and Vincennes Avenue. At the funeral he was praised as a "master party-giver"; his father told the *Defender,* "Little Willie did a few bad things. But all in all, he was a loving and caring son, husband, father, brother, and friend to people around the nation."

I had heard so much about the Stokes funeral that I wanted to talk with the people most closely involved—Stokes's parents and the funeral director.

Stokes's mother, Jean, said, "I wouldn't have traded that funeral for anything. I really liked the way it went."

She said that the family had decided on the Cadillac coffin after shopping around for caskets. "We were looking in the showroom, and there was just nothing that we liked," she said. "You know how it is, when the merchandise just doesn't appeal to you.

"That's when we thought it would be nice if Willie could be buried in a Cadillac, because he was so crazy about his car. My only disappointment is that the casket looked like a Seville. Willie drove an Eldorado."

She said that the design of the casket was a joint venture: "The wheels were made out of flowers, put together by Maxine's Florist on 47th Street. It was my husband who said that we should have a windshield put on the casket so it looked like a convertible."

She said that she appreciated the large number of mourners, although "personally, I generally don't like a crowd." She said she thought her son "left like he lived—in a lively manner."

The funeral director, Spencer Leak, said, "Mr. Stokes had let it be known that in the event of his demise, he would prefer a funeral that reflected his lifestyle. I called all around the country trying to find a casket company that could provide me with a casket that looked like a Cadillac. In Indianapolis, I found one. They said, 'How about a Seville?' I said, 'Perfect.'"

Leak said, "The family was elated. They said it was exactly what they wanted. This is a flashy family."

He said he had no problem with the question of tastefulness. "This was not a rowdy thing," he said. "It was very subdued and respectful. It was done with class. As a funeral director, my job is to honor the family's requests, reflect the lifestyle of the deceased, and relate to everyone's bereavement. This I did."

Stokes's father, Willie M. ("Flukie") Stokes, Sr., said that his own occupation, like his son's, was "professional gambler," although Chicago police have characterized him as one of the city's leading drug dealers. Stokes said that his son had been "a fine young man; he was very well liked and did a lot of gambling."

He said the funeral pleased him greatly. "Anyone who wants to criticize it can criticize it," he said. "But my son would have liked it. He liked anything I did for him."

He said he assumed it was the most unusual funeral in anyone's memory, but that he had no real way of knowing. "I don't go to funerals," he said. "Funerals aren't my thing. There's no dice at funerals."

He said that he personally put the thousand-dollar bills between his son's fingers in the casket because "he gambled for that kind of money."

I asked Stokes if there was any particular reason he had opted for such a flashy funeral.

"It's not flashy," he said. "It's just everyday living."

I asked why he thought other families didn't choose to have funerals like this one.

"I don't know," he said. "Maybe not everyone cares about their son the way I did."

The Coolest Guy
in the Room

There are men in this world who, since they were little boys, have had life beaten. There's one in every junior high school—the kid who's a natural on the playground, who's irresistible to the girls, who makes the other boys jealous.

Most of those boys lose it somewhere along the way; the high school heroes discover, twenty years later, that the best days of their lives were left behind in the cement-block football stadium of their teens. Some don't lose it, though. And among all those who didn't lose it, Frank Gifford stands out.

If all you know about Gifford is what you've seen on "Monday Night Football," you might be smirking a little by now. Gifford is clearly not the star of that show. Next to Howard Cosell and Don Meredith, Gifford's electronic image comes off a little bland, a little bloodless; he is just the play-by-play guy, and the casual television viewer might regard him as sort of vanilla.

There's a difference, though. Television makes celebrities out of virtually everyone who appears regularly on it. If you've been on television and people see you on the street, they stop. Some men who were the biggest jerks in their high school classes are sought after now merely because they are frequently televised.

Gifford, quite simply, would command attention if a television camera had never been trained on him. He is one of the few men on national TV who don't need TV for their self-esteem. Every step of his life, he has found himself doing the most glamorous thing a man can do. In the late Forties and early Fifties, when the desired thing was to be a big man on campus, Gifford was an all-American tailback at the University of Southern California. In the Fifties and early Sixties, when the desired thing was to play in the National Football League, Gifford was an all-pro left halfback for the New York Giants. In the Seventies and Eighties, when the desired thing is to be a network television personality, Gifford is a first-string announcer with ABC Sports.

I do some work for ABC News; I have been on the road in the same city with Gifford, and when he walks into a room something remarkable happens. People stop what they are doing and involuntarily focus their eyes on him—and it has virtually nothing to do with his video familiarity. There is something about his stunning looks, something about the absolute self-confidence with which he carries himself; there is something about him that gives off the message that this is no mere television star—this is that kid who ruled the playground, now grown older, but still having whatever it is the playground heroes used to have. Women look at Gifford and covet his company; men look at him and suddenly feel too fat or too bald or too short or too pale.

He apparently has had this effect on people all his life. Author Frederick Exley, in his book *A Fan's Notes,* recalled seeing Gifford in a campus coffee shop when they were both students at Southern Cal. The two had never met, but of course Exley knew who Gifford was. The two did not speak, but Exley recalled thinking: "Listen, you son of a bitch. Life isn't always a goddamned football game! You won't always get the girl! Life is rejection and pain and loss." Alex Karras, who worked in the announcing booth with Gifford briefly on "Monday Night Football," at the time said of Gifford: "Yesterday he had on a pair of Levi's and a T-shirt with MAMA written on it. I had on a five-hundred-dollar suit. I looked like Emmett Kelly and he looked like a guy in a tuxedo."

It's a fairly simple concept: for his whole life, whenever Gifford has walked into a room, he has been the coolest guy in the room. Most of us don't know what that's like. I always wondered about it; I had never had the opportunity to ask him, and I wasn't sure how he'd react to the question if I did.

Gifford greeted me at the door of his Manhattan apartment. He lives with his second wife and stepchildren in Connecticut, but keeps the New

York apartment for nights when he is working late or has to be in the ABC studios early. He motioned me inside; we sat at a dining room table. Gifford smoked Larks.

I tried to explain what I wanted to talk about. He showed no reaction to the request. He began to give me a brief autobiography: how his father had worked in the oil fields, and how the family had had to move often—sometimes fifteen times in a single year. The only way he and his brother were able to make friends with new schoolmates was to excel on the athletic field. "That's a way to fit in right away, when you move so often," he said.

I said that there must be thousands of other young boys who have to move a lot, but who aren't Frank Gifford on the playground.

"I can't help that," Gifford said. "You're talking about physical ability. I was born with that. I had nothing to do with it."

He ran through his life as a high school quarterback, a college tailback, a pro halfback. I brought up the Frederick Exley quote; I mentioned the section of *A Fan's Notes* in which Exley mused on his envy of Gifford.

"I think he was stuck on my girlfriend," Gifford said. "He'd seen her around campus."

But surely Gifford was accustomed to people reacting that way to who he was, and what he had.

"I suppose," he said. "People have always looked for things in me that they'd like to see in themselves. I've experienced a lifetime of it. I have never known what to think of it. It wasn't my fault that I was a good athlete. It was just genetic structure." He went to the kitchen and came back with some Oreo cookies and a cup of coffee.

I asked if he had ever had the moment, as an adolescent, that all adolescent boys have—the moment they look in the bathroom mirror and see all nose or all chin or all acne. That moment in every young boy's life when he realizes he looks awful, and there's nothing he can do about it.

"I guess not, because I don't recall it," he said.

I asked if he had always been so remarkably good-looking.

"I've been attractive all my life, and my looks have helped me all my life," he said. "Attractive, I guess, both to men and to women. Because men don't seem to be threatened by me. Guys will push their wives at me and say, 'Oh, my wife thinks you're adorable,' and I'll just say, 'Thank you very much.'"

And there was never a time, no matter how brief, when he was worried about the way he looked?

"I don't think I ever thought about it."

What about the other boys—the ones who were awkward, who were clumsy on the athletic field, who looked ugly in their bathroom mirrors? When Gifford was growing up, what did he think about those boys?

"Not a hell of a lot, because they weren't in my life," he said. "It's a matter of economy of time. Everyone associates with the people who were in their life. The people who were in my life were the guys who were playing football."

I said that a lot of men who didn't become famous via television until they had reached their forties or fifties seemed to make excuses to go out in public, just so they could reaffirm their fame every day. Was it different for someone who had always known the feel of admiring looks?

"Absolutely," Gifford said. "There are people who hire press agents, who run and try to get their pictures in the paper and to be written about. When you've had that on an ongoing basis all your life, you tend to find it less important. You don't go out frantically seeking love and attention and affection from strangers.

"When I'm on the road for 'Monday Night Football,' I'll get into town on a Sunday and just stay in my room. I'll order all my meals from room service, and study my notes for the game. Maybe I'll go out for a run, or if it's in a warm-weather city I'll go down to the pool and lie in the sun. But do I ever get a sudden flash of insecurity and feel I have to go down to the lobby to make sure everyone knows who the hell I am? No."

Gifford said that he was fifty-two now. "I just had a little grandson," he said. "I thought it might bother me—becoming a grandfather. I didn't know what it would be like. People would kid me and say, 'Here comes grand-daddy.' I wondered if it would make me feel old. They said 'granddaddy' as if it were a terrible disease. And people these days are so concerned about age; when you turn thirty or thirty-five you're regarded as an animal that's ready to be terminated.

"So I didn't know how I'd react to being a grandfather. But it's . . . really an interesting rush. My grandson is absolutely adorable. Seeing my daughter, who I held in my own arms, holding that baby in her arms . . . it's an interesting little lifestep. And I have no complaints about being fifty-two. A lot of guys didn't make it."

I said that fifty-two might mean one thing for most men; it meant something completely different in the context of Frank Gifford. When people saw him, they did not think "fifty-two-year-old man"; age seemed almost immaterial, and that fact undoubtedly unleashed the same flow of emotions in people that his being an all-American tailback did thirty years ago. I asked him if he had always been aware of the envy he aroused in others.

"There's really nothing I can do about that," he said. "I know what you mean. People thinking, 'You lucky son of a bitch.' If they want to think that, fine. But nobody works harder. I've found that the more you put into it, the luckier you are. Maybe they were lying on their ass drinking a can of beer, when I was getting done with football practice and then putting on a suit and tie so I could meet someone who might be able to help me in the off-season."

I asked him about the thought that had brought me to see him: the idea of walking into rooms his whole life and knowing the effect he would have on the people already in the room. Surely that must do something to a man.

"I enjoy walking into a room," Gifford said. "Most of the rooms I walk into, either I'm working, in which case I don't give a shit what the people think about me, or they're my friends, in which case I know what they think of me. So yeah, I'm comfortable. I've never had a problem walking into any room, if that's what you're asking."

We talked some more, and before I left I found out something that amazed me. I asked Gifford if there was ever anything in his life that he had wanted, and that he had not gotten.

And there was. It seems that he had once asked the New York Giants to let him switch from halfback to quarterback. The Giants had allowed him to try it in practice, but never in a game. All these years later, it turned out, Gifford still resented that.

"There wasn't a whole lot of doubt in my mind that I could have been an all-pro quarterback," he said. "I really felt I could have played the position."

I said that surely the slight couldn't have made much of a difference to him, even back then. After all, he was one of the most famous and successful players in the National Football League.

"Some people thought I wanted to do it for the publicity," he said. "Or for the glamour. But I was already the leading rusher, the leading scorer, the leading receiver. How could it have been more glamorous for me?"

Then why had he wanted to become a quarterback?

"I didn't want to *become* a quarterback," he said. "I *was* a quarterback. I was a quarterback in high school. USC recruited me to play quarterback. Halfback was forced on me."

But could it have made any real difference in his life? Considering the way things had turned out?

Thirty-seven floors below, the Manhattan traffic edged slowly along. Gifford ate another Oreo.

"Look, I don't want you to get the idea that I dwell on this," he said. "But always, in my own mind, I was a quarterback. I was never a halfback. I didn't *want* to be a quarterback. I *was* a quarterback. Nobody ever seemed to understand that."

Strangers on a Plane

On board United Airlines' Flight 1118, I waited for the jet to pull away from the gate. We were parked at Los Angeles International Airport; we were getting ready to take off for San Francisco.

The seat next to me was unoccupied. I was looking forward to stretching out during the flight. But just as the door at the front of the plane was closing, she rushed on. She excused herself and slipped into the seat directly to my left.

She was tall, in a tan dress. She wore diamond earrings. She appeared to be in her early thirties. It was clear that she had been in a big hurry; she was perspiring and breathing more rapidly than is normal, the way people breathe when they've been running down the airport concourse, trying to make a flight they can't afford to miss.

I didn't say anything. We taxied onto the runway, paused briefly, then picked up speed; in a few moments we were in the air.

She was the first to speak. "Are you a nervous flier?" she said.

"I am," I said. "How can you tell?"

She nodded toward my legs. "Your foot's going crazy," she said. I followed her stare. My left foot was indeed tapping away.

"How long has that been going on?" she said.

"Awhile," I said.

"Do you have to fly a lot?" she said.

"I do," I said.

The flight attendant came around and took drink orders. The woman said she'd have a Jack Daniel's and Seven-Up.

She was working on her drink, several minutes later, when she said, "Are you flying for business or pleasure?"

"Business," I said.

She seemed to be expecting me to pursue the line of questioning, so I said, "What about you? Are you flying for business or pleasure?"

"Neither," she said. "I'm just flying."

I didn't understand, of course. So I thought I'd ask it another way.

"How long were you in Los Angeles?" I said.

"About fifteen minutes," she said, and went back to her drink.

Before long she withdrew some pieces of paper from her purse and laid them on the tray table in front of her. I sneaked a look; they were United Airlines write-your-own-ticket passes, the kind that flight attendants carry with them so that they can board any plane they want.

"You fly for United, then?" I said.

"No," she said.

"Then what are the passes?" I said.

"They're spouse passes," she said. "I get them because of my husband."

"What does your husband do for United?" I said.

"He's dead," she said.

She kept ordering drinks, and she gradually told me her story. She lived in Colorado; her husband, she said, had been a baggage handler for United for fifteen years. He had died last December.

"Was it a long illness?" I said. "Did you know it was coming?"

"He killed himself," she said.

She said that since her husband's death, she had been flying. Not flying anywhere in particular; just flying.

"Today I got on the plane in Denver," she said. "What I usually do is walk into the terminal at the next airport, look around for the United flight board, and get onto the next flight, wherever it's going. This afternoon the next flight was going to San Francisco."

She said that, because of the spouse passes, the cost to her was minimal: maybe four dollars for a short flight, eight dollars for a longer one.

"You mean you just go anywhere the airplanes go?" I said.

"That's right," she said.

"How many flights in a row do you usually take?" I said.

She shrugged. "There's no plan to it, really," she said. "I just fly until I know it's time to stop flying. Then I go home."

She looked out the window and down at the Pacific Ocean. "It's so peaceful up here," she said. "Look at that boat in the water." I leaned over toward the window; the boat was barely visible far below, but you could, indeed, make it out if you looked hard enough.

I asked her when she had started her aimless flying.

"My husband and I used to travel together all the time," she said. "I got used to it then, and now that I'm alone I still do it."

I looked at her left hand, and she saw what I was doing. "Putting my wedding ring away was the hardest thing," she said. "That was like officially admitting it to myself, 'He's dead.' Until I put the ring away, it didn't seem final."

I asked her if the flying was a way to avoid thinking about her husband.

"That's not it at all," she said. "I don't want to avoid thinking about him. Actually, it's easier to think up here. You have more time."

The flight attendant came around again to see if we needed anything. She ordered another drink, handing the flight attendant her empty glass as she did so; I asked her if she was purposely trying to get drunk.

"I can get drunk on one drink," she said. "Getting drunk has nothing to do with it."

I said that there might be better ways to sort out her feelings than just getting onto airplanes at random.

"I like it this way," she said.

"But why?" I said.

"Just because," she said.

The seat-belt sign flashed on, and a voice on the plane's loudspeaker system announced that we were beginning our descent into San Francisco. It was nearing dinnertime; I asked the woman if she knew where she was going to sleep.

"I guess on a plane," she said. "I'll probably get an all-night flight, and I'll sleep on that."

"Is that what you always do when you're flying like this?" I said. "Sleep on all-night flights?"

"Sometimes," she said. "If I go to Hawaii, I might stay over for the night, just to say I've been there. But the plane's just as good. I prefer the plane."

I didn't know what to say to her. The runway of San Francisco International was within sight, and the landing gear locked into place, and I found myself for some reason saying, "Do you think one of these days you'll wake up and you'll be able to care about another person again?"

She smiled. "I'm really not into caring these days," she said.

We hit the ground and taxied toward the gate.

"You're nice to talk to," she said. "You're not a grumpo. I end up sitting next to so many grumpos."

A flight attendant, on the PA system, said, "Thank you for flying with us, and for choosing United Airlines. We hope that the next time your plans call for air travel, you'll think of the friendly skies."

The woman smiled again. "Little do they know," she said.

In the ensuing days I found myself thinking about her. I wondered . . . she had been drinking so much, and her story had been so unlikely; could the whole thing have been a put-on, a little airborne fantasy designed to break the boredom and get her through the afternoon? Could she have been just another businesswoman on her way to an appointment in San Francisco, or a housewife on her way to meet her husband?

I had asked her her name, and the name of her late husband; I had written them down on a paper napkin from the flight. I called a man I knew at United's executive offices in Chicago; his name was Joe Hopkins, and I asked him if he could see if United had ever had an employee with the same name as the man whose name was scrawled on my napkin.

He called me back within an hour. "Our records show that the man worked for us for about fifteen years," Hopkins said. "But he died last December."

I asked Hopkins if the records showed whether the death was a suicide. He said he was not at liberty to give out that kind of information. So I got in touch with the United operations center in Denver, where the man had supposedly worked. I asked around and eventually found a baggage handler named Dave Bellavance; Bellavance, forty-one, had been a colleague of the man.

"Yes, he killed himself last December," Bellavance said in a soft voice. "I had really enjoyed working with him. He was a guy who liked to have a good time. It was good knowing him. When I heard what had happened, I was sad and disappointed and even a little angry. I guess I was angry that he had decided to take himself away from the world."

Bellavance asked why I was bringing up these questions, so I told him about the woman on the plane. He didn't respond for a few seconds; I asked him if her story made any sense.

"Yeah," he said. "It makes sense. They were the kind of people who were always flying around. It's so cheap when you work for the airlines, some people do it all the time. They were the kind of people who would fly to Arizona just to pick up a T-shirt."

I asked him if he had seen his co-worker's wife since the suicide.

"No," he said. "But I'm not surprised to hear what she's doing."

Whenever I see a plane unloading into an airport concourse now, I take a look. Whenever I board a United flight, I can't help glancing around the cabin at my fellow passengers.

We all have our own ways of running away, I suppose; we all have our own ways of escaping the parts of our lives we'd rather not acknowledge.

I walk down the street and I hear the sound of a plane up above, and I stare at the sky and I think about her. She's up there somewhere; I don't know how long she'll keep running, or whether she'll ever stop. But I know she's up there, and I find myself wondering where she's sleeping tonight.

Western Reunion

It was a meeting without fanfare. This year's gathering was smaller than last year's; next year's, no doubt, will be smaller still.

The thirty men were gathered in a small room off the eighth-floor cafeteria in the Carson Pirie Scott & Co. department store in Chicago's Loop. They had all been telegraphers; each of them had operated telegraph keys back in the days when sending dots and dashes over the wires was the fastest, most efficient way of communication. They had worked for railroads, for brokerage houses, for Western Union, for the Postal Telegraph Company.

Now they are not needed. Computers and television and inexpensive long-distance phone lines have erased the requirement for telegraphers. There are no young men coming up to replace the men who had come to lunch in this room.

"You feel like an orphan," said Carl Sostak, eighty, who had gone to work for Western Union in 1923. "In the time it took us to send one character, an IBM computer screen can print pages. You don't feel as if you're a part of this generation. You're out of step. We just don't belong anymore."

Sostak, like his companions at lunch, had dressed in a nice business suit.

The men in the room call themselves the Morse Telegraph Club. There are approximately fifty chapters across the United States—and on this day all of the chapters were holding meetings simultaneously. Here in Chicago it was on the eighth floor of Carson's; in Aberdeen, South Dakota, it was at the Flame Restaurant; in Portland, Oregon, it was at the Mallory Hotel; in Terre Haute, Indiana, it was at Joy's Restaurant.

Western Union had set up a special wire connecting each of the chapter meetings for a few hours. On a table in this room there were a telegraph key and its sounder; by hitting the key, the men could communicate with their brethren around the nation. As the men filed in, the key and its sounder were alive; messages were arriving from Minneapolis, from Oklahoma City, from Cincinnati.

"We all have rabbit ears," said Bill Dunbar, and it seemed to be true; even as the old telegraphers were greeting one another, they were listening to the sounder, and silently translating the messages as they came across the wire. A red metal Prince Albert tobacco can had been attached to the key-and-sounder; the men explained that this was a telegraphers' tradition— the can made the messages louder, made their sound carry more distinctly.

"Someone's calling Seattle," said A. J. Long, sixty-nine, as the sounder clicked.

"We're a proud breed because there's nobody learning it today," he said. "We took a lot of care in the messages we sent out. I remember once, Harry Truman was passing through Salem, Illinois, on a train on his way to Washington. He had just heard that MacArthur was not going to run for President. The train was full of newsmen, and they had all written stories that had to be wired to their papers.

"I got a call at midnight. I was to be down at the station when the train rolled through. They tossed the stories off the train, and I transmitted them to newspapers all over the country until seven A.M. When I finally got home, that day's St. Louis *Globe-Democrat* had arrived at my house. And there was the story I had sent—perfect, right down to the letter."

The men in the room said they have trouble explaining to younger people just what it is they used to do. "It's a skill no one today would ever want to learn," said Glenn Keeney, seventy-nine, a railroad telegrapher. "There's no field for them to get into. We were proud, though; we were doing something that somebody else couldn't do. We felt like we were part of a profession."

Helner Ahlborg, seventy-nine, who worked for Western Union and Postal Telegraph, said, "There was a lot of braggadocio among telegraphers about the speed you could attain. Some of the fellows never did develop any speed, while others got to be terrific.

"The important thing was to know the capabilities of the fellow on the other end while you were sending. If he wasn't a speed demon at receiving, you knew to hold back a bit. You got to know the other fellow's way of sending. It was just like listening to his voice. Every man had a certain swing to his transmitting."

At ten minutes before noon, the sounder at the front of the room clicked again. The men, now sitting at tables, turned to it. Out in Lincoln, Nebraska, a retired telegrapher named Cecil Combs was saying grace on the wire. His prayer was clicking into all the chapters around the nation.

The metal arm on the sounder tapped against the Prince Albert can, and suddenly, in unison, every man in the room rose. They listened together; the sounder clicked some more, and they all closed their eyes and reached out to the men on either side of them. They held hands. The only noise in the room was the steady clicking. From Nebraska, Cecil Combs was telling them that it was time to give thanks; time to thank God that, despite all the changes in the world, they were all here again, together.

Alley Girls

The day had been a long one, and darkness had come early. It was enough to depress a fellow.

I was just getting ready to go home when I happened to glance at the calendar. It was Wednesday. Ah, Wednesday. I smiled at the very thought of it. If it's Wednesday, everything's all right.

On Wednesday the Greenettes bowl. I hailed a cab and headed for the lanes.

Most of us can never even dream of owning a professional sports franchise; being a big league owner is the province of multimillionaires, and we have as little chance of identifying with them as of identifying with the king of Saudi Arabia.

But I have discovered that you don't have to be a millionaire to feel like George Steinbrenner. All you really need is twenty-five bucks; for that paltry sum you can own a team that will make you happier than ten years of New York Yankees, with none of the headaches.

Twenty-five dollars is the sponsor's fee for the Wednesday Night Ladies' League at the Mont Clare Lanes bowling alley on the northwest side of Chicago. If you pay the twenty-five, a team is yours. Five frisky females who are as grateful and indebted to you as if you were keeping them in minks, champagne, and duplex condominiums.

The Greenettes are my team. I sponsor them; they wear my name on their bowling shirts. They mean the world to me, especially on dreary Wednesday nights when life is looking dismal. Tonight I needed to check out my girls.

When I arrived at Mont Clare Lanes, the Greenettes were just starting their match. They were pitted against a fivesome called Up Your Alley; the Greenettes and Up Your Alley were seated on a salmon-and-white bench that spanned two lanes.

Spectators are supposed to sit in chairs behind the alleys, but as owner of the team I am permitted to sit on the bench with the Greenettes themselves. When they saw me they let out a chorus of welcoming cheers; as I joined them they gathered around me.

I was wearing a coat and tie, as is my custom when visiting the Greenettes. I walked over to peruse the league standings; the girls, alas, were in eighth place in a fourteen-team division.

No matter. The season was young. I leaned back and took an appreciative gaze at my squad.

The Pindel sisters were looking fine. The Pindels are the heart of the Greenettes; there are three of them on the team. Angela Pindel, twenty-six, a telephone console operator for a newspaper publishing company, had a league average of 117 as of tonight. Helen Pindel-Costa, twenty-four, a secretary for a Loop manufacturing firm, was averaging 153. Jo-Ann Pindel Jasiak, twenty-eight, an employee of the cosmetics department of J. C. Penney, was averaging 135.

Corky Barnash, thirty-two, a bookkeeper for restaurants and bars, was averaging 128. The kid of the team, Sandy McCowan, twenty, a nursing student, was averaging 93.

Angela converted a spare, and pranced back to give a high-five handslap to each of the Greenettes, and to me. It is a custom on the team; when any member gets a strike or a spare, we smack palms. Some of the other teams think it's bush, but we like it.

As Jo-Ann got set to roll her ball I mused on how the fates deal us curious hands. Just one day before I found these five women, they had almost decided that they would not be able to recruit a sponsor. The Pindels' Uncle Norbert, sensing desperation in the girls, had agreed to underwrite the team if no one else could be found. They were going to be called Norb's Nieces.

But why dwell on what might have been? I had found them in time. They were the Greenettes, and they were mine.

All around us, other sponsors' teams were rolling away. Ogden and Carroll Service Station, Willoughby's Two bar, Sam's Finer Foods. As far as I could tell, no other sponsors were there in person—in the owner's box, as it were. This did not surprise me. I had learned that many sponsors are shockingly lackadaisical about providing on-site support. That burns me. They pop for the money, and they think that's their only obligation,

Helen was holding a vodka and orange juice as she waited her turn to bowl. One thing about the Wednesday Night Ladies' League: these women drink and they smoke. You have to accept that if you want to be a good owner. You're not likely to mistake your athletes for potential Olympians in training; if that's what you're looking for, you're best advised to find another sport.

So up and down the thirty-two lanes a haze of smoke hovered over the scoring consoles, and empty beer bottles were discarded in anticipation of a waitress who would pick them up and bring refills.

Jo-Ann was fuming. "If I had known that was the beer frame, I would have tried harder," she said. "I only got a nine. You really want to get a mark in the beer frame. You don't want to be the one who has the low score and who has to put the fifty cents into the pot."

On the Mont Clare's loudspeaker system, the recorded voice of Bobby Vinton could be heard singing "Mr. Lonely."

"Hey!" Angela said. "I saw a Bobby Vinton special on TV last night! Did you know that he wrote this song in three minutes? That's what he said on TV. He said he was in the Army when he wrote it and the words came to him just like that."

Sandy was standing off to the side. She is the quiet Greenette; I have a hunch it's because of her tender years. Whatever the reason, she doesn't say much. I asked her if she wouldn't rather be out chasing boys than bowling.

"Nah," she said. "Not on a weeknight." She lives at home with her mother; she said that her mom, if the truth be told, would prefer that she stay home and study rather than bowl with the Greenettes. She wandered toward the ball-return rack, ever the enigma.

Corky had overheard our brief conversation. She laughed. "Come hell or high water, I'm here," she said. "I have a two-year-old, and Wednesday night is my only night out. I bowl Wednesdays, my husband bowls Thursdays."

I glanced up at the scorecard, which was projected on a screen above the lanes. The Greenettes were ahead in the first game.

There had been a dramatic personal event in the life of one of the Greenettes just four weeks earlier. On the Thursday following a Wednesday night match, Helen had flown to Las Vegas with her boyfriend, Steve Costa, a filling-station employee and part-time rock musician, and had gotten married. The ceremony was still the major topic of the squad's between-frames chatter.

"Look at the pictures she brought back," said Angela, showing me some color snapshots. "She got married in the Silver Bell Wedding Chapel, right on the Strip."

I looked at the photos.

"Stars get married in this chapel," Angela said. "It's the chapel of the stars. Helen, who are the stars who got married there?"

"I don't know," Helen said. "It's on the card. I think I've got it in my purse." She rummaged through the purse, but did not find it. "I must have left the card on my dresser at home," she said.

"I think it said Diana Ross got married there," Angela said.

"Don't go saying that," Helen said. "I don't think it said that Diana Ross actually got married there. I think it might have said that Diana Ross just visited there once."

Sandy rolled her ball down the lane; the pins smacked off one another, and two were left standing.

"Man in your bedroom!" Corky yelled.

"That's just Corky's phrase," Angela explained to me. "It's what she calls it when one pin is hidden behind another. I don't know where she got that. Technically, it's called a sleeper."

I was noticing that, although my team was in fierce competition with Up Your Alley, the members of the two squads were not talking to one another.

They were sitting on the same bench, but not more than a dozen words had been exchanged between the two aggregations all night.

I decided to try to find out why. I scooted over next to the other team and started to ask them about it.

"What do you think of the Greenettes?" I said to Marge Wanat, one of their members.

"I don't know," she said. "This is the first time we ever played them."

"I'm their sponsor," I said.

"Yeah," she said. "We know."

"How come you're not talking to them?" I said. "Is there something you don't like about them?"

"No, they seem all right," she said. "Sometimes you play a team that's real crabby. Your team's not crabby."

Another member of Up Your Alley, Pat Grimes, said, "We don't really come here to socialize with the other teams. We come here to socialize with ourselves. This is the only chance we get to see each other all week long."

"They're like every other team here," said Colleen Mahoney. She avoided making eye contact with the Greenettes.

I had a sneaking suspicion that I knew what the problem was. "Who's your sponsor?" I said.

"We don't have a sponsor," Marge Wanat said, a little too quickly. "We sponsor ourselves."

Aha. It must be tough. Here they were—Up Your Alley, a team without an owner—and in walks the owner of the Greenettes himself, in person, on the scene, actually sitting on the bench, giving his girls encouragement. I couldn't say I really blamed Up Your Alley. I dropped the line of questioning and moved back down with my squad.

On the lane to our right, a team called Killer Bees Two was bowling. On top of their console was a stuffed toy bee.

"That's their mascot," Angela told me. "Both Killer Bees Two and Killer Bees One always bring their bees with them. Look down at lane thirty. See? That's Killer Bees One. See their bee?"

I peered over at them. The women of Killer Bees One seemed to be snacking on something.

"I don't know what it is about Killer Bees One," Angela said. "They always bring their own potato chips. Us, we use the vending machines provided by the lanes."

Next to us, the team that was bowling against Killer Bees Two—Willoughby's Two bar—had undertaken a new routine. Every time one of their members bowled, she would tie a blue plastic rain bonnet over her head. When she had finished her frame, she would give the rain bonnet to the next woman in the lineup. The rain bonnet kept passing from head to head. Apparently this was some sort of good-luck ritual.

"Where'd you get the hat?" Angela called to one of the women.

"She found it in her purse," the woman answered, pointing to a teammate.

I paced on the carpeting behind the alleys. The Greenettes were into their third game; they were far enough ahead that they were assured of being victors for the night. I was due back downtown. Things seemed to be in secure enough shape for me to leave.

I was down by the Lustre King ball-conditioning machine when I heard my women cheer. Jo-Ann had just rolled a strike; they were giving each other the high five. I hurried back so that I could join them.

I told them that I had to take off. We waved goodbye. As I was on my way out a buzzer went off back in the direction of the Greenettes' lane. I looked back; Corky, carrying a Stroh's, had walked past the foul line, setting off an alarm. Her ball was stuck in the gutter, and she was going out to retrieve it. I don't know how Steinbrenner feels when he's walking out of Yankee Stadium, but there's no way that it could be any better.

Bexley

WASHINGTON—I was supposed to deliver this year's commencement address at the high school from which I graduated in 1965. I got sick and didn't make it to the ceremony, so the speech never got made, but I've been giving some thought to what I might have said had I arrived on schedule, and I'm finding that I'm surprising myself.

Bexley, Ohio, is a town of 14,000. It is quiet and sedate, a suburb of

Columbus; the cliché "Middle America" probably fits. When I was going to Bexley High School, most of us talked about getting out. It was our obsession. Bexley was too small, too confined, too safe; we wanted the Real World.

Eight hundred students attend Bexley High School; in Chicago, the town where I now make my living, we kill more than that many people every year. In Bexley, there has not been a murder recorded since the town hired its first marshal in 1917. Bexley has five marked police cars; in Chicago, there are more than 11,000 men and women employed by the Police Department. I guess I found the Real World.

And yet as I sit here in Washington, where I'm making my temporary headquarters, my mind is on Bexley, and all of the other Bexleys across America. Chicago may be the Real World, and Washington may be the Power Center, whatever that means, but it seems to me that the Real Worlds and the Power Centers are mainly made up of those of us who decided to leave the Bexleys, and I'm trying to think what I might have told those students at that graduation ceremony.

Because more and more, as I learn of the realities of life in the so-called important locales of the United States, I find myself wondering about Bexley, and whether it was so smart to leave it in the first place. I see the cruelties and the horrors and the outrages that have become the norm in the supposedly sophisticated centers of my Real World, and suddenly Bexley seems pretty good. All of those high school hours spent dreaming of escape . . . and now the dreams are of Bexley.

I know that I'll probably never go back. All of us, the ones who made the decisions to leave the Bexleys and seek out the Chicagos and the Washingtons and the New Yorks, we may dream about it, but it will somehow never get done. The decisions and impulses of your youth have a way of hardening up on you.

But still, I would never have given up my years of boyhood in Bexley, not for anything. The very things we found so maddening as teenagers— the small-town atmosphere that seemed to hem us in and keep us from everything exciting that was happening Out There—are the things that I now treasure most. I think that the most important part of me was formed in Bexley, and it's something that men and women who grew up in the big cities of the land will never know.

For there is something to be said for being allowed to grow up in a world without real problems, something to be said for being allowed to learn about life in a world without crime and without strife and without open hatred on the streets.

I know that there is another side of this to be argued; to grow up in a Bexley is to be made vulnerable and innocent and open to a lot of hurts and truths that you never even suspected exist. Bexley was, and is, white; there aren't even enough blacks living in Bexley to be statistically measurable on a census scale. The families of Bexley are financially comfortable. When a major part of the human spectrum is kept away from you as a child, you grow up ignorant about what much of life is about.

And yet the privilege of being allowed to grow up in such a peaceful world, a world where you are not always looking over your shoulder in the darkness or listening for footsteps in the night—that is a privilege that is becoming more and more priceless in the new world I am seeing. In the Bexley where I grew up, trouble meant getting caught painting our initials on the Penn Central bridge, or tearing the hands off the clock on top of the elementary school. I've learned since then, but I don't know how far I've come.

The irony, of course, is that even now the students of Bexley High School are dreaming of getting out, of finding that same Real World that seemed so elusive to us back in central Ohio. Some of the students in this year's graduating class will make it out, and some of them won't; they will stay in Bexley, and raise the next generation to grow up in Bexley.

And I guess, had I made that speech, it's the getting-out students I would have been talking to—the ones who will leave, and who will make Bexley only a part of their memories. I couldn't have told them not to do it; when you want to get out, there is nothing that can stop you, and I suppose I know that as well as anyone else. But to those who leave Bexley, please at least believe this: you will miss it. Jesus, how you will miss it.

King of the Campus

This curious thing happened. Last summer I wrote a column about a career woman in her thirties who had a good job, a nice apartment, fine friends—but who was miserable because she had no husband. She said that, even with the rest of her life in precise order, she was unhappy every day because she had no one to come home to.

She was afraid that people would think her attitudes were outmoded and behind the times, but that's not how readers reacted. Many business and professional people—men and women—wrote and called to say they felt the same way.

Among the responses were a number of letters from men who said they wanted to meet the woman in question. I had not printed her name; the men sent me long letters directed to her, and asked me to pass the letters along.

As I was reading the letters from the men, I couldn't help but wonder what kind of fellows would express such longing toward a woman they knew almost nothing about. I suppose I was envisioning sad, lonely men who had never been part of the so-called good life,

And then one of the letters stopped me cold. I read it—it was as lonely and poignant as any of the others—and I got to the signature, and I couldn't believe it.

I knew the man.

I knew him from college. Back at Northwestern, he had been one of the freewheeling, good-looking fraternity studs who ruled the campus. He had been in one of the best houses; he was well known as an ace intramural athlete; he ran with the most desirable crowd at the university.

And here was his letter. He wrote to the woman:

"I come home at night to my small studio apartment and fix myself a tuna sandwich with melted cheese, and I sit down to eat it and I look across the table and there's no one there."

I must have read the letter a dozen times. More than any of the others, it affected me. I read the words, and I thought of his happy-go-lucky face as he jauntily strode across the Northwestern campus in the late Sixties.

I sent the letter on to the woman, but I kept thinking about it. Finally I sought him out; we talked. He is thirty-six now. After college he tried to become a part of the business world, but didn't fit in. He does manual labor for a living.

I told him what my impression of him had been back at college.

"I know what people thought of me," he said. "But that image really wasn't true. I never even dated that much in college."

I said I had remembered seeing him and his friends at fraternity-sorority exchanges; they had always been surrounded by the most attractive co-eds from the best sororities.

"I was fairly shy," he said. "I suppose you could say I was kind of afraid of women. You talk about the exchanges; do you remember . . ." [Here he named some of the best-known fraternity men and athletes at Northwestern.] I said that I did, indeed, remember them.

"They were my roommates," he said. "If there was going to be an exchange at a downtown hotel with the Kappas or the Thetas, we would go down there early in the afternoon before anyone else got there, and start drinking beer. That's how we got through the exchanges. At six o'clock, when everyone else was heading back to campus to get ready for their dates, we'd go to the Toddle House and that would be our evening. I remember one Homecoming when I spent the evening doing my laundry."

He said he sometimes worries about the way things have turned out. "Everyone around me, all my closest friends from college and high school, have successful careers in corporate America," he said. "They have families and everything you're supposed to have. They must be pulling down $100,000 plus.

"I don't know anyone who, like myself, has failed to make any money. All my old friends have nice homes; I live in this crummy little studio apartment. That's a hard notion to live with. You wonder, why haven't you grabbed the brass ring?"

I asked him what had prompted him to write the letter to the woman.

"I was just feeling pretty miserable that night," he said. "I was sitting here in the apartment, having dinner with myself. I guess I thought that by writing the letter, by letting one other person in this world know that I was hurting, maybe I'd feel a little better."

I asked him what he wanted out of life.

"Well, I'm thirty-six and I've never been married, and I love children, and I would love to have some of my own someday," he said. "There was this article in *Newsweek* a couple of years ago about how women are afraid of hearing their biological clock ticking—how they get afraid they'll never have children. Men can feel that fear, too. It's not the same thing with the biological clock, but I feel afraid about it.

"The image of men in their thirties, I think, comes pretty much from beer commercials. You know, the men leave their downtown office to go play rugby, and then they get together for beer and good fellowship. The message is that life is lived from one peak experience to another, every day. But I know my life isn't like that."

We talked about a lot of other things; there isn't space to go into them here. But I kept envisioning him back on campus, in those final years of the Sixties; I kept seeing him coming out of his north campus fraternity house on a crisp fall day, ready to go to class. I asked him if he ever wished he could be back there again.

"No," he said. "I know I can't change places with anyone else. There's no point in wishing. Things work out the way they were intended to work out. There's a plan for all of us, and here I am."

Never Travel For Food

Some people told me they wanted me to try the "best pizza in the world."

In a weak moment, I said I'd go with them. They made me promise not to mention the name of the pizzeria in the newspaper; they did not want to ruin the place by having people from all over creation coming to check it out. I said I'd go anyway; I like pizza.

We drove for an hour and ten minutes. Finally we arrived at the pizzeria. It was a nondescript, low-slung building.

We walked inside. There were a limited number of tables; customers were expected to place their orders as soon as they entered the place, then wait for a table to open up. With luck, their pizza and their table would be ready at about the same time.

I was asked what kind of pizza I wanted.

"Oh, I don't know," I said. As long as I was at the place that cooked the best pizza in the world, I was ready to try anything.

"Go ahead," I was told. "What kind do you want?"

"Double cheese with pepperoni," I said.

"We don't have pepperoni here," I was told.

I stood there dumbstruck. This was no joke; the place with the "best pizza in the world" was telling me that pepperoni was not a feature of its menu.

I could have screamed. I could have cried. I could have kicked the wall.

I did none of those things. What I did do is this: I made myself repeat in my head, twenty straight times, one of the most valuable rules of life—a rule I had no business violating:

Never Travel For Food.

It's basic; it's simple; it's essential. The fault was all mine, for I had willingly violated the rule. No one should ever travel for an hour and ten minutes for a meal. It doesn't matter how good the meal is alleged to be; if a person is foolish enough to travel for an hour and ten minutes, then that person deserves to end up at a pizzeria that does not serve pepperoni.

Never Travel For Food. The rule seems almost quaint in a society that treats restaurants the same way it used to treat ornate and majestic movie theaters, that offers vast fortunes for entrepreneurs who open the right restaurant at the right time, that has *restaurant critics*. It's apparent that Americans have learned to honor and kneel before restaurants, and to travel any distance for a chance at the Right Meal.

Some of us, though, have an attitude that is slightly different. We find nothing magical about food. We are cars, and food is gasoline. When we are empty, we go to the nearest station and fill up. Then we cruise along until we are empty again, at which time we look for a convenient station at which to fill up again. We would no sooner travel an hour and ten minutes to go to a particular restaurant than travel an hour and ten minutes to go to a particular gas station. Give us five bucks' worth of regular and get us on our way.

Food, it seems to us, can do only several things. It can make us feel bloated. It can make us feel sick. It can get us by for a number of hours at a time.

Don't get us wrong; food can taste good. But it's no big deal; whatever the effects of a certain meal are, they are sure to disappear by morning. Spend time traveling for food? How nonsensical.

Our rule of thumb is: If it's close, eat there. What restaurant do we recommend? Almost everyone has at least one restaurant or coffee shop within a few blocks of home. That's the one we recommend; eat there.

On the road, things get a little more complicated. When one checks into a hotel, the first choice for a meal should be room service. It's the closest of all; you don't have to move. If room service is not practical, then the next best thing is to eat in the hotel dining room. That way you don't have to go outside. If for some reason you must go outside, the best place to eat is the first restaurant you run into after walking out of the hotel. Forget the guidebooks that tell you which restaurants in town rate however many stars. The first restaurant you enter will be fine.

Never Travel For Food. Such an obvious and wise concept; yet millions flout it routinely. There are even people who get on airplanes and fly to foreign countries—mainly France—just to eat. They don't eat as a *part* of their trip; the whole purpose of the trip is to eat.

"Why don't you try sausage on your pizza?" the people who had driven me for an hour and ten minutes said.

"I hate sausage on pizza," I said.

"Then what will you have?" they said.

"Double cheese, sausage, and onion," I said.

"We thought you said you hated sausage," they said.

"I do," I said. "The onion will hide the taste."

I made myself eat it. It was punishment, and I deserved it. Never Travel For Food. This wasn't a case of being ignorant—I knew the rule and I paid no attention to it. There was no reason to hurry; the only thing waiting for me at the other end of the meal was an hour-and-ten-minute drive back home. Which is where I should have stayed in the first place; I already had in my refrigerator the same thing they were offering at the best pizzeria in the world: no pepperoni.

Nixon on Nixon

NEW YORK—"I was walking along the street the other day," said Richard Nixon. "I was going over to the Regency Hotel to get a haircut. A couple of young fellows were standing on the corner. And a Secret Service agent said to me, 'Smell that. It's a joint.' Marijuana. Actually, I hadn't smelled it before."

Nixon broke into a small grin.

"I suppose I'm a bit square on that," he said. "I realize that's old hat."

We were in a long conversation, which was nearing the end of its second hour. Nixon, dressed in a blue suit, sat in a corner of his office in a federal government building. The office is not listed on the building's directory board; its telephone number is unlisted, and it is behind a plain, unmarked door.

The idea had been—in this era during which political men somehow all seem somewhat dull and smaller than life—to seek out the one man who had stirred the passions of the nation like no other.

I did not want to talk to Nixon about Watergate, or about the current political season. Rather, I just wanted to see if he would spend time with me. I was not seeking to hear Nixon talk about government or to make him judge office seekers. I wanted to hear Nixon talk about Nixon.

He was wary at first. "I have never been one to do a very effective job of psychoanalysis," he told me. "I don't try to psychoanalyze others, and so I'm not that good at psychoanalyzing myself. I think, frankly, that those who engage in that activity—much of it is superficial and contrived, and most of it is useless."

But as the hours went by, he loosened up. He moved away from his desk—the one with two flags behind it, the American flag and a dark blue flag bearing the seal of the President of the United States—and he sat in a red patterned chair. And he began to talk freely—about his days in the White House, about his relationships with the news media, about his views on television, about his new life in New York, about his feelings on the "drug generation," about the public's perception of him.

"Walter Cronkite," Nixon said.

We had been talking about the fact that public opinion polls often had showed Cronkite to be the most trusted man in America—while the same polls just as often listed politicians among the least-trustworthy categories.

"Yeah," Nixon said. "I think it's probably just a reflection on the fact that television is so powerful. And I would say that whoever is President—if he's so concerned to please everybody, not to ruffle feathers, to be a kind and gentle Walter Cronkite—then God help the country."

The question of public personality seemed to be very much on Nixon's mind. He was aware that Cronkite had attained the status of a beloved and warm American figure—and just as aware that he, Richard Nixon, was destined to go down in history with a reputation as a stiff, cold, bloodless man. He said he realized that many people think that of him; he wondered why they did not think the same of other Presidents.

"Truman was considered to be a very down-to-earth fellow," Nixon said. "But believe me, he didn't want any familiarity with him, except from his close friends.

"Eisenhower with that famous grin and so forth—but he didn't like to be touched. That's right. What I mean by that is that, of course, he would shake hands and all the rest. But he didn't want people to come up and throw their arms around him and say, 'Hi, Ike.'

"Kennedy was the same way. Despite the fact that he had the reputation of being, you know, very glamorous and the rest, he had a certain privacy about him, a certain sense of dignity. Now, Johnson was . . . Johnson was one who believed in touching the flesh, and the rest.

"I, of course, was more like Kennedy."

Nixon seemed aware that, because of his formality, many people found him to be a distant figure, not to be embraced or thought of with warmth. He said that was a product of the way he grew up thinking of the Presidency.

"A President must not be one of the crowd," he said. "He must maintain a certain figure. People want him to be that way. They don't want him to be down there saying, 'Look, I'm the same as you.'

"The White House is a very formal place. One doesn't feel that he can really kick up his heels there. Now T.R. [Theodore Roosevelt], of course, was able to accomplish that very well. His family romped around the White House and the rest. Ours never romped.

"We found one of the reasons we liked Camp David and our place in Florida was that you could sort of put on a sport shirt and the rest and relax. For example—and may I say that this is not intended to say that others should not do it differently—but in all the years I was in the White House, I never recall running around in a sport shirt, let alone a T-shirt. Or sneakers and the rest. Others do it, but I just didn't feel that way.

"And Mrs. Nixon never wore jeans. Maybe they weren't that much in style at that point. But it wasn't because we were stuffy. It was just that we would not feel comfortable in that house unless we were somewhat formal.

"Now, I wear a coat and a tie all the time. It isn't a case of trying to be formal, but I'm more comfortable that way. I've done it all my life.

"I don't mind people around here in the office, particularly younger people—they usually take their coats off. But I just never have. It's just the way I am. I work in a coat and tie—and believe me, believe it or not, it's hard for people to realize, but when I'm writing a speech or working on a book or dictating or so forth, I'm always wearing a coat and tie. Even when I'm alone. If I were to take it off, probably I would catch cold. That's the way it is."

Of all the things that Nixon might ponder concerning the Presidency, surprisingly the one he chose to bring up is an astonishingly small one— the fact that some newspapers capitalize the word "President" in second reference, while other papers use the lower-case "president."

"Well, yes," he said. "You have what I think is a rather juvenile practice which has occurred in the last four or five years. You do not capitalize the word 'president' when you say 'the President.' Now, I've noted the very significant change. We still follow the British. The British started to capitalize about three years ago. Then the *Wall Street Journal* in this country. Now the *New York Times* does it. *Washington Post,* no. Now that, to me, is a little petty."

Nixon appeared to be puzzled by what he perceives as a growing lack of respect for the institution of the Presidency—as exemplified by newspapers that refuse to capitalize the word "President," and by First Families who dress casually inside the official residence.

"Again, it goes back to the way we were raised," he said. "I recall the first time Mrs. Nixon and I went to the White House. I was a new congressman. And they had, as every President does at the beginning of every new Congress, a reception for all the members of Congress.

"And we had very little then. A congressman, incidentally—when I entered Congress, his salary was $12,500 a year. Which we thought then was not bad. But Mrs. Nixon, she scrimped and she bought a new dress to wear to the White House. A formal.

"And she said to me, 'Well, this is going to be a little hard on the budget, but this may be the only time we'll ever be there.'"

"If I had feelings," Nixon said, "I probably wouldn't have even survived."

We were talking about the traumas of his years in the White House— the public disenchantment with him that intensified during the Vietnam War, and culminated with his forced resignation from office after the Watergate affair.

"I don't allow my feelings to be hurt," Nixon said. "I learned very early on that you must not allow it to get to you. And as the years have gone on—and this used to infuriate my critics during the White House years— I made the decision not to respond, no matter how rough the attacks were."

We were at a highly intriguing point in our visit. I had told Nixon that when I had been in college, and then in my early twenties in the years immediately following college, I had run with a crowd that, in the main, despised the very mention of his name.

"Yeah, most of them were like that," Nixon said.

I said that there were several phrases that people liked to fling about when talking of Nixon. I wondered if he had ever heard them: "Tricky Dick," and "Would you buy a used car from this man?"

"Oh my, yes," he said. "Yeah."

I asked him if, when he heard those things being said about him, his feelings became hurt. And he immediately said that he was immune to such hurt.

"What was difficult for me," he said, "was that I was trying to end the war and end it in an honorable way. And to go around and have the students yell . . . you know, they didn't say, 'One, two, three, four, how many . . .' no, it was 'LBJ, how many boys did you kill today?' And all that sort of thing. And at the end of it, looking at the period, the treatment of me was much rougher than what they gave Johnson.

"I remember very clearly something. I was speaking down in Williamsburg, Virginia, and this was right after I had become President. And I think we had made the first announcement about our first withdrawal of twenty-five thousand. And this very pretty girl, she was I guess sixteen, seventeen—came up and spit full in my face and said: 'You murderer.'

"I borrowed a handkerchief from a Secret Service man and wiped it off and then I went in and made my speech. It was tough.

"The point is, if I had not been schooled in defeat, then probably it would have gotten to me so deeply that I would not have done a good job. You move from one battle to another. And in order to do the job well, my best advice to someone sitting in this office is, don't be too sensitive to the criticism. I think President Johnson died of a broken heart. I really do.

"Here's Johnson, this big, strong, intelligent, tough guy, practically getting so emotional that he'd almost cry, because his critics didn't appreciate him. He, 'til the very last, thought that he might be able to win them. And the point was, rather than win them, rather than have them love him, he should have tried to do what he could have done very well—have them respect him. And in the end he lost. He neither gained the love nor retained the respect."

There was a momentary silence, as if Nixon might be pondering how those words applied to his own life. He seemed a bit uncomfortable talking about it, and became much more at ease when the conversation turned to his moment of triumph—the day when, after all the years of trying, he first walked into the White House as President.

"In the biographies of Presidents that I read and so forth, they say, 'Well, from the time he was in his mother's arms she looked down and said, "You're going to be President some day,"' and so forth and so on. But I never set my cap for it, so to speak. To say 'I'm going to be Vice-President and then President' and so forth and so on. Oh, my no, no way.

"When I was a kid, of course, I grew up in the Depression. We had it rough. There was a lot of illness in the family. We didn't have much time to dream about the future. We were just trying to keep our heads above water and survive. I would have thought being Justice of the Peace would have been a big deal.

"But what happened was, at a very early age in my career I became involved in a very big story, the so-called Hiss investigation. I was thirty-four years of age. And so I became a national celebrity very early, and I was a fairly good speaker, and I went around the country and people even at that time started to come up and say, 'You know, you could be President. You ought to be President.'"

We talked some more, and the subject of his very first night in the White House came up—the night after his inauguration, when he moved in as the offlcial resident.

"I had never been in the President's bedroom," Nixon said. "Except on one occasion—not when Eisenhower was there, but when Johnson was there. I came to a Gridiron Dinner, and after the dinner Johnson invited me to come up and have breakfast with him. He had stayed up late after the dinner. He had developed a terrible sore throat, laryngitis, and was in bed. So that was really the first time I was ever in that bedroom. Here was Johnson propped up on one of these big king-sized beds, and I sat there and had a cup of coffee with him."

For all the times he had been in the White House itself during the Eisenhower years, Nixon said that on his first night as President, he found himself wandering around, just looking at things and taking it all in.

"It was a new adventure," he said. "I explored it. When you're in there as a guest—it's presumptuous to sort of examine things. And when you're there on your own, you sort of look at it through different eyes.

"I never tired of walking around late at night. Sleep was a problem for me. Because you're moving in high tension all day long. In a period of war, it is tough, because no matter how you try to put it out of your mind, you're thinking about what is happening on the battlefield. Anybody in that job is going to get very charged up. And at night sometimes it's difficult to sleep. Eisenhower used to take sleeping pills. I used to take them. I didn't take them much—I liked to take just as little as possible, because I didn't want to have a hangover the next day.

"So I never tired of walking around late at night and looking at the paintings and so forth. Coming into the Oval Office, one has a feeling of the dignity of it and the history of it and the rest. You cannot walk in those old rooms without feeling or hearing the footsteps of those who have gone before you."

Imagining Nixon walking alone through the White House late at night, my mind immediately shifted to that famous picture: August 9, 1974, standing in the doorway of the military helicopter on the back lawn, waving his arms as he left the White House for the last time. He had obviously felt such love for living in that house; I asked him what thoughts were filling him as he waved farewell from the helicopter.

Nixon's eyes glazed over.

"I don't know," he said softly. "It's hard to recapture it all. At the time I was frankly so physically and mentally and emotionally exhausted that I really didn't have any profound thoughts. I mean, I knew I was leaving, and that was that."

"I never wanted to be buddy-buddy," Nixon said. "Not only with the press. Even with close friends. I don't believe in letting your hair down, confiding this and that and the other thing—saying, 'Gee, I couldn't sleep, because I was worrying about this or that and so forth and so on.'

"I believe you should keep your troubles to yourself."

We were talking about Nixon's public image. I had told him that many people considered him to be an icy, forbidding figure—not only because of his political policies, which they may have disagreed with, but because of his seeming inability to try to relate to others on human terms.

Nixon nodded his head affirmatively.

"That's just the way I am," he said. "Some people are different. Some people think it's good therapy to sit with a close friend and, you know, just spill your guts.

"I think of this nice gal—apparently, I don't know her, but she appears to be this very intelligent gal—who had to resign from Bendix. [Mary Cunningham.]

"Yeah, and obviously she had met with some press people and has gone into all of her private life. Now, to me, that would be a very embarrassing thing to do, but I know that's what's taught in schools today, so perhaps the younger generation should go in every time that they are asked by the press how they feel about this or that, and they should reveal their inner psyche—whether they were breast-fed, or bottle-fed.

"Not me. No way."

I asked him if that didn't bother him. Here he is, a man who has had more inches in the American press, more time on television, more covers of *Time* magazine, than probably any other political figure in history—and people still feel they don't know him. They have seen him for years, and yet in many ways he remains a mystery man.

"Yeah. It's true," Nixon said. "And it's not necessary for them to know.

"Not to make ambiguous comparisons, but who knew De Gaulle? Who knew Adenauer? People think they knew Eisenhower. Not really. There isn't a good biography on Eisenhower. They are either puff pieces or pieces that are totally frivolous. And he was a very complex fellow. People, when they talk about him as this nice, good man, who sort of presided in a genteel way—they forget that the guy who ordered the landing in Normandy when everything was on the line was no softhead."

I asked Nixon if he relaxed his attitude even around his closest associates—if, for example, during the White House years he had ever, in a personal moment, invited his top-echelon aides to call him by his first name.

"Never," he said. "And none did."

I asked him if it wouldn't have made him feel more comfortable to have someone close to him who could call him "Dick" or "Richard."

"None did," he said. "That was just the way I did it. And Eisenhower was exactly the same way. I perhaps learned a lot from Eisenhower. With President Eisenhower, it was always 'Mr. President' from me. I, of course, was younger than Eisenhower. I never called him 'Ike,' and I never referred to him in my conversations with others as 'Ike.' He was 'the President' or 'the General.'"

I said that surely Nixon's close friends—not his advisers, but his personal buddies—must have been allowed to call him by his first name.

"No," he said. "They didn't. Even my close friends like [Bebe] Rebozo, for example, did not refer to me that way."

I said I found that hard to believe. When Nixon and Rebozo were out on a fishing boat, in casual clothes, and Rebozo wanted to offer Nixon a beer—did he actually say, "Would you like a beer, Mr. President?"

"Yep," Nixon said. "That's right. That's the way."

He began to speak of his ambition—the driving force that took him to the top office in the land, and which, in the end, led to his downfall.

"We all can't be President of the United States, and we all can't be president of General Motors," he said. "Okay. How does it happen? Some of it is luck. Although I can say more of it is a case of taking advantage of opportunities presented.

"Above all, in political life, you must be willing to take great risks. You must risk greatly—I know, looking back on my own political career, of a number of very able people, very intelligent, a lot of mystique, a lot of charisma, etc., who stopped at Congress. Who never went to the Senate. Never went on to become governor. Who stopped at that level.

"Because they didn't want to risk a safe seat. The moment people begin to think of how they can be secure, they are never going to make it clear to the top.

"You've got to take great risks and lose if necessary. And maybe lose twice or three times and keep coming back. That's the secret.

"My public life has not been easy. For reasons that we don't need to go into. And it's very rough on the family, etc. I would say, however, that if I had known what was going to happen, that I would not have refused or declined to get into it.

"I think what you have—what is essential—let me put it this way. When you think of high office, there are two kinds of people: There are the men and the boys. The boys are those who want to be in high office to be somebody. The men are those who want to be in high office in order to do something. Now you have both. And again, not to put it solely in personal terms, I always felt that I wanted to do something."

I asked Nixon if he thought his personal style had hurt him—if he thought that had he presented himself as a looser, more accessible individual, some of the political criticism of him would have been muted.

"No, the problem in my case was not style," he said. "I mean, I could have had the press in for dinners. I could do those things. I never drank with the press, of course—I don't mind that others do, understand. But I don't think it's a good idea. And I don't think it's a good idea to drink with the Secret Service and that sort of thing.

"You've got to retain a certain . . . be that as it may, I could have had all sorts of little chatty dinners and the rest, and you might get a nice warm piece the next day. But deep down, the problems I had with the press— you're referring to what happened before the resignation period—the problems had to do with what I believed in. I believed in different things than what they did."

"I have never seen myself on television," Nixon said.

At first I thought he was kidding me. Nixon was probably the most televised public figure in the history of the country. But he said it was true.

"No, I don't engage in some of the practices of others," he said. "I've never watched a tape of myself. Oh, a flash on the news or something, if I'm looking at it. But during the White House years I deliberately read the news summaries, which had of course total coverage of what was on the evening news and that sort of thing.

"But I don't—I've never had a tape of myself, and then studied the tape and then gone out and practiced.

"Oh, never. I remember that many years ago, Tom Dewey—whom I greatly admired and I think would have been a great President, secretary of state, chief justice, anything, if the time would have been right—but Dewey was known as somewhat of a mechanical man. And I have heard that he sometimes would practice his speech before a mirror.

"I know that others of course will do that. I noticed, for example, at the last convention, a number of the people apparently went down to the convention hall and practiced their speeches. I've never practiced a speech in my life."

I said that surely, before delivering those famous televised addresses, he must have done a few run-throughs.

"No sir, never," Nixon said. "On TV, I do it live. I don't like to make a tape. I like to do it live, and maybe you flub a little but on the other hand it has more believability.

"I do a lot of the writing myself. When I've been through about twelve drafts, I've got a lot of it up here. But I never read it out loud. No, sir, never out loud. And I don't time it.

"I think if you read the thing out loud, or if you watch yourself on television, you become self-conscious and say, 'Gee, I should have this kind of a gesture rather than that,' and so forth.

"Now you will probably learn things, but on the other hand, your critics —family, close staff, and the rest—they will say, 'Look, I think you were speaking too fast, or you were speaking too slow, or you were looking too much here, there, or you were looking down too much, you should look up more, you should sit straighter'—all these things.

"You should listen. You should take that sort of criticism. But I think when the individual himself gets into that business where he practices it . . . it's very difficult, at least in my case, to retain spontaneity."

I said that it was difficult for me to believe that, before addressing the nation on momentous issues, he had not studied tapes of his previous performances.

"Let me put it in other terms," Nixon said. "I quit playing golf over a year ago—you know, I got so busy with my last book, now I probably won't play again. I've broken eighty, and that is as far as I'll ever go anyway. But I know that the golfers say that they have videotapes made of their golf swing, or they have pictures taken of their golf swing, and they go out and watch the pictures and they try to swing and so forth.

"I could no more do that and play a good game—I'd become so self-conscious, I'd miss the ball. So my point is, don't look at yourself."

For all his protestations about not watching himself on television, however, Nixon seemed to have almost an obsession with the institution of TV. Again and again during our conversation, he kept coming back to it.

"In your colleges and universities and in your speech courses," he said, "they believe that you should listen to your voice. The network people, they all—some are men and some are women—they all have the same lilt at the end, or the drop, and so forth. The same cadence—and to me it's as boring as the dickens. They would be much more interesting if they would talk in different terms.

"CBS, for example, which is a network I listen to a great deal—I also listen to NBC and ABC—but I notice each has a certain cadence, where they must say to some of these people, 'You're going to talk this way.' I think they lose something."

He began to talk about Lyndon Johnson, and suddenly television came up again.

"The trouble with Lyndon," Nixon said, "he had three television sets in the office, and he would look at them, the critics on television, and then call the heads of the networks. Those people were not elected—he was. Well, I took that to heart. One of the first things I did when I came to the Oval Office was to remove all the television sets.

"He even had them in his bathroom. And in the little room there, he had little television sets in the bathroom and he had one in the sitting room, the anteroom off the Oval Office, and three in his bedroom. I took all of them out.

"Yeah. Absolutely. Oh, I didn't have one in the bedroom. I don't have one there now. When I do look at television I usually go to look at sports, and I of course see the evening news. Although I generally get my news from reading—but these days, since eighty percent or ninety percent of the people do see the evening news, you'd better look at it to see what people are doing."

I said that with all the social problems in modern America—teenage pregnancies, widespread drug use, soaring divorce rate, open marital infidelity—I wondered what Nixon thought was the biggest potential problem.

"I would say I am concerned the most about the enormous power of television," he said. "When I read polls to the effect that the average American spends four hours in front of the tube, it to me is a very discouraging thing to see.

"I think the younger generation will come out less well educated than would be the case if they could read more. To be responsible in the world, you can't be looking at the tube and getting these pictures and flashbacks and pontifical comments and so forth and so on.

"I remember, for example, you take a presidential press conference.

You're supposed to answer twenty-five questions in thirty minutes. So they ask you the question, What are you going to do about Iran? And you're supposed to answer it in a minute and a half.

"No way. And yet that's the way it's done. So people get a superficial answer. Television commentators, of course—if you get a half a minute on the evening news, it's a big deal. How can you discuss inflation, how can you discuss a new program for drugs? How can you discuss anything intelligently in one-half a minute, and yet that is what the poor politicians have to do every night in order to get on the evening news."

He said that his great concern for his grandchildren's generation is that the legacy of books may be lost on them, replaced by the new legacy of television.

"There are so many good books out there to read. There are so many good articles that are thoughtful to read. It is something people have lost if they sit in front of the tube and turn off their minds.

"And the people who are leading them in television—not that they are bad people, but they may not know. They may not be that profound. And like an Eric Sevareid can sound profound, but it can be very superficial. That's an act with him.

"It's a question of discipline and parental leadership. I understand that parents park their kids in front of the television. They scream and holler until you put them in front of the television. I don't mind it, perhaps, when they're very young—but when they get in school, don't let them be before that tube.

"My best advice to any young person moving up is: Read more, look at television less."

"Somebody who has served as President," Nixon said, "there is nothing else that he can do."

We were nearing the end of our conversation. The talk had turned to Nixon's life today. I was getting the impression that some of his days were emptier than he would like.

"There is not the challenge and not the stimulation of being in office," he said. "And I'm sure there are people retired from any position, no matter what it is, low or high—I think we talked earlier about the problems of youth. I think probably just as great these days is the problems of age.

"We have early retirement. We now have people retiring at sixty and so forth. They may be in the prime of life then. They think they want to play golf and fish the rest of their life, and after about a month they get bored with it."

His days, as he described them, do not vary much. He rises each morning at 5:30, while his wife is still asleep. He eats breakfast alone. He goes out for a walk—usually a mile.

"I come down here [his office], arriving at 7:00 or 7:15," he said. "And then I'm here until about 11:30. Then I go back and have lunch with Mrs. Nixon. I spend the rest of the day there. That way I avoid the traffic both times. The traffic is murderous at 8:00 in the morning, and thereafter it's murderous at noon. So you'd better go at 11:30.

"I don't go to bed as late as I used to—unless the ball game is on, I'll stay up and listen to that, but I go to bed early, around 10:30."

He said that he and Mrs. Nixon have virtually no night life, by their own choice.

"We never go to a cocktail party," he said. "I'll never go to another cocktail party. Just don't like it. A cocktail party is an invention of the devil. The talk—it's so loud, and people drink too much, and talk too much, and think too little."

I said that Richard Nixon, in a room full of drinking, socializing people, must be like a lightning rod. Everyone must want their one scene with him.

"It's a bore," he said. "I just don't go. We say sorry, got another engagement."

Most of his evenings, he said, are devoted to solitary reading.

"I have books around that I can read," he said. "Newspapers. I don't read novels. The only one I read recently, but it's really somewhat true to life although a little too much sex, I thought, not because I'm prudish but because it got in the way of the plot—was *The Spike*.

"If I wake up at night, I don't read anymore. Reading does not put me to sleep, it stimulates me. And I cannot go to sleep if I have music on, because I concentrate on the music. I've never gone to sleep in a movie, nor a play. Even as dull as they can be at times."

The reason Nixon's walks come so early in the morning is that he is likely to be mobbed if he goes out while the streets are filled with people. He is still probably the most famous man in America, and when people see him they press toward him and it soon gets out of hand.

"If you walk and you stop, then you sign the autographs. . . . I've never turned down an autograph in my life. My name is not long, anyway. But I went down to Julie's for the new baby, and I must have had about three hundred at that little hospital. Which is fine, they're awful nice people.

"But New York is a city where you can either take it or leave it, and they leave you alone. Everyone is just pounding away at his own thing, and they have a deep sense of privacy themselves. They're sort of suckers for celebrities in a way. On the other hand, they will leave a celebrity alone.

"It's a cold town in that respect. It can be very cold here, or very warm. But it's up to the individual. You can come here and get lost, if you want. This can be the place where you can be . . . you can find more privacy here than you can in the deserts of California."

Nixon said that he spends a lot of time thinking about the moral decay of much of society. Something that bothers him especially is the widespread and casual use of drugs in America.

"There isn't any question that you'll find the breakdown of morality in terms of the use of drugs and excesses in any way," he said. "In the breaking up of marriages and so forth. That is a danger sign of decadence.

"I think the drug culture, of course, is widespread. It isn't something that is just a so-called low-class thing—that isn't who can afford it. It is in with the beautiful set of people in Hollywood.

"The further this goes, the less strong society is. You see our competitors in the world, and God knows when you look at the Soviets and you look at the Chinese—the Communist system in general—the system doesn't work. Doesn't work economically, the idea has lost its appeal. They stay in power only because of power.

"But it's interesting to note that these societies . . . taking the Chinese, particularly, it's a highly moral society. Even this nuthead Qaddafi in Libya, he runs a highly moral show. Looking at the Chinese—drugs are out. As I look at history, any society that is on the way down moves into the drug culture. The societies that are to survive and be vital move away from it.

"It's a very tough time to raise kids. Right across the street from us, for example, there is a fine Catholic school. Now they do a good job in one respect. Every day at noon they close the street off. For an hour. They don't let any cars in there, and the kids run around, you know, in the street. And this is a school that is grade school and high school. It's mixed, boys and girls. They wear uniforms and so forth. And it's totally integrated. It's really a delight to see the young black kids and white kids playing their games and squealing and so forth and so on.

"On the other side of the coin, on their side of the street, where the school is, no smoking is allowed. On our side of the street—I was walking up the other day at noon, and here were some girls, I am sure they were no more than thirteen. They were smoking, and they smoked cigarettes, and some of them were smoking marijuana. On our side of the street. Yeah, the kids from the school, and there is nothing the teachers can do about it.

"Well, I guess this is quite common, but we saw it firsthand. They were smoking cigarettes and they were smoking marijuana. These are girls. That's what surprised me. Boys you'd expect to engage in all sorts of shenanigans, but little girls—I don't know. But I suppose that's part of the whole women's lib movement. The girls are supposed to be as immoral or decadent as the boys. I hope not."

It was almost time for me to leave. As I sat there looking at Nixon, it struck me that one of these days this fascinating, complex, contradictory man who has been at the center of American life for more than thirty years will be gone. It almost happened once—when he was hospitalized shortly after he left office, and went into shock.

"Frankly, the sense of your mortality grows as you get older," Nixon said. "I mean, after all, you read the obituary page, and you read of people sixty-five, sixty-nine, seventy, seventy-three, seventy-four, seventy-five—all of my generation. They cut off. They die. Heart attacks, cancer, what have you.

"But I never get morbid about it. I never worry about it.

"I just figure that every day may be the last."

Top Dogs

A manufacturer of dog food, in conjunction with the 100th anniversary of the American Kennel Club, has sponsored a survey of the most popular names among American dogs.

The winner is Rover. Spot is second.

Somehow that is reassuring. If I had been asked to guess, I would have predicted that the most popular names for American dogs in the Eighties were probably Lance, Barry, Cyndi, Zoom-Zoom, Crawdaddy, Crochet . . . names like that.

I would have guessed, in other words, that the era of the good, solid, generic dog name was over.

It's nice to be wrong. I like the idea that of all the dogs scampering across the American landscape, Rover is the most popular name.

But I'm so surprised that I have a nagging suspicion that the competition was fixed. When was the last time that you met a dog named Rover? I don't think that Kal Kan, the dogfood manufacturer that sponsored the contest, wanted to tell the American people that it had combed the countryside and had found that the most popular name among dogs was Springsteen.

No, I can envision the folks at Kal Kan sitting around, looking at the legitimate list of favorite Eighties dog names—Taos, Spock, Trendola—and the chairman of the board of the company slamming his fist down on the conference table and saying:

"Gentlemen, we must take a stand! We owe it to our country to protect the citizens from this distressing information! Put out a press release! Damn the real results! We will tell the American public that the favorite dog name is . . ."

A silence. The chairman thinks back across the years, to the nostalgic memory of his happy boyhood.

". . . Rover!"

More silence at the table.

"And the second-favorite name is . . ."

More silence. More warm thoughts of boyhood.

". . . Spot!"

And so the press release was drafted, and the nation was informed that Rover and Spot were the favorite names for American dogs in the Eighties. At which point the Kal Kan board of directors went home and were greeted at their front doors by their own dogs: Jermaine, Ferraro, Tuna Melt, and Sid.

I know from my own experience that Rover, while perhaps the favorite dog name of the Thirties, Forties, and Fifties, is not really the favorite dog name of the Eighties. When we were growing up, we all lived next door to people whose dogs were named Rover; now, more often than not, our neighbors' dogs are named Guccione or Tennis.

When I was a boy, my first dog was a little white mutt named Fido. In the middle of Ohio in the middle of the 1950s, that was the perfect name for a dog. You would almost expect the summer fill-in mailman to stroll up the front walk for the first time, smile as he put the *Saturday Evening Post* in the mailbox, and say, "Hi, son! What's that dog's name? Bet it's Fido!"

But the era of Rovers and Spots and Fidos is long gone; now it is unlikely that a contemporary mail carrier ever would venture a guess that a homeowner's dog was named Fido, although it is not inconceivable that a large number of today's mail carriers are named Fido.

Today when a youngster goes to school and stands up during show-and-tell time to inform his classmates about his adventures with his dog, it is likely that he will be talking about the adventures of Taco or Spielberg or Sin.

And when he dreams of heroic dogs—dogs that belong in the movies, up there on the silver screen—he undoubtedly does not dream of Lassie or Lad or Rin Tin Tin. The superdogs that dance across his dreams at night probably are named Salad or Nautilus or Fern.

It's probably good for America, though, that the dog-food company is saying that the favorite dog names are Rover and Spot. We are supposed to be in an era of a return to traditional values, and maybe if people read enough stories saying that the favorite dog names are Rover and Spot, they will go home at night and say, "Cappuccino, you are now Rover!" or "Nike, you are now Spot!"

But even if people start doing that, there's no way it can last. We may go through a few new years of Rovers and Spots and Fidos, but then the trend will reverse itself again and you will start seeing dogs named Beach and Psychiatrist and Terrence.

So don't be too hard on that dog-food company for putting out the word that Rover and Spot are the most popular names for American dogs. The company is just doing its bit to raise the nation's morale, and that seems like a harmless enough thing to do. If the company wants us to believe that most people have dogs named Rover and Spot, then let's all tell the company that we believe it.

I would comment further on this subject, but right now I have to go home and feed my dog, Stir-Fry.

Lights, Camera, Clara

The most talked-about actress in America sat silently while her director determined whether the camera angle was right. Even though there was a flurry of activity all around her, she appeared to be so calm she might have been getting ready to go to sleep.

"We'll be set in just a minute," the director said to her.

The actress nodded her assent.

This was not Meryl Streep, Debra Winger, or Goldie Hawn. Who talks about them?

This was Clara Peller, eighty-two, who has rocketed to fame on the strength of one line of dialogue:

"Where's the beef?"

Mrs. Peller—a widow who used to work as a manicurist—is the star of the Wendy's Hamburgers commercial in which she uttered her now immortal line. In that commercial, Mrs. Peller—paired with two other elderly women—stood at a counter that was designed to look like part of one of Wendy's competitors' restaurants. When a tiny hamburger arrived on a huge bun, Mrs. Peller looked at it and said . . . well, you know what she said.

"Where's the beef?" quickly became a national catchphrase. Political cartoonists used it with their drawings. Bar patrons said it to one another as they wait for drinks. Crowds at college basketball games chanted it during timeouts. Ministers based their Sunday sermons on it.

And now Wendy's was preparing to shoot a sequel to the commercial. The cast had been reassembled; along with Mrs. Peller there were Elizabeth Shaw and Mildred Lane, the two women who had appeared with her in the first commercial. All eyes in the room were on Clara Peller, though; she was the one who had said the magic words in all of those living rooms, and she was the new superstar.

Joe Sedelmaier, the director of the "Where's the beef?" commercials, conferred quietly with his assistants and technicians. Off to the side, William M. Welter, executive vice-president of Wendy's, looked at the scene and marveled.

"This is amazing," Welter said. "Our business has increased dramatically as a direct result of these commercials, and there's no doubt that Clara is the big reason why. People just love her. She's not some thirty-two-year-old sexy broad; she's real. She appeals to everyone from two-year-olds to ninety-year-olds. We know because we see the fan mail."

Wendy's does not like to talk about it, but they almost lost Clara Peller last week. After the success of the first commercial she hired an attorney, and for a few tense days it seemed as if the Wendy's attorneys and Mrs. Peller's attorney might not be able to reach an agreement on a contract for the new commercial.

But things had been worked out. Now, as she waited for Sedelmaier to start shooting, she sat with her two fellow actresses.

"I heard they were going to make posters of us," Elizabeth Shaw said.

"I thought it was place mats," Mildred Lane said.

"Whatever," Elizabeth Shaw said. "I'll just talk to my agent." She turned to Clara Peller. "You're the star," she said. "We're just the background."

Mrs. Peller stared down at the floor, where a tape mark had been placed to show her where to stand when the shooting started. Behind the three women was a sign that said HOME OF THE BIG BURGER.

Sedelmaier was ready. Aides carried a Styrofoam cup of ice water to Mrs. Peller. She took a sip.

"All right," Sedelmaier said. "Let's do it."

The women stood up. The idea was that the three were supposed to be back in the restaurant again—this time trying to complain to the manager. In the commercial they stand at the counter, in front of a huge bun and a tiny burger, and Mildred Lane holds a telephone—ostensibly trying to call the manager.

The camera rolled. Mildred Lane said into the telephone, "We *know* it's a big, fluffy bun."

Elizabeth Shaw stage-whispered to her, "Talk to the manager."

Mildred Lane replied, "It *is* the manager."

Down on the floor, hidden from sight, a production assistant named Dwight Irwin sat with his right hand grasping the hem of Clara Peller's dress. Mrs. Peller is hard of hearing; it is difficult for her to hear her cues. So when it is time for her to speak, Irwin's job is to pull on her dress as a signal.

As soon as Mildred Lane had said, "It *is* the manager," Irwin pulled on Mrs. Peller's dress.

And Clara Peller blurted out, like an angry foghorn:

"Where's the beef?"

"Really let 'em have it," Joe Sedelmaier said. *"Where's the beef?"*

"Where's the beef?" Clara Peller bellowed again.

"Wait until he tugs on your dress," Sedelmaier said.

Wendy's is spending $11 million on the "Where's the beef?" campaign. Clara Peller, the most valuable part of that $11 million expenditure, readied herself for another take. America, America.

Words of Love

Traveling through Texas, I listened to local radio stations. In San Antonio I found myself listening to KISS-FM, a rock 'n' roll outlet.

On the air, one of the station's disc jockeys mentioned a promotion. "What would you do to meet the Crüe?" he said. He explained that a heavy-metal rock band called Mötley Crüe was coming to San Antonio. Listeners were invited to mail entries to the station. The winners would get free tickets to the concert; some would get to go backstage and meet the band.

I called the station. I said I would be interested in seeing the entries. I asked if there were any ground rules. I was told that the only rule was that listeners had to answer the one basic question: "What would you do to meet the Crüe?"

A week later, I read the entries.

We seem to have come quite a distance from Herman's Hermits fan clubs and "I Want to Hold Your Hand."

From a sixteen-year-old girl:

"What I Would Do To See Mötley Crüe:

"First, I would tie you up, spreadeagle and naked, with leather straps. Then I'd shave all the hair off of your chest, and if I should nick you I'll suck up all the blood as it slowly trickles over your body. Next I'll cover your body with motion lotion to get things really heated up. When it gets *too* hot, I'll cover your body in crushed ice and lay on top of you to melt it down and cool you off.

"Then I'll do things to your body with my tongue that you never thought humanly possible. Then when you are screaming for mercy and begging for more, telling me how you want it all, I'll slam the spiked heel of my right leather boot into your navel, call you a very naughty boy, and laugh as I slowly walk away, telling you I'm just not that kind of girl."

From a fifteen-year-old girl:

"I want to see Mötley Crüe so bad I'd wear black nail polish and body glitter. . . . When I see them I'd get on my hands & knees & give them my body & even tear my clothes off if I had to. If that didn't work I'd do like Ozzy did and bite a dove's head off & say, 'Okay, let's talk business.'"

From a thirteen-year-old girl:
"I'd do *it* with the Crüe till black and blue is all you can see."

From a fifteen-year-old girl:
"I'm really a big fan of Mötley Crüe's and I would do anything to meet them. Vince Neil and Nikki Sixx are so fine!! I love 'em all. I would even get fucked by the ugliest, fattest, most disgusting guy in the world to meet them. . . .

"My boyfriend gets mad at me because I like them so much, and listen to the radio all the time for their songs to come on! I had to beg him to let me write this letter to you. Hopefully, I will win, because I went through a lot of trouble begging my boyfriend to let me do this.

"That would be just terrific if I won. I would have a chance of meeting Vince Neil! God, he's so fucking fine!!! If it would mean losing my boyfriend, I would fuck his best friend to meet these gorgeous guys. It wouldn't matter, as long as I got to meet Vince Neil and see his fine ass and fine body!! God, I can just see it now! Fucking him would be my biggest fantasy in the world! Well, I hope I win! Thank you!"

From a thirteen-year-old girl:
"I'd leave my tits to Mötley Crüe."
From a seventeen-year-old girl:
"To get backstage to Mötley Crüe I think I'd give them *every* piece of action they wanted. I'd give them my body, money, or whatever they wanted."

From a nineteen-year-old girl:
"I would go down to the local hardware store and buy some chains, leather straps, and nails. I would then put together the most outlandish outfit made of nothing but the leather straps, chains, and nails. I would go to the concert in this Kiss-Ass outfit, because I would do anything to get close to 'Marvelous' Mick Mars, 'Luscious' Tommy Lee, Nikki 'Sexx,' and Vince 'Can't Say No' Neil. P.S. I would take a hammer so the guys (the Crüe) can loosen the nails off my outfit."

From a thirteen-year-old girl:
"What's up? Well, you asked what I would do to be a Mötley Crüe, so here it is. First, I'd spread whipped cream all *over* my body. Then, I'd let

Vince Neil *lick* it all off! I sure hope you enjoyed this cause I would love for it to happen."

From a fourteen-year-old boy:
"This is what I would do to join the KISS Mötley Crüe: I would give them my mother, who is very beautiful. She has red hair and brown eyes. She loves heavy metal and especially Mötley Crüe. My mother definitely has *the looks that kill.*"

I spoke with the sixteen-year-old girl who said she would tie the band members up with leather straps and shave their chests.
"I didn't let my boyfriend read it before I sent it in," she said. "It would make him wonder what he didn't know about me.
"Why did I write those things? I don't know. I just sat down and wrote what I thought. It took me about half an hour. I don't know where the ideas came from. They just came out."
I spoke with the girl's mother.
"Yes, I read the letter," the mother said. "Actually, I took it down to the radio station for her. I guess I was shocked in a way, but I'm sure she didn't mean anything by it. She's a very Christian girl.
"Did I think about not turning it in to the radio station? Well, it really wouldn't have been fair for me not to turn it in. I promised my daughter I would do it. It wouldn't have been fair for me to put it in the garbage."

I spoke with the fifteen-year-old girl who said she would get on her hands and knees for the band and give them her body.
"I was one of the winners of the contest, but I didn't get to go to the concert because I didn't have a ride," she said. "My father was supposed to take me, but he had to work late. I didn't speak to him for two days.
"I meant what I said. I'd get on my hands and knees and give them my body. I know that they're grown men and I'm fifteen, but so what? It would be worth giving them my body just to meet them. I think it would be neat.
"I heard that in ancient times women used to get on their hands and knees and not even be allowed to look at men. I think rock groups should be treated like that. They're like God, but they're even better. The reason I would take my clothes off and crawl to them is that I would hope that they liked that."

I spoke with the thirteen-year-old girl who said she would do "it" with the band until she was black and blue.

"I just love the group," she said. "I wrote what I wrote because they look like the type who would like that. They look like women-lovers."

I spoke with the fifteen-year-old girl who said she would go to bed with "the ugliest, fattest, most disgusting guy in the world" in order to meet the band.

"I like their hair," she said. "I just like them a lot. It's pretty boring in this town. I don't like school very much, I get C's and D's. I wrote those things because I thought it might help me win. I meant every word of it.

"I really like Vince Neil's body When he's onstage he wears a bunch of spikes and leather pants. I'd do whatever I had to do to meet him. I told my mother's boyfriend about it, and he said, 'Whatever turns you on.'"

I spoke with the thirteen-year-old girl who said she would "leave my tits" to the band.

"I really like the way their faces look," she said. "It makes me excited to see them onstage.

"I wrote what I did because I thought they might like it, and then I'd get to meet them. You can tell that they're like that. All rock groups know that they can have any girls' bodies that they want. That's one of the reasons they join a band."

I spoke with the seventeen-year-old girl who said she would give the band "*every* piece of action they wanted," and give the band money.

"They seem like a wild, outgoing bunch of guys to me," she said. "They seem like they'd do just about anything and not care about it.

"I'd give them whatever they wanted. They can do whatever they want with my body. They look wild and mean and evil. What I meant about giving them money is that first I'd try to convince them in other ways to take my body. I'd follow them where they went and tell them to do with me whatever they wanted to. I think I could convince them.

"But if they wanted money for it, I'd pay them to take me. It would be worth the money to me. I have some money saved from baby-sitting; plus my father is a truck driver, and I could borrow the money from him if I needed more.

"I'd do it with all four of them at once if that's what they wanted. If they said, 'Be with all four of us or get out,' I'd say, 'Okay, come on.' I'd be crazy not to if that was my only chance to be with them."

I spoke with the nineteen-year-old girl who said she would dress in chains, leather straps, and nails for the band.

"I think they're all gorgeous," she said. "When I see them, I just naturally think of leather and whips and chains. I think that means that they're aggressive. I happen to love that image; it's a neat image.

"I think it's that kind of aggressiveness that a woman is always looking for. Why did I put that thing in about bringing a hammer with me? Just like I said—they could use it to loosen the nails on my clothes."

I spoke with the thirteen-year-old girl who said she would let one of the band members lick whipped cream off her body.

"They're really good-looking," she said. "Good and mean. They just look like guys who are out to party and have a good time.

"I saw the band in a magazine and I thought they were pretty neat. I like Vince Neil the best of them. He's got the blondest hair; it's kind of long. He's not fat and he's not thin; he's just right.

"I wouldn't make the same offer to my boyfriend that I made to the band. It just wouldn't be the same with him. With the band, you think more of being wild and having a good time. My boyfriend is fifteen. We don't car-date yet; our mothers mostly drop us off at the movies and pick us up afterward."

I spoke with the fourteen-year-old boy who said he would give his mother to the band.

"I wrote that letter because I really wanted to get to go backstage and meet Mötley Crüe," he said. "My mom likes the band, too, and I thought if I offered her to them, I might have a good chance of winning.

"If the band told me that they really wanted my mother? I'd say, 'Take her.' I'd say, 'Here.' I really love my mom; I know she'd go with them."

I spoke with the boy's mother, who is thirty-four.

"Yes, I am a fan of the band," she said. "I sure am. I approved of his letter.

"We keep listening to the radio to hear their music. They're kind of wild; just a little wild.

"Billy and I have a good mother-and-son relationship. He's crazy about me and I'm crazy about him. When Billy said that he had offered me to the band, I said, 'Oh, Billy!' But I really do like them, and I would like to help Billy win the contest."

I was done with the interviews, and I knew it was time to sit down and write this story. First I went outside and took a long walk. Usually that helps to clear my head. For some reason this time it didn't seem to work.

Mother and Child

At thirty-six she is a high school teacher, living in the Chicago suburbs; she has never been married. She had driven to the southern part of the state to visit her parents; her mother, who had been suffering from cancer for three years, was not doing well.

It was a Friday night. Her mother was in bed; she was hooked up to an oxygen tank by a long cord. The daughter climbed onto the bed next to her mother, just as she had as a little girl. The two of them watched "Dallas" and "Falcon Crest." The daughter sensed that her mother was thinking something but not saying it.

The mother looked over. She said the words:

"I just don't want to leave yet."

The two women both started to cry. They held each other, and the daughter could not tell who was rocking whom: the mother rocking the daughter, as in days long ago, or the daughter rocking the mother? They spoke of death; the daughter said that she was afraid she would never get over missing this woman who had been there for her for a lifetime.

The mother said that in time, it happens; the hurt begins to let up. She said that she had been forty when her own mother died; all these years since, she had missed her. They kept rocking each other, the mother and the daughter, and they said all the words that needed to be said.

At the end of the weekend the daughter drove back to Chicago, to work. Within days the news came from downstate: the mother had taken a bad turn. She was in the hospital.

So the daughter made the drive again. A nurse stopped her in the hallway; the nurse warned that the mother looked much worse than she had even four days before. In the hospital room the daughter saw her mother propped up in bed, her eyes seeming to focus on someplace beyond the four walls.

The daughter's father and brother were there, too, as they had been all day. They said they were going to go away for a few hours; the daughter said she would stay with her mother. The mother drifted into a drugged sleep; once she woke up, apparently startled to find the daughter there. She asked: "How much longer will it be?" She didn't wait for an answer. Another time she opened her eyes and said that she was "ready."

"Dallas" was on the television set. The daughter thought: Had it really been a week since they had sat together and watched the show? She stroked her mother's hand and talked softly to her; her mother said that the daughter looked tired and should go home. The daughter said she would rather stay. A nurse came in and gave the mother a shot; it hurt, and she turned onto her side because her back was sore, and the daughter massaged her. Once the mother opened her eyes and the daughter smiled and said the mother was missing "Dallas."

At 11:00 P.M. the daughter's brother came back. The mother was having trouble breathing; the daughter let the mother rest her head on her shoulder, and the daughter held her up like a baby. Several hours later—about 2:00 A.M.—the mother sat upright and let her legs dangle over the side of the bed. She wouldn't lie back down.

The nurse who was present asked the mother if she knew her daughter and son were there. She nodded yes. She was awake, but this was clearly the end.

The daughter thought: So this is what death is like.

The two children embraced their mother for thirty or forty minutes. They could hear that she was having great difficulty breathing. No one really spoke; they just held on. Finally, with her tired back resting against her daughter's chest and her head leaning against her daughter's shoulder, she closed her eyes and died.

The daughter thought: This wasn't frightening and it wasn't awful and it wasn't terrible. A woman had died in the arms of her children, knowing that she was loved.

The daughter thought: I don't know how I will get over this. I have called this woman on the telephone every night of my life since I was in college. This woman has told me I am all right all of my life, even during times when I wasn't so sure myself. I always hoped that if I ever got married, this woman would be there. But she never bothered me about it. She always said, "You're doing fine; your life is great."

It was twenty-five minutes before the daughter's father arrived back at the hospital. For that whole time, the daughter continued to hold her mother in her arms.

Now that it is over, the daughter lies in bed in her apartment, and she feels as if her mother is still alive. She feels as if her mother is watching her life. "It's like my mother is still in on it," the daughter will think. "It's as if she's in me. She's a part of me."

Of course there are days when the daughter will think of her mother constantly. She will be watching television and suddenly she will start crying. She will see mothers and daughters on the street and again the tears will come.

But there are also days—more and more of them recently—when she will realize that she has not thought about her mother. This surprises her; she had assumed such a time would never come.

"It's the life-and-death of it," she says. "It's the life-and-death of it that spooks me. Life goes on. Oh, my, my."

Doing the Eastern Shuttle

I have just returned from being away for several weeks. I spent most of the time traveling, and as is usual when I am on the road, I discovered many new, amazing, and exotic things.

Nothing I saw, though, was quite so amazing and exotic as the Eastern Shuttle.

"The Eastern Shuttle." It is a phrase that has lurked somewhere near the back of my consciousness for years. I vaguely realized that the Eastern Shuttle was a form of air transportation available to people on the East Coast; I knew that the rules of the Eastern Shuttle were somehow different from the rules of regular airplane travel, but I didn't know precisely how.

I was secretly intimidated by the very idea of the Eastern Shuttle. About six months ago I had to get to Washington from New York at an early evening hour; a colleague in New York said, "That's no problem. Just go out to LaGuardia and catch the Eastern Shuttle." It turned out that the Eastern Shuttle was the only plane leaving from LaGuardia that would get me to Washington that night. Coward that I am, I took a cab to the more distant Kennedy Airport and took a more expensive Pan Am flight to Washington. At the time, I just didn't have the guts to deal with the Eastern Shuttle.

This time, though, I had no choice. I needed to get from New York to Boston in a hurry, and then get back in a hurry. My only option, I learned, was the Eastern Shuttle.

I did a little quick research. The Eastern Shuttle, it turned out, is an economical air service run by Eastern Airlines. It goes between New York and Washington, and New York and Boston. You don't need a reservation to get a seat on the Eastern Shuttle; as a matter of fact, you can't *make* a reservation on the Eastern Shuttle. The Eastern Shuttle operates on the hour, all day and all evening. You just show up at the gate. If the plane is already full, they'll bring another plane for you. Even if there are only five or six of you left over—theoretically, even if you're the *only* passenger left over—they'll bring a plane. You're guaranteed a seat.

Airplanes in the rest of the country, of course, don't operate this way. In the rest of the country, you phone for a reservation. If there are no seats available, you don't get to go on the flight. The Eastern Shuttle is unique; it is pure East Coast, which is probably why Midwesterners like myself are so suspicious of it.

Anyway . . . my cab pulled up to the Eastern Shuttle terminal at LaGuardia. [The Eastern Shuttle has its own building; if you are taking an Eastern Airlines flight to, say, Miami, you go to the regular Eastern building. If you are taking the shuttle, you go to the Eastern Shuttle building.]

I walked into the terminal. I asked a uniformed man where I should go to buy my ticket. He looked at me as if I had dropped my trousers.

"You write your own ticket on the Eastern Shuttle," the man said with great disdain.

I looked all around me. Indeed, men and women were scribbling away on blank ticket forms that they had retrieved from a table, like deposit slips at a bank. I stood next to one of the people and, like a school kid cribbing on a chemistry exam, copied what he was doing.

I followed him down a hallway and on board the plane. It was a huge, wide-bodied plane, and people were sitting anywhere they wanted, just like on a bus. I knew that I hadn't paid for my ticket, but nobody stopped me.

A few minutes after the hour, the plane taxied away from the gate. I looked around me. The passengers on the Eastern Shuttle were clearly business people; clearly *East Coast* business people. I hate to stereotype folks, but if I hadn't known where I was I would have assumed that I had been dropped into the middle of a George Bush look-alike contest.

We took off. A plurality of the passengers began to work on pocket calculators.

I looked at the man next to me. On his wrist he was wearing a watch with two faces: one set to New York time, one set to Los Angeles time.

The captain of the plane came onto the public address system. He seemed to share the East Coast business mind-set of his passengers. He did not wish us a nice day. He said:

"I hope all of you have had a real successful week."

And then he said:

"We'll be flying over to Boston at 22,000."

Not 22,000 *feet*; it was clear that the captain assumed that all of the passengers on the Eastern Shuttle were such world-weary, seasoned travelers that there was no need to waste words.

I looked for someone to talk to, but the people who weren't buried in their *Wall Street Journals* were buried in their "Business Day" sections of the *New York Times*.

I saw a small army of flight attendants heading down the aisles pushing carts. I assumed they were going to offer us refreshments. Boy, was I wrong.

On top of the carts were credit-card imprinting machines. The flight attendants on the Eastern Shuttle were collecting fares from the passengers four miles up in the air, as we hurtled toward Boston. They would grab a passenger's American Express Gold Card, run it through the machine, hand it back, and push the cart to the next row of seats.

The flight attendants finished collecting the fares just as we were descending into Boston. The passengers, looking just as bored and jaded as they had throughout the flight, filed off the plane. I followed them.

I got to my hotel. The person I was supposed to meet called my room. "When did you get in?" he said.

"About half an hour ago," I said with an exaggerated yawn. "Caught the Eastern Shuttle."

The Woman in the Photograph

The smartest person I know is my mother. During the years between my birth and the time my brother and sister and I left home, she never had a paying job; although she did voluminous amounts of volunteer work for various charitable organizations, if she had been asked to compile a resumé it would have been blank under the category marked "Employment."

Her job, as she saw it, was to be our mother—full-time. She did this by choice. I had never really thought about what this must have meant to her life; when the editors of *Esquire* told me that the magazine was devoting an entire issue to the American woman and asked me if there was a woman I would like to write about in that month's column, I said yes, there was.

There is a photograph of my mother and my father, taken in 1942, while they were on their honeymoon. They are seated at a table in a restaurant, my father wearing his Army uniform; in the picture my mother, I think, looks beautiful. She was twenty-three at the time.

Looking at that picture, I see a woman who had she been twenty-three in the 1980s would have had limitless options available to her. She is more than pretty; she is visibly bright and vibrant and interesting. I look at the picture, and I know that had she decided to pursue personal pleasure or professional accomplishment, doors would have been open to her. In the picture she is a person whom, had I been a young man in 1942, I would have wanted to know.

Her history bears this out; although she, like me, was born in Columbus, Ohio, she was educated at Wellesley College and graduated Phi Beta Kappa. When I said in the opening sentence that she is the smartest person I know, that was no exaggeration. Most of us secretly feel that we are innately sharper than the rest of the world; I accept for a fact that, even on my best days, my mother is brighter and more capable than I. I am thirty-seven years old and I have never heard her utter a stupid sentence; I have never seen her make a judgment that seemed wrong.

And yet we come back to a basic fact: she always defined herself as a wife and mother. She was honored in our hometown for her volunteer civic work, but if she was asked what she did, she unhesitatingly answered that she was Robert Greene's wife, and Bobby, Debby, and Timmy Greene's mother. You could see it in her signature: "Mrs. Robert (Phyllis H.) Greene."

Coming home for lunch from school; somehow, that is what I remember most clearly. We didn't live all that far from the school building, and I would come home most days rather than eat in the lunchroom. Invariably she was there; just after eleven o'clock she had started preparing our meal, and when the three of us would walk through the back door she would be putting it on the table.

I suppose today many women would find that to be a demeaning waste of their potential. Why should an intelligent, ambitious woman be satisfied making egg salad sandwiches and heating up cans of soup?

I can't answer that, at least not from a woman's point of view. But it must have counted for something if, all these years later, I can still literally feel what it was Iike to rush through that back door and see her there putting the lunch on the table. If I recall correctly, we children didn't even talk much to her during those hurried meals between our last class of the morning and our first class of the afternoon; mainly, I think, we talked to one another about things that were going on at school.

I don't know what she thought on all of those afternoons when we jumped up from the table and ran out the same door we had run in. I assume that even back then a woman must have thought—her husband at work, her children at school—that something was missing. But if she felt that way, she never let us know; it never occurred to us that she was supposed to be anywhere but at home, waiting for us.

Today she might be an executive or an entrepreneur or an author. If she ever considered those things in the Fifties and Sixties, she never said them out loud; the world had yet to change its assumptions about women, and we instinctively knew that because she was a woman, she was right where she belonged.

Of my best friends from my high school days—there were five of us—three have already been divorced. Of my parents' best friends—a dozen couples or more—none were divorced. It just didn't happen.

Did men and women love each other more strongly back then? Doubtful. Did they feel a sense of obligation to stay together, a sense of obligation that is missing in today's marriages? Probably. Were they cheating themselves back then? Were they missing out on opportunities for richer lives?

Maybe I'm not qualified to answer. But I am of a generation that, by and large, was brought up in families that stayed together, by mothers who stayed home all day. And I wouldn't trade it for anything. If my mother deprived herself by the way she spent those years, I suppose I am sorry, but I know that she did not deprive Debby or Timmy or me. Whatever good there is about us, much of it came because we had a mother who defined her job as being our mother.

I once knew a homicide detective in Chicago, a man who saw the absolute grisliest, meanest parts of humanity every day. You would expect a man like that to be tough beyond redemption, but I always sensed a soft center to him; a part of him that didn't jibe with his job. One day I sat down with him and asked him about it, and he told me that no matter where he went in his life, part of him remained a small boy—and that inside the small boy there was the memory of his mother.

He told me, "Even when I was in the service, when I'd be out on a pass at four in the morning, I could hear my mother's voice saying, 'Joe, get home,' and I'd go back to the barracks."

I knew exactly what he meant. I am not the best person in the world; there are things about me that I would change if I could, and that I would not particularly respect if I found them in other people. But I know this: whenever I am doing something I sense might be wrong, I can check myself out by asking myself whether I would be ashamed if my mother knew about it.

I'm not saying I ask that question all the time. But this is an age in which the concept of "conscience" sometimes becomes muddied; we are all supposed to be so sophisticated about the nuances and tangents of a full life that sometimes it seems we can explain away anything, make ourselves believe that anything is all right. So it is reassuring to know that a simple rule of thumb is always there: How would I feel if my mother were to see me right this instant?

In a way I think we are a whole generation of men who are living with that question; men who at times are able to fool ourselves into thinking that we can reinvent the world and change the rules on a daily basis, but who know, in the end, that we really haven't changed at all from the days when our mothers could look into our faces and tell what we had been up to without our uttering a word.

Curiously, sometimes it seems that most men spend much of their lives trying to symbolically deny the fact that their mothers' voices still sound in their heads.

In my business, there is an almost laughable premium put on the concept of hardness and grittiness. About the most flattering thing you can say about a reporter is that he is "street smart"; we love to tell stories in which we see dead bodies and do not flinch; in which we consort with criminals and think it only colorful. I am sure it is the same in other businesses, whether they be medicine or accounting or the law; if we can place enough distance between the men we are now and the little boys we used to be— if we can convince strangers that when we saw the dead bodies we did not cry—then maybe we can also convince them that no one can ever touch us, in any way.

There was a time, though, when we were not so afraid of being afraid. My mother tells me, and I vaguely remember, that as a small child I thought there were monsters in my closet. Before I could go to sleep, I would need for her to make the monsters leave my room. So every night she would say the words—she remembers them even now—"Ruley and duck and goose and wolf, car, airplane, hoo-hoo, and the one who burps—get out of here!" And I would sleep.

I cringe a little, typing that. But it seems that only by recounting the specific can I say what I mean: that in many ways there is nothing that affects a man so strongly as those childhood years spent with his mother; and that I doubt that children have changed so much by now that they are less needful of what their mothers can give them. For most of our lives it is our own responsibility to chase the monsters away; for a few brief years at the beginning, our mothers are there to do it for us.

But what of the woman in the photograph, sitting next to the man in the Army uniform? What of the choices she made, and the choices she might have made had the fates allowed her to be born half a century or so later?

Had she been a 1984 woman, she would have been a success; of that I am sure. I see them every day: women of achievement striding purposefully down the avenue, briefcases in hand, on their way to appointments and meetings. Had she been a young woman today, had she elected to go out into the world of commerce and ambition, I have little doubt that she would have fit right in.

So her salary would have risen, and her resumé would have grown, and maybe one day she would have awakened to find that she was one of the people running the company. She might have found herself going to work in a downtown high-rise where dozens—hundreds?—of other men and women labored for her, men and women whose own professional lives revolved around decisions that she would make.

And what about the end of the day? When she went home, would whatever she felt equal the emotions that she felt staying at home all those years with my father and my brother and my sister and me?

There are some who would argue that by never having the opportunity to know the answer to that question, she was robbed of a part of life that women today take for granted. That today's woman can make a decision to live the same life that my mother did—but can also make a decision to reject that life, a decision that was simply not open to my mother.

I don't know. Many women today, I think, would be afraid to live my mother's life. So much has happened, so much has changed, that for a smart and resourceful American woman to do what my mother did—to devote her life totally to her husband and children, and to fit in other things only when those things did not interfere with her home responsibilities—would seem not only confining, but a little dangerous, a little foolhardy. I think that even a woman who instinctively might want to lead my mother's life would feel pressured to reject it on principle.

Which doesn't matter; my mother is not a young woman any longer, and the choices that she made she will never have to make again. But I know this: Debby and Timmy and I grew up during a time when a life like my mother's was taken for granted, and I feel grateful beyond words for that. I hope that my mother feels contented; I hope that, looking back on her life, she feels she did the right thing.

There are questions and contradictions here; I know that much of this is troubling, and that I have not summed it up very neatly. All of us move through our grown-up worlds, pretending that we were never anyone else but the fully formed adults that our colleagues see at the office every day. We were, though; a lot of us were once little boys who hurried home for lunch knowing that someone was waiting. It mattered then, and it matters now, and I could not be happier that the woman in the photograph was the one who waited for me.

The Twitching of America

BOSTON—There is a restaurant here called Legal Sea-
foods, with three locations in the metropolitan area. The restaurant has a
unique policy about bringing diners their checks.

When you order your dinner or lunch, your waiter writes down what you
want. Then, before bringing you your food, he presents you with your check
and requests your money.

Legal Seafoods is not some fast-food operation; it is a respected Boston
restaurant, and you pay healthy prices for your meal and drinks. So the pay-
first policy is surprising to people who are eating there for the first time.

The reason for the policy is a simple one:

"A large part of our clientele consists of businessmen and business-
women," said Bruce Ota, the restaurant's manager. "They are always in a
hurry. They prefer not to wait around at the end of the meal. If they pay
before they eat, then they can get up and leave the moment they've finished with their meal."

Ah. It makes sense. It's not that the management of Legal Seafoods
doesn't trust the customers to pay at the end of the meal—it's that they
know the customers are twitching in their seats in anticipation of getting
back to work, or on their way to the next place they're supposed to be. To
wait two or three minutes for a check would drive them crazy.

It fits in with something that seems to be happening all over the country. For want of a better term, it might be called The Twitching of America.
All of a sudden, people seem to be in an insane hurry to get too much done
in too little time. A reluctance to enjoy a meal and then wait a few minutes
for the waiter to fetch the check is merely a symptom.

Time magazine recently touched on this phenomenon in a cover story
on stress. The magazine said that increasing numbers of people are running themselves so hard that their stress is starting to become a medical
problem; indeed, some men and women may even be becoming addicted
to the adrenaline that their own twitching bodies are producing.

If you look around you, you can see The Twitching of America everywhere. There are people who will punch a button for an elevator, and if
the elevator does not arrive within five seconds they will begin punching
the button again repeatedly—or they will begin looking for a staircase. There
are people whose faces become ruddy and flushed in traffic if the car in
front of them pauses even momentarily before starting up again after the
light turns green. There are people whose pulses begin to race if they call
Directory Assistance and the operator does not answer before the third ring.
There are people whose days are ruined if they have to stand in line at the
bank. There are even people who, while using a bank of pay telephones,
attempt to carry on conversations on two phones at once—if they are put
on hold on the first line, they will pick up a second line to start a new call
while they're waiting.

The so-called laid-back days of our society are definitely over. The Twitching of America is claiming more victims every day; no one really enjoys it,
but the inroads it is making are undeniable.

This trip of mine to Boston is probably a prime example. I caught the
first morning flight here; tonight I will catch one of the last flights back to
Chicago. A day trip like this, halfway across the country, is far from uncommon; businessmen who used to routinely stay overnight in a distant city
now check airline timetables so they can do their work and be back in their
hometown the same day.

This has nothing to do with saving on hotel bills. It has to do with a feeling that waking up in another city on the morning after you have completed
your work is wasteful of your time; you could be back in your office taking
care of important tasks. So now, instead of relaxing and having an enjoy-
able dinner after a hard day in the distant city, businessmen rush to airports so they can get back to their own towns late at night.

It is merely a permutation of the Legal Seafoods phenomenon; the people
who start tapping their feet and looking at their watches if the waiter does
not bring their check right away are the same people who feel guilty if they
waste another half-day traveling, when they could be working.

There is undeniably something deeply unhealthy about all of this; a society that has begun to value the clock so highly has got to be missing out on
certain other aspects of a normal life. The cliché, of course, is "Stop and
smell the roses"; now not only have people ceased stopping to smell the
roses—they resent it if someone who *is* smelling the roses happens to block
their path on the sidewalk for three seconds.

So they eat at Legal Seafoods, then hurry back to their offices to drum
their fingers on their desks as they impatiently wait for their Federal Express

packages to be delivered, inside of which are documents that had to reach them overnight. What would have happened if the packages had been sent via regular mail, and had taken three days instead of half a day to get there? Who knows. The important thing is, the phone has already rung twice, and the secretary hasn't picked it up yet. It's enough to drive a modern person right off the edge.

The Real Superman

If you can believe the newspaper ads, the reviews for this summer's *Superman III* movie have been pretty great.

One critic is quoted as saying: "Get in line fast! The funniest and most bracing of the *Superman* movies."

Another says; "*Superman III* is one of the summer's great escapes. Very funny and clever and strong on the old magic of special effects."

And a third weighs in with: "*Superman III* is the best yet. It's a hit. . . . It's a delight. . . . It's Supersequel! The most entertaining and affecting *Superman* yet."

I have no reason to doubt those critics. But I haven't seen any of the three modern-day *Superman* movies, and my reason is a simple one.

It's this: I was hopelessly addicted to the old "Superman" TV show. When I first heard that there were plans to make a big-budget Superman movie a few years ago, I was afraid that regardless of whether the movie was good or bad, it would forever overshadow the original TV series. And of course that is right; when future generations think of Superman, it will be in terms of the spectacularly successful new movies starring Christopher Reeve.

Which, I suppose, is only right. It must be admitted even by those of us who loved it that the old "Superman" TV series was pretty awful stuff, in terms of craftsmanship and production values. But millions upon millions of us, when we were children, would put down anything else we were doing, and stare at the TV screen whenever "Superman" came on—and we find that, as adults, we do the same thing anytime we come across a grainy rerun in syndication.

The main draw, of course, was George Reeves, the actor who played Clark Kent and Superman. It is hard to define the qualities that Reeves brought to the role. You would think that the character of Superman would demand strength, rock-jawed good looks, inner gentleness, a firmness of vocal tone . . . you would think that, but in the case of George Reeves you would be dead wrong.

The amazing thing about Reeves is that he had almost a mincing quality, and it showed through in every episode. I'm not sure whether we noticed it when we were kids—but for adults watching the reruns, it's almost impossible to ignore the fact that the casting of Reeves seems in retrospect like an inside joke perpetrated by Hollywood producers on the youth of America. All you have to do is watch Reeves put his hand to his chin and say, "Hmmm, Jimmy, you may be right," and you see what I mean. At times Reeves played Superman like a combination of Jack Benny and Gloria Swanson.

But somehow it worked. The character of Superman was so spectacular that it was impossible to dilute its effectiveness. Children wanted to believe in Superman—and if what Hollywood demanded was that we believe in an arch, coy, purse-lipped fellow who seemed more like a lummoxing great-aunt than like the man of steel, we were willing to give it a go.

Of course, Reeves was not the only draw. There was Noell Neill, who played Lois Lane, the first working woman many of us ever saw; Jack Larson, who played cub reporter Jimmy Olson; and, unforgettably, John Hamilton as Perry White, the dyspeptic editor of the *Daily Planet,* who kept shouting at Olson, "Don't call me chief!"

Looking back on it, it seems as if the *Daily Planet* had no other staffers; Clark Kent, Lois Lane, Jimmy Olson, and Perry White managed to put out the paper all by themselves, and the first three were hardly ever in the office.

But if that factor was designed to stretch our credulity, then what passed for "special effects" tested us even further. Any five-year-old could watch George Reeves flex his legs and get ready to leap from a window or off the sidewalk, and predict the exact point at which the director would snip the film so we didn't see Reeves fall back to the ground. We didn't care. We wanted to believe; we were on his side.

And when the "Superman" theme music swelled up, and George Reeves cradled a crippled girl in leg braces in the crook of his arms to give her a flying tour of the world, our eyes misted and our throats got tight. All the bad acting and lousy special effects in the world couldn't reduce the impact of that kind of scene.

George Reeves committed suicide in 1959; the rest of the cast of the

"Superman" TV series occasionally turn up as answers to trivia quizzes. The new multi-million-dollar *Superman* movies have been both critical and financial successes; it is almost a sure thing that when future Americans think of Superman, it will be in terms of Christopher Reeve, not George Reeves.

So I'm glad I have protected myself from that. Never having seen the new *Superman* films, my eternal image of the greatest hero the world has ever known is guaranteed to be the unlikely, hilarious, but ultimately lovable one I first saw on a black-and-white TV screen in the 1950s. Hmmm, Jimmy, you may be right.

Confessions of a Middle-Aged Man

I woke up in a hotel room on the road the other morning, and when the room-service waiter brought my breakfast he also dropped off a copy of the local newspaper. I glanced at Page One, and I noticed something interesting about the date: It was my thirty-sixth birthday.

That struck me as pretty weird. For the last year I had been living fairly comfortably with the notion that I was thirty-five; thirty-five never seemed all that far removed from thirty. But thirty-six was a different matter entirely. Being thirty-six means only one thing; being thirty-six means you are middle-aged.

So I had my breakfast and got dressed and went out to conduct my business. It was the first day of my life that I had ventured out into the world as a middle-aged man. It felt . . . different.

The problem is, the last time I noticed, I was seventeen. My most vivid and cherished memories are of the time I was seventeen; my closest friends are still the people who were closest to me when I was seventeen; the events of the years 1964 and 1965—when I was seventeen—still seem important and meaningful to me. There's nothing wrong with that; I think it's probably pretty healthy to feel good about the early years of your life.

But it's sort of jarring for a person like that to realize he is now thirty-six. Being thirty-six is much more than one year older than thirty-five. A person who is thirty-five is one year older than a person who is thirty-four, but a person who is thirty-six has entered a whole new ball game.

Fortunately, I have been getting ready for this for several years. The first time I started thinking about it was during one of my twice-a-year visits to the dentist. He got done looking at my mouth, and—as I had been doing for years—I asked him if I had any new cavities. He said no.

I was gleeful. The dentist very gently said, "You know, you really shouldn't be worrying about cavities. You're not going to get a whole lot more cavities in your life. Middle-aged people shouldn't be concerned with cavities. They should be concerned with gum problems."

On the way home from that visit, I tried to figure out how the dentist could have meant that without implying that I was a middle-aged person. I knew I was not a middle-aged person; at the time I was only thirty-four, and as far as I was concerned, that made me in my early thirties, not middle-aged. But clearly the dentist had been trying to tell me something.

The message took hold. From that point on, in stories where I was trying to describe someone, I began to delete two adjectives that once were routine parts of my lexicon: "middle-aged" and "aging." The two phrases had suddenly taken on new and different meanings to me. When I used to write "middle-aged," I now realized, I had done it in a somewhat patronizing way. To write that someone was "middle-aged" had the connotation that the person was somehow bland, tired, not on the cutting edge; I had used the phrase for years, but only now did I realize that it had always had a negative connotation.

And "aging"; it used to be a convenient term to use in giving a sentence a bittersweet tug: an "aging centerfielder," an "aging businessman." Now it struck me that the phrase was meaningless; everyone is aging, even a four-year-old. We are all aging every minute of our lives. The phrase seemed mean-spirited, imprecise, and ultimately unfair.

And now here I was. When I had started this trip, I had been a thirty-five-year-old man. Now the person who would be coming home was a middle-aged man. I wondered if my parents realized I was a middle-aged man? If it made me feel so strange, imagine how it must make them feel. How would you like to be the parent of a middle-aged man?

This is definitely going to take some getting used to. When I hear that a person is thirty-six or thirty-seven, that person seems—in my mind—to be a much older person than I am. If I'm making a telephone call to a man I have learned is thirty-six or thirty-seven, I will call that man "Mr." on the phone. A person who is thirty-six or thirty-seven has always seemed to be a person worthy of deference. Now I am that person.

There are almost certainly some positive aspects to this. I know instinctively that even though I am middle-aged, that does not mean I have had all the experiences in life that a person can have. For example, I have never had an olive; that little fact alone encourages me to keep on going and experience the world to the fullest. Who knows what is waiting?

On the day after I turned thirty-six, I packed my bags and headed to the airport for the trip home. On the airplane, I found myself sitting next to a personable woman I had never met. We began a conversation during the course of the flight.

At one point I said to her, "How old are you?" [I have always been known for the ease, wit, and appropriateness of my small-talk.]

"Twenty-seven," she said. "How old are you?"

"Thirty-six," I said, and I saw something in her eyes.

I knew what it was, even though she probably couldn't have put her finger on it. In that one instant, she had found out whom she was sitting next to; she was sitting next to some middle-aged man.

But hey, that was her problem, not mine. Someday soon she will be middle-aged, too; let's wait and see how she likes it.

Rules of the Road

Three years ago this month, "American Beat" started appearing regularly in *Esquire*. As you know if you stop by this space on occasion, you will not find any particular brand of expertise here. We have no special insights on personal fashion, participatory sports, outdoor living, high life, or ethics. All we do is go out and see things and write about them.

Going out and seeing those things, though, has given us—what the heck, me—an intimate look at one particular area of modern life. I stay in an awful lot of hotel rooms in pursuit of my livelihood, and it has been suggested to me that perhaps I should share some of my hotel theories with you. Chances are you stay in a hotel room or two yourself during the course of a month, and maybe you could use the guidance of a hotel-room pro.

Done. Here, for your edification: American Beat's Rules of the Road.

1. If your telephone and your clock are on a night table by the side of your bed, sleep on that side of the bed. It will help you regain your bearings if you wake up at 3:00 A.M. and have no idea where you are. If the phone is on a table on one side of the bed and the clock is on a table on the other side, sleep on the side with the phone.

2. Stay in hotels that offer twenty-four-hour room service. Even if you never order a meal after midnight—and I never have—you want to stay in a hotel with a kitchen that's open while you're sleeping. The reason is that hotels with twenty-four-hour room service are generally clicking on all cylinders in other areas, too; if they're willing to keep their staffs on hand all night for the few customers who might need them, then they're thinking about you in other ways you don't see or notice.

3. Do not leave your shoes outside your door when you stay in a hotel that offers complimentary shoeshines. You never know. It is far better to have dirty shoes in the morning than to wake up and discover that you have no shoes at all.

4. When you're making reservations at a hotel that's part of a chain, spend the couple of bucks to call the hotel directly, rather than dialing the chain's toll-free 800 number. This rule may be an example of naiveté on my part; but I have become convinced that you get more personal attention if you deal with the specific hotel rather than with the chain's computer bank. I will confess that this probably has more to do with superstition than with reality.

5. The size of your room is much more important than the view. Often a desk clerk will offer you a "lake view" or a "park view," and you arrive in the room to find that it is the size of a moderate closet. For some reason, travelers are perfectly willing to request a particular view, but are shy about asking how big the room is. Go ahead and ask; the clerks know. Almost always, the bigger the room, the better. Do not be fooled by front-desk euphemisms; there is no such thing as a "cozy" hotel room.

6. A corollary to the above rule: There is one set of hotel rooms in America that combine both amazing size with a beautiful view. This is the 02 tier at the Watergate Hotel in Washington. If you get any room there with a number that ends in 02, you are in luck.

7. The best measure of whether a hotel cares about you or not can be found in your room's lamps. If the hotel cares about you, the button to turn the lamp on and off will be found on the base of the lamp, within easy reach. If the hotel does not care, the button will be found somewhere up beneath the shade, or on a little plastic clicker attached to the cord—where you have to search to locate it.

If you are thinking that this is a ridiculous thing to be concerned about, and that you would not notice something like this at home: of course you wouldn't. Homes are never as nice as hotels. You should always expect more of a hotel room than you would of your home.

8. The other measure of whether a hotel cares about you or not can be found on your telephone. In some of the most expensive hotels in America, there is no red message light on the phone. Nothing is more important to a business traveler than knowing when he has received a phone call; yet many hotels that charge top dollar will not go to the expense of installing message lights.

The desk clerks in these hotels will invariably tell you that someone will always bring your message up promptly and slip it under your door. But of course "promptly" is a state of mind; if you are waiting for a particular call, and you find out three hours later that the call has come in, all the apologies in the world won't help. No message light on the phone is a perfectly valid reason for choosing another hotel the next time you are in town. More to the point, it is a perfectly valid thing to check into when you are making your reservations.

9. Some hotels have a feature that gives out a beeping sound when you are on the phone and someone else is trying to get through. This is useless; in almost all cases, the phones do not have the capability to disconnect from one call temporarily while you see who the other caller is.

One hotel—the Ritz-Carlton in New York—has come up with a surprisingly simple, yet ideal, solution to this. In every one of the Ritz's guest rooms the phones have two lines—just like the phones you may have at your office. The phones have buttons running across the bottom of the base; if you're talking to a person and someone else wants to reach you, the desk rings the second caller through to your second line, you put the first caller on hold, and you conduct your business. If this sounds like an unnecessary luxury on a short trip, then you don't realize how many calls you're missing in hotels when you're talking to someone else.

10. When you leave your room in the morning, always call housekeeping to request that a maid come by to make up your room right away. Do not rely on her coming automatically, and do not rely on the PLEASE MAKE UP ROOM EARLY signs you're supposed to leave outside your door. If you use your room for business, it does you no good to get back at 3:00 P.M. and find that they haven't gotten around to you yet. The housekeeping people don't mind hearing from you; it helps them get *their* business done as soon as possible, and they like that.

11. At a Holiday Inn, always request a King Leisure. At worst it's the nicest room in the house, and at best you'll think you're at a Westin or a Hyatt.

12. While traveling through America, do not read the *New York Times*; do not read the *Wall Street Journal*; do not read *USA Today*. Read the local papers. The whole point of being on the road is to feel like you're on the road.

13. If you find yourself booked into the Circus Circus in Las Vegas, bring tranquilizers.

14. A serious note: The first thing you should do after checking into your room is go back out into the hallway and familiarize yourself with the fire-exit route. This will take you thirty seconds. Not to overstate the obvious, but it's worth your time.

15. If you have been up all night and want to sleep all day, don't count on it. If you hang your DO NOT DISTURB sign during daylight hours, one of two things will happen: either the maid will knock on your door at 1:00 P.M., wake you up, and then say, "Just checking"; or your telephone will ring and a cheery voice will say, "Housekeeping. Did you want your room made up today?"

16. On the other hand, when those maids do wake you up, don't be short with them. On a slow day, they can make good conversation partners, and you can learn some interesting things. A maid at the Hi Ho Best Western Motel in Custer, South Dakota, told me that she had once made Harry Reasoner's bed.

17. Square foot for square foot, the most important area of your hotel room is the bathroom. If your bathroom is in good shape but your bedroom is mediocre, you can still have a good stay. If your bedroom is superb and your bathroom is horrible, your entire trip can be ruined. Pay special attention to shower heads.

18. As a modern business traveler, you are the beneficiary of a merchandising battle you may not even be aware of: Shampoo Wars.

For some reason, the general managers of America's hotels have decided to conduct their most intense competition in the area of the free shampoo that is provided in the rooms. This is never promoted or advertised, but if you look closely, you will see that it is so.

The nation's hotels are locked in an ever-escalating, never-ending game of one-upmanship to see who can provide guests with the most exotic, distinctive shampoo. Whether this is a matter of corporate hotel ego or of a secret perversity known only to a few lodging magnates, I have no idea; the only way to notice this is to examine the shampoo packets in your room to see what you're being offered. At the Century Plaza in Los Angeles, for example, you get Max Factor Honey and Almond shampoo; in Hyatt hotels you get shampoo manufactured from mink oil.

The most expert and sophisticated of travelers are well aware of this practice. I was in New York one evening, walking along 66th Street on my way to dinner with Bill Lord, the executive producer of "ABC News Nightline."

"Where are you staying tonight?" he said.

"The Helmsley Palace," I said.

"Ah," he said, not breaking stride. "Coconut shampoo."

19. Hotels are in business to make money, and thus can be excused for charging you for anything they feel like. Except one item. In recent months, freed from federal regulations, many hotels have for the first time added a surcharge on long-distance calls that you bill to your credit card or company number. Some hotels charge up to several dollars extra on each call for this; what it means is that you are now paying for something you got last year for free—and that you are paying a stiff penalty fee on top of a phone-company fee that is already increased significantly over the basic direct-dial fee. There are two ways to beat this: use the pay phone in the lobby, which seems silly when you're spending big bucks for a room; or complain bitterly to the manager. If enough people do, maybe this will stop as quickly as it started.

20. Unless your company gives you a credit card that is billed directly to them—and few companies do—get a cash advance and pay for everything on your trip with it. Put nothing on a credit card that will eventually be billed to you.

Once a business trip is over, it should be over; you don't want personal credit card bills coming in months later reminding you of where you have had dinner and where you have slept. By the time you receive those bills, often you have already been reimbursed by your company and have already spent the money. It ends up costing you out of your pocket.

Carry the cash. If your company balks about giving you that much cash up front, ask them for a credit card that's billed to them instead. You'll get the cash.

21. The nicest things about hotel rooms, expensive or modest, are the Gideon Bibles. It doesn't matter whether you're an especially religious person or not; just the idea that the Gideon International folks, year after year, have placed all those millions of Bibles in all those millions of rooms is sort of warming. I know, I know; you've stopped even noticing they're there. Next time, take a minute and read a verse. It won't kill you.

So there you have it. These particular Rules of the Road have been the standard model, for the average traveler. There is a set of advanced rules, too—one that comes to mind is the Style and Etiquette of Hanging Overnight Breakfast Orders on the Doorknob—but those rules are not for everyone, and should not be bandied about in a place like this. Happy trails; see you on the road.

Stranger at the Table

It's hard to make any sense of this story; but then, it's becoming increasingly hard to make any sense of these times.

On a recent Saturday night a man named David Gambill was returning to his home in Richmond, Virginia. Gambill and his wife, Ayer, had been on a week's vacation to Massachusetts; now they were tired, and were anxious to get back to their own house.

They pulled into the driveway. Gambill opened the back door. It struck him right away that something was amiss.

There was food on the stove, and the food was cooking. Chow mein and six fish sticks. But there was no one in the kitchen.

Gambill told his wife to wait by the back door. He began to walk around his house. In a bathroom, he found that a window had been broken. Now he was sure that someone was in his house.

He went from room to room. Later his friends would tell him that he was crazy to do that; the friends would say that he should have gotten out of the house and called the police. But Gambill was determined to find out who was in his home.

He went into his son's bedroom. The door to his son's closet was closed. Gambill opened the door.

Sitting in the closet, huddled behind Gambill's son's rolled-up sleeping bag, was a bedraggled-looking old fellow.

"He looked awful," Gambill said. "He needed a shave, and he was wearing what I can only describe as thrift-shop clothing. The thing I remember most clearly was his eyes. They were just staring back at me. I knew right away that I wasn't in any danger. In his eyes I saw fear—fear and relief that I wasn't going to hurt him."

Gambill stood there staring at the man. The man started to speak.

"I was hungry," the man said. "I was hungry, so I came on into your house."

Gambill didn't know what to say to the man.

"You can call the police if you want," the man said.

Gambill thought of what he should do: pounce on the man, tie him up, lock him in the closet.

But he realized that what he was feeling wasn't anger. It was sadness.

"You really broke in because you were hungry?" Gambill said.

"Yes," the man said.

Gambill knew that, in looking around the house, nothing had been stolen. The only things that had been disturbed, with the exception of the broken bathroom window, were the chow mein and the fish sticks that had been taken from the Gambills' refrigerator and put on the stove.

"You can go in and finish your supper," Gambill said.

So the man straightened up, walked out of the closet, and went to the kitchen. As Gambill and his wife watched, the man put the chow mein and the fish sticks onto a plate, and sat down at the kitchen table.

Gambill, almost as a second thought, picked up the telephone and called the Henrico County police. He told the dispatcher what had happened; the dispatcher said police officers would be over immediately.

"I couldn't believe how fast he ate that food," Gambill said. "He just kept putting it into his mouth as fast as he could.

"I know I probably shouldn't have let him do it. But when I thought about it—he was risking getting arrested so he could have a meal. He was risking his life, really. He could have got shot breaking into someone's house. If he was that desperate, I couldn't deny him the food."

The man finished his meal. He went over and got a water tumbler from the Gambills' shelf. He drew a glass of water from the kitchen sink. He gulped it down.

Gambill said he still felt no danger, being in the house with the man who had broken in. "He wasn't going to spring at me or anything," Gambill said. "There was no threat to me. He was very docile."

The police arrived. They entered the Gambills' kitchen, and Gambill immediately filled them in on what had happened. The police stared at the man, who was still in the kitchen, with the now-empty plate and glass. The man made no effort to flee.

The police began to read the man his Miranda rights.

"It was the most bizarre scene," Gambill said. "The old guy was standing there, and the police were reading his rights to him, and it was like something off a television show. I kept staring at the old guy, and I kept hearing these phrases the police were reading: 'right to remain silent,' and 'right to an attorney.' The guy was showing no visible reaction."

The police put the man in handcuffs and led him out to the squad cars.

As the man left, he said nothing to Gambill or his wife. Later, the police would charge the man—whom they identified as Allen Young, age approximately fifty-seven—with breaking and entering, and petty larceny.

"I've felt terrible ever since that night," Gambill said. "I make a pretty good living; hunger isn't a big issue for me. We read about hunger, and we know it's out there, but it takes something like this to bring it home."

Gambill said that, in the days following the incident, he has gone through all the emotions that people who are burglarized often feel: a sense of violation, a sense of being helpless against outside forces, a sense of his home not being entirely his own any longer.

But the dominant emotion was a different one.

"I don't know how to put this, but I almost felt like crying," he said. "Crying at the thought of what's going on out there for people like that fellow. Can you understand what I'm saying? I haven't been sleeping very well at night."

Copy

The journalistic and literary sin that has always puzzled me the most is plagiarism.

I think I know a little bit about why people write, and I have never understood why a writer would resort to stealing another writer's words. It's not so much a moral issue; after all, the world has plenty of people who murder and burglarize, so we ought to understand that some people have hazy ideas of morality.

But to be a writer, I have always thought, a person must have a healthy ego. If you are presumptuous enough to choose to sit down and put words on paper with the hope that other people will read them, you should have a good amount of self-confidence. To plagiarize—to print someone else's words under your own name—is to admit to yourself that your own words and your own thoughts are deficient. I have always wondered how any writer could do that; if he feels that way about his own abilities, then why is he a writer in the first place?

I bring this up because the other day I received a letter from Lt. Col. Henry C. Rilling, of the Fort Huachuca Army base in Arizona. The letter was quite apologetic; enclosed with it was a story from the Fort Huachuca base newspaper.

I read the story and immediately saw why Lt. Col. Rilling had sent it to me. Although the story ran under the byline of one of the Army base's employees, I had written it; it was virtually the same story as one by me that had appeared in a national magazine. Only a few words had been altered.

Lt. Col. Rilling said in his letter that base personnel had discovered the plagiarism only after the story had appeared in the paper. I read the story over several times; it was on an intensely personal topic, and it was a funny feeling, seeing my emotions, in my own words, expressed under another man's name.

I called Lt. Col. Rilling; I told him that I had no interest in bringing any legal action against the man who had "written" the story. But I said I had one favor to ask. I explained that I had never been able to understand why a person would plagiarize; I asked if he could put me in touch with the man, so that we could talk. I really wanted to know what had gone through his head as he had typed up that story.

So it was that, the other night, I called the man at home and introduced myself.

He said that he was embarrassed and sorry about what had happened. I asked him how it had come about.

"I am fifty years old," he said. "I retired from the Army as a chief warrant officer in 1975. Now I'm a civilian working on the base, doing clerical work.

"I don't have any legitimate excuse for what I did. I've been trying so hard to get recognized and be accepted in my job, and I haven't been doing that well. I thought to have a story published in the base newspaper would be an ego trip. I thought that people would see it, and that they would think well of me.

"I had intended to write something of my own. But then I saw your story, and I liked it, and for some reason I just changed a few things and put my name on top of it. I knew I was doing wrong, but I did it anyway."

I asked him if he had had any misgivings when he turned it in.

"I don't think I've ever felt this guilty in my whole life," he said. "My original intention was that I hoped some of the people in higher ranks would like the story, and would recognize my name if my name came up for a good job in their offices. But then the newspaper came out, and I started to get a good response to the story, and I couldn't sleep at night. I felt that I had taken something from someone else; but by this point I didn't know what to do."

I asked him if he had thought about confessing what he had done.

"I may have thought about it, but I didn't do it—until I got caught, of course," he said. "I wasn't used to the kind of recognition I was getting. People came up to me whom I had not even met, and they were commenting on 'my' story. Part of me felt good at the time because the people were noticing me—but part of me realized what I had done."

I asked him if he had even considered turning in some of his own work, and seeing if it would be accepted for publication.

"I think that was my intention, at first," he said. 'But I'd been having some problems—my fiancé and I had just broken up—and what can I say? I turned in your story.

"I truthfully don't think of myself as a generally dishonest person. I know that what I did was wrong. But I was at a point in my life when I wanted some positive attention paid to me; I thought it would be good for my sense of pride, and this seemed to be a good way to do it. I guess I didn't analyze it; I just did it."

He apologized again, and I told him again that I had no desire to take any action against him. He told me that he was afraid he was going to face disciplinary action on the Army base because of what had happened; he asked me if it would be all right to have his immediate superior call me and talk about the conversation we had just had.

I said sure. The older I get, the less certain I am about what makes this world of ours go around.

A Dying Cub Fan's
Last Request

The news we were hearing about Steve Goodman was not happy.

Goodman, thirty-six, was the Chicago-born folk singer and songwriter whose biggest national hit was the railroad ballad "City of New Orleans." In his hometown, though, Goodman was just as well known for some of his less commercially successful but equally wonderful songs: "Daley's Gone," "My Old Man," "Lincoln Park Pirates."

Goodman was known for something else, too: for being a truly lovely person who, despite his talent and his success, never went high-hat on his old acquaintances, and never lost the accessibility that has long been a hallmark of performers who get started in Chicago.

For years there was a barely concealed secret about Goodman: his long battle with leukemia. He never talked about it, and music writers did him the favor of not mentioning it in their stories. Goodman simply felt that it was not a piece of information he wished to trade on.

Several years ago, though, Goodman finally went public with the fact that he had been undergoing chemotherapy for the leukemia. He made it clear that he was telling people about it only because there was no longer any way to hide it; he didn't want any favors from anyone. He just wanted to make his music.

Goodman died on Thursday. For days we had been hearing that it was only a matter of time.

He had been in critical condition in the critical care unit of the University of Washington Hospital in Seattle. Hospital official Wendy Lippman said that Goodman was admitted in August suffering from "rapidly progressing acute leukemia"; later that month, she said, he received a bone marrow transplant from his brother David.

Knowing how bad things were, Goodman's admirers in Chicago were struck by a terrible irony about what was happening. If there was anything that Goodman was known for as well as his love of music, it was his love of the Chicago Cubs. He had been a Cub fan all his life; this year's upbeat Cubs anthem, "Go Cubs Go," was his composition.

But there is another song about the Cubs that Goodman was even more closely identified with. It was his warm, funny, bittersweet song about a longtime Cub fan who is near death. The song is called "A Dying Cub Fan's Last Request."

In the song, the dying Cub fan says to the friends gathered around his bed:

Do they still play the blues in Chicago
when baseball season rolls around?
When the snow melts away, do the Cubbies still play
in their ivy-covered burial ground?

When I was a boy they were my pride and joy.
But now they only bring fatigue
to the home of the brave, the land of the free
and the doormat of the National League.

Finally this is the year, of course, when the Cubs are threatening to bring a baseball championship to Chicago. And Goodman's Chicago friends and fans were haunted by the words near the end of his song, in which the Cub fan enunciates his last wish:

Now I fear that I might never get to go back there,
and I'd like to go one more time before I come to my
    eternal rest.
So, have your pencil and scorecard ready,
and I'll give you my last request.

I'd like a Dixieland funeral in Wrigley Field
on a double-header Saturday.
And the man at the organ plays the National Anthem
and "Na Na Na Na, Hey, Hey, Hey."
Get six bullpen pitchers to carry my coffin.
Let's get groundskeepers to clear my path.
And the umpires call me out as every base goes by,
and I vent my holy wrath.

Take a few of the Cubs out into the infield,
and have one of them drop an infield fly.
Then let everyone eat a Frosty Malt and a bag of peanuts,
and then I'll be ready to die.
It's a beautiful day for a funeral.
Hey, Ernie, Hey, Ernie, let's play two.
Have Jack Brickhouse call up Leo Durocher
to conduct my final interview.

Then build a fire with Danley Lumber and Louisville
*   Sluggers*
and toss my coffin in.
And let the ashes blow in a beautiful snow
from a 30-mile-an-hour southwest wind.
And as my last remains go flying over the left field wall,
I'll bid the Bleacher Bums adieu.
And come to my final resting place
out on Waveland Avenue.

In the midst of a baseball pennant race, there was a race of another sort
out in Seattle that weighed heavy on the minds of a lot of us in Chicago.

Louisville Slugger

At the newspaper where I work we have a rule that staff
members are not allowed to accept any gift of significant value from an
outside source. The rule probably makes sense; its purpose is to prevent
potential news sources from trying to influence news coverage through the
bestowing of lavish presents.

But I recently received something in the mail from an outside company,
and if the newspaper makes me give it back they're going to have to drag
me out of here kicking and screaming and holding onto it for dear life.

The package was long and narrow. I opened it. Inside was something that brought tears to my eyes and a funny feeling to my throat:

A Louisville Slugger baseball bat—a Bob Greene autographed model.

For five minutes I sat there looking at it and caressing it and speaking softly to it.

There, in the middle of the barrel, was the Louisville Slugger logo, and the famous copyrighted slogan: "Powerized." There, next to the logo, was the trademark of the Hillerich & Bradsby Co., which manufactures Louisville Sluggers.

And there—right at the end of the barrel—were the words PERSONAL MODEL—LOUISVILLE SLUGGER. And where Mickey Mantle's or Hank Aaron's autograph ought to be, the script words "Bob Greene."

I suppose there must be some item that an American boy might treasure more fiercely than a Louisville Slugger with his own signature on it, but I can't think of one. For all of us who grew up on sandlots and playgrounds, gripping Louisville Sluggers bearing the autographs of major league stars, the thought of owning one with our own name on the barrel is almost too much to comprehend.

In the box with the Louisville Slugger was a letter from John A. Hillerich III, president of Hillerich & Bradsby. In the letter Hillerich said that this is the centennial year for Louisville Sluggers; the first one was manufactured in the spring of 1884. Thus, the enclosed bat—a memento of the 100th anniversary.

When I started to show my new bat to people, the response I got was interesting. Women seemed not to care too much; generally they said something like, "Oh, a baseball bat." They would inspect it a little more closely, and then say, "What's your name doing on it?"

But men—men were a different story. First they would see the bat. They'd say something like, "A real Louisville Slugger. That's great." Invariably they would lift it up and go into a batting stance—perhaps for the first time in twenty or thirty years. Then they would roll the bat around in their hands—and finally they would see the signature.

That's when they'd get faint in the head. They would look as if they were about to swoon. Their eyes would start to resemble pinwheels. And in reverential whispers, they would say: "That is the most wonderful thing I have ever seen. Your own name on a Louisville Slugger. You are so lucky."

For it is true: a Louisville Slugger, for the American male, is a talisman—a piece of property that carries such symbolic weight and meaning that words of description do not do it justice. I have a friend who has two photographs mounted above his desk at work. One photo shows Elvis Presley kissing a woman. The other shows Ted Williams kissing his Louisville Slugger. No one ever asks my friend the meaning of those pictures; the meaning, of course, is quite clear without any explanation.

Hillerich & Bradsby has a photo in its archives that is similarly moving. In the photo, Babe Ruth and Lou Gehrig are standing in a batting cage. Gehrig, a wide smile on his face, is examining the bat. Perhaps you could find another photo that contains three figures more holy to the American male than those three—Ruth, Gehrig, and a Louisville Slugger—but I don't know where you'd look.

Hillerich & Bradsby has some intriguing figures and facts about Louisville Sluggers. The company manufactures approximately one million of them each year. That requires the use of about two hundred thousand trees each baseball season; the company owns five thousand acres of timberland in Pennsylvania and New York to provide the trees. Ash timber is the wood of choice for Louisville Sluggers. Years ago, the wood of choice was hickory.

According to the company, a professional baseball player uses an average of seventy-two bats each season—which comes as a surprise to those of us who always envisioned a major leaguer using the same special good-luck bat for years on end. The company says that, during World War II, some American sporting goods found their way to a German prison camp in Upper Silesia; the American prisoners of war there reportedly cried at the sight of the Louisville Sluggers. During the Korean War, an American soldier reportedly dashed out of his trench during a firefight to retrieve a Louisville Slugger he had left out in the open before the battle began.

As I sit here typing this, a colleague—a male—has just walked up next to my computer terminal, lifted my Louisville Slugger to his shoulder, and gone into a batter's crouch. In a moment, if I'm right, he'll start examining the bat—and in another moment he'll see the autograph.

I can't wait.

His Honor

We were the unlikeliest of friends. The first major story I ever covered as a newspaperman was the Chicago Seven conspiracy trial; Judge Julius J. Hoffman presided, and I thought he was a villain. I'm sure it showed up in my copy.

When you cover a long-running story, you tend to become attached to all the characters involved with it. About a year after the Chicago Seven trial ended—when everyone had moved on to other things—I got to thinking about Judge Hoffman, and about all the days I had sat in his courtroom, watching that bizarre drama unfold. I wrote him a letter saying that I regretted that, for all the words I had written about him, I had never met him personally; I had merely observed him on the bench.

Two days after I mailed the letter, he called. He invited me to his chambers; our visit lasted for hours. He was fascinating; pure ego, but with an overwhelming sense of what he perceived as the majesty of the federal judiciary. He led me around the office, showing me plaques and awards; although he knew his role in the Chicago Seven trial had made him a symbolic enemy of many, he was clearly pleased that, at least for a brief time, he had become the most famous judge in America.

I was amazed to find that we seemed to like each other. And we started to spend time together occasionally. Sometimes I would visit his chambers; sometimes we would have a drink in one of the barrooms of the Drake Hotel, near his home. I was happy just to serve as an audience for him, and he loved having that audience. Strangely, though, he always refused to go on television; he somehow felt that doing so would reflect badly on a man of his position. Once he told me, almost gloating:

"Wallace of '60 Minutes' called me up four times. Twice from New York, twice from Washington. I told him no four times. He told me, 'What? You're turning down an opportunity to be seen by fifty million people?' I told him that I was a federal judge, that I wasn't running for alderman of the Forty-second Ward."

When Hoffman died at eighty-seven last week, the first thing I thought of was a summer night in 1975, when the Public Broadcasting Service was scheduled to run a dramatization of the Chicago Seven trial, with actors portraying all the principals—the defendants, the attorneys, Judge Hoffman himself. I called him the day before the broadcast to ask if he would be watching; he said no. "That trial was five years ago," he said. "I have put it aside altogether. No, I think I'll let it pass."

But the next day he called me. He had changed his mind. "I don't suppose I can be accused of being excessively modest," he said. "Everyone likes to be noticed. Maybe I would like to see it after all."

He told me that his wife had been ill; he did not want to disturb her by watching the show at home. Did I have any suggestions?

I rented a room at the Drake. I told him I would meet him there just before the show began. He showed up right on time, still dapper and well turned out at eighty. I had pulled two chairs up to the room's television set; we sat down together to watch the show.

"Is the set working?" he asked. I assured him it was.

"I took pains to see what the competition is, by the way," he said. "There's not much on tonight on the other channels. I think we'll have a pretty respectable audience."

For me it was a remarkable evening. The screenplay was taken directly from the trial transcripts; all the heat and anger of the testimony were on the TV screen, and the actor playing Judge Hoffman ruled with all the haughty arrogance that Hoffman had exhibited in the trial itself. Hoffman stared at the screen; occasionally he would pull his chair closer to the set, to be sure he was not missing anything.

He seemed to be getting a kick out of the show. The actor portraying Black Panther leader Bobby Seale came onto the screen, and said: "I think there is a lot of racism involved, myself. . . . Look, old man, if you keep up denying me my constitutional rights, you are being exposed to the public and the world that you do not care about people's constitutional rights to defend themselves." And in the hotel room, the real Julius Hoffman chuckled.

When the TV Abbie Hoffman raged at the TV Julius Hoffman, the real-life judge in the hotel room laughed aloud and said, "He's a funny man, that Abbie. He used to wear his hair in a bun in the back. Tied it in a ribbon. We were very close. He used to call me 'Julie.' Not my Christian name, 'Julius,' but 'Julie.'"

At the end of the evening, as the program concluded, Hoffman said that he should be getting home to his wife. We prepared to leave the room, and he said to me:

"They can call me an old bastard if they want. Some people think I'm the greatest trial judge in the country. Others think I'm a rotten judge. . . . Franklin Delano Roosevelt, he was elected to the highest office in the land, and now you hardly ever hear his name. I like to be talked about. I think I'll get a pretty good obituary, don't you?"

Wanna Party?

There is a new verb form being used among the young and the allegedly young at heart: "to party."

You have probably heard the usage. Someone—usually someone who is a teenager or in his or her twenties—will say:

"I really want to party tonight."

Or:

"We're going to get together around eleven o'clock and party all night long."

Or:

"She's great. She really knows how to party."

Now, most of us grew up thinking that "party" was normally used as a noun. A "party" was a happy event to which we were invited.

When we were very young, a party usually meant a birthday party. We would be taken to a friend's house by our parents, and there would be cake, ice cream, crepe paper streamers, balloons, and—if we were really lucky—a pony.

A little later in our lives, a party usually meant some sort of dance. They were often held at the high school gym; we would take our shoes off so as not to mar the basketball court, and we would do steps such as the Pony or the Jerk to the sound of records or a live band.

Still later in our lives, a party usually meant a gathering at a fraternity house, sorority house, or hotel ballroom that had been rented for the night. At these parties we would meet other college students from the same university. Again, dancing was common.

We never used "party" as a verb; we never said, "I'm going to party my [obscenity] off tonight," which is what many current-day partyers say.

This is all heading somewhere; trust me.

The point is: "to party" seems to mean something totally different from what parties used to mean in the Fifties, Sixties, and early Seventies.

When people today say that they "love to party," they say it with a salacious gleam in their eyes. When they say that they "party with the best of them," it has a lewd ring to it; they seem to be hinting at something a little obscene; a little dirty; a little illicit; a little raunchy.

In short, it can be assumed that when they say a girl "really knows how to party," they are not saying that she is good at going to sorority parties.

I have never known precisely what "to party" means, but in the last few weeks I have made a vow to find out. Anytime I have overheard people say that they plan "to party" that night or that weekend, I have stopped them and asked them to tell me—exactly—what they will be doing while they are "partying." Most of these overheard conversations, by the way, have been in shopping malls.

For weeks, virtually none of the people I asked about "partying" answered me. Instead of explaining, they gave me weird looks, as if I were invading their privacy—which, I suppose, I was.

But last week I heard a teenaged girl say that she was looking forward to "partying" later that night. I excused myself for interrupting, then asked her what "partying" meant.

"You know," she said, not pausing in the chewing of her gum. "Drugs. Sex. Alcohol."

Aha. I had suspected as much. In fact, the first time I had heard "party" used as a verb was back when I was writing stories about rock and roll bands on the road. Outside the dressing rooms after the concerts each night, it was not uncommon to find teenaged girls who would invariably say, "Where are you guys staying? We want to party with you."

Naive as I was, I understood instinctively that these girls were not talking about birthday cake, ice cream, crepe paper streamers, balloons, or ponies. [Well, they might have been talking about ponies; on those rock and roll tours, you never knew.]

What they were talking about—it was true, it was true—were drugs, sex, and alcohol.

Now, midway into the Eighties, the verb those backstage girls used— "to party"—is rapidly becoming part of the language. I suppose I can't blame people for using that term in public; after all, it is far more acceptable to say, "I'm going to party tonight" than to say, "I'm going to take drugs, have sex, and drink alcohol tonight."

But I am concerned that I may be wrong. Perhaps I am judging the party people too harshly. Maybe "to party" does not, indeed, mean to take drugs, have sex, and drink alcohol. Maybe "to party" merely means, as in days of old, to go to the high school gym and kick one's shoes off to the strains of a Lesley Gore record. [The record I have in mind is "It's My Party and I'll Cry If I Want To"; somehow I can't imagine Miss Gore, then or now, singing "It's My Drugs, Sex, and Alcohol and I'll Cry If I Want To."]

So today I have a request for all of you party people:

Please, tell me what you mean. Drop me a line at the newspaper. If you can't bear the thought of writing a whole letter [writing is a very unpartying thing to do], call me. Tell me what you mean when you say you're going "to party tonight." Convince me I'm wrong. If I am, I will write a column explaining the error of my ways. If I'm right, though, I will have to go public with the fact that all of you really are spending all that time in the company of drugs, sex, and alcohol.

When I'm finished with this project, I have another, more specialized question I want to ask you:

What do all of you mean when you say you like to "party hardy"?

I'm not sure I even want to know the answer to that one.

The Party Animals Respond

Some things I've learned about partying since I asked you last week what you meant when you said you "like to party":

- You might not be all that interested in presidential politics, the situation in Lebanon, the nuclear freeze issue, or the state of the national economy, but you sure get enthusiastic about so-called partying. The response to the column was so heavy that there's no way I'm going to be able to write back to all of you individually; I've read all the letters, though, so everything that all of you said got taken into consideration.

- In the column I quoted a teenaged girl as saying that "partying" means drugs, sex, and alcohol. A lot of you disagreed. You said that partying was simply a euphemism for smoking marijuana—period. You said that if someone inquires, "Does she party?" what they mean is, "Does she smoke marijuana?" This definition was especially prevalent among college students who wrote.

- Curiously, a lot of you seem to equate vomiting with having fun. A significant portion of the letters reported that you knew you were having a great time partying if you threw up at some point during the evening; a number of correspondents thoughtfully advised me to "party 'til you puke."

- If your letters are any indication, there is a game called "quarters" being played in hundreds of thousands of suburban basements and college dormitories on any given night. Quarters seems to consist, basically, of trying to bounce a quarter off the surface of a table and into a beer glass; if you make the shot, you can then command someone else to drink a full glass of beer. The glass is continuously refilled. The person who drinks the beer is also supposed to catch the quarter between his or her teeth. Apparently this is supposed to be fun.

- A lot of you seem to have a different definition of drugs and alcohol from the rest of the world's definition. A typical conversation with you went something like this. You: "Partying doesn't mean drugs and alcohol." Me: "Then what does it mean?" You: "You know, you might go out with some friends and have a few beers and dance, and then later you might smoke some pot, which is as far as it usually goes unless someone has some cocaine." Me: "But you don't consider beer and marijuana and cocaine to be alcohol and drugs?" You: "Well, not really . . ."

- About the highest compliment you can give a friend is to say that he or she is a "party animal." You seem to confer this title with great affection and pride; to be a "party animal" appears to be the Eighties version of having a Phi Beta Kappa key.

- Not only do you cling to the traditions of the Sixties, you seem to cling to the paraphernalia of the Sixties, too. A large number of your letters mentioned that you own "bongs," which, fifteen years ago, were popular items designed to pull marijuana smoke through a liquid. More than one high school student reported that he or she enjoyed smoking marijuana through a bong filled with Jack Daniel's whiskey. This is probably as good a place as any to mention that I am simply reporting the facts of the response to the column.

- Close to 100 percent of you said that "partying" has nothing to do with sex. You said that when you partied, sex almost never took place.

- However, a few of you pointed out that "to party" may have originated among prostitutes, who often approach potential customers with the question, "Do you want to party?" So it can be assumed that at least some portion of America's partyers are, indeed, having sex—although they may be paying for it.

- On the subject of "party hardy"—most of you accused me of getting the spelling wrong. You said that the phrase was "party hearty," and that it meant, basically, to party excessively. Correspondent Ben Hollis, however, points out that "party hardy" is, indeed, the correct phrase. He lists a dictionary definition of "hardy": "stalwart and rugged; strong; brazenly daring; audacious; hotheaded; capable of surviving unfavorable conditions such as cold weather or lack of moisture."

- To the teachers who assigned their classes to write essays on what the students thought "partying" meant, and who then forwarded those essays to me: I'm not sure that was the appropriate response to the column.

- To give you some idea of the mind-set we're dealing with here, the following is a verbatim excerpt from one of the responses: "'To party' means fun. Dance till you drop and boogie till you puke! You know—WE AIN'T LEAVIN' TILL WE'RE HEAVIN'! You can't *explain* 'to party'—you just have to *party.*"

- Seven young men from the suburbs sent me a booklet they had written, titled "So You Wanna Be a Party Animal." If you are the parent of a teenager and you want to browse through something that is guaranteed to depress you to the point of despair, I highly recommend it.

Memories Are Made of This

My father ran the company that bronzes baby shoes. During the summers of my growing up, while my friends were earning money by caddying at golf courses or mowing lawns or painting center stripes for the Ohio Department of Highways, I toiled in a warm room on the first floor of the Bron-Shoe Company, opening packages. Inside the packages were baby shoes—baby shoes from all over the world. The parents of the babies had sent the shoes to Columbus—to the Bron-Shoe Company—so that the shoes could be bronzed.

I recall that most of the shoes were white. I recall that I was always surrounded by literally thousands of them—tiny shoes everywhere. I recall that I was the youngest person in the receiving department; the other workers were middle-aged men who smoked cigarettes and made funny sounds in their throats in rebellion against the crack-of-dawn mornings and the prospect of encountering all those little shoes before it was time to punch out. Mostly, though, my memory of the Bron-Shoe Company is pretty hazy.

I decided to go back and take a look. My father is retired now, and the Bron-Shoe Company has moved to newer, more modern headquarters than the place where I worked. It's still in Columbus, though, and when I called the two men who are now its top executives—Robert J. Kaynes and William P. Moser—they said to drop on by.

The first thing I did when I arrived was ask to see the receiving room. Kaynes and Moser took me there. Twenty years later, there were still thousands upon thousands of shoes stacked all over the room, waiting to be bronzed. Twenty years later, most of the shoes were still white.

"It never changes," Kaynes said. "We're still in the business of memories."

"People may think that bronzing baby shoes is a corny thing to do," Moser said. "But then they have their first child, and that child outgrows his or her first shoe, and the parents can't bear the thought of throwing it away. And so they end up sending it to us."

There was one obvious difference in the new receiving room: each baby shoe that arrived at the Bron-Shoe Company was now listed in a computer. There were video terminals around the room with screens to display the information.

"We plate more than half a million baby shoes a year," Kaynes said. "The computer has been a great help in keeping track of them. We give every shoe a job number when it comes in, and mark it twice—on the bottom of the shoe, and inside the shoe. Very seldom do we misplace one, but when we do, we can track it down right away."

I asked whether parents, when they received their bronzed shoes, could really tell if they were the wrong ones.

Moser laughed. "Are you kidding?" he said. "They know within two seconds. A mother knows her baby's first shoe."

We walked through the plant. Here, in a nineteen-step process, the shoes are plated. Tanks of bubbling solution were arranged over the length and width of the floor; on the periphery, as far as the eye could see, were racks of plated baby shoes.

"We offer several finishes," Kaynes said. "As you can see, each has a different look. There's bronze. There's antique bronze. There's silver. There's pewter. There's gold. And there's porcelain. People always talk about 'bronzing' their baby's shoes, but when they see all the finishes that are available, sometimes they choose one of the others."

I picked up some of the completed shoes from a rack. The detail was amazing. Every little flower design, every crease, every wrinkle showed up through the metal plating.

"That's the whole point," Kaynes said. "The parents want the shoe exactly as the baby wore it. We get castigated if we take a crease or a scuff out. The imperfections are part of the memories."

The three of us went back to Kaynes's office. I asked what people said to these men when they found out what line of work they were in. "People say, 'You bronze shoes? Do they still do *that*?'" Kaynes said. "When I assure them that we do, indeed, still do that, they say, 'Can you actually make a living doing that?'"

"We have one hundred and forty full-time employees," Moser said. "We'll probably always have the reputation of being a very old-fashioned business. We realize that we're perceived that way. But an awful lot of people apparently still want what we do."

I said that it must be an eerie feeling, walking through that factory and being surrounded by so many thousands of people's tangible memories.

"For me, that really doesn't come up too often," Kaynes said. "I suppose I'm like a surgeon—I realize that each of those shoes means the whole world to some family somewhere, but after a while they just become numbers to me. We don't know the babies. We just bronze the shoes."

Moser said that, for all the market studies and all the advertising strategies, there is one key to selling bronzed baby shoes: If a person has had bronzed shoes in his own house when he was growing up, he is likely to have his baby's shoes bronzed. If he hasn't, he is likely not to.

"They even like the older styles," Moser said. "They like the shoes mounted on the old-fashioned flowery metal base, for example. They don't like the new styles, like the Lucite base. They say, 'I want these shoes done the same way my mother had mine done.'"

In the summer of 1960, my father, sitting at the dinner table, pulled a golf ball from his pocket.

"What do you think this is?" he said.

"A golf ball," I said, a trained observer even then.

He handed it to me. "Look closer," he said. "What is it?"

I looked. "A used golf ball," I said.

"That golf ball," my father said, "is the golf ball Arnold Palmer used to win the Masters."

And indeed it was. In addition to bronzing baby shoes, the Bron-Shoe Company has always been willing to bronze virtually anything anyone might want to preserve in metal. On Kaynes's desk, for example, was a bronzed pretzel. "I just keep it here to make me think of possibilities," he said.

In the Bron-Shoe plant on the day I visited were the following items waiting for bronzing: A railroad spike. A horseshoe. A pacifier. A belt buckle. An electric razor. A first baseman's mitt. A nurse's cap. A drill sergeant's hat. Three chocolate-chip cookies. A set of dental impressions. A dice cup. A set of barber's tools. A dog biscuit.

I asked Kaynes and Moser to recall additional items the company had bronzed. A partial list: Athletic supporters. Stethoscopes. Underwear. Blue jeans. Red Skelton's cigar butt. Turkey feet. A Big Mac. Armadillo skulls. Horse manure.

I asked if there was anything they would not attempt to bronze.

"Teddy bears," Kaynes said.

"Teddy bears are the worst," Moser said. "The fur won't hold the plating solution. The solution seeps into the bear, and the metal slowly turns green for the next two years. And then the plating solution comes oozing out."

"We once had a teddy bear here for a year, trying to get it to dry out," Kaynes said. "It just wouldn't dry."

"Teddy bears are miserable," Moser said.

Teddy bears, cigar butts, and horse manure notwithstanding, it is baby shoes that have made the Bron-Shoe Company prosper. And the woman who started the company in the baby-shoe-bronzing business, Violet Shinbach, still lives in Columbus. She is eighty-one now.

"It was 1933," Mrs. Shinbach said. "When my daughter Ibby was a baby, I had taken one of her shoes to a store to have it bronzed. It seemed like a good idea. So I decided to go into business having other people's shoes bronzed.

"I would go door to door. I would look for children's bicycles, or for swings and playthings, outside the house. Then I would ring the doorbell and say, 'How old is your child? We do something that is very novel.' And then I would show them Ibby's shoes."

Mrs. Shinbach's husband, Sam, was in the pants business; she ran the shoe-bronzing enterprise out of the basement of their home, contracting the work out to a metal plater. Eventually it became so successful that Sam gave up his pants store and joined her in founding the Bron-Shoe Company—which, in addition to taking orders for the shoes, would do the plating itself.

She said that she doubts the business could evolve in the same way if it were starting today: "Everyone treated me so cordially. Today, I don't think they'd let a stranger into their house—especially if the stranger was asking about their children."

But, she said, the same emotions that made people like the idea of bronzed shoes in the first place are still at work now.

"When people heard I could bronze their babies' shoes, there wasn't a doubt in their minds," she said. "People never throw a baby's first shoes away. They just don't do it. They used to keep them in a closet, or hang them from their car's rearview mirror. But once they were able to bronze them, they all wanted to do it. A baby's first pair of shoes is like a baby's first tooth. You want to keep it.

"Actually, that's not quite true. At one point I tried to expand the company into bronzing babies' first teeth. It was a failure. The parents didn't want to preserve the first teeth. But the first shoes—yes."

Before I left the Bron-Shoe Company, I stopped in the receiving department again and went through the bins of arriving baby shoes.

Each shoe was marked with a tag identifying the parents of the babies; I wrote some down, and later I called the parents to see what had been on their minds when they had placed their orders.

"It's the traditional thing in my family," said Patricia Franck, thirty-two, of Roswell, Georgia. "It's a way to freeze a moment in time.

"My son, Ryan, is just about a year old, and you can see his personality in his first shoe. He's *worn* it. He's been *in* it. I want to keep that.

"I suppose some people might think that's a little old-fashioned or a little corny, but I don't care. I've ordered the shoes to be bronzed unmounted; when they come back, I'm going to mount them myself, with a pen set in between. That way every time I reach for my pen I'll think of Ryan."

Debbie Watters, thirty-five, of Cuyahoga Falls, Ohio, said, "We had a lot of trouble having our first child. We tried for ten years. There were tests, and there was surgery involved, and finally we were able to have Patrick. So I think he means something a little extra special to us.

"We were at a store called Miller's Jr. Shoe Port when we saw the display for bronzed shoes. We've ordered the shoes to be mounted on both sides of a picture frame in which we'll put Patrick's picture. I used to go through stores, and I'd see baby shoes and baby clothes, and I'd think about the possibility that we'd never have a baby. So there was never any question that we'd have Patrick's shoes bronzed. What else do you do with your baby's first shoes?"

John Manelski, twenty-two, of Wilmington, Delaware, said, "I work at the General Motors plant. I spray-paint Chevettes. When John Junior was born it was one of the greatest days of my life.

"When I was a baby my parents had my first shoes bronzed. They kept them on display in the china closet in our house. That's what I'm going to do with John Junior's shoes. I'm going to keep them in our china closet, or on top of our TV set, right where everyone can see them.

"And then when he grows up I'm going to give them to him. I'm going to tell him that they're his to do with as he pleases, but that he has to follow two rules: He has to put them somewhere where people can always see them. And he should never disrespect those shoes."

The Tradin' Times They Are A-Changin'

Maybe you're familiar with a publication known as *Tradin' Times*. It's a folksy, nuts-and-bolts newspaper that is devoted to helping its readers sell their unwanted bedroom furniture, camping equipment, stoves, refrigerators . . . anything a person might have around the house.

Each issue of *Tradin' Times* consists of classified ads inserted by people who want to get rid of those things. The paper is bought by other people who might want to buy them. Most of the readers of *Tradin' Times* are suburban or rural; the newspaper has been likened to "a garage sale on newsprint," and is considered to be one of the staples of Middle America.

However . . . recently, there has been a twist in what is available through *Tradin' Times*. If you peruse the pages of the Chicago-Northwest Indiana edition of *Tradin' Times,* you will soon discover that one can now arrange to sell the old lawn mower and have an extramarital affair at the same time.

Tradin' Times now runs—along with the ads for pool tables, end tables, and sofas—ads from married men and women requesting the company of other women and men for the purpose of romance.

Sexual advertisements in the personals sections of certain publications are not new, of course. The so-called underground press pioneered this practice; now it is fairly common to see single people advertising their desire to meet other single people.

But married people? In *Tradin' Times*? *Tradin' Times* is purchased right along with the eggs and chewing gum at suburban supermarkets and rural drugstores. And yet here are some of the ads:

NW Suburbs, wht. married male, affectionate, clean, gentle, sincere, 37, seeking loving married female, 23-39, for discreet, romantic companionship, long term. [The advertiser concluded his ad with a *Tradin' Times* box number to which replies were to be directed.]

Attractive wht. sophisticated married male, 32, great sense of humor, looking to meet an attractive married female, 25-40, for honest, warm, caring, fun-filled relationship. Letter, phone, picture, discretion assured.

Attractive, wht., high-class married female, 32, would like to meet a warm, sincere, sensitive, wht. married male, 30-40, for honest & caring long-term friendship. Insensitive or uncaring persons please don't write.

Certainly the *Tradin' Times* ads are nowhere near as salacious as the bizarre offerings seen in some less-than-reputable publications. But still . . . this is *Tradin' Times,* not *Hot Love Weekly.* Finding the ads in there is akin to going to the weekly Rotary Club meeting and being informed that the after-lunch speech has been replaced by a screening of "Debbie Does Dallas."

The suburban housewife who pointed this out to me—*Tradin' Times* reader Barbara Tomasek, of Lockport, Illinois—said that she was not naive enough to think that married people in neighborhoods like hers didn't sometimes fool around.

"But silly me," she said. "I always thought that sort of thing . . . well, just happened. I didn't know that you were supposed to advertise in *Tradin' Times* for it."

I told Mrs. Tomasek that this was news to me, too. I said that I would do my best to contact *Tradin' Times* and find out what the story was.

Getting through to *Tradin' Times,* it turned out, is not the easiest thing in the world; the publication's phone lines are constantly tied up by people placing ads trying to sell slipcovers, adding machines, armchairs, etc. When someone did answer, I asked to talk to the boss—and was transferred to Patricia Fry, the newspaper's sales manager for classified advertising.

I explained why I was calling. Mrs. Fry sighed. "I know what you're talking about," she said. "All I can say is that I have no control over what people want. As long as the ads are not dirty or off-color, we print them."

I asked Mrs. Fry if she was sure the ads were legitimate.

"Oh, yes," she said. "We don't make up ads. We are a very reputable firm. The company's feeling is that if the language in the ads is not pornographic or kooky, then we'll run them. These people are being very honest in their ads. They're saying, 'I'm married, but I'm looking for someone.'"

I asked her if anyone responded to the ads I was inquiring about.

"You would not believe it," she said. "We don't open the replies—we just forward them. But it's not uncommon for a person who placed one of those ads to get ten or fifteen responses a week."

Mrs. Fry—who said that she was "over fifty," and that she has been happily married for thirty-seven years—said she tried not to pass judgment on the morality of the people who place and answer the ads.

"I guess times are changing," she said. "I know that in the last year, these kinds of ads have picked up tremendously in *Tradin' Times*. I suppose it's better for a person to admit he's married in one of these ads than for a young girl to fall for an old duffer she meets who claims he's single."

I asked whether there was some lesson here about the sexual revolution finally hitting mainstream America with full force, but Mrs. Fry said:

"I don't think it's anything new. Remember Cleopatra, back on the Nile? I'm afraid it can't be stopped."

I called Mrs. Tomasek, the lady who had alerted me to the new material in *Tradin' Times,* and told her what I had found out.

She paused to reflect on all this.

"I wonder what happens," she said, "when some fellow in the suburbs places one of those ads, and he gets a response that turns out to be his own wife looking for a little action?"

Grandma at the
Playboy Club

I received a letter the other day; the return address on the envelope said it was from Heritage House, in Columbus, Ohio. I knew immediately who had sent me the letter; Heritage House is a senior citizens' residence in Columbus, and my grandmother, who is ninety-six years old, lives there.

So I was ready for a newsy little note from Grandma. I opened the envelope—and what dropped out but a Playboy Club key with my name on it.

There was a letter, too. It began:

Dearest Bobby—
When I went to the Playboy Club and told them who I was, you would have thought I had become Queen for a Day! The managers and the Bunnies couldn't have been nicer. At the end of the meal they gave me a membership key for myself—plus keys for you and your father! So now I am a member of the Playboy Club. . . .

My head swam. Last month I had visited Columbus, my hometown, and had been surprised to find a new Playboy Club there. When I was growing up in Columbus, we had always assumed that if you were in search of certain things, you would have to leave central Ohio—and one of those things was a Playboy Club. Now Columbus and Playboy apparently were ready for each other.

I visited the Columbus Playboy Club; I wrote a column about the visit, and I thought that was the end of it.

Now, though . . . this letter from Grandma . . . the Playboy Club key . . .

I called the Playboy Club in Columbus and asked to talk to Steve Smith, the club's director of entertainment. I had met him during my visit there.

"Steve," I said, "I don't know how to put this—"

"Hi!" Smith said. "Your grandmother was in the other day!"

"That's what I was afraid of," I said.

"She seemed to be having a great time," Smith said. "She was with a party of four other women, and we gave them a table in the VIP Room, and I decided to make her a member."

"Steve, my grandmother is ninety-six years old," I said. "Why would she want to be a member of the Playboy Club?"

"She said she was thrilled," Smith said. "She told me she thought the food was delicious; she said it was the first time in years she had finished her sandwich for lunch. I told her that we have dancing at night, and she promised she'd be back."

"Steve . . ." I said.

"Here," Smith said. "I'll let you talk to the person who served her."

A female voice came onto the line. The owner of the voice identified herself as "Bunny Jill."

"Your grandmother couldn't have been cuter," Bunny Jill said. "When we gave her the key, she said that now she had a place she could go when she didn't have anything to do."

This was getting out of hand. I called Heritage House.

"Grandma . . . ," I said.

"Bobby!" she said. "Did you get your Playboy Club key?"

"I did, Grandma, and that's what I have to talk to you about," I said.

"You should have seen it," she said. "As soon as I came in, all the Bunnies gathered around me. I was basking in glory."

"Grandma, I don't think it's appropriate that you be hanging around the Playboy Club," I said.

"Why not?" she said.

"Well, it's just not the kind of place for a ninety-six-year-old woman," I said.

"Nonsense," she said. "I thought the Bunnies were gorgeous. I had heard about them, but I never thought I would ever see one in person. Grandpa's eyes would have fallen out! The dining room was filled with men—and they were all eating their lunch! I thought, what a bunch of fools! They can eat anytime. They should have been looking!"

"Grandma, have you ever even seen a copy of *Playboy*?" I said.

"Of course I have," she said.

"Where?" I said.

"In your room, when you were a little boy," she said. "You had it hidden."

"Look," I said. "I suppose it's fine that you went once. But you're not planning on going again, are you?"

"Of course I'm going again," she said. "I'm a member, aren't I? I'm going to take your Aunt Violet as my guest."

I was resigned to it then. Grandma was going to be a regular at the Playboy Club. I knew there was one more call I had to make.

I placed the long-distance call to Hugh Hefner in California. Naturally, Hefner was still asleep; I should have known—it was only four o'clock in the afternoon out there.

But a few hours later, Hefner called me back. I gave him a rundown of how my grandmother happened to be the newest Playboy Club member.

"Well, she's certainly welcome," Hefner said. "If she feels comfortable as a member of the club, we feel comfortable having her."

I asked him if he didn't think it was a little odd for a ninety-six-year-old woman to be a member of the Playboy Club.

"It's completely up to the individual involved," Hefner said. "It's obvious that you have a very special lady for your grandmother. My own mother is eighty-six, and she often goes to the club in Phoenix for lunch. I hope your grandmother enjoys it as much as my mother does.

"Age should not be a limiting factor in the way you lead your life. This is evidence of that, and I think it's wonderful."

Hefner said that he knew it was unlikely that my grandmother would be making a trip to California—but that if she ever did, he wanted her to know she would be welcome as his guest at the Playboy Mansion West.

"We'll be waiting for her in the Jacuzzi," he said.

For Members Only

In this country there is a certain prestige attached to becoming a member of celebrated organizations. Probably the most desirable of all is the United States Senate; when an American is elected to that body, he or she can take comfort in being part of what has been called the most exclusive club in the world.

Other associations carry their own particular symbolism and weight. Be it a college fraternity, a local Rotary, or a suburban country club, there always seems to be a particular organization with the power to make people strive for entry.

Those sorts of clubs aren't the only ones in America, though. According to Denise Akey—who, as editor of the *Encyclopedia of Associations,* keeps track of such matters—there are at least 18,414 organizations in the United States. That's only the ones she knows about; she thinks there are undoubtedly many more.

So if you haven't filed for a run at the U.S. Senate in next fall's campaign, and if the golf club in your city hasn't responded to your application, you might want to keep some of the following in mind. All of them are more than willing to take new members.

The North American Tiddlywinks Association, with headquarters in Gaithersburg, Maryland, is the only national organization dedicated to that sport. Its secretary-general, Larry Kahn, estimates its membership at approximately one hundred.

"The biggest problem we have is our image," Kahn said. "It's almost impossible to recruit new members. They think of tiddlywinks as a children's game. We think of it as a war game that happens to be played on a six-feet-by-three-feet felt mat."

Most members of the North American Tiddlywinks Association, Kahn said, own standard sets of winks—the little red, blue, green, and yellow disks that are propelled around the mat. Top tournament players, though, own many squidgers—the larger disks that are used to shoot the winks.

"I have eight squidgers," Kahn said. "They're like golf clubs; you use different squidgers to make different shots. Some people have as many as twenty squidgers, but they're just showing off, if you ask me. There's no way you need twenty squidgers."

Although the North American Tiddlywinks Association has never been compared to the National Football League, Kahn maintains that tiddlywinks can keep a person in shape. "During a tournament you can be on your feet for eight hours," he said. "At the end of the day you really feel it in your legs."

"We haven't been able to find all of us," said Emma Bishop, president of the Rockette Alumnae Association. "The Rockettes have been in existence for over fifty years, and there were always thirty-six dancers on stage at any given moment, so I think there are probably hundreds of former Rockettes we don't know about."

As it is, there are 320 members of the organization, which has its headquarters in Maplewood, New Jersey. Any woman who has ever been a member of the famed Radio City Music Hall dance troupe or its early predecessor, the Missouri Rockets, is eligible. Major annual functions are a fall luncheon and a spring charity ball.

"We were never thought of as sex symbols," Mrs. Bishop said. "We weren't like Playboy Bunnies. Our image was the all-American, apple-pie, girl-next-door type. The founder of the Rockettes got very angry if we were referred to as a 'chorus line.' He insisted on the term 'precision dancers.' 'Precision dancers' has a more wholesome connotation."

The first question a Rockette alumna is always asked, Mrs. Bishop said, is, "Did you ever make a mistake?"

"I'm sure we all made mistakes," she said. "I know I did. No one's perfect. But we were known for all making every move in unison, so I guess that's what people think about when they think of us."

"It's just what it sounds like," said James H. Smith, Jr., of Camp Hill, Pennsylvania, president of the Jim Smith Society. "It's an organization of people named Jim Smith."

The purpose of the club, which has 1,218 members, is to give people named Jim Smith pride in their name. "When your name is Jim Smith, the tendency is to feel pretty ordinary," Smith said. "Our goal is to make Jim Smiths stick out their chests and stand tall."

One of the problems about being a Jim Smith, Smith said, is that people often assume you are traveling under an alias. "When my wife and I were first married, we used to get strange looks from hotel desk clerks. Her name is Jane Smith."

Smith feels that Jim Smiths often turn out to be overachievers—perhaps as a means of trying to compensate for their names. "I think there may be a subconscious desire for a person named Jim Smith to show the world he's special in other ways," Smith said. "Although I won't kid you—not all Jim Smiths are great success stories. I have had appeals from two Jim Smiths to help get them out of jail."

Smith said that the members of the organization feel quite comfortable when they all get together for outings. "We have an all-Jim Smith softball game every year," he said. "Jim Smiths travel five hundred miles to play. The only problem is what to call each other. You can't just yell 'Jim' or 'Smith.' We usually call each other by the name of the state or town we're from. They call me 'Camp Hill.'"

The Dogs on Stamps Study Unit, with headquarters in Newark, New Jersey, is dedicated to the study of postage stamps that have dogs on them.

"There are more than two thousand stamps worldwide with dogs on them," said Morris Raskin, secretary-treasurer of the organization. "Whenever a new stamp with a dog on it is issued, or we discover a dog on an old stamp, our one hundred seventy-five members communicate with each other about it."

Although most people might be surprised to learn there are so many stamps with dogs on them, Raskin said that the members of his club are hardened to the phenomenon. "We don't get excited about it," he said. "We kind of expect it. The average person might be shocked to look at a stamp and find a dog, but that's what we're always looking for."

The main challenge for the study group, Raskin said, is to find stamps where dogs may or may not be—and then to document that there is, indeed, a dog on the stamp. "Say there's a stamp with a picture of a famous person in a rocking chair," he said. "There's a dark object under the chair. Now, is that dark object a dog? Is it the hair on the head of a dog? Is the dog curled up there? Or is it just another dark object, and not a dog? Our job is to find out."

The Nineteen Thirty-Two Buick Registry is a club made up of people who own Buick automobiles manufactured in 1932. Its registrar, McClellan G. Blair, of Indiana, Pennsylvania, estimates the membership at "a couple of hundred."

Blair himself said that he owns "quite a few" 1932 Buicks. "I suppose I own a couple of dozen. I've never really counted. Some are hard to call cars—they're just parts. I can't tell if some of them are cars, or half-a-cars, or pieces of cars."

He said the members of the organization hold no illusions that the 1932 Buick was the finest car ever built. "We just like them. Nothing in particular about them. They're just nice. They look sort of oldish, but they're mechanically modern enough that you can drive them and they won't fall apart."

He said that the concerns of his members are generally the same: "We're all looking for the same kinds of parts." He said that 1932 Buick owners are not fanatics. "I don't think that you could accuse us of having rapturous love affairs with our cars. But we do like them a lot."

"Basically, we just want to make Americans better educated about aardvarks," said Thomas P. Byrne, president of the National Association for the Advancement of Aardvarks in America.

Byrne, of Waukesha, Wisconsin, said that he has never seen an aardvark in person—but that he has long been attracted to photographs and paintings of aardvarks.

"Even in Africa, you can live for years and never see an aardvark," he said. "The most fun our members have is exchanging photographs and drawings of aardvarks. We have more than six hundred card-carrying members, but I have a suspicion that a lot of them aren't that serious about aardvarks. I'd say that the hard-core membership is only a hundred or a hundred-fifty."

Byrne said that he is an admirer of aardvarks for their abilities. "The aardvark is the fastest-burrowing animal alive," he said. "They dig faster than six men with spades. They also have tremendous hearing. There's no way to really know, but it's been said that aardvarks can hear army ants while on the march, and from quite a distance, too."

The long-range goal of the association is to hasten the day when aardvarks are accepted as household pets in the United States, Byrne said. "They have certain qualities that would make them better pets than cats and dogs," he said. "For example, they're pretty incapable of taking offensive action. Instead, they'll just roll over on their backs and stick out their feet, adopting a defensive posture. To a person who is deathly afraid of dogs, this could be a big advantage."

The International Barbed Wire Collectors Historical Society has headquarters in Sunset, Texas. Its secretary-treasurer, Jack Glover, said its six hundred active members are devoted to collecting and passing on barbed wire lore.

"Barbed wire is part of our history, just like guns," Glover said. "Do you know what settled the West? Barbed wire and windmills settled the West."

Although many people probably assume there is only one kind of barbed wire, Glover said that there are 898 different patents for barbed wire, each for a different variety. "We display our barbed wire collections on boards," he said. "The wire is cut in eighteen-inch strips. Anyone who would display a piece of wire less than eighteen inches is not a true collector. The eighteen inches are enough to show you at least two or three barbs."

Glover is rather jingoistic about barbed wire. "People from all over the country call me and ask me what kind of barbed wire to buy," he said. "You can buy cheap barbed wire overseas. But then winter's going to come, and that foreign wire is going to stretch and snap. Or if it doesn't it's going to stretch and then sag. In my opinion foreign barbed wire just doesn't have the tensile strength of domestic barbed wire."

He said that he sees nothing particularly unusual about his dedication to the collection of barbed wire. "But you know what I can't understand?" he said. "I can't understand people who collect buttons. Sometimes I think the biggest collectors in the world are button collectors. Me, I wouldn't have a button."

"I probably own twenty thousand buttons," said Lois Pool, of Akron, Ohio, the president of the National Button Society.

"The typical button you will see on a man's or a woman's shirt is not a collectible button," Miss Pool said. "It's not unique enough. We look for the button that is remarkable enough to want to preserve."

The National Button Society has more than two thousand members, Miss Pool said. "We publish the *National Button Bulletin*," she said.

"It comes out five times a year, and features full-page photographs of buttons, so that we can examine the buttons in detail. We are just about to go to color photos in one issue a year, so that we can study the true colors of the buttons."

She said that members of the society sometimes can't help themselves from looking a person up and down when they meet. "I work as an office manager in a funeral home," she said. "When my boss walks in and he's wearing a new suit, my eyes go immediately to the buttons. It happened just the other day. The buttons on his suit were plastic, encircled in brass, with initials in the center. I couldn't help myself. I said to him, 'When that suit is worn out, I would like the buttons.'"

Why Fathers Are a Cut Above Their Sons

There is only one major difference between my generation of men and my father's generation of men:

My father's generation knew how to carve a roast.

This occurred to me the other day when a male friend of mine, in a state of panic, was frantically looking through cookbooks. The reason was that he and his wife were having people over for dinner, and he was going to have to carve the turkey.

My friend had no idea how to carve a turkey, just as he had no idea how to carve a roast. Ever since his wife had casually announced that the dinner menu would consist of turkey, he had been losing sleep and imagining how he would react at the big moment. The guests would be seated at the dinner table, the wife would carry the steaming turkey from the kitchen, everyone would lean expectantly toward their plates . . . and my friend would stand there, carving utensils in his hands, without a clue about where to start cutting.

I sympathized. Like my friend, I haven't the foggiest idea how to carve a turkey. And let's be honest: turkeys are generally eaten only on special occasions. The real test of a man's carving skills is whether he can carve a roast. I can't do that, either.

I have taken an informal survey of men in their late twenties, their thirties, and their early forties. It is almost unanimous: Virtually none of us can carve a roast.

Carving a roast used to be the very definition of manhood. If you were a husband and father, you were the person who was responsible for hacking up the meat. Maybe you never went near the kitchen—but when the meat was carried out to the dining table, it was your turn at bat.

Most of my memories of childhood tend to get a little foggy, but in the meat department the scenes are crystal clear:

We would be at the dinner table. The meat would be hunkered down on a wooden base; it seems to me now that the meat and the base were placed on some sort of separate small table right next to the dining table itself, but I can't be sure about that. In any event, there were little troughs cut into the wooden base, to catch the juices from the roast.

This whole setup was just to my father's left; my father, of course, sat at the head of the table. He had been home from work for about forty-five minutes; he was still wearing his white shirt and tie from the office, although he had taken off his suit jacket, and now he had another duty—he had to carve the roast.

I recall him holding utensils in both hands; this is getting dim, but it seems that there was a long, wooden-handled knife in one hand, and in the other hand an elongated rod used to sharpen the knife. I sense him running the knife back and forth over the sharpener; logically the sharpener should have been replaced by a fork or another knife at some point, but I'm not sure. Not knowing how to carve a roast, I have no idea of what the correct tools were, or are.

My father would ask each of us how much we wanted. Then he would carve. We would each pass our plate to him, he would carve precisely the right amount of meat, then put it on the plates. And then we would eat.

This all sounds simple enough. It's deeply symbolic, though. What happened between generations? One day there was a whole country filled with men who knew how to carve roasts. The next day the same country was filled with men who couldn't carve a roast if a gun was held to their heads. Who taught our fathers? Why didn't our fathers teach us?

Social custom undoubtedly has had a lot to do with this. During our fathers' generation, families did not eat meals that were boiled inside plastic bags in individual portions; families did not eat meals that were heated up under tinfoil coverings. As odd as it sounds now, families shared meat cut from the same slab of beef; there was actually food that didn't come precut and enclosed in cardboard with a colorful picture of itself printed on top.

Also—and I may be wrong here—it seems that people did not eat out as much then as people do now. Today restaurants have become almost an entertainment medium; people have become used to eating in restaurants so often that restaurants are reviewed and rated by critics just like movies and plays. And of course the fast-food places have added a dining alternative that simply didn't exist during our fathers' generation.

Still, those are just weak excuses. When the final score is tallied up, the men of my generation are going to have to hang their heads and meekly admit it. Our fathers could carve, and we couldn't, and that is the legacy we will pass on to future generations.

I know for a fact that this must cause great glee among the men of my father's generation. For years, the message they got from us was that we knew everything there was to know about politics, education, sex, and virtually every other area of life that mattered. Most of the time we made them feel as if we thought we had invented all of those things.

Now, finally, it is their turn to gloat. Our fathers are getting old now, and we are the ones who are moving into society's mainstream. Finally it really is our turn to take over the world.

But that doesn't matter. Anytime our fathers want to show us who's still boss, they don't have to say a word.

All they have to do is roll a simmering, steaming roast into the room. And then say to us:

"All right, smarty. Let's see who can cut it."

A View from the Bridge of My Nose

Most people, it seems, are entranced by the music video craze. If they're not watching MTV they're watching one of the dozens of spin-offs that have proliferated on networks and local stations; the combination of intricately edited videotape and hot new music is the media phenomenon of the Eighties.

When other men and women mention a specific new video to me, I smile and nod. Undoubtedly I leave them with the impression that I, too, am hooked on videos.

But I have decided to confess. I do not watch music videos, just as I did not play computerized video games when those games were said to be the raging new fad. I get my entertainment elsewhere.

What I do is . . . oh, I might as well just come out and say it. My chosen medium of entertainment is the View-Master.

I spend hours with my View-Master, and I never tell anyone about it. Do you blame me?

You know what View-Masters are; you may have forgotten about them, but you used to use them when you were a kid.

View-Master viewers are those binocularlike devices that you press against your nose and eyes, then turn toward a light source and peer into. Into the View-Masters are inserted little disks (called "reels" in the industry), each approximately the size of a cocktail coaster. Around the circumference of each reel are fourteen tiny color transparencies; when you look into your View-Master the fourteen transparencies become seven 3-D scenes. You advance from scene to scene by depressing a little lever on the right side of the View-Master.

I openly admit that being hooked on View-Masters is not the most sophisticated thing that can happen to a man, especially in this media-wise age. I can't help it, though; somehow, secure in my room, my View-Master smashed up hard against my face until the bridge of my nose hurts, my eyes turned toward a table lamp, I feel contented. Those three-dimensional scenes make me happy, whether I am looking at "The Seven Wonders of the World" or "The Butterflies of North America," there is something peaceful and calm about the View-Master experience—something that shifting, changing images on a television screen can't provide.

Maybe it has something to do with the idea that I can advance the pictures at exactly my own rate; maybe it's simply the fact that I know that twenty million other Americans aren't looking at precisely the same thing at precisely the same moment I am looking at it. Whatever the reason, I spend more time with my View-Master than is probably healthy.

The first View-Masters went on sale just before Christmas in 1938. They were manufactured by a company called Sawyer's Inc. in Portland, Oregon. In the Twenties, Sawyer's was the nation's largest producer of scenic postcards; the introduction of the View-Master was an immediate success, and within a year more than one thousand dealers were selling all of the View-Masters that Sawyer's could produce.

During the Forties and Fifties, View-Masters became an American institution. Virtually every child who grew up during that era can remember using a View-Master. In 1966, at the beginning of the modern media explosion, GAF Corporation of New York City purchased the View-Master business from Sawyer's. With many exotic new forms of entertainment available to the American public, View-Master did not fare well; in the late 1970s, the View-Master division of GAF began posting losses. In 1981, View-Master was purchased by a limited partnership formed by a businessman named Arnold Thaler.

"Some people questioned the wisdom of my buying the company," Thaler, sixty-one, told me. "But I was convinced that not everything revolves around the video tube. When you look at something with your own eyes and you see it in 3-D, that's still special."

Thaler said that he has returned the View-Master business to profitability. "The secret is to make the subject matter of the View-Master reels contemporary," he said. "We have purchased the rights to some of the most popular movies and television series. We have *Close Encounters* on View-Master reels, we have *E.T.*, we have "The A-Team," we have "Knight Rider," we have the Smurfs. And now we are getting into rock groups. We have Menudo on View-Master reels, and we are negotiating with Van Halen and Adam Ant and Culture Club.

"And the View-Master is still one of the world's most economical entertainment buys. The viewer costs four dollars, and a packet of three reels costs three dollars. Where can you beat that?"

Thaler didn't need to convince me; I was already one of the converted.

But as we talked I took silent exception to one of his major points. He seemed to truly believe that the TV and movie characters were the key to View-Master's continued popularity.

Speaking for myself, though, I much prefer the old, traditional reels. View-Master has more than six hundred active titles in its "reel library," as it refers to its catalog, and another six hundred in storage. I get much more pleasure out of the vintage reels than out of the new, pop-culture-oriented ones.

For example, I am a big fan of "Coronation of Queen Elizabeth II." The three View-Master reels in the coronation packet were shot in London on June 2, 1953, and I defy any television documentary to tell the story of an event any better.

Another nice one is "Grand Canyon National Park," which, for my money, is just as good as a visit to the canyon. And for bedtime viewing, nothing can beat "Hans Christian Andersen's Fairy Tales." The three reels in that packet (No. B305) are "The Little Mermaid," "The Steadfast Tin Soldier," and "The Emperor's New Clothes." Tune in to the adult movie channel on your cable setup if you will; when midnight rolls around at my house I'll stick with that flaxen-haired View-Master mermaid.

As a writer, I am in awe of the View-Master wordsmiths. Anyone can do a creditable job when they have a couple of pages in a magazine to fill, or a whole book; the View-Master staff writers face the challenge of getting their whole story into the little opening near the top of the View-Master—the hole in the machine that reveals the text printed on each reel. The writers have only seven short sentences—one per 3-D scene—to tell their tales.

The writers are masters of compression. Here, for example, is the entire text of "Little Red Riding Hood" (Packet B310):

"Little Red Riding Hood went to her Grandmother's." "She told a friendly wolf where she was going." "The wolf ran on ahead to Grandmother's house." "'Come in, my dear,' said the wolf in a high voice." "'Grandmother, what large teeth you have!'" "'The better to eat you with,' the wolf shouted." "A woodcutter saved Little Red Riding Hood."

Whoever wrote that could make a fine living as an editor of *Reader's Digest,* or at least on the rewrite bank of *USA Today*.

I was skeptical when I heard about a new product called the Talking View-Master. The company announced that each Talking View-Master would contain "a microprocessor-controlled unit with a constant-speed motor, linear tracking tone arm, and self-cleaning sapphire needle." This sounded suspiciously like the media modernism I was trying to get away from. My warning signals grew especially loud when I learned that the premiere title for the Talking View-Master was "Michael Jackson's 'Thriller.'"

But—although personally I plan to stick with the old silent, four-dollar, hand-operated View-Master—I must admit that the Talking View-Masters have promise, if you like that sort of thing. Watching Mr. Jackson's little drama on my Talking View-Master (it is heavier and larger than the standard model and runs on penlight batteries), I was impressed with the sound quality and the overall effect of the whole production. I tried another talking reel—"Popeye in 'Paint Ahoy'"—and the spoken dialogue drew me viscerally into the house-painting contest between Popeye and Brutus.

Sometimes it seems as if there's no way to avoid the future.

The senior photographer for View-Master is Hank Gaylord, sixty-four. He has been shooting pictures for View-Master reels for twenty-one years.

"The business has changed," Gaylord said. "For years we emphasized tabletop models of fairy-tale stories. It was such intricate work—we would make as many as thirteen or fourteen exposures on a single frame of film.

"We had three artists on the staff who did nothing but create sculptures for those tabletops. They built sets, just like in the movies. Sometimes we would use a dozen mirrors during a shot, to focus the lighting exactly right on each figurine on the table. It was a real team effort.

"Now it's different. We're out in the field much more. We're shooting on location, and that's a different feeling. I just got back from a Van Halen concert, for example. I was shooting the band for their reel. I used twin Nikons mounted on a bar; there was a belt drive between the cameras, so that when I focused one of the cameras I was automatically focusing the other one, too. That's how you get your precise 3-D.

"When I was shooting 'Thriller,' Michael Jackson walked up to me and asked if I was the photographer from View-Master. I said that I was. He said, 'You know, this was my idea.' It seems that he started collecting View-Master reels when he was a kid, and for all the fame he has, he really wanted to be photographed in 3-D for View-Master."

Sometimes when he is on assignment, Gaylord said, he feels slightly awkward announcing whom he represents. "We were traveling with the Pope in 1979, for example," he said. "We did a set of reels on his tour. There I was with photographers from UPI, and *Time* magazine, and the Associated Press. And when they asked me who I was with, it sounded a little odd to say, 'View-Master.'

"But when people hear it, they usually react positively. They say something like, 'Oh, I had one of those when I was a kid.' And they're genuinely surprised that we're still out there shooting. I just tell them, 'Yep, we're still here.'"

The View-Master people are quick to provide numbers and statistics designed to make us View-Master addicts feel a little less alone. For example, according to the company, View-Master products are currently sold in more than 116 countries, in seventeen languages. Since the development of the device, the company says, more than one billion View-Master reels and more than one million View-Masters have been sold worldwide.

Still, those of us who repair to our rooms to share a few quiet moments with our View-Masters continue to feel slightly out of synch with the rest of the world. Everyone else is lining up at the local theater to see the latest Steven Spielberg or George Lucas film; we're staring at a light source and flipping through "Williamsburg Colonial Restoration" (Packet 181).

I talked about this with Gary Evans, forty-three, one of View-Master's top executives. I thought that Evans might be sympathetic; when your title is Creative Director for View-Master, you're most likely able to justify the way you spend your life.

"I don't want to be too poetic about this," Evans said. "But View-Masters provide classic entertainment, in that they leave a lot to the imagination. I don't think it's going too far to compare a good View-Master reel to 'Ode on a Grecian Urn.' We're talking about images that are stopped in time; elements of real timelessness."

Perhaps. Regardless of what it all means, though, I'm glad that I've gotten this off my chest. Next time my colleagues see me in the morning with red indentations around my nose and eyes, they'll know what I was doing the night before. When you're hooked on View-Masters, you can spot a fellow user ten yards away.

Alice Doesn't Live
There Anymore

There is a delicatessen near where I work; it has a service bar in the back, and sometimes at the end of the day I will stop in there.

One night I did. The bartender said, "A friend of yours was in the restaurant the other day."

"Oh?" I said. "Who's that?"

"Alice Cooper," the bartender said.

That seemed odd. "Are you sure?" I said.

"It was him, all right," the bartender said. "He had his wife and daughter with him."

"What do you suppose he was doing in Chicago?" I said.

"Somebody asked him that," the bartender said. "He said he was living here now."

"Alice Cooper is living in Chicago?" I said.

"That's what he said," the bartender said. "I'm right about him being a friend of yours aren't I?"

Yes, he was right. For a brief period of time—not that long, no more than a month, really—I suppose you could even have said that we were best friends.

In 1973, in an effort to take a look at the world of rock 'n' roll from the inside, I made arrangements to join a band as a performing member. The band I became a part of was Alice Cooper, named after its lead singer, a former high school athlete from Arizona who had changed his name from Vincent Furnier and subsequently became one of the biggest pop stars in the world.

The Seventies were a time when planned outrage was in fashion, and Alice Cooper was taking full advantage of it. He was a forerunner of today's fascination with violence, harsh sexuality, and androgyny; his stage show featured simulated bloodletting, raw, suggestive song lyrics, and leering incitements of his young audiences. Alice appeared onstage every night wearing grotesque facial makeup and outlandish costumes; his show was the epitome of calculated tastelessness.

It was working to perfection. The year I joined up, the band took in more than $17 million; they played before more than eight hundred thousand customers in live performance. There wasn't a week that Alice's name failed to appear in one national publication or another. In Britain a member of Parliament, Leo Abse, attempted to have the Alice Cooper show banned. He based his position on what his teenage children had told him about Alice. "They tell me Alice is absolutely sick," he said, "and I agree with them. I regard his act as an incitement to infanticide for his subteenage audience. He is deliberately trying to involve these kids in sadomasochism. He is peddling the culture of the concentration camp. Pop is one thing; anthems of necrophilia are another."

I joined the band and sang background vocals on one of their albums; I went on a nationwide tour with them and played a role in their violent stage show every night. My purpose was to try to see the rock 'n' roll road from their vantage point—from the stage, from the limousines, from the chartered jets—and to write a book about it.

I can't exactly say that Leo Abse's summation of the Alice Cooper show was wrong; actually, it was a fairly accurate appraisal. But I found something out about Alice: he was one of the brightest, funniest people I had ever met. He realized what the tone of the decade was; he was selling his young audiences what they were eager to buy, but he was full of a sense of irony about it. He was as appalled by their avid acceptance of his show's bloodlust as was the most conservative fundamentalist minister; the difference was, even though he was appalled, he was becoming wealthy from it.

On the tour I joined, his original band was in the process of falling apart. There were rampant jealousies among the members; they resented the individual fame that Alice was attaining. Alice was becoming uneasy about having to go onstage and be Alice every night; he seemed to sense that he had created a monster, and that he was that monster. He was drinking heavily and staying barricaded in his hotel rooms between performances.

He wasn't speaking much with his fellow band members, and he wasn't going out, so he and I became unlikely friends. He was twenty-five; I was twenty-six. We would spend hours every day and night just sitting in his room talking and drinking and watching television while bodyguards kept fans away. We came to genuinely like each other, and our companionship grew to be a welcome one. It was destined not to continue; when the tour ended he went to live in California, and I went back to my home in Chicago. But we had each found someone of whom we were genuinely fond.

I have to say, that tour was one of the most interesting things that ever has happened to me. Standing onstage every night, the Super Trouper spotlights glaring in my eyes, looking out at twenty thousand screaming people—there's no way you can put a price on an experience like that. The tour, as it turned out, was the last ever by the original Alice Cooper band; the divisions I was seeing on the road caused them to break up soon after.

It wasn't long before I stopped hearing the name Alice Cooper altogether. New bands came to the forefront of the young public's attention; new records became number one. I read something about Alice admitting his alcoholism and going to a private clinic to seek help for it; once in a while I would see a story in which the members of a new band, their image based on outrage, would pay tribute to what they had learned from Alice Cooper. But it had been ten years since I had spoken with him or seen him; it had been almost as long since I had thought much about him.

And now the bartender was saying that he was living in Chicago.

On a Saturday night an Alice Cooper called my office and left a local phone number. When I returned the call he said that he had, indeed, moved to town; would I like to join him and his wife for dinner the following week?

We met in front of the maitre d's desk at an Italian restaurant called Spiaggia. We were both closer to forty than to thirty; we both wore sport jackets and ties. Alice was accompanied by his wife, Sheryl.

After some initial, awkward banter, we were led to a table by the window. I asked him the obvious question first: What was he doing living in Chicago? If there was ever a person who seemed perfect for the entertainment-industry ambience of southern California, it was Alice Cooper. Why had he left?

"My daughter is three and a half years old now," Alice said. "Sheryl is pregnant again. We were living in Beverly Hills, but we just decided that that's no environment to bring up children. It's crazy in Los Angeles—the drugs, the fast life. There are too many negative temptations. I just couldn't see risking bringing my children up in that kind of atmosphere."

Alice's wife said, "There is something less jaded about the Midwest. And my parents live in the Chicago suburbs—Oak Park. We thought it would be nice to be near them."

"The in-laws make nice free baby-sitters," Alice said.

He said he loved being a father. "It puts your whole life in perspective," he said. "The moment your child is born, you feel a chemical response— you become a person you've never been before. All of a sudden there's someone other than yourself who's important to think about and take care of.

"I spend most of every day with my daughter. I'll put a videotape of one of my old performances on the TV, and she'll know that the person on the TV is Alice, and the person sitting with her is Daddy.

"I take her to Sunday school every week. I think it's important to her that Daddy takes her there. Daddy and Mommy do it together—the family feeling is a big part of Sunday."

I asked him what had happened to him professionally in the almost twelve years since his last number-one hit. I hadn't heard a thing about him; had he stopped recording?

He shook his head. He talked of a dispute with his record company; he felt that they had torpedoed any chance his albums had of becoming successes. "I made six albums that no one ever heard of," he said. "That started to kill me.

"I started getting pretty depressed. I knew intellectually that in rock 'n' roll there is no such thing as something more than a two-year run. I had had my run. Michael Jackson, Prince—I don't care who you name, nobody ever got more publicity than Alice Cooper did. And I missed it. It got to the point where I couldn't watch a video or listen to the radio. I'll admit it, it was jealousy. You realize everyone gets their own shot, and that you're not the only person on the planet. But it's almost like a fighter knowing that he can knock another guy out, but not being given the chance. That's how I would feel every time I heard a hit record."

He said he had decided to try to become a leading star again. "The worst thing in the world is to be considered an oldie," he said. "To be sitting in a hotel room and hear the radio come on and hear them say that you're an oldie—look, I don't want to be Chuck Berry. It's easy to say, 'Well, I was good back then.' But I feel more like an old gunslinger. If the young guys think they're faster than me—bring 'em on."

He said that he was working on a plan. He was going to write the music for all hour-long video, in which he would costar with some of the top heavy-metal bands of the Eighties—the young musicians who grew up emulating Alice Cooper. "The video will be like *The Magnificent Seven* of rock 'n' roll," he said. "And I'll be playing the Yul Brynner role.

"Then, when the video comes out, I'll go back on the road. Now the challenge is going to be whether I can do it again. You know, the first time around we were in competition with the Rolling Stones, with the Who. Now I'll be going up against bands that I never heard of. The rock 'n' roll road used to be like the National Football League—everybody was a known quantity. It was like, 'Who do we play this Sunday? The Washington Redskins?' Now, because of videos, a band that has never even been on tour can have a number-one album. A band with no Holiday Inn knowledge at all."

I asked him if people still recognized him when they saw him. He smiled.

"Yeah, sometimes they do," he said. "But the other day, I was shopping at Marshall Field's, and these two young boys were whispering to each other and looking at me. And finally one of them came up to me and said, 'Excuse me, but are you really Boy George?'

"I'm not looking forward that much to going on the road again. I'm not drinking at all now, and if you recall, there was a time when I couldn't be more than eight inches away from a bottle of V.O.

"But I have to try, to see what happens. I don't kid myself, though—the most important thing in the world to me is being a good father. Sheryl will be out of the house, and it will just be my daughter and me at home. And I'll say, 'Who's the best rock star in the world?' And she'll say, 'Daddy!' And I'll say, 'Who makes the best records?' And she'll say, 'Daddy!'

"That's all I want, really—to be her hero. You can be a hero to millions of kids, but what you really want is to be a hero to your own."

We sat in the restaurant for hours. We talked of our time together on the road all those years ago, and of what had become of the former members of his band, and of the nature of gigantic stardom. He said that he had once met Elvis Presley in Las Vegas; Elvis had invited Alice to his hotel suite. Elvis handed Alice a gun and told him to point it at him. Alice did; immediately Elvis threw a karate move on him, and the next thing Alice knew he was flat on his back on the floor, with the gun lying by his head and Elvis's foot on his throat.

"And all l could think was: What a great album cover this would make," Alice said.

We laughed, and the talk got to shopping malls and automobiles, to potty training and cesarean sections. The waiter arrived and placed desserts in front of each of us.

Alice looked down at his.

"I don't know," he said, turning to his wife. "This looks awfully rich."

"Oh, Alice," she said. "Go ahead. Live a little."

The Meaning of Culture

CHARLESTON, W. VA.—I had been spending time in New York, which prides itself, with some justification, as the cultural capital of the nation. New York is the home of the country's most prestigious book publishers, of the Broadway theater, of the three major television networks, of the most influential national magazines.

On the way home, I stopped off here in Charleston. And I can't help it; when I think about culture, and about literary life in its truest meaning, what I saw in this West Virginia town is what will stay in my mind long after this trip is over.

I stopped off in Charleston to attend the annual Library Appreciation Day Dinner sponsored by the West Virginia Library Association. That may sound pretty boring to you, but you ought to know what it means.

West Virginia is one of the poorest states in America. It is one of the first states to feel bad economic times, and one of the last to feel the beginnings of economic recovery. There are 1.9 million people in West Virginia's fifty-five counties—far fewer people in the entire state than in the city of New York or Los Angeles or Chicago. Needless to say, no one has ever mentioned West Virginia in the same breath with New York when talking about culture or literary tradition.

And yet the people of West Virginia have deep feelings about their libraries. There are 164 public libraries throughout the state, and often the local library is the major source of cultural enrichment for an entire West Virginia county. This is a relatively recent phenomenon in the state; since 1965 there have been 128 library building projects in West Virginia.

"Most of our people are rural," said Frederick Glazer, director of the West Virginia Library Commission. "It is impossible to overestimate the sense of isolation. There is not a single city in West Virginia with a population of one hundred thousand. There are counties without movie houses. There are communities down in the hollows that are so isolated they cannot pick up television broadcast signals."

This is where the libraries come in. "Sometimes a library is the only connection with the outside world for people down in West Virginia coal country," Glazer said. "The library can become the only way for people to experience something other than their own walls."

For the Library Appreciation Day Dinner, more than eight hundred West Virginia citizens came to Charleston. For some it was a seven-hour drive or bus ride each way; people came two hundred miles, two hundred and fifty miles, three hundred miles. They weren't lobbyists; most weren't even library workers. They were just people who wanted the state legislature to know that they cherished the state's libraries.

They had dinner in a big room inside the Charleston Civic Center. Their purpose was to ask the legislature to appropriate three dollars for every person in West Virginia to go to the library system. According to officials here, that would make West Virginia the one state among the fifty with the highest per capita commitment to libraries.

"We can't be Number One in many areas," one man at the dinner said. "But we can try to be Number One in libraries."

The politicians of West Virginia took note of this turnout, and of this seriousness of purpose toward libraries. The three top politicians in the state were at the dinner: Governor John D. Rockefeller IV; Clyde See, speaker of the House of Delegates; and Warren McGraw, president of the Senate. So were more than one hundred other West Virginia legislators.

They all met for a cocktail hour, and then for a dinner catered by a company that used fresh-faced Charleston high school girls among its waitresses. Again, I couldn't help but notice the contrast between the typical Manhattan restaurant dining experience and the experience of the church-supper-type dinner being served in West Virginia. But I also couldn't help wishing that some of the high-powered New York publishing executives could have seen this outpouring in support of books and libraries.

"You just don't see this kind of turnout unless people feel very intensely and very personally about something," Fred Glazer told me. "It sounds corny to say it, but these people are here because they know that their libraries make their lives better.

"We've found that, especially in the most isolated parts of the state, people use the libraries to discover and follow their own pursuits. Maybe it's something as simple as someone deciding to spend his lifetime reading Westerns. Or maybe it's more sophisticated than that; a woman down in the hollows will never be able to see the Royal Ballet, or the New York Opera. But from her library she can borrow films of the ballet, or records of the opera or books about them both.

"What it means, I think, is that a person's life does not have to be dictated by where he or she happens to live. I had one woman tell me that she would prefer the legislature to spend money on libraries rather than highways. She said that the highway projects never seem to make it out to her part of the state. But she said that she sees people taking books home from their local library in shopping bags every day."

There are 3.6 million books in West Virginia's 164 libraries, I was told. Figures like that aren't what I'll remember from this visit, though. What I'll remember are the eight hundred people who traveled for much of the day to say that they appreciated their libraries, and wanted those libraries to prosper. That may not be the dictionary definition of "culture," but it's good enough for me.

Fashion Plate

The men's magazines are beginning to feature fashion stories with titles along the lines of "A Return to Elegant Dressing for the Fall."

Drat. Foiled again.

There's not a whole lot in this life that one can accurately predict, but I think it's safe to say that I will not be dressing elegantly this fall. Winter will probably roll around with me dressing approximately the same way I have dressed since 1965. I can't help it. It's part of me, like having a bad personality.

People who see me on the street probably think I have no idea of how to dress. This is not true. I have eyes. I know how people dress when they want to look nice. I just can't do it.

I have three basic uniforms.

The first is what I wear ninety-nine percent of the time. It is a blue shirt with the tie yanked loose and the sleeves rolled up; a pair of old jeans; and Weejuns.

The second is what I wear if I have to have lunch with a boss, or make a speech, or appear on TV. It is a blue shirt with the tie pulled up to the throat, a pair of brown corduroy pants, a blue blazer, and Weejuns. The sport coat is holding up remarkably well; it doesn't look a day older than when I bought it to cover the Richard Nixon—George McGovern presidential campaign of 1972.

The third is what I wore to Gene Siskel's wedding. It is a dark blue suit with stripes in it. I purchased it for the wedding, and planned to wear it on other special occasions, but there haven't been any.

I take no pride in this, and I'm not trying to prove anything. I will be the first to admit that a man my age should not show up at work every day in a pair of jeans and a blue shirt with the tie yanked loose It's a stupid way to dress. When I see other people who are dressed the way I am, my immediate instinct is that they are dressed badly.

But I simply can't wear nice clothes. I physically can't do it. If I put on elegant clothes, I can't write. There is no way for me to sit down at a typewriter or a word processor if I have on an expensive, well-pressed pair of pants. I could no more write wearing a suit than I could take a shower wearing a suit.

The best way I can describe this is to say that, for me, wearing nice clothes feels like being in prison. All I want to do is break out of there. At Siskel's wedding, for example, all I could think about was getting home and throwing that suit on the floor, where it belonged.

I wasn't always like this. Before I went away to college for my freshman year, I made a point of buying the back-to-school issue of *Gentlemen's Quarterly* and purchasing everything that the magazine's editors recommended for the well-dressed man on campus. I recall, for example, that I was in a near-panic when the day to leave Ohio for Northwestern rolled around, and it suddenly struck me that I had neglected to buy a yellow shirt. I had never owned a yellow shirt in my life, nor had I known anyone who had owned a yellow shirt; but *Gentlemen's Quarterly* said that a yellow shirt was essential for the college man's wardrobe, and so before I set off for campus the last thing I did before departing my hometown was to buy that yellow shirt.

About six weeks into fall quarter I stored all the *Gentlemen's Quarterly* clothes in my closet in my dormitory, and started to dress the way I dress now. I've never changed.

I may not look good, but you have to grant me consistency. I glance at snapshots from the last two decades; the people who are with me in the pictures reflect the changing fashions and tastes of the Sixties, Seventies, and Eighties, but I always am dressed the same way I am dressed this morning, which is the same way I was dressed my sophomore year in college.

There, in the snapshots, are the others in wide lapels, narrow lapels, fat ties, skinny ties, bell-bottomed trousers, cuffed trousers, button-down shirts, big-collared shirts, scruffy revolutionary clothing, conservative business clothing. And there I am. Blue shirt, tie yanked loose, sleeves rolled up, jeans, Weejuns.

There is one great advantage to this; you never have to spend a moment in the morning deciding what you will wear. It is predetermined; your office is redecorated more frequently than you are. To your colleagues at work, you become like a painting that is hung on the wall. You are going to look the same every day of the year.

You'd think I'd get bored with this, but I'm not yet. On principle, though, I know I should change. During the year I was twenty-six I sat down and had a serious heart-to-heart talk with myself; I told myself that this was no way for a twenty-seven-year-old man to dress, and that on my twenty-seventh birthday I would go out and buy some good clothes and start to change. But time seems to have gotten away from me; ten more years have passed, and I'm wearing the same stuff.

Reading those men's magazines that are predicting the return of elegance for fall makes me a little melancholy. I think those men in the magazines look great; I wish I could wear those clothes. Truly I do. If I could put on those clothes and walk out the door to work wearing them, all of the people in my life would be delirious with joy. But I might as well try to leap into the air and fly.

I wonder what I did with that yellow shirt?

Streep

We walked down West Fifty-seventh Street in Manhattan. We passed beneath the marquee above the main entrance to Carnegie Hall. "The problem with walking a baby in New York City is that the strollers are at exactly the height of the exhausts on the cars," said Meryl Streep.

She did not have either of her two children with her on this afternoon. We made our way through the sidewalk crowds; we saw an ice-cream parlor and stepped inside.

We each ordered a chocolate soda with vanilla ice cream. I fetched them from the man behind the counter; we sat on stools near the store's front window.

Streep's presence was causing more of a stir inside the ice-cream shop than it had on the street. Out there the New Yorkers were all in such self-absorbed hurries, were so reluctant to make eye contact with their fellow pedestrians, that only a few people had noticed Streep among them. In the ice-cream store, though, the patrons had relinquished their customary defenses for long enough to look across the room and realize who was here.

They began to approach her for autographs. She obliged, each time putting down her orange-and-white paper cup so that she could sign another napkin. At one point, as she was picking up the cup again, it tipped over; she spilled part of the soda on her bare left arm.

I got up to get some napkins from the dispenser on the counter. When I came back, there were more people waiting to talk to Streep, her arm still wet. As they spoke to her and stared at her, it struck me that there was quite a bit of deference in the air. The people were not reacting to her as they might to this year's most famous athlete, or most notorious rock star. Mixed with their curiosity was an almost palpable feeling of respect; if these people could bestow honors, what they would be giving Streep at this moment was not an Oscar or an Emmy, but some sort of Lifetime Achievement Award. They reacted to her as they might react to, say, Katharine Hepburn; and as I looked at Streep's face, lit by the sun coming through the window, I found it worth thinking about that she was only thirty-five years old.

"My mother and father always thought I was great," Streep said. We were sitting in an office in midtown Manhattan, a place that belonged to one of Streep's business associates. The business associate had said that Streep could borrow the office for the afternoon; now we were talking.

"My parents thought I was just fine," Streep said. "My Aunt Jane, though . . . Aunt Jane, I think, has only come to like me in my older years. She tells me that I was a terrible-looking little kid, and bossy besides."

Streep laughed. I had read references to her ugly-duckling childhood; she always seemed to make light of it. I said that surely it couldn't have been very funny to her back then. Looking good is important to little girls.

"Yes, it's very important for little girls," she said. "It's very important for grown-up women, too, especially if they're in the movies. There aren't so many roles for a female Spencer Tracy, if you know what I mean."

I had also read that Streep had blossomed during high school; that she had become a cheerleader and, eventually, homecoming queen.

"I think that came from an acting instinct," she said. "My first successful characterization is what I devised for myself in high school. I laid out my clothes for the week every Sunday so that I wouldn't repeat. That sounds pretty sick and obsessive, but that's what I did."

On the wall of the office was a framed cover of *Time* magazine, dated September 7, 1981. On the cover of the magazine was a color photograph of Streep; the article coincided with the release of her movie *The French Lieutenant's Woman*. The cover line was MAGIC MERYL.

I looked over at the cover. "That's really an American icon," I said.

Streep seemed uncomfortable. "It's just a role," she said.

"No," I said, "it really is sort of an important part of America."

Streep was shaking her head. "It's the lighting," she said. "The photograph was very well lit."

"I'm not talking about the picture itself," I said. "I'm talking about being on the cover of *Time* magazine."

Now she was blushing, still shaking her head. "Everybody's on the cover of *Time*," she said.

"Everybody's on the cover of *Time*?" I said.

It was clear that she would rather have been talking about something else. "I didn't mean it that way," she said. "What I meant is that they have fifty-two covers a year that they have to fill, and they've got to have somebody on the cover every week. When it happened to me, I didn't feel anything. But my next-door neighbor had her picture on the cover of the *New York Times Magazine*. It was an article about working women. The cover showed her kissing her child goodbye as she headed for work. That was impressive to me. It made me feel that I knew someone famous. When something like that happens to me . . . I don't know, it has no impact."

Every superlative, of course, has been used to describe Streep's acting skill. Her thumbnail biography is known by virtually every man and woman who wants to become an actor. Born in suburban New Jersey. College at Vassar, where acting coaches began to notice her remarkable giftedness. Membership in a small repertory company in Vermont, then three years at the Yale School of Drama, where the praise for her work grew.

Stage work in New York; more plaudits. Then a string of movie roles that transformed her into the most admired actress of her generation: *The*

Deer Hunter, Manhattan, The Seduction of Joe Tynan, Kramer vs. Kramer, The French Lieutenant's Woman, Sophie's Choice, Silkwood. Two Academy Awards, and an Emmy for her performance in the television miniseries "Holocaust." And with every acting assignment, a recognition on the part of the public that she was doing things the hard way; that she was choosing unconventional parts, parts that were not guaranteed to automatically please everyone who had seen her last movie. Streep was developing a reputation for unpredictability in what she was willing to try; it was unpredictability in a positive sense—the unpredictability of a person willing to continually test her limits.

Now, on this afternoon, she had recently completed filming a new movie called *Falling in Love,* in which she starred with Robert De Niro. In a few days she would be leaving for London, where another movie project was waiting.

"The packing is driving me crazy," she said. "Winter shoes, summer shoes, medicine, toys, books . . ."

Her husband, Don Gummer, a sculptor, and her two young children, Henry and Mary Willa, would be accompanying her on the trip to England. "I feel like Coach Landry lately," she said. "The unsmiling statistician."

I asked her if her current success was the culmination of some long-hidden childhood dream. "It never occurred to me that I might be a movie star," she said. "I looked at television, and there were the Mouseketeers getting bosoms, and they were all so pretty. And there was Sandra Dee, and she was what a movie star was supposed to be. I watched all of this . . . but I never wanted to be inside the box. I say 'the box' because what I mainly did was watch TV. I didn't go to movies very much. Still don't.

"As a matter of fact, when I was little I never let myself hope for very much, in general. Never let myself hope for very much of anything. If I didn't hope for much, then I wouldn't be disappointed when I didn't get it.

"I remember in high school, walking into the room where you took the SAT tests. What I remember thinking is that you got three hundred points just for writing your name on the test. I have no idea whether that's true or not, but that was the rumor at our high school. So I thought to myself, 'At least I'll make a three hundred.' It turned out that I did okay on the SATs. But my attitude was 'Who cares. It doesn't matter.' The same with people. 'If they like me, fine. If not, that's fine, too.'"

I said that I had a stupid question. How hard was it to memorize lines? After all the years of watching thousands of actors and actresses in the movies and on television, I still couldn't figure out how they managed to memorize all of those words that someone else had written. Was there a trick to it?

"Two weeks ago, I was in London for a brief visit, and it turned out that my mother was in London, too," Streep said. "She was staying at a sublet. She gave me her phone number, and I wrote it down on the pad at the hotel where I was staying.

"Yesterday I wanted to call my mother. And I thought of that pad in that hotel room . . . and I remembered the number. It's a sort of idiot's memory I have, and it's what got me through college.

"I've always felt a little guilty about being able to do that. I'd read a script two or three times, and I'd have my lines. The others were staying up at night studying their scripts. It's nothing I felt particularly good about, though. It's sort of like when I was at Yale, and they would post the cast lists for all of the plays. I was always worried when the lists went up. Not because I was afraid I wasn't going to be on them. I was worried that I was going to be cast in the lead again. I was worried about how the rest of the class would feel about that."

I said that surely those kinds of emotions must be mixed with a fierce sense of pride in herself.

"You know what makes me proud of myself?" she said. "I'm proud of myself when all of these things are set next to each other. If I make a false step, it's only one step. It's like the string of beads in a necklace. One stone may not be as interesting as the next, but the whole necklace is a good necklace."

She said that her plan is to work in spurts—do two or three movies at a time, then take a year or so off to be with her family, then do some more movies. She said she can never be sure how long she will be valuable to movie producers; one of these days, she said, she may wake up to find that she is too old to command the kinds of roles she is offered now.

"I'm going to be sort of, maybe, relieved at that point," she said. "Making movies is hard work. The theater is something I like better. And it's more welcoming to women.

"There's something about movies that I need, though. Making movies is sort of like exercise for my imagination. I turn slovenly very easily. I like the family kind of interaction that comes when you're working on a movie.

"Being a housewife and a mother is much more difficult, though. To be a good housewife and mother, you have to be more self-generated. You have to create your own playground of the imagination and the mind. To be a really good, creative mother you have to be an extraordinary woman.

You have to keep yourself involved with your child during great periods of the day when it's just the two of you and you feel that at any moment you may literally go out of your mind.

"I'm lucky, because I get to go in spurts. I do great chunks of work, and then I can concentrate on being a mother. The spark of electricity is always there when you're making a movie; you sit down at a script conference, and it's easier to feel that you're participating because it's not just you. Other people pick up the slack. It's not like that when you're a mother, and that's what's so impressive about good mothers."

I asked her how the concept of ambition fit into all of that. Did she consider herself to be an ambitious person?

"It's changing, the idea of what you're supposed to be," she said. "You're supposed to have teeth and nails now. In pursuit of what, really? There was a time when I was bewildered that other people perceived me as incredibly ambitious. I resented the fact that I was thought of as being self-effacing or coy because I said that a lot of what had happened to me had happened because of luck.

"I would hear from friends that 'So-and-so has this real thing about you— you're the reason that she didn't get this part or that part.' And I would find it hard to believe that people would spend so much time worrying about the course of someone else's career.

"I think you can only be as good as the task at hand. If Jascha Heifetz plays 'Frère Jacques,' it will be very good. But it will only be as good as 'Frère Jacques' can be. Does that make sense?

"My whole attitude is that whatever the task at hand is, as long as I'm doing it, then I might as well try to do it better. If you're washing the floor, at some point the question is going to come up: Do you go in the corners or not? I'm the kind of person who wants the floor clean. The corners, too. It's not a perfectionist thing."

"Then what is it?" I said.

"I guess it's an impatience with being half-assed," she said.

I asked her about being famous. How much did she like it?

"I have a friend who has a son, and the son wants to be a rock 'n' roll star," she said. "He doesn't want to play well. He doesn't want to compose music. He just wants to be a famous rock star.

"I think there's a lot of that out there. People who have no interest in doing anything well—they just want to be famous. And I think, well, they should just spend two weeks with someone who's famous.

"I like some aspects of it. I like the aspects that make New York seem like a small town. Strangers smile at you.

"But I don't like what it does to someone who is with me, and who is not famous. It's gotten to the point where I prefer being with someone who is famous, because it takes the weight off my shoulders. If I'm walking down the street with someone I know, and I'm stopped five times by people who recognize me, I can't help a little corner of my heart curdling for the other person.

"With my children, they're young enough that they don't realize what my situation is yet. They're growing up thinking that New York is an incredibly friendly place. Everyone says hello and smiles. I don't know what it's going to be like when they're old enough to understand."

I asked her if she ever walked into a movie theater where one of her films was showing, took a seat in the back of the house, and watched the show along with the other paying customers.

"No," she said.

"Never?" I said.

"Never," she said. "The first time I watched one of my movies with any audience at all was *Sophie's Choice,* and that was a benefit arranged by the studio.

"But buy a ticket and walk into a theater? I could never do that. If you do that, you really lay yourself open. What if the people laugh at the serious part? What if they snore during the part that's supposed to be funny? I don't know why you'd want to be there to be wounded by that.

"I'll tell you something, though. We don't have HBO on our TV at home, but the HBO movies show up on the screen all scrambled. One night *Sophie's Choice* came on. I could hear it, but I couldn't see it. And I sat there for twenty minutes, and I looked at it—all scrambled and fuzzy, with little corners of the movie showing up on the screen.

"We had just bought a video camera to record the kids growing up. Home movies. And it occurred to me as I was watching the scrambled-up *Sophie's Choice* . . . you know, I have my own home movies. They're my real movies. When other people see them, they may see the plot and the scenery and the actors. When I see them, though . . . I see something else. I'm watching a different movie. I see them and I think about the place where I lived when we were filming the movie, and where we ate, and the arguments we had about different scenes. . . .

"That's what I was thinking about when I was watching the jumbled-up *Sophie's Choice.* I have my own home movies, but everyone else gets to see them. They're reminders of my life, and they're right out there."

We rode through the late-afternoon crosstown traffic. Streep had an appointment with Sydney Pollack, the director; they were supposed to talk about a future movie project. If Streep agreed to do it, she would begin to work on it immediately after the movie in London was completed.

"Do you ever wish that any of this was any different?" I said.

"Well, I think about my children," she said. "When I was a little kid, I was the star in my household. That's how it should be for all little kids. When you're a little kid, you should be the light of the house."

"And in your house?" I said.

"Sometimes, in my situation, it gets a little difficult," she said.

"Did you ever think about moving to a smaller town?" I said. "Just to get away from the New York City atmosphere?"

"I've thought about it," she said. "But I don't know if I'll ever do it."

"Does it appeal to you?" I said.

"I suppose, but you never know what's going to happen," she said. "I mean, a small town sounds great for children. But then you have idiots racing their cars up and down the streets at 120 miles an hour in those small towns. I know. I was in that car when I was growing up. And I didn't say anything. I could have said, 'Jerome, turn the engine off. I'm scared and I want to go home.' But I didn't say a word.

"I guess that's how it is, isn't it? You're scared to death and you don't say a thing."

Letters from Laura

I don't know why this makes me feel so sad, but it does.

About a year ago I wrote a story about a twenty-six-year-old woman named Laura Thomas, who had come up with a rather original idea. Thomas was a fan of television soap operas, and she started thinking: What if people could receive a continuing soap opera through the mail?

Her plan was to write a continuing series of adventures in the form of letters. People would be able to subscribe to the letters; in each letter would be news of a fictional heroine, one "Laura Alexander."

The fictional Laura Alexander, according to Thomas, would be "in her early twenties. She is very naive, very innocent. She is a virgin. She has moved to Chicago from a small town in Iowa, and now she is trying to make her fortune in the big city."

Actually, the personality of the fictional Laura Alexander reminded me a little of Laura Thomas. Laura Thomas seemed to be a wide-eyed, hopeful, trusting sort herself—and she had great aspirations for her "Letters from Laura" idea.

"Each letter will carry a personal salutation," Laura Thomas told me at the time. "I want the person who receives it to feel that he or she is really receiving a letter from a friend."

She said that she hoped there would be a big market for "Letters from Laura" among senior citizens, "A lot of them really treasure it when they get mail," she said. "And I would hope that 'Letters from Laura' would remind them of what their own wholesome, nice granddaughters might be going through in a similar adventure of moving to the big city. I would hope that they would really begin to care about what happens to Laura Alexander."

Well . . . I talked with Laura Thomas again the other day. "Letters from Laura," it seems, was a total flop.

She took out advertisements promoting the service, and did all she could to let people know about it. Her grand total of subscribers: fewer than fifty.

"I guess people just weren't interested," she said. "It seemed like a good idea to me, but there doesn't seem to be a market for the adventures of an innocent young woman in the city."

And then Thomas showed me the new project upon which she has embarked.

It is a reincarnation of "Letters from Laura."

Only this time Laura isn't a naive young virgin.

This time Laura is a porno queen.

"Now Laura Alexander is a gorgeous, sexy, experienced, uninhibited young woman who is the biggest movie porno star of all time," Thomas said. "She loves sex. She will do anything. Her letters are totally X-rated—they are very hot."

She showed me a sample of the new "Letters from Laura."

The letter was one of the filthiest things I had ever read. To say it was hard-core would be to engage in massive understatement. This new version of "Letters from Laura" was raw pornography, pure and simple. There is no way I can quote any of it here

"I'm doing this because I was pretty devastated when the original 'Letters from Laura' failed," Thomas said. "I felt that I was a bad business-woman.

"Actually, it was my own father who helped me come up with the new idea. He told me that people just didn't want to pay good money to read about the adventures of some nice, innocent girl. He said, 'Sex sells.' And I decided he was right."

So Thomas has taken out advertisements for the new "Letters from Laura" in some of the raunchiest men's magazines. She has also begun writing a monthly version of "Letters from Laura" for one of the hardest-core of the porno magazines; the editors are not paying her for it, but are running the "Letters from Laura" post office box number so that she can get subscribers.

"I had no idea how to do this," Thomas said. "I'm more like the old Laura Alexander—I'm naive about a lot of things, and I don't have a lot of experience with men. But I went to an adult bookstore and bought some of the dirtiest porno magazines, and I read them and studied the writing. It wasn't that hard to learn to write like that."

She said that she feels the new "Letters from Laura" will do much better in the marketplace than last year's version. "The original Laura Alexander—the nice young woman in the big city—must have been too boring for people," she said. "I guess if you want people to read something like this, it has to be taboo and nasty."

She said she is writing to her original fifty subscribers to tell them that the old "Letters from Laura" are coming to an end. "I'll miss writing for those people," she said. "Sometimes they'd write to Laura Alexander. They seemed very middle-class and conservative. They seemed like nice, decent, home-oriented, down-to-earth, warm people. But there just weren't enough of them."

And now she will begin writing the hard-core, X-rated "Letters from Laura" to see if more people want them.

I told Laura Thomas that I had a question for her:

Last year, when she had begun "Letters from Laura," she had told me that she hoped people would become interested in what became of Laura Alexander. So I wondered: What did become of Laura?

Laura Thomas paused.

"I guess she sold herself," she said.

Then she said:

"That sounds awful, doesn't it? Let's just say that she decided to become a different person."

Yippie vs. Yuppie

It was a scene that stretched credulity.

Sitting backstage in a warmup room for the "Donahue" television show, Jerry Rubin and Abbie Hoffman marked time.

Fifteen years ago, they were in the midst of the Chicago Seven trial—the conspiracy trial that stemmed from their involvement in the street disruptions during the 1968 Democratic National Convention. The trial made them the most famous radicals in America. With their painted faces and angry outbursts, they became better known than all but a few U.S. senators.

Everything changes. Today Jerry Rubin, forty-six, backstage at "Donahue," was sipping from a bottle of Perrier. He was the picture of a successful young businessman—clean-shaven, tailored sport coat, tie, gray slacks, tasseled loafers.

Across the room Abbie Hoffman, forty-seven, slumped in a leather chair. He was bearded and tieless, in corduroy pants and boots.

The two former compatriots were launching a national tour. They plan to crisscross the United States appearing on college campuses, in town halls, and clubs; their act is being billed as "The Yippie vs. the Yuppie."

Also backstage at "Donahue" was one Don Epstein, the president of a New York firm called Greater Talent Network, Inc. Epstein is the agent for Rubin and Hoffman; his job is to get them as many bookings as he can. The fee for a Rubin-Hoffman appearance is five thousand dollars per night, plus expenses.

"We're just beginning the tour, and already I have sixteen cities booked," Epstein said. "I'm confident that I can book as many cities as Jerry and Abbie are willing to work. If they're willing to do one hundred appearances in the next year, I should have no problem lining one hundred appearances up."

The idea is to market the fact that Rubin and Hoffman have gone their separate ways. Rubin has become an entrepreneur, Hoffman still espouses many of the causes that he believed in as a Sixties radical; thus, the premise for "The Yippie vs. the Yuppie" tour.

"It's a classic confrontation," Jerry Rubin explained. "A passionate set of disagreements between two personalities who are connected in people's minds."

Abbie Hoffman said, "The colleges today are so boring and bland—they remind me of hospital food. I really hold college students' feet to the coals."

"And I disagree," Rubin said. "I tell college students that I promote the entrepreneurial ethic and working within the system. I tell the students that they should become powerful businesspeople and take over the country with the money they earn."

Whatever . . . the point is, Rubin and Hoffman have become business partners themselves. Their joint venture is the lecture tour, and they knew that their success on the road would depend, in large part, on how well they did on "Donahue." The show is perhaps the most powerful in the country in terms of reaching consumers—and Rubin and Hoffman knew that if the sparks flew on TV today, Don Epstein's booking job would be made much easier.

A visitor to the anteroom wondered: Did today's college students even remember Jerry and Abbie?

"They remember, they remember," Hoffman said.

"Of course the kids remember," Don Epstein said. "Jerry and Abbie are a part of history. We should get, at the least, between a thousand and fifteen hundred people everywhere we go."

It was almost time for the show to begin. Out in the studio, a "Donahue" producer was talking to the audience.

"Do you remember the Sixties here in Chicago?" she said. "How many remember what went on in Chicago in the Sixties?" There were some hands raised, and a smatter of applause.

The producer said: "You remember the Chicago Seven trial, right?"

There was silence.

"No?" she said.

Hoffman and Rubin were led to chairs that were placed on a riser. Microphones were pinned to their shirts.

The producer, reading from a card, introduced the two to the audience, and called them "two of the Sixties' wildest radicals and most entertaining activists."

Phil Donahue appeared one minute before air time. A floor manager counted down the final seconds, and the show began. Rubin and Hoffman did their best to disagree vehemently with each other and make the point that they were now on different sides of the political fence; at one point Hoffman said, "If you scratch Jerry Rubin, you're going to find Ronald Reagan."

After some heated exchanges, Donahue broke for a commercial. The houselights dimmed.

Jerry Rubin craned his neck, as if looking for someone. He found who he was looking for: Don Epstein, sitting in the back row.

"Donny, how is it?" he called out.

The agent meshed his fingers together and held them up for Rubin to see.

"Interact more, Jerry," he said. "Interact more."

"I'm trying to," Rubin said. "But Phil moved away."

The commercial ended. The houselights went back up. Donahue began his questions again. Rubin and Hoffman resumed their arguing. Coming soon to an auditorium near you.

Set Point

Along with millions of other Americans, I watched the telecasts of the recently concluded U.S. Open tennis tournament. It struck me how much tennis has changed in such a short time.

When I was a boy, I harbored a dream of becoming a world-class tennis player. I never made it, but I tried hard enough for a number of years; the last paying job I had before becoming a newspaperman was as a teaching pro at some local public courts, and that's as close as I got.

Tennis was the last major sport to change. It was rooted in politeness and tradition; you were not allowed on the courts unless you dressed completely in white, and even on schoolyard courts players obediently wore their "whites." The major tennis tournaments were for amateurs only; professional tennis players had their own circuit, but the prestigious events, including the U.S. national championships, were available only to amateurs.

There was no such thing as a "U.S. Open"; if you got paid for playing tennis, then you were disqualified from the U.S. championship.

It was as if the men who ran the tennis establishment believed that there was something holy in amateurism. Frankly, it was kind of nice. Tennis paid for this anachronism, of course; even the loftiest tournaments were seldom televised, and you were lucky if you could find a tennis story on the sports pages. Those of us who dreamed tennis dreams assumed that we could never attain the fame, never mind the money, of the stars in sports like football and baseball. But we didn't care that much. There was something special about tennis.

I was thinking about this as I watched John McEnroe and Ivan Lendl and Jimmy Connors play in this year's U.S. Open.

Some of the players were like walking billboards; they seemed to be selling any available inch of their clothing to sponsors who would pay to paste their logos on a tennis star. Their clothes were colorful and distinctive; the era of "whites" is long past. The U.S. Open was being telecast to live audiences all over the world.

What it got me thinking about was a Davis Cup sectional match back in 1962. The United States was playing another country; I'm not sure, but I think it was Canada. The series was being held at some courts up in Cleveland, and like most tennis events, it was no big national deal. No television; little press coverage.

A friend of mine named Bruce Friedman and I rode the train up to Cleveland to watch the matches. He had the tennis dream, too, and there was no way that we were going to let the country's best amateur players be that close to where we lived, and not see them.

We hung around for the first day of competition. The crowd was small; really no more people than you would get for the end-of-summer finals at a good-sized country club. It was great to see the U.S. team, but that's not what truly excited us. What was really exciting was that Pancho Gonzales—one of the greatest tennis players in American history—was serving as a coach for the U.S. Davis Cup team.

Gonzales was a pro by this time. From our seats in the stands, we watched him watching the team. He was tall and brown and lean; he was everything an athletic hero should be. The day's matches ended, and the players wandered off into a combination locker room area and snack bar.

My friend and I hung around. At dusk, walking out of the locker room, we saw Gonzales. He was in tennis whites now; he carried several racquets in his hand. He was accompanied by a player named Chuck McKinley, and it was clear that the two were going to play; they were going to have an impromptu workout.

My friend and I walked over to the court; there was virtually no one else around. Gonzales and McKinley started hitting back and forth, and one of us got up the nerve to ask Gonzales if they needed ball boys.

Gonzales nodded and motioned the two of us to opposite ends of the court. For the next two hours, as we shagged balls and tossed them back to the players, we got a priceless gift: we got to watch the great Gonzales up close.

You talk about the best tennis lesson a person could ever get. Gonzales was famed for his serves—both the booming flat serve, and an American Twist that leapt skyward as soon as it hit the court. We crouched down and watched how he did it; we studied his ground strokes and took note of how he moved across the court. Who would have guessed, just one day earlier, that we would ever have gotten an opportunity like this?

Gonzales wasn't the sweetest guy in the world; a few times, when we were watching him too intently and not chasing the balls rapidly enough, he cursed at us and reminded us that we were supposed to be ball boys. We didn't mind; we were a couple of suburban teenagers and he was Pancho Gonzales, and if he wanted to chew us out, that was his privilege.

It strikes me that something like that probably couldn't happen today. Somehow, with the publicity and the commercial endorsements and the marketing strategies and the telecasts, I can't imagine, say, John McEnroe walking out onto a solitary court at the end of the day during a big tournament, and allowing the only two kids left in the area to chase balls for him. The crowds would be too big today; the time schedule would be too regimented.

That's what I was thinking about as I watched the U.S. Open. On that day in Cleveland, after Gonzales had finished, he started walking back toward the locker room. Almost as an afterthought he called out in our direction; when we looked back at him, he tossed us the tennis balls with which he had been playing. That's what I was thinking about.

The New Generation Gap

I was talking with an eighteen-year-old girl, a senior in high school. She said she wanted to ask me something.

"Who was Ed Sullivan?" she said.

I said I didn't think I understood the question.

"I mean, who was he?" she said. "Was he, like, your generation's David Letterman?"

Not precisely, I said.

"Well, what did he look like?" she said.

I asked her if she meant that, were Ed Sullivan to walk into the room at that very moment, she would not recognize him?

"No," she said. "I wouldn't."

Then she said:

"Did he look like this?"

She stood up and let her arms hang in front of her like an orangutan.

I said that actually he had, indeed, looked a little like that. Where had she seen him?

"I think I saw him in a Beatles video," she said.

The Beatles hadn't made videos, I said; they had made movies.

"Let me ask you something else," she said.

I said to go ahead.

"Is it true that Elvis Presley and the Beatles made their first appearances on the Ed Sullivan show?" she said.

I said that basically that was true.

"Well, why did you watch them, then?" she said. "If they hadn't been on TV before, how did you know that you wanted to see them?"

I said that we watched Ed Sullivan every week.

"You mean you watched his show no matter what was on it?" she said.

I said yes.

"I see," she said. "Kind of like MTV."

Alas . . . it has come to pass. My generation, which alienated the rest of America in the Sixties and Seventies by acting as if we had created the concept of youth, is now on the far side of a generation gap that excludes millions of our younger countrymen who have no real memory of Ed Sullivan.

The young woman is not alone; there are millions upon millions of bright, intelligent young people out there who are no more familiar with Iron Butterfly or Dobie Gillis than we were with Rudy Vallee or Jack Armstrong, the All-American Boy. To them Lyndon Johnson is as distant a figure as FDR was to us; to them the idea of watching Jack Paar on television is as unimaginable as our thoughts of listening to Fred Allen on network radio.

This shouldn't be so surprising, of course; it happens to every generation, and it is probably a healthy thing.

But there has never been a generation that seemed so happily, smugly sure that it was inventing the world for the first time than those of us in the so-called Baby Boom. Because we represented a big hump in the country's demographic profile, we always felt comfortably surrounded by others just like us; there were so many members of our generation that often we felt important just by being alive.

Which makes it all the bigger a shock when we now realize that a completely new generation has come along—a generation that frankly regards us as middle-aged and sort of quaint. The fact that they're right doesn't help any.

This phenomenon has even extended to politics. Those of us who grew up during the war in Indochina and were still relatively young when Watergate happened view the universe with a gimlet-eyed perspective that we always considered sort of weatherbeaten and world-weary. We may have assumed that the generations that came along after us would eagerly imitate our political attitudes

But as my eighteen-year-old acquaintance said to me:

"I'm real sorry about Vietnam and everything, but I don't see why your generation hates the government and hates America so much."

Although she was oversimplifying, I knew exactly what she meant; it is far more likely that a member of her generation will join the Marines than end up marching on a picket line protesting some bit of American foreign policy.

My conversation with her was not the first time I have seen this new set of attitudes come up. A few months ago I was talking to another teenager— this one seventeen years old—and she mentioned that her parents liked to play tapes in their car.

I asked her what kind of music her mom and dad played.

"You know, classical stuff," she said.

Like what? I asked.

"The Grateful Dead," she said.

And my old college roommate called me the other day to ask me if I'd seen the current issue of *Playboy*—the one that features a pictorial about young men being romantically involved with older women.

"The 'older women' in the article are younger than we are!" he said. "The 'older women' are thirty-five years old!"

Oh, well. My eighteen-year-old acquaintance asked me another question about what Ed Sullivan's show had been like.

I was going to tell her about Topo Gigio, but I didn't have the heart.

Book 'em

Friends have asked me to name the most bizarre moment of all. At first I was tempted to say it came in Los Angeles, when I found that there were going to be two of us on a morning talk show—just me and Britt Ekland, who was there to discuss her theory of "sensuous beauty."

Then I was tempted to say it came in Washington, when I stepped into the makeup trailer and found that the person being worked on before me was Little Richard.

Then I was going to say it came in New York, when I reported for a radio interview at which the person who would be answering the questions was me, and the person who would be asking the questions was Howard Cosell.

But I decided that the most bizarre moment probably came early one morning in Aurora, Ohio. "The Morning Exchange"—a Cleveland television program—was broadcasting live on location from Sea World, located in Aurora. It was a chilly, stormy day; thunderclouds covered the sky, and rain was descending in harsh sheets.

The show was being telecast outdoors. I was sitting on a canvas director's chair, between the two hosts of the program, Fred Griffith and Jan Jones.

To protect us from the weather, we had been positioned under a stone ledge halfway up the side of a man-made cave. Across the way from us, sitting in a covered grandstand, were several hundred northern Ohio housewives.

And between us was the otter pool. The otters were sticking their noses up through the surface of the water, attempting to leap into the rainy dawn. There we were—Fred, Jan, and me—up on the ledge of the cave. There they were—the audience—beneath the roof of the grandstand. And separating us were the storm and the agitated otters.

I clutched a wireless microphone in my right hand and spoke into it. I heard my voice echoing back from the grandstand and bouncing off the wet walls of our cave. It struck me that, when I had first decided I might like to grow up to be a writer, I had not quite imagined this.

The book tour is a staple of modern literary life. Sadly, the day is long past when you could count on large numbers of people strolling casually into a bookstore, browsing at their leisure until they have spotted a title that intrigues them, then deciding, on an impulse, to give that title a try.

People are in a hurry today. In most cases, they will purchase a book only if they have heard of it. How do they hear of it? Media.

So a little community of sorts has sprung up. The main players—the publicists who work for the publishing companies, and the "bookers" who work for the television and radio shows—change relatively infrequently. They deal with one another on virtually a daily basis. The publishers call and say who will be coming through a particular town in a given week, and the bookers decide if the literary travelers sound interesting enough to put on the air.

The variables—the folks whose names change with the seasons—are the authors. On a given day, there may be scores of authors on tour somewhere in America. Armed with photocopied itineraries, plane tickets, and pocket cash, they have been put on the road for a simple reason. A book will not sell unless people know about it. The way most people know about things in the Eighties is by watching their television sets, listening to their radios, and reading their newspapers. Thus, the book tour.

In a recent twelve-month period it happened that I was sent on three separate national book tours. I visited thirty-six cities. It was unlike any experience I have had before.

First, a disclaimer: I have read stories in which touring authors have moaned and complained about the long hours, the bad hotels, the indifferent interviewers, and the general pain that come with going on a book tour. I can't quite buy that.

Maybe it's just me, but I can't help feeling flattered every time I learn that someone actually has said he or she is willing to interview me. Because I wrote stories for a living. I'm always a little surprised when someone agrees to turn the tables, and do an interview with me. In that sense, a book tour is one continuing ego trip—how often does a writer get to hit the road and talk about himself all over the country?

Having said that, I must quickly add that a book tour is probably the most disorienting thing I have ever been a part of. It lifts you out of your daily life, plops you into a world that you were previously only vaguely aware of, then drops you back into your daily life again. Your job is to retain some sense of equilibrium, which is a challenge you quickly learn you may not be up to.

Sometimes it all happens in a flash. You wake up in your own bed in your own town, have breakfast, then head for the airport to catch a flight to Los Angeles. Upon arriving you take a cab to Vine Street, to a television studio inside which you are scheduled to appear on "The Merv Griffin Show." A makeup artist dabs liquid on your face, you are led to a lounge equipped with a bar and a television monitor, and soon enough the monitor flashes to life and you hear an announcer's voice say that tonight Merv's guests will be Susan Anton, Erica Jong, a stand-up comedian, and you. Before too long you are led onto the set, where Merv Griffin greets you, an audience full of strangers applauds, and you talk to Merv for eight minutes. After you finish, the audience leaves and so do you; the next day you are back in the town where you live again, working at your own desk again.

Sometimes it happens in slow motion, so repeatedly that you begin to feel like a tired old boxer who is being beaten against the ropes by a healthy young stud eager for an early knockout. The schedule for one day in Detroit: 9:00 A.M., "Kelly and Company" talk show, WXYZ television; 10:20 A.M., interview with J. P. McCarthy, "Focus" show, WJR radio; 11:00 A.M., "The Sonya Show," WDIV television; 11:45 A.M., "Midday" show, WWJ radio; 12:15 P.M., "Metro Magazine" show, WOMC radio; 1:00 P.M., "Mark Scott" show, WXYT radio; 2:30 P.M., taped interview for early evening news, WDIV television; 3:30 P.M., newspaper interview with *Ypsilanti Press,* Detroit Metro Airport. Immediately following interview: flight to next city.

Again: all this attention is gratifying; all this attention is more than any writer has a right ever to ask for. And perhaps that is the thing that makes a book tour so confusing—so exhilarating, yet so exhausting—to be a part of. I know that on each of my three recent tours, I found myself thinking: this is a part of America that everyone should get to experience once. Few people are even aware it's out there, yet it's going on every day.

There is a relatively new phenomenon that has become a part of book tours: the "media escort."

Media escorts are men and women who take visiting authors around to their various interviews. They live in the towns the authors pass through; they charge considerably less money than limousine services, and are more reliable than cabs. Take another look at that Detroit schedule. Without an escort waiting with his car and knowing his way around the city, a schedule like that one would be impossible to book.

Media escorts see a side of the literary world that few others do. They become acquainted with a far greater number of prominent authors than even the most gregarious Manhattan editor or agent. They sometimes escort a different author every day; they spend up to twelve hours a day with "their" authors, and therefore can tell author stories far more intimate and revealing than the stories garnered by the broadcasters who do the quick interviews in the studios while the escorts wait outside.

Often the media escort is the only person whom an author will leave a given town with a real memory of. By the time the author reaches the next town, though—usually late at night, in order to be present for the next morning's first talk show—the next media escort will have left a message at his hotel, giving instructions about where to meet just after dawn. My favorite instruction, delivered on a pink hotel message slip: "Look for an aging blonde in a silver Mercedes."

An author on a book tour learns to look for familiar sights. One of these, he realizes early on, is his book. It is often the only thing that he can recognize as being a part of his real life. So when he arrives at each ensuing television or radio station, his eyes involuntarily begin to search for his book. The sight of it begins to give him a warm feeling, like a letter from home.

The other familiar thing a touring author learns to look for is other touring authors. Over the course of a year there may be hundreds and hundreds of them on the road, but during a given week, in a specific section of the country, you are likely to find the same people. So when I saw Jane and Michael Stern, the authors of *Square Meals,* in the San Francisco airport, it did not seem at all odd that I had seen them only hours before in the lobby of KRLD radio in Dallas. And when I ran into a psychologist named Elliot Weiner, the author of something called *The Love Exam,* no fewer than seven times in two cities during one twenty-four-hour period, I did not question it; it was sort of like in high school, when you used to see the same people in the hallways between classes every day.

In an effort to maintain my sanity, I started keeping notes during my book tours. In the margins of my daily schedule, I would scribble my impressions about the people who were interviewing me.

So while Don Miller of the *Santa Cruz Sentinel* was asking me questions in my hotel room in San Francisco, I was writing on my schedule: "Why is the photographer lying on my bed?" While Marcia Alvar was talking to me on KUOW radio at the University of Washington in Seattle, I was writing: "This woman is really good." While Jim Bohannon, sitting in for host Larry King, was interviewing me on Mutual Radio's syndicated "The Larry King Show," I was writing: "Why are all of these obviously intelligent, apparently well-read people up at three o'clock in the morning making phone calls to a person they have never met?"

Sometimes something would happen that required me to turn the schedule over and write on the back. After a live interview on "Midday L.A." at KTTV television in Los Angeles, I wrote: "A producer came up to me on the set and said, 'You'll have to clue me in on who you are.' I said, 'I'm a writer.' She said, 'Like an author?' I said, 'Yes.' Her eyes glazed over and she said, 'Oh, interesting.' I could tell she was expecting someone else. I asked her who she had thought I was. She said, 'A water commissioner.'"

Between 9:00 A.M. and 10:00 A.M. Eastern Time every Thursday morning, there is a telephone number—it is in the 556 exchange in Manhattan—that constantly rings busy. That is because virtually every author on the road—and representatives of virtually every publishing house back home—is trying to get through.

This is the telephone line on which the editors of the *New York Times Book Review* place a tape recording of their best-seller lists, both hardback and paperback. On Thursday mornings a new tape is put on the machine; on it a voice announces the fresh best-seller list that will appear in the Sunday *Times* ten days hence.

In Seattle, it's 6:00 A.M. In Denver, it's 7:00 A.M. In St. Louis, it's 8:00 A.M. In Boston, it's 9:00 A.M.

In hotel rooms everywhere, groggy authors punch the New York telephone number, get a busy signal, hang up, and punch the number again.

Soon they will be out in a new city, for a new day. Right now, though, they can't face the morning without hearing the tape. If book touring is a game, the tape is the scoreboard.

When my third tour of the year was over, I went back to my newspaper office in Chicago. One of the first telephone callers was a woman from the publicity department of a publishing house in New York.

"We've got a very interesting author who will be in your town next week," she said. "He's written an important new book, and I think it would make a great story for you. . . ."

I closed my eyes and thought of airports. And otters.

Wedding Story

Olive Johnson, who went through the first seventy-seven years of her life as a single woman, got married the other afternoon. After a lifetime of hearing people call her Miss Johnson, now she is being called Mrs. Lange. That may not be front-page headline news, but it is making her very happy.

"Mr. Lange . . . Harold . . . and I both live here in the retirement community," the new Mrs. Lange said. She was explaining how she had met her husband, who is seventy-five. The retirement community is called the Holmstad, and is located in Batavia, Illinois.

"One day about four years ago I was working in the garden," she said. "I was breaking up some sticks to mark off the garden, and Mr. Lange . . . Harold . . . was in the next garden. He started bawling me out; he said, 'If you do it that way, you're going to get slivers in your hand.' He went and got me some other sticks to use."

Olive Johnson had accepted the fact that she would never marry. "I suppose I thought about it when I was a young girl," she said. "I felt bad when all my girl friends were getting married, and I wasn't. I missed the companionship. But my mother was ill, and so I lived with my parents to take care of her. Then my father became ill, and I took care of him, and after a while I didn't think about getting married anymore."

Harold Lange and Olive Johnson began to become good friends. He was married before, but his wife died; Olive Johnson did not let herself think about the possibility that, so late in her life, she might finally wed. But as the two of them began participating in more activities together at the retirement community, she realized she was beginning to feel emotions she had never felt before.

"I didn't know what it was like to be in love," she said. "But other people began to say to me, 'You're in love.' They said that they could tell by looking at my eyes."

At seventy-seven, her days and nights had developed a pattern.

"In the morning I would get up, and I would go to the breakfast table," she said. "I have a studio apartment; I would fix myself some cereal and some fruit or orange juice. I'd sit there by myself and listen to Wally Phillips on the radio.

"The days would be spent with the other people here in the community. I would have good company, but I never lost sight of the basic fact that I was alone. At night, before bed, sometimes I'd fix a snack for myself. I'd listen to the radio again, and I'd get into bed and read. When my eyes closed and my book dropped out of my hands, I'd know it was time to sleep."

More and more, she found that she was looking forward to the hours she spent with Harold Lange. "We have so much in common," she said. "We love our gardens, we enjoy classical and religious music, we both enjoy church. Mostly, though, we simply enjoy each other's company."

When it finally happened, it caught her by surprise. "He had driven me to an appointment I had with my doctor," she said. "He waited for me, and as we left we were driving through the parking lot, and he stopped the car. He pulled a ring out of his pocket, and he said it: 'Will you marry me?'

"I looked at him and I handed him my hand, and that was how I said yes."

So the other afternoon, in front of almost five hundred guests, including more than three hundred fellow residents from the Holmstad retirement community, Olive Johnson became the bride of Harold Lange.

"I feel like a young kid," she said. "I feel like years have dropped away. I feel like I'm on Cloud Nine."

She said she is realistic about the future: "I know there's no guarantee of how long we'll have each other. But we'll love each other and enjoy each other as long as we can. I hope that we can give each other some years of happiness. I'm so grateful that there will be no more lonely nights."

As I said it, it's not headline news. The new Mr. and Mrs. Lange will be living in his apartment; she is moving out of her studio and into his home. That will happen in a few weeks, though; right now they are on their honeymoon. They are driving through Wisconsin and Canada to see the leaves turn colors.

"That's something I always wanted to do," the new Mrs. Lange said. "I always wanted to get a chance to go north and see the colors of autumn, to see the leaves turn.

"But I never did it, because I didn't want to take a trip like that by myself. I never felt that I cared to do it alone. Well, I'm not alone now, and I'm going to see the colors."

Platinum Card

He had an embarrassed, furtive sound to his voice. He said he had a confession to make.

"I got the American Express Platinum Card," he said. He was referring to the new credit cards that are sold for $250 a year to the top echelon of American Express's charge-card customers.

"You really have one?" I said.

"You can't use my name," he hurriedly said. "I'm a funeral director, and it wouldn't look good for the families around here to think that I'm spending their hard-earned money on something like the Platinum Card."

I asked him to tell me the whole story. Start at the beginning, I said.

"Well, first I just had the regular American Express green card," he said. "I thought that was a pretty good card to have. Then we were at lunch at Kon-Tiki Ports, and the bill came. I gave the waiter my card. He came back and said, 'I'm sorry, but it's going to be a while. There's a problem with the phone lines, and we have to wait to get verification on your card.'

"My friend who was with me whipped out his Gold Card. He said, 'Will we have to wait with this?' The waiter said, 'No, *sir*! Right away!'

"They said *sir* to him. They never said *sir* to me. I thought, 'Phooey on this. I need a Gold Card!'"

So he applied for one and he got it. American Express's regular green cards cost $35 a year; the Gold Cards cost $65 a year. But he figured it was worth it.

Then, earlier this year, he looked at an American Express imprinting machine in a restaurant. There were decals on it showing the regular green card and the Gold Card. But there was a new decal, too: the Platinum Card.

"I asked the person at the restaurant about it," he said. "He told me that the Platinum Card costs $250 a year, and only the very elite of American Express's customers could get one.

"I had to do it. I called American Express and asked how I could get a Platinum Card. The person on the phone was very snotty about it. The person said, '*We* will determine who receives a Platinum Card. You cannot *apply* for it. You must be *invited*.' Very aloof.

"Part of me realized that there is something very warped about a society that tells you that you can pay $250 for a charge card that has a different color to it than your regular charge card—and you actually want the $250 card anyway.

"But each day I looked in my mail for an invitation. It didn't come and it didn't come. I felt brokenhearted. I wasn't good enough for the Platinum Card. I wondered what I had done to get American Express mad at me.

"Each day I woke up and thought, 'Maybe this is the day.' Each day passed, and I wasn't one of the chosen people.

"But then it happened. In October, it came. The envelope was like parchment. There were platinum lines all over it. It made me feel like someone was asking me to marry their daughter.

"I opened it up. It was an invitation to obtain a Platinum Card. Not an application—an invitation.

"I sent my check for $250 in. When the card came, it was in an envelope from Fort Lauderdale. This is no kidding—I took it in the bathroom to open it up. I didn't want anyone else around.

"Inside me, a little voice was saying: 'You're living a double standard.' I told the little voice to shut up.

"I had to use it right away. So I went down to a Toys-R-Us store to buy a video game cartridge for one of my kids. Very casually, I handed my new Platinum Card to the girl behind the counter.

"All she said is, 'I'm new here, I've never done an American Express card before. I have to get the manager.' The manager came up and he just processed the card. No big reaction. No bells ringing. People were standing behind me in line—no reaction from them, either. I felt like I wanted to cry. I had just laid a Platinum Card on them—and nothing.

"I went home and walked in the house with a big smile on my face. I said to my wife, 'Guess what I got?' I whipped out my Platinum Card. She said, 'That's nice, dear.' I said, 'No, honey, you don't understand. This is a *Platinum Card.*' She said, 'Yes, honey. An American Express Card.'"

He said it was all downhill from there. So far, there has been virtually no reaction to the Platinum Card he spent $250 for. Once he took a friend to lunch, and when he paid for it with his Platinum Card, he thought he noticed the two men at the next table looking over and smiling.

"But after lunch I kept asking myself: Were they smiling or were they smirking? Did they think I was one of life's special few for having a Platinum Card? Or did they think I was a jerk for putting out $250 for a credit card?"

In his dark moments, he has had a troubling thought: "I see them sitting around in the American Express boardroom, and suddenly one of the big corporate bosses says: 'I need a new pool in my back yard. Let's color some of our cards platinum and see if we can get some suckers to pay $250 for them.'"

He said that every time he pulls out his Platinum Card now, he's not sure how he should feel. "It doesn't exactly give you a warm feeling, like sex or a hot toddy," he said. "But there's a definite twinge you feel in your ego."

So what was the final answer, I asked. Did his Platinum Card make him feel like a special person or like a sucker?

"I feel like a special type of sucker," he said.

Where Have You Gone, Dick and Jane?

There are dozens of theories about why children today don't read with the same fervor as earlier generations of children. Television gets the blame, and family structure gets the blame, and a lack of discipline throughout society gets the blame.

There's another possibility, though. When you look at the way we learned to read in the Thirties, Forties, Fifties, and Sixties, and you compare it with the way children are learning to read today, one glaring difference makes itself evident:

The Dick and Jane books have gone out of print.

The Dick and Jane books were published by Scott, Foresman and Company; they were a series of preprimers and primers, used in the lower grades of elementary school. For millions upon millions of us, the first words we ever read by ourselves were contained in the Dick and Jane books.

The scene repeated itself in classrooms all over America. The first-grade teacher would call us to the front of the room, where she had gathered a semicircle of chairs around a huge stand-up version of the first preprimer: *We Look and See.* She would open the book; there, beneath a brightly colored picture, was the first word we were to be taught: "Look."

There were only seventeen words in the version of *We Look and See* that was used in schools in the Fifties: *look, oh, Jane, see, Dick, funny, Sally, Puff, jump, run, Spot, come, Tim, up, and, go,* and *down.* Those seventeen words, though, were enough to start us on a lifetime of reading pleasure.

Even back then, every time we would read a new story in *We Look and See* and a brand-new word would be introduced, it would feel like a minor electrical jolt. We had never seen the word "jump" before; we turned a page, and it entered our lives, and by the end of the day it would be a part of our reading vocabulary forever. At the time we might not have realized how important that was—but we knew it was essential enough to talk about excitedly at the dinner table that night.

In addition to *We Look and See,* the other preprimers were *We Work and Play* and *We Come and Go.* When we had mastered those, we were ready for our first genuine reader: *Fun with Dick and Jane.*

None are available for use in schools in the Eighties.

Of the authors whose bylines appeared in the Dick and Jane books that were in use in the Fifties, only one is alive today. He is A. Sterl Artley, seventy-seven; he lives in Columbia, Missouri.

When asked if he realized that, in a way, he was the most influential author in the lives of uncounted millions of American men and women— being, as he was, the first author in their lives—Artley laughed it off.

"I've never really thought of myself as being influential in any way," he said. "We tried to do an honorable job of devising a reading program that would teach children the first words they would ever know. We were very serious about our work, but influential? We didn't think in those terms."

Artley was part of a team of educators who worked on the Dick and Jane books. "The method was solid," he said. "That's what you should remember. The method was built around word identification and word perception. The vocabulary was carefully controlled in the stories. Only one new word was allowed to be introduced per page. And once a word had been introduced, it had to be repeated a certain number of times. There was never a word introduced that was 'lost'; once it was a part of the text, it remained a part of the text.

"With Dick, Jane, and Sally, we knew we had something very, very special. We knew that, as simple as the books seemed, what we were doing would reflect on how generations of American children would learn to read. And I can't imagine too many things that are more basic to a culture than that."

Artley said that, in his mind, Dick, Jane, and Sally had distinctive personalities, each clearly defined:

"Dick was sort of the hero of the family. He was the one whom the children followed. He set the pace for all of their activities. The leader of the gang.

"Jane was the typical American girl. She never got dirty—but then, I guess none of the children in the books ever got dirty. Jane was very school oriented. She wasn't quite so much a leader as Dick. I guess you'd say she was a mother in miniature.

"Sally was sort of the tagalong. She was the baby of the group. She was a lovable little youngster; in today's terms, you would say that she was very sensitive. She tended to emulate Dick."

Although the very mention of the Dick and Jane books brings a rush of warm nostalgia to today's older generations of Americans, Artley said that there was some vocal criticism of the books' methods back when they were being used.

"We were attacked for using so much repetition," he said. "Some educators said that children just didn't talk that way in real life—'Run, Sally, run,' and 'Jump, Dick, jump.' We tried to explain: the teachers were instructed to 'read' the pictures first—they were supposed to explain to the class what was going on in the pictures. Then they were supposed to read the words aloud—the words were the words of Dick, Jane, and Sally, going along with what they were doing in the pictures. It was very natural."

Artley said that, by design of the team of authors, the behavior of Dick, Jane, and Sally was always exemplary. "They never fought. They never got into real trouble of any kind; they were models of good behavior. This was a conscious decision on our part. We knew that the books were going to be a part of the curricula of so many millions of children; we wanted to portray a behavior pattern that would deserve the approval of the parents.

"Because of that, Dick, Jane, and Sally became role models for American children. Teachers and parents would say to children: 'Would Dick have done that? Would Jane have done that? Let's do what Dick and Jane would have done.'

"So in a way, I suppose, we did more than teach children how to read. We helped set a cultural pattern for the times. You could probably say that we helped create several American generations of Dicks, Janes, and Sallys.'"

The last surviving editor who was in charge of the Dick and Jane books is Lee Horton, eighty-two, who now lives in Wilmette, Illinois.

"The popularity of the Dick and Jane books peaked in the mid-Fifties," Miss Horton said. "I think we had eighty-five percent of the market then.

"People wondered what our secret was. It wasn't really that complicated. First, the Dick and Jane books told a real story. Every story, no matter how short, had a beginning, a middle, and an end. The story may have been as simple as Dick and Jane playing, and Sally gets hold of a wagon, and the wagon rolls down the sidewalk. But even in a story that elementary, the children who are reading it retain interest because there is some suspense; they know that something is going to happen, and they want to find out what it is.

"The second thing was that we took a position on the educational argument over phonics. The big question was, do you teach children sounds— phonics—or do you start with meaningful language? The Dick and Jane books started with meaningful language, and I think time has shown that we made the right decision."

Miss Horton said that the first Dick and Jane books were published in the Thirties; the last revised editions were published in 1965, and by the early Seventies virtually all of the books were out of print.

"With all the revisions, some things never changed," she said. "'Look' was always the first word the children learned, for example. People may laugh at that, but I'll tell you something: studies used to be taken among college English students, in which they were asked to name the characters they best remembered from all the literature to which they had been exposed. And Dick, Jane, and Sally ended up on every list.

"You should have seen the response from children back in the heyday. I would get literally thousands of letters a year from children writing to Dick, Jane, and Sally. The letters were piled up in my office in boxes. I must have had a thousand letters just asking one question: What was Dick and Jane's last name? We never answered that. What would you choose? An Irish name? A Polish name? An Italian name? We didn't want to say.

"Why did the books go out of print? By the Seventies our culture had changed. Dick and Jane were based on the structure of the family as it existed in the Twenties. There was a father, and a mother, and two or more children, and pets. The mother kept house and the father worked.

"That was fine, but then the American family began to break up. There was a lot of divorce. We had pressure groups telling us that we had to show the mother going to work, and the father staying home to take care of Dick and Jane. We were told that the other way was a bad stereotype and we had to get rid of it.

"Then there were the other pressure groups demanding that we make the Dick and Jane stories multiethnic. They had a good point; near the end of the series we had a character named Mike and his twin sisters move in next door to Dick and Jane. The new family was black. I was told by our Southern office that we'd never sell another copy south of the Mason-Dixon line, although we did, of course.

"But things were getting so complicated . . . even I had to admit that Dick and Jane no longer really represented the culture. People just did not all live in houses with white picket fences and two children and the mother staying home and the father going to work anymore.

"I suppose everything has to change. But I see these poor little young-sters today, stretching their necks so they can see a computer screen that gives them no human response. . . . I have to say, I miss Dick and Jane."

It is not widely recalled, but Dick and Jane had competition.

"Some school systems used books other than the Dick and Jane books," said Darrel Peterson, now seventy-three, who used to be a top Scott, Foresman salesman and rose to become chairman of the board before retiring in 1976.

"I remember one of our competitors had a series of Alice and Jerry books. And when I was out on the road, my job was to persuade the schools that Dick and Jane were superior to Alice and Jerry. Dick and Jane won out; we had more of the reading business than all of our competitors put together."

At Scott, Foresman today, the editorial vice president for reading is Roxane McLean, forty-three.

"Dick and Jane just kind of came to an end," she said. "The sales started falling off in the 1960s. By 1970 we had started a new reading program that contained no mention of Dick and Jane at all.

"The women's groups and civil rights groups that started campaigning against Dick and Jane were pretty fervent. They made the argument that Dick and Jane represented a middleclass white American disposition that just didn't speak for the country anymore. They said that Dick and Jane ought to be replaced because they were no longer effective.

"So we replaced them. We still get requests from school systems, asking us to ship them Dick and Jane books. They can't get them, though, because they don't exist. When they place those orders they get a computerized form saying 'Out of print.'

"Would we ever bring Dick and Jane back as they were? I have to say no. It's just not going to happen.

"But I'll tell you . . . I can still remember sitting in my first-grade class-room and learning to read from the Dick and Jane books. I loved those books. I learned a love for reading back then, and I still have that love for reading today. So when people talk about whether Dick and Jane did their job or not . . . well, I think there are a lot of us out here who are living proof that they did just fine."

The Strange Case of the Beatles' Bedsheets

When the Beatles first came to America twenty years ago, it seemed that everything they touched turned to gold.

But that wasn't quite true. There was the strange case of the Beatles' bedsheets. Now the story can be told.

When the Beatles made their first concert tour of America in 1964, two enterprising young directors at WBKB television in Chicago sat down and tried to figure out a way to cash in on the hysteria the group was causing. The men were Richy Victor and Larry Einhorn.

They hit on what they thought was a perfect scheme. They would contact the managers of several of the hotels where the group was staying, and arrange to purchase the bedsheets and pillowcases slept on by the Beatles. Then they would cut the bed linens up into one-inch-square pieces and sell them for a dollar each.

"We thought it was a magnificent idea," Victor recalls now. "Can you imagine anything more exciting for a young fan than an actual sheet that was slept on by an actual Beatle?"

So when the Beatles arrived in Detroit, and then in Kansas City, for performances, Victor and Einhorn called the managers of Detroit's Whittier Hotel and Kansas City's Muehlebach Hotel. The men made cash offers. They would pay $400 for the Beatles' bed linens at the Whittier, and $750 for the Beatles' bed linens at the Muehlebach. [The group spent two nights at the Muehlebach, Victor said. Hence, two sets of sheets; hence, a bigger price.]

"The managers accepted our offers," Victor said. "We told 'em to plug the rooms up as soon as the Beatles left. Seal 'em up like a murder scene."

Victor and Einhorn went to the hotels with lawyers and witnesses. They procured signed affidavits vowing that the Beatles had, indeed, slept on those very sheets.

Then they cut the sheets up and mounted the one-inch swatches on copies of letters from the managers of the hotels. The letter from the manager of the Whittier began:

To whom it may concern: This is to certify that the "Beatles" stayed at the Whittier Hotel, arriving at 1:17 A.M. Sept. 6, 1964 [Detroit Time], occupying Executive Suite No. 1566, checking out at 2:05 P.M. Sept. 6, 1964. This is also to certify that the bed linen so designated is authentic and factual as to each of the "Beatles" using same.

And underneath the manager's signature was a small piece of bedsheet or pillowcase. Next to each piece of linen was a notation: either "John Slept Here" or "Paul Slept Here" or "George Slept Here" or "Ringo Slept Here."

"Actually, that part was not quite truthful," Victor said. "We had no idea which of the Beatles slept on which sheets. We were just given bags full of sheets. We had to guess who slept on which sheets. For all we know, all four of them slept in the same bed with four girls."

National news outlets picked up the story of the two entrepreneurs who were selling the Beatles' bedsheets. Victor and Einhorn thought they were going to become rich. They figured out that they could cut 164,000 little squares out of the sheets and pillowcases they had purchased. They could almost feel the $164,000 in their pockets.

Then two things happened.

The first was that no one bought the pieces of the Beatles' sheets.

"Don't ask me why," Victor said. "I've never understood it. I think it was because people thought we were phonies. There was so much Beatle junk being sold those days—the drugstores were full of it. I don't think anyone really believed that we had bought the Beatles' actual bedsheets."

The second thing that happened to Victor and Einhorn was that they received a letter from a New York attorney named Walter Hofer. Hofer's letter said:

Gentlemen: Please be advised that this office represents the interests of Paul McCartney, George Harrison, Ringo Starr, John Lennon, individually and collectively known as the Beatles.

It has come to our clients' attention that you are advertising and offering for sale certain linens allegedly used by the Beatles; and in connection therewith using the name of our clients. We are advised that you have not received authority or permission from the Beatles in connection with same.

Your activities in this connection are causing great damage to our clients, and unless you immediately cease and desist this improper and unauthorized activity, we shall have no alternative but to proceed in accordance with our clients' instructions.

So on the one hand Victor and Einhorn had 164,000 pieces of Beatle bedsheets that no one believed were real, and no one wanted to buy; and on the other hand they had the Beatles' attorney threatening to sue them.

"I think we sold between 700 and 800 of the pieces of sheets," Victor said. "We lost money. We didn't even get back what we paid for the sheets."

And now twenty years have passed. Victor dropped by the other day. He gave me four pieces of Beatle bedsheets.

"Richy," I said to him, "after I write about this, and people start wanting to contact you so they can get pieces of the Beatles' bedsheets, what should I tell them?"

"No one's going to call you," Victor said. "You know how many calls you'll get? Zilch.

"There has been publicity about this over the years. Nobody ever wants the sheets. Walter Cronkite mentioned the sheets when they first came out. The only response we got was from Walter Cronkite himself. He said he wanted a piece of the sheets for his kid."

I asked Victor how many pieces of the Beatles' sheets he had left.

"Bags and bags of them," he said. "I keep them in shopping bags. They're going to be with me for the rest of my life."

Off the Wagon

I dimmed the lights.

I put on my best suit. I placed an album of classical music on the stereo. I lit a candle and set it upon the table.

I brought out a crystal goblet and filled it with ice.

And then I did it—I poured a Coca-Cola into the goblet.

My hands were shaking. I reached for the goblet. For a moment I hesitated; did I have the guts to really do it? Something inside was telling me no, but my heart was telling me yes.

It has been a year. One entire, agonizing year.

One year ago I went on a diet. In a relatively brief time, I lost twenty-two pounds. I did this by drastically reducing the number of calories I consumed each day.

Surveys say that for every hundred pounds that Americans lose, they regain ninety of them within a calendar year. That hasn't happened with me; the twenty-two pounds have stayed off. And one of the most dramatic reasons is that, exactly one year ago, I gave up Cokes.

This may seem like a simple thing to you; logical, even. Coca-Cola is laden with wasteful calories; diet colas contain only one calorie per serving.

But I was a Coke addict. Had been for most of my life.

From the time I was six years old, I drank—on the average—three bottles of Coke a day. Back in 1975, during a slow period, I sat down and figured out how much Coke I had swallowed up to that point in my life. It came out to 4,893 quarts—the equivalent of 9,786 pounds.

Clearly, if I was going to lose weight, I would have to give up Coke. Which was like asking Buddy ("Nature Boy") Rogers to give up wrestling.

But I did it. The major problem was learning how to request a substitute. Every time I asked for "one Tab" I felt like a stewardess. Nevertheless, I persevered; for twelve long months I did without Coke, and the twenty-two pounds stayed off.

And now it was my anniversary: one year from the day I had last tasted a Coke.

As a reward to myself, I vowed that I would have one. Just one; one couldn't do that much damage, and I felt I was entitled. For old times' sake.

So there I was, in a darkened room with a candle glowing and violins playing on the turntable.

I reached for the goblet. I lifted it to my lips. I tilted it toward me. And the Coke coursed down my throat.

My body shivered and shook. It was as if someone had plunged an intravenous tube into my arm and shot me full of some rich medicine. The sensation was almost too much to bear. My teeth even hurt.

I had expected to be disappointed; I had expected that either the Coke would taste exactly like Tab, or—on the other end of the spectrum—that it would taste so syrupy and sugary that I would ask myself what I had ever seen in it in the first place.

Oh, I was so wrong. It was nectar from the gods, that's what it was; it was the most divine liquid that has ever flowed among us.

In that instant—the instant I swallowed my first mouthful of Coke in a year—the entire previous 365 days disappeared. It was as if I had never lived them. Instead, with the taste of the Coke still on my tongue, my mind was filled with memories:

Coming home from elementary school in the Fifties, rushing into the kitchen, ripping open a bag of potato chips, and then going into the refrigerator and pouring a Coke into a jelly glass with Howdy Doody's picture painted on it.

Cruising by the lake at dusk on summer nights in the Sixties, the radio playing, a cold 6½-ounce bottle of Coke in my left hand, the glass of the bottle clinking against the metal of my high school class ring.

Staying up all night to study for college finals, sitting at long tables in the basement of the fraternity house, friends on all sides, the TV playing in the background, a Coke from the vending machine resting on the Formica next to my books.

The feeling was so intense—and I had finished only one gulp of the Coke.

I took a few more tentative sips. I knew I must stop before this went too far. No wonder that addicts instinctively know that they must never, never go back to the fruit of their addiction, no matter how great the temptation; the aftertaste of the Coke in my throat [so much more real than the aftertaste of Tab, never mind Diet Rite!] warned me that if this continued, I might never be the same man again.

I stood up and walked around the room. I held the goblet of Coke in front of me, pausing every few minutes to look down at its undulating surface, the ice cubes protruding like so many miniature glaciers. It was as moving and as beautiful a sight as I have ever experienced.

But I knew what I had to do. Feeling the moisture coming to my eyes, I walked to the kitchen, leaned over the sink and—before I had time to stop myself—poured the remainder of the Coke down the drain. I could hear it gurgling away.

In a moment it was gone. I let out a deep breath. It had been a long year, and the future stretched drearily out ahead. I turned the lights up to full brightness and blew out the candle. Welcome back to the brave new world. One Tab, please.

Farewell to Hef's Pad

You've probably heard: the Playboy Mansion in Chicago is going to be turned into a dormitory for art students. The Playboy Mansion— a seventy-two-room, four-story house on the city's Near North Side—has sat virtually vacant since the mid-1970s, when its principal inhabitant, Hugh Hefner, moved to Holmby Hills, California, and purchased an estate that he began calling the Playboy Mansion West.

Apparently Hefner liked life in California; the West Coast mansion featured outdoor fish ponds and meandering wildlife and tennis courts and hiking paths, providing the owner with a fresh-air atmosphere he had never known before. After settling in at his Playboy Mansion West, he never really returned to the original Playboy Mansion, at least not on a permanent basis. Night after night the huge Chicago house at 1340 North State Parkway would sit with its lights darkened.

And last summer the official announcement was made: Playboy Enterprises Inc. would donate the original Playboy Mansion to the School of the Art Institute of Chicago. Beginning next January, approximately fifty Art Institute students will use the mansion as a dormitory. Playboy will eventually receive tax credits as a result of the donation. From here on in, it was announced, the building will be known as Hefner Hall.

I know I'm not the only one; I know, in fact, that I am merely one man among millions.

I grew up sneaking copies of *Playboy* out of my father's shirt drawer, where each month the magazine was hidden beneath a pile of white shirts with the expectation that the children would not be able to find it. *Playboy*, at the time, was considered racy almost to the point of sinfulness; it was not displayed out on the magazine racks along with *Time* and *Newsweek*, the way it is today, and responsible parents most certainly did not just leave it lying around the house.

There were a lot of fantasies in that magazine every month, starting with the beautiful women. But the fantasy that hit me the hardest was a more basic one. I may have been just a naive, skinny teenager in central Ohio, but I knew what I wanted. All I wanted to do was move to Chicago and be Hugh Hefner's friend so that I could be invited to—as it was called in the magazine—Hef's Pad.

Hef's Pad was the Playboy Mansion, of course, and I do not think any single edifice has ever been more successfully promoted in the pages of a magazine or newspaper. I had never been there, obviously; I was a kid, and I had never even been to Chicago. But I had seen it and read about it so often in the magazine, I knew the Playboy Mansion as well as I knew the homes of some of my closest uncles and aunts.

There was the brass plaque welcoming visitors, inscribed in Latin: SI NON OSCILLAS, NOLI TINTINNARE ("If you don't swing, don't ring"). There was the massive living room, decorated with suits of armor and LeRoy Neiman paintings, where all of Hef's friends were always dancing the Watusi—the men wearing expensive Italian-cut suits, the women wearing cocktail dresses or bikinis. In the magazine, everyone at Hef's Pad was always smiling and having the time of their lives.

A typical article from the magazine in the 1960s summarizes the atmosphere at one of the parties at Hef's Pad; this is the vision we Midwestern lads were being served up:

> No phase of the good life at the Mansion matches in reputation the far-flung fame of Hefner's legendary parties—Gatsbyesque whee-for-alls in the grand manor (and the grand manner) that leave the launching pad at midnight and orbit until dawn, with a passenger list of four hundred or five hundred revelers aboard. No sooner will you enter the main room—arriving at a fashionable three or four, when the revelry has reached its apogee—than you'll find yourself swept up in the heady atmosphere that prevails at these sumptuously swinging galas, and greeted by a phantasmagoria of sight and sound: crimson-liveried housemen threading their way through the throngs bearing trays of hot and cold canapés, mixed drinks, and champagne; the throbbing go-go beat of the combo in the corner, where Sal Mineo's sitting in on drums tonight; June "The Bosom" Wilkinson, in a skintight sheath, frugging up a storm in the middle of the dance floor; Hugh O'Brian chatting over cocktails with an elegantly gowned Chicago socialite just arrived from an evening at the opera; bikinied beauties still dewy from a dip in the pool, checking out the action in the ballroom. . . .

That was just the beginning, though. There was the pool itself, down in the basement, with a hidden cranny where Hefner's lust-crazed pals liked to take their dates. The cranny was called the Woo Grotto, and all of those devilish bachelors thought they were guaranteed total privacy when they swam into it. But were they in for a surprise! Hef and his other gag-loving friends had a secret trapdoor above the Woo Grotto, in the living room, that they could open and spy on the unsuspecting couple below.

There was the game room, stocked with all of the latest pinball machines, pool tables, slot-racing courses, and the like. There was the underwater bar, built in a subbasement level, featuring a window revealing the depths of the pool. To reach this barroom you could either climb down some narrow, winding stairs—or slide down a fire pole that led directly into the midst of all the revelry.

And of course there was Hefner's bedroom, with the circular, motor-driven, rotating, vibrating bed. Here, we were told, Hefner worked as well as played, often never going outside the building for months at a time. The Bunny dormitory—where two dozen Bunnies from the Chicago Playboy Club lived and paid a nominal rent—was only steps away.

Cruising the streets of our hometowns, it seemed to many of us that all the fun in the world was being had at Hef's Pad. In later years many of us would question some of the values that went along with life inside the mansion, and question some of the messages that the magazine had been selling us; but if the truth be told, to a generation of boys whose night-time horizons extended no further than softball diamonds and Dairy Queens and suburban recreation centers, the image of life at the Playboy Mansion seemed like Christmas morning every day.

It so happened that I did make it to Chicago and, eventually, to Hef's Pad. In 1973, working on a Sunday magazine story for the newspaper where I was employed, I talked Playboy into allowing me to live in the Playboy Mansion for a week.

Arriving for the assignment, I had an eerie feeling. I was giddy over the prospect of finally seeing the place I was so familiar with from the magazine. But once I got there, it struck me that there was nothing I hadn't already seen. There didn't seem to be a square foot of the place that hadn't been photographed and published repeatedly; everywhere I wandered, it felt like a movie set—this seemed like a scale model of the Playboy Mansion, not the real thing.

I was assigned to a bedroom called the Blue Room; it fronted on the mansion's ballroom, and shared a bathroom with the adjoining Red Room.

It turned out that the Red Room was occupied by a young woman who had come to town for her Playmate of the Month photo session; we had to work out a series of knocks to let each other know who was using the bathroom, and she seemed as unnerved and daunted by the mansion as I was.

Hefner himself was on the premises. Invariably clad in pajamas and velvet slippers that bore his initials, he would play Monopoly all night with a group of his friends. He had compiled a handwritten list of all the properties on the Monopoly board—which ones were the most potentially profitable, which were a waste of money. There was a stereo nearby; Hefner had a mammoth supply of albums to choose from, but he kept playing the same two over and over: a collection of old ballads by Harry Nilsson and another collection of old ballads by Peggy Lee. The two records would play, they would click off, and Hefner would start them over again. If the repetition was bothering his friends, they didn't say anything. When I turned in for the night, Hefner would be sitting at the Monopoly board and singing along with Nilsson: "Maybe I'm right and maybe I'm wrong . . ." When I would wake up the next morning and leave my room for breakfast, Hefner would still be there, still singing along: "Maybe I'm right and maybe I'm wrong . . ."

But this story isn't supposed to be about the reality of what I found at the Playboy Mansion; this is supposed to be about the fantasy of that mansion held by earlier generations of American teenaged boys, and the fact that the fantasy is now officially past tense.

A few days after it was announced that the Playboy Mansion would be turned into the art students' dorm, I went over to take one last look. Already the transformation into Hefner Hall had begun; young men wearing green-and-white T-shirts bearing the legend THE ART INSTITUTE OF CHICAGO were trimming the shrubbery in front.

I was met at the front door by Eileen Harakal, a member of the Art Institute's administration, who was going to show me around. Since she really wasn't yet familiar with the building, she had enlisted the help of Marv Meadors, sixty-four, the Playboy Mansion's longtime chief engineer and handyman.

Meadors looked a little sad. We entered the building; the "If you don't swing, don't ring" plaque had already been taken down. The furniture looked pretty much the way it had in all those magazine layouts past, but everything had red or green inventory tags attached in preparation for removal.

We walked past the swimming pool. I asked Eileen Harakal if the Art Institute planned on keeping it.

"We just don't know," she said. "We have to look into the insurance requirements. The safety of the students has to be foremost in our minds."

Marv Meadors had a wistful expression on his face.

We moved on past the famous fire pole that led down to the underwater bar. I could almost close my eyes and see all those color magazine photos with happy men and women hoisting cocktails and sliding down the pole to join their friends.

"This definitely gets taken out," Harakal said. "We'll take the pole out and cover up the opening. What possible function could it serve for the students? There is a real risk of broken legs. It will go."

Marv Meadors looked off in the other direction.

We went to Hefner's bedroom. In the middle of the white carpeting there was a circular impression where the bed had once been. It had been removed. All that remained were some electrical cables that had presumably been used to make it revolve and vibrate.

"This is a nice room," Harakal said. "I like the size of it. I think we will use it as a classroom, for programs that are open to the community."

Marv Meadors and I sneaked a brief glance at each other.

We passed through the mansion's living room.

"Marv," I said, "will you do one thing?"

"What's that?" Meadors said.

"Will you open up the trapdoor so that we can look down into the Woo Grotto?"

A soft smile crossed Meadors's face. He went to the wall, found a hidden button, and pressed it. Slowly, a square piece of the floor began to lift up; as it did so a stereo tape player was automatically activated, and from down below romantic music wafted up.

We peered down. There was the Woo Grotto, all right: a secluded little corner of the pool hidden behind a man-made cave, where no one could see what was going on—save for the people up here in the living room.

"Well," said Eileen Harakal, "this is a surprise. I can guarantee you that this will be sealed up. That's all we need, a student bumping into the button by mistake and falling into that hole in the floor."

I don't know what Marv Meadors was doing right then; I was gazing off somewhere in the distance, and I didn't see him.

So Long, Davies

Nothing is as good as running a college newspaper. No matter how much luck you have later on, in the real world, it can never top the feeling you have on your college campus when, for the first time, you are part of a daily newspaper, and it belongs to no one but you and your friends, and whatever successes or failures it achieves are yours and yours alone.

Later on the pleasures and the pains will be diluted; when you work for a large organization there are plenty of people to share your triumphs and your mistakes. The process of putting out the paper becomes institutionalized; it is safer, but it is also less personal.

Five of us put out the *Daily Northwestern* in 1968 and 1969. There were many more on the staff, of course, but we were the seniors; it was our year. John Walter was the editor; Steve Sink, Bill Harsh, Tom Davies, and I were the other editors. Davies and I wrote columns.

It was pretty heady stuff for both of us. We would walk around campus and people we had never met before would stop us—they would recognize us from the pictures in our column logos—and they would tell us what they thought of that day's story. The first few times that happens to you you think you are in heaven.

Davies and I had a friendly rivalry; I would try to get fancier in my column than he would in his, and I would come into the newsroom to hear him telling the rest of the staff, "That Greene has no idea how to write a *news* story." Our columns alternated. We were constantly trying to outdo each other.

One day Davies had a pretty good column, and through a mistake at the printing shop, my logo appeared above it. I was upset about it until, that evening, a co-ed stopped me in the library and told me how much she had liked it. I didn't correct her; as I recall, Davies was not amused the next day.

The five of us who put out the *Daily* thought we were all going to be world beaters; we had marvelous plans for ourselves. Davies considered himself to have a leg up on the rest of us because he was a stringer for the *New York Times;* he hoped to convert that into a full-time job.

But something happened. Right after graduation Davies married Betty Jean Peters, a girl he had known since kindergarten. On their honeymoon in Fort Lauderdale he became violently ill. He thought it was the flu, or at worst bronchitis. They went back to their hometown of Toledo, Ohio. The doctors took tests. Davies had a deadly disease—systemic lupus erythematosus.

The doctors told the newlyweds: "You will not have a long life together. You will not grow old together." Gone were the plans to try to be a journalistic whiz kid. Davies and his wife settled down in Toledo, and he went to work for his hometown paper, the *Blade.* The editors of the *Blade* had known Davies since he was in high school. They hired him even knowing that he had the disease. He would often remark, later, that probably no other paper in the country would have been kind enough to offer him a chance at employment knowing what they knew.

For the next eight years Davies wrote for the *Blade.* He was often in terrible pain; he was in and out of hospitals, and it was not uncommon for him to miss sixty, seventy, eighty days of work a year. He became depressed; he was afraid that the other reporters and editors would think he was taking advantage of the newspaper.

The rest of us from the college paper went out and traveled the country and the world and did the best we could. Davies, meanwhile, eventually went off the full-time staff at the *Blade*; he had to spend more and more time in bed, so he worked on a part-time basis at home. When he would go out to conduct an interview, sometimes the strain would be so great on him that it would put him back in bed for another three or four days after the story was completed.

He never got tired of seeing his name in print, though; when the paper boy delivered the *Blade* to his house, he would rip it open to his stories. It still meant something to him, to see his work in a newspaper.

The rest of us were a little awkward whenever we talked to him; we knew the troubles he was having, and we could never find the right words to express what we were thinking. In 1979 we had our tenth *Daily Northwestern* reunion in Chicago. Davies seemed to be in good spirits at dinner, but he was drinking heavily. Near the end of the meal he called me aside.

"Greene, I'm a dead man," he said. "I won't be at the next reunion."

I knew he wasn't kidding, and he wasn't. Tom Davies died the other day; he was only thirty-five years old.

"He loved to follow what the rest of you were doing with your lives," Betty Jean Davies told me. "He knew that it wasn't destined to happen with him, so he took great pride in what the rest of you accomplished.

"You, though, Bob . . ." she said. She laughed. "Sometimes he would see something you had written, and he would hold it up in the air and say, 'That boy *still* can't write a news story.'"

Toward the end, she said, Davies sometimes talked about a fantasy he had. "He would say that he was thinking what it would be like if you guys all bought your own newspaper somewhere," she said. "What it would be like if you got to put out your own paper together again. Those days turned out to be the best of his life."

She did a very nice thing for his funeral. She found an old feature story he had written, and she had the reverend read it aloud during the funeral services. It was a funny story; everyone in the congregation laughed. Ah, Davies, those days were pretty good for the rest of us, too.

Icebreaker

A weary, road-battered traveler—Mr. Greene himself— pulled into Cleveland at the end of a long evening. I decided that it might be a nice idea to have one quick drink before bed.

A bar called the Shalamar looked inviting. I prepared to enter, when a perky young woman seated at a table next to the front door said, "Which initials would you like?"

"Huh?" I said.

"Which initials?" she repeated.

I decided it was best to ignore her. "I don't want initials," I said. "I just want a drink." I walked into the bar.

It didn't take a genius to see that something unusual was going on. Oh, the bar was typical enough in most respects—tables, muted lighting, music from a live band whose members wore red Vegas-style jackets.

But the customers . . . they all had big initials pinned to their chests.

There was a woman marked "A.N." A man marked "J.B." Another woman marked "L.T." Another man marked "T.Z." All around the room, the people wore the letters.

I selected the last available table in the bar and looked for a waitress. As I peered around the room, I noticed that everyone else's eyes seemed to be focused on an area just above the bandstand, near the ceiling.

What they were looking at was a computerized screen—a long screen that featured messages trailing across it, kind of like the weather bulletins the television stations sometimes feature at the bottom of the TV screen during a show.

I read the messages:

FROM T.G. [MALE] TO B.B. [FEMALE]—LET ME TAKE YOU AWAY FROM THIS AND GET CRAAAAAZY! I'M SITTING UP ON THE LEDGE.

FROM L.L. [FEMALE] to T.K. [MALE]—I LIKE THE WAY YOU LOOK IN THOSE JEANS. LET ME SEE THEM UP CLOSE ON THE DANCE FLOOR.

FROM T.T. [MALE] TO M.Z. [FEMALE]—ARE YOU ALL TALK AND NO ACTION? I GUESS THERE'S ONLY ONE WAY TO FIND OUT FOR SURE!

The messages moved across the screen, one after another. This was pretty bizarre; apparently all these men and women with the initials pinned to their chests were somehow sending the messages to one another.

I made a reconnaissance cruise around the room. Sure enough, at the different tables men and women were checking each other out through the smoky haze. They were writing down their thoughts about specific members of the opposite sex who wore specific initials.

I kept walking. At the far end of the room, I found a computer operator sitting at a keyboard. In front of the operator was a wooden box; the men and women in the bar were dropping their messages into a slot in the top of the box. Periodically the operator would empty the box, then punch the messages onto the keyboard. Soon, the messages would come flashing across the screen.

This was hard to believe. I had never seen this before. I had heard about the "personals" in newspapers—the classified ads designed to help the people who placed them find romance. And I knew, of course, that this was the computer/video age.

But could this be happening? Could people really be coming to a bar, sizing up men and women across the room, then trying to seduce those men and women via this computerized, live "personals" setup?

I wandered, fascinated. The people seldom looked away from the screen. They all seemed to be looking for their own initials to come scooting across.

The man in charge of the bar was a fellow named Jim Gauss. He confirmed that this was, indeed, precisely what was going on.

"This is the fourth week we've been using this setup," Gauss said. "We're getting a very positive response from everyone. The word-of-mouth is great. People hear about it and come to try it."

He said that the customers are given the initials when they first arrive at the Shalamar. The initials are not necessarily the person's real initials; one can choose any combination. But once a set of initials is taken, that same set cannot be used by anyone else that night.

I asked Gauss why on earth anyone would do this—send computerized messages to someone else who might be standing a mere five feet away.

"There are some individuals who are sort of shy," Gauss said. "Maybe they don't have the nerve to say something, or to ask someone to dance. With this system, they can do it on the computer. It makes it easier."

"So there's no fear of rejection?" I said.

"Oh, there's a lot of rejection," Gauss said. "You should see the people who send a message to someone they're attracted to; they wait for their message to be returned, and when it never is, you can see the reaction on their faces."

As the night grew later, the messages grew bolder. Gauss told me that the keyboard operator was instructed not to process messages that were too racy; but there seemed to be a definite correlation between the lateness of the hour, the consumption of alcohol, and the borderline lewdness of the messages that crawled along the screen.

There was probably a lesson here—about human nature, or the depersonalization of society, or the unspoken distance that still exists between men and women. Instead of thinking about that, though, I dropped a message into the wooden box next to the keyboard operator:

B.G. [MALE] IS CONFUSED. SEEKS SYMPATHETIC CHEESEBURGER. GRILLED ONIONS PREFERRED.

We all have our own definition of romance, and the road is long.